Topical Index

D1496725

Use this index to quickly locate some of the most critical topics covered in this book.

Tom Swan's Mastering Borland C++ 5

Tom Swan

SAMS
PUBLISHING

201 West 103rd Street
Indianapolis, Indiana 46290

To Anne. May all your dreams come true.

Copyright © 1996 by Tom Swan

FIRST EDITION

International Standard Book Number: 0-672-30802-9

Library of Congress Catalog Card Number: 95-72923

99 98 97   4 3 2

Interpretation of the printing code: the rightmost double-digit number is the year of the book's printing; the rightmost single-digit, the number of the book's printing. For example, a printing code of 96-1 shows that the first printing of the book occurred in 1996.

Composed in Agaramond and MCPdigital by Macmillan Computer Publishing

Printed in the United States of America

Publisher and President:	Richard K. Swadley
Acquisitions Manager:	Greg Wiegand
Development Manager:	Dean Miller
Managing Editor:	Cindy Morrow
Marketing Manager:	John Pierce
Assistant Marketing Manager:	Kristina Perry

Acquisitions Editor
Kim Spilker

Development Editor
Anthony Amico

Software Development Specialist
Steve Straiger

Production Editor
Ryan Rader

Technical Reviewers
Greg Guntle
Lilly Shrager
Wade Evans

Editorial Coordinator
Bill Whitmer

Technical Edit Coordinator
Lynette Quinn

Formatter
Frank Sinclair

Editorial Assistants
Carol Ackerman
Andi Richter
Rhonda Tinch-Mize

Cover Designer
Tim Amrhein

Book Designer
Alyssa Yesh

Copy Writer
Peter Fuller

Production Team Supervisor
Brad Chinn

Production
Carol Bowers
Jason Hand
Sonja Hart
Mike Henry
Louisa Klucznik
Ayanna Lacey
Clint Lahnen
Paula Lowell
Erika Millen
Erich J. Richter
Laura Robbins
Bobbi Satterfield
SA Springer
Colleen Williams

Overview

Contents

xiii

Preface

Some time ago, when Borland announced plans for Borland C++ 5, I immediately began revising the second edition of my book, *Mastering Borland C++ 4.5*. When, however, I learned the extent of the changes and new features that Borland had in store for this popular C++ development system, I realized that a mere revised edition of this book would hardly cut the mustard.

So, rather than hold the pickles and onions, I decided to rewrite this book from scratch and throw in all the fixings. In these pages, you will find many new chapters on ANSI C++ programming—from simple to advanced topics—including classes, object-oriented programming, I/O and file streams, new data types, and key words. There are full explanations of the ANSI C++ standard template library's strings, containers, and algorithms. I've added new material on programming Windows 95 applications using Microsoft Foundation Classes, on writing database systems with Borland's new visual database tools, on customizing the IDE with Object Scripting (a new language in its own right), on mixing Borland C++ 5 with Delphi 2.0, and on getting started with Java programming to create interactive Internet Web pages.

But that's not all. Included are introductions to ObjectWindows 5.0 (OWL), Windows 95 programming techniques (using whiz-bang OWL classes to manage controls such as dockable toolbars and splash screens), OLE2, Borland's template class library, memory management, and so much more that the head of marketing at Sams was actually seen cartwheeling down the hall.

Okay, that was an unconfirmed rumor, but there *is* a lot of good stuff here. For example, with the help of the publisher, I have included on the accompanying CD-ROM the complete electronic, indexed text of *Mastering Borland C++ 4.5*. Of course, all source code listings for this book *and* its predecessor are also on the CD-ROM. Together, this book and CD-ROM bring you hundreds of sample program listings and over 2,500 pages of printed and electronic text on C++ programming!

Much of the new material in this book comes from reader suggestions, and I owe a huge thank you to all who have taken time to write. So don't be a stranger—let me know what you think of *Mastering Borland C++ 5*. I'm excited about the scope of this book and about the future direction of computer programming as developers everywhere move from a text-based world to one of striking visual interfaces, 32-bit Windows operating systems, and a global network that has already linked programmers and computer users together in ways unforeseen only a few years ago. This book represents a new beginning for the publisher and me in bringing you up-to-date information on C++ programming. In these pages, I hope that you find what *you* need to master Borland C++ 5.

Tom Swan
Key West, Florida
CompuServe ID: 73627,3241

Acknowledgments

In writing this book, I'm extremely proud to have been a member of the finest team of individuals ever assembled for a publishing project, including at Sams, Kim Spilker, Tony Amico, Ryan Rader, Steve Straiger, and Richard Swadley. Thanks also to everyone at Borland, especially Nan Borreson, for providing me with software and encouragement, and to Jerry and Alice at the Key West Office Center for service with a smile despite the fact that a hurricane would probably make my office look *more* organized. Thanks and lots more to Elizabeth Saenger for helpful suggestions, chocolate breaks, and sushi. And last but not least, special thanks, and sweeping bows, to all of my CompuServe correspondents who have once again helped me to keep my feet out of my mouth and firmly on the floor where they belong.

PART

Introductions

CHAPTER

1

Introducing This Book

Borland C++ 5 and Visual Database Tools is a highly sophisticated programming system for DOS, Windows, and database developers. How can you learn to use this tremendously capable package? Where do you begin?

Experienced developers probably welcome the complexity of Borland C++ 5. PC programming isn't getting any easier, and as developers, we need all the help, tools, and utilities that we can cram onto our disks. Gone are the days when compilers took only a few thousand bytes of disk space.

Gone also are the days when mastering programming simply meant spending a few days studying a tutorial and learning a text editor's commands. It's no longer enough to master a programming *language.* Today's software developers also have to master a programming *environment* consisting of editors, debuggers, project and resource managers, expert application generators, class and function libraries, database engines, and an army of related utilities. To that end, *Mastering Borland C++ 5* now focuses less on programming fundamentals and more on today's critical software-development techniques.

Readers of past editions of *Mastering Borland C++* will recognize only a few chapters from the earlier texts. In response to reader requests (the publisher calls this "market pressure"), I completely rewrote this book from scratch, while keeping only those sections and chapters that remain relevant to today's fast-paced world of programming. For readers who don't have an earlier edition, the entire cross-referenced text of the second edition of *Mastering Borland C++ 4.5* is included on the accompanying CD-ROM. Refer to these online documents if you need help with DOS programming, DOS graphics, standard library functions, and ANSI C programming. All source code files for this book *and* the second edition are also included on the CD-ROM.

To get the most out of this book, you should be familiar with the fundamentals of C. For those who need a refresher course, a full ANSI C tutorial is provided on CD-ROM. The C++ tutorial chapters in Part II pick up where C leaves off, concentrating mostly on classes and object-oriented programming. Many more sections explain templates, exception handling, strings, and other advanced topics. You'll find complete tutorials and tips for using Borland's container class library and the new ANSI C++ standard template library (STL), which includes a string template, numerous container classes, and algorithms. You'll learn how to use the newest release of Borland's ObjectWindows (OWL) 5.0 class library for programming Windows 3.x, Windows 95, and Windows NT 16- and 32-bit applications. Alternatively, Borland C++ 5 now supports Microsoft Foundation Classes (MFC) for Windows development, as explained in Chapter 24. New chapters also cover Borland's Visual Database Tools, the new Object Scripting language for customizing the integrated development environment (IDE), how to mix Delphi 2 with Borland C++ 5, and how to get started with Java programming for the Internet.

In short, despite its familiar title, *Mastering Borland C++ 5* is substantially new, and more than half of its content has never before been published.

Following are hardware and software requirements, instructions on using the CD-ROM packaged inside the back cover, and summaries of the book's parts and chapters.

Requirements

You can use this book's programs with a wide variety of software, hardware, and memory capacities. No single configuration is right for all. If you can install Borland C++ 5, you're ready to begin. Following are minimum hardware and software requirements you'll need to get the most out of this book.

Hardware

To compile and run most sample programs in this book, you need to have some or all of the following hardware components:

- An 80486 or a Pentium-based PC with 16M RAM (24M or more is recommended). When in doubt, get the fastest PC you can beg, borrow, steal, or preferably, purchase legally. I used a desktop multimedia 100MHz Pentium-based PC with 32M RAM to write this book and compile all sample programs.

- A hard disk drive with about 100M free space available for installing Borland C++ 5 and Visual Database Tools. A full installation, including the 32-bit Windows-based IDE plus add-ons such as Java and the BDE, can use as much as 175M. A minimal, DOS-only, 16-bit installation uses about 25M. You can use a minimum installation with this book to learn C++ programming, but you won't be able to use the Windows-based IDE, and you'll need more room to compile and run this book's Windows, database, MFC, and Java examples. In addition to space for Borland C++ 5, you'll need about 2M free disk space to install the sample programs on this book's CD-ROM, and another 5M to 10M to compile those programs. In round numbers, if you have 200M free space available before installing Borland C++, you're in business. If you have about 75M, you can get by, but you might not be able to install the full system including online documentation, examples, and source code files.

- A Windows-compatible mouse or similar device, such as a trackball.

- A CD-ROM drive for installing this book's sample applications and viewing the online hypertext version of this book, the text of the second edition, and other documents.

- Optional equipment: A printer, modem, sound card, and high-resolution SVGA display. On my main development system, I normally configure Windows 95 to display 800×600 pixels, but you can use any other resolution.

> **NOTE**
>
> Most developers I've talked to agree that a resolution of 800×600 offers the ideal compromise between screen size and readability. Because dialog windows are scaled according to font sizes, 1024×768 font substitutions can complicate software development, especially in arranging dialog box controls. Designing dialogs under 800×600 and then *testing* the results in lower and higher resolutions usually produces more reliable results.

Software

Now for the best part: the software. To compile and run this book's sample programs, you need some or all of the following software components:

- Microsoft Windows 95, or Windows NT 3.51 or 4.0. Although you may use this book and Borland C++ 5 to develop 16-bit DOS and Windows 3.x applications, the 32-bit IDE requires Windows 95 or Windows NT. You can run either the retail version of Windows 95 or the debugging version provided on Microsoft's SDK for Win95.

- Borland C++ 5. A few sample programs *might* work with earlier versions, but you should upgrade to the new compiler as soon as possible to make full use of this book's information. *I tested this book's programs only with Borland C++ 5.*

- Visual Database Tools. This includes 16- and 32-bit versions of The Borland Database Engine (BDE) plus other tools such as the Database Desktop. *You do not need to purchase additional software to make use of this book's new database programming information.* As I'll explain, Borland C++ 5 now contains all you need to create, maintain, and develop applications for Paradox, dBASE, ODBC-compliant, and client-server databases.

- Optional: Turbo Assembler 5.0. (You may also be able to use another version such as 4.0.) This stand-alone assembler is available separately from Borland, and you'll need it only for portions of Chapter 19, "Mixing C++ and Assembly Language." As that chapter explains, Borland C++ 5 directly supports inline assembly; so unless your applications require extensive assembly-language capabilities, you do not need to purchase Turbo Assembler.

Installing Borland C++ 5

Read the instructions that come with Borland C++ 5 to install the compiler and related files. You must use Windows 95 or Windows NT to install Borland C++ 5 and run the Windows-based 32-bit IDE. Following are a few tips that will help settle questions during installation and thereafter:

- I assume that you have installed Borland C++ in the default C:\BC5 directory. If you installed to a different base directory or drive letter, you'll have to modify all of the project files on this book's CD-ROM and you'll also have to regenerate all Make files. This is a lot of work, so for best results, you should install Borland C++ 5 in the default directories on drive C:.

- Inspect your system path (type **path** at a DOS prompt). The installer inserts a path to the compiler's executable code files into Autoexec.bat with a command such as the following. (By the way, BIN stands for *binaries*.)

  ```
  PATH=C:\WINDOWS;C:\WINDOWS\COMMAND;C:\DOS;C:\BC5\BIN;
  ```

- If you have enough disk space, install everything. You can always delete (or copy to floppy disks) files that you don't need. It's much easier to install every component now than it is to install only some files and then reinstall others later.

- If you receive errors when compiling, check whether you have defined an INCLUDE environment variable. (Type **SET** at a DOS prompt.) Utilities such as Make, but not the compiler or linker, recognize INCLUDE, which may cause mysterious conflicts, especially if you have other compilers that also depend on INCLUDE.

- Don't configure your system to use Borland C++ and other compilers such as Visual C++ at the same time. If you must do this, however, create separate Autoexec.bat and Config.sys files for each C and C++ development system installed on your system. You might also have to modify the Windows 95 registry, or the System.ini and Win.ini files, to remove conflicting virtual device drivers and DLLs. *For best results, remove all other C and C++ compilers from your computer before installing Borland C++ 5.*

Installing This Book's CD-ROM

Source code files for this book's sample programs are stored by chapter number in subdirectory Source. For example, the files for Chapter 12 are in the directory Source\C12. Some chapter directories also have additional subdirectories.

The sample files are not compressed. You can view them using a text editor or the Borland C++ IDE. To compile and run the sample programs, copy them to your hard drive. For best results, use the Windows 95 Explorer utility to copy the entire Source directory to your hard drive. If you receive errors during compilation, check all .ide project file path names, and then from a DOS prompt, enter the following command to reset all read-only settings:

```
cd \Source
attrib -R *.* /S
```

Please refer to the last page of this book for additional instructions on installing and using the accompanying CD-ROM.

Part and Chapter Summaries

This book's chapters build on one another. I've tried to place simpler subjects before advanced topics so that you can read the book from front to back as a tutorial. However, depending on your needs and programming skills, you can also browse for interesting subjects, so feel free to hop around as you please. The following brief summaries of each part and chapter will help you find the subjects you need.

Parts

Five parts divide *Mastering Borland C++ 5* into logical boundaries:

- Part I, *Introductions,* introduces this book and gets you started on programming with C++ and using Borland C++ 5.

- Part II, *C++ Tutorials,* covers the C++ programming language. I assume in this part that you know the fundamentals of C programming, but even experienced C++ programmers will want to read the updated information on ANSI C++. The emphasis in this part's chapters is on using classes and object-oriented programming techniques. Exercises at the end of each chapter test your knowledge as you master C++.

- Part III, *Class Libraries,* builds on the information in Part II. Chapters in this part explain how to use Borland's template container class library, the new standard C++ standard template library (STL), the new string template, standard containers, and standard algorithms.

- Part IV, *Windows Development,* introduces Object Windows 5.0 (OWL), the newest version of Borland's application framework class library for Windows programming. Chapters in this part explain how to write 16- and 32-bit applications for Windows 3.x, Windows 95, and Windows NT. Also covered are OLE and Object Component Frameworks (OCF).

- Part V, *Developer's Toolbox,* explains how to use the IDE's project manager, how to mix C++ and assembly language, how to use process control and memory models, how to develop database systems with Borland's new 32-bit visual database tools, how to customize the IDE with object scripting, how to mix Delphi 2 with Borland C++ 5, how to compile Microsoft Foundation Class programs, and how to get started with Java programming for the Internet.

NOTE

The standard function library reference from *Mastering Borland C++ 4.5* is now provided on this book's CD-ROM in cross-indexed format for fast searching. A streamlined version of the reference is in Chapter 26.

Chapters

In its five parts, this book's 26 chapters cover a wide variety of ANSI C++, DOS, Windows, database, and other programming topics. The following notes briefly describe each chapter's contents.

- Chapter 1, "Introducing This Book," as you are discovering, suggests how to make the most of this book.

- Chapter 2, "Introducing Borland C++ 5," provides installation tips and suggests methods for setting up and using the Borland C++ 5 IDE (Windows) and command-line (DOS) environments.

- Chapter 3, "Introducing C++ Programming," is the first of several chapters on C++. Read this chapter for an overview of C++ and to learn how C++ differs from C.

- Chapter 4, "Programming with Classes," introduces the class, used in C++ to create encapsulated data structures for object-oriented programming (OOP).

- Chapter 5, "Investing in Inheritance," explains the key OOP concepts of inheritance and virtual member functions for deriving new classes from existing ones and for creating polymorphic objects that behave according to their types.

- Chapter 6, "Handling Exceptions," shows how to create robust applications that handle errors and other abnormal conditions using C++ exceptions.

- Chapter 7, "Overloading Your Friends," explains all about friends and operator overloading, which are OOP techniques for advanced C++ programming.

- Chapter 8, "Advancing Your C++ Knowledge," covers additional and miscellaneous C++ topics ranging from I/O and file streams to namespaces and runtime type information.

- Chapter 9, "Mastering Borland's Template Class Library," explains how to use Borland's template container classes for efficient object-oriented data storage.

- Chapter 10, "Mastering the Standard Template Library," guides you through the all-new standard template library (STL), licensed from Rogue Wave and provided with Borland C++ 5.

- Chapter 11, "Mastering Standard Strings," digs deeply into this new addition to ANSI C++, a highly capable string template that eliminates many of the snafus associated with common C-style null-terminated strings.

- Chapter 12, "Mastering Standard Containers," shows the ins and outs of using ANSI C++ standard container class templates for data storage in OOP and conventional applications.

- Chapter 13, "Mastering Standard Algorithms," combines the information in the preceding three chapters with examples that demonstrate how to use standard algorithms from the STL for performing a variety of operations on data in OOP and conventional applications.

- Chapter 14, "Introducing OWL," explains how to develop 16- and 32-bit Windows applications with this newest release of Borland's popular ObjectWindows (OWL) class library.
- Chapter 15, "Developing Windows 95 Applications," covers OWL programming techniques for developing 32-bit applications for Windows 95. (Information in this chapter is also applicable to the upcoming release of Windows NT, version 4.0.)
- Chapter 16, "Introducing OLE and OCF," explains the basics of Object Linking and Embedding for constructing compound documents and provides complete instructions for developing OLE container and server applications.
- Chapter 17, "Creating OLE Applications," explains how to use OCF and OWL with OLE automation.
- Chapter 18, "Managing Projects," explores how to use the IDE's project manager for developing multiple-file and multiple-target applications.
- Chapter 19, "Mixing C++ and Assembly Language," tours the ins and outs of using the Borland C++ inline assembler and, optionally, the stand-alone Turbo Assembler for adding fast, low-level assembly language code to C++ functions.
- Chapter 20, "Using Process Control, Optimizations, and Other Tools," offers numerous tips on background compilation, code optimizations, and memory-model management.
- Chapter 21, "Developing Database Applications," illustrates how to create relational databases using nonvisual and visual component classes, which provide object-oriented interfaces to the Borland Database Engine (BDE) supplied with Borland C++ 5.
- Chapter 22, "Customizing the IDE with Object Scripting," demonstrates how to use this all new feature—a programming language in its own right—to customize the IDE.
- Chapter 23, "Mixing Borland C++ 5 and Delphi 2," fully explains the four ways to mix C++ and Delphi 2 to create applications that use elements of both systems.
- Chapter 24, "Compiling MFC Applications," explains how to write and compile Windows applications using Microsoft's Foundation Classes (MFC), such as those supplied with Visual C++.
- Chapter 25, "Jumping Into Java," introduces the exciting new world of Java programming for the Internet. Java is a new programming language, similar to C++, that is provided in full with Borland C++ 5. This chapter gets you started writing Internet applets that you can insert into Web Page HTML documents.
- Chapter 26, "Mastering Standard Functions," is a streamlined, alphabetic reference to C++ standard functions, complete with many program examples.

In addition to its main course of chapters, the book serves up five appendixes for dessert:

- Appendix A, "Character Sets," lists extended ASCII character sets for DOS and Windows.

- Appendix B, "Compiler Options," lists command-line compiler options for Borland C++ versions 3.0, 3.1, 4.x, and the current version (5).

- Appendix C, "Linker Options," lists command-line linker options for Turbo Linker versions 5.0. 5.1, 6.x, 7.0, and the current version. (Because I'm using a prerelease linker at this time, it is unclear whether the final Turbo Linker version number will be 7.x or 8.0.)

- Appendix D, "Operator Precedence and Associativity," lists C++ operators and their left-to-right or right-to-left associativity.

- Appendix E, "C and C++ Keywords," lists standard ANSI C++ and nonstandard Borland C++ keywords and other reserved symbols.

Last but hardly least are the answers to exercises, a bibliography, and a subject index. However, as big as this book is, it can't possibly cover every topic in PC and Borland C++ programming. Consult the bibliography for references in which you can find additional information on DOS and Windows programming techniques. Also look up unfamiliar terms, functions, and classes in the online help files supplied with Borland C++ 5.

> **NOTE**
>
> Turn to the last page of this book, "What's on the Disc," for detailed instructions on installing and using the book's CD-ROM.

Summary

- Borland C++ is a sophisticated software-development system for DOS and Windows programming. *Mastering Borland C++ 5* is virtually a new book, with many new chapters that address the rapidly changing demands placed on today's C++ programmers.

- You need to know C (and perhaps some C++) to fully understand the information in this book. A complete ANSI C tutorial is on the book's CD-ROM. Part II provides complete C++ tutorials.

- This book has many new chapters on Windows 16- and 32-bit development, OWL 5.0, Visual Database Tools, Microsoft Foundation Classes, the ANSI C++ standard template and string library, Delphi 2, assembly language, Java, and more. All other chapters are updated for Borland C++ 5.

- Borland C++ 5 requires an 80486 or Pentium processor and at least 16M RAM (24M or more is recommended). Windows 95 or Windows NT 3.51 or 4.0 are required to run the new 32-bit integrated development system (IDE).

- The full text of the second edition to Mastering Borland C++ 4.5 is included in hypertext-indexed form on the CD-ROM, plus full source code for both books. The CD-ROM also contains the standard function reference from the second edition.

2

CHAPTER

Introducing Borland C++ 5

In a word, the Borland C++ 5 Integrated Development Environment (IDE) is sensational. You can use it to write, compile, and debug DOS and Windows applications of many different kinds. You also can use the IDE's text editor to view and edit any plain ASCII text file.

Borland's User's Guide fully documents every IDE command and feature. This chapter adds to that information with tips and hands-on tutorials that demonstrate many of the IDE's features. The chapter also suggests ways to compile this book's program listings using DOS or Windows.

Integrated Development Environment

The IDE requires Windows 95 or Windows NT 3.51, or a later version, and a mouse or a compatible point-and-click device, such as a trackball. Some of the features that make the IDE a wonderful workhorse for programmers include the following items, introduced in this chapter:

- *TargetExpert* selects a target code file—to choose whether to generate a DOS or a Windows EXE file, for example. With TargetExpert, it takes only a few seconds to switch between DOS and Windows development.

- *Settings Notebooks* make option selection much easier than in past IDE designs. Borland C++ 5 has hundreds of interrelated options. Settings Notebooks help you find and select the options you need.

- *Speed Menus* and a customizable *SpeedBar* give expert users fast alternative methods for issuing commands such as loading files and compiling multiple-file projects.

- *Context-sensitive online help* provides full references to the IDE and to all function library components. This book's online reference to standard functions supplements Borland's online reference material with complete examples for nearly all functions.

- *Text Editor with Brief and Epsilon emulations* is the IDE's central component. You use it to write and edit source-code files, and to load this book's sample listings from disk, but you also can use it to edit any plain ASCII text file. The newly revised editor includes sophisticated features such as multiple-pane windows, column cut and paste, and syntax highlighting.

- *Message Window* informs you about errors detected by the compiler and linker, and also shows the output of external tools and utilities. The Message Window automatically appears when the IDE has a message to deliver.

- *Tools Menu* is ideal for running external utilities such as GREP, a regular-expression search utility that searches text files. Using the Tool Menu, you can transfer to a stand-alone debugger and run other external programs.

Some other major IDE features covered elsewhere in this book include the following:

- *Integrated GUI debugger* helps you explore a program's code and data. Using the debugger, you can single-step through statements, seeing their effects in slow motion, and you can inspect variables, objects, and other structures. You also can set breakpoints to halt a program at a strategic location so you can inspect its output. See "The Art and Science of Debugging" in this chapter for tips on using the debugger to explore how programs operate.

- *Hierarchical Project Manager* simplifies the daunting task of organizing the many modules and related files that go into the making of a commercial-level application. Many of this book's sample programs use projects to organize their files. Chapter 18 explains how to use the IDE's Project Manager for your own applications.

- *Object Browser* enables you to trace relationships among classes, functions, and structures.

- *Integrated 16- and 32-bit Resource Editor* makes it possible to create and edit Windows resources such as menus and dialog boxes directly in the IDE. It is no longer necessary, as it was in the past, to run a separate program such as Resource Workshop, which is no longer supplied with Borland C++ 5. (The older 16-bit version of RW is available with Borland C++ 4.5, which is supplied with Borland C++ 5.0. You may use this version of RW to create and edit resources for Windows 95 and Windows NT, but the integrated editor is superior and fully supports all new Windows 95 controls as well as visual database components.)

- *Script Compiler* for customizing the IDE. Chapter 22, "Customizing the IDE with Object Scripting," explains how to use the new Object Scripting language to write your own IDE commands.

Getting Started

Figure 2.1 shows the IDE's display with an as-yet-unnamed file open in an editor window. As Figure 2.1 shows, new files are initially named something like Noname00.cpp, with 00 automatically incrementing to 99 if you create more than one new, unnamed file in a directory. When you save the file with the *File|Save* or *File|Save as* commands, the IDE prompts you to enter a filename. It's usually best to supply a different name, but for quick tests you can use the default name.

Figure 2.1.
The Borland C++ 5 Integrated Development Environment.

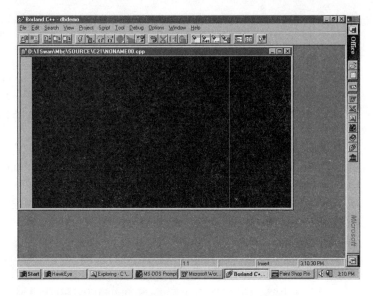

Entering Commands

You probably already know how to select IDE menu items and click SpeedBar buttons to enter commands. If you know your way around Windows, you can learn most IDE commands on your own. If, however, the IDE's operations are foreign to you, you may need to take a Windows tutorial before continuing.

Unlike in past versions, the new IDE's *File|Open* command now opens all types of files. Use this command to open projects, source code files, resource script files, and other text files. Aside from this change, most commands are intuitive and will be familiar if you have used Borland C++ before.

> **TIP**
>
> Use *Options|Environment* to configure the IDE's display and keyboard commands. Then, select Preferences and enable the Environment, Desktop, and Project (and optionally the Editor files) check boxes. These settings preserve your working environment when you exit the IDE so that you can quickly get back to work on a project.

The Bottom Line

Always pay close attention to the IDE's *Status Line* at the bottom of the display. Brief messages, called *hints,* appear from time to time in the space at the left. Move the mouse cursor over a toolbar button for a sample hint. Abbreviated hints also appear in a small yellow box when you move the mouse cursor over a button and wait a second or two.

When you move the mouse inside an editor window or to the IDE desktop, or during typing, the IDE displays other information at the right in the Status Line.

First are the current line and column numbers, separated by a colon. Next is the word *Modified* when the current editor window contains changes that you haven't saved. If all changes are saved, this section in the Status Line is blank.

The next panel tells you the current typing mode—*Insert* to insert text at the cursor position; *Overwrite* to replace text at the cursor. Press the Ins key to toggle between the two modes. Last in the Status Line at far left is the current time. (I really needed another reminder on how late I am on my deadlines.)

Closing the IDE prompts you to save any changes not written to disk, but it's still important to watch for the *Modified* indicator in the Status Line. While developing new programs, you may experience strange and wonderful happenings—or, in less euphemistic terms, the operating system along with your code may crash and burn. If that happens, you could lose any changes you didn't save, so it's always wise to save your files before running untested programs.

Opening Sample Listing Files

You may open any of this book's sample listings ending with the filename extension .cpp. Simply select *File|Open* and browse directories until you find the file you want. This book's sample programs are stored in the Source directory on the CD-ROM, under subdirectories according to chapter (C03, C17, and so on). Copy these directories from the CD-ROM to your hard drive.

Applications that have multiple related files, however, are stored in additional named directories. In those cases, you'll find a *project file* with the extension .ide in the directory. When a file ending with .ide is in a directory, always open it and then use the resulting project manager window to open the project's individual files.

> **TIP**
>
> The Windows Explorer and File Manager simplify browsing and viewing all files in directories. You may want to use these utilities, as I do, instead of the *File|Open* command to open files and projects in the IDE.

Settings Notebooks

Settings Notebooks are interactive dialog boxes that simplify the often confusing task of selecting from the IDE's hundreds of options. You'll come across many different Settings Notebooks as you learn your way around the IDE. All use commands similar to those described here.

For practice using Settings Notebooks, select the *Options\Environment* command to open the dialog displayed in Figure 2.2.

Figure 2.2.
Environment Options dialog.

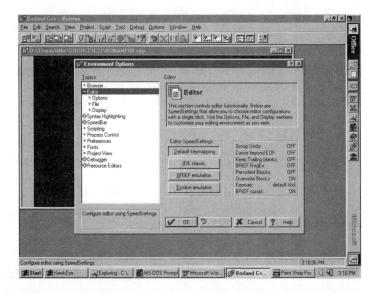

Each Settings Notebook dialog has two main parts. A list of *Topics* appears at left. Individual settings for the selected topic appear at right. The individual settings, collectively called a *page*, may consist of various controls, input fields, buttons, and read-only descriptions. The dialog also has several buttons—*OK* to accept your settings, *Undo Page* to restore this page's original values, *Cancel* to throw away any changed settings, and *Help* for instructions. You can also press Enter to select OK or press Esc to select Cancel.

To view different pages in a Settings Notebook dialog, select a topic. Try selecting Editor, Syntax Highlighting, and SpeedBar now to see the different pages for these topics.

If a topic has a plus sign to its left, additional subtopics are available by single-clicking on the plus symbol. If a topic has a minus sign, all its subtopics are visible. If a topic has a dot, it has no further subtopics. Try selecting the plus sign now for the Editor topic. You should see three subtopics indented under Editor: Options, File, and Display.

In general, subtopics take you deeper into the individual pages for a main topic. Here, for example, with the main Editor topic selected, you can click one of the *Editor SpeedSettings* buttons to choose default configurations for standard (Default keymapping), IDE classic (similar to past IDE key mappings), or Brief and Epsilon emulations. For finer control over these configurations, select an Editor subtopic. For example, the Brief emulation button turns on an underline cursor. If you want a similar cursor with a different configuration, select the Display subtopic and check the box labeled BRIEF Cursor Shapes.

I won't explain all possible options here; that information is in your manuals. And besides, you can probably figure out most options on your own. For safety, however, you might want to enable Editor files, Environment, Desktop, and Project under SpeedBar, Preferences, Auto-Save. This ensures that any changes you make to environment options, project options, files, and desktop windows are automatically saved. If you don't select these options, you must remember to use the *Options|Save* command to save environment, project, and desktop settings. You also have to save changes made to text files, which as I mentioned, is a wise idea before running untested programs.

Speed Menus

A Speed Menu, otherwise known in Windows jargon as a "floating popup menu," makes it easy to select context-sensitive commands. Move the mouse cursor to a window and click the right mouse button to open a Speed Menu of commands you can issue for this window.

For example, open the file Welcome.cpp in the C03 directory. Position the cursor on the header file iostream.h. Move the mouse into the window, click the right mouse button, and then select *Open source* to open the header file. Click the window close buttons to close the files before continuing.

SpeedBar

Called a *toolbar* in many Windows programs, the IDE's SpeedBar offers point-and-click buttons to select various commands. The SpeedBar displays different sets of buttons depending on which window is active. Let the mouse cursor rest (don't click) on a SpeedBar button for a second to see a popup hint that describes the button. Also read the status line for a lengthier description.

> **TIP**
>
> Throughout this book, I suggest various menu commands to give, but it might be faster to issue those commands using the SpeedBar. Try to memorize the buttons for the commands you use most frequently. This will save you a ton of time.

You can also customize the SpeedBar to show buttons for other commands, or you can remove buttons you don't use. The SpeedBar is completely programmable. For practice, add a new button to the SpeedBar by following these steps. The button gives you a point-and-click command to exit the IDE:

1. Select *Options|Environment* to open the Environment Options Settings Notebook.
2. Single-click the plus sign next to the SpeedBar topic. You should see a single subtopic, Customize. Single-click the Customize subtopic to open its settings page. This may take a few seconds the first time you use the command.

3. Select the type of window to view its collection of SpeedBar buttons. For example, choose Desktop to view the SpeedBar displayed when no windows are open in the IDE. In this case, select Desktop now, and then return to this step to add the same button to the Message, Project, and Editor windows.

4. To add the new icon to the SpeedBar, first select a button such as File Save under Active Buttons that you want to appear to the right of the new button. Next, from the Available Buttons list, select a new button such as General Exit. Click the right-facing arrow between the two lists to add the button to the SpeedBar.

5. To change the new button's location, select it and click the up or down arrows below Active Buttons. To add some space between button groups, click Separator.

6. Repeat from step 3 for other SpeedBars; then when you are finished, select OK to close the dialog window and return to normal operation.

Text Editor

The IDE's text editor is easy to use, and you can probably pick up most commands on your own. You can open up to 32 windows in the IDE editor. Each window can display the contents of a different file, or you can display the same file in multiple windows—to view different portions of a file, for example, at the same time. If you open a file this way, you can edit the text in any window. All other windows are automatically updated.

That works because a window is just a *view* of the file's contents. The file's text is stored in a *buffer*. An editor view window shows you, and lets you modify, the text in a buffer.

Another, and perhaps more convenient, way to view different parts of the same file is to divide a window into panes. Do that by clicking the *Split view horizontally* or *Split view vertically* buttons at far right in the SpeedBar. A text editor window must be active. Click inside the divided window to work on and view the text there. To get rid of a pane, click and drag its border to another pane or window boundary. Figure 2.3 shows a sample text editor window divided horizontally.

Consult your printed or online references if you need help with typing commands. For editing and compiling the programs in this book, you probably need no further instruction. If you are familiar with WordStar keys, you can use them in the editor (as you can in all Borland IDEs). You might also want to select Brief or Epsilon emulations, using the Options menu, if you are familiar with those editors. In this book, all commands refer to the IDE's default key mappings.

TIP

To make it easier to perform various operations on multiple text editor windows, use the *Edit/Buffer* list command. For example, open several text files. Select the command and use the resulting dialog box buttons to save, edit, and delete selected buffers. (Deleting a buffer does not delete its associated file; it just removes the buffer from memory.)

Figure 2.3.
An IDE text editor divided horizontally into panes.

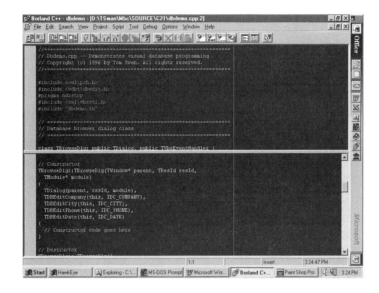

Message Window

When you compile a program, or at other times, the IDE opens a Message window to show any errors, warnings, and other information. As Figure 2.4 shows, this window has Buildtime, Runtime, and Script tabs that show different information. From time to time, you'll see error and warning messages in this window, and you'll find its runtime event history essential in tracking down bugs.

Figure 2.4.
The message window shows information about Buildtime, Runtime, and Script events.

Closing the Message window does not disturb its contents. To get it back, select *View\Message*. Click the right mouse button inside the window for other commands. For example, you can use this menu to save a copy of the window in a text file, which you can print for reference or save for posterity.

How To Compile the Sample Programs

I was going to begin this paragraph with "There's more than one way to skin a cat," but come to think of it, I'm not sure that's true. Besides, I like cats. On the other hand, there have been times when I've wanted to skin my computer alive. Let me count the ways.

So you aren't similarly tempted, following are suggestions for compiling this book's sample programs using DOS, Windows, or a combination of both. First, though, are some notes on common troubles that regularly flow through my email in-box.

When Things Go Wrong...

This book's first and second editions generated a number of letters from readers who reported problems compiling programs. In every case, errors were due to one of the following causes:

- *Improper configuration.* If you did not install Borland C++ 5 in the default C:\BC5 directory, you must modify path names in all project files ending in .ide. Use *Options\Project* to inspect your Directories settings.

- *Improper path.* You must place C:\BC5\bin on the system PATH. Insert a PATH statement such as the following in your Autoexec.bat file (which you can edit using the IDE). You can, of course, add other path names. For best results, let the BC5 installation program revise Autoexec.bat for you. For database development, you also need the C:\Iblocal\bin and C:\Idapi directories, and optionally C:\Interbas\bin, on the path.

  ```
  PATH=C:\Windows;C:\Windows\command;C:\Dos;C:\BC5\bin
  ```

- *Too many compilers.* It is difficult, if not impossible, to configure your system for more than one compiler at a time. All C and C++ compilers use similarly named files that differ internally, and each compiler *must* be able to locate its own files. Never place more than one C or C++ compiler's directories on your system PATH. Better still, never install more than one C or C++ compiler on the same drive partition. Beware of environment variables created with SET commands that can cause directory conflicts.

- *An improper version.* You must use Borland C++ 5 with this book's sample programs. You might be able to use another compiler or version, but I offer no guarantees on that score. Borland C++ 5 includes many features that have been recently added to the C++ language and to various libraries. Another compiler, even one sold by Borland, may not recognize those same features.

- *Attempting to run a non-program file.* Every file is not a program. Some programs consist of multiple files, which the linker combines to create a finished code file. You can't open any file at random and create a working program. Carefully follow instructions here and in the listings to compile and run the sample programs printed in this book and provided on the CD-ROM.

Compiling Under Windows

You can use Windows to compile all programs in Chapter 3's introduction to C++ and also in Part II's C++ tutorials. You can also use Windows to compile many single-file sample programs in other chapters. Follow these steps to compile programs as EasyWin applications that display output in a graphical window:

1. Use *File|Open* to open the program's source code file, ending in .cpp. Try this now by opening Welcome.cpp in the C03 directory.

2. Open a Speed Menu by pointing the mouse cursor to the editor window and single-clicking the right mouse button. Select the TargetExpert command.

3. Select the EasyWin target type. The platform should be Windows 3.x (16), and the target model should be Large (these are the default settings). Select the OK button to close the TargetExpert dialog.

4. Select *Options|Project* and choose the *Linker, General* topic. Enter 3.10 into the Subsystem version input box. This is the default setting. Select OK to close the Project Options dialog.

5. Press Ctrl+F9 to compile and run the example. Close the output window when its title indicates the program is "inactive." Alternatively, press F9 or Alt+F9 to compile (or select the *Project|Make all* command), and then run the resulting .exe code file using the Windows Explorer or File Manager.

6. If you receive a "fixup" error, or if compilation fails for another reason, use the *Project|Build all* command instead of the preceding step. This compiles the entire program from scratch, which might be necessary if you previously attempted to compile using a different code-file target.

NOTE

Only standard C and C++ programs can be run as EasyWin applications. Programs that include certain library files, or that require a DOS text-mode display (the CD-ROM's BGI graphics examples from the second edition, for instance), are incompatible with EasyWin. You must compile these programs using a suitable target type—for example, Application with a Platform set to DOS (Standard). Windows programs should of course be targeted as Applications with the Platform set to Win32 or another Windows operating system.

Compiling Under DOS

You may compile all programs in this book from a DOS prompt. If you are using Windows 95, you may also run all programs from DOS, even the Windows examples. Of course, if you are not running Windows, you can run only the simpler programs in this book that use standard input and output.

Even so, for the C++ introduction in the next chapter and for the chapters in Part II, you might find the going easier by compiling and running programs from DOS and viewing output on a full-screen text display. Also use the following steps if you experience trouble compiling programs as EasyWin targets. (Remember first, however, to try the *Build all* command.)

1. Get to a DOS prompt. You can quit Windows (or use the Windows 95 Shutdown command to restart in DOS), or you can open a DOS-prompt window under Microsoft Windows (my preferred method).
2. Change to the appropriate directory such as Source\C03, which you copied from the CD-ROM.
3. Enter **bcc welcome** or specify another filename. You don't have to type the .cpp filename extension but it doesn't hurt if you do. If this fails, check your system path.
4. Type **welcome** to run the resulting .exe code file.
5. If you experience trouble, you may have attempted to compile only one file from a multiple-file project. In such cases, use the supplied Makefile in the directory to compile—simply type **make** and stand back.

NOTE

If the preceding steps fail, edit the path names in the Rootdir.inc file, found in the Source directory, which you must copy from the CD-ROM to your hard drive. If you still have trouble, check that no files are set to read-only, which may happen when copying from the CD-ROM. Type the command `attrib -r *.* /s` to turn off the read-only attributes.

Compiling Under Windows for DOS

You may use the Windows IDE to compile DOS applications, which you may then run either from DOS or Windows. This method allows you full use of the IDE editor and other facilities, but makes it easy to view the output of programs that simply display a line or two of text in the course of illustrating a programming technique. Follow these steps:

1. Use *File|Open* to open the program's source code file, ending in .cpp.
2. Open a SpeedMenu by pointing the mouse cursor at the editor window and single-clicking the right mouse button. Select the TargetExpert command.

3. Select the Application target type. The Platform should be DOS (Standard), and the Target Model should be Large. Select the OK button to close the TargetExpert dialog.

4. Press F9 to compile and link the program, creating an executable code file ending with .exe. You can also use the Project menu's *Make all* or *Build all* commands.

5. Open a DOS prompt window and change to the directory that contains the compiled and linked .exe code file. Type the program name to run it. Alternatively, you can run DOS programs from the Windows File Manager or Windows 95 Explorer, but because many sample programs in this book merely display something and end, the output window might close before you have a chance to see it. Running programs from a DOS prompt avoids this problem.

> **NOTE**
>
> As with EasyWin applications, if you experience troubles compiling, linking, or running applications, the cause may be an earlier attempt to compile the program as a different target. Use *Project|Build all* before looking for other causes.

Compiling Under DOS for Windows

DOS prompt lovers (they're the ones who speak in Grep expressions at parties) may want to compile all programs, including the Windows samples, under DOS. These steps are the simplest of all:

1. Change to the chapter or project directory.

2. Type **make**.

3. Run the resulting .exe code file by typing its name, or if you are not running Windows 95 and it's a Windows program, run the file by using the File Manager or Explorer.

> **NOTE**
>
> If the preceding steps fail, check the path names in the Source\Rootdir.inc.

Compiling Projects

If a directory has a project file ending with .ide, open that file using the *File|Open* command. A project lists multiple files that are required to create some of the book's sample programs (all the Windows examples, for instance). If you find a project file in a directory, use these steps to compile the program:

1. Close any open windows.

2. Select the *Project|Open project* command to open the .ide project file. (You may also use *File|Open*.) You should see the project window. If not, select *View|Project*.

3. Press F9 to compile, or use the Project menu's *Make all* or *Build all* commands.

4. You can run Windows programs directly from the IDE (press Ctrl+F9), or by selecting the compiled .exe code file with the File Manager or the Windows 95 Explorer.

TIP

If you automatically save the desktop for a project with all windows closed, the next time you open that project, all of its windows, including the Project window, will be invisible. If you open a project file and nothing seems to happen, use *View|Project* to bring the Project window back into view. You can then open individual files in the project by double-clicking their names.

The Art and Science of Debugging

Borland C++ 5 provides four debuggers that can help you locate the causes of program errors. A debugger can halt programs at a specific instruction, called a *breakpoint*, and it can view the values of variables in memory. You can also use a debugger to perform numerous other diagnostic operations such as single stepping through a program's instructions and viewing the processor code that the compiler generates. In addition, a debugger makes a marvelous tool for learning how programs work. The four debuggers supplied with Borland C++ 5 are as follows:

- *Integrated debugger.* When you run a program from the IDE, it actually runs under the control of the integrated debugger. You can also use this debugger to single step instructions, set breakpoints, and view variables.

- *Turbo Debugger for DOS.* Use this debugger from a DOS prompt to debug DOS applications.

- *Turbo Debugger for Windows.* Use this debugger to debug 16-bit Windows programs.

- *Turbo Debugger for Win32.* Use this debugger to debug 32-bit Windows programs for Windows 95 and NT.

Don't wait for me to suggest using the integrated debugger. Use these commands to investigate most of the tutorial programs in this book.

All four debuggers understand similar commands. The integrated debugger has fewer features than the other three stand-alone versions, but it is still useful for most debugging chores. Following are some suggestions that will help you get started.

Preparing To Debug

After loading a program or project, select the *Options|Project* command and check that the following two settings are enabled. These check boxes insert debugging information into compiled code files, which the debugger uses to perform its commands. Technically, you can debug programs without debugging information, but you won't be able to track source code lines or view structures, so for all practical purposes, you must enable these options before debugging:

- *Compiler, Debugging.* Enable the *Debug information in OBJs* check box. This inserts debugging information into intermediate .obj (object code) files that the compiler creates.
- *Linker, General.* Enable the *Include debug information* check box. This copies debugging information from .obj files to the final .exe code file.

The reason there are two settings is to permit you to add debugging information to only some .obj code files. This is especially valuable in very large applications, where the amount of debugging information uses too much memory, possibly even preventing loading into the debugger.

> **TIP**
>
> Turn off the second option to exclude debugging information from your production .exe code files. This will save disk space. Alternatively, run your finished code files through the DOS utility Tdstrip, which strips debugging information from code files.

Single Stepping

Normally, programs operate at full speed—far too fast to inspect the program's individual instructions. *Single stepping* a program executes its instructions one at a time so you can learn exactly what each instruction does. There are two single-stepping commands:

- Press F8 to *step over* one instruction. *Stepping over* means to execute an instruction and stop.
- Press F7 to *step into* an instruction and stop. If that instruction calls a function, the program halts at the first instruction inside that function.

The first time you press F7 or F8, the IDE compiles the program in the active window if necessary. This creates the executable code file and runs the program. After this, pressing F7 or F8 again reuses the compiled code.

While single stepping, your application is running under control of the debugger, but is paused. Press Alt+Tab to switch to the program's window—if it has become visible, that is. During debugging, the mouse cursor becomes a Stop sign, indicating that this program is halted in progress.

Always try to run programs to completion (press Ctrl+F9 while viewing the application in the IDE, and F9 in the stand-alone debuggers). If an error prevents running a program to its end, try the Reset and Terminate commands in the Debug menu to recover. You may still leave some objects suspended in memory, which won't be recovered until next time you reboot—but that's life in software development.

Inspecting Data

Use a debugger to inspect the values of data, and to view structures and objects. Think of this feature as a kind of microscope that you can use to peer into memory and view values that belong to programs.

The stand-alone debuggers have more extensive inspection capabilities, but you can view many variables and structures effectively in the integrated debugger. Select the Add watch command from the Debug menu and enter a variable name in the Expression input box. When you single step and run the program, the Watches window shows the variable's value.

> **TIP**
>
> I often use the Watches window to view the results of test functions and other processes rather than write output statements. For example, some of the programs in this book produce no on-screen output, but you can use the Watches window to view their variables and you can single step through the code to better understand how it works.

Setting Breakpoints

A *breakpoint* is a temporary stopping place in a program. After setting a breakpoint, you can run a program at full speed. The debugger halts execution at the breakpoint, just *before* executing that marked instruction. You can then single step the program and view its data from this strategic location.

There are several ways to set a breakpoint. In the integrated debugger, click the left mouse button in the gray area to the left of a source code line. A red dot appears to remind you that a breakpoint is set on this line.

In a stand-alone debugger, move the flashing text cursor to a source code line and press F2. This toggles a breakpoint on and off, shown by highlighting the entire line in red.

In either case, with a breakpoint set, you can run the program by pressing F9. When execution reaches the breakpoint, the debugger halts the program so that you can inspect variables or begin single stepping from that point.

Summary

- The sensational Borland C++ 5 IDE gives you a highly sophisticated programming environment. You can use the IDE to write, compile, and debug DOS and Windows applications of many different kinds.

- Main features in the IDE include TargetExpert for selecting a program's output target. Settings Notebooks simplify option selection. Speed Menus (displayed by clicking the right mouse button) and a SpeedBar of buttons offer alternative methods for choosing among IDE commands and operations.

- The IDE's text editor is capable of emulating the popular Brief and Epsilon programming editors.

- Four debuggers, one integrated into the IDE and three stand-alone models, help you explore applications by single stepping program statements, viewing variables, and setting breakpoints. A debugger is useful, not only for tracking down the source of program errors, but also for learning how programs operate.

3

CHAPTER

Introducing C++ Programming

Many programmers think of C++ as an object-oriented version of C, but that's not an entirely accurate description. Although the major contribution of C++ is the class—a special kind of structure that can have data and function members—C++ is unique in many other, non-object-oriented, ways. In the next chapter, "Programming with Classes," you explore classes and learn how to use them for object-oriented programming. In this chapter, you tour other less profound, but no less important, features that make C++ special.

The language's name, C++ (pronounced "C plus plus"), is something of a pun—a play on the increment operator (++). The C++ language is literally "one step beyond C." Early on, C++ was known as "C with Classes," but the modern name C++ quickly won popularity. It is the perfect title for this enhanced flavor of C.

The inventor of C++, Bjarne Stroustrup, calls the language "a better C." In addition to the class, C++ adds to ANSI C several new keywords and operators, inline and overloaded functions, overloaded operators, new memory management techniques, and other odds and ends. In every instance, these C++ features were designed to correct an oversight or inconsistency in C, or to add new tools for building solid code. If C is an ice cream cone, C++ is a fudge sundae.

Since the humble beginnings of C++ in the early 1980s at AT&T Bell Laboratories, some of the language's unique features have spilled back into ANSI C, thus muddying the waters that divide C++ from its direct ancestor, Classic C. Today, ANSI C and C++ are as close as kissing cousins, and most ANSI C programs are compatible with C++. Many of C++'s more advanced features, however, such as classes, are not found in ANSI C.

Anatomy of a C++ Program

Most of what you know about C programming applies to C++. C and C++ programs look pretty much the same. They use nearly identical syntax, as well as the same kinds of loops, data types, pointers, structures, and other elements.

Because the Borland C++ compiler can tackle ANSI C and C++ programs, you must tell the compiler which of these languages you intend to use. The easiest way to fulfill this requirement for C++ programs is to name your source code files with the extension .cpp rather than .c. From a DOS prompt, the command `bcc file.c` compiles file.c as an ANSI C program. The command `bcc file.cpp` compiles file.cpp as a C++ program. Because .cpp is the Borland C++ default file extension, the commands `bcc file` and `bcc file.cpp` give the same results. From the IDE, to compile C++ programs, save them with the extension .cpp and compile normally.

> **NOTE**
>
> You can also use the -P option to force Borland C++ to compile in C++ mode. Naming your source files with .cpp is simpler, however, and helps to distinguish C program files from those that use C++ features.

Listing 3.1, Welcome.Cpp, is one of the simplest C++ programs in this book. Even so, it demonstrates several important techniques. Choose one of the compilation methods in the sidebar. You can use these same methods to compile all programs in this chapter.

Listing 3.1. Welcome.Cpp (A simple C++ program).

```
//===============================================================
// Welcome.cpp -- A simple C++ program
// To compile:
//   bcc welcome
// To run:
//   welcome
// Copyright (c) 1996 by Tom Swan. All rights reserved.
//===============================================================

#include <iostream.h>

void main()
{
  cout << "Welcome to Borland C++ 5 programming!\n";
}
```

COMPILATION METHODS

From a DOS prompt, enter `bcc welcome` to compile and link the source code file and create Welcome.exe. Run the program by typing its name.

To compile all programs in this chapter, from a DOS prompt change to the C03 directory and enter `make`. If you receive errors, edit the path in Source\Rootdir.inc, and then try again.

For Windows from the IDE, right-click the mouse and select TargetExpert. Choose the EasyWin Target Type, and click OK. Select *Options/Project,* and under *Linker,General,* enter 3.10 in the Subsystem version input box. Click OK. Press Ctrl+F9 to compile and run. If this produces an error, select *Project/Build all* and then run by pressing Ctrl+F9.

For DOS from the IDE, right-click the mouse and select TargetExpert. Choose the Application Target Type, and set Platform to DOS (Standard) and Target Model to Large. Select *Project/Make all* to compile. If this produces an error, select *Project/Build all*. Get to a DOS prompt, change to the C03 directory, and run the program by typing its name.

Welcome.cpp begins with an `include` statement that reads the iostream.h header file. This enables stream input and output, the rough equivalent in C++ of standard I/O as provided by including the stdio.h header in a C program. (You can include both of these headers if necessary.) I'll discuss stream I/O at length eventually, but for now, we need only some simple input and output capabilities for demonstration purposes.

For example, in function main, a stream-output statement displays a line of text using the iostream library's cout ("character out") standard output stream object. To send information

33

to a destination (in this case, to the display), iostream uses the C++ "put to" operator <<. Think of << as an arrow that tosses some data, such as the literal string in the sample program, to an I/O stream object, such as cout.

You can also write multipart iostream statements. If firstName and lastName are char * pointers to strings, the statement

```
cout << lastName << ", " << firstName << endl;
```

writes the two names, last name first, separating the two strings with a comma and ending with a new line. Writing the endl *manipulator* starts a new output line. You can do the same by writing the string "\n" or the character '\n'. Some programmers prefer to write each section of a multipart iostream on a separate line. Despite appearances, the following is one statement, not four:

```
cout << lastName
<< ", "
<< firstName
<< endl;
```

An iostream statement can output a wide variety of data types, including all built-in types such as int, long, and double, and also types of your own making. If count is type long, the statement

```
cout << "Count == " << count << endl;
```

displays a string followed by count's value and a new line.

> **NOTE**
>
> You may mix stdio and iostream techniques, and you may still use printf and other standard-library functions in C++ programs. However, as you'll learn in Part II, iostreams can be extended to accommodate new data types. Function printf can handle only built-in types, and its output formats, while extensive, are not programmable.

Before turning to more interesting topics, Welcome.cpp demonstrates another important, and somewhat controversial, subject: function main's return type. In the listing, main returns void, which as you know, means "no value." You may also declare main with no return type, in which case its type defaults to int:

```
main()
{
...
  return 0;
}
```

In that case, you must add a return statement or you'll receive the following warning from the compiler. Warnings are not fatal errors, and the program still compiles and runs; however, the results might be unexpected, and you should never ignore compiler warnings such as this:

Function should return a value in function main()

I prefer never to rely on default features (another compiler might change them), so if you need a return value from main, it's better to declare one explicitly:

```
int main()
{
...
  return 0;
}
```

Again, the return statement is needed to prevent a warning. However, in this book, unless a return value is needed, I'll use void for main's return type, which eliminates the unnecessary return statement and does not produce a warning:

```
void main()
{
...
}
```

Be aware that this version of main potentially returns a value at random to the operating system; but in Borland C++, this value is always zero.

Comparing C and C++

Before beginning to learn about the features of C++, you need to memorize a few rules that alter some of the facts you know about C. Following are some key differences between C and C++:

- C and C++ generally use the same syntax, operators, expressions, built-in data types, structures, arrays, unions, loops, functions, and pointers. These fundamental elements are used identically in both languages.
- C++ has several new reserved keywords, listed in Table 3.1. Words marked with an asterisk are specific to C++ and are not available in C. See Appendix E for a complete list of reserved words that includes other symbols reserved specifically by Borland C++.

Table 3.1. C and C++ keywords.

asm	auto	bool*	break	case	catch*
char	class*	const	continue	default	delete*
do	double	else	enum	explicit*	extern
false*	float	for	friend*	goto	if
inline*	int	long	mutable*	namespace	new*
operator*	private*	protected*	public*	register	return
short	signed	sizeof	static	struct	switch
template*	this*	throw*	true*	try*	typedef
typename	union	unsigned	using	virtual*	void
volatile*	while				

- C++ also has a few operators that are not found in C. You've already seen one of these, the put-to operator <<. Eventually, you'll meet them all in this chapter and in Part II. See Appendix D for a complete list of C++ operators.

- C++ requires all functions to have formal prototypes. C encourages, but does not require, function prototypes.

- Type checking in expressions is more strictly performed by C++. In general, values in expressions must be of the same types, or they must be readily convertible to appropriate types. Where C gives an incompatible type warning, C++ tends to generate a compiler error. However, ANSI C and ANSI C++ are much closer in their type-checking rules than are Classic C and C++.

- The need for `typedef` declarations is greatly reduced in C++. You can declare a `struct` like

```
struct mystruct {
...
};
```

and then declare variables such as `mystruct x;`. To do the same in ANSI C, you need to write `struct mystruct x;`, or you need to use a `typedef` alias for `struct mystruct`.

- In C++, a `char` is an 8-bit byte. In C, a `char`'s size is not defined, although in Borland C++, chars are *always* 8 bits long.

- In C, character constants are type `int`, and the expression `sizeof('X')` equals `sizeof(int)`. In C++, character constants are type `char`, and the expression `sizeof('X')` equals `sizeof(char)`.

- C++ supports object-oriented programming, using the `class`, an enhanced `struct` that encapsulates data and code declarations and supports the concept of inheritance (one class derived from another).

- C++ supports additional features such as templates (a kind of class schematic) and object-oriented exception handling for robust error handling.

- C++ now provides a standard template library (STL) along with a string template. These features help programmers write code that is compatible with other ANSI C++ compilers.

C++ Comments

C++ supplements C comments with a new comment style, resurrected from the Classic C predecessor language, BCPL. In a C++ program, a double slash // begins a comment. The compiler ignores every character from // to the end of the line. In C, the comment

```
/* This is a comment */
```

can also be written in C++ as

```
// This is a comment
```

The C comment, which you can use in C++ programs, requires two delimiters: /* to begin the comment and */ to end it. The C++ comment requires only one // symbol; it ends at the end of the line. C comments may continue for two or more lines; C++ comments occupy single lines only. Either kind of comment may come at the end of a line. In C, you can add a comment to a statement like this:

```
count++;  /* Increment count */
```

In C++, that line might also be written

```
count++;  // Increment count
```

Only C comments may be embedded in a statement. The following is a valid (though confusing) C or C++ statement:

```
result = count /* Embedded comment */ + 100;
```

However, the statement

```
result = count // Embedded comment??? + 100;
```

causes a syntax error because C++ comments extend to the end of the line, and they cannot be embedded inside statements.

NOTE

By the way, throughout this book, I use three question marks in a C++ comment (//???) to indicate a questionable technique or to point out a statement that will not compile due to an error.

Mixing Comment Styles

You may mix C and C++ comments in the same program. Listing 3.2, Comments.Cpp, shows several examples.

Listing 3.2. Comments.Cpp (Compares C and C++ comment styles).

```
//==============================================================
// Comments.cpp -- Compares C and C++ comment styles
// To compile:
//    bcc comments
// To run:
//    comments
// Copyright (c) 1996 by Tom Swan. All rights reserved.
//==============================================================

#include <iostream.h>
```

continues

Listing 3.2. continued

```
// ------------------------------------------
// Author   : Tom Duck
// Company  : Ugly Duckling Software (very Ltd)
// Revision : v2.0 and counting
// ------------------------------------------

void main()
{
  cout << "A Brief C++ Commentary\n";  // Display title
  cout << "\n";  // Display blank line under title

/* This paragraph demonstrates that C-style
comments can occupy more than one line.
C++ comments are restricted to single lines. */

  cout << "// This is not a comment.\n\n";  // This is a comment
  cout << "/* This also is not a comment.*/ \n\n";
  cout /* This is a comment. */ << "This text is displayed.\n";
}
```

Comments.cpp uses C++ comments for a small information header that describes the program. Many programmers like to "sign" their source listings with a uniquely styled header, which might list facts about the program, bug repairs, version numbers, modification dates, and so on.

The program shows the classic way to end C++ statements with explanatory comments. The three-line comment in the middle of the program uses C-style comment delimiters because C++ comments are single lines only. Of course, you could begin each of the three lines with the C++ delimiter //.

Comments of any style cannot occur in the middle of character strings. Although the last statement in the program demonstrates that C-style comments may be embedded inside statements, this commenting style is more confusing than helpful, and is best avoided.

Debugging with Comments

You can nest C++ comments inside C comments, a fact that leads to a useful debugging trick. Consider this fragment:

```
char buffer[128];          // Input buffer
gets(buffer);              // Get string into buffer
cout << endl;              // Start new display line
cout << buffer << endl;    // Display buffer and start new line
```

Suppose these statements do not produce the expected results, and you decide to test what happens if you delete the third statement, which begins a new line before displaying buffer. Rather than delete the line, you can remove its effect by turning it into a C-style comment:

```
char buffer[128];       // Input buffer
gets(buffer);           // Get string into buffer
/*
cout << endl;           // Start new display line
*/
cout << buffer << endl; // Display buffer and start new line
```

The `/*` and `*/` brackets "comment out" the surrounded statement. The compiler ignores all characters between the brackets, including the C++ comment at the end of the line. You can now recompile and run the temporarily modified program. If you decide to restore the original statement, simply delete the C comment delimiters. This trick is especially useful for commenting out multiple-statement blocks.

Introducing I/O Streams

A few sample programs demonstrate the power of the C++ iostream library. As in C, input and output in C++ is not part of the language but is provided by external library functions. This means programmers writing code for embedded systems or special-purpose computers are free to devise their own I/O functions and techniques—one of the reasons C and C++ are popular for low-level programming tasks. Most programmers, however, may as well take advantage of the standard libraries. These libraries have been tweaked to the hilt by superb software specialists, and it would be difficult to outdo their efforts.

An iostream object behaves much like the standard input and output file streams you have used in C programs. However, the `cout` (character out) and `cin` (character in) streams have many unique capabilities. To display a character `c`, you can write

```
cout << c;
```

or you can write

```
cout.put(c);
```

Function `put` is a *member function* of `cout`—a new concept that you'll encounter frequently in the coming chapters. To call a member function, separate it from `cout` with a period, which is similar to the dot notation used to access `struct` members. The `cout` stream is an instance of a *class,* also called a *class object,* which can have associated functions such as `put`. (The next chapter, "Programming with Classes," covers this notion in greater depth.) You must call member functions in reference to an object such as `cout`. Alone, the statement

```
put(c);  // ???
```

attempts to call a separate `put` function. The statement

```
cout.put(c);
```

calls the `put` function that *belongs* to `cout`.

To read a character from the standard input, use the input stream `cin` along with the >> (get from) operator. The statement

```
cin >> c;
```

reads one character from the standard input and assigns that character to c. You also can call `cin`'s `get` member function to do the same:

```
cin.get(c);
```

As with standard I/O, a C++ iostream uses the system's standard input and output files, and can be used to write filter programs. Listing 3.3, Filter.cpp, demonstrates the basic technique. Because Windows doesn't support the concept of a filter, you must compile Filter.cpp as a DOS application and run it from a DOS prompt.

Listing 3.3. Filter.cpp (A basic C++ iostream filter).

```
//=================================================================
// Filter.cpp -- A basic C++ iostream filter
// To compile:
//   bcc filter
// To run:
//   filter <filter.cpp
// Copyright (c) 1996 by Tom Swan. All rights reserved.
//=================================================================

#include <iostream.h>

void main()
{
  char c;

  while (cin.get(c))
    cout.put(c);
}
```

NOTE

If Filter seems to hang, it's probably expecting input from the console. Press Ctrl+Z and Enter, the DOS end-file code, to exit the program.

Run Filter as you do other DOS filters, redirecting I/O with less-than and greater-than symbols. For example, to display the program's own source code file, enter this command:

```
filter <filter.cpp
```

To send console input to a printer, enter

```
filter >prn
```

To print a file, enter

```
filter <filename.ext >prn
```

Filter calls `cin.get(c)` to obtain a character. The expression `cin.get(c)` returns an `int` value or null upon reaching the end of the input source. The program passes every character from the source to the standard output using the expression `cout.put(c)`.

Reading Built-In Types

Reading and writing multiple data types are main attractions under the big tent of the C++ iostream library. Listing 3.4, Getval.cpp, tames a few iostream statements into reading integer and floating-point values. Compile and run the program as an EasyWin application in Windows, or as a DOS program, and then enter values as prompted. Try entering mistakes (XXX rather than a floating-point value, for example) to see how the program handles errors.

Listing 3.4. Getval.cpp (Uses iostreams to read built-in types).

```
//================================================================
// Getval -- Uses iostreams to read built-in types
// To compile:
//   bcc getval
// To run:
//   getval
// Copyright (c) 1996 by Tom Swan. All rights reserved.
//================================================================

#include <iostream.h>
#include <stdlib.h>

void test(void);

void main()
{
  double fp;  // A floating point value
  long k;      // A long int value

  cout << "Enter a floating point value: ";
  cin >> fp;
  test();
  cout << "Value entered is: " << fp << endl;
  cout << "Enter an integer value: ";
  cin >> k;
  test();
  cout << "Value entered is: " << k << endl;
}

void test(void)
{
  if (!cin.good()) {
    cout << "Error detected";
    exit(1);
  }
}
```

Function `main` prompts for a floating-point value, read by an iostream input statement into a `double` variable `fp`. A similar input statement reads an integer. Unlike standard I/O, which requires you to specify data types in `scanf` statements or to call functions that can read and convert specific types, iostreams automatically detect the types of variables used in I/O statements. Because you don't have to specify the data type in advance, you can't make a data-type selection mistake as you can with standard I/O. It's very hard in C++ to input data into the wrong kind of variable!

Calls to local function `test` demonstrate another important quality of iostreams. The `test` function examines `cin.good`, a member function that returns true if no unresolved errors exist for the specified stream. Use `cout.good` to do the same for output streams. In the sample program, if `cin.good` is false, the function displays a message and halts the program by calling `exit`.

You don't have to halt a program upon detecting an error. To clear a pending error, use a statement such as

```
cin.clear();
```

Reading Character Strings

You have learned how iostreams can output character strings. For example, the following declaration assigns to a `char` pointer `s` the address of a literal string:

```
char *s = "Gently down the iostream";
```

After that, this statement sends the string `"Gently down the iostream"` on its way to the system's standard output, usually the display:

```
cout << s;
```

To read a string, reverse the process using the `cin` input stream identifier and the `>>` ("put to") operator:

```
char buffer[128];   // Declare string buffer
cin >> buffer;      // ???
```

This works, but it poses a hidden danger: If the user enters more than 127 characters, the input statement overwrites the end of the buffer, possibly destroying code or data after the array. *Statements like this might crash your system!*

Fortunately, there is a safer way to enter strings, as demonstrated by Listing 3.5, Getstr.cpp. Compile and run the program, and then enter a string longer than 24 characters, which is safely truncated to fit in the program's string buffer.

Listing 3.5. Getstr.cpp (Uses iostreams to safely read character strings).

```
//=================================================================
// Getstr.cpp -- Uses iostreams to safely read character strings
// To compile:
//    bcc getstr
```

```
// To run:
//   getstr
// Copyright (c) 1996 by Tom Swan. All rights reserved.
//=============================================================

#include <iostream.h>

void main()
{
  char s[25];
  char c;

  cout << "Enter a 24-char string safely: \n";
  cin.get(s, 25, '\n');
  cout << "You entered: " << s << endl;
  if (cin.get(c) && c != '\n')
    cout << "Maximum line length reached\n";
}
```

The second statement in main shows the safe way to read strings with iostream statements. Call member function `cin.get` with three arguments:

- The destination address of a char array. The resulting string read into this array is null-terminated.

- The size of the array in bytes.

- The character that, when typed, should end input. If not supplied, this character defaults to `'\n'`.

Reading input as shown here is safe as long as you correctly specify the size of the destination buffer. However, one problem remains. The newline or other character that ends input is left in the stream and must be read by another `cin.get` statement as shown by the final `if` statement. If `cin.get` does not read a newline character, input has been truncated—a fact that may be important for some programs to determine.

The problem of a leftover newline character can be solved differently by calling a member function, `cin.getline`. To read a 24-character string into a 25-byte buffer (leaving one byte for the null terminator), use these statements:

```
char buffer[25];
cin.getline(buffer, 25);
```

Writing Values

In general, you can write any kind of variable in an output stream statement. For a variable v, regardless of type, the statement

```
cout << v;
```

should write something reasonable to the system's standard output. The exact form of some kinds of data may not be as you expect, and this advice does not apply to structures or arrays.

However, you can display the values of pointers. Given a pointer declared as int *p (or as another pointer type), the statement

```
cout << p;
```

displays p's value as a long integer. This may be useful for debugging, but it's probably not a good idea to expect similar results with all C++ compilers and operating systems.

Formatting iostream Output

An iostream understands a variety of output formatting commands. Listing 3.6, Convert.cpp, shows how to use three output stream identifiers—dec, hex, and oct—to write integer values in decimal, hexadecimal, and octal formats.

Listing 3.6. Convert.cpp (Uses iostreams to display formatted output).

```
//================================================================
// Convert.cpp -- Uses iostreams to display formatted output
// To compile:
//    bcc convert
// To run:
//    convert
// Copyright (c) 1996 by Tom Swan. All rights reserved.
//================================================================

#include <iostream.h>
#include <stdlib.h>

#define SIZE 35

void main()
{
  int value;
  char s[SIZE];

  cout << "Value? ";
  cin.get(s, SIZE, '\n');
  value = atoi(s);
  cout << "Decimal=" << dec << value
    << "  Hexadecimal=0x" << hex << value
    << "  Octal=0" << oct << value << endl;
}
```

The final statement in main is a single output stream statement with many parts. Some of those parts are literal strings. Others write an int variable value. Just before writing that value, the identifiers dec, hex, and oct modify the output stream's current format, changing the result. On screen, the program displays output such as

```
Value? 123
Decimal=123  Hexadecimal=0x7b  Octal=0173
```

You can also specify output width by calling cout.width(n), where n is the number of columns you want. For example, to have your output right-justified in 15 columns, use programming such as

```
int value = 1234;   // Value to be formatted
cout.width(15);     // Specify 15-character column
cout << value;      // Output value in 15 columns
```

It may not always be convenient to use iostream formatting. Complex iostream statements might be difficult to read. Judging from published listings, expert C++ programmers prefer a mix of standard C and C++ formatting methods. Listing 3.7, Convert2.cpp, shows a typical case, and produces the same output as Convert.cpp.

Listing 3.7. Convert2.cpp (Uses sprintf to prepare formatted output).

```
//==============================================================
// Convert2.cpp -- Uses sprintf to prepare formatted output
// To compile:
//    bcc convert2
// To run:
//    convert2
// Copyright (c) 1996 by Tom Swan. All rights reserved.
//==============================================================

#include <iostream.h>
#include <stdio.h>
#include <stdlib.h>

#define SIZE 35

void main()
{
  int value;
  char s[SIZE];
  char buffer[80];

  cout << "Value? ";
  cin.get(s, SIZE, '\n');
  value = atoi(s);
  sprintf(buffer, "Decimal=%d  Hexadecimal=%#x  Octal=%#o\n",
    value, value, value);
  cout << buffer;
}
```

The complex output stream statement from Convert.cpp is replaced by a call to sprintf. The sprintf function, prototyped in stdlib.h, prepares a character string with values formatted according to the same rules for printf and related functions. A literal string specifies %d (decimal), %#x (hexadecimal), and %#o (octal) formats to be inserted at these locations in the output buffer. A single output stream statement writes the completed string to the system's standard output.

Which is the better method? It depends on your needs, and there's no single right answer. However, the `printf` family of formatting functions are so handy, I prefer to use them to format string buffers for writing in output stream statements rather than use the pure C++ approach.

Scope and Variable Definitions

Scope ambiguities are always a headache. Here's what you can do to resolve them. For example, given a global variable `int count`, a function can declare a local variable of that same name without producing an error:

```
int count;    // Global variable
void AnyFunction()
{
  int count;  // Local variable
...
}
```

The local `count`'s scope extends to its declaring function. In that function, local `count` effectively hides the global variable of the same name. In C++, you can use the scope resolution operator, `::`, to unhide the global name. Writing the above function as follows assigns 1234 to the local count and 4321 to the global count:

```
int count;    // Global variable
void AnyFunction()
{
int count;       // Local variable
count = 1234;    // Assign value to local count
::count = 4321;  // Assign value to global count
}
```

The expression `::count` instructs C++ to refer to the count in the outer scope rather than the count in the local scope (see Figure 3.1).

Figure 3.1.

The scope resolution operator can unhide a global variable.

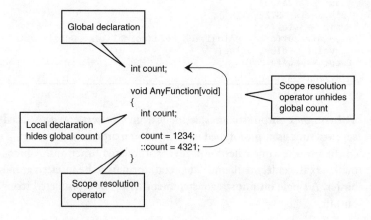

Listing 3.8, Scope.cpp, shows how to use the C++ scope resolution operator. This listing also illustrates a related concept: C++ declarations may appear anywhere inside a statement block, not only globally or at the beginning of a function as in C. You must, however, declare variables before you can use them.

Listing 3.8. Scope.cpp (Demonstrates scope resolution operator, ::).

```
//=================================================================
// Scope.cpp -- Demonstrates scope resolution operator (::)
// To compile:
//   bcc scope
// To run:
//   scope
// Copyright (c) 1996 by Tom Swan. All rights reserved.
//=================================================================

#include <iostream.h>

int k = 100;      // Global variable

void main()
{
  int i = 200;   // Local variable

  cout << "Global k == " << k << endl;
  cout << "Local i  == " << i << endl;
  {
    int k = 300;
    cout << "Local k  == " << k << endl;
    cout << "Global k == " << ::k << endl;
  }
}
```

Running Scope produces the following output:

```
Global k == 100
Local i  == 200
Local k  == 300
Global k == 100
```

A global variable k is initialized to 100. Variable i, local to main, is assigned the value 200. Two output statements display the values of k and i. There's no need to use the C++ scope resolution operator because there is only one k declared at this point.

Braces at the end of main form a new, nested statement block. Usually, such blocks belong to a control structure such as if or while, but technically, you may nest statement blocks as shown here, though the technique is of little practical value. I use it here to demonstrate that a block may declare a local variable, in this case, another k, initialized to 300. Now there are two ks. Because the new local k hides the global variable of the same name, the program uses the scope resolution operator ::k to refer to the outer (global) variable. Without the operator, k refers to the variable declared within the statement block's scope.

Variables declared inside a statement block exist only within that block. In other words, their scope is limited to the place of their declaration. The compiler rejects code such as

```
if (expression) {
  int count = 0;    // Declare variable within if's scope
...
}
cout << "count == " << count << endl;  // ???
```

The last line does not compile because count is declared within the scope of the if statement, and the variable does not exist outside of that scope.

A useful related trick is to declare and initialize a for loop's control variable at the same time. As you probably know, C for loops are typically written like this:

```
void f()
{
  int i;
  for (i = 0; i < MAX; i++)
...
}
```

In C++, you can declare the loop index directly inside the for loop, shortening the code to

```
void f()
{
  for (int i = 0; i < MAX; i++)
...
}
```

Up until recently, a variable declared inside a control loop as in the preceding example did not exist within the scope of a for or other statement block. A recent change in ANSI C++ now specifies the exact opposite. For example, this code used to display the final value of i:

```
for (int i = 0; i < MAX; i++)
  cout << i << endl;
cout << "Final i == " << i << endl;  // ???
```

The final statement is no longer permitted because i's scope is limited to the block in which it is defined, in this case, the extent of the for loop. Outside of that block, the variable does not exist.

Constants

The const identifier is a C++ innovation, which was subsequently adopted back into ANSI C. Declaring variables with const throws a force field around them, preventing changes to their values at runtime. If you declare an integer count like this

```
const int count = 1234;
```

the compiler rejects the statement:

```
count++;  // ???
```

Some C++ programmers recommend using `const` declarations rather than symbolic constants created with `#define`. The symbolic constant

```
#define MAX 100
```

declares a macro named MAX associated with the text 100 (*not* an integer value 100). If MAX appears in an expression such as

```
for (int i = 0; i < MAX; i++)
...
```

the compiler replaces MAX with the text digits 100 and compiles the statement as though you had typed those digits at this location.

Some C++ experts argue that symbolic constants such as MAX are too easily misused. Proponents of `const` would have you declare MAX like this:

```
const int MAX = 100;
```

The `for` loop remains the same, but with MAX declared as a true constant rather than a macro symbol, you gain two supposed advantages:

- The compiler can perform stricter type checking on MAX. C++ knows that the constant MAX is an `int` value; the compiler doesn't know any such type information about the text macro MAX.

- Turbo Debugger recognizes the true constant MAX. The debugger does not recognize symbolic macro constants created with `#define`.

These are important considerations. Unfortunately, however, the true constant MAX requires permanent storage in the program's data segment. Numerous constants in a program can take up hundreds or thousands of bytes, wasting memory. Worse, using those values may require time-wasting memory references. Using `#defined` symbolic constants typically generates efficient instructions that load values directly into registers.

True `const` constants are useful for declaring values that behave like variables, but must not change at runtime. However, the advantages are not so great to warrant giving up `#define`.

Inline Functions

One of the sad truths of programming languages such as C and C++ is that function calls waste time. Although a function call takes place in the barest flutter of an eyelash, numerous function calls can shave points off a program's performance. Avoiding functions is not an acceptable solution to this problem! Functions make programs modular and easier to maintain. Without functions, it's extremely difficult, perhaps impossible, to write even medium-size programs that run correctly.

On the other hand, unrolling loops and removing multiple function calls are time-honored techniques for improving a program's runtime performance. Consider this hypothetical `for` loop:

```
for (int i = 0; i < MAX; i++) {
  AnyFunction();
...
}
```

If `MAX` is very large, the numerous calls to `AnyFunction` might steal precious time from the program's overall performance. Suppose that `AnyFunction` is written like this:

```
void AnyFunction(void)
{
  cout << AnyValue << endl;
  AnyValue++;
}
```

All of this is hypothetical, but one fact is apparent: Inserting `AnyFunction`'s statements directly into the `for` loop should speed up the program:

```
for (int i = 0; i < MAX; i++) {
  cout << AnyValue << endl;
  AnyValue++;
...
}
```

The amount of time saved should equal the value of `MAX` times the amount of time it takes to execute one function call. An even better solution is to unroll the loop completely, doing away with the `for` statement's overhead altogether:

```
cout << AnyValue << endl;
AnyValue++;
cout << AnyValue << endl;
AnyValue++;
...
cout << AnyValue << endl;
AnyValue++;
```

Never mind that you have to type `MAX` * 2 statements, and if `MAX` is large, the compiled code will probably grow to elephantine proportions. No matter—you have improved the program's performance by at least a millisecond or two!

Ridiculous? Yes, but even though saving time is important, giving up functions and loops is too high a price to pay for a small improvement. Luckily, C++ offers an alternative. Rather than do away with function calls, you can declare functions *inline*, injecting their statements directly into the code stream. Listing 3.9, Inline.cpp, shows how.

Listing 3.9. Inline.cpp (Demonstrates inline functions).

```
//============================================================
// Inline.cpp -- Demonstrates inline functions
// To compile:
//    bcc inline
// To run:
```

```
//   inline
// Copyright (c) 1996 by Tom Swan. All rights reserved.
//===============================================================

#include <iostream.h>

inline int max(int a, int b)
{
  if (a >= b)
    return a;
  else
    return b;
}

void main()
{
  int x, y, z;

  cout << "X? ";
  cin >> x;
  cout << "Y? ";
  cin >> y;
  z = max(x, y);
  cout << "max(a, b) == " << z << endl;
}
```

Running the program prompts you for two integers, and then displays the greater of the two values:

```
X? 45
Y? 99
max(a, b) == 99
```

To declare an inline function, precede it with the C++ inline keyword. Implement the function normally, but usually, before function main. There is nothing special about an inline function's contents—anything that can go in a normal function can also go in one declared inline. Usually, inline functions such as max in the sample program are declared in header files and included in each module that needs to use the functions. Regardless, an inline function must appear in full before that function may be used.

Use inline functions the same way you use normal functions. For instance, "call" max to determine which of two integers is greater, assigning that value to z. Actually, however, the compiler replaces max with its inline statements, and does not actually call a function. In this example, the call to max and assignment to z are actually compiled as these statements:

```
if (x >= y)
  z = x;
else
  z = y;
```

The amount of time saved in this small example is minuscule. If max were called thousands of times in a loop, however, the program's performance might gain a significant boost from the inline code.

51

> **NOTE**
>
> Inline functions are akin to register variables. When you declare an `inline` function, you are telling the compiler that, *if possible,* the function's statements should be inserted directly where the function is used. The compiler is not an obedient genie, however, and there is no guarantee that it will carry out your every wish. If the inline code is very large, the compiler might refuse to inject it into the code stream, and in such cases the compiler will generate a common function call. Also, when compiling programs for Turbo Debugger, all inline functions are converted to callable functions so they can be traced. Well-written C++ programs should work correctly whether or not their inline functions are actually compiled inline.

Managing Memory with `new` and `delete`

You may use the same memory techniques in C++ that are commonly used in C. Functions `malloc`, `farmalloc`, `calloc`, `farcalloc`, `free`, `farfree`, and others are available to all C and C++ programs. C++, however, offers alternate memory allocation *operators* `new` and `delete`, which can do everything standard memory functions can do—and more.

Use `new` to allocate space for dynamic variables. Use `delete` to free space allocated by `new`, reclaiming allocated memory for use in subsequent `new` expressions. Keep in mind that `new` and `delete` are unary operators, not functions. This fact is significant because, as you'll discover in later chapters, C++ makes it possible to reprogram most operators, including `new` and `delete`. Using these operators rather than the standard memory functions makes it possible to take over memory-management details if that should be necessary. The operators also play important roles in object-oriented programming, a topic for the next chapter, "Programming with Classes."

To allocate memory for a `double` variable and assign its address to a pointer, you can write

```
double *dp = new double;
```

You might often see similar declarations written as

```
double *dp = new(double);
```

which makes `new` appear to be a function. It's not, and the extra parentheses are ignored. Use `dp` as you do any pointer allocated by `malloc` or a similar function. To assign a value to the memory addressed by `dp`, write

```
*dp = 3.14159;
```

When you are done using a dynamic variable, delete it like this:

```
delete dp;
```

Deleting the pointer reclaims the memory allocated to `dp`, making that memory available for other uses. Always use `delete` to free memory allocated by `new`. Dynamic variables allocated by `malloc` or other memory-allocation functions should be freed by `free` (or perhaps `farfree`). You may use `malloc` and `new` in the same program, but you must not mix standard C and C++ memory management techniques.

Detecting Out-of-Memory Errors

When creating dynamic variables, your main concern is whether enough memory is available. If `new` is successful, it returns a pointer to reserved memory of the requested size. If unsuccessful, one of two actions occurs:

- `new` throws an exception, or
- `new` returns null (zero)

In past versions of C++, `new` returned null if the operator failed to allocate memory for any reason, usually because enough free space is not available. ANSI C++ specifications now require `new` to *throw an exception*—a technique I explain in Chapter 6, "Handling Exceptions."

You can reprogram `new` to revert to its original action of returning null for memory allocation errors. This is useful for compiling C programs that depend on this feature, and also for short examples such as many of the sample programs in this book. To do that, include the new.h header in your program and add the following statement to `main`, or anywhere before the first use of `new`:

```
set_new_handler(0);
```

The `set_new_handler` function assigns the address of a runtime subroutine, called a *handler,* used by `new`. The default handler causes `new` to throw an exception for errors. Setting the handler's address to zero tells `new` to instead return null for errors.

TIP

When updating an existing C++ program to Borland C++ 5, you might have to call `set_new_handler(0)` before the program will work correctly. Make this modification if the program ends unexpectedly with an "abnormal termination" message, which can be caused by `new` throwing an exception for an out-of-memory error.

Listing 3.10, Memerr.cpp, explains how to use `new` to allocate memory for structures, and also demonstrates what happens when the program runs out of memory. You can compile and run the program as an EasyWin application from the IDE, or from a DOS prompt.

Listing 3.10. Memerr.cpp (Demonstrates new and out-of-memory error).

```
//================================================================
// Memerr.cpp -- Demonstrates new and out-of-memory error
// To compile:
//   bcc memerr
// To run:
//   memerr
// Copyright (c) 1996 by Tom Swan. All rights reserved.
//================================================================

#include <iostream.h>
#include <new.h>
#include <stdlib.h>

struct q {
  int ia[1024];   // 2048-byte structure
};

void main()
{
  struct q *qp;            // Pointer to structure q

  set_new_handler(0);      // Tell new to return 0 on failure
  for (;;) {               // Do following statements "forever"
    qp = new q;            // Allocate new struture of type q
    cout << qp << endl;    // Display structure address
    if (qp == 0) {         // If new returned 0, do the following
      cout << "Out of memory\n";  // Display error message
      exit(1);             // Exit program with error code 1
    }
  }
}
```

A structure q with an array of 1,024 integers gives the program some data to use. Passing this structure to new allocates a 2,048-byte block of memory (assuming an integer occupies two bytes). Repeating that operation eventually causes the program to run out of RAM, demonstrating what happens when new can't find enough free memory.

So that new returns null for that error condition, the program passes 0 to set_new_handler. After that, a "do-forever" for loop executes several statements. The first statement calls new to allocate a 2,048-byte structure, and assigns the structure's address to pointer qp. Next, an output statement displays qp's address. If qp is null, then new failed to find enough memory, and the program halts by calling exit after displaying an error message. Here's a portion of what my display showed (the addresses are probably different on your screen):

```
0x1366
0x1b6a
...
0x0000
Out of memory
```

If the program did not call set_new_handler, new throws an exception instead of returning null. To demonstrate the difference, comment out or delete the set_new_handler statement, recompile, and run. Now the program displays

```
0x1366
0x1b6a
...
0xf3d6
Abnormal program termination
```

In the former test, the program itself detected the out-of-memory condition and halted by calling exit. In the new test, new throws an exception, which causes an abnormal shutdown. In part II, you'll learn how to trap this and other exceptions to provide robust error handling.

Using Simple Dynamic Variables

Although Memerr.cpp demonstrates what happens when new runs out of memory, the program is not a good example of how to allocate memory. Using a "do-forever" for loop, for instance, is usually a poor programming practice, though it is necessary here to force a memory error regardless of how much memory your computer has.

More often, you will use new to allocate memory for a variable, a structure, or an array, as follows. For example, you might declare a structure:

```
struct q {
  int ia[1024];  // 2048-byte structure
};
```

You can then use new to allocate space for a variable of type q:

```
struct q *qp;  // Define pointer to a struct q variable
qp = new q;    // Allocate memory for a struct q variable
```

If new succeeds, qp addresses a dynamic instance, in other words an object, of type struct q. You can use this object as you would if it were declared as a local or global variable. For example, you can use the struct addressed by qp to assign values to its member array, and to display those values with statements such as

```
qp->ia[10] = 1234;
cout << qp->ia[10] << endl;
```

When you are done using the dynamic variable, free its memory with the delete operator. The freed memory is then available for future uses of new:

```
delete qp;  // Delete and free memory addressed by qp
```

If you don't delete your program's dynamic variables, you run the risk of filling memory and causing future out-of-memory errors. Memerr.cpp, which never deletes any memory it allocates, demonstrates the inevitable outcome of this serious mistake.

> **NOTE**
>
> When a program halts, all allocated memory is automatically freed. Still, it's a good program-ming practice to delete dynamic variables when you are finished using them. This is especially true of multitasking operating systems such as Windows in which dynamic objects are not necessarily freed automatically when the program ends.

By the way, it is always okay to delete a pointer, even if it equals null. After deleting a pointer, however, the memory that it formerly addressed is no longer reserved for the program's use. Deleting that same pointer again, or using its addressed memory in any way, can cause serious bugs. Never write code such as this:

```
double *dp;          // Define pointer to double
dp = new double;     // Allocate memory and address with dp
*dp = 3.14159;       // Assign value to addressed memory
delete dp;           // Delete the allocated memory. Okay so far.
...
*dp = 9.9999;        // ??? Serious error! Don't do this!
delete dp;           // ??? Serious error! Corrupts heap!
```

The preceding fragment is correctly programmed up to the last two statements. After deleting dp, you must not reuse the pointer because the deleted memory might have been allocated to another variable. Deleting the same pointer again, as the last statement does, is also a serious mistake because this might corrupt the heap by double-linking the same memory block into the heap's list of free spaces. The hard and fast rule is: *after deleting a pointer, never use it for any purpose.* You may, however, reuse a pointer to address memory newly allocated by new:

```
dp = new double;     // Allocate memory for a dynamic variable
*dp = 3.14159;       // Assign value to dynamic variable
delete dp;           // Delete the memory. Don't use dp after this!
...
dp = new double;     // You may, however, allocate another variable
*dp = 9.99999;       // Assign value to the newly allocated variable
delete dp;           // Delete the memory. Again, don't use dp after!
```

Using Dynamic Strings

You can use new to allocate dynamic character strings of any practical size. Listing 3.11, Newstr.cpp, demonstrates the technique for common null-terminated string buffers.

Listing 3.11. Newstr.cpp (Creates dynamic string using new).

```
//=================================================================
// Newstr.cpp -- Creates dynamic string using new
// To compile:
//   bcc newstr
// To run:
//   newstr
```

```
// Copyright (c) 1996 by Tom Swan. All rights reserved.
//===============================================================

#include <iostream.h>

#define SIZE 80

void main()
{
  char *sp;

  sp = new char[SIZE];
  cout << "String? ";
  cin.getline(sp, SIZE);
  cout << "You entered: " << sp << endl;
  delete[] sp;
}
```

The program uses new to allocate a char array of SIZE bytes, and assigns the address of the array's first byte to sp. Stream input and output statements then prompt you to enter a string and display your typing.

The final statement deletes the dynamic char array. Borland C++ permits this statement to be written without brackets as

```
delete sp;  // ???, but okay in Borland C++
```

To stay in tune with strict C++ protocol, the empty brackets should be used in the expression delete[], which tells the compiler that an array, rather than just a simple variable, is being deleted. (In Borland C++, the brackets are required only when deleting arrays of class objects, but more on that later.)

> **NOTE**
>
> Early versions of C++ required specifying the number of elements when deleting an array. In C++ Version 2.0, for example, line 15 would be written delete[SIZE] sp;. Borland C++ ignores SIZE in this case, and displays a warning if you attempt to use this older form of delete.

Using Dynamic Arrays

You're not limited to allocating dynamic null-terminated strings, which of course, are merely arrays of characters. Unsurprisingly, new and delete also can be used to create and free dynamic arrays of other types. Listing 3.12, Newarray.cpp, demonstrates.

Listing 3.12. Newarray.cpp (Creates dynamic array using new).

```
//==============================================================
// Newarray.cpp -- Creates dynamic array using new
// To compile:
//    bcc newarray
// To run:
//    newarray
// Copyright (c) 1996 by Tom Swan. All rights reserved.
//==============================================================

#include <iostream.h>

#define COUNT 100  // Number of integers

void main()
{
  int *array;  // Array of integers
  int i;       // Array index

  array = new int[COUNT];

// Fill array
  for (i = 0; i < COUNT; i++)
    array[i] = i;

// Display array contents
  for (i = 0; i < COUNT; i++) {
    cout.width(8);
    cout << array[i];
  }
  delete[] array;
}
```

First, function main declares an int pointer named array. It also declares an integer index, i. Operator new allocates space for 100 int values, and the statement assigns to array the address of the allocated memory's first byte. The program then fills the array with values from 0 to 99, displayed in 8-character columns by a for loop. Finally, the program deletes the array, using empty brackets in the expression delete[], as in the preceding listing, to tell the compiler that an array, and not just one int, is being deleted.

Multidimensional Dynamic Arrays

To declare a pointer to a two- or three-dimensional array (or one with more dimensions), specify the number of elements in the second and subsequent positions. For example, suppose you want to allocate space for a 10-by-20 array of double values. You begin by declaring

```
int (*matrix)[20];
```

which states that matrix is a pointer to an array of 20 integers. You must use parentheses around (*matrix) because the array brackets have higher precedence than the pointer symbol *. The integers don't exist just yet; all you've done is tell the compiler that matrix *potentially* addresses an array of a certain size. To allocate memory for an actual 10-by-20 matrix and assign the array's address to matrix, use the statement

```
matrix = new int[10][20];
```

Operator new allocates memory for the array. The resulting address is assigned to matrix. To create an 8-by-8-by-8 cube, use the statements

```
int (*matrix)[8][8];
matrix = new int[8][8][8];
```

This declaration of matrix specifies the second and third array dimensions, telling the compiler that matrix is to address an 8-by-8 array of integers. The new expression specifies all three dimensions, allocating space for a specific *number* of 8-by-8 arrays—in other words, a three-dimensional cube.

When allocating space for a multidimensional array, the first subscript may be a variable, but the second and subsequent subscripts must be constants. If an int v equals 40, for instance, the statements

```
int (*matrix)[20];
matrix = new int[v][20];
```

allocate space for a two-dimensional, 40-by-20 array of int values addressed by matrix. Delete multidimensional arrays of any size as though they had only one dimension:

```
delete[] matrix;
```

Function Overloading

All programmers face the demandingly creative job of thinking up new function names. Sure, you can invent any old name for a function—the compiler greets a function named f29q with the same enthusiasm as it greets one named BattingAverage. Humans, however, tend to comprehend the latter name.

In a large program, coming up with good function names is no joking matter. Consider a drawing program that has to draw umpteen shapes. Each drawing function needs a unique name, leading to programs strewn with functions such as DrawEllipse, DrawCircle, DrawSquare, DrawLine, and so on. The code probably also has numerous variables named ellipse, circle, square, and line, and the resulting code looks as though it has developed a bad stammer:

```
DrawEllipse(ellipse);
DrawCircle(circle);
DrawSquare(square);
DrawLine(line);
```

Wouldn't it be great if you could use the *same* function name—let's call it Draw—to draw all shapes? Then, you could simply write

```
Draw(ellipse);
Draw(circle);
Draw(square);
Draw(line);
```

This is the kind of clarity that function overloading can bring to programs. In C++, multiple functions may have the same names as long as they differ in at least one parameter. The functions are "overloaded" because, though named the same, they perform multiple jobs. The many Draw functions in our hypothetical graphics program are still separate and distinct, and are written just as other non-overloaded functions, but the C++ compiler recognizes them *by the way they are used,* not only by their names.

A simple example demonstrates how function overloading can help simplify a program's text. Listing 3.13, Overload.cpp, uses overloaded functions to display the square of three values, each of a different type.

Listing 3.13. Overload.cpp (Demonstrates overloaded functions).

```
//=================================================================
// Overload.cpp -- Demonstrates overloaded functions
// To compile:
//    bcc overload
// To run:
//    overload
// Copyright (c) 1996 by Tom Swan. All rights reserved.
//=================================================================

#include <iostream.h>

int square(int a);
double square(double a);
long double square(long double a);

void main()
{
  int x = 10;
  double y = 20.5;
  long double z = 30.75;

  cout << square(x) << endl;
  cout << square(y) << endl;
  cout << square(z) << endl;
}

int square(int a)
{
  return a * a;
}

double square(double a)
{
```

```
  return a * a;
}

long double square(long double a)
{
  return a * a;
}
```

Running the program displays the square of three different types of variables, producing on screen these lines:

```
100
420.25
945.562
```

Three overloaded `square` functions are prototyped above function `main`. Each function has the same name, but is considered distinct because each differs in at least one parameter. The program implements each function separately, just as each would be if their names were not the same.

Overloaded functions can clarify a program's meaning. Despite the different data types involved, it's obvious that each output statement in `main` displays the square of an argument. This is much neater than having separate `squareInt`, `squareDouble`, and `squareLongDouble` function names. Of course, it's up to you to overload functions that perform more or less the same jobs. If you name *every* function in your program the same (provided each one differs by at least one argument), your code might be as incomprehensible as a novel written using only one word.

Default Function Arguments

An important C++ technique provides default argument values to function parameters. This can be useful when function calls need to supply only some, but not always all, arguments. Suppose you need a function that returns the sum of four `int` values, like this:

```
int sum(int a, int b, int c, int d)
{
  return a + b + c + d;
}
```

To call the function with only two argument values—let's call them `v1` and `v2`—you need to supply zeros to the other two unused parameters:

```
cout << sum(v1, v2, 0, 0);
```

This is no great imposition, but it does require you to look up `sum`'s documentation to determine what values to supply to unused parameters. Mistakenly passing -1 or another value to parameters `c` and `d`, which a careless programmer might do, causes the function to return the wrong sum.

Default function arguments are designed to guard against this condition by supplying values for unspecified arguments. To declare a default value, follow the parameter with an equal sign and a value in the function's prototype:

```
int sum(int a, int b, int c = 0, int d = 0);
```

Declared like this, sum requires only two arguments, but can have up to four. The default values must come last in the function's parameter list, and must appear only in the function's prototype. If arguments are not specified for c and d, those parameters are given the default values listed in the prototype. These statements are now allowed:

```
cout << sum(1, 2);       // a == 1, b == 2, c == 0, d == 0
cout << sum(1, 2, 3);    // a == 1, b == 2, c == 3, d == 0
cout << sum(1, 2, 3, 4); // a == 1, b == 2, c == 3, d == 4
```

The next program, Center.cpp, shows a more practical example of default function arguments. The program centers an input string by copying it to an output string buffer, surrounded by one or two fill characters. Use the sample program's Center function to prepare strings such as

```
**** Error: You goofed big time! ****
<<<<<<< Press any key to continue >>>>>>>
```

Compile Center.cpp in Listing 3.14 as an EasyWin or DOS application. Run the program and enter a string, which is displayed in several different ways by function Center, which also demonstrates how to use default function arguments.

Listing 3.14. Center.cpp (Demonstrates default function arguments).

```
//================================================================
// Center.cpp -- Demonstrates default function arguments
// To compile:
//    bcc center
// To run:
//    center
// Copyright (c) 1996 by Tom Swan. All rights reserved.
//================================================================

#include <iostream.h>
#include <string.h>

#define SIZE 128

void Center(const char *instr, char *outstr,
  int width = 0, char lFill = '-', char rFill = '-');

void main()
{
  char instr[SIZE];  // Input string
  char outstr[SIZE]; // Output string
  int length;        // Length of string in characters

  cout << "Enter a string: ";
  cin.getline(instr, SIZE / 2);
  length = strlen(instr);
```

```
    Center(instr, outstr);
    cout << outstr << endl;
    Center(instr, outstr, length + 8);
    cout << outstr << endl;
    Center(instr, outstr, length + 16, '*', '*');
    cout << outstr << endl;
    Center(instr, outstr, 78, '<', '>');
    cout << outstr << endl;
}

// instr:    Input string pointer
// outstr:   Output string pointer
// width:    Final desired output string width
// fill:     Fill character for output string

void Center(const char *instr, char *outstr,
    int width, char lFill, char rFill)
{
    if (outstr == 0)    // The output string must not be null
        return;         // Return immediately if it is null

    if (instr == 0) {   // If input is null
        *outstr = 0;    // Make output into null string,
        return;         // and return.
    }

    // Calculate variables for filling output string
    int len = strlen(instr);
    if (width < len)
        width = len;
    int wd2 = (width - len) / 2;

    int i;  // String index and for-loop control variable

    for (i = 0; i < wd2; i++)
        outstr[i] = lFill;
    for (/*i = i*/; i < wd2 + len; i++)
        outstr[i] = instr[i - wd2];
    for (/*i = i*/; i < width; i++)
        outstr[i] = rFill;
    outstr[i] = 0;       // Terminate string with null
}
```

The program declares a prototype for function Center with three default arguments:

```
void Center(const char *instr, char *outstr,
    int width = 0, char lFill = '-', char rFill = '-');
```

The first two parameters address input and output strings. The input string is declared const to prevent it from being changed by the function. The last three parameters are given default argument values, initializing those parameters if arguments are not supplied by the statement that calls Center. As the first such call in the program demonstrates, you can call the function with as few as two arguments:

```
Center(instr, outstr);
```

Values for the other arguments are supplied by the default values in the function prototype. The other calls to Center supply one or more arguments, overriding the default values. Each statement produces a different output string, with the input centered and surrounded by various fill characters.

References

A reference is an alias for a pointer that does not require dereferencing to use. For example, these statements declare an int variable i initialized to 1234, and an int pointer ip, initialized to the address of i:

```
int i   = 1234; // Create variable i
int *ip = &i;    // Create pointer to i
```

The expression &i is a reference to i. It *refers* by address to the object named i. C++ carries this concept one step further by permitting you to declare reference variables. These are similar to pointers, but do not require dereferencing. For example, you can define a reference ir to the variable i:

```
int &ir = i;     // Create reference to i
```

Internally, the reference ir and the pointer ip are both pointers to i. However, only the pointer requires dereferencing. The reference variable is a true alias—you use it exactly as though it were the object it addresses. Consider these three output statements:

```
cout << "i   == " << i   << endl;
cout << "*ip == " << *ip << endl;
cout << "ri  == " << ri  << endl;
```

Each of those statements displays the value of i. The first statement refers to i directly. The second dereferences the pointer ip. The third uses the reference ri as though it were i.

References are safer than pointers because you cannot reassign reference addresses. Pointers are more flexible, but run the risk of being used incorrectly (as most C and C++ programmers are all too aware).

There are three main uses for references: as variables, as function parameters, and as function results. Let's take a look at these valuable techniques.

References as Variables

As a variable, a reference *refers* to another value. You probably won't use references this way in practice, but the technique demonstrates how references work. Compile and run Listing 3.15, Refvar.cpp, as an EasyWin or DOS application. The program shows four ways to address and display an integer value.

Listing 3.15. Refvar.cpp (Demonstrates reference variables).

```
//================================================================
// Refvar.cpp -- Demonstrates reference variables
// To compile:
//   bcc refvar
// To run:
//   refvar
// Copyright (c) 1996 by Tom Swan. All rights reserved.
//================================================================

#include <iostream.h>

void main()
{
  int ivar = 1234;    // Variable assigned value
  int *iptr = &ivar;  // Pointer assigned ivar's address
  int &iref = ivar;   // Reference associated with ivar
  int *p = &iref;     // Pointer assigned iref's address

  cout << "ivar  == " << ivar << endl;
  cout << "*iptr == " << *iptr << endl;
  cout << "iref  == " << iref << endl;
  cout << "*p    == " << *p << endl;
}
```

Function main declares four variables. First is a simple int, ivar, initialized to 1234. Next is a pointer to int, named iptr, and assigned the address of ivar. The third declaration creates a reference iref that refers to i. The fourth declaration creates another pointer, p, assigned the address stored in iref.

Pointers to objects and pointers to references are one and the same as this program's output statements demonstrate. Each of the four stream statements displays the value of i. The first refers directly to ivar. The second dereferences pointer iptr. The third uses the reference iref as though it were ivar. The fourth dereferences pointer p, previously assigned the address of iref.

Figure 3.2 illustrates the relationships of the variables in Refvar.cpp. As the illustration suggests, using iref is similar to using a dereferenced pointer such as *p. Both expressions access ivar's value, 1234.

Remember one rule when using references: *Once initialized, a reference may not be reassigned.* In Refvar.cpp, you cannot declare a new integer variable and set iref to refer to it:

```
int anotherInt;
iref = anotherInt;  // ???
```

This does not cause iref to refer to anotherInt. It assigns anotherInt's value to the object to which iref refers—in other words, to ivar. The second statement is identical to the assignment:

```
ivar = anotherInt;
```

Figure 3.2.
Relationships of variables in Refvar.cpp.

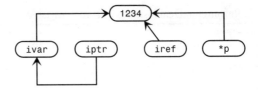

You may also assign new literal values to the object of a reference. For example, the statement

```
iref = 4321;
```

changes ivar's value to 4321. You might find these rules easier to memorize if you think of references as unchanging aliases, similar—but not identical—to pointer aliases.

As a related rule, references must be initialized in their declarations. For example, this is never allowed:

```
int &iref;   // ???
```

Unlike a pointer, which can be declared in an uninitialized state, or set to null if the pointer does not address valid data, a reference must always refer to an object. There is no equivalent of a null pointer for a reference.

> **NOTE**
>
> There are some exceptions to the preceding rule. References do not have to be preinitialized in four special cases: when declared extern, when used as function parameters, when used as function return types, or when used in class declarations.

No operators apply directly to references. Operators apply only to referenced objects. For instance, you can increment ivar by using its reference:

```
iref++;
```

The compiler generates code to increment ivar, the variable to which iref refers. The statement does not affect iref directly in any way.

References may also refer to constants; however, you may not assign literal constant values directly to a reference. The following declaration does not compile because 1234 is not an object to which iref can refer:

```
int &iref = 1234;   // ???
```

You may, however, declare a const reference to a legitimate object with programming such as this:

```
int x = 1234;        // Declare and initialize int object
const int &iref = x; // Declare const reference iref for x
```

The technique is important because it effectively converts a variable into a constant, which cannot be altered. You can, for example, write the value of x by reference in an output stream statement:

```
cout << "iref == " << iref << endl;  // Okay
```

You can also change variable x's value:

```
x = 4321;  // Also okay
```

Because iref is constant, however, you cannot assign a new value to x by reference:

```
iref = 4321;  // ??? Not allowed
```

Attempting to compile that statement produces the error message "Cannot modify a const object in function main()."

References as Function Parameters

Despite having intriguing properties, on their own, reference variables as described in the preceding section are rarely of much practical use. Rather than use a reference to refer to another variable, you may as well just use the variable itself.

As function parameters, however, references are far more versatile and offer a handy alternative to pointer parameters. References are especially useful in functions that return multiple objects—one that prompts for two or more input values, for example. Listing 3.16, Tax.cpp, demonstrates the technique. Compile and run the program as an EasyWin or DOS application, and then enter an amount paid and a sales tax rate when prompted. The program displays the list price and amount of tax based on your input.

Listing 3.16. Tax.cpp (Demonstrates function reference parameters).

```
//==============================================================
// Tax.cpp -- Demonstrates function reference parameters
// To compile:
//    bcc tax
// To run:
//    tax
// Copyright (c) 1996 by Tom Swan. All rights reserved.
//==============================================================

#include <iostream.h>
#include <stdlib.h>
#include <stdio.h>

double GetDouble(const char *prompt);
void GetData(double &paid, double &rate);
void Calculate(const double paid, const double rate,
```

continues

Listing 3.16. continued

```c
  double &list, double &tax);

void main()
{
  double paid, rate, list, tax;
  GetData(paid, rate);
  Calculate(paid, rate, list, tax);
  printf("List price = $%8.2f\n", list);
  printf("Tax paid   = $%8.2f\n", tax);
}

// Return one double value
double GetDouble(const char *prompt)
{
  char s[20];          // Input string
  printf(prompt);      // Display prompt string
  scanf("%20s", s);    // Input data as string
  return atof(s);      // Return double equivalent of input
}

// Get amount paid and tax rate double values
// Note: Changes values of paid and rate
void GetData(double &paid, double &rate)
{
  paid = GetDouble("Price paid? ");
  rate = GetDouble("Tax rate (ex: .06)? ");
}

// Calculate list price and tax paid from amount and rate
// Note: Changes values of list and tax
void Calculate(const double paid, const double rate,
  double &list, double &tax)
{
  list = paid / (1 + rate);
  tax = paid - list;
}
```

The program prototypes three functions. The first function prompts for and returns a double value—the usual way of writing a function that returns a single item:

```c
double GetDouble(const char *prompt);
```

The second function shows how to use reference parameters to return two or more values. Notice that the function's two parameters are prefaced with the symbol &, indicating that they are passed to the function by reference (that is, their addresses rather than their values are passed to GetData):

```c
void GetData(double &paid, double &rate);
```

Examine the code for GetData farther down in the listing. Its two statements call GetDouble with a string to display, and assign the returned value to the reference parameters paid and rate:

```
paid = GetDouble("Price paid? ");
rate = GetDouble("Tax rate (ex: .06)? ");
```

Because `paid` and `rate` are references, the assigned values are stored in the objects passed to `GetDouble`. In the `main` function, for example, this statement inputs values into two variables, also named `paid` and `rate`:

```
GetData(paid, rate);
```

The third and final function in the sample program calculates the list price and tax paid based on the actual price and tax rate. The first two parameters, `paid` and `rate`, are the function's input values. Because the function doesn't change them, the parameters are declared `const`, and are passed by value (that is, a *copy* of each actual value is passed to the function). The second two parameters, `list` and `tax`, are the function's output. These values are changed by the function, and therefore, they are passed by reference:

```
void Calculate(const double paid, const double rate,
  double &list, double &tax)
```

Function `Calculate` assigns new values to `list` and `tax` with the statements

```
list = paid / (1 + rate);
tax = paid - list;
```

Because the parameters are references, they refer back to the variables passed to `Calculate`. Assigning expression results to the references therefore changes the actual variables when `main` calls the function with the statement:

```
Calculate(paid, rate, list, tax);
```

Again, there's no way to tell which arguments are passed by value and which are passed by reference. Good documentation for the `Calculate` function is vital to avoid costly mistakes.

Reference and pointer parameters are closely related. In fact, references can be implemented internally by a C++ compiler as pointers. To hammer home the idea, consider this small function:

```
void f(int *ip)
{
  *ip = 1234;
}
```

Inside the function, pointer `ip` addresses an argument passed to the function with a statement such as

```
f(&ivar);   // Pass ivar by address
```

In the function, the statement `*ip = 1234;` assigns 1234 to `ivar`, which is passed by address to `f`. Now consider the same function using a reference parameter:

```
void f(int &ir)
{
  ir = 1234;
}
```

Pointer `ip` is replaced by a reference `ir`, to which the function assigns 1234. Assignments like this give values to the referenced object. The statement

```
f(ivar);  // Pass ivar by reference
```

passes `ivar` *by reference* to `f`, causing `ir` to refer to `ivar`, thus setting `ivar` to 1234.

References as Function Results

Functions may return references to objects, provided those objects persist when the function is not active. (In other words, functions may not return references to local automatic variables.) A function declared as

```
double &ref(double d);
```

requires one `double` argument and returns a reference to a `double` object, presumably one that is declared elsewhere.

Listing 3.17, Reffunc.cpp, demonstrates how to use reference functions to hide a data structure's internal representation. The technique is important in large projects, especially when data structures might change, possibly causing a conventional ANSI C program to require extensive modifications. C++ reference functions can reduce these kinds of maintenance chores by providing access to structures such as arrays without tying the code to the data's physical properties. Compile and run the program, and when prompted, enter an index value from 0 to 9, and then enter a floating-point value. The program inserts your entry into an array of `double` values. To end the program, press Enter at the prompt.

Listing 3.17. Reffunc.cpp (Demonstrates function reference return values).

```
//=================================================================
// Reffunc.cpp -- Demonstrates function reference return values
// To compile:
//    bcc reffunc
// To run:
//    reffunc
// Copyright (c) 1996 by Tom Swan. All rights reserved.
//=================================================================
```

```
#include <iostream.h>
#include <stdlib.h>
#include <string.h>

#define FALSE 0
#define TRUE 1
#define SIZE 10
#define BUFLEN 20

double &ref(int index);
void ShowArray(void);

double array[SIZE];

void main()
{
  int done = FALSE, index;
  char buffer[BUFLEN];

  for (index = 0; index < SIZE; index++)
    ref(index) = index;  // Assign to reference function!
  while (!done) {
    ShowArray();
    cout << "\nEnter index from 0 to 9, Enter to quit: ";
    cin.getline(buffer, BUFLEN);
    done = (strlen(buffer) == 0);
    if (!done) {
      index = atoi(buffer);
      cout << "Enter floating point value: ";
      cin.getline(buffer, BUFLEN);
      ref(index) = atof(buffer);
    }
  }
}

double &ref(int index)
{
  if ((index < 0) || (index >= SIZE))
    index = 0;
  return array[index];  // Return reference to array element
}

void ShowArray(void)
{
  cout << "\nArray:\n";
  for (int i = 0; i < SIZE; i++)
    cout << "[" << i << "] == " << array[i] << endl;
}
```

The program uses a global array of double values for storage. Although the program displays and inserts values into this array, it does so without referring directly to the global data structure anywhere in function main. Thanks to a reference function, it would be possible to change the internal storage of the double values (perhaps using a linked list rather than an array), and the program will still operate as before, without a single change to any of main's statements.

Examine the prototype for the reference function named ref:

```
double &ref(int index);
```

The function returns a reference to a double object identified by an int parameter index. Because the function returns a reference to a double object, the function name may appear on the left side of an assignment operator, as shown by the assignment statement in the program's for loop:

```
ref(index) = index;
```

This is probably the most common use for reference functions. The statement assigns a value to the double object referred to by ref(index). Exactly how that object is stored is immaterial. The reference function hides the data's internal representation.

The program shows another use for reference functions when it assigns the double result from function atof to ref(index) at the end of the if statement inside the while loop:

```
ref(index) = atof(buffer);
```

If ref were an array, this statement might be written as

```
ref[index] = atof(buffer);
```

A change to the data's storage mechanism, then, would require a corresponding change to the code, which in turn would require additional testing, debugging, and so on. Reference functions can help reduce such undesirable changes.

The reference function implementation follows main. An if statement forces index into the proper range, after which the function returns a reference to one of the double values in the global array. It's important to understand that the return statement does *not* return a double value. It returns a *reference* to a double object. Consequently, ref may appear on the left side of an assignment operator as demonstrated in main.

Summary

- C++ is more than just an object-oriented version of C. C++ has many features that improve and extend C. Most of what you know about C applies to C++, and most C programs are C++ compatible. C++'s more advanced features, however, are not available in C.

- Compiling a program file named with the extension .cpp indicates to Borland C++ that the file contains C++ programming.

- C++ recognizes all C keywords, operators, and other language elements. C++ adds several new keywords and operators to C.

- Function prototypes are required in C++ programs. Before a statement may call a function, the compiler must have processed that function's prototype.

- Other new C++ features include stricter type checking, a reduced need for `typedef`, and the definition of a `char` as an 8-bit byte. In C++, literal characters such as `'X'` are type `char`. In ANSI C, literal characters are type `int`.

- Use the C++ comment symbol, `//`, to begin a comment that extends to the end of the current line. C++ and C comments (using brackets `/*` and `*/`) may be mixed in the same program. C++ comments may be nested inside C comments.

- I/O streams use the `<<` (put to) and `>>` (get from) operators to write and read data. The output stream `cout` is tied to the system's standard output. The input stream `cin` is tied to the standard input. Use output stream `cerr` to display error messages on the console.

- The safest way to read character strings into buffers is to call an input stream's `get` member function. Use `cin.get` or `cin.getline` to read strings from the system's standard input.

- Use member functions such as `cout.width` to set the column width for a subsequent output stream statement. Use modifiers `dec`, `hex`, and `oct` to specify decimal, hexadecimal, and octal output formats. You can also call standard functions such as `sprintf` to prepare strings for writing to output streams.

- Declarations may appear anywhere in any C++ statement block. You can, for example, declare a variable inside a `for` loop statement's braces. Such a variable's scope extends only to its declaring block. You must declare variables, however, before you can use them.

- When a local variable has the same name as a global variable, the local name hides the global name. Use the scope resolution operator `::` to unhide a global variable. If a local variable is named `count`, the expression `::count` refers to a global `count`.

- Some C++ authorities recommend using `const` rather than `#define` to declare symbolic constants. The compiler can check the data types of `const` objects in expressions. Also, Turbo Debugger recognizes `const`, but not `#defined`, names. Global `const` values, however, occupy space in the program's data segment and require time-wasting memory references to use. In practice, and despite published advice to the contrary, C++ programmers use `#define` just as successfully as C programmers do.

- An inline function's statements are injected directly into the compiled code in place of a function call. Use inline functions to avoid making function calls, which can waste time inside tight loops that must run as fast as possible. Be aware that the `inline` keyword, such as register, is only a suggestion to the compiler, not an ironclad command. An inline function may or may not be compiled inline. (Inline functions are never compiled inline when preparing code for debugging.)

- Use the operators `new` and `delete` to allocate and free heap memory for dynamic variables. In C++ programs, new and delete take the place of conventional memory-management functions such as `malloc`, `calloc`, `free`, and others. You may still use these functions in C++ programs. Memory allocated by new, however, *must* be freed by `delete`. Memory allocated by `malloc` must be freed by `free`.

- Function names may be overloaded. That is, a program may have two or more functions of the same names as long as those functions differ in at least one parameter. Function overloading helps reduce the need to invent arbitrarily unique function names such as `DrawCircle` and `DrawEllipse`. It's your responsibility to use function overloading sensibly.

- Default function arguments supply values for parameters. Declare default values after any other parameters listed in the function's prototype.

- A reference, declared with `&`, *refers* to another object. Unlike a pointer alias, which also can refer to an object, a reference must be initialized when declared (except in certain cases), and a reference may not be made to refer to a different object later on.

- References are typically used to declare function parameters that refer to the actual arguments passed to the function. In this way, references are similar to pointer parameters, but are easier to use. References can be returned as function results.

Exercises

3.1 Using I/O streams, write a filter program that converts a text file to all uppercase.

3.2 Revise Getval.cpp, to repeat its prompt upon detecting an error on the input stream.

3.3 Design and test an inline function `min`, which returns the lesser of two integer values.

3.4 Using the `min` inline function from the preceding exercise, write a benchmark program that reports the amount of time saved compared to a normal function call.

3.5 Design a set of overloaded functions that return the absolute value of an `int`, a `long`, and a `double` value.

3.6 Write a program using C++'s new operator and I/O streams to read a string into a dynamic variable created on the heap.

3.7 Modify Reffunc.cpp to store `double` values in a linked list rather than an array. The program should operate exactly as before, and thanks to the use of a reference function, statements in `main` should not require any modifications.

PART

C++ Tutorials

4

CHAPTER

Programming with Classes

You'd have to be living face down in a moon crater not to have heard about object-oriented programming, or OOP as it is comically known. OOP is the programming paradigm of the 1990s, the model (some say) upon which all the world's software soon will be built. There are still a few doubters who resist the move to OOP, but the predictions of OOP's wide acceptance appear to be coming true, and those who ignore OOP risk missing the major contribution of C++ to programming—the *class*.

Simply stated, a class is an object-oriented tool for creating new data types. C++ has many built-in types such as int, double, and char. Classes give you the means to create new types that, due in part to OOP principles, behave in ways nearly identical to those built into C++.

Why Use Object-Oriented Programming?

Many experts agree that OOP and C++ classes help reduce complexity, especially in large programs. OOP encourages programmers to reuse existing code rather than rewrite functions from scratch. It's common for conventional C programmers to rewrite the same code over and over because *it's too much trouble to reuse existing, tested modules*. C++ classes are easy to reuse and extend, and OOP code tends to evolve from existing modules the way trees grow by extending their branches. Rather than replant low-level code into every new program, with OOP you write programs that grow naturally from your current crop of tested modules.

If this is your initial exposure to OOP, don't be concerned if OOP's advantages elude you at first. C++ lets you learn OOP at your own speed. Unlike so-called "pure" OOP languages such as SmallTalk and Actor, C++ is a hybrid programming language that combines conventional and OOP methods. This means you can use what you already know about C++ while you learn OOP; you don't have to choke down all of OOP's details at once. Three concepts distinguish OOP from conventional programming:

- Encapsulation
- Inheritance
- Virtual functions

In this chapter, you learn how encapsulation combines data and functions in a class. The next chapter introduces inheritance and virtual functions.

Understanding the importance of encapsulation requires a brief trip back to conventional C programming. As you will learn, C++ classes and encapsulation can unclog one of the most common and most constricting bottlenecks that conventional programmers face—a change to a fundamental data structure in a program nearing completion.

Trouble in Paradise

Conventional C programming techniques often make programmers work harder than necessary. For instance, consider how you might represent the date and time—a typical task that many, if not most, programs need to do. In C, you could declare a struct like this:

```
struct TTime {
  int year;
  int month;
  int day;
  int hour;
  int minute;
};
```

TTime's members store the member values of a single date and time. The initial T in TTime stands for *type*, an optional naming convention that I like to use to help distinguish data type names from others. (This conforms to Borland's class naming style.) Given this structure, you can declare a TTime variable such as

```
TTime appointment;
```

Notice that C++ does not require the struct keyword before TTime as does C. Given this declaration, a program can assign values to appointment's members with statements such as

```
appointment.year = 1996;
appointment.month = 7;
appointment.day = 14;
appointment.hour = 8;
appointment.minute = 30;
```

A program that uses lots of TTime structures probably needs functions to display dates and times, to change structure members, to compare two dates, and so on. You could write a display function like this:

```
void Display(struct TTime *tp)
{
  char buffer[32];
  sprintf(buffer, "Date: %02d/%02d/%04d  Time: %02d:%02d\n",
    tp->month, tp->day, tp->year, tp->hour, tp->minute);
  cout << buffer;
}
```

To display a date and time, a statement can pass to Display the address of a TTime structure such as appointment:

```
Display(&appointment);
```

So far, all is well in paradise. Consider, however, a typical problem that can cause carefully written conventional code to fall from grace. After designing a struct like TTime and writing a zillion date and time functions, you discover a superior way to store the date and time that would greatly improve your program's runtime speed. For example, you might use a long integer that represents the number of seconds from a fixed date. This change also makes it possible to use date and time library functions that recognize the date and time stored in this way.

Too bad you didn't think of this great idea earlier! To change the program's representation at this late stage, you have to perform these laborious steps:

1. Modify the TTime structure, deleting the current members and adding a single new long integer member. (You might even decide not to use a structure after all.)

2. Revise all functions such as `Display` that declare `TTime` parameters or that return `TTime` structures, pointers, or references.

3. Hunt for and modify statements that assign or use component values in `TTime` structures. These statements must be revised to use the new date and time format.

In a large program with thousands of lines, the prospect of tracking down every use of `TTime` is disheartening. The change in the data's structure forces you to revise code that has already been tested, thus requiring new debugging sessions and wasting valuable development time. The old rule of thumb, "let the data structure the code," doesn't always work well in the real world where data specifications are likely to change during a program's development, making extra work for programmers.

With conventional programming, the data representations you choose early in a program's development limit your freedom to make changes later. With OOP, data may change in form with only limited effects on the code. C++ classes can restrict a program's access to internal data storage details, so changes to data representations do not necessarily propagate modifications throughout the program's modules. The larger the program, the greater the potential benefit.

Introducing the Class

Consider how you might store the date and time in a class and take advantage of OOP's benefits. A class is a kind of structure that encapsulates data and functions into a handy package. (See Figure 4.1.)

Figure 4.1.
A class encapsulates data and functions.

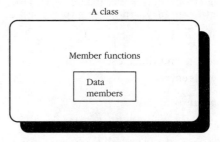

Here's the previous `TTime` structure rewritten as a class that encapsulates data and functions:

```
class TTime {
public:                 // Access specifier
  int year;             // Data member
  int month;            //     "     "
  int day;              //     "     "
  int hour;             //     "     "
  int minute;           //     "     "
  void Display(void);   // Member function
};
```

The class looks very much like the TTime struct, except that it begins with the class keyword. Technically, a class *is* a struct with added capabilities. Again, by convention, the initial T in the class name indicates that TTime is a data type. Braces enclose the six members of the class, which are preceded by public, one of three *access specifiers* that define the ways statements may use members of a class. Later, you'll examine two other access specifiers, private and protected. The public access specifier makes the members that follow available to all users of the class. Access specifiers end with a colon.

Data members in a class are exactly like data members in a struct. Data members such as year, month, and day may be variables, pointers, references, arrays, structures, and so on. They may also be class objects. However, members may not use the storage class specifiers auto, extern, or register.

Class member functions such as Display are declared as function prototypes. Presumably, member functions such as Display in TTime perform some kind of operation on the class's data members. The actual function statements are provided at another place in the program.

Listing 4.1, Class1.cpp, uses the TTime class in a C++ program and demonstrates how to implement a member function. Compile the program and run it to display a date and time.

Listing 4.1. Class1.cpp (Demonstrates a simple class).

```
//===============================================================
// Class1.cpp -- Demonstrates a simple class
// To compile:
//    bcc class1
// To run:
//    class1
// Copyright (c) 1996 by Tom Swan. All rights reserved.
//===============================================================

#include <iostream.h>
#include <stdio.h>

class TTime {
public:                   // Access specifier
  int year;               // Data member
  int month;              //    "    "
  int day;                //    "    "
  int hour;               //    "    "
  int minute;             //    "    "
  void Display(void);     // Member function
};

void main()
{
  TTime appointment;  // Object of type TTime

  appointment.month = 7;       // Initialize object data members
  appointment.day = 14;
  appointment.year = 1996;
```

continues

Listing 4.1. continued

```
  appointment.hour = 8;
  appointment.minute = 30;
  cout << "Appointment == ";
  appointment.Display();       // Call member function
  cout << endl;
}

void TTime::Display(void)
{
  char s[32];
  sprintf(s, "Date: %02d/%02d/%04d  Time: %02d:%02d\n",
    month, day, year, hour, minute);
  cout << s;
}
```

Typically, class declarations are written in header files and included into program modules, but you may also insert them directly into a program module as done here for demonstration purposes. The TTime class declaration is the same as the one you examined a moment ago.

Skip to the end of the listing where the Display member function is implemented. There are two main differences between a member function's implementation and the implementation of a common function:

- The member function name is prefaced by the class name and a scope resolution operator. The function header tells the compiler that Display is a member of the TTime class and that the function returns void. The class name uniquely qualifies the member function's name, and as a result, other classes may have Display functions without producing a naming conflict.

- Inside the member function, statements have direct access to the class's members. For example, sprintf uses the month, day, year, hour, and minute data members to format a string buffer, written in an output stream statement.

- Function main uses the TTime class much as it would any other data type. First, it defines appointment as a *class object,* or *instance,* of type TTime. The class merely describes the format of the class members. You must create an object such as appointment of the class type in order to use the class.

After constructing the appointment object, the program assigns values to the object's data members, initializing a date and time. Again, this is similar to the way you use a struct. After making all assignments, the program calls the Display member function, which displays the appointment's date and time. All these statements use dot notation to reference class object data members and to call member functions.

You may create as many objects of a class as your program needs. For example, a program might define other TTime class objects such as

```
TTime today;
TTime tomorrow;
TTime yesterday;
```

These objects could be assigned values and then displayed with the statements

```
today.Display();        // Display value of today class object
tomorrow.Display();     // Display value of tomorrow class object
yesterday.Display();    // Display value of yesterday class object
```

> **NOTE**
>
> C++ permits structs and unions as well as classes to have member functions. In fact, in Class1.cpp, if you change class to struct and remove the public access specifier, the program works as before. (Members of a struct or union are public by default.) In practice, however, member functions are rarely of much practical use in structures and unions, and are therefore more commonly declared in classes.

Class1.cpp is not a very good example of a class. For example, the program does nothing to prevent the problems associated with changes to data representations mentioned earlier. All data members in the TTime class are public, and are therefore directly accessible by all statements in any modules that use the class.

Listing 4.2, Class2.cpp, declares a new and improved TTime class that uses member functions to access a class object's data members. The data members are made private to the class, thus restricting their use and improving the code's modularity.

Listing 4.2. Class2.cpp (Demonstrates private and public access specifiers).

```
//==============================================================
// Class2.cpp -- Demonstrates private and public access specifiers
// To compile:
//    bcc class2
// To run:
//    class2
// Copyright (c) 1996 by Tom Swan. All rights reserved.
//==============================================================

#include <iostream.h>
#include <stdio.h>

class TTime {
private:
  int year;
  int month;
  int day;
  int hour;
```

continues

83

Listing 4.2. continued

```
  int minute;
public:
  void Display(void);
  void GetTime(int &m, int &d, int &y, int &hr, int &min);
  void SetTime(int m, int d, int y, int hr, int min);
};

void main()
{
  TTime appointment;
  int month, day, year, hour, minute;

  appointment.SetTime(7, 14, 1996, 8, 30);
  cout << "Appointment == ";
  appointment.Display();
  appointment.GetTime(month, day, year, hour, minute);
  appointment.SetTime(month, day, year, ++hour, minute);
  cout << "Next hour   == ";
  appointment.Display();
}

void TTime::Display(void)
{
  char s[32];
  sprintf(s, "Date: %02d/%02d/%04d  Time: %02d:%02d\n",
    month, day, year, hour, minute);
  cout << s;
}

void TTime::GetTime(int &m, int &d, int &y, int &hr, int &min)
{
  m = month;      // Return data members to caller
  d = day;
  y = year;
  hr = hour;
  min = minute;
}

void TTime::SetTime(int m, int d, int y, int hr, int min)
{
  month = m;      // Assign arguments to data members
  day = d;
  year = y;
  hour = hr;
  minute = min;
}
```

The new TTime class has three additions. First, the private access specifier makes the int data members private to the class. Because of this change, only class member functions Display, GetTime, and SetTime may use these data members. Remember this rule: *A class's private members are available only to members of their class. Private members are not accessible to functions outside of the class.*

NOTE

Members of a class are private by default, and technically speaking, the `private` access specifier in Class2.cpp is redundant. For clarity, however, it's a good idea to mark members with explicit access specifiers. Members of a `struct` are public by default—a key difference between classes and common structures.

A class may have multiple private and public sections, which may be in any order. You can repeat the private and public access specifiers as many times as you want in a class declaration. Member functions are commonly public, but they may also be private to a class. You'll investigate a third access specifier, `protected`, in the next chapter.

Two other additions to TTime are the `GetTime` and `SetTime` member functions. Along with `Display`, the three member functions provide controlled access to the class's private parts. The only way for functions outside of the class to use TTime's private data members is to call one of the class's public member functions. The data and functions are encapsulated in the class, and as a direct result, if the data representation changes, only the class's member functions need to be rewritten. Similarly, if a problem develops, debugging can begin with an examination of the class member functions because no other functions or statements in the program have access to TTime's private members. Figure 4.2 shows these concepts with arrows indicating access paths to a class's public and private members. Thus any problems with those members are likely caused by class member functions.

The program implements the class member functions following `main`. The class name and scope resolution operator `TTime::` preface the function names, informing the compiler that these functions belong to the class.

TIP

A typical error is to forget to preface function headers with the class name and scope resolution operator. If you receive one or more "Undefined symbol" errors, this is the likely cause.

Inside the member function implementations, statements have direct access to the class's data members `month`, `day`, `year`, `hour`, and `minute`. (See Figure 4.2.) In function `GetTime`, for example, statements pass the values of the class object's component members back to the caller's arguments by way of the five `int` reference parameters. In `SetTime`, value parameters are assigned to the class object's data members.

In the main program, because TTime's data members are private to the class, it is no longer possible to assign values directly to a class object. For example, the statement

```
appointment.month = 7;   // ???
```

from the previous example, Class1.cpp, does not compile in Class2.cpp because `month` is private to the `TTime` class and is therefore directly usable only by members of that class. If you try to compile that statement, the compiler complains that "`TTime::month` is not accessible in function `main`."

Figure 4.2.

Classes restrict access to private members.

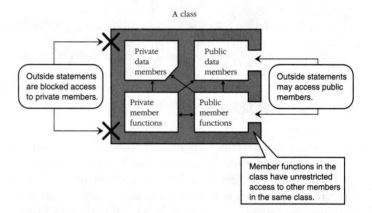

In the new program, to assign values to the appointment class object requires calling a member function. For example, `main` executes the statement

```
appointment.SetTime(7, 14, 1996, 8, 30);
```

to set appointment's date and time to July 14, 1996, at 8:30. Similarly, another statement in `main` calls `GetTime` to copy appointment's data member values to local variables. The program then passes these values back to `SetTime` with the hour incremented, thus upping the appointment's hour. (This is hardly the ideal way to change a date and time, but we'll improve `TTime`'s design later.)

Using Member Functions

Most classes are best declared in header files, ending with the file name extension .h, which various modules can include to share the same classes. Member function implementations are best written in separate source code modules, ending in .cpp, that are linked to a host program to create a finished executable code file.

The next several listings expand the `TTime` class and illustrate how to declare and implement classes in separate modules, and how to link those modules to host programs. Although this takes more work, programs with many classes greatly benefit from a modular design. Separate modules are easier to reuse and maintain. In fact, many professional programmers religiously follow a rule of one class per module.

The header file in Listing 4.3, Time1.h, declares a new TTime class, similar to the one in Class2.cpp, but with a couple of additional member functions. As before, the new class has several private data members. Like most software projects under development, this program has a few inefficiencies. No matter—we'll deal with any problems as we improve the class design in subsequent revisions.

Like all good header files, Time1.h is not a program. It is purely declarative, and you can't compile and run it. Other program modules (see the next two listings) include the header, making its declarations available to statements. Using headers is an optional, but recommended, method for better organizing a program's parts and pieces.

> **NOTE**
>
> For simplicity, this book's sample programs don't always declare classes in header files, but you should follow this design technique in your own application programs. Declare classes in header files; implement them in separate modules; and link those modules to host programs as explained in the following sections.

Listing 4.3. Time1.h (Declares the TTime class version 1).

```
//=============================================================
// Time1.h -- Declares the TTime class version 1
// Copyright (c) 1996 by Tom Swan. All rights reserved.
//=============================================================

#ifndef __TIME1_H
#define __TIME1_H  1  // Prevent multiple #includes

class TTime {
private:
  int month;
  int day;
  int year;
  int hour;
  int minute;
public:
  void Display(void);
  void GetTime(int &m, int &d, int &y, int &hr, int &min);
  void SetTime(int m, int d, int y, int hr, int min);
  char *GetSTime(void);
  void ChangeTime(long nminutes);
};

#endif  // __TIME1_H
```

The conditional compilation instructions—#ifndef, #define, and #endif—prevent the Time1.h header file from being compiled more than once. This optional convention makes it possible for multiple modules to include the header without causing multiple-declaration errors. The first time a module includes Time1.h, the symbol __TIME1_H is defined. On any subsequent includes of this same header, the #ifndef instruction causes the compiler to skip the entire file down to the final #endif. This also helps keep compilation speeds fast by not feeding declarations to the compiler that it has already digested.

Listing 4.4, Time1.cpp, implements the TTime class member functions in a separate module. This module is not a program (it lacks a main function), and therefore, you cannot run it. Use the -c (compile-only) switch to compile the module from a DOS prompt. This creates the object-code file Time1.obj, which you will later link to a finished host program (in Listing 4.4) that uses the module's class.

> **NOTE**
>
> I recommend you compile all programs in this chapter from a DOS prompt by following instructions at the beginning of each listing. The listings are in the Source\C04 directory, which you can copy from the CD-ROM. Even simpler, change to that directory and type make to compile all programs. If you prefer to use the IDE, open the .ide project files to compile each sample program and associated modules as EasyWin applications.

Listing 4.4. Time1.cpp (Implements the TTime class version 1).

```
//=================================================================
// Time1.cpp -- Implements the TTime class version 1
// To Compile:
//    bcc -c time1
// Copyright (c) 1996 by Tom Swan. All rights reserved.
//=================================================================

#include <iostream.h>
#include <stdio.h>
#include <dos.h>
#include <string.h>
#include "time1.h"

// Display date and time
void TTime::Display(void)
{
  char s[30];
  sprintf(s, "Date: %02d/%02d/%04d  Time: %02d:%02d",
    month, day, year, hour, minute );
  cout << s << endl;
}
```

```
// Return current date and time data members
void TTime::GetTime(int &m, int &d, int &y, int &hr, int &min)
{
  m = month;      // Pass object's data members to caller
  d = day;
  y = year;
  hr = hour;
  min = minute;
}

// Set date and time data members
void TTime::SetTime(int m, int d, int y, int hr, int min)
{
  month = m;      // Assign arguments to object's data members
  day = d;
  year = y;
  hour = hr;
  minute = min;
}

// Return string representation of date and time
char *TTime::GetSTime(void)
{
  char buffer[40];  // Plenty of space
  char *cp;  // Pointer to function result

  sprintf(buffer, "Date: %02d/%02d/%04d  Time: %02d:%02d\n",
    month, day, year, hour, minute );
  cp = strdup(buffer);  // Trim to smallest possible size
  return cp;
}

// Add nminutes (which may be negative) to current time
void TTime::ChangeTime(long nminutes)
{
  struct date ds;
  struct time ts;
  long timeinsecs;

  ds.da_year = year;
  ds.da_mon = month;
  ds.da_day = day;
  ts.ti_hour = hour;
  ts.ti_min = minute;
  ts.ti_sec = 0;
  ts.ti_hund = 0;
  timeinsecs = dostounix(&ds, &ts);
  timeinsecs += (nminutes * 60);
  unixtodos(timeinsecs, &ds, &ts);
  year = ds.da_year;
  month = ds.da_mon;
  day = ds.da_day;
  hour = ts.ti_hour;
  minute = ts.ti_min;
}
```

Before examining how Time1.cpp implements the TTime class, compile and run Listing 4.5, Appoint1.cpp, a sample host program that uses the module's class to display a page from a fictitious appointment calendar. (Lucky for you, I gave you the day off and your calendar shows no appointments. You can thank me later.)

Listing 4.5. Appoint1.cpp (Demonstrates the TTime class version 1).

```
//===============================================================
// Appoint1.cpp -- Demonstrates the TTime class version 1
// To compile:
//    bcc -c time1
//    bcc appoint1 time1.obj
// To run:
//    appoint1
// Copyright (c) 1996 by Tom Swan. All rights reserved.
//===============================================================

#include <iostream.h>
#include <stdio.h>
#include "time1.h"

void main()
{
  TTime appointment;

  appointment.SetTime(7, 21, 1996, 8, 30);
  for (int slots = 1; slots <= 17; slots++) {
    appointment.Display();
    appointment.ChangeTime(30);
  }
}
```

The program includes Time1.h, which makes the TTime class declaration available. Function main begins by declaring an appointment class object of type TTime. A statement then calls SetTime to assign date and time values to the object, after which a for loop displays a series of time slots, 30 minutes apart. The important observation here is that, in all cases, the program calls member functions to perform actions on appointment. On screen, the program displays lines such as

```
Date: 07/21/1996  Time: 08:30
Date: 07/21/1996  Time: 09:00
Date: 07/21/1996  Time: 09:30
Date: 07/21/1996  Time: 10:00
...
Date: 07/21/1996  Time: 16:30
```

Now that you've seen how to use the TTime class, skip back to Time1.cpp, which implements the class member functions. Some of the programming is repeated from before. New member functions are GetSTime, which returns a string representation of a TTime object's date and time, and ChangeTime, which adds or subtracts a specified number of minutes from an object's date and time.

These two new member functions are prefaced with `TTime::` to identify them to the compiler as members of the `TTime` class. Member function `GetSTime` calls `sprintf` to prepare a string with the private data members `month`, `day`, `year`, `hour`, and `minute` inserted with the appropriate punctuation. The function then calls `strdup` to copy this raw string to a new one on the heap, The final statement returns a pointer to this string, which the program can delete by calling `free`.

Member function `ChangeTime` calls two library functions, `dostounix` and `unixtodos`, to convert the class object's date and time to and from a long integer format. This makes it easy to add or subtract the specified number of minutes passed to the member function as parameter `nminutes`. In the main program, the statement

```
appointment.ChangeTime(30);
```

calls the `ChangeTime` member function for the appointment class object to advance the object's time by 30 minutes.

When a statement such as this calls a member function, C++ passes to the function the address of the object, in this case, the address of `appointment`. Inside the member function, that object's address is available through a special, undeclared, keyword named `this`. All member functions receive a `this` pointer, which addresses the class object for which the member function was called. In Appoint1.cpp, calls to `SetTime`, `Display`, and `ChangeTime` pass `this` so the functions can operate on the object's data members.

In a member function, you may use `this` as a pointer to an object of the class type. For example, in Time1.cpp, function `GetTime`, this statement

```
m = month;
```

is exactly equivalent to

```
m = this->month;
```

Translated to plain English, the statement assigns to reference parameter `m` the value of the month data member in the class object addressed by `this`. Although you'll rarely need `this`, it's often valuable as a function argument. For example, given a function `f` that operates on an object of the `TTime` class, a statement could pass to `f` the object for which a member function was called. That function might be declared as follows to accept a reference to a `TTime` object:

```
void f(TTime &theTime);   // Requires passing f a TTime object
```

Elsewhere, the program creates a `TTime` object, and calls a `MemberFunction` in the class:

```
TTime anObject;            // Create TTime object
anObject.MemberFunction(); // Call TTime member function for object
```

`MemberFunction`'s implementation calls function `f` and passed `this` as an argument to give `f` the address of `anObject`, for which `MemberFunction` was called:

```
TTime::MemberFunction()  // Receives anObject's address as "this"
{
  f(this);  // Passes anObject by reference to function f
  ...
}
```

Modifying Private Data Members

Better ways to represent data often become apparent midway in the mad dash to a software project's deadline. For example, storing the date and time as the number of seconds from a fixed date (typically January 1, 1970, on DOS systems) is more convenient than using individual integer fields, and this format allows the use of other conforming library functions.

Member function ChangeTime in Time1.cpp converts the date and time data members to a long integer (timeinsecs), thus wasting time and effort if this function is called frequently. Obviously, this function could be simplified if the date and time were already in long integer format.

Listings 4.6, Time2.h, 4.7, Time2.cpp, and 4.8, Appoint2.cpp, make this improvement to TTime's data representation. As in the preceding example, Time2.h declares the class, which is implemented in Time2.cpp. These files are not programs—you have to compile them to create Time2.obj, and then link that object code file to the Appoint2.cpp host program. See the beginning of Appoint2.cpp for compilation instructions.

Listing 4.6. Time2.h (Declares the TTime class version 2).

```
//=================================================================
// Time2.h -- Declares the TTime class version 2
// Copyright (c) 1996 by Tom Swan. All rights reserved.
//=================================================================

#ifndef __TIME2_H
#define __TIME2_H  1  // Prevent multiple #includes

class TTime {
private:
  long dt;  // Date and time in seconds from January 1, 1970
public:
  void Display(void);
  void GetTime(int &m, int &d, int &y, int &hr, int &min);
  void SetTime(int m, int d, int y, int hr, int min);
  char *GetSTime(void);
  void ChangeTime(long nminutes);
};

#endif  // __TIME2_H
```

Class TTime in Time2.h is identical to TTime in Time1.h, but declares only a single long private data member, dt. Gone are the individual month, day, year, hour, and minute data members.

Despite this change, however, *the public member functions are the same,* and thus, statements that use the TTime class need no modifications.

Of course, the member functions themselves must be revised to use the new data, but at least the revision work is limited to a set of easily identified functions. Consider a typical case of a dozen modules that use this class. Only the following module, Listing 4.7, Time2.cpp, needs revision to implement the new data format.

Listing 4.7. Time2.cpp (Implements the TTime class version 2).

```
//==============================================================
// Time2.cpp -- Implements the TTime class version 2
// To compile:
//   bcc -c time2
// Copyright (c) 1996 by Tom Swan. All rights reserved.
//==============================================================

#include <iostream.h>
#include <time.h>
#include <dos.h>
#include <string.h>
#include "time2.h"

// Display date and time
void TTime::Display(void)
{
  cout << ctime(&dt);
}

// Return current date and time data members
void TTime::GetTime(int &m, int &d, int &y, int &hr, int &min)
{
  struct date ds;
  struct time ts;

  unixtodos(dt, &ds, &ts);
  y = ds.da_year;
  m = ds.da_mon;
  d = ds.da_day;
  hr = ts.ti_hour;
  min = ts.ti_min;
}

// Set dt data member
void TTime::SetTime(int m, int d, int y, int hr, int min)
{
  struct date ds;
  struct time ts;

  ds.da_year = y;
  ds.da_mon = m;
  ds.da_day = d;
  ts.ti_hour = hr;
```

continues

93

Listing 4.7. continued

```
   ts.ti_min = min;
   ts.ti_sec = 0;
   ts.ti_hund = 0;
   dt = dostounix(&ds, &ts);
}

// Return string representation of date and time
char *TTime::GetSTime(void)
{
   char *cp = strdup(ctime(&dt));
   return cp;
}

// Add nminutes (which may be negative) to current time
void TTime::ChangeTime(long nminutes)
{
   dt += (nminutes * 60);
}
```

The new module greatly improves the old, and it has shrunk in size. Now that the date and time are stored as a long integer, function Display can simply call the library function ctime to convert the date and time to a null-terminated string. Member functions GetTime and PutTime are somewhat more complex than before, because they now have to convert the date and time to and from individual parameters, using the unixtodos and dostounix library functions described earlier. We've gone two steps forward and one back. So it goes.

On the bright side, member functions GetSTime and ChangeTime are vastly improved. GetSTime passes the result of ctime directly to strdup to return the date and time as a string. Best of all, ChangeTime is now reduced to a single statement. Because the date and time are in the proper form, there's no need for all the conversion statements in the former version.

Changing data formats to simplify code is a time-honored programming optimization technique. With OOP and C++ classes, a change to a fundamental data structure does not necessarily require corresponding changes to statements that use that information. As demonstrated by Listing 4.8, Appoint2.cpp, the main program in the sample project is oblivious to the major modifications made to the TTime class.

In fact, the new program, Appoint2.cpp, is identical to Appoint1.cpp, except that it includes header Time2.h rather than Time1.h. It doesn't take much imagination to realize the benefits of this fact in a larger program, although in this small example, the advantages are practically nil. Even a 10,000-line program with hundreds of TTime class objects would require no more effort to modify than this simple example! Encapsulating data and functions in a class localizes changes to code by restricting access to data, thus minimizing the potential amount of revisions required later if the data representation changes.

Listing 4.8. Appoint2.cpp (Demonstrates the TTime class version 2).

```
//=============================================================
// Appoint2.cpp -- Demonstrates the TTime class version 2
// To compile:
//    bcc -c time2
//    bcc appoint2 time2.obj
// To run:
//    appoint2
// Copyright (c) 1996 by Tom Swan. All rights reserved.
//=============================================================

#include <iostream.h>
#include <stdio.h>
#include "time2.h"

void main()
{
  TTime appointment;

  appointment.SetTime(7, 21, 1996, 8, 30);
  for (int slots = 1; slots <= 17; slots++) {
    appointment.Display();
    appointment.ChangeTime(30);
  }
}
```

Inline Member Functions

So far, you've seen relatively simple examples of class declarations, but C++ offers many other goodies that you can use in classes. For example, using member functions to access class data members rightly brings up the concern of efficiency. Calling a member function like SetTime to assign values to a class object's data members takes more time than simply assigning values directly to those members—if, that is, they were public.

Although that observation is true, remember that one of the major goals of using classes is to restrict access to data, which simplifies maintenance. How much are a few function calls worth to the stability of your program and the ease of making future modifications?

In most cases, calling member functions instead of accessing class data members directly has little significant impact on a program's performance. There are times, however, when utmost efficiency is required. For those times, C++ permits classes to declare *inline member functions*. Though inline member functions are used exactly as others, no function calls are made in the compiled code. Rather, an inline member function's statements *are inserted directly into the compiled program.* (See Figure 4.3.)

Figure 4.3.

An inline member function's statements are inserted directly into the program.

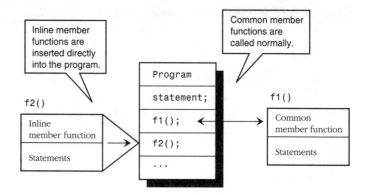

Listing 4.9, Time3.h, redeclares the TTime class using a few inline member functions. As with the preceding examples, you must compile and link the next three listings together to produce a working program. Follow instructions near the top of the Appoint3.cpp listing.

Listing 4.9. Time3.h (Declares the TTime class version 3).

```
//==============================================================
// Time3.h -- Declares the TTime class version 3
// Copyright (c) 1996 by Tom Swan. All rights reserved.
//==============================================================

#ifndef __TIME3_H
#define __TIME3_H  1  // Prevent multiple #includes

#include <iostream.h>
#include <time.h>
#include <string.h>

class TTime {
private:
  long dt;  // Date and time in seconds from January 1, 1970
public:
  void Display(void) { cout << ctime(&dt); }
  void GetTime(int &m, int &d, int &y, int &hr, int &min);
  void SetTime(int m, int d, int y, int hr, int min);
  char *GetSTime(void)
  {
    char *cp = strdup(ctime(&dt));
    return cp;
  }
  void ChangeTime(long nminutes) { dt += (nminutes * 60); }
};

#endif  // __TIME3_H
```

As a result of the inline member functions in Time3.h, the class's implementation in Listing 4.10, Time3.cpp, is much simpler than before. This is because most of the code-generating statements are now in the header file.

> **NOTE**
>
> C programmers are frequently told, upon pain of endless bugs, never to insert code statements into header files. Inline functions, however, are a necessary exception to this rule. They must be declared in headers so other modules can include them for compilation. (Modules can declare inline functions directly as well.) Inline functions are still purely declarative, and it's fully appropriate to store them in header files.

Listing 4.10. Time3.cpp (Implements the TTime class version 3).

```
//============================================================
// Time3.cpp -- Implements the TTime class version 3
// To compile:
//    bcc -c time3
// Copyright (c) 1996 by Tom Swan. All rights reserved.
//============================================================

#include <dos.h>
#include "time3.h"

// Return current date and time data members
void TTime::GetTime(int &m, int &d, int &y, int &hr, int &min)
{
  struct date ds;
  struct time ts;

  unixtodos(dt, &ds, &ts);
  y = ds.da_year;
  m = ds.da_mon;
  d = ds.da_day;
  hr = ts.ti_hour;
  min = ts.ti_min;
}

// Set dt data member
void TTime::SetTime(int m, int d, int y, int hr, int min)
{
  struct date ds;
  struct time ts;

  ds.da_year = y;
  ds.da_mon = m;
  ds.da_day = d;
  ts.ti_hour = hr;
  ts.ti_min = min;
  ts.ti_sec = 0;
  ts.ti_hund = 0;
  dt = dostounix(&ds, &ts);
}
```

Because inline member functions are used no differently than normal member functions, the main program requires no significant modifications. Listing 4.11, Appoint3.cpp, is identical to Appoint2.cpp, but includes Time3.h rather than Time2.h. See the beginning of the listing for compilation instructions.

Listing 4.11. Appoint3.cpp (Demonstrates the TTime class version 3).

```
//================================================================
// Appoint3.cpp -- Demonstrates the TTime class version 3
// To compile:
//    bcc -c time3
//    bcc appoint3 time3.obj
// To run:
//    appoint3
// Copyright (c) 1996 by Tom Swan. All rights reserved.
//================================================================

#include <iostream.h>
#include <stdio.h>
#include "time3.h"

void main()
{
  TTime appointment;

  appointment.SetTime(7, 21, 1996, 8, 30);
  for (int slots = 1; slots <= 17; slots++) {
    appointment.Display();
    appointment.ChangeTime(30);
  }
}
```

Time3.h shows a typical inline member function declaration. So you don't have to flip pages, here's a shortened version:

```
class TTime {
private:
  long dt;
public:
  void Display(void) { cout << ctime(&dt); }
  ...
};
```

Member function Display's statements are written directly in braces after the member function header in the class declaration. Notice the placement of the semicolon, which comes after the cout output stream statement. This format is consistent with C and C++ rules, which state that semicolons terminate declarations and statements. You might find this format easier to learn by writing the inline member function using an indented style:

```
class TTime {
private:
  long dt;
public:
```

```
  void Display(void)
  {
    cout << ctime(&dt);
  }
...
};
```

Either format works equally well, but to save space, inline functions are typically written on one or two run-together lines, as shown earlier.

Statements that call the inline `Display` member function do not necessarily generate a function call in the compiled code. For example, if you declare a class object and assign it a date and time using code such as

```
TTime today;
today.SetTime(4, 19, 1998, 6, 0);
```

you can then call the `Display` member function for the `today` class object:

```
today.Display();
```

Despite appearances, the program is compiled as though the preceding statement had been written

```
cout << ctime(&today.dt);
```

Of course, you can't actually write such a statement into the program because `dt` is a private data member of `TTime`, and it therefore cannot be accessed outside of the class. However, the compiler can do so because no access rules can be violated during compilation.

> **NOTE**
>
> As with common inline functions, C++ may or may not inject inline member functions directly into the compiled code. For example, if an inline member function is too complex, the compiler may choose to compile it as a normal member function. Keeping your inline member functions as short as possible is the best way to ensure that their statements are actually inserted inline.

Most inline member functions are declared directly in a class, as demonstrated in Time3.h. However, you may also declare inline member functions by using the inline keyword in the module's implementation. For example, to convert `TTime`'s `GetTime` to an inline member function, you can revise the function implementation in Time3.cpp to the following. (I show only the new declaration—the function content is unchanged.)

```
inline void TTime::GetTime(int &m, int &d, int &y, int &hr, int &min)
{
  ...
}
```

Simply tacking on inline to a member function, however, may not produce the expected results because *an inline member function's implementation must be seen by the compiler before that function is called.* In most cases, inline member functions are best encoded directly in class declarations stored in header files.

Overloaded Member Functions

In the previous chapter, you learned how to overload functions by declaring multiple functions of the same names that differ in at least one parameter. You may use a similar technique to overload a class's member functions.

Overloaded member functions are particularly useful when some (but not all) of a member function's parameters are needed. For example, as currently designed, TTime's SetTime function requires five integer arguments. To set the date and time to January 15, 1997, at 11:45, you must write

```
TTime anyTime;  // Define anyTime object
anyTime.SetTime(1, 15, 1997, 11, 45);  // Set object's date and time
```

Suppose, however, you want to set only the date, letting the class default to the current time. Currently, there is no easy way to initialize TTime in this way. Overloading SetTime with differing numbers of parameters makes it possible for the program to pass zero or more arguments, as in the statement

```
anyTime.SetTime(1, 15, 1997);
```

Listing 4.12, Time4.h, shows the new TTime class with several overloaded SetTime member functions.

Listing 4.12. Time4.h (Declares the TTime class version 4).

```
//===============================================================
// Time4.h -- Declares the TTime class version 4
// Copyright (c) 1996 by Tom Swan. All rights reserved.
//===============================================================

#ifndef __TIME4_H
#define __TIME4_H  1  // Prevent multiple #includes

#include <iostream.h>
#include <time.h>
#include <string.h>

class TTime {
private:
  long dt;  // Date and time in seconds from January 1, 1970
public:
  void Display(void) { cout << ctime(&dt); }
  void GetTime(int &m, int &d, int &y, int &hr, int &min);
  void SetTime(int m, int d, int y, int hr, int min);
  void SetTime(int m, int d, int y, int hr);
  void SetTime(int m, int d, int y);
  void SetTime(int m, int d);
  void SetTime(int m);
  void SetTime(void);
```

```
  char *GetSTime(void)
  {
    char *cp = strdup(ctime(&dt));
    return cp;
  }
  void ChangeTime(long nminutes) { dt += (nminutes * 60); }
};

#endif  // __TIME4_H
```

The header file declares six overloaded SetTime member functions in the TTime class. Each member function has the same name and differs in at least one parameter—the minimum requirements for the compiler to distinguish among them. Even though each member function has the same name, however, each is distinct and must be implemented separately, as Listing 4.13, Time4.cpp, shows.

Listing 4.13. Time4.cpp (Implements the TTime class version 4).

```
//===============================================================
// Time4.cpp -- Implements the TTime class version 4
// To compile:
//   bcc -c time4
// Copyright (c) 1996 by Tom Swan. All rights reserved.
//===============================================================

#include <dos.h>
#include "time4.h"

// Return current date and time data members
void TTime::GetTime(int &m, int &d, int &y, int &hr, int &min)
{
  struct date ds;
  struct time ts;

  unixtodos(dt, &ds, &ts);
  y = ds.da_year;
  m = ds.da_mon;
  d = ds.da_day;
  hr = ts.ti_hour;
  min = ts.ti_min;
}

// Set dt data member
void TTime::SetTime(int m, int d, int y, int hr, int min)
{
  struct date ds;
  struct time ts;

  getdate(&ds);  // Get current date and time
  gettime(&ts);
  if (y >= 0) ds.da_year = y;
  if (m >= 0) ds.da_mon = m;
  if (d >= 0) ds.da_day = d;
```

continues

101

Listing 4.13. continued

```
  if (hr >= 0) ts.ti_hour = hr;
  if (min >= 0) ts.ti_min = min;
  ts.ti_sec = 0;
  ts.ti_hund = 0;
  dt = dostounix(&ds, &ts);
}

void TTime::SetTime(int m, int d, int y, int hr)
{
  SetTime(m, d, y, hr, -1);
}

void TTime::SetTime(int m, int d, int y)
{
  SetTime(m, d, y, -1, -1);
}

void TTime::SetTime(int m, int d)
{
  SetTime(m, d, -1, -1, -1);
}

void TTime::SetTime(int m)
{
  SetTime(m, -1, -1, -1, -1);
}

void TTime::SetTime(void)
{
  SetTime(-1, -1, -1, -1, -1);
}
```

The first SetTime member function calls library functions getdate and gettime to obtain the system's current date and time. This new version of the function assigns to the class object's data members any parameter values that are greater than or equal to zero, thus leaving the current default values alone for any parameters that are less than zero. If today is a class object of type TTime, the statement

```
today.SetTime(1, 15, 1998, -1, -1);
```

sets today's date to January 15, 1998, but uses the current hour and minute because those two arguments are set to -1.

Because the function is overloaded, there's no need to enter the two negative argument placeholders. You can simply write

```
today.SetTime(1, 15, 1998);
```

In this case, the overloaded member function with three int parameters is called, which supplies the missing negative values. The compiler knows which of the overloaded SetTime member functions to call based on the number and types of arguments used in the statement. The other overloaded member functions are similarly implemented in terms of the five-parameter, fully equipped SetTime. For example, the statement

```
today.SetTime();
```

calls the no-parameter overloaded SetTime member function (the last one implemented), which calls the five-parameter version to set today to the system's current date and time.

Listing 4.14, Overmf.cpp, demonstrates how to use the overloaded TTime member functions. See the listing for compilation instructions.

Listing 4.14. Overmf.cpp (Demonstrates the TTime class version 4).

```
//================================================================
// Overmf.cpp -- Demonstrates the TTime class version 4
// To compile:
//    bcc -c time4
//    bcc overmf time4.obj
// To run:
//    overmf
// Copyright (c) 1996 by Tom Swan. All rights reserved.
//================================================================

#include <iostream.h>
#include <stdio.h>
#include "time4.h"

void main()
{
  TTime appointment;

  appointment.SetTime();
  appointment.Display();
  appointment.SetTime(8);
  appointment.Display();
  appointment.SetTime(8, 1);
  appointment.Display();
  appointment.SetTime(8, 1, 1996);
  appointment.Display();
  appointment.SetTime(8, 1, 1996, 8);
  appointment.Display();
  appointment.SetTime(8, 1, 1996, 8, 30);
  appointment.Display();
}
```

The test program calls each of the overloaded SetTime member functions, passing from zero to five arguments. When you run the program, the interspersed calls to Display show the results of each overloaded function call.

Default Member Function Parameters

Numerous overloaded member functions such as those in Time4.h and Time4.cpp are useful, but they often lead to confusing code. In some cases, default member function parameters can reduce the number of member functions required while still permitting statements to specify a variable number of arguments.

The previous chapter, "Introducing C++," explained how to use default parameters for common functions. Default member function parameters are exactly the same, but they appear in a class declaration. Listing 4.15, Time5.h, revises the TTime class's SetTime member function to use default parameter values.

Listing 4.15. Time5.h (Declares the TTime class version 5).

```
//=================================================================
// Time5.h -- Declares the TTime class version 5
// Copyright (c) 1996 by Tom Swan. All rights reserved.
//=================================================================

#ifndef __TIME5_H
#define __TIME5_H  1  // Prevent multiple #includes

#include <iostream.h>
#include <time.h>
#include <string.h>

class TTime {
private:
  long dt;  // Date and time in seconds from January 1, 1970
public:
  void Display(void) { cout << ctime(&dt); }
  void GetTime(int &m, int &d, int &y, int &hr, int &min);
  void SetTime(int m = -1, int d = -1, int y = -1,
    int hr = -1, int min = -1);
  char *GetSTime(void)
  {
    char *cp = strdup(ctime(&dt));
    return cp;
  }
  void ChangeTime(long nminutes) { dt += (nminutes * 60); }
};

#endif  // __TIME5_H
```

Each of SetTime's parameters is assigned a default value of -1, which is used for any unspecified arguments in calls to this member function. Default parameter values must follow any other parameters in the member function's declaration. Given a TTime class object named today, the statement

```
today.SetTime(1, 15, 1998);
```

passes January 15, 1998, to SetTime's first three parameters. Because unspecified parameters assume the declared default values, the last two arguments are invisibly set to -1, and the preceding statement is compiled as though it had been written

```
today.SetTime(1, 15, 1998, -1, -1);
```

Implementing the new TTime class is now much simpler than with the overloaded SetTime member functions. Listing 4.16, Time5.cpp, shows the result.

Listing 4.16. Time5.cpp (Implements the TTime class version 5).

```
//===============================================================
// time5.cpp -- Implements the TTime class version 5
// To compile:
//   bcc -c time5
// Copyright (c) 1996 by Tom Swan. All rights reserved.
//===============================================================

#include <dos.h>
#include "time5.h"

// Return current date and time data members
void TTime::GetTime(int &m, int &d, int &y, int &hr, int &min)
{
  struct date ds;
  struct time ts;

  unixtodos(dt, &ds, &ts);
  y = ds.da_year;
  m = ds.da_mon;
  d = ds.da_day;
  hr = ts.ti_hour;
  min = ts.ti_min;
}

// Set dt data member
void TTime::SetTime(int m, int d, int y, int hr, int min)
{
  struct date ds;
  struct time ts;

  getdate(&ds);  // Get current date and time
  gettime(&ts);
  if (y >= 0) ds.da_year = y;
  if (m >= 0) ds.da_mon = m;
  if (d >= 0) ds.da_day = d;
  if (hr >= 0) ts.ti_hour = hr;
  if (min >= 0) ts.ti_min = min;
  ts.ti_sec = 0;
  ts.ti_hund = 0;
  dt = dostounix(&ds, &ts);
}
```

In the implementation module, the default member function parameter values are not again listed in the function's header. Default values may appear only in the member function's declaration, never in the function's implementation.

Listing 4.17, Default.cpp, uses the new TTime class, demonstrating that in this case, the default member function parameters allow a variable number of arguments to be passed to SetTime. The end result is the same as the overloaded example presented earlier, but the class implementation is far simpler. See the compilation instructions at the beginning of the listing.

Listing 4.17. Default.cpp (Demonstrates the TTime class version 5).

```
//===============================================================
// Default.cpp -- Demonstrates the TTime class version 5
// To compile:
//    bcc -c time5
//    bcc default time5.obj
// To run:
//    default
// Copyright (c) 1996 by Tom Swan. All rights reserved.
//===============================================================

#include <iostream.h>
#include <stdio.h>
#include "time5.h"

void main()
{
  TTime appointment;

  appointment.SetTime();
  appointment.Display();
  appointment.SetTime(8);
  appointment.Display();
  appointment.SetTime(8, 1);
  appointment.Display();
  appointment.SetTime(8, 1, 1996);
  appointment.Display();
  appointment.SetTime(8, 1, 1996, 8);
  appointment.Display();
  appointment.SetTime(8, 1, 1996, 8, 30);
  appointment.Display();
}
```

Constructors and Destructors

Until now, the programming examples you've examined have created uninitialized class objects. Consider any one of the preceding TTime classes. The declaration

```
TTime anyTime;
```

creates a class object anyTime of type TTime, but does not initialize that object's data members. If you forget to initialize the class object, the statement

```
anyTime.Display();
```

is likely to output garbage, or at the very least, an incorrect date and time.

Classes may declare one or more *constructors* to initialize class objects automatically when the object is created, thus eliminating errors caused by using uninitialized data. Classes may also declare a *destructor* (but only one) that is called to perform clean-up duties when a class object is destroyed—deleting memory allocated to an object, for example. Constructors and destructors are similar to common member functions, but are rarely called directly by program statements. C++ calls constructors and destructors automatically to initialize and clean up class objects.

Listing 4.18, Time6.h, declares yet one more version of the TTime class. The new class has two constructors to initialize newly created TTime class objects. It also has a destructor to clean up old TTime class objects that are about to be destroyed.

Listing 4.18. Time6.h (Declares the TTime class version 6).

```
//=============================================================
// Time6.h -- Declares the TTime class version 6
// Copyright (c) 1996 by Tom Swan. All rights reserved.
//=============================================================

#ifndef __TIME6_H
#define __TIME6_H  1  // Prevent multiple #includes

#include <iostream.h>
#include <time.h>
#include <string.h>

class TTime {
private:
  long dt;     // Date and time in seconds from January 1, 1970
  char *dts;   // Date and time as a string
  void DeleteDts(void);  // Delete dts pointer
public:
  TTime();                                // Constructor
  TTime(int m, int d = -1, int y = -1,    // Constructor
    int hr = -1, int min = -1);
  ~TTime();                               // Destructor
  void Display(void) { cout << ctime(&dt); }
  void GetTime(int &m, int &d, int &y, int &hr, int &min);
  void SetTime(int m = -1, int d = -1, int y = -1,
    int hr = -1, int min = -1);
  const char *GetSTime(void);
  void ChangeTime(long nminutes)
    { dt += (nminutes * 60); DeleteDts(); }
};

#endif  // __TIME6_H
```

Declare a constructor as you do a member function, but without a return value. Constructors may have zero or more parameters of any type (but not of the constructor's own class). Constructors are typically declared in a public section, but technically speaking, you may insert them anywhere in a class. Constructors always have the same name as the class in which they are declared. They may optionally be coded inline or implemented separately, just as other member functions.

Just below the `public` access specifier, the class declares a default `TTime` constructor. It's a *default constructor* because it declares no parameters. The next two lines declare a second overloaded constructor, also named `TTime`. This constructor declares five `int` parameters, the last four of which are given default values of `-1`. The `TTime` class also declares a destructor, prefaced with the tilde character (~), but more on that later.

In addition to its two constructors and destructor, the new `TTime` class has two other new features. A second private data member, `dts`, adds a `char` pointer to the class. This pointer is intended to address a string representation of the date and time. As you'll see later, keeping the date and time in string form helps lighten the class's memory management duties, and improves runtime performance. The private section also adds a new member function, `DeleteDts`, which deletes any memory addressed by the `dts` pointer. Member functions that are private may be called only by other member functions in the class. There is no way, then, for an errant program statement to call `DeleteDtr` and delete the memory addressed by `dts`. Only members of the class are so privileged.

Before looking at an example of a constructor in use, examine `TTime`'s implementation in Listing 4.19, Time6.cpp.

Listing 4.19. Time6.cpp (Implements the `TTime` class version 6).

```
//================================================================
// Time6.cpp -- Implements the TTime class version 6
// To compile:
//   bcc -c time6
// Copyright (c) 1996 by Tom Swan. All rights reserved.
//================================================================

#include <dos.h>
#include "time6.h"

// Default constructor
TTime::TTime()
{
  dts = NULL;  // No current string
  SetTime(-1, -1, -1, -1, -1);
}

// Overloaded constructor
TTime::TTime(int m, int d, int y, int hr, int min)
{
  dts = NULL;  // No current string
```

```
    SetTime(m, d, y, hr, min);
}

// Destructor
TTime::~TTime()
{
    delete dts;  // Delete string owned by object
}

// Delete dts pointer
void TTime::DeleteDts(void)
{
    delete dts;  // Delete string owned by object
    dts = NULL;  // Set pointer to null
}

// Return current date and time data members
void TTime::GetTime(int &m, int &d, int &y, int &hr, int &min)
{
    struct date ds;
    struct time ts;

    unixtodos(dt, &ds, &ts);
    y = ds.da_year;
    m = ds.da_mon;
    d = ds.da_day;
    hr = ts.ti_hour;
    min = ts.ti_min;
}

// Set dt data member
void TTime::SetTime(int m, int d, int y, int hr, int min)
{
    struct date ds;
    struct time ts;

    getdate(&ds);  // Get current date and time
    gettime(&ts);
    if (y >= 0) ds.da_year = y;
    if (m >= 0) ds.da_mon = m;
    if (d >= 0) ds.da_day = d;
    if (hr >= 0) ts.ti_hour = hr;
    if (min >= 0) ts.ti_min = min;
    ts.ti_sec = 0;
    ts.ti_hund = 0;
    dt = dostounix(&ds, &ts);
    DeleteDts();  // Delete any current string
}

const char *TTime::GetSTime(void)
{
    if (dts)         // Return current string if there is one
        return dts;
    dts = strdup(ctime(&dt));
    return dts;
}
```

The module implements TTime's default constructor. As with all member functions, the implementation's header is prefaced with the class name and a scope resolution operator. Although the header TTime::TTime appears to suffer from a bad case of mirror imaging, it properly identifies the TTime constructor as belonging to the TTime class (see Figure 4.4).

Figure 4.4.
A default constructor's parts and pieces.

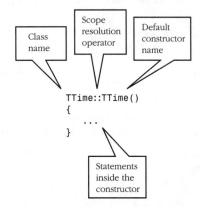

Statements in a constructor may use the same kinds of programming as found in other member and nonmember functions. Typically, however, a constructor limits its duties to assigning initial values to class data members, to allocating memory owned by class objects, and so on. In this case, the default constructor sets char pointer dts to NULL, indicating that the pointer does not yet address a valid string. Because C++ calls the constructor automatically to initialize an object of the TTime class, all such objects are guaranteed to have initialized dts pointers. The constructor also calls the SetTime member function with default arguments of -1, thus initializing the class object to the current date and time.

The module next implements the second constructor. Similar to the default constructor, but declaring date and time parameters, this constructor can be used to assign any initial values to a class object. Overloaded constructors are similar to overloaded member functions. In any class, you can declare as many constructors as needed, provided they differ from one another by at least one parameter. Constructors must have the same name as their declaring class, and multiple constructors are therefore overloaded by definition.

Using Constructors

Not all classes need constructors, but most classes have at least one. Other classes might have a dozen constructors or more. The purpose of a constructor is to provide clearly defined initializations for class objects. Listing 4.20, Construc.cpp, demonstrates how TTime's constructors initialize TTime objects. Compile the program by following instructions at the beginning of the listing.

Listing 4.20. Construc.cpp (Demonstrates TTime version 6 constructor).

```
//==============================================================
// Construc.cpp -- Demonstrates TTime version 6 constructor
// To compile:
//    bcc -c time6
//    bcc construc time6.obj
// To run:
//    construc
// Copyright (c) 1996 by Tom Swan. All rights reserved.
//==============================================================

#include <iostream.h>
#include <stdio.h>
#include "time6.h"

void main()
{
  TTime t1;
  TTime t2(8);
  TTime t3(8, 1);
  TTime t4(8, 1, 1996);
  TTime t5(8, 1, 1996, 8);
  TTime t6(8, 1, 1996, 8, 30);

  t1.Display();
  t2.Display();
  t3.Display();
  t4.Display();
  t5.Display();
  t6.Display();
}
```

Function main declares six class objects, t1 through t6, of type TTime. In each declaration, C++ calls a constructor that matches the types and number of arguments. For example, when the program allocates storage for t1, the default constructor is called to initialize the object. When the program allocates storage for t4, the second constructor is called with three integer arguments and two default values equal to -1.

> **TIP**
>
> Use the IDE's built-in debugger to examine how the sample program calls the TTime class's multiple constructors. Open Construc.ide, and then select Construc.cpp from the project window to open that file. Click in the gray area to the left of the first statement in main to set a breakpoint at that line. Set breakpoints also for the next five lines. All six lines should be prefaced with red dots and are highlighted in red. When you compile and run the program, execution pauses at the first breakpoint. To investigate which constructor this statement calls, press F7 to step into the constructor's implementation. This brings up the class's default constructor. Press Ctrl+F9 to continue running the program up to the next breakpoint, and once again, press F7 to step into the function call—this time, bringing up the class's second constructor. Repeat these steps, and examine each constructor call, until the program's output appears.

Using Destructors

Another sample program uses the TTime class from Time6.h and Time6.cpp, and shows how a destructor can clean up class objects immediately before they are destroyed. Compile Listing 4.21, Destruc.cpp, by following instructions in the listing.

Listing 4.21. Destruc.cpp (Demonstrates TTime version 6 destructor).

```
//=============================================================
// Destruc.cpp -- Demonstrates TTime version 6 destructor
// To compile:
//    bcc -c time6
//    bcc destruc time6.obj
// To run:
//    destruc
// Copyright (c) 1996 by Tom Swan. All rights reserved.
//=============================================================

#include <iostream.h>
#include <stdio.h>
#include "time6.h"

void f(void);

void main()
{
  f();
}

void f(void)
{
  TTime today;
  const char *sp;

  sp = today.GetSTime();
  cout << "First time: " << sp;
  sp = today.GetSTime();
  cout << "Second time: " << sp;
}
```

The program's main function calls another function f, implemented after main. That function declares an automatic TTime class object, today, local to the function. Because local automatic objects are created when their declaring functions are called, C++ calls the TTime default constructor for today as part of the function's startup duties. *This action occurs every time the function is called.* (You might want to verify this fact by running the program in a debugger.)

After constructing the TTime object and a char pointer, the function calls GetSTime to get the object's string representation of the current date and time. The address of that string is saved in the character pointer sp. Examine Time6.cpp, where GetSTime is implemented. The member function first checks whether data member dts is null. If not, it returns dts; otherwise it calls strdup and ctime to convert the current date and time to a string, saving the string's address in char pointer dts, a private data member of the class. Subsequent calls to GetSTime therefore use a previously allocated string. This reduces the number of times the same date and time string is allocated space on the heap, a refinement that should reduce heap fragmentation and help keep the code running quickly.

Because a TTime class object owns a dts pointer to a memory block allocated on the heap, the class must carefully manage this memory. Objects of type TTime must not be destroyed before their memory allocations are freed, or that memory would be unrecoverable. Also, if a TTime class object's date and time change—by calls to ChangeTime and SetTime, for example—a non-null dts pointer must be deleted and set to null, so it will be reallocated on the next call to GetSTime.

Skip back to Time6.h and examine the class destructor declaration. Destructors are usually declared in a class's public section, but they don't have to be. A class may have only one destructor, which is named the same as its declaring class (as are any constructors), but is preceded by a tilde character (~). Destructors are the antithesis of constructors—what a constructor constructs, a destructor should destroy.

Implement a destructor as you do other class member functions. You may optionally code a destructor inline, or you can implement it separately. Time6.cpp implements the TTime class destructor, repeated here so you don't have to flip pages (which always flips *me* out when I read big books like this one):

```
TTime::~TTime
{
  delete dts;  // Delete string owned by object
}
```

As with constructors and member functions, the destructor's name ~TTime is prefaced by the class name and a scope resolution operator TTime::, identifying the destructor as a member of the TTime class. The single statement in TTime's destructor deletes dts. (It's not necessary to test whether dts is null because the delete operator ignores null pointer arguments.)

Just before an object of the TTime class is destroyed, C++ automatically calls that object's class destructor if it has one. This gives objects the opportunity to clean up any memory allocations or other critical items before the object goes to that big bit bucket in the sky.

> **TIP**
>
> Remember: constructors build; destructors destroy. A class may have many constructors, and programs may therefore build objects in many different ways. However, a class may have only one destructor, which is called automatically when an object is destroyed. If you need different ways to destroy objects, a destructor can call member functions, use a switch statement, or take other actions to change how the destructor operates based on various conditions.

Constructing Class Objects

Class objects can be global or local to a function. As you can with variables of built-in types such as int and double, you can refer to class objects using pointers and references. Think of classes as new data types, and use them accordingly, just as you do variables of other types.

The nature of an object—that is, whether it's global, local, addressed by a pointer, and so on—affects when that object's class constructors and destructor are called. When an object is created, C++ automatically calls that object's default constructor, or it calls another constructor that you specify in the object's declaration. When an object is destroyed, C++ calls that object's destructor if its class declares one.

The following notes help clarify exactly when constructors and destructors are called for class objects of various kinds, and also demonstrate more about constructing objects.

Global Class Objects

A global class object's class constructor is called before function main begins to run. This action ensures that all global class objects are initialized before the program formally starts. Using the TTime class from Time6.h and Time6.cpp, the global declaration

```
TTime today;
```

creates a global object today of the class TTime. Before calling main, C++ calls TTime's default constructor for today, which assigns the current date and time to the object.

To initialize a global TTime class object for a specific date and time, declare the object like this:

```
TTime someTime(9, 4, 1953, 10, 45);
```

The presence of an initializer list in parentheses causes C++ to search TTime for a constructor that can accept the specified initializing arguments. In this case, C++ calls TTime's overloaded constructor, which initializes someTime to September 4, 1953, at 10:45. Again, this action occurs before main is called.

A global object's class destructor is normally called as part of the program's shutdown duties after any atexit functions finish. (If you're not familiar with atexit, look it up online and also in this book's function reference on the CD-ROM.) Destructors are not called, however, if the program ends by calling abort.

Local Class Objects

Automatic class objects declared locally to a function are created when the function is called and destroyed when the function ends. Like variables of common types, automatic class object data members are stored on the stack. In the function

```
void anyFunction(void)
{
```

```
  TTime now;  // Initialized on each entry to function
  ...
}
```

the default TTime constructor is called to initialize the class object now to the current date and time each time a statement calls the function.

When the function ends, C++ calls TTime's destructor for the now object, thus giving the object the chance to clean up after itself before it is permanently destroyed.

If you call exit to end a program, global class object destructors are called normally, but destructors for any existing automatic variables local to a function (including those local to main) are *not* called.

Pointers to Objects

A pointer may address a dynamic class object, which is typically allocated heap memory by new. You can declare a pointer pToday to a class object of type TTime:

```
TTime *pToday;
```

This might be a global declaration or it might be local to a function. Like all pointers, pToday must be initialized before use, usually by using new:

```
pToday = new TTime;
```

Alternatively, you can perform both steps in one easy statement:

```
TTime *pToday = new TTime;
```

Probably, this is the most common method for declaring and initializing a pointer to a class object. In this statement, operator new allocates memory for an object of type TTime. The address of that object's first byte is assigned to pToday. In addition, C++ calls the object's default constructor, which, in this example, initializes the object to the current date and time.

To use another constructor, add parameters after the class name. For example, this allocates memory for a TTime object and initializes it by calling the class's 5-parameter constructor:

```
TTime *pToday = new TTime(9, 4, 1953, 10, 45);
```

To use pointers to class objects, dereference them as you do pointers to objects of other types. For example, this statement displays the date and time for the TTime class object addressed by pToday:

```
pToday->Display();
```

Classes resemble structures, so when using pointers to class objects, you'll most often use the -> operator to refer to an addressed object's member. However, you can also use the * dereference operator with class object pointers. For example, the statement

```
sp = (*pToday).GetSTime();
```

assigns to sp (declared as const char *sp;) the result of member function GetSTime for the class object addressed by pToday. However, the statement

```
sp = pToday->GetSTime;
```

is easier to write, clearer to read, and performs the identical service.

C++ calls a dynamic class object's destructor when that object is deleted. The statement

```
delete pToday;
```

deletes the object addressed by pToday, returning that object's memory to the heap's available pool. Just before the object is destroyed, C++ calls the class destructor, which can delete any memory that the object happens to own. In this case, for instance, the destructor can delete a string buffer addressed by pointer dts.

> **NOTE**
>
> Do not confuse the life of a pointer with the life of an addressed object. A global pointer exists for the duration of the program, but it may address a multitude of class objects created by new and destroyed by delete. Similarly, an automatic pointer declared locally to a function is created when the function runs and destroyed when the function ends. However, the objects addressed by pointers have global scope and must be deleted explicitly. In a function f, if you call new to create a dynamic object, that object remains in memory even after the function ends. You must *explicitly* delete any such object if you don't want it to remain in memory after the local pointer is destroyed.

Reference Objects

You may declare references to class objects. Here's a sample. First declare a global TTime class object such as

```
TTime today;  // Global today object
```

Later in the program, you can declare a reference to today like this:

```
TTime &rToday = today;  // Reference to today
```

The reference rToday is an alias for today, and may be used in today's stead. For example, each of these two statements displays today's date and time:

```
rToday.Display();
today.Display();
```

Because references refer to an existing object, the class constructor is not called when the reference is initialized, nor is the destructor called when the reference is destroyed. These actions occur only when the object itself is created and destroyed.

Parameter Objects

You may pass class objects, pointers to class objects, and class object references as arguments to functions. Classes are data types, and you can declare function parameters of them as you do other parameters. Here's a sample:

```
void anyFunction(TTime t)
{
  t.Display();
}
```

Function anyFunction has a single parameter t of type TTime. The function calls t's Display member function to display the parameter's date and time. A program can define a class object of type TTime:

```
TTime today;
```

Then it can pass that object by value to anyFunction:

```
anyFunction(today);
```

Passing large class objects by value to functions causes those objects to occupy an undesirable amount of stack space. In such cases, a pointer parameter is more efficient:

```
void anyFunction(TTime *tp)
{
  tp->Display();
}
```

To call this version of anyFunction, a statement passes the address of a TTime class object rather than the object itself:

```
anyFunction(&today);
```

This is one of the most common methods for passing objects to functions. However, parameters may also be declared as references. The results are similar to what you can achieve with pointer parameters, but inside the function, no pointer dereferences are required. Here's yet one more version of anyFunction, this time using a reference parameter to an object of class TTime:

```
void anyFunction(TTime &tr)  // tr is a reference parameter
{
  tr.Display();  // Call Display for object that tr references
}
```

Elsewhere in the program, you can pass a TTime class object directly to anyFunction's reference parameter:

```
anyFunction(today);
```

> **NOTE**
>
> One disadvantage of reference parameters is that statements such as this appear to pass an argument by value. The fact that a reference to today is passed to anyFunction is not clear from the text.

Object Function Results

Functions may return a class object directly, as a pointer, or as a reference. Least common is a function that returns a TTime class object directly:

```
TTime newTime(void)
{
  TTime t;
  return t;
}
```

Local object t (initialized automatically by a constructor call when the function begins) is returned directly as the function result. A statement could call newTime like this:

```
TTime anotherTime = newTime();
```

which copies newTime's function result to anotherTime. This technique offers few advantages, and it's just as easy to create a new TTime object without calling a function:

```
TTime anotherTime;   // Same as above
```

Furthermore, object function results are passed on the stack, which can slow the program and waste precious stack space for large objects or deeply nested function calls.

More commonly, functions return pointers and references to class objects. For instance, here's a function that allocates a new TTime class object in memory and returns the object's address:

```
TTime *newTimeP(void)
{
  TTime *p = new TTime; // Allocate and initialize object
  return p;  // Return address of object as function result
}
```

Inside the function, a TTime pointer p is assigned the address of a TTime class object allocated by new. The pointer exists only inside the function, but the object addressed by the pointer has global scope; therefore, the function may return its address. A statement can call newTime to obtain a new object and assign the object's address to a TTime pointer such as tp:

```
TTime *tp = newTimeP();
```

Finally, functions may return references to class objects. You might use a reference function to refer to an existing object such as a global TTime today:

```
TTime &newTimeR(void)
{
  return today;
}
```

Elsewhere, you can declare a TTime reference and assign newTimeR's result to it:

```
TTime &tr = newTimeR();
```

Reference tr is now an alias for today, and can be used in a statement:

```
tr.Display();
```

The reference function also can be used directly in a statement. For example, the program can call newTimeR to display today's date and time:

```
newTimeR().Display();
```

This technique is especially useful when a function such as newTimeR performs a search operation, perhaps returning a reference to one of several TTime class objects based on some specified criteria.

Arrays of Class Objects

Just as you can declare arrays of common data types, you can declare arrays of class objects. For example, this declaration creates an array of 10 TTime objects:

```
TTime tenTimes[10];
```

There's only one hard-and-fast rule to remember: *Class objects to be stored in arrays must have default constructors.* When an array of class objects such as tenTimes comes into being, C++ calls the class default constructor once for *each* object in the array. In the case of tenTimes, C++ calls TTime's default constructor 10 times, thus initializing objects tenTimes[0] through tenTimes[9] to the current date and time.

A sample program, Listing 4.22, Obarray1.cpp, demonstrates how to use simple arrays of class objects. The program uses the TTime class defined earlier in Time6.h. See the listing for compilation instructions.

Listing 4.22. Obarray1.cpp (Demonstrates arrays and default constructor).

```
//================================================================
// Obarray1.cpp -- Demonstrates arrays and default constructor
// To compile:
//    bcc -c time6
//    bcc obarray1 time6.obj
// To run
//    obarray1
// Copyright (c) 1996 by Tom Swan. All rights reserved.
//================================================================

#include <iostream.h>
#include <stdio.h>
#include "time6.h"

void main()
{
  TTime tarray[6];

  for (int i = 0; i < 6; i++)
    tarray[i].Display();
}
```

Function main declares an array tarray of six TTime objects. When you run the program, you see six equivalent dates and times, indicating that C++ called the class constructor to initialize each array element. You might also run the program in Turbo Debugger and press F7 repeatedly to trace the statements, verifying that TTime's constructor is called six times.

If you want C++ to call a different constructor for arrayed objects, you must explicitly initialize each array element. You can do this directly in the array's declaration as Listing 4.23, Obarray2.cpp, demonstrates. The listing includes compilation instructions.

Listing 4.23. Obarray2.cpp (Demonstrates arrays and constructors).

```
//================================================================
// Obarray2.cpp -- Demonstrates arrays and constructors
// To compile:
//    bcc -c time6
//    bcc obarray2 time6.obj
// To run:
//    obarray2
// Copyright (c) 1996 by Tom Swan. All rights reserved.
//================================================================

#include <iostream.h>
#include <stdio.h>
#include "time6.h"

void main()
{
  TTime tarray[6] = {
    TTime(),
```

```
    TTime(8),
    TTime(8, 1),
    TTime(8, 1, 1996),
    TTime(8, 1, 1996, 8),
    TTime(8, 1, 1996, 8, 30)
  };

  for (int i = 0; i < 6; i++)
    tarray[i].Display();
}
```

This program declares an array of six TTime objects, just as in the preceding demonstration. In this case, however, the arrayed objects are initialized by specifying constructors inside braces, similar to the way you would initialize elements in an array of structs.

There's no easy way to initialize some arrayed class objects using the default constructor and some using an alternate constructor. If you need to do that, it's probably best to declare the array as in Obarray1, and then reinitialize selected objects as needed. Except for small arrays, the technique illustrated in Obarray2 may be too unwieldy to be of practical use.

Arrays of class objects may also be stored on the heap and addressed with pointers. Some extra care is needed in this case to manage the array. Listing 4.24, Obarray3.cpp, demonstrates the idea. The listing shows compilation instructions.

Listing 4.24. Obarray3.cpp (Demonstrates dynamic arrays and delete[]).

```
//==============================================================
// Obarray3.cpp -- Demonstrates dynamic arrays and delete[]
// To compile:
//    bcc -c time6
//    bcc obarray3 time6.obj
// To run:
//    obarray3
// Copyright (c) 1996 by Tom Swan. All rights reserved.
//==============================================================

#include <iostream.h>
#include <stdio.h>
#include "time6.h"

void main()
{
  TTime *tarrayP;

  tarrayP = new TTime[6];  // Allocate dynamic array
  for (int i = 0; i < 6; i++)
    tarrayP[i].Display();
  delete[] tarrayP;  // Note special form of delete[]
}
```

To create an array of six TTime objects, this variation uses the new operator to allocate a block of memory, and assign the resulting array's address to a TTime pointer, tarrayP. In conjunction with the call to new, C++ automatically calls TTime's default constructor six times to initialize each of the arrayed objects.

As you should with other dynamic objects, you should delete dynamic class object arrays after you are done using them. However, deleting such arrays leads to a problem. Due to the inability in C++ (and also C) to distinguish between pointers and arrays, programs must use a special form of delete[] with trailing square brackets to ensure that, when deleting a dynamic array of class objects, any destructor for those objects' class is properly called. Deleting tarrayP as follows is a very bad error:

```
delete tarrayP;   // ???
```

From that statement, the compiler cannot determine whether tarrayP addresses a single TTime class object or an array of them. To inform the compiler that tarrayP addresses an array, add empty brackets to delete:

```
delete[] tarrayP;   // Delete array of TTime class objects
```

This special command ensures that the class destructor is called for each object in the array. The compiler can easily calculate how many objects the array holds simply by dividing the size of the allocated memory by the size of one TTime object. This is why you don't have to specify the number of objects to delete.

Summary

- Object-oriented programming, or OOP, helps programmers to reduce complexity and to reuse existing code.

- In C++, the principles of OOP are embodied in the class, a tool for creating new data types that behave much as built-in types such as int and double. Use objects of a class as you do objects of other data types.

- Classes are similar to structures, but may have data and function members and can use additional features such as virtual functions and inheritance, topics not yet introduced. Classes encapsulate data and functions, thus controlling access to a program's data. Structs can also have data and function members, but most C++ programmers would use a class rather than a struct for this purpose.

- Use the public access specifier to make class members available to all users of a class. Use the private access specifier to make class members private. Only the class's own member functions may directly access private data members and call private member functions. The next chapter, "Object-Oriented Programming," introduces a third access specifier, protected.

- Members of a class are private by default. However, for clarity, it's best to use the private access specifier to identify private members. Members of a struct are public by default. This is a key difference between structures and classes.

- Class member functions are implemented like normal functions, but their headers include the class name and a scope resolution operator. For a class T, a member function declared as void f(void); is implemented using the header void T::f(void), identifying to the compiler that function f is a member of class T.

- Every class member function receives an undeclared parameter named this, which addresses the object for which the member function is called. For an object x of class T, in a member function T::f(), this addresses x. Usually, it's not necessary to use this in statements because member functions can directly access a class object's members.

- Class objects may be declared globally or locally to functions. Class objects may also be created dynamically by new, stored on the heap, and addressed by pointers. You may also declare references to class objects.

- Functions may declare class object parameters, which can be value parameters, pointers, or references. Functions may also return class objects, but they more commonly return pointers and references to class objects.

- Inline member functions inject their statements directly into the compiled code. The inline keyword, however, is merely a suggestion to the compiler, which may or may not take the hint to compile inline functions in line. Writing short inline functions is the best way to prevent the compiler from converting inline declarations into common member functions.

- Like common functions, member functions may be overloaded. A class may declare an unlimited number of functions that have the same name, provided each function differs in at least one parameter. Overloaded member functions help reduce the number of symbols you have to think up for similar operations. However, overloaded member functions are distinct from one another, and you must implement them individually.

- Member functions may declare default parameter values for unspecified arguments.

- A class may declare one or more constructors to provide automatic initialization for class objects. A constructor is named the same as its class and has no return type. A class's default constructor has no parameters. Other constructors may declare one or more parameters, usually to provide initial values to class objects. Constructor parameters may be of any type, but not of the constructor's own class. C++ calls one of a class's constructors when an object of the class is created.

- A class may declare a destructor (but only one). A destructor typically deletes pointer variables addressed by class object data members, but it may perform other cleanup duties. C++ calls the class destructor just before an object of the class is destroyed.

- Programs may create arrays of class objects. The class must have a default constructor, which C++ calls once for each object in the array. Arrays may also be declared and initialized with explicit calls to overloaded constructors.

- Just before arrays of class objects are destroyed, C++ calls the class destructor for each arrayed object.

- Dynamic arrays of class objects may be created by `new`, stored on the heap, and addressed by pointers. However, because C and C++ do not distinguish between pointers and arrays, you must use `delete[]` (with empty brackets), not `delete` (without brackets), to delete dynamic class object arrays. This form of `delete` ensures that the class destructor is called for each arrayed object.

Exercises

NOTE

For all exercises that refer to the TTime class, use the declaration in Time6.h and implementation in Time6.cpp in the Source\C04 directory. Copies of these files are also in the Source\Answers directory.

4.1 Invent a button class such as you might use in a simulation that requires on/off switches. Your class should have appropriate member functions to control button class objects.

4.2 Using the TTime class, write a program Dt.cpp that displays the current date and time.

4.3 Starting with your answer to Exercise 4.2, write a statement to change your object's date to tomorrow at the same time.

4.4 Using the TTime class, write a program named Day.cpp that reports the day of the week for any date entered on the DOS command line. For example, the command `day jan 5 1997` should report the specified date's day of the week.

4.5 Add member functions to the TTime class to get and change the date and time using a long integer argument representing the number of seconds from January 1, 1970. Also add a constructor to initialize a TTime class object using a long integer seconds value. You may use inline member functions in your answer.

4.6 Create a class that can store a string on the heap. It should be possible to pass a string to an object of your class, and later, to retrieve a pointer to that same string. It should also be possible to modify a class object's string. Use constructors and a destructor to provide for any necessary automatic object initialization and deinitialization.

4.7 Write a program that uses your string object from Exercise 4.6 to read and display a text file.

5

Investing in Inheritance

In the preceding chapter, you learned how classes encapsulate data and functions into one handy package. As you will discover in this chapter, classes can do much more. Using an OOP technique called *inheritance,* you can build new classes from existing ones just as a builder constructs a skyscraper out of brick, stone, and other relatively simple building materials. You'll also investigate virtual member functions—a method technically known as *polymorphism*—that make it possible to redirect function calls at runtime based on an object's type.

Single Inheritance

Single inheritance describes the relationship between one class that is derived from another. (See Figure 5.1.) The class at the top of the hierarchy is the *base class.* The other class is the *derived class.*

Figure 5.1.
Single inheritance.

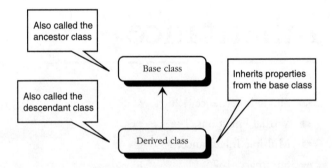

Many classes might be derived from a single base class. Even so, as Figure 5.2 illustrates, such relationships are still of the single-inheritance variety because each new class derives from a single base. Later in this chapter, you'll investigate *multiple inheritance,* in which one class is derived from multiple base classes.

Figure 5.2.
Multiple classes derived from a single base.

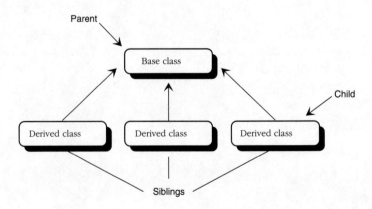

A variety of terms describe classes that are related through inheritance. A base class is often called an *ancestor*, and a derived class is often called a *descendant*. *Grandparent*, *parent*, and *child* also conveniently describe class relationships. In Figure 5.2, the derived classes are called *siblings* because they share the same parent. Terms used less frequently include *subclass* (base) and *superclass* (derived), but these technical words are usually more confusing than helpful.

A derived class may itself be a base class from which additional classes are derived. Despite the apparent complexity of the class hierarchy in Figure 5.3, all the illustrated relationships use single inheritance because all derived classes possess only one parent each. There is no set limit on the number of classes that may be derived from one another. You can build derivations of classes upon classes until they reach the sky.

Figure 5.3.
A derived class may be a base class for other derivations.

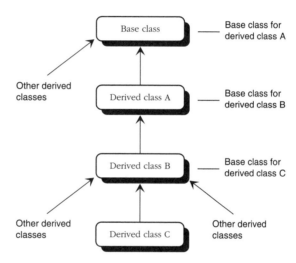

A derived class inherits data members and member functions from its base class. However, a derived class does not inherit any constructors or destructor. In Figure 5.3, for instance, derived class A inherits properties from the base class at the top of the hierarchy. Derived class B inherits those properties plus any new ones in class A. Derived class C inherits properties from the top base class and from derived classes A and B. Later, you'll encounter some refinements to this rule. In general, though, a derived class begins its existence with a copy of its base class's members, including any members inherited from more distantly related classes.

Declaring Derived Classes

A few examples demonstrate the mechanism of inheritance. Consider a base class, TBase, declared as

```
class TBase {
private:
  int count;  // Represents private class data
public:
```

```
  TBase() { count = 0; }
  void SetCount(int n) { count = n; }
  int GetCount(void) { return count; }
};
```

Though not of any practical use, TBase's members resemble those typically found in C++ classes from which new classes might be derived. Member count represents the class's private data. Only TBase member functions may refer directly to count. The default constructor, TBase, initializes count to zero. Member function SetCount assigns count a new value. Member function GetCount returns count's present value. To keep the code simple, TBase's constructor and two member functions are written inline and require no separate implementations.

Suppose you need a new class that contains all of TBase's properties yet can increment and decrement a class object's value by a specified amount. You could rewrite the original class, but that might not be practical in a large project, especially when many programmers are involved. Such a change might not even be possible if TBase is part of a commercial class library to which the source code is unavailable. Rather than modify TBase, you can derive a new class from it and add the features you need:

```
class TDerived: public TBase {
public:
  TDerived(): TBase() { }
  void ChangeCount(int n) { SetCount(GetCount() + n); }
};
```

The derived class is named TDerived. Immediately following the derived class name are a colon and one of the keywords public, protected, or private. After those elements comes the name of a base class (TBase) from which TDerived receives its inheritance. Figure 5.4 illustrates the parts and pieces of TDerived and its constructor.

Figure 5.4.

Some parts and pieces of a derived class.

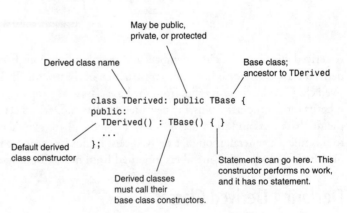

A public base class's public members remain public in the derived class. In a derived class declaration that begins as

```
class TDerived: public TBase {
```

all of TBase's public members become public members in TDerived. Any private members in TBase remain private to their original declaring class, and TDerived may not access those members in TBase. You may also declare a base class to be private:

```
class TDerived: private TBase {
```

In this case, all public members in TBase become private members in TDerived. Subsequent derivations of TDerived may not access any members in TBase. Later in this chapter, you'll look at a third type of base class specifier, protected.

Using Derived Class Constructors

Closely examine TDerived's constructor, which is named the same as its class. A derived class typically provides a constructor if its base class has one. Also, in that case, a derived class constructor must call its base class constructor. In TDerived, the declaration

```
TDerived(): TBase() { }
```

states the derived class's constructor TDerived and calls the base class constructor using the special form : TBase(). You don't call base class constructors in statements; you call them by specifying their names following a derived class constructor declaration.

In this example, the new TDerived class constructor performs no new duties and accordingly is implemented as a null inline function with an empty pair of braces. A constructor may execute statements, however. For instance, TDerived's constructor might be declared inline as

```
TDerived(): TBase() { cout << "I am being initialized" << endl; }
```

However, you do not have to implement derived constructors inline, and you could also declare TDerived like this:

```
class TDerived: public TBase {
public:
  TDerived();   // Derived constructor
  void ChangeCount(int n) { SetCount(GetCount() + n); }
};
```

You must then separately implement the declared constructor. If the new constructor has no new tasks to perform, you could write it like this:

```
TDerived::TDerived()   // Constructor header
  : TBase()            // Calls base class constructor
{
  // Derived constructor's statements go here
}
```

The first line of this constructor's implementation begins with the class name and a scope resolution operator (TDerived::), followed by the constructor's name (TDerived). Because the TDerived class is derived from class TBase, the new constructor must call the base class constructor as shown. This call ensures that any data members inherited from the base class are properly initialized. In this case, for example, the base class constructor sets the private count member to zero.

Using Derived Class Member Functions

Our derived class inherits count from the base class. Because count is private to TBase, however, TDerived cannot directly access that member. Only members of the declaring class may access a class's private members. TDerived can, however, declare its own private members. For example, suppose you declare the class as

```
class TDerived: public TBase {
private:
  int secondCount;
public:
  TDerived();  // Derived constructor
  void ChangeCount(int n) { SetCount(GetCount() + n); }
};
```

To its inherited members, TDerived adds a new private member secondCount. To initialize the new data, you might now implement the constructor as

```
TDerived::TDerived()  // Constructor header
  : TBase()           // Initialize TBase data member(s)
{
  secondCount = 0;    // Initialize TDerived data member
}
```

The call to constructor TBase initializes any data from the TBase ancestor class. The derived class constructor's assignment to secondCount initializes the new data added to TDerived. The base class constructor must be called first, thus ensuring that any inherited members are initialized before initializing any new members in the derived class. Figure 5.5 illustrates this typical relationship between TBase and TDerived.

Figure 5.5.
The relationship between TBase *and* TDerived.

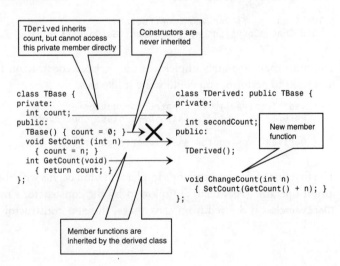

130

The new `TDerived` class also declares a `ChangeCount` public member function for incrementing or decrementing the `count` value inherited from `TBase`. However, because `count` is private to `TBase`, `ChangeCount` cannot access that member directly. You could *not* write `ChangeCount` as

```
void ChangeCount(int n) { count += n; }   // ???
```

That statement won't compile because `count` is private to the base class, and only members of `TBase` can access `count` directly. To modify `count`, `ChangeCount` must call the public inherited member functions such as `SetCount` and `GetCount`:

```
void ChangeCount(int n) { SetCount(GetCount() + n); }
```

Introducing Protected Members

A *protected class member* is a cross between a private and a public member. Like private members, protected members are accessible only to other class member functions. Protected members are not available to statements outside of the class. Like public members, protected members are inherited by derived classes and are accessible to member functions in the derived class. Figure 5.6 illustrates the relationship between derived and base classes and their private, protected, and public members.

Figure 5.6.
Private, protected, and public members in base and derived classes.

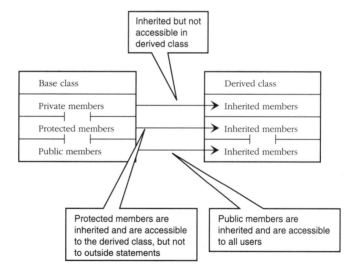

Keep the following rules in mind when deciding whether to make members private, protected, or public:

- A private member is accessible only to members of the class in which the private member is declared.
- A protected member is accessible to members of its own class and to any members in a derived class.

131

- A public member is accessible to the class's own members, to a derived class's members, and to all other users of the class.

You may have as many private, protected, and public sections in a class as you need, and the sections may occur in any order. (However, if an inline member function refers to another member, that member must be declared before the inline member function is implemented.) Consider this class:

```
class TAnyClass {
private:
   int A;          // Accessible only to TAnyClass members
   void fa(void);  //     "         "         "        "
protected:
   int B;          // Accessible to TAnyClass and derived class members
   void fb(void);  //     "         "         "        "
public:
   int C;          // Accessible to all members and users
   void fc(void);  //     "         "         "        "
};
```

Data member A is private to TAnyClass and is accessible only to other members of the class—that is, member functions fa, fb, and fc may access A directly. However, outside statements and even member functions in a derived class may never refer directly to A. In addition, member function fa may be called only by other members of TAnyClass. No outside statement may call fa, which is the exclusive and private property of TAnyClass.

Data member B and member function fb are protected. These members are accessible to other members of TAnyClass and to any members in a derived class. However, outside the class, protected members have private status. No outside statements may access B or fb.

Data member C and member function fc are public, and may be accessed directly by all TAnyClass members, by members in a derived class, and by statements outside the class. Public members are always accessible to all users of the class.

The private, protected, or public access specifiers may also preface a base class name in a derived class declaration. Using TAnyClass, a derived class can be declared as

```
class TDerived: public TAnyClass {
   // New data members, member functions, constructors, etc.
};
```

The public specifier may be replaced by private or protected. If none of these specifiers is used, members of the inherited class default to private status. The specifier affects the status of inherited members. In a derived class,

- A public base class's members retain their public, protected, and private access specifications.

- A protected base class's public members become protected members of the derived class. Protected and private members retain their original access specifications.

- A private base class's members all become private members in the derived class, regardless of those members' original access specifications.

The third case—a base class declared as private to a derived class—has the most profound effect on inherited members. In the following base class:

```
class TBase {
protected:
  int x;
public:
  int y;
  ...
};
```

if you derive a new class like this:

```
class TDerived: private TBase {  // Note "private" status
public:
  void f(void);
};
```

member function f may access members x and y inherited from TBase. However, because TBase is declared as a private base class of TDerived, the status of members x and y change to private. In a subsequent derivation such as

```
class TDescendant: public TDerived {
public:
  void g(void);
};
```

member function g may not access members x and y, despite these members' original protected and public status.

Qualifying Selected Members

A base class specifier potentially affects all inherited members. For instance, given the class A

```
class A {
public:
  int x;
  A() { cout << "Inside A's constructor " << endl; x = 0; }
  void Display(void) { cout << "x == " << x << endl; }
};
```

class B can inherit A as a private base class:

```
class B: private A {
public:
  B(): A() { cout << "Inside B's constructor" << endl; }
};
```

133

Because A is declared private to B, all of A's formerly public members are now private members of B. This means that subsequent derived classes of B or any statements outside of B cannot call the `Display` member function inherited from A. These lines compile and run correctly:

```
A objectA;
objectA.Display();  // Okay. Display() is public to A
```

But the following lines cause the compiler to complain that "'A::Display()' is not accessible..."

```
B objectB;
objectB.Display();  // ??? Display is private to B
```

If you want to make only some inherited members private to a derived class, you can selectively qualify one or more members. Suppose you want class A's public `int x` member to become a private member of B, but you want A's public `Display` member function to remain public in B so that outside statements can call it. To do this, specify base class A as a private member of B as you did before, but in B's public section, qualify the inherited members you want to remain public:

```
class B: private A {
public:
  A::Display;  // Selectively qualify Display
  B(): A() { cout << "Inside B's constructor" << endl; }
};
```

The expression `A::Display;` in B's public section tells the compiler that this member, which was declared in A, should retain its public status. The inherited `int x` data member becomes a private member of B as it did before, but `Display` remains public. The earlier attempt to call `Display` for a B class object now compiles and works correctly:

```
B objectB;
objectB.Display();  // Display is a public member of B
```

Using Constructors and Destructors

As I mentioned, a derived class typically provides a constructor if its base class has one, and a base class constructor must be called in order to initialize any data members in the base class.

Destructors, on the other hand, do not require such strict handling. A derived class needs to supply a destructor only if the derived class has any members that require deleting when an object of the derived class is destroyed. Consider a base class declared as

```
class TBase {
private:
  char *basep;
public:
  TBase(const char *s) { basep = strdup(s); }
  ~TBase() { delete basep; }
  const char *GetStr(void) { return basep; }
};
```

This `TBase` class has one private data member, a pointer `basep` to a character string. The class constructor calls library function `strdup` to copy a string argument to a dynamic variable, assigning the address of the allocated memory to basep. The destructor ~TBase deletes this memory when an object of type TBase is destroyed. Creating a class object such as

```
TBase president("George Washington");
```

passes the string "George Washington" to the class constructor, which copies the string and assigns the string's address to president's basep data member. To display president's string, you could use the statement

```
cout << president.GetStr();
```

When the president object is destroyed, the class destructor deletes the string that was copied onto the heap by the constructor. Figure 5.7 illustrates how president exists in memory.

Figure 5.7.
The president object of type TBase.

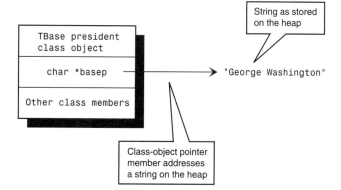

Consider what happens in a new class derived from TBase. The derived class might be declared as

```
class TDerived: public TBase {
private:
  char *uppercasep;
public:
  TDerived(const char *s);
  ~TDerived() { delete uppercasep; }
  const char *GetUStr(void) { return uppercasep; }
};
```

To its inheritance from TBase, TDerived adds a private char pointer data member named uppercasep to address an uppercase copy of the string stored by TBase. The derived class destructor deletes this new string. TDerived's constructor might be implemented as

```
TDerived::TDerived(const char *s)
  : TBase(s)  // Call base constructor
{
  uppercasep = strupr(strdup(s));  // Initialize TDerived data
}
```

The constructor calls TBase's constructor, which copies the string addressed by s to the heap and initializes the basep pointer to address the copied string. After completing this step, the derived class constructor makes another copy of the string, converts its characters to uppercase by calling `strupr`, and assigns to `uppercasep` the address of the copied string.

If you now create an object of type `TDerived`, you create two copies of a string, one unchanged and one in uppercase. You might use a declaration such as

```
TDerived president("George Washington");
```

and then execute statements like these:

```
cout << "Original string: " << president.GetStr() << endl;
cout << "Uppercase string: " << president.GetUStr() << endl;
```

The first output statement displays the original unchanged copy of the string `"George Washington"`. The second output statement displays the copy of that string in uppercase as initialized by the derived class constructor:

```
Original string: George Washington
Uppercase string: GEORGE WASHINGTON
```

Figure 5.8 illustrates how this new `president` class object is organized in memory.

Figure 5.8.

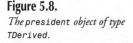
The president object of type TDerived.

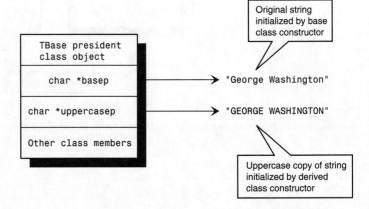

A derived class object such as `president` must carefully delete any memory that it allocates. In Figure 5.8, `president` owns two memory blocks. When the object is destroyed, its destructor deletes this memory and returns it to the heap for reuse.

The `TBase` class destructor deletes the memory addressed by data member `basep`. For simplicity, the destructor is coded inline:

```
~TBase() { delete basep; }
```

Similarly, the `TDerived` destructor deletes the memory addressed by data member `uppercasep`. Again, an inline declaration keeps the code simple:

```
~TDerived() { delete uppercasep; }
```

Unlike constructors, a destructor in a derived class does not explicitly call the base class destructor. (It is possible, however, for a program to call a destructor as a common member function, an advanced technique covered in Chapter 7.) C++ calls destructors automatically when objects of a class are destroyed. In Figure 5.8, for example, when `president` is destroyed, C++ first calls the derived class destructor, which executes the statement

```
delete uppercasep;
```

Next, C++ calls the base class destructor, which executes the statement

```
delete basep;
```

As you can see, the two strings are deleted in the reverse order in which they were constructed. An easy way to remember the order in which constructors and destructors are called is to think of a hierarchy of base and derived classes as floors in a building (see Figure 5.9). Base class constructors are called before derived class constructors, thus constructing derived objects from the ground up—similar to the way skyscrapers are built from the foundation to the clouds. When a derived class object is destroyed, its destructors run in the reverse order, tearing an object apart by calling derived class destructors before destructors in base classes, much as a destruction crew demolishes a real building from the penthouse down.

Figure 5.9.
Like buildings, objects are constructed from the ground up and destroyed from the top down.

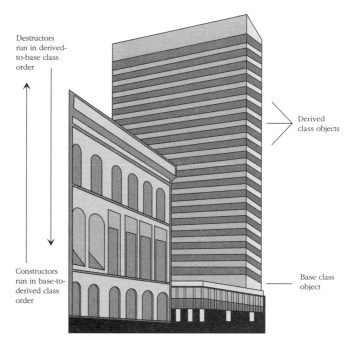

Destructors run in derived-to-base class order

Derived class objects

Constructors run in base-to-derived class order

Base class object

Using Replacement Member Functions

As you've seen, a derived class typically provides new data and function members. But it may also replace member functions inherited from a base class. Suppose you declare class TBase like this:

```
class TBase {
private:
  char *sptr;
public:
  TBase(const char *s) { sptr = strdup(s); }
  ~TBase() { delete sptr; }
  void Display(void) { cout << sptr << endl; }
};
```

The class is similar to others you've examined in this chapter. The TBase constructor calls strdup to copy a string argument to the heap and addresses the allocated memory with private member sptr. The destructor ~TBase deletes this addressed memory when a TBase object is destroyed. Member function Display displays the addressed string using an inline output stream statement. You could declare a TBase object as

```
TBase state("California");
```

and then display state's string with the statement

```
state.Display();
```

Later in this program's development, suppose you decide that all such strings should be labeled with the string "State:". You could accomplish that with the two statements

```
cout << "State: ";
state.Display();
```

but you would have to make similar modifications throughout the program. A better solution is to derive a new class from TBase and replace the inherited Display member function with a modified version. You could write the derived class as

```
class TState: public TBase {
public:
  TState(const char *s): TBase(s) { }
  void Display(void);  // Replacement function
};
```

In addition to a constructor, the derived class declares a member function Display. Because this member is identical to the base class Display, the new member function replaces the inherited one. You might implement the replacement member function as

```
void TState::Display(void)
{
  cout << "State: ";  // New statement
  TBase::Display();    // Call replaced member function
}
```

The replacement `Display` member function outputs the `"State:"` preface and calls the base class's `Display` to finish the string. Prefacing `Display` with `TBase::` tells the compiler to call the member function in `TBase`.

Declaring and using a class object like

```
TState state("Ohio");
state.Display();
```

displays the string `"State: Ohio"`.

A similar trick applies to constructors in derived classes. Suppose you need a few classes for various state names. You could design a class for each state, such as this one:

```
class TPennsylvania: public TState {
public:
  TPennsylvania(): TState("Pennsylvania") { }
};
```

The `TPennsylvania` class is derived from `TState`. The new constructor, which declares no parameters, passes the literal string `"Pennsylvania"` to the base class constructor. The statements

```
TPennsylvania Pennsylvania;
Pennsylvania.Display();
```

create an object named `Pennsylvania` and display the state's name.

Constructors also might add additional parameters. Perhaps you need a class that, in addition to recording a state's name, also stores its population. You could derive the new class from `TState`:

```
class TPopulation: public TState {
private:
  long population;
public:
  TPopulation(long n, const char *name);
  void Display(void);
};
```

`TPopulation`'s constructor specifies a long parameter for the state's population and a `const char` pointer for its name. You could write the constructor as

```
TPopulation::TPopulation(long n, const char *name)
  : TState(name)
{
  population = n;
}
```

The derived class calls the base class constructor, passing name to `TState` to initialize the string portion of the derived class object. After that step, the constructor saves the long parameter n in the derived class's private `population` data member.

To display the state's name and its `population`, you could write the replacement `Display` member function as

```
void TPopulation::Display(void)
{
  TState::Display();
  cout << "Population == " << population << endl;
}
```

Elsewhere in the program, you could create and use a TPopulation class object to display a state's name and population:

```
TPopulation Nebraska(1570000, "Nebraska");
Nebraska.Display();
```

Using Inheritance

So far, this chapter has presented several academic facts about inheritance, derived classes, constructors, and destructors. A real-life example illustrates how to put these concepts to work in real programs. With inheritance, you can derive a new class that augments the properties of an existing class. Rather than write code from scratch, with classes and inheritance you can build programs that take advantage of existing code more easily than with conventional function libraries.

Borland C++ contains an extensive class library, covered in Part III of this book. However, the next program uses one of the library's classes named TTimer, which is tailor-made for timing events. In this section, you'll build a derived class that enhances TTimer through inheritance to create a general-purpose benchmark class, which you might use to test algorithms, I/O throughput, or other speed-sensitive code.

> **NOTE**
>
> TTimer (two Ts) was named Timer (one T) in Borland C++ 3.1. Because of TTimer's low-level nature (it directly accesses the computer's hardware to provide timing services), you may use the class only in DOS, not in Windows, programs.

Ignoring the class's private members—which a derived class can't use anyway—the TTimer class is declared in file Timer.h located in the BC5\Include\Classlib directory as follows. I added the comments to clarify how to use the class:

```
class TTimer
{
public:
  TTimer();       // Constructor
  void Start();   // Start timing
  void Stop();    // Stop timing
  void Reset();   // Reset the timer
  int Status();   // 0==not timing; 1==timing in progress
  double Time();  // Elapsed time in milliseconds
  static double Resolution();  // See note
private:
  ...
};
```

NOTE

Chapter 8, "Advancing Your C++ Knowledge," describes the purpose of static member functions such as `Resolution` in `TTimer`.

Interestingly, the `TTimer` class module has a built-in test program that you can compile and run. To try this program from DOS, change to the directory that contains Timer.cpp (C:\BC5\Source\Classlib on my system) and enter the following command (*carefully type all spacing exactly as shown*):

```
bcc -DTEST_TIMER -DBI_OLDNAMES -IC:\BC5\INCLUDE timer
```

Defining the symbol `TEST_TIMER` with option `-D` compiles a `main` function in the Timer.cpp module, which allows the module to serve as its own test program. Defining the symbol `BI_OLDNAMES` is necessary because the test program seems to have been copied from Version 3.1, and evidently, was not updated since then. You need to specify an *include* path with `-I` only if your default configuration doesn't already do that.

After compiling, run Timer by typing its name. The program displays a report of the timer's accuracy. Here's what my system showed:

```
Resolution: 8.39e-07
   0 ms., actual time = 0.032770 seconds.
 100 ms., actual time = 0.133741 seconds.
 200 ms., actual time = 0.224728 seconds.
 300 ms., actual time = 0.306451 seconds.
 400 ms., actual time = 0.432790 seconds.
 500 ms., actual time = 0.604048 seconds.
 600 ms., actual time = 0.601715 seconds.
 700 ms., actual time = 0.754305 seconds.
 800 ms., actual time = 0.841970 seconds.
 900 ms., actual time = 0.919024 seconds.
```

These figures suggest that Timer isn't precisely accurate, but it's still useful for timing events to an accuracy of about one-tenth of a second, which is good enough for many benchmarking jobs.

Building a Benchmark Class

Now that we have located and tested a base class, the next step is to derive a new class from `TTimer`. The class needs a constructor along with member functions to call a test function and to report the elapsed time for a specified number of tests. Listing 5.1, Bench.h, shows one way to design a class with these characteristics. Because this is just a header file, you can't compile it.

Listing 5.1. Bench.h (Declares the TBench class).

```
//================================================================
// Bench.h -- Declares the TBench class
// Copyright (c) 1996 by Tom Swan. All rights reserved.
//================================================================

#ifndef __BENCH_H
#define __BENCH_H    // Prevent multiple #includes

#include <classlib\timer.h>

typedef void (* testfn)(void);

class TBench: public TTimer {
public:
  TBench(): TTimer() { }
  void Benchmark(long numTests, testfn tf);
  void Report(void);
};

#endif  // __BENCH_H
```

Class TBench is derived from TTimer. The TBench constructor calls the base class TTimer's constructor, but adds no new statements to construct TBench objects. Member function Benchmark lists two parameters: numTests, equal to the number of tests to perform, and tf, a pointer to the test function, which must return void and have no parameters (see the typedef declaration for this function's prototype). A second member function, Report, displays test results.

Listing 5.2, Bench.cpp, implements the TBench derived class. A later program shows how to use this module, but you may compile it to create Bench.obj if you want. Instructions are in the listing.

Listing 5.2. Bench.cpp (Implements the TBench class).

```
//================================================================
// Bench.cpp -- Implements the TBench class
// To compile:
//    bcc -c bench
// Copyright (c) 1996 by Tom Swan. All rights reserved.
//================================================================

#include <stdio.h>
#include "bench.h"

// Call testfunction tf a total of numTests times
void TBench::Benchmark(long numTests, testfn tf)
{
  printf("Running %ld tests...", numTests);
  Reset();     // Reset timer to zero
  Start();     // Start timing
  while (--numTests >= 0)
    (* tf)();  // Call user test function
```

```
  Stop();        // Stop timing
  puts("\nTests completed");
}

// Display test results
void TBench::Report(void)
{
  double result = Time();
  if (result < Resolution())
    puts("Results too small for accuracy");
  printf("Elapsed time == %6f sec.\n", result);
}
```

The implementation of member function Benchmark begins by displaying the number of tests to perform. The function then resets and starts the timer by calling inherited member functions Reset and Start. A while loop counts down the number of desired tests, and repeatedly calls the test function addressed by pointer tf. After the final test is performed, another inherited member function, Stop, halts the timer. A final puts statement displays a brief message to let users know the tests are finished.

Member function Report is implemented next. The function first assigns to result the value of inherited member function Time. An if statement then displays a message if the elapsed time is too small to be trustworthy. (If you see this message, try increasing the number of tests.) Finally, a printf statement displays the benchmark's results in seconds.

To use the class, create a TBench object and pass to member function Benchmark the number of tests to perform. Also pass the address of a test function. Calling Benchmark runs the test. Call Report for the results. Listing 5.3, Tbench.cpp, demonstrates these steps and serves as a shell for your own benchmarks. Compiling Tbench.cpp and the Bench.cpp module requires linking to the library file Bidss.lib, which contains the TTimer class's compiled code. Compilation instructions are in the TBench.cpp listing. If you receive an error, enter the following two lines into a file Turboc.cfg in the current directory and try again:

```
-IC:\bc5\include
-LC:\bc5\lib
```

Listing 5.3. Tbench.cpp (Tests the TBench class).

```
//================================================================
// Tbench.cpp -- Tests the TBench class
// To compile:
//    bcc -c bench
//    bcc tbench bench.obj bidss.lib
// To run:
//    tbench
// Copyright (c) 1996 by Tom Swan. All rights reserved.
//================================================================
```

continues

Listing 5.3. continued

```cpp
#include <iostream.h>
#include <stdio.h>
#include "bench.h"

#define NUMTESTS 20000

void Testfn(void);

void main()
{
  TBench test;

  cout << "Testing sprintf() function" << endl;
  test.Benchmark(NUMTESTS, Testfn);
  test.Report();
}

void Testfn(void)
{
  char buffer[80];
  double d = 3.14159;

  sprintf(buffer, "%lf", d);
}
```

The test program declares a TBench object named test. Because C++ calls the object's constructor (which calls the base class Timer constructor), you can be certain that the test object is properly initialized and is therefore ready for use. After displaying a brief message, the program calls member function Benchmark and passes the number of tests to perform and the address of a test function. After that, the program calls Report to display the test results. The test function, Testfn, calls sprintf just for demonstration. For a different time trial, replace Testfn's contents with other statements. Running the program displays the following report:

```
Testing sprintf() function
Running 20000 tests...
Tests completed
Elapsed time == 4.118690 sec.
```

Virtual Functions

Simply stated, a virtual function is one that is called based on an object's type. Understanding virtual functions is the key that unlocks the secret to successful object-oriented design. In classic programming, statements typically pass data objects to functions, which require you to specify the object types *when you write the code.* In OOP, you can write virtual functions so that objects determine which functions to call *when the program runs.*

In short, with virtual functions, *objects determine their own actions.* If there's a rainbow in C++, the pot of gold at its end is filled with virtual functions.

To understand virtual functions, you first need to learn an important principle of C++ classes that are related through inheritance. By the rules of C++, *a base class pointer may address an object of that class or an object of any class derived from the base class* (see Figures 5.10 and 5.11).

Figure 5.10.

A base class pointer may address a derived class object.

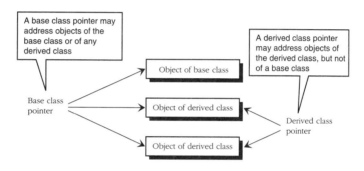

Figure 5.11.

A base class pointer can address data members inherited by a derived class.

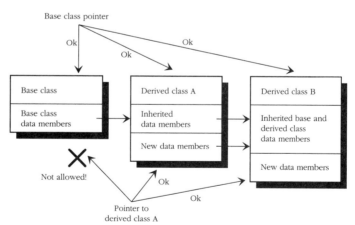

Understanding this rule is the key to learning how to use virtual functions. Consider a series of classes A, B, and C, where B is derived from A and C is derived from B. The program can define objects of classes A, B, and C using statements such as

```
A aObject;  // Define an object of type A
B bObject;  // Define an object of type B
C cObject;  // Define an object of type C
```

145

By definition, a pointer of type `A*` can address any of those three objects because they are related through inheritance. You can, for example, assign the address of `cObject` to a base-class pointer, `p`:

```
A *p;          // Define a base class pointer p of type A*
p = &cObject;  // Assign address of cObject to p
```

Even though pointer `p` is of type `A*`, not `C*`, it may address an object of type `C` because that class is derived from `A`. The rule may be clearer if you think of a `C` object as a *special kind* of `A` object—the way a goldfish is a special kind of fish, but it's still a fish.

The relationship of objects and pointers, however, works in only one direction. An object of type `C` is a special kind of `A` object, but an object of type `A` is not a special kind of `B` or `C` object.

If the principle is still unclear, assume that *you* are a class object derived from your parents. You possess many characteristics such as your hair and skin color inherited from your mother and father, along with other properties inherited from their parents. Your parents and grandparents are part of you, but you are not part of them.

This principle becomes especially valuable when related classes define virtual member functions. The functions look like, and are programmed identically to, normal functions, but are preceded by the keyword `virtual`. For example, class `A` might define a virtual function `vf`:

```
class A {
public:
  virtual void vf();  // A virtual function declaration
};
```

A virtual function can declare parameters and it can return a value, just as any other function can. It differs from common member functions only in the addition of the `virtual` keyword. A class may declare as many virtual functions as needed. Virtual functions may be `public`, `protected`, or `private` class members.

Class `B`, derived from `A`, might also declare a virtual function, again named `vf`:

```
class B: public A {
public:
  virtual void vf();  // replacement virtual function
};
```

When a class such as `B` defines a virtual function of the same name as a virtual function in its ancestor class, the function is called a *replacement function*. The virtual function `vf` in `B` *replaces* the virtual function of that name in `A`.

Class `C` might also define a replacement virtual function:

```
class C: public B {
public:
  virtual void vf();
};
```

In this case, the `virtual` keyword is not strictly required because C is at the end of the inheritance line. If, however, another class D will be derived from C, and if D needs to replace function `vf`, then C should define `vf` using the `virtual` keyword.

Get ready—here's where the neat part comes. Recall the pointer, p, of type A*, which addresses an object, cObject, of type C*. Carefully examine this statement, which calls the virtual function `vf` for an object addressed by p:

```
p->vf();
```

Pointer p may address an object of type A, B, or C. At runtime, this statement therefore calls the virtual function for the addressed object's class. If p addresses an object of type A, the statement calls A's `vf` function. If p addresses an object of type B, it calls B's `vf`. If p addresses an object of type C, it calls C's `vf`. The *same* statement calls the function in the class of the addressed object, an action that is determined at runtime.

Virtual Functions in the Real World

The preceding section describes the theory of virtual functions in general terms. Another classic example helps explain their practical value in the real world of programming.

Imagine you are writing a graphics program, and you want to design various classes for shapes such as circles, squares, and lines. Because all of these classes are related (they are all shapes), you first create a base class, Shape, like this:

```
class Shape {
public:
  // ... various members
  virtual void Draw();
};
```

You don't know all of the actual types of shapes you need, and besides, you probably want to add new shapes at a later date. You do know, however, that you need to store a collection of Shape objects, perhaps in an array of pointers (assume this definition is global so that all pointers are initialized to null):

```
Shape *picture[100];  // Array of Shape-object pointers
```

As defined, a `picture` array may address up to 100 Shape objects. Each element of the array is a Shape* pointer, which, from the preceding section, you know can address an object of type Shape *or of any derived class.* Because Shape defines a virtual Draw function, you can program a loop that calls Draw for pointers in the `picture` array:

```
int i = 0;
while (i < 100 && picture[i] != 0) {
  picture[i]->Draw();  // Call virtual Draw function
  i++;
}
```

You have just written the code that draws a picture *before* you have any actual shapes to draw! If that doesn't strike you as a valuable technique, consider that you can compile this code and store it in a library or .Obj file. Later, you (or other programmers) can derive new classes from Shape, stuff objects of those types into the picture array, and the while loop will call those objects' virtual Draw functions to draw specific images.

Notice especially that this code does not require you to specify the exact data types of the objects that picture's pointers address—only that all such objects are of classes derived from Shape. *The objects determine at runtime which Draw functions to call.* Suppose, for instance, you derive Circle and Line classes from the Shape class:

```
class Circle: public Shape {
public:
  virtual void Draw();
};

class Line: public Shape {
public:
  virtual void Draw();
};
```

You would also program the replacement Draw functions in Circle and Line to draw their respective shapes. When the program runs, the drawing loop calls the correct virtual function based on the type of addressed objects. You can, for example, add shapes to the picture array, something like this:

```
picture[0] = new Circle;
picture[1] = new Circle;
picture[2] = new Line;
picture[3] = new Circle;
picture[4] = new Line;
```

Or, you might read Shape objects from a disk file, or add new shapes to the array as users draw them on-screen. Obviously, in such cases, there's no way to predict in advance what kinds of objects the picture array will hold, but that doesn't matter to the drawing loop, which can draw *any* object of a class derived from Shape.

Virtual and Nonvirtual Member Functions

Keeping in mind the class pointer rules stated in the preceding section, consider another simple class, which declares a data member, a constructor, and a member function:

```
class TValue {
protected:
  int value;
public:
  TValue(int n) { value = n; }
  int GetValue(void) { return value; }
};
```

You can declare and use a TValue object, which stores and regurgitates an integer value on demand:

```
TValue x(10);                  // Initialize TValue object x
cout << x.GetValue() << endl;  // Displays 10
```

Next, derive a new class from TValue. For demonstration purposes, the derived class multiplies the base class value by a specified amount. Let's call the class TMult:

```
class TMult: public TValue {
protected:
  int multiplier;
public:
  TMult(int n, int m): TValue(n) { multiplier = m; }
  int GetValue(void) { return value * multiplier; }
};
```

TMult replaces its inherited member function GetValue with a new function that returns value * multiplier. If you declare an object of type TMult and call its GetValue member function, the result—as you might expect—is the product of the two values used to initialize the object:

```
TMult y(10, 2);                // Initialize TMult object y
cout << y.GetValue() << endl;  // Displays 20
```

Consider what happens now if you address a TSingle or a TDouble object with a pointer. You can declare and initialize a TValue pointer tvp like this:

```
TValue *tvp = new TValue(10);
```

And then you can call the GetValue member function for the addressed object:

```
cout << tvp->GetValue() << endl;  // Displays 10
```

Of course, you can also declare a pointer to the derived class TMult and call the replacement GetValue member function:

```
TMult *tmp = new TMult(10, 2);
cout << tmp->GetValue() << endl;  // Displays 20
```

Applying the C++ rule about pointers and derived classes, you also can declare a pointer to the base class:

```
TValue *basep;  // Pointer to a TValue object
```

Then you can assign the address of a derived object to that pointer:

```
basep = new TMult(10, 2);  // !!! Address a derived object
```

Pointer basep was declared to address an object of class TValue, but this statement creates a derived TMult object and assigns the object's address to basep. What do you suppose happens if you execute the following statement?

```
cout << basep->GetValue() << endl;  // ??? Displays 10
```

This statement compiles, but it does not produce the expected result, 20. As far as C++ knows, pointer basep addresses a TValue object. Therefore, C++ calls the GetValue member function in the base class TValue. But we want C++ to call the GetValue member function for the derived object that the pointer actually addresses.

149

The solution to this predicament is to declare GetValue as a virtual member function. Calls to virtual member functions are linked at runtime (by a technique known as *late binding*). Calls to run-of-the-mill member functions are linked at compile time (*early binding*). Virtual member functions and late binding make it possible for objects to determine their own behavior at runtime.

> **NOTE**
>
> Borland C++ statically links virtual member functions if it can safely do so without negatively affecting any uses of those functions. The compiler performs this optimization automatically.

Listing 5.4, Virtual.cpp, declares the TValue and TMult classes as described earlier, but with one change. In the new classes, GetValue is declared as a virtual member function. Compile and run the program following directions in the listing.

Listing 5.4. Virtual.cpp (Demonstrates virtual member functions).

```
//================================================================
// Virtual.cpp -- Demonstrates virtual member functions
// To compile:
//    bcc virtual
// To run:
//    virtual
// Copyright (c) 1996 by Tom Swan. All rights reserved.
//================================================================

#include <iostream.h>

class TValue {
protected:
  int value;
public:
  TValue(int n) { value = n; }
  virtual int GetValue(void) { return value; }
};

class TMult: public TValue {
protected:
  int multiplier;
public:
  TMult(int n, int m): TValue(n) { multiplier = m; }
  virtual int GetValue(void) { return value * multiplier; }
};

void main()
{
  TValue *basep;
```

```
    basep = new TValue(10);
    cout << basep->GetValue() << endl;    // Displays 10
    delete basep;

    basep = new TMult(10, 2);            // !!!
    cout << basep->GetValue() << endl;    // !!! Displays 20
    delete basep;
}
```

The two classes preface GetValue's declaration with the keyword virtual. This informs the compiler that calls to GetValue are to be linked at runtime. Technically, the addresses of the two GetValue virtual member functions are stored in an internal table. When statements call virtual member functions, C++ looks up the correct function addresses from this table. If you think this lookup action takes time, you are correct. Using virtual member functions might reduce the program's performance, although in practice, any negative effect is small enough to ignore.

Virtual member functions are inherited by derived classes, as are common member functions. However, once declared virtual, a member function's declaration may not change. In other words, to add new programming to GetValue, derived class TMult *must* declare this member function exactly as TValue does. You may, however, delete the virtual keyword from the last of a series of derived classes.

When you run the program, you see two values, 10 and 20, on-screen—the results of calling the two GetValue virtual member functions. The main function declares a pointer basep to class TValue. It then calls new to create a TValue object, which is initialized to the value 10.

After deleting this object, the program creates an object of the derived class TMult. Because of C++'s class-pointer rule, basep may address an object of this derived class, even though the pointer was declared to address a TValue object. Because basep addresses a TMult object, the final output statement displays the value 20.

Carefully compare the two output statements in the program. Ignoring the comments at the ends of the lines, obviously the two statements are identical. Question: If the two statements are the same, how can they produce different output? Answer: The addressed objects determine for themselves which of the two virtual GetValue member functions to call. Even more importantly, this decision is made by the program at runtime, not by the compiler or programmer.

Pure Virtual Member Functions

A pure virtual member function is an unfinished placeholder that a derived class is expected to complete. Declare a pure virtual member function as you normally would, but follow its declaration in a class with = 0. For example, in this class

```
class AbstractClass {
public:
  virtual void f1(void);       // Normal virtual member function
  virtual void f2(void) = 0;   // Pure virtual member function
  ...
};
```

`f2` is a pure virtual member function. The compiler does not require the implementation of `f2` as it does of other member functions declared in a class.

When a class contains one or more pure virtual member functions, it is called an *abstract class*. Like an abstract idea, an abstract class describes an unrealized concept. An abstract class is a kind of schematic from which you are expected to build one or more derived classes. With C++, you cannot create objects of an abstract class type. For example, you could not declare an object of type `AbstractClass`. If you try to compile the line

```
AbstractClass myObject;  // ???
```

the compiler tells you that it "Cannot create an instance of class 'AbstractClass.'" However, other member functions in `AbstractClass` may call a pure virtual member function. For instance, you can write code in member function `f1` to `f2`:

```
void AbstractClass::f1(void)
{
  f2();  // Call pure virtual member function
  ...    // Other statements in f1()
}
```

To use the abstract class, you must derive a new class from it:

```
class MyClass: public AbstractClass {
public:
  virtual void f2(void);  // Former pure virtual member function
  ...
};
```

The derived `MyClass` inherits the pure virtual member function, but declares it without `= 0`. (Including the suffix would cause `MyClass` to become an abstract class.) Elsewhere, you must implement member function `f2`:

```
void MyClass::f2(void)
{
  ...  // Statements in member function
}
```

Calls to the original pure virtual member function—as made in this case by `AnyClass::f1`, for example—are now redirected to `MyClass::f2`. Simply by implementing a pure virtual member function in a derived class, you can plug in code that other members can call, without requiring those other members to be revised or even recompiled. Pure virtual member functions operate like hooks onto which you can attach code in derived classes.

Now that all pure virtual member functions are accounted for, the compiler accepts objects of type `MyClass`:

```
MyClass myObject;
```

Executing the statement

```
myObject.f1();
```

calls the inherited f1, which calls f2 in MyClass.

The next several listings show a practical example of a pure virtual member function and an abstract class. The class, TSet, can store simple sets of objects of an unspecified type. Listing 5.5, Set.h, declares the class in a header file along with a few other items.

Listing 5.5. Set.h (Declares the TSet class).

```
//================================================================
// Set.h -- Declares the TSet class
// Copyright (c) 1996 by Tom Swan. All rights reserved.
//================================================================

#ifndef __SET_H
#define __SET_H      // Prevent multiple #includes

class TElem;
typedef TElem* PTElem;
typedef PTElem* PPTElem;

class TSet;
typedef TSet* PTSet;

class TSet {
private:
  int max;        // Maximum number of elements
  int index;      // Set array index
  PPTElem set;    // Pointer to array of PTElem pointers
protected:
  virtual int CompareElems(PTElem p1, PTElem p2) = 0;
public:
  TSet(int n)
    { max = n; index = 0; set = new PTElem[n]; }
  virtual ~TSet()
    { delete[] set; }
  void AddElem(PTElem p);
  bool HasElem(PTElem p);
};

#endif   // __SET_H
```

To make TSet as versatile as possible, the class needs to store objects of an unspecified class. As the header file shows, C++ permits incomplete class declarations that have no bodies:

```
class TElem;   // Incomplete class declaration
```

Given this declaration, TElem objects can be listed in function parameters, returned by functions, and so on. Eventually, the program must specify a real class for TElem. However, the incomplete class declaration makes it possible to write the TSet class without knowing in advance what kind of class objects are to be stored in the set.

Two `typedef` declarations declare optional symbols, which help keep program listings easy to read. `PTElem` is declared as an alias for `TElem*`. In other words, `PTElem` is a pointer to an object of type `TElem`. Similarly, `PPTElem` is declared as an alias for a `PTElem` pointer—that is, a pointer *to a pointer to* a `TElem` object. The `TSet` class uses `PPTElem` to create a dynamically sized array of `PTElem` pointers.

The next two lines use similar declarations to specify an incomplete `TSet` class and an alias symbol `PTSet` as a pointer to a `TSet` object. The only reason for declaring `TSet` incompletely is to permit the subsequent `typedef` declaration to compile.

The `TSet` class declaration comes next. Three private data members hide the class's inner details. In this version of `TSet`, a set is stored as a dynamically sized array of `PTElem` pointers, using a `PPTElem` pointer to address the array. (Member `set` is literally a pointer to an array of pointers to `TElem` objects.) Members `max` and `index` are used to manage this array.

Because all `TSet`'s data members are private to the class, they could be changed at a later time without affecting statements that use objects of the class. When designing classes, it's often useful to choose a simple, if not ideally efficient, method for storing class data. As long as you make that data private to the class, you can always change it later without affecting any programming outside the class.

Examine the pure virtual member function, `CompareElems`, in `TSet`'s protected section. Pure virtual member functions also can be public, but are often protected because a derived class is expected to furnish them. `CompareElems` is supposed to return zero if two `TElem` objects addressed by pointers `p1` and `p2` are identical. Obviously, you can't complete `CompareElems` yet because you don't know what a `TElem` class contains. However, by using pure virtual member functions, you can at least finish the generic programming needed by `TSet`.

That programming is declared and partially implemented in the class's public section. An inline class constructor initializes private data members and uses `new` to allocate an array of `PTElem` pointers. The destructor deletes this memory, cleaning up any `TSet` objects before they are destroyed.

Member functions `AddElem` and `HasElem` are too lengthy for inline implementations. Listing 5.6, Set.cpp, completes these functions. You can compile this much of the program by following instructions in the listing, but to use the class, you must supply a host program. An example follows in the next section.

Listing 5.6. Set.cpp (Implements the `TSet` class).

```
//================================================================
// Set.cpp -- Implements the TSet class
// To compile:
//   bcc -c set
```

```
// Copyright (c) 1996 by Tom Swan. All rights reserved.
//==============================================================

#include <iostream.h>
#include <stdlib.h>
#include "set.h"

// Add element to set. (Aborts program on error!)
void TSet::AddElem(PTElem p)
{
  if (set == NULL) {
    cout << endl << "ERROR: Out of memory";
    exit(1);
  }
  if (index >= max) {
    cout << endl << "ERROR: Set limit exceeded";
    exit(1);
  }
  set[index] = p;
  ++index;
}

// Returns true if element at p is in the set
bool TSet::HasElem(PTElem p)
{
  if (set == NULL)
    return false;  // No elements in a null set
  for (int i = 0; i < index; i++)
    if (CompareElems(p, set[i]) == 0)
      return true;  // Element is in set
  return false;  // Element is not in set
}
```

Set.cpp implements TSet's two member functions, AddElem and HasElem. Interestingly, it's possible to write these functions *without knowing* the design of the elements on which they operate. All that's known about the elements is that they are of an unspecified class named TElem.

Even so, AddElem adds a TElem object addressed by parameter p to the set. Statements check for error conditions and halt the program if insufficient memory is available or if the set is full. (A more sophisticated class would provide better error handling, perhaps using exceptions, but this minimal design will do for the example.) The next to last statement in the function stores the TElem object addressed by p in the set array. The function then increments the index value.

Member function HasElem returns the bool value true if the passed TElem object is currently in the set. HasElem calls the class's pure virtual member function CompareElems. Although this function does not yet exist, it's okay to write calls to it! However, a derived class must eventually supply the real programming in order to compare two elements.

The next program, Tset.cpp, Listing 5.7, supplies the missing pieces in TSet and TElem to create a set of strings equal to the names of the months that have 30 days: April, June, November, and September. To create the finished program, compile and link Tset.cpp to its supporting Set.cpp module by following instructions in the listing.

155

Listing 5.7. Tset.cpp (Tests the TSet class).

```
//==============================================================
// Tset.cpp -- Tests the TSet class
// To compile:
//    bcc -c set
//    bcc tset set.obj
// To run:
//    tset
// Copyright (c) 1996 by Tom Swan. All rights reserved.
//==============================================================

#include <iostream.h>
#include <string.h>
#include "set.h"

class TElem {
private:
  char *sp;  // Pointer to element string
public:
  TElem(const char *s) { sp = strdup(s); }
  virtual ~TElem() { delete sp; }
  virtual const char *GetString(void) { return sp; }
};

class TMySet: public TSet {
protected:
  virtual int CompareElems(PTElem p1, PTElem p2);
public:
  TMySet(int n): TSet(n) { }
};

void Test(const char *s, PTSet setp);

void main()
{
  TMySet thirties(12);  // A set of 12 TElem objects

  thirties.AddElem(new TElem("Sep"));
  thirties.AddElem(new TElem("Apr"));
  thirties.AddElem(new TElem("Jun"));
  thirties.AddElem(new TElem("Nov"));
  Test("Jan", &thirties);
  Test("Feb", &thirties);
  Test("Mar", &thirties);
  Test("Apr", &thirties);
  Test("May", &thirties);
  Test("Jun", &thirties);
  Test("Jul", &thirties);
  Test("Aug", &thirties);
  Test("Sep", &thirties);
  Test("Oct", &thirties);
  Test("Nov", &thirties);
  Test("Dec", &thirties);
}

// Report whether string s is in the set at setp
void Test(const char *s, PTSet setp)
{
```

```
  TElem testElem(s);

  if (setp->HasElem(&testElem))
    cout << s << " is in the set" << endl;
  else
    cout << s << " is not in the set" << endl;
}

// Return zero if two TElems are equal; nonzero if not
int TMySet::CompareElems(PTElem p1, PTElem p2)
{
  return (stricmp(p1->GetString(), p2->GetString()));
}
```

The first step in using the TSet class is to create a TElem class. This provides the format of objects to be stored in the set. In this case, the program declares a TElem class that can store a string value. For convenience, I declared all of the class's member functions inline.

Next, the program creates a new class, TMySet, derived from the abstract TSet. The new class constructor performs no new duties, so it simply calls the base class TSet constructor. Most importantly, the class's protected section declares a virtual member function CompareElems, which as you recall, was declared as a pure virtual member function in TSet.

Skip to the end of the listing where CompareElems is implemented. The completed function calls library function stricmp to compare two strings. These strings are obtained by calling the TElem GetString member function. When you run the completed program, calls to CompareElems in the original TSet class's member functions are redirected at runtime to the string-comparison function in the test program. (For an education in virtual member functions, single step this code in Turbo Debugger and follow these calls.)

This example of virtual member functions and abstract classes leads to some interesting observations:

- You can compile the Set.cpp module separately and insert its code into a library file. Class users do not require the source code file Set.cpp of the TSet class. To use the class, host programs need only the compiled code and the header file Set.h.

- Another program can use the same TSet class to store a set of *different* TElem class objects. You do not need to recompile Set.cpp for such new uses. TSet provides rudimentary set operations. It's up to a user of the class to fill in the details.

- On the downside, when designing abstract classes such as TSet, it's tempting to add numerous virtual member functions just in case they are needed. Resist this urge, and try to provide only the minimum required members instead of attempting to cover every possible base. If your classes are too complex, other programmers (or even you at a later date) may be discouraged from deriving new classes from them.

Virtual Destructors

Member functions and destructors—but not constructors—may be virtual. A virtual destructor typically is used when one class needs to delete objects of a derived class that are addressed by pointers to a base class. For example, consider this class, which can store a string value:

```
class TBase {
private:
  char *sp1;
public:
  TBase(const char *s)
    { sp1 = strdup(s); }
  virtual ~TBase()
    { delete sp1; }
};
```

The TBase class constructor allocates space for a string by calling strdup and stores the new string's address in sp1. The virtual destructor deletes this memory when an object of type TBase goes out of scope.

Next, derive a new class from TBase:

```
class TDerived: public TBase {
private:
  char *sp2;
public:
  TDerived(const char *s1, const char *s2): TBase(s1)
    { sp2 = strdup(s2); }
  virtual ~TDerived()
    { delete sp2; }
};
```

The new class stores a second string that sp2 addresses. The new constructor calls TBase, passes one string to the base class, and allocates some additional memory for a second string, which is deleted by the class destructor.

When a TDerived object goes out of scope, it's important that both strings be deleted. Suppose you declare a pointer to TBase but assign it the address of a TDerived object—this is perfectly allowable because, as you've learned before, a base class pointer may address an object of that class or of any derived class. The program at this stage looks like this:

```
TBase *pbase;
pbase = new TDerived("String 1", "String 2");
```

Consider what happens later when the program deletes the object addressed by pbase:

```
delete pbase;  // !!!
```

The compiler was told that pbase addresses a TBase object, and the program normally would call TBase's destructor when the addressed object is deleted. However, pbase actually addresses a TDerived object, and that class's destructor must be called as well as the one in the base class.

Because the destructors are declared to be virtual, calls to them are linked at runtime, and the object itself determines which destructor should be called. If the destructors were not virtual, however, only the base class destructor would be called, leaving the second string in memory, which might cause a serious bug.

Multiple Inheritance

So far in this chapter, derived and base classes have been related by single inheritance. Multiple inheritance describes a more complex relationship in which a single class inherits the data members and member functions from more than one base class. Figure 5.12 illustrates the concept of multiple inheritance.

Figure 5.12.
Multiple inheritance.

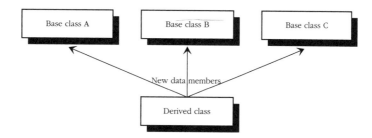

Loading the Bases

To derive a new class from multiple base classes, list the base class names after the new one. If A, B, and C are classes, a new class D could inherit all of them like this:

```
class D: public A, public B, public C {
  ...
};
```

You can also declare multiple base classes as private or protected to a derived class. Or, you can use a mix of specifiers:

```
class D: protected A, public B, C {
  ...
};
```

Base class C defaults to private status, but for clarity, it's best to state explicitly a base class's private, protected, or public status. The same rules listed earlier for single inheritance apply to multiple inherited base classes.

The difference in multiple inheritance is that a derived class receives all of the inheritable properties from all of its base classes. In the event of a name conflict (two base classes declaring a member function of the same name, for example) use the scope resolution operator to specify which member you intend to use. For instance, suppose classes A and B each have a public Display member function. In the derived class

```
class D: public A, public B {
public:
  void f(void);
  ...
};
```

member function f must specify which of the conflicting Display functions to use. It does this by prefacing function calls with the appropriate class name and a scope resolution operator:

```
void D::f(void)
{
  Display();      // ??? Ambiguous; won't compile
  A::Display();   // Call A's member function
  B::Display();   // Call B's member function
}
```

Using Multiple Base Class Constructors

A class derived from multiple base classes might also need to call multiple base class constructors. If A, B, and C are classes with default constructors, a derived class D can call those constructors like this:

```
class D: public A, public B, public C {
public:
  D(): A(), B(), C() { }  // Inline constructor
  ...
};
```

Or, the constructor can be declared

```
class D: public A, public B, public C {
public:
  D();  // Externally implemented constructor
  ...
};
```

and implemented separately, typically in another file:

```
D::D()
  : A(), B(), C()
{
  ... // Statements in constructor D()
}
```

Of course, the constructors may have various parameters not shown here. The constructors are called in the order in which their base classes are declared. However, it's generally unwise to devise classes that depend on other class objects to be constructed in a particular order. As a rule, classes should operate as independently of each other as possible.

Using Virtual Base Classes

Derived classes and their bases form a class hierarchy that can grow tremendously complex even in relatively simple programs. A base class can be inherited by one or more other classes that in turn can become base classes for still more classes. All of these classes are consequently related by single or multiple inheritance as though they were biblical characters begetting one another until no one can tell who is related to whom.

It's easy to understand how conflicts arise in a complex class hierarchy, especially when multiple inheritance is involved. One of the most common conflicts occurs when a derived class inherits too many copies of a particular base—like lottery winners, for example, who suddenly acquire more "cousins" than they previously knew existed.

To demonstrate how derived classes can get into inheritance trouble, examine the classes from the following program in Listing 5.8, Franch.cpp. The program uses familiar relationships between fictitious companies and three fictitious franchisees: Bob, Ted, and Alice. The program may seem a bit silly, but borrowing familiar relationships from the real world helps to explain a typical and often exasperating problem with multiple inheritance.

Listing 5.8. Franch.cpp (Shows a problem with multiple inheritance).

```
//============================================================
// Franch.cpp -- Shows a problem with multiple inheritance
// To compile:
//    bcc franch
// To run:
//    franch
// Copyright (c) 1996 by Tom Swan. All rights reserved.
//============================================================

#include <iostream.h>
#include <string.h>
```

continues

Listing 5.8. continued

```cpp
class Company {
private:
  char *name;
public:
  Company(const char *s) {
    name = strdup(s);
    cout << " In constructor for ";
    Display();
  }
  virtual ~Company() {
    cout << " In destructor for ";
    Display();
    delete name;
  }
  void Display(void) { cout << name << endl; }
};

class Jennys: public Company {
public:
  Jennys(): Company("Jenny's") { }
};

class McDougles: public Company {
public:
  McDougles(): Company("McDougles") { }
};

class BurgerQueen: public Company {
public:
  BurgerQueen(): Company("BurgerQueen") { }
};

class Bob
  : public Jennys,
    public McDougles {
};

class Ted
  : public McDougles,
    public BurgerQueen {
};

class Alice
  : public Jennys,
    public McDougles,
    public BurgerQueen {
};

void main()
{
  Bob *bobp;
  Ted *tedp;
  Alice *alicep;

  cout << endl << "Initializing Bob's restaurant" << endl;
  bobp = new Bob;
  cout << "Initializing Ted's restaurant" << endl;
```

```
    tedp = new Ted;
    cout << "Initializing Alice's restaurant" << endl;
    alicep = new Alice;

    cout << endl << "Deleting Bob's restaurant" << endl;
    delete bobp;
    cout << "Deleting Ted's restaurant" << endl;
    delete tedp;
    cout << "Deleting Alice's restaurant" << endl;
    delete alicep;
}
```

Figure 5.13 illustrates the relationships among the classes in Franch.cpp. At the root of the hierarchy is the Company class, which serves as a base class for three derived classes: Jennys, McDougles, and BurgerQueen. Each of these "company" classes is derived from Company, and each class therefore inherits a name data member and a Display member function.

Figure 5.13.
Class hierarchy in program Franch.cpp.

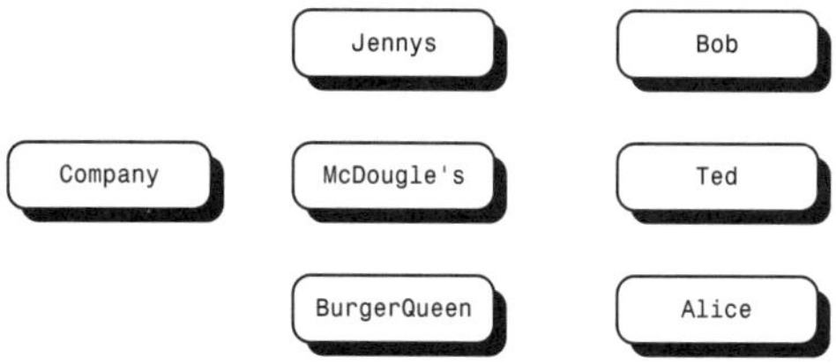

The three adventurous investors, Bob, Ted, and Alice, are declared as classes. Class Bob derives his culinary empire from two Company classes, Jennys and McDougles. Class Ted derives his fortunes from McDougles and BurgerQueen. Alice, the most ambitious soul in the group, takes on the three Company classes: Jennys, McDougles, and BurgerQueen. When you run the program, you see a report that indicates which constructors and destructors run at what times as they initialize and destroy three class objects, one for each franchisee.

> **TIP**
>
> When debugging your own code, you might use output statements similar to those in Franch.cpp. Displaying a message in a constructor, destructor, or member function often provides useful feedback about a complex class hierarchy's organization.

The class hierarchy in Franch.cpp seems simple enough. But a subtle problem with the class relationships arises if another class is derived from the group of companies and investors. Suppose another corporation purchases some of the parent companies and selected franchisees. As in the real world of corporate finance, the complex relationships among companies and people can easily get out of hand. Consider a Corporation class that attempts to inherit the McDougles company along with franchisees Ted and Alice:

```
class Corporation
  : public McDougles,   // ???
    public Ted,
    public Alice {
public:
  ...
};
```

Refer back to Figure 5.13 and you can see why this Corporation can never get off the ground. (The code does not even compile.) Ted and Alice already derive in part from McDougles. When Corporation attempts to do the same, it ends up with multiple McDougles base classes. At this point, the compiler warns you that "McDougles is inaccessible because [it is] also in Ted."

When you receive a similar warning for a complex set of related classes, try to identify those base classes which require only a single object. In the case of Corporation, it makes sense to have only one McDougles company. Even though Ted is derived from McDougles, it is the same McDougles from which Corporation is attempting to derive. In the process of acquiring Ted's assets, the Corporation does not end up with two separate McDougles parent companies. There's only one such parent, which is related to Corporation directly and indirectly through Ted.

In similar (but less frivolous) situations, in which a multiple-derived class requires only one copy of a multiple-inherited base class, you can reduce those bases to one instance by declaring them all to be virtual base classes. In a class hierarchy, there is only one copy of a virtual base class object, even when that object's class is inherited more than once.

Listing 5.9, Conglom.cpp, demonstrates how to form a Corporation class that uses virtual base classes and solves the problem of a proliferation of McDougles base classes. Compile the program by following instructions in the listing. (If you want to use the IDE browser to investigate the program's class relationships, however, compile the program as an EasyWin application.)

Listing 5.9. Conglom.cpp (Demonstrates virtual base classes).

```
//================================================================
// Conglom.cpp -- Demonstrates virtual base classes
// To compile:
//   bcc conglom
// To run:
//   conglom
// Copyright (c) 1996 by Tom Swan. All rights reserved.
//================================================================

#include <iostream.h>
#include <string.h>

class Company {
private:
  char *name;
public:
  Company(const char *s) {
    name = strdup(s);
    cout << " In constructor for ";
```

```
    Display();
  }
  virtual ~Company() {
    cout << " In destructor for ";
    Display();
    delete name;
  }
  void Display(void) { cout << name << endl; }
};

class Jennys: public Company {
public:
  Jennys(): Company("Jenny's") { }
};

class McDougles: public Company {
public:
  McDougles(): Company("McDougles") { }
};

class BurgerQueen: public Company {
public:
  BurgerQueen(): Company("BurgerQueen") { }
};

class Bob
  : virtual public Jennys,
    virtual public McDougles {
};

class Ted
  : virtual public McDougles,
    virtual public BurgerQueen {
};

class Alice
  : virtual public Jennys,
    virtual public McDougles,
    virtual public BurgerQueen {
};

class Corporation
  : virtual public McDougles,
    public Ted,
    public Alice {
private:
  char *name;
public:
  Corporation(): McDougles(), Ted(), Alice()
    { name = "Conglomerate Industries"; }
  void Display(void) { cout << name << endl; }
};

void main()
{
  cout << endl << "Forming a corporation" << endl;
  Corporation *cp;
```

continues

Listing 5.9. continued

```
    cp = new Corporation;
    cp->Display();
    delete cp;
}
```

Class `Company` is unchanged, as are `Jennys`, `McDougles`, and `BurgerQueen`. `Bob`, `Ted`, and `Alice`, however, require modifications to prevent future derivations from ending up with too many copies of their parent base classes. For example, `Bob` is now declared as

```
class Bob
  : virtual public Jennys,
    virtual public McDougles {
};
```

Adding virtual to the listed base classes tells the compiler that, in a subsequent derivation, which also inherits either `Jennys` or `McDougles`, there should be only one instance of those two base classes. Similarly, `Ted` and `Alice` specify their base classes to be virtual.

You can now form class `Corporation`. As before, the class inherits bases `McDougles`, `Ted`, and `Alice`. By specifying `McDougles` as a virtual base class, however, only one copy of that `Company` class exists in the final result, despite the fact that `Ted` and `Alice` are also derived from `McDougles`.

> **NOTE**
>
> `Ted` and `Alice` could also be declared as virtual base classes. This is required only if a subsequent derivation of `Corporation` also inherits those classes.

Using Borland's Object Browser

There's nothing like a few diagrams to help explain the relationships among a set of derived classes. If you are running the Windows IDE, you can use Object Browser in the IDE to display related classes and their members. You can use the browser whether you are writing a Windows or a DOS application, but you must use Windows as your development system to run the IDE.

The browser is easy to use. For example, after compiling Conglom.cpp as an EasyWin application (see Chapter 2 if you are having trouble), select *View|Classes* to see a graphic chart of the program's classes and their relationships (see Figure 5.14). Because the program also uses I/O streams for output, the chart shows the `ios`, `streambuf`, and other classes from the standard library supplied with Borland C++.

Figure 5.14.
Conglom's classes and their relationships.

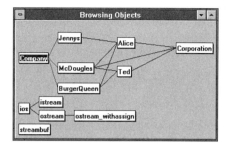

Double-click any class (McDougles, for example) to open a window that shows the class's contents (see Figure 5.15). You can further select any content line to see its definition. Also try selecting the filters—F (functions), V (variables), I (inherited declarations), and V (virtual functions)—to alter the kinds of information the window displays.

Figure 5.15.
McDougles contents in the object browser.

Summary

- Single inheritance describes the relationship between one class that is derived from another. Many classes may be derived from a single base class.

- Multiple inheritance describes the relationship of a class that is derived from more than one base class.

- Derived classes may serve as base classes for subsequent derivations. There is no set limit on the number of classes that may be derived from other classes.

- A protected class member is a cross between a private and a public member. Like a private member, a protected member is not accessible outside the class. Like a public member, a protected member is available to a derived class that inherits that member from a base class.

- A derived class inherits all present data members and member functions—but not constructors or destructors—from a base class.

- A derived class must call a base class constructor—if it has one—to initialize data members in the base class portion of a derived object.

- A base class's public and protected members are inherited and are accessible in a derived class. The private members of a base class remain private to the base class and are not accessible in the derived class.

- Derived classes may declare public, protected, or private base classes. These access specifiers can change the access status (public, protected, and private) of inherited members.

- You may selectively qualify inherited members. For example, if a derived class declares a private base class, all of the base class's members become private to the derived class. Selected inherited members, however, may be qualified to retain their original access status.

- Destructors are normally provided in derived classes only if those classes declare data members that require deletion when an object of the derived class goes out of scope. However, destructors may perform other cleanup chores. C++ automatically calls class destructors (and default constructors) as needed.

- Constructors in a base class are called before constructors in a class derived from that base. Destructors are called in the opposite order: a derived class destructor is called before a base class destructor. Objects of derived classes are constructed in base-to-derived class order and destroyed in derived-to-base class order.

- Derived classes may provide replacements for member functions inherited from a base class. These member functions have the same names as their inherited functions, but may possess the same or a different set of parameters.

- A pointer to a base class may address an object of that class or of any class derived from that base. Using such a pointer, a statement may call a virtual member function, which is linked at runtime to the actual object that the pointer addresses.

- Destructors and member functions may be virtual, but constructors may not. C++ links virtual member functions and virtual destructors at runtime.

- A pure virtual member function declaration ends with = 0. Any class that contains one or more pure virtual member functions is called an abstract class, of which you cannot create objects. A derived class is expected to inherit an abstract class and provide programming for all pure virtual member functions.

- Multiple inheritance can lead to highly complex class hierarchies. One of the most common problems with multiple inheritance is a derived class that inherits too many copies of a distant base-class relative. To fix this problem, you may declare the base class virtual, limiting to one the number of base class objects existing in derived class objects.

Exercises

5.1 Write a series of related classes appropriate for a screen entry program such as a name-and-address database. Aim for generic classes that can prompt for and return values of a variety of data types at specified locations on-screen. (The purpose of this exercise is for you to think about class hierarchies. Your answer does not need to read and write information in disk files.)

5.2 Derive a new class from the TBench class (Listings 5.1 and 5.2) that performs a series of tests for a specified number of repetitions and reports the average elapsed time for all tests.

5.3 Design and test a class that can store a set of integer values from 0 to 15 using one bit per value. The class should have member functions to add, delete, extract, and display set values. Use virtual member functions, constructors, and destructors where appropriate. The class should display a binary value such as 0100100011001011, where 1 represents items in the set.

5.4 Design a class that can store a list of objects of an unspecified class type.

5.5 Using your answer from Exercise 5.4, write a program that can store and display a disk directory as a list of string objects.

5.6 Starting with the classes in the answer to Exercise 5.5, use multiple inheritance to derive a new class that displays a directory and can store a wildcard string. For example, initializing the new directory object with the string "*.cpp" should display all .Cpp files in the current directory and should also store this wildcard string for future reference.

6

CHAPTER

Handling Exceptions

Exceptions are the new darlings of ANSI C++, but until you get used to them, you might consider exceptions more devilish than dear. After you learn how to use them, however, you'll appreciate how exceptions make it possible to write robust code that handles all errors and other exceptional conditions. Also, Borland's class libraries such as ObjectWindows (OWL) and the template class library use exceptions extensively, so it's important for all C++ developers to understand how they work.

A Few Good Terms

Exceptions come with their own terminology and concepts. Following are some overviews that will help you to read and understand this chapter:

- An *exception* is just that—it's an *exceptional condition* that requires special handling. Exceptions are best used for a program's error handling, but they are not limited to that use.

- To create an exception, a statement *throws* an object that describes the nature of the exception. The object can be a literal value, a string, an object of a class, or any other object. An *exception object* is not necessarily a *class* object, but in practice, it usually is.

- To handle an exception, a statement *catches* a condition thrown by some other process. Statements that catch exceptions are called *exception handlers*.

- Programs prepare to catch exceptions by *trying* one or more statements that might throw exceptions. In general, to use exceptions, you *try* one or more statements and you *catch* any exceptions those statements *throw*.

Introducing Exceptions

Now, let's see what exceptions actually look like in C++. Upon detecting an error condition, a function can *throw an exception*. This produces two effects:

- It announces that an exceptional condition has been detected. This might be an error condition, but it could be any other circumstance that requires special handling.

- It requests that an exception handler deal with the problem. The handler, if it exists, is called automatically in response to throwing an exception object.

A program throws an exception by executing a throw statement, usually somewhere inside a function:

```
throw 1;
```

Normally, however, you shouldn't throw literal integers around—they don't mean much out of context. A better object to throw is a string:

```
throw "overflow";
```

That's more meaningful. Elsewhere in the program, a string-exception handler can catch and display the thrown object. The handler specifies the object's type (const char* in this example) in a catch expression:

```
catch (const char* message) {
  cout << "Error! - " << message << endl;
  // ... Other actions in response to the exception
}
```

The catch statement catches the thrown string-exception object, and displays it in an output stream statement. What happens next is up to you. If you take no further actions, the program continues after the catch. Or, you could halt the program, call another function, or continue a loop to restart the condition that caused the problem. An exception is a mechanism for reporting and dealing with exceptional conditions—it does not dictate a course of action. That's still your job.

> **NOTE**
>
> It's especially important to understand that exceptions are not limited to error handling—despite conflicting information you may have read elsewhere. For instance, an empty list object could report its bare cupboards as an exceptional condition. Whether that's an "error" depends on how you define a program's runtime faults. You would probably agree that not being able to open a file is an error. But is the absence of a specific string inside that file an error, or is that merely one of many possible, and unexceptional, results that a search function may report? Depending on your answer, exceptions may or may not be appropriate for dealing with failed searches or empty lists.

Because of their potential for ambiguous application, exceptions are probably best used for dealing with actual errors—those that force the program to cancel a process, or those conditions that if ignored, would cause the program to fail or produce faulty output. Limiting exceptions to truly exceptional conditions helps separate normal statements from those that perform critical error handling—one of the most difficult goals to achieve in any but the smallest of programs.

Using Exceptions

What exactly is an exception? A good definition is this: *Exceptions are objects that closely resemble function arguments.* Exceptions can be objects of any type, but they are most conveniently represented as instances of a class. For example, you might declare an Overflow class—it doesn't need any substance; just a name will do nicely:

```
class Overflow { };
```

You can throw an instance of this disembodied class as an exception (assume this is inside a function):

```
throw Overflow();
```

That statement constructs an object of the Overflow class, and it throws that object back to the function's caller. Elsewhere, the program can catch the exception in a catch statement:

```
catch (Overflow) {
  cout << "Overflow detected!" << endl;
}
```

The mere presence of an Overflow object indicates that an exception has been thrown. The object doesn't have to do anything, and it doesn't have to possess any content.

Be sure to understand that the preceding throw statement *throws an object of the* Overflow *class,* which is caught by the catch statement at another place in the program (never mind exactly where for the moment). The concept might be easier to fathom by giving the caught object a name, using the same syntax employed in function parameter lists:

```
catch (Overflow overObject) {
  // ...
}
```

This time, the catch statement gives the exception object a name, overObject. Other statements inside the catch statement may use overObject in exactly the same way a statement uses a function parameter.

Typically, for example, an exception class provides member functions that a catch expression can call. Here's an example:

```
class Overflow {
  void Report()
    { cout << "Error: overflow" << endl; }
};
```

Class Overflow declares a member function Report, which displays an error message. (I used an inline function for demonstration purposes, but it could also be a separately implemented member function.) The catch statement can call Report for the exception object to display an error message:

```
catch (Overflow overObject) {
  overObject.Report();  // Calls Report function for thrown object
}
```

Throwing Multiple Exceptions

Functions can throw *different types* of exception objects to represent various exceptional conditions. Here's a hypothetical example that reports two different kinds of problems:

```
int AnyFunction()
{
  if (conditionA)        // If conditionA is true,
```

```
    throw "Big trouble!";  // throw a string object.
  if (conditionB)          // If conditionB is true,
    throw Overflow();      // throw an Overflow class object.
  return 123;              // If no problems, return normally
}
```

If conditionA is true (whatever that means), the function throws a string exception, reporting *Big Trouble!* If conditionB is true, the function throws an object of the Overflow class, constructed in this case by calling that object's default class constructor. If the function detects no error conditions, it returns normally, passing a return value 123 to its caller.

The three most important lessons to learn from this example are as follows:

- Functions can throw one or more exceptions of various types representing *different exceptional conditions.*
- Throwing an exception *immediately terminates* the function that executes the throw statement.
- As the preceding two observations suggest, an exception provides functions with an *alternate return mechanism.*

That last point is key. AnyFunction normally returns an int value, but if an exception occurs, it returns either a string or an object of the Overflow class. Only catch statements can receive these special return values. If no exceptions are thrown, the function returns normally, optionally passing a value of the function's declared type back to the function's caller.

You can handle multiple types of exception objects with a series of catch statements. For example, to handle Error class and string exceptions, simply write two catch statements back-to-back:

```
catch (Error e) {
  // Handle Error class exception objects
}
catch (const char* message) {
  // Handle string exception objects
}
```

Introducing try Blocks

Now it's time to toss in another wrinkle—try *blocks,* which seem to confuse everybody the first time they use them. To receive exception objects, call a function from inside a try block:

```
try {
  int x = AnyFunction();  // Try calling this function
}
catch (Error e) {         // If function throws an exception
  e.Report();             // call the Error objects Report function
  exit(-1);               // and exit the program.
}
```

A try block contains one or more statements for which you want to catch exceptions. One or more catch statements *must* follow the try block. You cannot have a try block in one place

175

and `catch` statements elsewhere. That would be like having a ball game's pitcher on the mound and the catcher in the parking lot. In all cases, you must follow a `try` block with one or more `catch` statements that catch any exceptions thrown by the tried statements.

Multiple `try` blocks and their associated `catch` statements also can be nested, although the syntax can produce messy-looking code. A `try` block, for example, can have a nested `try` block and `catch` statement as in the following hypothetical example. In this example, if `FunctionA` throws an exception, the program skips the nested `try` block entirely:

```
try {
  FunctionA();         // Try this function in outer block
  try {                // Nested try block. Skipped on exception
    FunctionB();       // Try this function in inner block
  }
  catch (Error e) {    // Catch exceptions thrown by FunctionB()
    e.Report();        // Call exception object's Report()
  }
}
catch (Error e) {      // Catch exceptions thrown by FunctionA()
  e.Report();          // Call exception object's Report()
}
```

Using try Blocks

Some additional examples help clarify what `try` blocks are and how to use them. A `try` block may have multiple statements (and it usually does):

```
try {
  cout << "Here we go! << endl;
  int x = AnyFunction();
  cout << "x == " << x << endl;
}
```

The sample `try` block first displays a message. Next, it calls `AnyFunction`, assigning the function's result to an `int` variable, `x`. If `AnyFunction` throws an exception, *the try block immediately ends.* Any exceptional conditions, in other words, skip the assignment to `x` and the final output statement.

> **NOTE**
>
> Especially important is the fact that, in the preceding code fragment, if `AnyFunction` throws an exception, the assignment to `int x` does not take place.

A `try` block must be followed by one or more `catch` statements (otherwise, there's no reason to use `try`). Here's a more complete example of how you can handle multiple exceptions that a function such as `AnyFunction` might throw:

```
try {
  cout << "Here we go! << endl;
  int x = AnyFunction();
```

```
  cout << "x == " << x << endl;
}
catch (char* message) {
  cout << "Error! - " << message << endl;
  exit(-1);  // Optional
}
catch (Overflow) {
  cout << "Overflow!" << endl;
  exit(-2);  // Optional
}
// Program continues here normally
```

The expanded code first *tries* to call AnyFunction. If the function returns normally, its result is assigned to x, which a subsequent statement writes to the standard output. If no exceptions are thrown, both of the catch statements are skipped because there are no exception objects of the declared types to catch. If AnyFunction throws an exception, however, *the try block is immediately terminated,* and the object thrown is caught by an appropriate catch statement—that is, the one that declares a parameter of the thrown object's data type.

In this example, the catch statements call the library function exit to halt the program. This response is optional. It's up to you to decide what to do in response to a caught exception.

You may insert one, two, three, or more catch statements after a try block to catch exceptions of different types. In this example, two catch statements handle string and Overflow exceptions. Any other types of exceptions that are not handled in a catch statement are *passed upward in the call chain.* Suppose, for instance, that AnyFunction also throws an exception of type NewException. If a function g had called the preceding code, that exception object is passed upward to g because only char* and Overflow exceptions are handled here.

Eventually, if no catch statement of the appropriate type exists anywhere in the call chain that led to the exception, the program terminates by calling a special runtime handler. To prevent this unhappy occurrence, you should program a catch statement for every possible type of thrown object.

NOTE

Exceptions eliminate the need to reserve special error return values. For example, in classic C and C++ programming, a function that returns int might specify that a return value of -1 indicates an error; otherwise, the return value is legitimate. There's nothing wrong with this technique, but reserving a special value isn't always possible. Consider a function that sums a list of integers. In that case, all return values must be legitimate, and it is impossible to reserve any single value as a special case. Most programmers solve that kind of impasse by defining a global error flag or variable, which the program must check to detect errors after function calls. Exceptions do away with this sort of messy error handling by returning objects that represent exceptional conditions without conflicting with a function's normal return values.

Programming with Exceptions

A sample program, Listing 6.1, Except.cpp, demonstrates how to use C++ exceptions. You may compile and run the program from DOS or Windows. Follow instructions in the listing. At a DOS prompt, enter bcc except, and then type the program's name to run the resulting Except.exe code file. Or, from the IDE, compile and run the program as an *EasyWin* application.

> **NOTE**
>
> For demonstration purposes, Except.cpp has a statement that never executes, causing the compiler to warn you about "Unreachable code in function Power(double, double)." I included this throw statement as a debugging device. If you make a mistake typing the program (of course, it's on CD-ROM, so you don't have to do that), the throw statement constructs an object of the Error class by calling its default constructor. This is a useful development tool that can help identify typing errors. If constructed by default, the Error object displays a message that indicates an error in the source code.

Listing 6.1. Except.cpp. (Demonstrates C++ exceptions).

```cpp
//================================================================
// Except.cpp -- Demonstrates C++ exceptions
// To compile:
//    bcc except
// To run:
//    except
// Copyright (c) 1996 by Tom Swan. All rights reserved.
//================================================================

#include <iostream.h>
#include <math.h>

// Function prototypes
void Instruct();
double Pow(double b, double e);
double Power(double b, double e);

// Exception class
class Error {
  double b;     // Base
  double e;     // Exponent
public:
  Error()
    { cout << "Error in source code!" << endl; }
  Error(double bb, double ee)
    : b(bb), e(ee) { }
  void Report();
};

int main()
```

```
{
  Instruct();
  try {
    double base, exponent, result;
    cout << "base? ";
    cin >> base;
    cout << "exponent? ";
    cin >> exponent;
    result = Power(base, exponent);
    cout << "result == " << result << endl;
  }
  catch (Error& e) {
    e.Report();
    return -1;
  }
  return 0;
}

void Instruct()
{
  cout << "Power Demonstration" << endl << endl;
  cout << "This program displays the result of raising" << endl;
  cout << "a value (base) to a power (exponent). To" << endl;
  cout << "force an exception, enter a negative base" << endl;
  cout << "and a fractional exponent (e.g. -4 and 1.5)" << endl;
  cout << "Or, enter a zero base and an exponent less than" << endl;
  cout << "zero." << endl << endl;
}

// Subfunction to Power
double Pow(double b, double e)
{
  return exp(e * log(b));
}

// Final b raised to the e power
double Power(double b, double e)
{
  if (b > 0.0) return Pow(b, e);
  if (b < 0.0) {
    double ipart;
    double fpart = modf(e, &ipart);
    if (fpart == 0) {
      if (fmod(ipart, 2) != 0)  // i.e. ipart is odd
        return -Pow(-b, e);
      else
        return Pow(-b, e);
    } else
      throw Error(b, e);
  } else {
    if (e == 0.0) return 1.0;
    if (e < 1.0) throw Error(b, e);
    return 0.0;
  }
  throw Error();  // Unreachable code warning expected
}
```

continues

Listing 6.1. continued

```
// Display values that caused an exception
void
Error::Report()
{
  cout << "Domain error:"
    << " base:" << b
    << " exponent:" << e
    << endl;
}
```

Except.cpp implements a Power function that can raise any real number to any real-number power. (By the way, this is a useful function to extract for your function library.) Two exceptional conditions cause the function to throw an exception:

- Raising a negative base to a fractional exponent.
- Raising zero to an exponent less than zero.

Those conditions are exactly the kind of problems that exceptions are best at handling. The alternatives are to halt the program (not pretty), return a special value (not practical), or set a global error flag (not good programming).

Instead of those relatively poor error-handling solutions, Power throws an exception as an object of an Error class. For example, on attempting to raise a negative base to a fractional exponent, Power executes the following statement, which constructs an object of the Error class, initialized with the values of b and e:

```
throw Error(b, e);
```

Back in main, the program calls Power in a try block, repeated in part here:

```
try {
  double base, exponent, result
  // ... prompt for base and exponent
  result = Power(base, exponent);
  cout << "result == " << result << endl;
}
```

If Power throws an exception, the assignment to result and the final output statement are skipped, and the try block immediately ends. A catch statement immediately following the try block catches the exception object:

```
catch (Error& e) {
  e.Report();
  return -1;
}
return 0;
```

If Power throws an exception, Error object e is caught by reference. The catch statement calls Error's Report member function for the exception e, displaying the values that caused Power to fail.

At this point, the program has complete control over how to handle the exception. The example returns -1 for errors, or 0 if no exceptions occurred. This is standard practice, even though DOS and Windows ignore program return values.

In many cases, however, it may not be desirable to end the program. Instead, you might want to repeat the statements that led to the exception—in this case, prompting for new input values. Later in this section, I explain how to use exceptions this way, but first you need to learn about an alternate declaration form for functions that throw exceptions.

Declared Exceptions

Using an alternate function-declaration format, you can declare exactly the types of exceptions that a function is permitted to throw. This format is especially valuable in function libraries for which it is important to handle all possible error conditions. A function AnyFunction, for example, can state its exception types:

```
void AnyFunction() throw(Error);
```

Following the function name and parameter list (empty in this case) with a throw expression indicates that AnyFunction might throw an Error object. More important, the declaration states to the compiler that AnyFunction *is not permitted to throw exceptions of any other kind.* When you encounter a function declared in this way, you do not need to hunt through the function's throw statements (and its documentation) to find all of its possible exceptions. The declaration tells you that, if AnyFunction throws an exception, it will be an object of the Error class.

To specify that a function can throw exceptions of multiple types, list each exception object data type in parentheses, separated by commas:

```
void AnyFunction() throw(Error, char*, OtherType);
```

Writing Exceptional Error Handlers

The preceding listing, Except.cpp, handles all possible exceptions, but it still ends the program when an error occurs. A better program repeats the statements that led to the exception, so that users can enter correct values. The modified program listed next also demonstrates how to write code that handles all possible exceptions, even unexpected ones thrown by third-party function libraries.

Compile and run Listing 6.2, Except2.cpp, as you did the preceding one (from DOS or as an EasyWin application). Enter bad input values as suggested by the program's instructions. Figure 6.1 shows a sample program run.

Figure 6.1.

Sample output from Except2.cpp.

```
Power Demonstration
This program displays the result of raising
a value (base) to a power (exponent). To
force an exception, enter a negative base
and a fractional exponent (e.g. -4 and 1.5)
Or, enter a zero base and an exponent less than
zero.

base? -4
exponent? 1.5
Domain error: base:-4 exponent:1.5
Error detected: Try again!
base? 0
exponent? -9.99
Domain error: base:0 exponent:-9.99
Error detected: Try again!
base? 2
exponent? 16
result == 65536
Program is ending normally.
```

Listing 6.2. Except2.cpp (Demonstrates error handling using exceptions).

```cpp
//================================================================
// Except2.cpp -- Demonstrates error handling using exceptions
// To compile:
//    bcc except2
// To run:
//    except2
// Copyright (c) 1996 by Tom Swan. All rights reserved.
//================================================================

#include <iostream.h>
#include <math.h>

// Exception-object class declared in advance by name only
// so that Power() can refer to it
class Error;

// Function prototypes (note Power's declared exception)
void Instruct();
void Run();
double Pow(double b, double e);
double Power(double b, double e) throw(Error);

// Exception-object class declared in full
class Error {
  double b;      // Base
  double e;      // Exponent
```

```
public:
  Error()
    { cout << "Error in source code!" << endl; }
  Error(double bb, double ee)
    : b(bb), e(ee) { }
  void Report();
};

int main()
{
  Instruct();
  for (;;) {
    try {
      Run();
      cout << "Program is ending normally." << endl;
      return 0;  // Only if no exceptions thrown
    }
    catch (...) {
      cout << "Error detected: Try again!" << endl;
    }
  }
}

void Instruct()
{
  cout << "Power Demonstration" << endl << endl;
  cout << "This program displays the result of raising" << endl;
  cout << "a value (base) to a power (exponent). To" << endl;
  cout << "force an exception, enter a negative base" << endl;
  cout << "and a fractional exponent (e.g. -4 and 1.5)" << endl;
  cout << "Or, enter a zero base and an exponent less than" << endl;
  cout << "zero." << endl << endl;
}

// Run program (called by main() repeatedly)
void Run()
{
  try {
    double base, exponent, result;
    cout << "base? ";
    cin >> base;
    cout << "exponent? ";
    cin >> exponent;
    result = Power(base, exponent);
    cout << "result == " << result << endl;
  }
  catch (Error& e) {
    e.Report();  // Display error message
    throw e;     // Rethrow the exception to Run()'s caller
  }
}

// Subfunction to Power
double Pow(double b, double e)
{
  return exp(e * log(b));
```

continues

Listing 6.2. continued

```
}

// Final b raised to the e power
double Power(double b, double e) throw(Error)
{
  if (b > 0.0) return Pow(b, e);
  if (b < 0.0) {
    double ipart;
    double fpart = modf(e, &ipart);
    if (fpart == 0) {
      if (fmod(ipart, 2) != 0)   // i.e. ipart is odd
        return -Pow(-b, e);
      else
        return Pow(-b, e);
    } else
      throw Error(b, e);
  } else {
    if (e == 0.0) return 1.0;
    if (e < 1.0) throw Error(b, e);
    return 0.0;
  }
}

// Implement Error() class's Report() member function
// Display values that caused an exception
void
Error::Report()
{
  cout << "Domain error:"
    << " base:" << b
    << " exponent:" << e
    << endl;
}
```

The revised listing makes several modifications. First, it declares Error using an incomplete class declaration. This permits functions to refer to the class, even though it is declared only by name at this point. The Power function, for example, uses a throw expression to indicate that it may throw an exception object of the Error class (and *only* an object of that class).

After the program's function prototypes, the Error class is fully declared. This is the same class used in the original listing.

TIP

Incomplete class declarations and function prototypes are more practical in large programs composed of multiple headers and modules. I used these methods here just to demonstrate their forms—they are not strictly required in simple demonstrations such as Except2.cpp.

To repeat the prompt for input values, function main uses a "do-forever" for loop, in the form:

```
for (;;) {
  // .. do this "forever"
}
```

The statements inside for execute until reaching a return or other statement that ends the program. This ensures that the program retains control over all possible exit paths.

Inside the for loop, a try block followed by a catch statement calls function Run, newly added to the demonstration. To guard against the possibility that an exception wasn't handled elsewhere in the code, the try block that calls Run uses a single catch statement with an ellipsis in parentheses:

```
try {
  Run();
  // any normal statements or a return
}
catch (...) {
  // catch-all handler statements
}
```

If no exceptions come back from Run, statements following the call to this function execute. These statements can be anything you like—a return statement, for example, can end the program, or you can call a library function such as exit.

When written with ellipsis in parentheses, the catch expression executes its statements for any and all exceptions that are not handled elsewhere. These exceptions are passed back through Run (since this is the only function that main calls). The technique therefore guarantees that no exceptions can halt the program through a default runtime subroutine.

In the listing, function Run is similar to the original main. It calls the Pow function (which calls Power), using a try block to catch any reported exceptions. The catch statement is a little different, however:

```
catch (Error& e) {
  e.Report();  // Display error message
  throw e;     // Rethrow the exception to Run()'s caller
}
```

If Power throws an Error exception, the catch statement calls the class's Report function to display an error message. After that, catch *rethrows the exception.* This exits Run immediately, and passes the error object back to Run's caller. The catch-all catch (the one with the ellipsis) in main receives this error message, skipping the return statement that ends the program and causing the for loop to repeat.

Unhandled Exceptions

The preceding section demonstrates how to catch all possible exceptions, but in other programs, you might wonder: What happens to exceptions that are thrown but not caught? The answer is simple and logical. Unhandled exceptions are passed upward in the call chain (that is, the

185

chain of functions that have called one another, linked by their return addresses on the stack) until they are handled by a catch statement, or until there are no more exception handlers left. If that happens, one of three runtime functions, automatically attached to every C++ program that uses exceptions, is called to deal with the exception. The three functions are unexpected, terminate, and abort. They are called according to the following rules:

- Exceptions that are not handled by a catch statement cause the program to call unexpected. An *unexpected exception* is defined as any exception that isn't handled by a catch statement. By default, unexpected calls terminate, explained next.

- Unexpected exceptions for which the program detects a corrupted stack or that result from a class destructor that throws an exception (a dangerous practice to be reserved only for the most critical of problems) cause the program to call the terminate function. By default, terminate calls abort, explained next.

- The abort function is lowest on the totem pole. As you might expect, abort ends the program immediately. It is never called directly. Unless you handle all possible exceptions, or unless you take additional measures to reprogram unexpected and, possibly, terminate, an unhandled exception will halt the program through abort. If the program gets to this stage, there is nothing you can do to prevent it from ending. (Conversely, if a program halts unexpectedly, you need to work on your error handling code!)

> **NOTE**
>
> From the Borland C++ runtime source code, terminate apparently does not call abort as ANSI C++ dictates. In BC45, terminate simply ends the program. Because you cannot replace abort, this tiny discrepancy has no negative effects, and it's useful to think of terminate as calling abort, if only to maintain the standard conceptually.

For a demonstration of what happens when a program fails to handle all possible exceptions, save a copy of Except2.cpp to another file. (I use X.cpp for these kinds of throw-away tests.) Rewrite function main as

```
int main()
{
  Instruct();
  Run();
  return 0;
}
```

Compile the program with the DOS-prompt command, bcc x, and run it by typing its name. Enter values to force an exception (-4 and 1.5, for example). Any unhandled exceptions from Run cause the program to call unexpected, which calls terminate, which calls abort, which ends the program. DOS applications that end this way display the message "Abnormal program termination." Windows and EasyWin applications end by displaying an error dialog box.

Except for simple examples and tests, you should do everything possible to prevent programs from unexpectedly ending this way.

You can replace `unexpected` and `terminate` with new code to deal with unhandled exceptions in whatever way you wish. It might make sense, for example, to replace `unexpected` to notify you of any unhandled exceptions during a program's development. This might also help identify a deficiency in the program's error handling. In other cases, you might want to replace `terminate` with diagnostic software to inspect memory in hopes of locating statements that corrupt the heap, or for investigating the cause of a class destructor that throws an exception.

You cannot replace `abort`. Calling `abort` always ends the program with no ifs, ands, buts, or tomorrows.

Replacing unexpected and terminate

Use the `set_unexpected` function, declared in the Borland C++ header Except.h, to assign the address of a custom unexpected-exception handler. The function must be of type `unexpected_function`, which requires no arguments and returns `void`.

Your unexpected-exception handler may throw an exception, in which case the search for an exception handler (that is, a `catch` statement) begins at the location that originally caused your handler to be called.

Use the `set_terminate` function, also declared in Except.h, to assign the address of a custom terminate handler. The function must be of type `terminate_function`, which requires no arguments and returns `void`.

Both functions, `set_unexpected` and `set_terminate`, return the address of the current handler. You can save and restore the existing handlers by storing these addresses in variables and passing them back to the functions. For example, first, declare a prototype for the handler:

```
void unexpectedHandler();
```

You would also have to implement the function (a more complete example follows). Next, enable the handler with this statement:

```
set_unexpected(unexpectedHandler);
```

Or, you can optionally save and restore the old handler's address:

```
unexpected_function savedAddress;  // Define address variable
savedAddress = set_unexpected(unexpectedHandler);  // Install handler
// ... Custom handler is used for unhandled exceptions
set_unexpected(savedAddress);  // Restore original handler
// ... Custom handler is no longer used
```

Set a custom `terminate` function similarly, but call `set_terminate`, which returns an address of type `terminate_function`.

187

Listing 6.3, Unexpect.cpp, demonstrates how to set unexpected-exception and terminate handlers. The program also shows a good technique for dealing with unexpected exceptions of unknown types as might be thrown by a poorly documented library function. You may compile and run the program as a DOS or EasyWin application.

Listing 6.3. Unexpect.cpp (Sets unexpected and terminate handlers).

```
//================================================================
// Unexpect.cpp -- Sets unexpected and terminate handlers
// To compile:
//    bcc unexpect
// To run:
//    unexpect
// Copyright (c) 1996 by Tom Swan. All rights reserved.
//================================================================

#include <iostream.h>
#include <except.h>

#define MAXERR 10

// Exception class used when errors exceed limit
class MaxError
{
};

// Normal error exception class
class Error {
public:
  Error();        // Constructor
  void Say();     // Report static error count
private:
  static int count;  // Only Error class can access this
};

// Prototype for function that throws an exception
void Run() throw(Error);
void trapper();
void zapper();

// Global static counter for Error class objects
int Error::count;

void main()
{
  set_unexpected(trapper);
  set_terminate(zapper);
  for (;;)
  {
    try {
```

```
    Run();
    }
    catch (Error e) {
      e.Say();
    }
  }
}

// Function that throws an exception
void Run() throw(Error)
{
  throw Error();
//  throw "An unknown exception object";
}

// Our unexpected error handler
void trapper()
{
  cout << endl << "Inside trapper function" << endl;
  throw Error();
}

// Our terminate error handler
void zapper()
{
  cout << endl << "Inside terminate function" << endl;
  cout << endl << "Exiting program with error code -1" << endl;
  exit(-1);
}

// Error class constructor
Error::Error()
{
  count++;
  if (count > MAXERR)
    throw MaxError();
}

// Error class reporting function
void Error::Say()
{
  cout << "Error: count = " << count << endl;
}
```

When you run Unexpect, it displays 10 error reports before terminating. Figure 6.2 shows the program's output.

Figure 6.2.
Sample output from UNEXPECT.CPP.

```
Error: count = 1
Error: count = 2
Error: count = 3
Error: count = 4
Error: count = 5
Error: count = 6
Error: count = 7
Error: count = 8
Error: count = 9
Error: count = 10

Inside trapper function

Inside terminate function

Exiting program with error code -1
```

The program uses two exception classes. MaxError, which has no data or functions, is thrown when the count of errors exceeds MAXERR, set to 10 here. Objects of the Error class are thrown as you have learned in previous examples.

The Error class constructor near the end of the listing increments the class's static count. Because count is static, only one copy of this value exists, and it persists throughout the life of the program. Making count a private member of the class ensures that no statement in the program outside the class can access this critical variable. Only the Error class has access to the program's error counter. Member function Say displays count's value.

In the course of constructing an Error object, if count equals or exceeds MAXERR, the constructor throws an exception of type MaxError. When a constructor throws an exception, the object is *not* constructed—that is, in this case, the construction of the Error object is aborted (more on this detail later).

Function main installs handlers that replace the default unexpected and terminate functions. The main program then executes a "do-forever" for loop, similar to the one you examined earlier. Inside the loop, a try block calls Run, and a catch statement catches any Error—class objects that Run throws. In the event of an exception, catch displays the current error count by calling the class's Say function for the thrown object.

The Run function always throws an exception, simulating multiple errors that a more extensive program might have to handle. The custom unexpected-exception handler, trapper, displays a message, which indicates when the function is called. As Figure 6.2 shows, this happens after 10 exceptions are thrown.

An unexpected-exception handler may throw another exception to continue the program. In the example, the following statement throws a new instance of the Error class.

```
throw Error();
```

Because our unexpected-exception handler isn't called until 10 exceptions occur, however, constructing the Error object causes its class constructor to throw another exception of type MaxError (see Error's constructor). This type of error is not handled by a catch statement, and therefore, the program's terminate handler, zapper, is called. A terminate function must *not* throw an exception. (An unexpected or terminate function also must not execute a return statement.)

At this stage, there doesn't seem to be much point in having both an unexpected and a terminate handler, both of which are called just before the program ends. What's really needed is a method for catching unexpected exceptions of unknown types, which will still permit the program to continue. You still want the terminate handler to be called only when the program exceeds its error limit.

To simulate this common requirement of complex error handlers, reprogram Run to throw an unknown type of exception. For example, throw a string by rewriting Run as follows:

```
void Run() throw(Error)
{
  throw "An unknown exception object";
}
```

When you compile and run the modified program, the unexpected handler, trapper, is now called for each exception that Run throws. This happens because there's no catch statement for exception objects of type const char* or char*. The trapper function, however, *translates* the unrecognized exception object by throwing one of a known type, in this case Error. The newly thrown exception continues the program's execution at the catch statement inside main, which handles the translated exception.

Eventually, the program exceeds its maximum error count, and a MaxError object is thrown by Error's constructor. This causes the terminate handler to be called, ending the program with a call to the exit library function.

Exceptions and Local Objects

Using a special compiler option, local objects left on the stack following an exception are automatically destroyed—that is, their destructors are called. To enable autodestruction, specify -xd for the command-line compiler. Or, in the IDE, select *Options|Project*, open the *C++ Options* topic, and select the topic sublevel *Exception Handling/RTTI*. (RTTI stands for *Runtime Type Information*.) Make sure *Enable exceptions* and *Enable destructor cleanup* are enabled.

In general, autodestruction is required for functions that

- Construct a local object
- Throw an exception after constructing the object

A simple example illustrates why you should be concerned with these two issues. The following function might leave an object of `AnyClass` floating on the stack:

```
int AnyFunction()
{
  AnyClass object(123);
  // ...
  if (condition) throw Error();
  return object.Value();
}
```

The function constructs the `AnyClass` `object` on the stack. In the normal course of events, when the function ends, `object`'s destructor is called. If, however, an exception ends the function, `object`'s destructor is *not* called, which in some cases might cause serious problems—if the program fails to delete memory allocated to `object`, for instance.

Using the `-xd` switch or equivalent IDE setting certifies that, in cases such as this, `object`'s destructor is called if the function ends due to an exception. Normally, this is desirable, but the switch adds a certain amount of overhead that you can eliminate if you don't have any local objects in functions that throw exceptions. (Remember, however, you must enable autodestruction for OWL programs.)

Notice that pointers to objects *are not automatically deleted.* If you construct a dynamic object, before throwing an exception, it's your responsibility to delete the object:

```
int AnyFunction()
{
  AnyClass *p = new AnyClass(123);
  // ...
  if (condition) {
    delete p;        // You MUST delete p here!
    throw Error();   // Immediately exits AnyFunction
  }
  delete p;      // Not executed if condition was true
  return 123;    // Normal return. Not executed if exception thrown
};
```

The only way to prevent duplicating the use of `delete` is to postpone throwing an exception until after disposing of all dynamic objects:

```
int AnyFunction()
{
  AnyClass *p = new AnyClass(123);
```

```
// ...
delete p;
if (condition) throw Error();
return 123;
}
```

Use a flag such as condition to indicate any errors, delete all dynamically allocated objects, and then throw the exception.

Exceptions and Constructors

Class constructors may throw exceptions to indicate that they cannot successfully construct an object. Up until recently, this was a serious deficiency in C++, which provided no means of indicating a faulty object construction. A typical work-around was to call a member function that returns true or false based on whether the object was properly constructed. Exceptions eliminate the need for this kind of kludgy code.

To throw an exception from inside a constructor, use the throw keyword as shown in other examples:

```
class AnyClass {
public:
  AnyClass()
    { if (condition) throw Error(); }
  ~AnyClass() { }
};
```

The key concept here is that if a constructor throws an exception—meaning that the constructor ends abnormally—*that object's destructor is not called.* Only fully constructed objects are destroyed by destructors, a fact that has especially important consequences in classes that own objects of *other* classes. Consider this case:

```
class AnyClass {
  OtherClass x;
public:
  AnyClass(): x(123)
    { if (condition) throw Error(); }
  ~AnyClass() { }
};
```

Object x of type OtherClass is constructed by AnyClass's constructor *before* the constructor's statements are executed. If the OtherClass constructor throws an exception, then AnyClass's constructor statements *are not executed.* Because that code never runs, the AnyClass object is not constructed, and therefore, the AnyClass destructor is also not called. The same mechanism applies in classes that own multiple objects:

```
class AnyClass {
  OtherClass a, b, c;
public:
  AnyClass: a(), b(), c() { }
  ~AnyClass() { }
};
```

193

If object b's constructor throws an exception, object c *is not constructed,* and neither is the AnyClass object. Object a's destructor is called normally (because a was fully constructed before b threw an exception), but the destructors, if any, in b, c, and AnyClass are not called.

Raising an Exception

A class can also throw an exception object of its own class type. Usually, this is done by a member function, often called Raise. You might, for example, design an exception class like this:

```
class Error {
public:
  void Raise()
    { throw Error(); }
};
```

If e is an object of the Error class, the statement

```
e.Raise;   // Throw fresh Error object
```

throws *another* object of that class. Depending on the other services that Error provides, throwing a fresh exception object might suit your purposes better than rethrowing the same exception with

```
throw e;     // Rethrow existing Error object
```

Exceptions and Memory Management

As mentioned elsewhere, operator new throws an exception if it can't fulfill a memory-allocation request. This differs from how new in earlier C++ releases returned null (zero) if enough memory was unavailable.

> **TIP**
>
> If you want new to act as it did in the past, returning null for out-of-memory errors, include the new.h header file, and add this statement to main:
>
> ```
> set_new_handler(0);
> ```

In the past, you probably wrote code such as this:

```
AnyClass *p;         // Pointer to AnyClass structure
p = new AnyClass();  // Allocate an AnyClass object; address with p
if (p == 0) Error(); // Call error routine if out of memory
```

After using new to allocate memory for an AnyClass object, if p is null, then new could not find enough memory to create the object. The trouble was that you had to perform this test on new's result after *each* use of the operator.

Exceptions change how you use new. Now, if enough memory is not available, new throws an exception of type xalloc, defined in EXCEPT.H as

```
class xalloc : public xmsg {
public:
  xalloc(const string &msg, size_t size);
  size_t requested() const;
  void raise() throw(xalloc);
private:
  size_t siz;
};
```

To use exceptions with new, encase memory allocation statements in a try block followed by a catch statement for an object of the xalloc class. For example, you can write

```
try {
  p = new AnyClass();
  // ... other memory allocation statements
}
catch (xalloc x) {
  cout << "Memory error: " << x.why() << endl;
  exit(-1);
}
```

The xalloc class is derived from another class, xmsg, also declared in Except.h. The ancestor class holds a text message of type string (described later in this chapter). Use the class's why member function to access this string as the preceding code fragment demonstrates in the catch's output statement. Call x.requested for the size in bytes of the failed memory request.

You can also use a *single* try block in main to trap all memory errors. For example, you can structure main something like this:

```
void main()
{
  for (;;) {
    try {
      Run();      // Run program
    }
    catch (xalloc x) {
      cout << "Out of memory" << endl;
      exit(-1);  // End program or take another action
    }
  }
}
```

The idea here is to call a single function, Run, that runs the program. Any exceptions must either be handled by Run (or by another function that Run calls), or those exceptions end up back in main where you can handle them with a catch statement.

Listing 6.4, Memerr.cpp, demonstrates how to use exceptions and the new operator. The program recovers gracefully from out-of-memory errors, which in the absence of exceptions, typically cause an abnormal program termination. You may compile and run the program as a DOS or EasyWin application. See instructions for DOS in the listing.

> **WARNING**
>
> Because Memerr allocates all memory, you should save all documents and close other applications before running the program. It is possible, but unlikely, for Memerr to crash DOS, Windows, and extended memory managers. (I have experienced all of these problems.) This is especially true if you modify the program's parameters. Be especially careful when running this program.

Listing 6.4. Memerr.cpp (Demonstrates exceptions and the new operator).

```
//================================================================
// Memerr.cpp -- Demonstrates exceptions and the new operator
// To compile:
//    bcc memerr
// To run:
//    memerr
// Copyright (c) 1996 by Tom Swan. All rights reserved.
//================================================================

#include <iostream.h>
#include <new.h>
#include <except.h>
#include <cstring.h>
#include <stdlib.h>

struct q {
  int ia[1024];   // 2048-byte structure
};

char *pool;       // Reserved memory pool pointer

void main()
{
  struct q *qp;              // Pointer to structure q

  try {
  pool = new char[512];    // Reserve small amount of memory
  }
  catch (xalloc) {
    cout << "Not enough RAM to run program" << endl;
    exit(-1);
  }

  for (;;) {                 // Do following statements "forever"
    try {                    // Use try block to catch exceptions
      qp = new q;            // Allocate new struture of type q
      cout << qp << endl;    // Display structure address
    }
    catch (xalloc x) {       // Catch exception from new
      delete pool;           // Delete reserved RAM for next line
      cout << "Error: " << x.why() << endl;   // Display message
      exit(-1);              // Exit program (or another action)
    }
  }
}
```

Memerr.cpp shows a potential danger that, when dealing with memory errors, you must consider. In its "do-forever" `for` loop, the program allocates 2048-byte structures of type q repeatedly until new throws an `xalloc` exception. A `catch` statement receives this error, and calls the object's `why` function (inherited by `xalloc` from `xmsg`) to display the cause of the problem.

The problem with this technique is that, upon running out of memory, there's no guarantee that the output statement before `exit` will work. In fact, as a general rule, after running out of RAM, you should be extremely wary of performing any I/O or other activity that might require some memory. In this case, simply outputting a string and calling the `why` function can crash the operating system and cause a loss of data.

The answer to this dilemma is to reserve a small pool of RAM at the program's start. Upon receiving an out-of-memory error, delete the pool to give any output statements some RAM to use. You can then exit the program, or if you decide to continue operation, allocate the memory pool again in case of future memory problems.

> **WARNING**
>
> If you want to attempt to reproduce the problem described in the preceding section, change the size of the reserved memory pool from 512 bytes to 1 or 2, recompile, and run. The modified program may crash your computer with a General Protection Fault (GPF) and cause a permanent loss of data. Try this experiment only with extreme caution.

Summary

- C++ exceptions provide a mechanism for writing robust code that handles all errors and other exceptional conditions.
- A function may `throw` an exception, indicating that an exceptional condition has occurred. Usually, exceptions report errors, but they can also be put to other uses. To use exceptions, call exception-throwing functions in a `try` block, followed by one or more `catch` statements.
- An exception object may be of any type—for example, an integer, a character string, or a class object.
- Unhandled exceptions cause the program to call a default `unexpected` function. Normally, `unexpected` calls `terminate`, which calls `abort` to halt the program. You may replace `unexpected` and `terminate` functions with your own exception handlers. You may not replace `abort`.
- A C++ operator, `typeid`, provides runtime type information for any object. The operator returns an object of the `Type_info` class, which describes the object's type. You can also use `typeid` to compare the types of objects.

Exercises

6.1 Write a program that uses the standard `memcmp` to compare two blocks of memory. Report any discrepancies using exceptions.

6.2 Design a `range(min, max, value)` function that uses exceptions to report `value`s that are out of the range of `min` to `max`. Is this a good use for C++ exceptions?

6.3 Write a string-concatenation function that throws an exception if the destination string would exceed a specified buffer length. Is this a good use for C++ exceptions?

6.4 If you didn't already, redesign your function from Exercise 6.3 to specify a declared exception in the function's prototype.

6.5 Show the steps required to implement a function that handles any unexpected exceptions that might occur at runtime.

6.6 *Advanced.* Design a function that indicates it throws no exceptions of any kind. Hint: The answer is an extension of the technique for declaring functions that throw only specific functions as described in this chapter.

CHAPTER

7

Overloading Your Friends

The topics of *operator overloading* and *friends* have been smothered in a lot of unnecessary mumbo jumbo. Simply stated, operator overloading makes it possible to define actions for class objects in expressions that use common operators such as plus (+) and minus (-). Friends modify class access rules, a fact that contributes to making overloaded operators logical and natural to use.

This chapter explains the techniques and practical value of operator overloading. Before getting to that subject, however, you first need a little help from your friends.

Friends

One of OOP's main gifts is the encapsulation of data and functions in classes. Typically, class member functions provide controlled access to data hidden within objects, which helps to eliminate common errors caused by the misuse of data. You've seen many examples of this *data-hiding* concept in this book's listings, and you've considered its benefits of reduced maintenance chores and easier debugging.

Like many rules in life and programming, however, those of data hiding are made to be broken. In C++, you break encapsulation's rules by using *friends*, although you do so at some risk to your program's welfare. Declaring a friend of a class is like giving a pal a copy of your house key. If you go away for the weekend, don't be surprised on your return to discover your buddy asleep on the couch and the refrigerator seriously depleted.

C++ classes can declare two kinds of friends. An entire class may be a friend of another class, or a single function may be declared as a friend. The following sections describe both of these friendly C++ techniques.

> **NOTE**
>
> If friends have a counterpart in C++, it's the goto statement. Like goto, a friend enables you to break the rules intended to help you write reliable code. Don't interpret the following sections as a blanket endorsement of friends. Top C++ programmers avoid using friends unless absolutely necessary.

Friend Classes

A class may declare another class as a friend. The first class (the one that declares the friend) gives another class (the friend) permission to access all private and protected members of the first class. Public members are always accessible, so you don't need to declare a class as a friend to give it access to public members.

Typically, friend classes are used when two unrelated classes require access to the class's private or protected parts. Suppose you declare this class:

```
class AClass {
private:
  double value;  // Private data member
public:
  AClass() { value = 3.14159; }
};
```

Class AClass contains a single private member, value, of type double. To that member, the class constructor assigns the value 3.14159. Except for that action, the class provides no means to change or even to inspect a class object's value. The private data member is as safe from harm as a bear cub by its mother's side.

Next, suppose you declare another class that contains an object of AClass as a data member:

```
class BClass {
private:
  AClass anObject;  // AClass object data member
public:
  void ShowValue(void)
    { cout << anObject.value; }   // ???
};
```

Member anObject of type AClass is private to BClass. Member function ShowValue attempts to display anObject's value. However, the declaration doesn't compile because value is private to AClass, and only member functions in AClass may access value.

Changing value's private access specifier to protected in AClass would not solve the problem. A protected member is available to its declaring class and to any derived class. Although BClass owns an object of type AClass, the two classes are unrelated, and BClass's members cannot access AClass's private and protected members. Of course, you could make value public in AClass, but that would also make value available to all statements, and would eliminate the advantages gained by hiding that critical piece of data.

A better solution is to make BClass a friend of AClass. Objects of BClass can then access value and any other private and protected members, but statements outside the two classes are still prevented from using AClass's restricted members. To make this change, use the friend keyword inside the class to which the other class needs access. In this example, BClass needs to use the private value data member inside AClass. So to give BClass permission to use that private data, AClass declares BClass as a friend. Here's the new AClass declaration:

```
class AClass {
  friend class BClass;  // BClass is a friend of AClass
private:
  double value;  // Accessible by AClass and BClass members!
public:
  AClass() { value = 3.14159; }
};
```

The only difference from the previous declaration is the declaration `friend class BClass`. This tells the compiler to grant `BClass` access to `AClass`'s private and protected members. Other statements in other classes and elsewhere in the program still can't use `AClass`'s private and protected declarations. Only `BClass` gets a backstage pass to `AClass`'s private dressing rooms. In this manner, you may declare any number of classes as friends. The only restriction is that the `friend` keyword must appear inside a class declaration. A few other facts are worth remembering:

- A class must name all of its friends in advance. You cannot create friends at runtime.

- The class containing the private and protected data is the one that declares another class to be a friend, thus giving that friend special access to the normally hidden members of the declaring class. A class can never declare itself to be a friend of another class.

- The friend class may be declared before or after the class that declares the friend. The order of the declarations is unimportant, but the friend class is typically declared last so the friend's inline member functions can refer to the other class's private or protected parts.

- Derived classes of the friend do not inherit special access to the original class's private and protected members. Only the specifically named friend has that permission.

- A derived class may be a friend of its base class, although in such cases, using protected members in the base accomplishes the same goal of giving the friend access to restricted members in a base class.

Listing 7.1, Friend.cpp, demonstrates how a friend class can access another class's private and protected members.

Listing 7.1. Friend.cpp (Demonstrates using a friend class).

```
//===============================================================
// Friend.cpp -- Demonstrates using a friend class
// To compile:
//   bcc friend
// To run:
//   friend
// Copyright (c) 1996 by Tom Swan. All rights reserved.
//===============================================================

#include <iostream.h>

class Pal {
  friend class Buddy;  // Buddy is a friend of Pal
private:
  int x;     // Accessible to Pal and Buddy members
protected:
  void doublex(void) { x *= x; }  // Accessible to Pal and Buddy
public:
  Pal() { x = 100; }     // Accessible to all users
```

```
  Pal(int n) { x = n; }  //   "   "   "   "   "
};

class Buddy {
private:
  Pal palObject;  // Accessible only to Buddy's members
public:
  void ShowValues(void);  // Accessible to all users
};

void main()
{
  Buddy aBuddy;
  aBuddy.ShowValues();
}

void Buddy::ShowValues(void)
{
  Pal aPal(1234);

  cout << endl << "Before, palObject.x == " << palObject.x;
  palObject.doublex();
  cout << endl << "After, palObject.x  == " << palObject.x;
  cout << endl << "aPal.x == " << aPal.x << endl;
}
```

Friend.cpp begins by declaring a class named Pal. The first declaration in Pal states that a second class Buddy is a friend of Pal. Because of this declaration, Buddy's member functions may access the private and protected members of Pal objects. However, Pal may not access any private or protected members in Buddy.

Farther down in the listing, the Buddy class declares a private object of the Pal class named palObject. When you run the program, even though Buddy is unrelated to Pal, member function Buddy::ShowValues can directly access Pal's private member x and protected member function doublex. Carefully examine how this works in the ShowValues function at the end of the listing. If Buddy were not a friend of Pal, the compiler would not allow expressions such as palObject.doublex and aPal.x.

Mutual Friend Classes

Two classes can declare each other as friends, giving each class access to the other's private and protected members. Of course, this also destroys the barriers that prohibit access to a class's restricted members. The frequent need for classes to befriend other classes signifies a poorly designed class hierarchy. Most classes are better off as strangers to one another.

Even though rarely needed, however, this technique is useful to know. For two classes to become mutual friends, each class must list the other as a friend, giving both classes access to each other's private and protected members. For AClass and BClass to be mutual friends, you could write their declarations as

```
class BClass;  // Optional incomplete class declaration

class AClass {
  friend class BClass;    // BClass may access all AClass members
  // ... other members
};

class BClass {
  friend class AClass;    // AClass may access all BClass members
  // ... other members;
};
```

Any member functions in either class may now access the private and protected members in an object of the other class. If the first class refers to the second class by name—in a member function parameter, for example—you may need to use an incomplete class declaration as done here for BClass. This allows AClass to declare BClass data members and member function parameters even though BClass's complete declaration comes later.

Friend Functions

A friend function is similar to—but less onerous than—a friend class. Declaring a function as a friend of a class gives that function access to private and protected members in class objects. The friend function may be a common C++ function or a class member.

In a typical design, a friend function declares parameters of classes to which the function owes its friendship. Inside the friend function, statements can then access normally hidden members in class-object arguments that are passed to the function.

Listing 7.2, Friendfn.cpp, demonstrates how to declare and use a typical friend function for two classes.

Listing 7.2. Friendfn.cpp (Demonstrates using a friend function).

```
//================================================================
// Friendfn.cpp -- Demonstrates using a friend function
// To compile:
//    bcc friendfn
// To run:
//    friendfn
// Copyright (c) 1996 by Tom Swan. All rights reserved.
//================================================================

#include <iostream.h>

class Two;  // Incomplete class declaration

class One {
  friend void Show(One &c1, Two &c2);
private:
  char *s1;  // Accessible to One and Show()
public:
```

```
  One() { s1 = "Testing "; }
};

class Two {
  friend void Show(One &c1, Two &c2);
private:
  char *s2;  // Accessible to Two and Show()
public:
  Two() { s2 = "one, two, three"; }
};

void main()
{
  One c1;
  Two c2;
  Show(c1, c2);
}

void Show(One &c1, Two &c2)
{
  cout << c1.s1 << c2.s2 << endl;
}
```

Friendfn.cpp declares two classes, One and Two. An incomplete class declaration allows One's members to refer to Two before the Two class is defined. Both classes identically declare a friend function named Show. Because of these declarations, statements in Show are granted access to the private and protected members in classes One and Two. (The classes listed here have no protected sections, but if they did, the friend declaration also would allow access to those members.)

Function Show declares reference parameters c1 and c2 of the two class types, a typical design. Because Show is a friend of those classes, statements inside Show can access private and protected members in class-object arguments that are passed to Show.

For example, the implementation for Show at the end of the listing displays the values of the strings addressed by pointers s1 and s2. Because Show is a friend of the two classes, it can refer directly to the s1 and s2 data members, which are private to their respective classes. Other "unfriendly" functions would not be allowed similar access to those hidden members.

Friend Member Functions

A friend function can also be a class member. In a typical case, a class declares a member function of another class as a friend. The friend member function can access the declaring class's private and protected members.

Listing 7.3, Friendmf.cpp (that's *mf* for member function), shows the basic strategy for using friend member functions.

Listing 7.3. Friendmf.cpp (Demonstrates using a friend member function).

```
//================================================================
// Friendmf.cpp -- Demonstrates using a friend member function
// To compile:
//    bcc friendmf
// To run:
//    friendmf
// Copyright (c) 1996 by Tom Swan. All rights reserved.
//================================================================

#include <iostream.h>

class One;  // Incomplete class declaration

class Two {
private:
  char *s2;  // Accessible to Two's members
public:
  Two() { s2 = "one, two, three"; }
  void Show(One &c1);
};

class One {
  friend void Two::Show(One &c1);
private:
  char *s1;  // Accessible to One and Two::Show
public:
  One() { s1 = "Testing "; }
};

void main()
{
  One c1;
  Two c2;
  c2.Show(c1);
}

void Two::Show(One &c1)
{
  cout << c1.s1 << s2 << endl;
}
```

As in the previous listing (Friendfn.cpp), the new program Friendmf.cpp declares two classes, One and Two. In this case, however, class Two declares Show as a common public member function. Class One declares that same member function as a friend using the class name and a scope resolution operator (Two::) to tell the compiler where it can find Show.

The order of the two classes is reversed from the earlier listing because the class that prototypes the member function must be declared before the class that specifies the member function as a friend. In order for One to declare Two::Show as a friend of the class, the compiler must already have seen Two's declaration.

Another difference is the way Show refers to private data in the two classes. (Refer to the function implementation at the end of the listing.) The function now declares only one reference parameter, &c1, of the One class. Because Show is a member of class Two, it can access all members of Two directly. However, the expression c1.s1 in the output stream statement is allowed because Show is a friend of class One, of which s1 is a private data member. Show can refer to s2 directly because this member belongs to class Two, the same class that declares Show.

Because Show is a member of Two, the member function now also has an undeclared this pointer that addresses the class object for which the member function was called. Consequently, function main must define an object of class Two and then call Show for that object.

Operator Overloading

As you are about to discover, friends and operator overloading cooperate fully with one another—as should all good friends. Operator overloading can greatly contribute to a program's organization and clarity. For example, with appropriately overloaded operators, you can declare a class such as TAnyClass and define some objects of that class type:

```
TAnyClass c1, c2, c3;
```

You can use these objects in expressions such as

```
c3 = c1 + c2;
```

In many cases, statements such as that are more understandable, and potentially easier to create, than are equivalent function calls. This isn't always true, but when it is, operator overloading is an appropriate tool.

To understand operator overloading, it helps to review what you know about operators in general. The common plus-sign operator (+), of course, sums two values. The minus sign (-) subtracts two values. These and other symbols are called *binary operators* because they require two arguments. Others, such as the not operator (!), are *unary* because they require only one argument. Unary minus (-) is another example. The expression -count negates count's value, the same as if you had a function Negate to which you passed count:

```
Negate(count);  // Conceptually equivalent to -count
```

Operator overloading makes it possible to add new data types to the built-in types that C++ operators are designed to handle. Depending on their intended uses, overloaded operators are typically declared as common friend functions or as class member functions. The following sections explain how to write and use overloaded binary and unary operator member functions.

Overloading Operator Functions

A simple example illustrates operator overloading for a hypothetical class named ZZ:

```
class ZZ {
public:
  friend ZZ operator+(ZZ a, ZZ b);
  friend ZZ operator-(ZZ a, ZZ b);
  friend ZZ operator*(ZZ a, ZZ b);
  friend ZZ operator/(ZZ a, ZZ b);
  // ... other public, private, and protected members
};
```

ZZ declares four overloaded operator friend functions. (In practice, ZZ might declare other public, private, and protected members.) The function names are operator+, operator-, operator*, and operator/. Normally, you can't use symbols like +, -, *, and / in identifiers, but for the purpose of overloading operators, in C++ a function name can consist of the key word operator and one of the symbols from Table 7.1.

Table 7.1. Operators that may be overloaded.

*	/	+	–	%	^	&	¦
~	!	,	=	<	>	<=	>=
++	--	<<	>>	==	!=	&&	¦¦
*=	/=	%=	^=	&=	¦=	+=	-=
<<=	>>=	->	->*	[]	()	new	delete

Operators +, -, *, and & may be overloaded for binary and unary expressions. Operators ., .*, ::, ?:, and sizeof may not be overloaded. In addition, =, (), [], and -> must be implemented as nonstatic member functions. (You examine static member functions in the next chapter.)

The hypothetical class ZZ declares operator functions for the first four operators in the table. Each function has the general form

```
friend ZZ operator+(ZZ a, ZZ b);
```

The function is declared as a friend of the class, which gives operator+ access to the class's private and protected members. The function returns type ZZ (it could return another type) so that its result may be assigned to another ZZ object. (Assigning one object to another brings some tricky subjects into play as discussed in the next chapter.) Most important, the function's name operator+ identifies the function as the method by which expressions that use the plus operator can process objects of the class. Presumably, operator+ adds two objects in a way that is appropriate for the ZZ class.

The `operator+` function name bothers some people upon first encounter. Remember, `operator+` is simply the function's name. If you named the function `feeblewitz` rather than `operator+`, you could write a statement such as

```
feeblewitz(a, b);
```

where a and b are objects of type `zz`. Replacing `feeblewitz` with `operator+`, you can call an overloaded operator function with the statement

```
operator+(a, b);  // Same as feeblewitz(a, b)
```

There is no difference between those two function calls—only the function names differ. However, as an overloaded operator, `operator+` *can also be called in an expression that uses a plus sign.* For example, this statement is exactly equivalent to the preceding function call:

```
a + b;  // Same as operator+(a, b);!
```

The expressions a + b and `operator+(a, b)` perform exactly the same jobs, and they generate exactly the same code. The only reason for using one form over the other is clarity. Operator overloading adds nothing to C++ that you don't already know. It simply enables you to use objects in expressions rather than pass objects to functions.

A working example of a class that uses overloaded operators helps illustrate these concepts. Listing 7.4, Strops.cpp, contains the beginnings of a class that can store integer values in string form. By using overloaded operators, the program can evaluate expressions that add and subtract strings as their equivalent numeric values.

Listing 7.4. Strops.cpp (Demonstrates overloaded operator functions).

```
//===============================================================
// Strops.cpp -- Demonstrates overloaded operator functions
// To compile:
//    bcc strops
// To run:
//    strops
// Copyright (c) 1996 by Tom Swan. All rights reserved.
//===============================================================
```

continues

Listing 7.4. continued

```
#include <iostream.h>
#include <stdlib.h>
#include <string.h>

class TStrOp {
private:
  char value[12];
public:
  TStrOp() { value[0] = 0; }
  TStrOp(const char *s);
  long GetValue(void) { return atol(value); }
  friend long operator+(TStrOp a, TStrOp b);
  friend long operator-(TStrOp a, TStrOp b);
};

void main()
{
  TStrOp a = "1234";
  TStrOp b = "4321";

  cout << endl << "Value of a == " << a.GetValue();
  cout << endl << "Value of b == " << b.GetValue();
  cout << endl << "a + b +  6 == " << (a + b + 6);
  cout << endl << "a - b + 10 == " << (a - b + 10)
       << endl;
}

TStrOp::TStrOp(const char *s)
{
  strncpy(value, s, 11);
  value[11] = 0;
}

long operator+(TStrOp a, TStrOp b)
{
  return (atol(a.value) + atol(b.value));
}

long operator-(TStrOp a, TStrOp b)
{
  return (atol(a.value) - atol(b.value));
}
```

Before examining the program's class and its overloaded operator functions, take a look at function main. It first defines two objects, a and b, of type TStrOp. The objects are initialized with literal strings, and these statements could also have been written as

```
TStrOp a("1234");
TStrOp b("4321");
```

Although the objects obviously represent string values, other statements in `main` add and subtract the objects as though they were binary values:

```
(a + b + 6)
(a - b + 10)
```

You normally can't use strings or objects in such expressions. However, operator overloading *enhances* C++'s knowledge of the kinds of data types it can add and subtract. In effect, Strops.cpp teaches C++ how to add and subtract strings!

Two friend functions overload the plus and minus operators for pairs of `TStrOp` class objects. The declarations are similar to those in the hypothetical `ZZ` class explained earlier, and appear at the end of the `TStrop` class's public section. In this case, the functions return type `long`. Typically, overloaded operator functions return the same type as their class (or a reference to a class object), but that's not a requirement. Overloaded operator functions, just like other functions, can return any data types.

Examine the overloaded operator implementations following function `main`. Because the functions were declared friends and not member functions, their implementations are identical to other common C++ functions. That is, they are not preceded by the class names. The function names, `operator+` and `operator-`, permit the compiler to evaluate expressions that use plus and minus operators and `TStrOp` class objects.

Because the operator functions are friends, they can access the private and protected parts of `TStrOp` objects. This fact enables the functions to convert the `value` string member in the two parameters `a` and `b` to a long integer. Those conversions are handled by calling the standard `atol` (ASCII to `long`) function prototyped in Stdlib.h. The functions simply return the addition or subtraction of the converted values.

Overloading Operator Member Functions

Overloaded functions also can be members of a class, as demonstrated in Listing 7.5, Strops2.cpp. This program is similar to Strops.cpp, but illustrates how to overload operators as member functions.

Listing 7.5. Strops2.cpp (Demonstrates overloaded operator member functions).

```
//=============================================================
// Strops2.cpp -- Demonstrates overloaded operator member functions
// To compile:
//    bcc strops2
// To run:
//    strops2
// Copyright (c) 1996 by Tom Swan. All rights reserved.
//=============================================================
```

continues

Listing 7.5. continued

```cpp
#include <iostream.h>
#include <stdlib.h>
#include <string.h>

class TStrOp {
private:
  char value[12];
public:
  TStrOp() { value[0] = 0; }
  TStrOp(const char *s);
  long GetValue(void) { return atol(value); }
  long operator+(TStrOp b);
  long operator-(TStrOp b);
};

void main()
{
  TStrOp a = "1234";
  TStrOp b = "4321";

  cout << endl << "Value of a == " << a.GetValue();
  cout << endl << "Value of b == " << b.GetValue();
  cout << endl << "a + b +  6 == " << (a + b + 6);
  cout << endl << "a - b + 10 == " << (a - b + 10)
       << endl;
}

TStrOp::TStrOp(const char *s)
{
  strncpy(value, s, 11);
  value[11] = 0;
}

long TStrOp::operator+(TStrOp b)
{
  return (atol(value) + atol(b.value));
}

long TStrOp::operator-(TStrOp b)
{
  return (atol(value) - atol(b.value));
}
```

Examine the overloaded operator member functions declared in the new TStrOp class. Because the functions are members of class TStrOp, they already have access to the class's private and protected members, so there's no need to specify them as friends of the class. In addition, the overloaded operator member functions receive a this pointer to the object for which the functions are called. The functions therefore need only single parameters, not two as before. To add two string values, operator+ sums the long-integer equivalents of the expressions this->value and b.value.

Operator functions and member functions require the proper numbers of parameters. You cannot declare operator+ in this case as

```
long operator+(TStrOp a, TStrOp b);   // ???
```

That declaration does not compile because operator+ is a member of the TStrOp class, and as a member function it receives a this pointer to a class object. Counting this and the parameters a and b totals three arguments, but an overloaded binary operator such as operator+ is permitted only two. For example, to add two TStrObj objects, the implementation of function operator+ sums *this.value and b.value. (An explicit reference to *this is understood, and you don't have to write that part of the expression.) The function doesn't need a third parameter. Member function operator- similarly receives a this pointer, and therefore needs only one other parameter to overload the binary subtraction operator.

Overloading Unary Operators

Unary operators such as unary plus and unary minus require only one argument. You can overload these and other unary operators with techniques similar to those illustrated in the preceding sections.

As with binary operators, you can declare an overloaded unary operator function as a friend or as a member of a class. An overloaded unary operator friend function declares only one parameter of the class type (it needs only one value on which to operate). For example, add this declaration to class TStrOp in file Strops2.cpp just above private: access specifier:

```
friend long operator-(TStrOp a);
```

Even though the class already overloads the minus operator, because the new declaration specifies only one parameter, there is no conflict. (Remember: overloaded functions may share the same name as long as their declarations differ in at least one parameter.) The existing operator- member function in the class's public section receives an undeclared this parameter. The friend function that you added does not receive this. To finish the friend function, add its implementation following main:

```
long operator-(TStrOp a)
{
  return -atol(a.value);
}
```

Because unary operator- is a friend of the class, the return statement may directly access the private value data member in the TStrOp parameter a. The function is now complete, and the compiler can evaluate unary minus expressions involving objects of the class type. For an example, insert the following statement into main:

```
cout << endl << "-a    == " << -a;
```

Compile the modified program and run. The expression -a is replaced by the long negation of -a's string member. You have taught C++ how to negate a long value that's represented in string form!

As with overloaded binary operators, you can also declare overloaded unary operators as member functions. Start with a fresh copy of Strops2.cpp and add the following declaration to the public section just before class TStrOp's closing brace:

```
long operator-(void);
```

This member function declaration is similar to the friend unary function you added a moment ago. Because all member functions receive a this pointer, the new operator- member function declares no parameters because it operates directly on the long equivalent of this->value. This is demonstrated in the function's implementation, which you can insert after main:

```
long TStrOp::operator-(void)
{
   return -atol(value);  // i.e. -atol(this->value)
}
```

The overloaded member function returns the long negation of value. Use the operator in expressions such as the following, which you can insert into main:

```
cout << endl << "-a    == " << -a;
```

Type Conversions

Using operator overloading, you can supply your own type-conversion rules to convert objects automatically to other types. For example, suppose you declare and initialize an object of the TStrOp class from Strops2.cpp:

```
TStrOp myValue = "9876";
```

The TStrOp class stores a string that can be used as an equivalent long integer in addition and subtraction expressions. Knowing this fact, you might logically attempt to assign the myValue object to a long variable:

```
long x = myValue;  // ???
```

That, however, doesn't compile because TStrOp does not provide for converting a string to a long integer. One solution to this problem is to declare an overloaded conversion operator that *translates* a TStrOp object to another data type.

Conversion operators take the form

```
operator type()
```

where type is the data type to which you want to convert objects of the class. For example, to provide a type conversion rule for translating TStrOp objects to type long, insert this inline function inside the class's public section:

```
operator long() { return atol(value); }
```

This is a special use for the `operator` keyword that C++ provides specifically for creating new type-conversion rules. With the new rule in place, it's now possible to assign an object of type `TStr0p` to a long variable, pass a `TStr0p` object to a long function parameter, and perform other operations that require translating `TStr0p` objects to long integers.

Array Subscript Operator

You can overload the array subscript operator `[]` to provide array-like access to a class's data members, even though that data might be stored as individual members or in a linked list. A simple example, Listing 7.6, Ssop.cpp, demonstrates how to overload `[]` for a class that stores four integer values as separate data members.

Listing 7.6. Ssop.cpp (Overloads the array subscript operator).

```
//=============================================================
// Ssop.cpp -- Overloads the array subscript operator
// To compile:
//   bcc ssop
// To run:
//   ssop
// Copyright (c) 1996 by Tom Swan. All rights reserved.
//=============================================================

#include <iostream.h>

class PseudoArray {
private:
  int value0;
  int value1;
  int value2;
  int value3;
public:
  PseudoArray(int v0, int v1, int v2, int v3)
    { value0 = v0; value1 = v1; value2 = v2; value3 = v3; }
  int GetInt(unsigned i);
  int operator[](unsigned i);
};

void main()
{
  PseudoArray pa(10, 20, 30, 40);

  for (int i = 0; i <= 3; i++)
    cout << "pa[" << i << "] == " << pa[i] << endl;
}

int PseudoArray::GetInt(unsigned i)
{
  switch (i) {
    case 0: return value0;  // Note: break not needed
    case 1: return value1;  //  "    "    "    "    "
    case 2: return value2;  //  "    "    "    "    "
```

continues

215

Listing 7.6. continued

```
    case 3: return value3;  // "    "    "    "    "
  default: return value0;
  }
}

int PseudoArray::operator[](unsigned i)
{
  return GetInt(i);
}
```

Although simplistic, class PseudoArray illustrates the basic requirements for overloading the array subscript operator. The class declares four private int data members, value0 through value3. The overloaded operator member function operator[] declared one unsigned parameter, i. This parameter serves as the array index, and it can be any data type. For example, you could pass to operator[] a char pointer to create an associative array, indexed by strings.

For comparison, member function GetInt shows the usual method for accessing a class's private data. For example, you might declare an object of the class and display its second value with the statements

```
PseudoArray pa(10, 20, 30, 40);
cout << "Value #2 == " << pa.GetInt(1);  // Call member function
```

Calling a function such as GetInt is the usual way to "get to" a class's private data. However, because the class overloads the array-subscript operator, you can also use this statement:

```
cout << "Value #2 == " << pa[1];  // Use pa as an array!
```

The expression pa[1] is more natural to most programmers than pa.GetInt(1). However, the end results of both expressions are the same.

Function main shows another example. The expressions pa[1] and pa[i] appear to access pa as an array, although pa is actually a class object. Overloading the subscript operator makes it possible to use array indexing (a handy and clear way to access multiple values) rather than call member functions for an object of a class.

Keep in mind that overloaded array indexes can be any data types. For example, you can re-place the overloaded operator declaration in the class with

```
int operator[](char c);
```

You can then use character array indexes such as 'A' to 'D' to index the array, with 'A' being the initial index—an atypical construction that is not allowed in common arrays, which are always indexed with zero-based integers. In a sense, by overloading [] and using characters for indexes, you are establishing an association between a set of characters and a set of values, cre-ating what's known as an *associative array*. You might implement the overloaded operator[] member function like this:

```
int PseudoArray::operator[](char c)
{
  return GetInt(c - 'A');
}
```

You can then use a char variable as an array index. For example, after making the preceding changes, you can write a for loop in main such as this:

```
for (char c = 'A'; c <= 'D'; c++)
  cout << "pa[" << c << "] == " << pa[c] << endl;
```

Function Call Operator

Overloading the function call operator() effectively makes a class object appear to be a callable function. The overloaded operator() may return a typed value or void, and it may optionally declare parameters. It must be a nonstatic class member. Here's a sample class with an overloaded function call operator that returns an int value:

```
class TAnyClass {
  int x;
public:
  int operator()(void);
  TAnyClass(int n) { x = n; }
};
```

TAnyClass overloads the function call operator() with the declaration int operator(void);. In place of void, you may declare one or more typed parameters. Implement the overloaded member function in the usual way:

```
int TAnyClass::operator()(void)
{
  return x;
}
```

In this example, operator() returns the int x data member of a TAnyClass object. A program might use the class like this:

```
main()
{
  TAnyClass object = 100;
  int q = object();  // Looks like a function call!
  cout << q;
  return 0;
}
```

The second statement appears to call a function named object, but it actually executes the statement

```
object.operator()();
```

Class-Member-Access Operator

The unary class-member-access operator, ->, is overloaded as `operator->`. It must be a nonstatic class member function. Here's how you might overload -> for `TAnyClass`:

```
class TAnyClass {
  int x, y;
public:
  TAnyClass(int xx, int yy) { x = xx; y = yy; }
  TAnyClass* operator->();
  int GetX(void) { return x; }
  int GetY(void) { return y; }
};
```

The `operator->` member function must return an object, a reference, or a pointer to an object of the class type. In this case, it returns a `TAnyClass` pointer. You might implement the operator as

```
TAnyClass* TAnyClass::operator->()
{
  cout << endl << "Accessing member: ";
  return this;
}
```

This also shows how to use an overloaded -> operator as a debugging device. The overloaded operator displays a brief message before returning `this`, which addresses the object for which the member function is called. The `main` program can apply the overloaded operator to a `TAnyClass` object as shown here:

```
void main()
{
  TAnyClass t(100, 200);
  cout << t->GetX() << endl;
  cout << t->GetY() << endl;
}
```

The two output stream statements use the overloaded -> operator to access member functions `GetX` and `GetY` for a `TAnyClass` object t. These statements actually execute as though they had been written in this far less understandable way:

```
cout << (t.operator->())->GetX() << endl;
cout << (t.operator->())->GetY() << endl;
```

Consequently, the program displays labels before the values returned by `GetX` and `GetY`:

```
Accessing member: 100
Accessing member: 200
```

Increment and Decrement Operators

In early versions of C++, it was not possible to define separate overloaded operations for postfix and prefix ++ and -- operators. The distinction is now possible, as `TAnyClass` shows:

```
class TAnyClass {
  int x;
public:
  TAnyClass(int xx) { x = xx; }
  int operator++() { return ++x; }      // Prefix ++object
  int operator++(int) { return x++; }   // Postfix object++
  int operator--() { return --x; }      // Prefix --object
  int operator--(int) { return x--; }   // Postfix object--
  int GetX(void) { return x; }
};
```

Member function `operator++` defines a prefix increment operator for an object of type `TAnyClass`. This member function has no parameters. Member function `operator++(int)` defines a postfix increment operator for a `TAnyClass` object. C++ assigns zero to the single `int` parameter. This parameter permits the compiler to distinguish between the postfix and prefix operators.

The demonstration functions are implemented inline, but you could implement them separately. For an object v of type `TAnyClass`, the expression ++v calls the overloaded prefix ++ operator, in effect executing the statement `x.operator++;`. The expression v++ calls the overloaded postfix ++ operator, and executes as though written `x.operator++(0);`. The decrement operators work similarly.

To experiment with the above class, add it to a C++ program with the following main function:

```
void main()
{
  TAnyClass t(100);
  cout << "t == " << t.GetX() << "; ++t == " << ++t << endl;
  cout << "t == " << t.GetX() << "; t++ == " << t++ << endl;
  cout << "t == " << t.GetX() << "; --t == " << --t << endl;
  cout << "t == " << t.GetX() << "; t-- == " << t-- << endl;
}
```

Running the program should produce the following report:

```
t == 100; ++t == 101
t == 101; t++ == 101
t == 102; --t == 101
t == 101; t-- == 101
```

The value of object t is shown before applying the ++ and -- operators, followed by the values of the expressions with the operators applied.

NOTE

Due apparently to a bug in Borland C++ 4.5, using that compiler did not produce the preceding results. If you experience this problem, repaired in Borland C++ 5, use the following main function, which divides the multipart output statements and ensures that the expressions are evaluated in strict left-to-right fashion:

```
void main()
{
  TAnyClass t(100);
  cout << "t == " << t.GetX();
  cout << "; ++t == " << ++t << endl;
  cout << "t == " << t.GetX();
  cout << "; t++ == " << t++ << endl;
  cout << "t == " << t.GetX();
  cout << "; --t == " << --t << endl;
  cout << "t == " << t.GetX();
  cout << "; t-- == " << t-- << endl;
}
```

Other Operator Overloading Concerns

As you learn more about operator overloading, keep the following facts in mind:

- C++ does not "understand" the meaning of an overloaded operator. It's your responsibility to provide meaningful overloaded operator functions.

- C++ is not able to derive complex operators from simple ones. In a class with overloaded operator functions operator* and operator=, C++ can't evaluate the expression a *= b unless you also overload operator*=.

- Never change the syntax of an overloaded operator. Binary operators must remain binary. Unary operators must remain unary. It is not possible, for example, to create a unary division operator because no such built-in capability exists for division in C++.

- You can't invent new operators. You can overload only the operators listed in Table 7.1.

- You can't overload preprocessing symbols # and ##.

Overloading and Memory Management

C programmers use functions such as malloc and free to allocate and deallocate dynamic memory. By contrast, C++ programmers use operators new and delete. Below the hatch, many if not most C++ implementations define new and delete internally by calling malloc and free. It is a mistake, however, to conclude that no significant differences exist between C and C++ memory management.

One reason this is so is because new and delete are *operators,* not functions. As operators, new and delete may be overloaded to provide customized memory management capabilities for objects of specific classes. By overloading new and delete, you gain total control over how objects are allocated memory in a way that malloc and free cannot duplicate.

Overloading new

You can overload `new` just as you can other operators such as + and =. Overloading `new` in a class declaration tells the compiler that from now on you will take care of memory allocation requests for objects of the class.

To overload `new`, insert a function prototype of the form

```
void * operator new(size_t size);
```

Future uses of `new` to allocate space for class objects are directed to the overloaded function. The function should return the address of space allocated for the object. If no space is available, the function should return null (zero), or it should throw an `xalloc` exception.

Listing 7.7, Overnew.cpp, is a simple but complete example that overloads `new` to allocate memory for class objects. Instead of storing the objects on the heap, the program stuffs them into a global buffer. You could use a similar technique to allocate space for objects stored in other locations—on disk, for example, or in custom memory hardware.

NOTE

Overnew.cpp issues a `#pragma warn -aus` command, which instructs the compiler to turn off warnings for unused variables that are declared in the program for demonstration purposes only.

Listing 7.7. Overnew.cpp (Overloads the new operator).

```
//===============================================================
// Overnew.cpp -- Overloads the new operator
// To compile:
//    bcc overnew
// To run:
//    overnew
// Copyright (c) 1996 by Tom Swan. All rights reserved.
//===============================================================
```

continues

Listing 7.7. continued

```cpp
#include <iostream.h>

// Following "pragma" turns off the compiler's warning about unused
// variables, which appear in the program for demonstration only

#pragma warn -aus

class BrandNew {
private:
  int x;
public:
  BrandNew();
  void * operator new(size_t size);
};

char buf[512];
int index;

void main()
{
  cout << endl << "Creating local instance";
  BrandNew b1;

  cout << endl << "Allocating space via new";
  BrandNew *b2 = new BrandNew;
  BrandNew *b3 = new BrandNew;
  BrandNew *b4 = new BrandNew;
  BrandNew *b5 = new BrandNew;
}

BrandNew::BrandNew()
{
  cout << endl << "Inside constructor";
  x = index;
}

void *BrandNew::operator new(size_t size)
{
  cout << endl << "Inside overloaded new. Size == " << size;
  if (index >= 512 - sizeof(BrandNew))
    return 0;
  else {
    int k = index;
    index += sizeof(BrandNew);
    return &buf[k];
  }
}
```

The overloaded new function declared in the program's BrandNew class checks whether space is available in the global buffer. (See the function's implementation at the end of the listing.) If no space is available, the function returns 0, which causes `new` to return null. (The program doesn't check for this condition, but you should do that in a real setting, of course.) If space is available, the global index is incremented by the size of the memory request that is passed to the new function in the `size` parameter. The function then returns the address of the newly allocated space.

Overloading `delete`

The `delete` operator is the other side of the memory allocation coin. As with `new`, you can overload `delete` to trap deletions of objects addressed by pointers.

An overloaded `delete` operator function's prototype must be in the form

```
void operator delete(void *p);
```

where `p` is the address of the object being deleted. Alternatively, you may declare the function using the form

```
void operator delete(void *p, size_t size);
```

With this second form, C++ passes in `size` the number of bytes to dispose.

To add an overloaded delete function to the `BrandNew` class from Overnew.cpp, add the following declaration to the class's public section:

```
void operator delete(void *p);
```

Next, append the function's implementation to the end of the listing:

```
void BrandNew::operator delete(void *p)
{
  cout << endl << "Deleting object at " << p;
}
```

An output statement displays the address of each object being deleted. Because the example program's objects are not stored on the heap, the overloaded `delete` operator doesn't actually delete any memory. You also need a few statements to delete some objects. Insert these lines at the end of function `main`:

```
delete b2;
delete b3;
delete b4;
delete b5;
```

When you run the program, the messages tell you exactly when the overloaded `delete` operator is called to action. This example is just for demonstration, and in a complete application, `delete` should dispose of deleted memory blocks for future uses of the overloaded `new`. (See also the section "Placing Objects at Specific Addresses" in the next chapter.)

> **NOTE**
>
> To use the C++ memory manager to allocate heap space for objects that override new, preface the operator with a double colon. For example, the line `BrandNew *x = ::new BrandNew` bypasses the overloaded new operator for `BrandNew` objects. Similarly, `::delete` calls the C++ default memory deallocator.

Setting the new Error Handler

Normally, if new can't fulfill a request for memory, the operator throws an `xalloc` exception, or it returns null. To change these default actions, you can assign a custom error-function address to the C++ `_new_handler` pointer, defined as

```
typedef void (*vfp)(void);
vfp _new_handler;
```

Using a `typedef` is optional, but it improves the clarity of the declarations. The error function returns void and requires no arguments. Assign an error function by calling `set_new_handler`, prototyped in new.h as

```
vfp set_new_handler(vfp);
```

Design your error handler as an ordinary C++ function. You might, for example, halt a program with an out-of-memory error message:

```
void memerr(void)
{
  fputs("\n\nOut of memory\n", stderr);
  exit(1);
}
```

To have new call `memerr` for memory errors, pass the function's address to `set_new_handler` like this:

```
set_new_handler(memerr);
```

Summary

- Friends of a class are granted access to that class's private and protected members. Public members are always accessible; any friends may access them as well.
- Two classes may declare each other as friends. These mutual friends have full access to one another's private and protected members.
- A friend function is granted access to a class's private and protected members. Friend functions may be garden variety functions or members of a class.

- Overloading operators extends the kinds of built-in data types that C++ operators recognize. You can overload binary operators such as divide (/) and times (*), and you can overload unary operators such as minus (-) and not (~). With few exceptions, most C++ operators can be overloaded to permit objects of a class to be used in expressions involving those operators.

- Because new and delete are operators, they too can be overloaded to provide custom memory management facilities for class objects.

- Normally, new throws an xalloc exception, or it returns null, if the operator can't satisfy a memory allocation request. You can modify this action by calling set_new_handler.

Exercises

7.1 Your mission is to write a simulation of an internal combustion engine. Devise two classes, one named TEngine, and one named TFuel with a private double data member level, which measures how much "fuel" is stored in a class object's tank. Using friends, declare your TFuel and TEngine classes so that TEngine can refer directly to Fuel's private level.

7.2 Add times (*) and divide (/) overloaded operator functions to the TStrOp class in Strops.cpp.

7.3 Add ++ and -- overloaded operators to the TStrOp class in Strops2.cpp. Implement prefix and postfix forms of these operators.

7.4 Declare and implement a double type-conversion operator for class TStrOp in Strops2.cpp.

CHAPTER

8

Advancing Your C++ Knowledge

Learning to program a computer is like learning to walk. When you can stand without top-pling over, the real work begins—figuring out how to get from point A to point B.

Now that you've learned most of what C++ has to offer, you might be wondering about your next step. With the knowledge you have acquired so far, you should be able to write a sizable application. But don't end your studies just yet. In this chapter, you'll meet advanced C++ topics such as I/O streams, manipulators, copy constructors, templates, file iostreams, runtime type information, namespaces, Borland's string class, and other techniques that may prove invaluable to your future programming treks.

Copying Class Objects

When copying one class object to another object of a compatible type, the results can be unex-pected, especially for classes that declare pointer data members. There are four trouble spots to consider:

- When one object is used to initialize a new object of the same class.
- When an object is passed to a function's value parameter of the class type.
- When a function returns a class object (as opposed to an object reference or pointer).
- When a statement assigns one object to another.

The first three cases construct and initialize new copies of class objects from existing objects. The fourth case assigns an existing object to another previously defined object. It's important to carefully consider the effects of these operations, which are not always as obvious as they might seem.

> **NOTE**
>
> Keep in mind one important distinction between *copying* and *assigning* objects. The first three cases listed here construct new objects by calling a class constructor. In the fourth case, assigning one object to another does not construct a new object, and therefore no constructor is called.

After copying an object, all may seem well, but troubles might arise if the class objects contain pointer data members. Copying such objects might cause duplicate pointers to address the same locations in memory. Deleting one of those pointers might cause others to address freed memory. Worse yet, deleting the same space more than once in a destructor might corrupt the heap.

C++ provides two mechanisms for ensuring that classes with pointer members are copied and assigned safely: *memberwise initialization* and *memberwise assignment*.

Memberwise Initialization

When an object is used to initialize a new object of a class, C++ copies each data member from the existing object to the new one. For example, here's a simple class with no pointer members:

```
class TAnyClass {
private:
  int i;
  double r;
public:
  TAnyClass()
    { i = 0; r = 0; }
  TAnyClass(int ii, double rr)
    { i = ii; r = rr; }
};
```

In practice, TAnyClass needs other member functions to access its private data members i and r, but the example illustrates how object copying works. The class declares two inline constructors. The default constructor, TAnyClass(), initializes members i and r to zero. An alternate constructor initializes a class object with explicit values. The constructors make it possible to define TAnyClass objects v1 and v2 in the following two ways:

```
TAnyClass v1;
TAnyClass v2(100, 3.14159);
```

You also can use an existing object such as v2 to initialize a new object v3:

```
TAnyClass v3 = v2;
```

This copies v2 to v3 by performing a memberwise initialization of v3's data members. In other words, v2's data members are copied one by one to v3's members as though you had written the following code:

```
TAnyClass v3;
v3.i = v2.i;    // For illustration only
v3.r = v2.r;    // "    "    "    "
```

> **NOTE**
>
> The second and third statements in the preceding example are for illustration only. Because the class data members are private, these statements do not compile, but they show what the compiled code performs.

Memberwise initialization of a new class object occurs also when you pass an object to a function's value parameter and when a function returns a class object. If any of these actions cause a pointer data member to be duplicated, a serious bug might arise. The next section explains how to stay out of duplicate-pointer trouble.

The Copy Constructor

You should usually provide a *copy constructor* for constructing objects that are copied from other objects. The constructor can perform whatever actions are needed to create a safe object copy— one that doesn't accidentally duplicate a pointer, for example.

Declare a copy constructor using the form

```
TClassName(const TClassName &copy);
```

Parameter &copy refers to the object to be copied. Because copying an object should rarely if ever alter the source object, this parameter is normally const. However, this is optional.

Like all constructors, a copy constructor cannot be virtual and is not inherited by a derived class. Here's a new version of TAnyClass class with a pointer data member and a copy constructor:

```
#include <string.h>
class TAnyClass {
private:
  int i;        // Private data member
  double r;     // Private data member
  char *s;      // Private pointer member!
public:
  TAnyClass()
    { i = 0; r = 0; s = NULL; }
  TAnyClass(int ii, double rr, const char *ss)
    { i = ii; r = rr; s = strdup(ss); }
  ~TAnyClass() { delete s; }
  const char *GetStr(void) { return s; }
  TAnyClass(const TAnyClass &copy);  // Copy constructor
};
```

The copy constructor has the same name as its class and declares a const reference &copy to a TAnyClass source object. Elsewhere in the program (or inline with the declaration), implement the copy constructor with code such as

```
TAnyClass::TAnyClass(const TAnyClass &copy)
{
  cout << "Inside TAnyClass's copy constructor" << endl;
  i = copy.i;
  r = copy.r;
  if (copy.s)
    s = strdup(copy.s);
  else
    s = NULL;
}
```

The output stream statement isn't necessary. It is useful, however, during debugging and for showing exactly when the copy constructor runs. The next two statements copy members i and r from copy to the new object. To deal with a string addressed by pointer s, strdup allocates fresh heap memory for a copy of the original string. Or, if copy's pointer is null, the new object's pointer is assigned NULL. For copied TAnyClass objects, there is no longer any danger that two or more s pointers might accidentally address the same memory. The program can now use statements such as

```
TAnyClass v1;
TAnyClass v2(1, 2, "A test string");
TAnyClass v3 = v2;  // Calls copy constructor
```

C++ calls the TAnyClass copy constructor automatically for the first three situations listed earlier: when an object is used to initialize a newly constructed TAnyClass object (illustrated by the third line above), when a statement passes an object to a function parameter, or when a function returns a class object.

Unfortunately, the class still is not completely safe. When a statement directly assigns one object to another, you must again consider what happens if those objects contain pointer members. The next section explains how to handle this problem.

NOTE

C++ calls copy constructors also for class object arguments passed by value to functions, and for functions that return class objects.

Memberwise Assignment

Assigning a class object to another object might cause pointer data members to address the same locations in memory—a dangerous situation to avoid at all costs. Consider this program fragment, which uses TAnyClass from the preceding section:

```
TAnyClass v1;
TAnyClass v2(1, 2, "A test string");
v1 = v2;  // ???
```

After defining v1 with default values and defining v2 with explicit arguments, an assignment statement copies v2 to v1. But look out! The assignment does not call any class constructor for v1, not even the class's copy constructor. If the class declares or inherits any pointer data members, the copied pointers now address the same locations in memory, almost certainly causing a major bug if that memory is deleted in a destructor.

A copy constructor can't solve this problem because the objects involved have already been constructed. C++ calls constructors to initialize new objects, not when assigning one object to another.

Fortunately, you can easily cure this problem by overloading the assignment operator, =. Use a declaration of the form

```
void operator=(const CLASS&);
```

For example, to add an overloaded assignment operator function to TAnyClass, modify the class from the preceding section as follows:

```
class TAnyClass {
private:
  int i;        // Private data member
  double r;     // Private data member
  char *s;      // Private pointer member!
public:
  ...           // See preceding TAnyClass declaration
  void operator=(const TAnyClass &copy);  // Assigment operator
};
```

The operator= declaration overloads the assignment operator, specifying a const reference parameter, named copy, of type TAnyClass. The parameter refers to the object being copied. In other words, if a and b are TAnyClass objects, in the assignment a = b, copy refers to b. Implement the overloaded assignment function like this:

```
void TAnyClass::operator=(const TAnyClass &copy)
{
  cout << endl << "Inside TAnyClass's operator= function";
  if (this == &copy)
    return;
  delete s;
  i = copy.i;
  r = copy.r;
  s = strdup(copy.s);
}
```

As before, the output statement is just for illustration. The first if statement compares the this pointer to the address of the copy reference parameter. This catches an accidental assignment of the same object to itself. If you attempt to execute

```
TAnyClass v1, v2;
v1 = v1;
```

the overloaded assignment operator simply ends without performing any actions. (It is of course a silly mistake to assign an object to itself! But, in a complex program with many pointers to various objects, this situation can occur more frequently than you might imagine, and it's good to guard against the possibility.)

The second if statement deletes the space (if any) currently allocated to pointer s. (It is not an error to delete a null pointer, so it is not necessary to first check whether s is null.)

The other assignments in the overloaded function are identical to those in the copy constructor presented earlier. The next section explains how to avoid this kind of duplicated code with a copy constructor and overloaded assignment operator that work together.

Calling `operator=` from a Copy Constructor

You can easily avoid wasteful duplications in a copy constructor and overloaded assignment operator. Inside the copy constructor, simply call the overloaded `operator=` function by assigning the copied object to `*this`:

```
TAnyClass::TAnyClass(TAnyClass &copy)
{
  s = NULL;       // Initialize any pointers to null!
  *this = copy;   // Calls overloaded assignment operator
}
```

It's vital to initialize any members (usually pointers) that the overloaded assignment operator inspects. If s were not assigned NULL, for example, that pointer might have an unpredictable value, causing the overloaded assignment function to delete unallocated memory. Needless to say, that's likely to cause a few problems.

Advanced I/O Streams

By overloading the input and output stream operators >> and <<, you can add one or more classes to the kinds of data types that the compiler recognizes for I/O stream statements. The following sections explain how to create streamable classes. I'll also introduce a few other useful I/O stream techniques.

Formatting Output

The Borland C++ header file Iostream.h declares one input and three output stream objects as follows:

```
extern istream_withassign _RTLENTRY cin;  // Input stream object
extern ostream_withassign _RTLENTRY cout; // Output stream object
extern ostream_withassign _RTLENTRY cerr; // Error output stream object
extern ostream_withassign _RTLENTRY clog; // Buffered error output object
```

The classes `istream_withassign` and `ostream_withassign` are ultimately derived from the granddaddy I/O stream class, `ios`. The macro, `_RTLENTRY`, modifies the declarations depending on various options such as the target platform, memory model, and so on. You don't need to study every detail about these declarations to use them in programs, but if you are interested in digging deeper, Borland C++ includes the complete and extensive source code for I/O streams.

I/O stream classes perform formatted input and output with built-in error-handling. I/O streams support the fundamental data types `char`, `short`, `int`, `long`, `char*` (a null-terminated string, for example), `float`, `double`, `long double`, and `void*` (displayed as an address value).

Keep in mind that `cin`, `cout`, `cerr`, and `clog` are *objects*. Their respective classes define overloaded input and output stream operators, making I/O stream statements such as the following possible:

233

```
cin >> v;    // Read variable v from standard input
cout << v;   // Write v to the standard output
```

As you've seen in many of this book's listings, you can cascade multiple-part I/O stream statements using a statement such as

```
cout << "Balance == $" << balance << " (dollars)" << endl;
```

To format output, you can set one or more flags in an I/O stream object (see the declaration for class ios in Iostream.h). Use the class `flags`, `setf`, and `unsetf` member functions to manipulate these flags directly. For example, to output an unsigned value in hexadecimal, you can set cout's hex flag by calling the ios class member function `setf()`:

```
unsigned v = 12345;
cout << "Before: " << v << endl;  // Output in default (decimal)
cout.setf(cout.hex);              // Modify output stream
cout << "After:  " << v << endl;  // Output in hexadecimal
```

Although this works, there are easier methods for formatting output streams, as demonstrated next.

Using Manipulators

Including the Borland C++ Iomanip.h header file (which includes Iostream.h if necessary) makes available several *manipulators* that are useful for constructing formatted output and reading formatted input. For example, you can use the `hex` manipulator to output a value in hexadecimal:

```
unsigned v = 12345;
cout << "In hexadecimal v == " << hex << v << endl;
cout << "In decimal v == " << dec << v << endl;
```

The last statement uses the `dec` manipulator to return cout's output format to decimal. You can also manipulate input streams. These statements read a value in hex and display that same value in decimal:

```
cout << "Enter value in hex: ";
cin >> hex >> v;
cout << "Value in decimal == " << dec << v;
```

Table 8.1 lists the I/O manipulators defined in Iomanip.h and Iostream.h.

Some manipulators accept a parameter. For example, `setbase(int n)` formats a value using radix n. (If n is zero, output defaults to decimal and input defaults to ANSI C specifications for literal integers.)

Table 8.1. Input and output stream manipulators.

Manipulator	Effect
dec	Decimal conversion.
endl	Inserts new line; flushes stream.
ends	Inserts null-terminator in string.
flush	Flushes output stream.
hex	Hexadecimal conversion.
lock(ios &ir)	Lock file handle for I/O stream reference ir.
oct	Octal conversion.
resetiosflags(long f)	Clears formatting bits specified by f.
setbase(int n)	Sets radix to n (0, 8, 10, or 16).
setiosflags(long f)	Sets formatting bits specified by f.
setfill(int c)	Uses c for justification fill character.
setprecision(int n)	Sets floating-point precision to n.
setw(int n)	Sets field width to n.
unlock(ios &ir)	Unlock file handle for I/O stream reference ir.
ws	Extract whitespace characters.

An output-stream manipulator function returns type ostream&—in other words, a reference to an ostream object. You can write your own manipulators by including Iostream.h and defining an ostream& reference function. For example, here's how you might define a bell manipulator for an output stream:

```
ostream& bell(ostream& os) {
  return os << "\a";  // '\a' is the bell escape code
}
```

The bell function returns ostream& and declares an ostream& parameter, os. This design allows the function to be cascaded in a multipart output stream statement:

```
cout << bell << "Ding!";
```

You can also call a stream object's member functions to adjust formatting. For instance, to display an int variable v right-justified in an 8-character column, you can write code such as

```
cout.width(8);
cout << v << endl;  // Displays v in 8 columns
cout << v << endl;  // Displays v using default justification
```

The width modifier is short-lived, and affects only the next output statement. Other member functions include `fill(char c)`, which sets justification filler to character c, and `precision(int n)`, which sets floating-point precision to n.

Overloading Output Streams

Normally, output streams can handle only simple data types—`int`, `long`, `double`, `char *`, and so on. By overloading the output stream operator `<<`, you can easily add your own classes to the data types that output stream statements are designed to use.

Listing 8.1, Pointout.cpp, creates a streamable class named `TPoint` with two int values, x and y, representing a coordinate, perhaps on a graphics display. The program overloads the output stream operator so it can write `TPoint` objects in output stream statements.

Listing 8.1. Pointout.cpp (Demonstrates output streams).

```
//===============================================================
// Pointout.cpp -- Demonstrates output streams
// To compile:
//    bcc pointout
// To run:
//    pointout
// Copyright (c) 1996 by Tom Swan. All rights reserved.
//===============================================================

#include <iostream.h>

class TPoint {
private:
  int x, y;
public:
  TPoint() { x = y = 0; }
  TPoint(int xx, int yy) { x = xx; y = yy; }
  void PutX(int xx) { x = xx; }
  void PutY(int yy) { y = yy; }
  int GetX(void) { return x; }
  int GetY(void) { return y; }
  friend ostream& operator<<(ostream& os, TPoint &p);
};

void main()
{
  TPoint p;

  cout << p << endl;
  p.PutX(100);
  p.PutY(200);
  cout << p << endl;
}

ostream& operator<<(ostream& os, TPoint &p)
{
  os << "x == " << p.x << ", y == " << p.y;
  return os;
}
```

The last declaration in the TPoint class overloads the output stream operator by declaring the friend member function:

```
friend ostream& operator<<(ostream& os, TPoint &p);
```

The function returns ostream& (that is, a reference to an output stream object) and declares two parameters: os, of type ostream&, and p, a reference to a TPoint object.

Because operator<< is a friend of TPoint, statements may directly access the x and y data members in the object addressed by reference p. For example, turn to the function implementation at the end of the listing. The first statement in the function is itself an output stream statement, which writes the values of the two data members plus two literal strings to the ostream reference os. Finally, the function returns os, a requirement that enables multiple-part stream statements. Running the program displays

```
x == 0, y == 0
x == 100, y == 200
```

Because operator<< returns an ostream reference, it's possible to cascade multiple objects in a single output stream statement. For example, if p1, p2, and p3 are TPoint objects, you can display their values with

```
cout << p1 << "; " << p2 << "; " << p3;
```

Internally, such statements are executed by making multiple function calls to the overloaded output-stream operators. The preceding line is executed as though it were written

```
(((((cout << p1) << "; ") << p2) << "; ") << p3;
```

Aren't you glad you don't have to type all those parentheses?

Overloading Input Streams

Overloading the input stream operator >> is also possible and effectively teaches C++ how to input objects of a class. Listing 8.2, Pointin.cpp, adds input streamability to the Pointout.cpp program in the preceding section.

Listing 8.2. Pointin.cpp (Demonstrates input streams).

```
//================================================================
// Pointin.cpp -- Demonstrates input streams
// To compile:
//    bcc pointin
// To run:
//    pointin
// Copyright (c) 1996 by Tom Swan. All rights reserved.
//================================================================

#include <iostream.h>
```

continues

Listing 8.2. continued

```cpp
class TPoint {
private:
  int x, y;
public:
  TPoint() { x = y = 0; }
  TPoint(int xx, int yy) { x = xx; y = yy; }
  void PutX(int xx) { x = xx; }
  void PutY(int yy) { y = yy; }
  int GetX(void) { return x; }
  int GetY(void) { return y; }
  friend ostream& operator<<(ostream& os, TPoint &p);
  friend istream& operator>>(istream& is, TPoint &p);
};

void main()
{
  TPoint p;

  cout << p << endl;
  p.PutX(100);
  p.PutY(200);
  cout << p << endl;
  cout << endl << "Enter x and y values: ";
  cin >> p;
  cout << endl << "You entered: " << p;
}

ostream& operator<<(ostream& os, TPoint &p)
{
  os << "x == " << p.x << ", y == " << p.y;
  return os;
}

istream& operator>>(istream& is, TPoint &p)
{
  is >> p.x >> p.y;
  return is;
}
```

The new TPoint class declares an output and also input stream friend member functions. The new function is declared

```cpp
friend istream& operator>>(istream& is, TPoint &p);
```

The function is similar to the overloaded output stream operator, but uses istream in place of ostream.

The function's implementation at the end of the listing reads values for x and y using the istream reference s. The function returns is so it can be cascaded in multiple-part input stream statements.

Running the program prompts you to enter x and y values. Type two integers separated by a space. The input stream statement in function main stores both values you enter in the class object, which an output stream statement then displays for confirmation.

Templates

Just as a class is a schematic for building objects, a *template* is a schematic for building functions and classes. Templates are especially useful in class libraries that are shared among many programmers. Also called *parameterized types,* templates provide specifications for functions and classes, but not the actual implementation details.

Template Functions

A function template describes the generic properties of a function—similar to a recipe for a cake. Typically declared in a header file, a template function has the general form

```
template<class T> void f(T param)
{
   // Function body
}
```

The template begins with template<class T>, which specifies to the compiler that T is a user-defined function name. You can change T to another name if you want. The word class here does not necessarily refer to a C++ class. At least one T parameter in parentheses is needed to give the function some data on which to operate. You may specify value (T param), pointer (T *param), and reference (T &param) parameters. The template also can declare multiple parameters of these types and return a value of type T, as in the following example:

```
template<class T> T f(int a, T b)
{
   // Function body
}
```

This version of template function f returns an object of type T and receives two parameters: an int named a and an object named b of type T. To use the template, you specify the actual data type for T. The C++ compiler then uses the template to fashion the real function, which you can then call as you do any other function. For example, to use the preceding template, declare the following prototype:

```
double f(int a, double b);
```

If f were a common function, you would have to supply its implementation. However, because f is a template function, the compiler implements the function's code—in this case replacing the placeholder T with double.

A complete example clarifies how templates can reduce the size and complexity of programs by providing generic functions that are implemented by the compiler. Listing 8.3, Minmax.h, declares two useful function templates, min and max. This is just a header file, so you can't compile and run it. I'll show you how to do that in a moment.

Listing 8.3. Minmax.h (Declares function templates for min and max).

```
//================================================================
// Minmax.h -- Declares function templates for min and max
// Copyright (c) 1996 by Tom Swan. All rights reserved.
//================================================================

#ifndef __MINMAX_H
#define __MINMAX_H    // Prevent multiple #includes

template<class T> T max(T a, T b)
{
  if (a > b)
    return a;
  else
    return b;
}

template<class T> T min(T a, T b)
{
  if (a < b)
    return a;
  else
    return b;
}

#endif   // __MINMAX_H
```

Study the first template declaration closely:

```
template<class T> T max(T a, T b)
```

This states that T is an unspecified type. The template function max returns an object of type T. In addition, max requires two value arguments, also both of type T. In the body of the function, its statements are schematics for the real statements that are generated later when you specify T's actual type in a function prototype. Function template min is declared similarly. Either template function can be used with *any* type of data that can be compared, including simple data types such as int and double, as well as complex objects of classes.

You can use more than one placeholder data type in a template. To create a max function that can receive two different types of parameters, you could write its declaration as follows:

```
template<class T1, class T2> T2 max(T1 a, T2 b)
```

This version of max returns a value of type T2 and requires two arguments, one of type T1 and one of type T2. These types could be the same, or they could be different. For example, to create a max function that can compare int and long values, simply declare the function prototype:

```
long max(int a, long b);
```

A program uses template functions simply by issuing prototypes, which the compiler uses to write the actual function bodies. Listing 8.4, Ftemplat.cpp, illustrates how this works and demonstrates the min and max templates.

Listing 8.4. Ftemplat.cpp (Demonstrates using the minmax.h templates).

```
//===============================================================
// Ftemplat.cpp -- Demonstrates using the minmax.h templates
// To compile:
//    bcc ftemplat
// To run:
//    ftemplat
// Copyright (c) 1996 by Tom Swan. All rights reserved.
//===============================================================

#include <iostream.h>
#include "minmax.h"

int max(int a, int b);
double max(double a, double b);
char max(char a, char b);

void main()
{
  int i1 = 100, i2 = 200;
  double d1 = 3.14159, d2 = 9.87654;
  char c1 = 'A', c2 = 'z';

  cout << "max(i1, i2) == " << max(i1, i2) << endl;
  cout << "max(d1, d2) == " << max(d1, d2) << endl;
  cout << "max(c1, c2) == " << max(c1, c2) << endl;
}
```

The program declares three prototypes. Because the program does not implement the functions, the compiler searches for a template that matches the function return type and its parameters. Finding such a template, the compile implements three overloaded max functions. Function main calls these functions in three test output statements.

Template Classes

Template classes are even more powerful than template functions. A class template provides the skeleton for a generic class to be implemented with user-specified data types. As with template functions, template classes are typically declared in header files. For example, Listing 8.5, Db.h, demonstrates how to write a template class—in this case, one that can store a small database of records. Again, this is just a header file—you have to write a host program to use it, as I'll explain a bit later.

Listing 8.5. Db.h (Declares the TDatabase template class).

```
//============================================================
// Db.h -- Declares the TDatabase template class
// Copyright (c) 1996 by Tom Swan. All rights reserved.
//============================================================

#ifndef __DB_H
#define __DB_H    // Prevent multiple #includes

template<class T>
class TDatabase {
private:
  T *rp;        // Records pointer
  int num;      // Number of records
public:
  TDatabase(int n)
    { rp = new T[num = n]; }
  ~TDatabase()
    { delete[] rp; }
  void DoNothing(void);
  T &GetRecord(int recnum);
};

template<class T>
void TDatabase<T>::DoNothing(void)
{
}

template<class T>
T &TDatabase<T>::GetRecord(int recnum)
{
  T *crp = rp;   // Current record ptr = records pointer
  if (0 <= recnum && recnum < num)
    while (recnum-- > 0)
      crp++;
  return *crp;
}

#endif  // __DB_H
```

Declare a template class using the general form:

```
template<class T> class TDatabase {
  // private, protected, and public members
}
```

T refers to an unspecified type that you must supply to use the class. You can name T something else if you want. As it is in a template function, T is a *placeholder* that you can replace with a built-in type, a class, a pointer type, a reference, or any valid C++ data type. TDatabase is the name of the template class. For clarity, it's usually best to declare the template's header on separate lines:

```
template<class T>
class TAnyClass {
  ...
}
```

You can also specify more than one placeholder:

```
template<class T1, class T2, class T3>
class TAnotherClass {
  ...
}
```

Inside the template class body, declarations can use T to declare data members, member function return values, parameters, and other items of this as-yet unspecified type. For example, the TDatabase class declares a pointer named rp of type T like this:

```
T *rp;
```

At this stage, T's real nature is unknown, and the program can use T only in completely generic ways. Nevertheless, TDatabase's constructor allocates an array of T objects, assigning the address of the array to rp and also setting a data member num equal to the number of requested records. (For simplicity, this demonstration ignores any memory-allocation errors that might occur.) The class destructor deletes the array's allocated memory, using the special form delete[] to ensure that a destructor is called in case the array holds class objects.

The TDatabase class also declares a member function GetRecord, which returns a reference to an object of type T:

```
T &GetRecord(int recnum);
```

This states that GetRecord returns a reference to an object of type T, identified by record number recnum. This is another totally generic operation and does not require any knowledge of T's actual type.

You can implement template class member functions inline as demonstrated by TDatabase's constructor and destructor. Or, you can implement them separately, just as you can other member functions. However, because these template class member functions are still only declarations, you normally insert them in a header file, not in a separate module. For example, function DoNothing—which, as its name implies, doesn't do much—shows the format to use for implementing a non-inline template class member function separately:

```
template<class T>
void TDatabase<T>::DoNothing(void)
{
}
```

The member function's header is prefaced with `template<class T>`. Next comes the function return type (`void`, but it could be any type), the class name (`TDatabase<T>`), and a scope resolution operator (`::`). Last are the function declaration (`DoNothing(void)`) and body (empty in this case). Use this sample as a guide to writing your own template class member functions.

`GetRecord`'s implementation illustrates a more sophisticated template class member function, which contains statements that perform the function's activities. `GetRecord` returns a reference to an object of type `T`. Inside the function, a `T` pointer `crp` is assigned `rp`. In other words, `crp` addresses the first record stored in the `TDatabase` object. An `if` statement checks whether `recnum` is in the proper range. If so, a `while` loop decrements `recnum` to zero as it advances `crp` through each record in the database.

Examine the increment statement carefully. Incrementing a typed pointer `crp` with the expression `crp++` advances the pointer by the number of bytes of the object that the pointer addresses. In `TDatabase`, even though the type of object addressed by `crp` is unknown, the expression `crp++` is perfectly acceptable. Later, when an actual type is supplied for the template class, the compiler can generate the proper instructions to increment `crp` by `sizeof(T)`.

The final statement in `GetRecord` returns the dereferenced value of `crp`—in other words, a reference to whatever object `crp` addresses after the preceding `while` loop finishes. This might not be the most efficient search method to look up records in a database, but it demonstrates typical uses for template class member functions.

The final step uses the `TDatabase` class template to create a real database class that can store some actual records. Listing 8.6, Ctemplat.cpp, puts the `TDatabase` template class to work.

Listing 8.6. Ctemplat.cpp (Demonstrates class template in db.h).

```
//===============================================================
// Ctemplat.cpp -- Demonstrates class template in db.h
// To compile:
//    bcc ctemplat
// To run:
//    ctemplat
// Copyright (c) 1996 by Tom Swan. All rights reserved.
//===============================================================

#include <iostream.h>
#include <string.h>
#include "db.h"

class TRecord {
private:
  char name[41];
public:
  TRecord()
    { name[0] = 0; }
  TRecord(const char *s)
```

```
        { Assign(s); }
    void Assign(const char *s)
        { strncpy(name, s, 40); }
    char *GetName(void)
        { return name; }
};

void main()
{
    int rn;                     // Record number index
    TDatabase<TRecord> db(3);   // Database of 3 TRecords
    TDatabase<TRecord*> dbp(3); // Database of 3 TRecord pointers
    TDatabase<TRecord> *pdb;    // Pointer to db of TRecords
    TDatabase<TRecord*> *ppdb;  // Pointer to db of TRecord ptrs

    cout << endl << endl << "Database of 3 TRecords" << endl;
    db.GetRecord(0).Assign("George Washington");
    db.GetRecord(1).Assign("John Adams");
    db.GetRecord(2).Assign("Thomas Jefferson");
    for (rn = 0; rn <= 2; rn++)
        cout << db.GetRecord(rn).GetName() << endl;

    cout << endl << endl << "Database of 3 TRecord pointers" << endl;
    dbp.GetRecord(0) = new TRecord("Billary Clinton");
    dbp.GetRecord(1) = new TRecord("Robert Doleful");
    dbp.GetRecord(2) = new TRecord("Newt Garbich");
    for (rn = 0; rn <= 2; rn++)
        cout << dbp.GetRecord(rn)->GetName() << endl;

    cout << endl << "Pointer to database of 3 TRecords" << endl;
    pdb = new TDatabase<TRecord>(3);
    pdb->GetRecord(0).Assign("John Adams");
    pdb->GetRecord(1).Assign("Thomas Jefferson");
    pdb->GetRecord(2).Assign("Aaron Burr");
    for (rn = 0; rn <= 2; rn++)
        cout << pdb->GetRecord(rn).GetName() << endl;

    cout << endl << endl << "Pointer to database of 3 TRecord pointers" << endl;
    ppdb = new TDatabase<TRecord *>(3);
    ppdb->GetRecord(0) = new TRecord("Walter Mundane");
    ppdb->GetRecord(1) = new TRecord("Albert Bore");
    ppdb->GetRecord(2) = new TRecord("George Mush");
    for (rn = 0; rn <= 2; rn++)
        cout << ppdb->GetRecord(rn)->GetName() << endl;
}
```

After including the TDatabase template class header file Db.h, the program declares a class TRecord. This is the class that the program uses to store objects in a TDatabase instance. The TRecord class is simplistic and declares only a single name character array as a data member. But TRecord could be any class, as the TDatabase template makes no assumptions about the kinds of objects it can store.

For example, function main uses TDatabase four different ways to create class objects from the template. The declaration

```
TDatabase<TRecord> db(3);
```

defines an object named `db` of the template class type `TDatabase` and specifies `TRecord` as the class that is to replace `T` throughout the template. The parenthetical `(3)` is `db`'s initializer, passed to the `TDatabase` constructor.

You can also define a database of other types of values—you don't have to use class types such as `TRecord`. For example, the following defines a database of 100 double values:

```
TDatabase<double> dbd(100);
```

Because it is designed to store objects of any type, `TDatabase` is called a *container class.* Usually, the best template container classes are fully generic, although that ideal is often difficult to achieve.

Function `main` also shows how to create some other kinds of template class instances. For example, the statement

```
TDatabase<TRecord*> dbp(3);
```

declares a `TDatabase` object `dbp` containing three `TRecord` pointers. The next declaration

```
TDatabase<TRecord> *pdb;
```

defines `pdb` as a pointer to a `TDatabase` object that contains an unspecified number of `TRecord` objects. Finally in `main`, the declaration

```
TDatabase<TRecord*> *ppdb;    // Pointer to db of TRecord ptrs
```

combines the preceding two definitions to create a pointer to a database of `TRecord` pointers that address `TRecord` objects.

TIP

Use the four sample `TDatabase` declarations in Ctemplat.cpp's function `main` as guides to creating objects of most types of class templates.

The Ctemplate.cpp program uses the `TDatabase` object as it would any nontemplate. For example, the statement

```
db.GetRecord(0).Assign("George Washington");
```

calls `GetRecord(0)` to obtain a reference to record number zero. The line then calls that object's `Assign` member function to give it a string value.

Other statements in the demonstration program show how to use the other `TDatabase` objects. This one is particularly interesting:

```
dbp.GetRecord(0) = new TRecord("Billary Clinton");
```

Because `GetRecord` returns a reference to an object, it can be used on the left side of an assignment statement. Behind the scenes, the statement constructs a new `TRecord` object for record number zero as referred to by `GetRecord`.

Note that in all of these examples, you do not need typecasts to inform the compiler about the data types used by `TDatabase`. Despite the template's generic nature, it is possible to avoid using typecasts yet still create classes that can handle a variety of data types.

> **TIP**
>
> Writing templates from scratch is often a difficult chore, and it can complicate debugging. For these reasons, it's usually easiest to create a working class that operates on real data, and then convert the class to a template by replacing actual data types with `<class T>` placeholders.

File Streams

File streams provide an object-oriented way to read and write information in disk files. Trouble is, the file stream library supplied with most C++ compilers is designed to work only with text files. But don't let this limitation turn you off from using streams for file handling. This section explains how to use file streams to read and write binary values, text, structures, or any other objects.

> **NOTE**
>
> The following information, which is updated for Borland C++ 5, is excerpted from my book *Code Secrets*.

File Stream Class

To use file streams, include the fstream.h header file, usually along with iostream.h, and begin your programs like this:

```
#include <iostream.h>
#include <fstream.h>
```

Here are some additional points to keep in mind while learning how to use file streams:

- All file stream classes except `filebuf` are ultimately derived from class `ios`. Because of their heritage, file streams can use iostream member functions, manipulators, state flags, and other stream-handling techniques.

- Use the `ifstream` class ("input file stream") for reading data from files. The `ifstream` class is derived from `istream`. It is literally an input-stream expanded to work with files.

- Use the `ofstream` class ("output file stream") for output files. The `ofstream` class is derived from `ostream`. It is literally an output-stream expanded to work with files.

- Use the `fstream` class for reading and writing data in the *same* file.

- The `filebuf` class provides buffered I/O services to the `ifstream`, `ofstream`, and `fstream` classes. You'll rarely, if ever, directly use the `filebuf` class. To keep programs portable, use the file I/O services provided by the `ifstream`, `ofstream`, and `fstream` classes.

Text File Streams

Text file streams are simple and easy to use. They make a great introduction to file streams in general, so let's begin there. There are three main areas to cover:

- Creating text files
- Writing to text files
- Reading from text files

In most cases, you should use the `ifstream` and `ofstream` classes to carry out these tasks. Because text files are usually organized in variable-length lines, it's best not to attempt simultaneous reading and writing to the same file using the `fstream` class.

Creating and Writing Text Files

To create a new text file, define an object of the `ofstream` class. Pass two arguments to the class constructor: a filename, and an *open mode* value:

```
ofstream ofs("Newfile.txt", ios::out);
```

Constructing the `ofstream` object creates the file Newfile.txt, with a length of zero, if that file doesn't already exist. Notice how different this is from conventional file handling where you might define a file handle, and then call a function to create the file. With file streams, you create the file object and its associated disk file in one stroke. If the file exists, constructing the `ofstream` object as shown here overwrites the file.

The actual format, number of characters, and other characteristics of the filename string might differ among various operating systems, but a similar statement should work with any ANSI C++ compatible compiler. The second argument, `ios::out`, selects an access mode for the file. The `ios` class declares `out` and other modes as `open_mode` enumerated constants, listed in Table 8.2 in alphabetical order. Specify multiple options by combining constants in logical-OR expressions. The header file Iostream.h defines the `ios` class and constants in the table.

Table 8.2. The `ios` class's `open_mode` constants.

Constant	Standard	Effect
app	no	The next write operation appends new information to the end of the file.
ate	yes	Seeks to the end of the file when opened. The word "ate" stands for "at end." It has nothing to do with "eating" data, as often supposed.
binary	yes	Might be spelled `bin` in some implementations. Opens file in binary (nontext) mode.
in	yes	Opens the file for input (reading).
nocreate	no	If the file does not already exist, does *not* create a new file.
noreplace	no	If the file already exists, does *not* overwrite the file.
out	yes	Opens the file for output (writing).
trunc	no	Opens and truncates an existing file. New information written to file replaces the file's current contents.

Unfortunately, the constants in Table 8.2 are not the same in all implementations of the `ios` class. The `open_mode` type identifier might even be named `openmode` with no underscore between the two words. The standard names marked with a bullet in the table should be universally available. The others may or may not be defined, and there might be other constants added for special purposes.

To help ensure portability, it might be wise to define symbolic constants for use as file mode selectors. For example, you can define a symbolic constant such as `OFSMODE`:

```
#include <iostream.h>
...
#define OFSMODE ios::out ¦ ios::app
```

Or, even better, you can instead define a `const` value of type `open_mode`:

```
const ios::open_mode OFSMODE = ios::out ¦ ios::app;
```

Whichever method you choose, pass the `OFSMODE` constant to the `ofstream` class constructor:

```
ofstream ofs("Newfile.txt", OFSMODE);
```

In this chapter, I'll continue to use `ios` `open_mode` constants directly. In a major software project where portability matters, however, I'd define constants for this purpose.

After creating or overwriting a file, always check that the ofstream object is ready for use. Perform this check using an if statement like this:

```
#include <stdlib.h>  // for exit()
...
ofstream ofs("Newfile.txt", ios::out);
if (!ofs) {
  cerr << "Error: unable to write to NEWFILE.TXT" << endl;
  exit(1);
}
```

The first line constructs an object named ofs of the ofstream class, creating or overwriting a file named Newfile.Txt. The parameters passed to the class constructor specify the filename and ios::out open_mode value.

The if statement tests whether the file was properly attached to the ofs object. If not, the program writes an error message to cerr and exits by calling the exit function, usually declared in stdlib.h.

The form of the if statement bothers a lot of programmers on a first meeting. If ofs is an object of the ofstream class, you might wonder, how can the expression (!ofs) make any sense? After all, the object isn't an int value, so what exactly is being evaluated here?

The secret is buried in ios class, which overloads the *not* operator (!). The statement

```
if (!ofs) {
...
}
```

calls the operator! function in ios for the ofs file-stream object. That function is probably implemented inline something like this:

```
int operator! () { return fail(); }
```

The operator! function, in other words, simply returns the result of the stream's fail function. Consequently, the statement

```
if (!ios) { }
```

is exactly equivalent to

```
if (ofs.fail()) { }  // Same as preceding example
```

Create an input file stream using similar techniques, but construct the file object from the ifstream class. For example, use these statements to open a file named Oldfile.txt:

```
ifstream ifs("Oldfile.txt", ios::in);
if (!ifs) {
  cerr << "Error: unable to open Oldfile.txt" << endl;
  exit(1);
}
```

Object `ifs` is constructed from the `ifstream` class and initialized with a filename and `open_mode` constant. The `if` statement uses the overloaded `operator!` function on the object to test whether the operation was a success. If so, the object is ready for reading data from the file; otherwise, the program halts with an error message.

That covers the basics of file streams. If you are familiar with conventional methods—opening, creating, and closing files by calling functions—at this stage, you might think some critical factors are missing. Remember, however, that *file streams are object-oriented.* To open a file, simply create an input file stream object, and then use stream statements to read from the file. To write or create a file, construct an output file stream object and use stream statements to write to the file. When the file stream object goes out of scope or is deleted, the file is automatically closed.

Next, let's examine some sample programs that read and write text files using the techniques outlined so far. There are four important methods to master:

- Reading text a character at a time
- Writing text a character at a time
- Reading text a line at a time
- Writing text a line at a time

Reading Text a Character at a Time

Listing 8.7, Rchar.cpp, demonstrates how to use a file stream to read a text file one character at a time. Just to keep things interesting, the program also counts the number of characters and lines in the file. Such requirements always come with built-in ambiguities—should the definition of a "character," for example, include the newline symbol at the end of a line? I decided not to count end-of-line characters; thus the total character count reported by Rchar.cpp probably won't match the file's size in the directory.

Listing 8.7. Rchar.cpp (Reads a text file a char at a time).

```
//============================================================
// Rchar.cpp -- Reads a text file a char at a time
// To compile:
//    bcc rchar
// To run:
//    rchar rchar.cpp
// Copyright (c) 1996 by Tom Swan. All rights reserved.
//============================================================

#include <iostream.h>
#include <fstream.h>
#include <stdlib.h>
```

continues

Listing 8.7. continued

```cpp
int main(int argc, char *argv[])
{
  if (argc <= 1) {
    cerr << "Error: filename missing" << endl;
    exit(1);
  }

  ifstream ifs(argv[1], ios::in);
  if (!ifs) {
    cerr << "Error: unable to open " << argv[1] << endl;
    exit(2);
  }

  char c;
  long nc = 0, nl = 0;
  while (ifs.get(c)) {
    if (c == '\n')
      nl++;  // Count number of lines
    else
      nc++;  // Count number of characters
    cout.put(c);
  }
  cout << endl << endl << "Total characters : " << nc;
  cout << endl << "Number of lines  : " << nl;
  return 0;
}
```

The `main` function begins by checking whether you supplied a filename. If not, an error message reminds you to run the program by typing a command such as

```
rchar rchar.cpp
```

which reads and displays the program's own source file. The following statement attempts to open the file specified as a command-line argument:

```cpp
ifstream ifs(argv[1], ios::in);
```

If this works, the `ifs` object is available for use as a source in an input stream statement. A simple `while` loop, for example, reads all the characters from the file and displays those characters by passing them to `cout.put`:

```cpp
while (ifs.get(c))
  cout.put(c)
```

Writing Text a Character at a Time

Creating and writing a text file is equally simple, as Listing 8.8, Wchar.cpp, shows.

Listing 8.8. Wchar.cpp (Writes a text file a char at a time).

```
//=================================================================
// Wchar.cpp -- Writes a text file a char at a time
// To compile:
//    bcc wchar
// To run:
//    wchar filename.txt
// Copyright (c) 1996 by Tom Swan. All rights reserved.
//=================================================================

#include <iostream.h>
#include <fstream.h>
#include <stdlib.h>

int main(int argc, char *argv[])
{
  if (argc <= 1) {
    cerr << "Error: filename missing" << endl;
    exit(1);
  }

  ifstream ifs(argv[1], ios::in);
  if (ifs) {
    cerr << "Error: " << argv[1] << " already exists" << endl;
    cerr << "       Specify a different filename" << endl;
    exit(2);
  }

  ofstream ofs(argv[1], ios::out);
  if (!ofs) {
    cerr << "Error: unable to write to " << argv[1] << endl;
    exit(3);
  }

  ofs << "1: A string\n";
  ofs.put('2');
  ofs.put(':');
  ofs.put(' ');
  ofs.put('C').put('h').put('a').put('r').put('s');
  ofs << endl;

  return 0;
}
```

Here again, the first job is to display an error message if the filename is missing. Try running the program with a command such as

```
wchar test.txt
```

To prevent Wchar.cpp from destroying Test.Txt if that file already exists, the program creates an input stream object for the specified file. If no errors are detected, the program assumes that

253

Test.Txt exists and halts with an error message. This part of the program shows how to detect whether a file exists, using an `if` statement such as

```
ifstream ifs("Test.Txt", ios::in);
if (ifs) {
  // ... File exists
}
```

After constructing the input file stream object, `ifs`, the `if` statement tests whether that operator succeeded. As before, this expression might strike experienced C++ programmers in the audience as extremely odd. Just what does `if (ifs) { }` accomplish?

Testing the `ifs` stream object in an `if` statement's expression this way is permitted because the `ios` class overloads the `operator void *` function inline as

```
operator void *()
  { return fail() ? 0 : this; }
```

In other words, the *value* of a file-stream object such as `ifs` equals zero (false, or null) if `fail` is true; otherwise, the value equals a pointer to the object. Thus, with these overloaded operators, the following `if` statement expressions are exact opposites:

```
if (!ifs)...  // Calls overloaded operator! function
if (ifs)...   // Calls overloaded operator void * function
```

Getting back to Wchar.cpp, if the file does not exist, the program creates the file and constructs an output stream object, `ofs`, ready for use in stream statements:

```
ofstream ofs(argv[1], ios::out);
if (!ofs) {
...
}
```

Again, the result of constructing the object is tested by an `if` statement, using the overloaded `operator!` function in the `ios` class. If no errors occur, you can use the constructed file-stream object as you do any output sink. For example, this writes a line of text to the file:

```
ofs << "Write me to disk" << endl;
```

You can also write individual characters:

```
ofs << 'X';
```

Or, you can pass characters to the `put` member function:

```
ofs.put('X');
```

By the way, because `put` returns `ostream &` (a reference to an object of the `ostream` class), you can string multiple `put` function calls together in an odd-looking construction such as this:

```
ofs.put('A').put('B').put('C');
```

You might see similar `put`-`put` statements in published listings, but there seems to be little reason to use this cryptic trick. However, perhaps a smart compiler could optimize the compiled code to keep the object references in a register.

Reading Text a Line at a Time

You can usually speed up the show by reading and writing text files a line at a time. On most operating systems, calling a single function to read an entire line of text is faster than executing multiple function calls to read characters one at a time.

Listing 8.9, Rline.cpp, operates like Rchar.cpp, but reads a text file a line at a time. Like its counterpart, the program totals the number of characters and lines in a file.

Listing 8.9. Rline.cpp (Reads a text file a line at a time).

```
//================================================================
// Rline.cpp -- Reads a text file a line at a time
// To compile:
//   bcc rline
// To run:
//   rline rline.cpp
// Copyright (c) 1996 by Tom Swan. All rights reserved.
//================================================================

#include <iostream.h>
#include <fstream.h>
#include <stdlib.h>
#include <string.h>

#define BUFLEN 128

int main(int argc, char *argv[])
{
  if (argc <= 1) {
    cerr << "Error: filename missing" << endl;
    exit(1);
  }

  ifstream ifs(argv[1], ios::in);
  if (!ifs) {
    cerr << "Error: unable to open " << argv[1] << endl;
    exit(2);
  }

  char buffer[BUFLEN];
  long nc = 0, nl = 0;
  while (!ifs.eof()) {
    ifs.getline(buffer, sizeof(buffer), '\n');
    if (!(ifs.eof() && strlen(buffer) == 0)) {
      nc += strlen(buffer);
      nl++;
      cout << buffer << endl;
    }
  }
  cout << endl << endl << "Total characters : " << nc;
  cout << endl << "Number of lines  : " << nl;
  return 0;
}
```

As when prompting for text interactively, it's best to call the `getline` member function to read strings from text files. If you simply write

```
ifs >> buffer;  // ???
```

you risk overwriting the end of `buffer` if that array isn't big enough to hold the line at the current file position. Instead of using an input stream statement, read a single line like this:

```
ifs.getline(buffer, sizeof(buffer), '\n');
```

Or, use the `setw` manipulator. To read the file one word at a time—words being broken by any white space or the ends of lines—include the iomanip.h header and read strings using this input stream statement:

```
#include <iomanip.h>
...
ifs >> setw(BUFLEN) >> buffer;
```

Check whether the program has reached the end of the file by calling the `eof` member function in reference to the file stream object. The function makes it easy to write a simple `while` loop that ends after reading the last smidgen of data from the file.

```
while (!ifs.eof()) {
  ifs.getline(buffer, sizeof(buffer), '\n');
  // Process line in buffer
}
```

Writing Text a Line at a Time

The last of the four fundamental text-file techniques writes text files a line at a time. Listing 8.10, Wline.cpp, demonstrates the method.

Listing 8.10. Wline.cpp (Writes a text file a line at a time).

```
//==================================================================
// Wline.cpp -- Writes a text file a line at a time
// To compile:
//    bcc wline
// To run:
//    wline filename.txt
// Copyright (c) 1996 by Tom Swan. All rights reserved.
//==================================================================

#include <iostream.h>
#include <fstream.h>
#include <stdlib.h>
#include <string.h>

#define STR "2: Another literal string"

int main(int argc, char *argv[])
{
```

```
  if (argc <= 1) {
    cerr << "Error: filename missing" << endl;
    exit(1);
  }

  ifstream ifs(argv[1], ios::in);
  if (ifs) {
    cerr << "Error: " << argv[1] << " already exists" << endl;
    cerr << "        Specify a different filename" << endl;
    exit(2);
  }

  ofstream ofs(argv[1], ios::out);
  if (!ofs) {
    cerr << "Error: unable to write to " << argv[1] << endl;
    exit(3);
  }

  ofs << "1: A literal string" << endl;
  ofs.write(STR, strlen(STR));
  ofs << endl;
  char *c = "String addressed by pointer";
  ofs << "3: " << c << endl;

  return 0;
}
```

As in Wchar.cpp, the program begins by checking for a filename and halting if a file by that name already exists. The program then creates the file by constructing an ofstream object, ofs.

To write lines of text to the file, you have two choices. One, you can write a literal string like this:

```
ofs << "Write me to disk!" << endl;
```

Remember to append a new-line, either by writing the endl manipulator, or by ending the string with a new-line character:

```
ofs << "Write me to disk!\n";
```

At times, it might also be useful to call the write member function, which requires two arguments: a pointer to a string (char *) and the number of characters to write. This writes an entire string addressed by a char pointer s:

```
ofs.write(s, strlen(s));
```

Usually, however, you'll use this kind of statement to write only a specified number of characters from a string. To write the first five characters, for example, use a statement like this:

```
if (strlen(s) >= 5)
  ofs.write(s, 5);
```

Binary File Streams

Don't look for binary file operations in the C++ file stream library. There aren't any. Although you can open a file for binary access—a capability provided by most disk operating systems—reading and writing binary data such as floating point values in their native form is a summit left for programmers to conquer.

The required steps are almost nonexistent in C++ tutorials. To use file streams for reading and writing binary data files, you need to add a few basic capabilities to the stock file stream classes. Extra programming is needed to

- Write one or more bytes of any values to a file.
- Read one or more bytes of any values from a file.
- Translate an object of any size into bytes.
- Translate a collection of bytes to any object.

Using Binary File Streams

Construct binary file stream objects in almost the same way as text files, but specify the ios::binary (or ios::bin in some other C++ compilers) mode constant. To create a new binary file, construct an ofstream object like this:

```
ofstream ofs("Newfile.Dat", ios::out | ios::binary);
if (!ofs) {
  cerr << "Error: unable to create or write to Newfile.Dat" << endl;
  exit(1);
}
```

To open an existing binary file for reading, construct an ifstream object this way:

```
ifstream ifs("Oldfile.Dat", ios::in | ios::binary);
if (!ifs) {
  cerr << "Error: unable to open Oldfile.Dat" << endl;
  exit(2);
}
```

Unfortunately, the ofs and ifs objects are not yet ready for use with binary data. The next sections explain how to complete the steps needed to read and write binary values using these file objects. First, however, let's take a look at the *wrong* way to proceed—it reveals the reason file objects can't be used directly with binary values.

The Wrong Solution

Constructing input and output file streams as in the preceding section might seem to work—until, that is, you attempt to use those objects to read and write binary values in files. Consider what happens, for example, if you create a new file like this:

```
ofstream ofs("Test.Dat", ios::out | ios::binary);
```

You then attempt to write a couple of `double` floating point values to the file using these output stream statements:

```
double d = 3.14159;
ofs << d;        // ???
ofs << d * d;    // ???
```

The program compiles and seems to run correctly. Later, however, you reopen the file by executing:

```
ifstream ifs("Test.Dat", ios::in ¦ ios::binary);
```

You then attempt to read the file's values with these statements:

```
long count = 0;
ifs >> d;   // ???
cout << d << endl;
ifs >> d;   // ???
cout << d << endl;
```

The program's health (and possibly your happiness in the programming profession) are now in serious jeopardy. Instead of the expected two values, `3.14159` and `9.8695877` (pi squared), on screen the program displays the same value twice:

```
3.14159
3.14159
```

What's wrong? Examining the first several bytes in the file provides a clue to solving the mystery (see Figure 8.1.)

```
2F54:0100   33 2E 31 34 31 35 39 39-2E 38 36 39 35 38 38 08   3.141599.869588.
2F54:0110   83 C4 06 EB 06 4F 7C 03-E9 7B FF C4 34 00 43 2F   .....O¦..{..4.C/
2F54:0120   1F 26 F7 47 0A 86 00 75-37 83 7E FC 00 74 31 FF   .&.G...u7.~..t1.
```

Figure 8.1. *Examining the file's data reveals a bug in the way file streams read and write binary values.*

The first several bytes in the file are ASCII characters (see the first line's character representations at far right). Despite the programmer's intentions, the stream wrote the `double` values in text form, and it didn't even bother to separate one value from the next. Although the program opened the file using the `ios::binary` constant, the iostream library *still translates binary data to and from text*. That is, after all, the library's primary job.

This approach for reading and writing binary values in files obviously won't work. Fortunately, the puzzle is not too difficult to solve.

The Right Solution

To read and write binary data *in its native form*, first derive your own binary file-stream classes from `ifstream` and `ofstream`. Because a `char` in C++ is stored in one byte, the array can be used as a buffer for holding a series of bytes representing any value in binary form. To write a binary double value to disk, the program copies the value to the array, which is then written to the file. To read a double value, the program reverses these steps. It reads bytes from the file into the character buffer, and then copies those bytes into the memory reserved for the double value.

In practice, you can dispense with the byte array and just pretend that a double or other value is an array of bytes. *Any* value of any kind fits that description, so the same technique can be used to read and write data of all types in binary form.

Listing 8.11, Wdouble.cpp, demonstrates how to use this method to create a file stream class for writing double values in binary to a disk file. Compile the program and run it. You won't see any screen activity (unless an error occurs). Unlike earlier programs in this chapter, the program writes to a predetermined filename, Test.dat. You don't have to type a name on the command line.

Listing 8.11. Wdouble.cpp (Writes a double binary file).

```
//=================================================================
// Wdouble.cpp -- Writes a double binary file
// To compile:
//    bcc wdouble
// To run:
//    wdouble
// Copyright (c) 1996 by Tom Swan. All rights reserved.
//=================================================================

#include <iostream.h>
#include <fstream.h>
#include <stdlib.h>

class bofstream: public ofstream {
public:
  bofstream(const char *fn)
    : ofstream(fn, ios::out | ios::binary) { }
  void writeBytes(const void *, int);
  bofstream & operator<< (double);
};

inline bofstream & bofstream::operator<< (double d)
{
  writeBytes(&d, sizeof(d));
  return *this;
}

int main()
{
  bofstream bofs("Test.dat");
  if (!bofs) {
    cerr << "Error: unable to write to Test.dat" << endl;
    exit(1);
  }

  double d = 3.14159;
  bofs << d;
  bofs << d * d;
```

```
    bofs << 9.9999999;
    d = 4.7E-8;
    bofs << d;

    return 0;
}

void bofstream::writeBytes(const void *p, int len)
{
    if (!p) return;
    if (len <= 0) return;
    write((char *)p, len);
}
```

To provide a binary output-file class, I derived a new class, bofstream, from ofstream. The class declares three public members:

- bofstream is the class constructor. For simplicity, it requires only a filename and passes a fixed open_mode expression to the base class constructor.

- writeBytes writes one or more bytes to the stream from the address specified by void *

- operator<< overloads the output stream operator so stream statements can be used to write values in binary.

> **TIP**
>
> The overloaded stream operator function in bofstream does not have to be a friend of the class because its initial hidden this parameter is of the correct type, bofstream *. Here, bofstream is a file stream object to be used as a sink or source, not as a vessel for the data to be stored in a file—an important distinction to keep in mind. You may overload operators << and >> as member functions in a file stream class, but you must overload those operators as friend functions in classes of objects to be *stored* in files.

An inline function implements the overloaded operator. The function simply calls writeBytes, passing the address of a double value and its size in bytes. The function returns *this so it can be used in cascaded output stream statements. (Dereferencing this in this case gives a reference to a bofstream object.)

Use bofstream as you do any other file stream class. After opening the file by constructing a bofstream object, this simple statement writes a double value in binary to disk:

```
bofs << d;
```

This statement and the similar ones listed in the program transfer the bytes from d directly to the file (the bytes might be buffered by the file object, however, so a disk write does not necessarily occur immediately).

The binary value is written to disk by member function writeBytes, which calls the inherited write function:

```
write((char *)p, len);
```

Listing 8.12, Rdouble.cpp, flips the coin and shows how to read binary double values from Test.dat into memory. Running the program displays the values that Wdouble.cpp wrote to disk:

```
1: 3.14159
2: 9.86958773
3: 9.9999999
4: 4.7e-08
```

Listing 8.12. Rdouble.cpp (Reads a double binary file).

```
//============================================================
// Rdouble.cpp -- Reads a double binary file
// To compile:
//    bcc rdouble
// To run:
//    wdouble
//    rdouble
// Copyright (c) 1996 by Tom Swan. All rights reserved.
//============================================================

#include <iostream.h>
#include <fstream.h>
#include <stdlib.h>

class bifstream: public ifstream {
public:
  bifstream(const char *fn)
    : ifstream(fn, ios::in | ios::binary) { }
  void readBytes(void *, int);
  bifstream & operator>> (double &);
};

inline bifstream & bifstream::operator>> (double &d)
{
  readBytes(&d, sizeof(d));
  return *this;
}

int main()
{
  bifstream bifs("Test.dat");
  if (!bifs) {
    cerr << "Error: unable to open Test.dat" << endl;
    cerr << "       compile and run Wdouble first" << endl;
    exit(1);
  }

  double d;
  long count = 0;

  cout.precision(8);
```

```
  bifs >> d;
  while (!bifs.eof()) {
    cout << ++count << ": " << d << endl;
    bifs >> d;
  }

  return 0;
}
void bifstream::readBytes(void *p, int len)
{
  if (!p) return;
  if (len <= 0) return;
  read((char *)p, len);
}
```

To provide a binary input-file stream, I derived class `bifstream` from `ifstream`. To the new class, I added a constructor (similar to `bofstream`'s), a function `readBytes`, and an overloaded input stream operator.

The inline `operator>>` member function calls `readBytes` to copy bytes from a binary file stream directly to a `double` object in memory. After opening a file, a simple statement reads a `double` value:

```
bifs >> d;
```

The `readBytes` member function is similar to `writeBytes` in Wdouble.cpp. This time, however, the function calls the inherited `read` function to read characters from the stream to the address indicated by `void *p`.

Classes for Binary File I/O

Expanding the concepts in the preceding two sections leads to versatile versions of the `bofstream` and `bifstream` classes that you can use to read and write all native C++ data types in binary form. Listing 8.13, Bstream.h, declares the two classes. (This is just a header file—you can't compile and run it.)

Listing 8.13. Bstream.h (Declares the `bofstream` and `bifstream` classes).

```
//=============================================================
// Bstream.h -- Declares the bofstream and bifstream classes
// Copyright (c) 1996 by Tom Swan. All rights reserved.
//=============================================================

#ifndef __BSTREAM_H
#define __BSTREAM_H      // Prevent multiple #includes

#include <iostream.h>
#include <fstream.h>
```

continues

Listing 8.13. continued

```cpp
// Binary output file stream

class bofstream: public ofstream {
public:
  bofstream(const char *fn)
    : ofstream(fn, ios::out | ios::binary) { }
  void writeBytes(const void *, int);
  friend bofstream & operator<< (bofstream &, signed char);
  friend bofstream & operator<< (bofstream &, unsigned char);
  friend bofstream & operator<< (bofstream &, signed short);
  friend bofstream & operator<< (bofstream &, unsigned short);
  friend bofstream & operator<< (bofstream &, signed int);
  friend bofstream & operator<< (bofstream &, unsigned int);
  friend bofstream & operator<< (bofstream &, signed long);
  friend bofstream & operator<< (bofstream &, unsigned long);
  friend bofstream & operator<< (bofstream &, float);
  friend bofstream & operator<< (bofstream &, double);
  friend bofstream & operator<< (bofstream &, long double);
};

// Binary input file stream

class bifstream: public ifstream {
public:
  bifstream(const char *fn)
    : ifstream(fn, ios::in | ios::binary) { }
  void readBytes(void *, int);
  friend bifstream & operator>> (bifstream &, signed char &);
  friend bifstream & operator>> (bifstream &, unsigned char &);
  friend bifstream & operator>> (bifstream &, signed short &);
  friend bifstream & operator>> (bifstream &, unsigned short &);
  friend bifstream & operator>> (bifstream &, signed int &);
  friend bifstream & operator>> (bifstream &, unsigned int &);
  friend bifstream & operator>> (bifstream &, signed long &);
  friend bifstream & operator>> (bifstream &, unsigned long &);
  friend bifstream & operator>> (bifstream &, float &);
  friend bifstream & operator>> (bifstream &, double &);
  friend bifstream & operator>> (bifstream &, long double &);
};

template<class T>
inline bofstream & operator<< (bofstream &bofs, T q)
{
  bofs.writeBytes(&q, sizeof(T));
  return bofs;
}

template<class T>
inline bifstream & operator>> (bifstream &bifs, T &q)
{
  bifs.readBytes(&q, sizeof(T));
  return bifs;
}

#endif  // __BSTREAM_H
```

The new `bofstream` and `bifstream` classes are similar to the ones listed earlier, but include overloaded input and output operators for all 11 native data types, from `signed char` to `long double`. If the thought of implementing all 22 friend functions in both classes horrifies you (as it does me), take heart. With C++ templates, you can write those 22 functions literally in two strokes.

Rather than implement each overloaded function in the `bofstream` and `bifstream` classes, the templates provide schematic-like designs for these functions, all of which are nearly identical except for the data type of one parameter. Specifying that parameter as `template<class T>` gives the compiler the information it needs to implement the functions with no help from you or me. The compiler does most of the work, and who can argue against the merits of that?

Templates must be classes or functions, so it was necessary to return to making the overloaded operator functions friends of the class (rather than class members). Listing 8.14, Bstream.cpp, implements the two remaining member functions. The `writeBytes` and `readBytes` member functions are the same ones you examined earlier. Because this is a separate module, you must compile it with the -c (compile-only) option, and link the resulting Bstream.obj code file to a host program, as the next section demonstrates.

Listing 8.14. Bstream.cpp (Implements the `bofstream` and `bifstream` classes).

```
//=============================================================
// Bstream.cpp -- Implements the bofstream and bifstream classes
// To compile:
//    bcc -c bstream
// Copyright (c) 1996 by Tom Swan. All rights reserved.
//=============================================================

#include "bstream.h"

void bofstream::writeBytes(const void *p, int len)
{
  if (!p) return;
  if (len <= 0) return;
  write((char *)p, len);
}

void bifstream::readBytes(void *p, int len)
{
  if (!p) return;
  if (len <= 0) return;
  read((char *)p, len);
}
```

Writing Binary Files

Include the Bstream.h header in your program to read and write binary data of all standard types. Listing 8.15, Tbdouble.cpp, demonstrates how to use the Bstream.obj module from the preceding section.

Listing 8.15. Tbdouble.cpp (Writes and reads double values in a binary file).

```
//================================================================
// Tbdouble.cpp -- Writes and reads double values in a binary file
// To compile:
//   bcc -c bstream
//   bcc tbdouble bstream.obj
// To run:
//   tbdouble
// Copyright (c) 1996 by Tom Swan. All rights reserved.
//================================================================

#include <iostream.h>
#include <stdlib.h>
#include "bstream.h"

#define FILENAME "tbdouble.dat"

int main()
{

// Construct binary output file
  bofstream bofs(FILENAME);
  if (!bofs) {
    cerr << "Error: unable to write to " << FILENAME << endl;
    exit(1);
  }

// Write values and close file
  double d = 3.14159;
  bofs << d << d * d << d * d * d;
  bofs.close();

// Construct binary input file
  bifstream bifs(FILENAME);
  if (!bifs) {
    cerr << "Error: unable to open " << FILENAME << endl;
    exit(2);
  }

// Read and display values from file
  long count = 0;
  cout.precision(8);
  bifs >> d;
  while (!bifs.eof()) {
    cout << ++count << ": " << d << endl;
    bifs >> d;
  }

  return 0;
}
```

Run Tbdouble.exe to write and read three floating point values in a file named Tbdouble.dat. The next program, Listing 8.16, Tbstream, writes and reads 11 C++ native data types in the same binary file.

Listing 8.16. Tbstream.cpp (Writes and reads native types in a binary file).

```
//================================================================
// Tbstream.cpp -- Writes and reads native types in a binary file
// To compile:
//    bcc -c bstream
//    bcc tbstream bstream.obj
// To run:
//    tbstream
// Copyright (c) 1996 by Tom Swan. All rights reserved.
//================================================================

#include <iostream.h>
#include <stdlib.h>
#include "bstream.h"

#define FILENAME "tbstream.dat"

void writefile();
void readfile();
void showvalues();

// Program reads into the following variables
// declared globally to set them to zero

signed char sc;
unsigned char uc;
signed short ss;
unsigned short us;
signed int si;
unsigned int ui;
signed long sl;
unsigned long ul;
float f;
double d;
long double ld;

int main()
{
  writefile();
  readfile();
  showvalues();
  return 0;
}

// Write test file of all data types
// Does not use the global variables
void writefile()
{
  signed char sc = 'Q';
  unsigned char uc = '@';
  signed short ss = 123;
  unsigned short us = 255;
  signed int si = -1;
  unsigned int ui = 65535U;
  signed long sl = -99999L;
```

continues

Listing 8.16. continued

```
  unsigned long ul = 99999L;
  float f = 3.14159;
  double d = 3.14159;
  long double ld = 3.14159;

  bofstream bofs(FILENAME);
  if (!bofs) {
    cerr << "Error: unable to write to " << FILENAME << endl;
    exit(1);
  }
  bofs << sc;
  bofs << uc;
  bofs << ss;
  bofs << us;
  bofs << si;
  bofs << ui;
  bofs << sl;
  bofs << ul;
  bofs << f;
  bofs << d;
  bofs << ld;
  bofs.close();   // Not required
}

// Read test file into global variables
void readfile()
{
  bifstream bifs(FILENAME);
  if (!bifs) {
    cerr << "Error: unable to open " << FILENAME << endl;
    exit(2);
  }
  bifs >> sc;
  bifs >> uc;
  bifs >> ss;
  bifs >> us;
  bifs >> si;
  bifs >> ui;
  bifs >> sl;
  bifs >> ul;
  bifs >> f;
  bifs >> d;
  bifs >> ld;
  bifs.close();   // Not required
}

// Display global variables
void showvalues()
{
  cout << "sc == " << sc << endl;
  cout << "uc == " << uc << endl;
  cout << "ss == " << ss << endl;
  cout << "us == " << us << endl;
```

```
    cout << "si == " << si << endl;
    cout << "ui == " << ui << endl;
    cout << "sl == " << sl << endl;
    cout << "ul == " << ul << endl;
    cout << "f  == " << f  << endl;
    cout << "d  == " << d  << endl;
    cout << "ld == " << ld << endl;
}
```

To write values to a data file, construct a `bofstream` object similar to the way you constructed other output files:

```
bofstream bofs("Myinfo.dat");
if (!bofs) {
  cerr << "Error: unable to write to Myinfo.dat" << endl;
  exit(1);
}
```

You can then write *any* C++ native object to the file. If `v` is a `double` value and `k` is an `int`, write them to `bofs` with stream statements:

```
bofs << v;
bofs << k;
```

Read binary data similarly. Construct a `bifstream` object, and then use input stream statements to read values from the file into memory.

```
bifstream bifs("Myinfo.dat");
if (!bifs) {
  cerr << "Error: unable to open Myinfo.dat" << endl;
  exit(2);
}
bifs >> v;
bifs >> k;
```

NOTE

Using the binary file techniques described here, it's your responsibility to read and write values in the correct order. If you write `double`, `char`, and `long int` values in that order, you must read those values back *in the same order.*

Storing Other Objects in Binary Files

Using the code and techniques from the preceding sections, you also can store class objects in binary files. Listing 8.17, Tbclass.cpp, demonstrates.

Listing 8.17. Tbclass.cpp (Writes and reads class object in a binary file).

```cpp
//================================================================
// Tbclass.cpp -- Writes and reads class object in a binary file
// To compile:
//    bcc -c bstream
//    bcc tbclass bstream.obj
// To run:
//    tbclass
// Copyright (c) 1996 by Tom Swan. All rights reserved.
//================================================================

#include <iostream.h>
#include <stdlib.h>
#include "bstream.h"

#define FILENAME "Tbclass.dat"

class TAnyClass {
  int x;
  int y;
  friend ostream & operator<< (ostream &, TAnyClass &);
  friend istream & operator>> (istream &, TAnyClass &);
  friend bofstream & operator<< (bofstream &, TAnyClass &);
  friend bifstream & operator>> (bifstream &, TAnyClass &);
public:
  TAnyClass(): x(0), y(0) { }
  TAnyClass(int X, int Y): x(X), y(Y) { }
};

int main()
{
  TAnyClass original, copy;

  cout << "Enter X and Y values" << endl;
  cin >> original;
  cout << "Your values are:" << endl;
  cout << original;

  cout << "Creating " << FILENAME << endl;
  bofstream bofs(FILENAME);
  if (!bofs) {
    cerr << "Error: unable to create " << FILENAME << endl;
    exit(1);
  }
  bofs << original;  // Write class object to disk
  bofs.close();

  cout << "File written" << endl;
  cout << "Opening " << FILENAME << endl;
  bifstream bifs(FILENAME);
  if (!bifs) {
    cerr << "Error: unable to open " << FILENAME << endl;
    exit(2);
  }
  bifs >> copy;       // Read class object from disk

  cout << "Copy of class object:" << endl;
  cout << copy;
```

```
    return 0;
}

ostream & operator<< (ostream &os, TAnyClass &c)
{
  os << "x == " << c.x << endl;
  os << "y == " << c.y << endl;
  return os;
}

istream & operator>> (istream &is, TAnyClass &c)
{
  cout << "Enter value for X: ";
  is >> c.x;
  cout << "Enter value for Y: ";
  is >> c.y;
  return is;
}
```

To make TAnyClass streamable, include the bstream.h header described in the preceding sections, and overload the << and >> operators:

```
#include "bstream.h"
...
class TAnyClass {
// data members
  friend bofstream & operator<< (bofstream &, TAnyClass &);
  friend bifstream & operator>> (bifstream &, TAnyClass &);
...
};
```

The overloaded operators, created from the Bstream.h header file templates, use file stream statements to read and write the class data members. You might also overload the input and output operators so you can read and write TAnyclass objects in stream statements—to prompt for values, for example, or to display file data. These functions are overloaded in the program as

```
friend ostream & operator<< (ostream &, TAnyClass &);
friend istream & operator>> (istream &, TAnyClass &);
```

Because the operator function parameters differ, the compiler can distinguish among the duplicate operator<< and operator>> functions. Implement the new output stream operator as shown here:

```
ostream & operator<< (ostream &os, TAnyClass &c)
{
  os << "x == " << c.x << endl;
  os << "y == " << c.y << endl;
  return os;
}
```

Implement the output operator to prompt for values interactively:

```
istream & operator>> (istream &is, TAnyClass &c)
```

```
{
  cout << "Enter value for X: ";
  is >> c.x;
  cout << "Enter value for Y: ";
  is >> c.y;
  return is;
}
```

You can now prompt for TAnyClass objects from cin, write those objects to cout, and use binary file streams to read and write the objects in disk files. All of these actions use relatively simple stream statements. Define a couple of TAnyClass objects:

```
TAnyClass original, copy;
```

Then, prompt for, read, and confirm object original with these statements:

```
cout << "Enter X and Y values" << endl;
cin >> original;    // Prompt for and read values
cout << "Your values are:" << endl;
cout << original;   // Display values entered into object
```

Next, to write the object in binary form to disk, first construct a binary output file stream. I'll call it bofs:

```
bofstream bofs("Tbclass.dat");
if (!bofs) {
  cerr << "Error: unable to create Tbclass.dat" << endl;
  exit(1);
}
bofs << original;   // Write class object to disk
bofs.close();       // Close file, flushing data to disk
```

The next to last statement writes the original object to the stream, storing its data on disk by virtue of the overloaded << function in the class. The final statement closes the file—necessary only if you need to access the file data while bofs remains in scope.

To reread the object, after closing the output file construct an input file stream and read a copy of the original object like this:

```
bifstream bifs("Tbclass.dat");
if (!bifs) {
  cerr << "Error: unable to open Tbclass.dat" << endl;
  exit(2);
}
bifs >> copy;   // Read class object from disk into copy
```

The final statement reads the file and, by calling the overloaded class >> operator function, loads the object's data from disk into a TAnyClass object named copy. Display copy's value with these statements:

```
cout << "Copy of class object:" << endl;
cout << copy;
```

8

Seeking in Streams

For database work, programs need to pick and choose specific records in files. You can do that with input file streams by calling one of two overloaded member functions, inherited from the `istream` class:

```
istream & seekg(streampos)
istream & seekg(streamoff, ios::seek_dir);
```

The `streampos` and `streamoff` data types are typically defined as equivalent to `long` values:

```
typedef long streampos;
typedef long streamoff;
```

> **TIP**
>
> Another C++ compiler might define `streampos` and `streamoff` using a different data type, so don't pass `long` values directly to `seekg`.

The first overloaded form of `seekg` positions an input stream to a specific byte. The second form positions the stream to an offset from one of three positions defined by `ios::seek_dir` (see Table 8.3).

Table 8.3. The `ios::seek_dir` constants.

Constant	Value	Description
beg	0	Seek from beginning of file
cur	1	Seek from current file position
end	2	Seek from end of file

Always supply positive offsets for `ios::beg`. Supply positive offsets for `ios::cur` to seek forward toward the end of the file, or use negative offsets to seek backward toward the beginning of the file. Always supply negative offsets for `ios::end`.

To position the internal file pointer for output streams, use the following two overloaded output file stream functions, inherited from the `ostream` class:

```
ostream & seekp(streampos);
ostream & seekp(streamoff, ios::seek_dir);
```

A few examples demonstrate how to use these functions. (I'll use `seekg` here. The `seekp` function works identically with output streams.) Listing 8.18, Seek.cpp, demonstrates the basic techniques. The program uses the same `TAnyClass` class from Tbclass.cpp.

Listing 8.18. Seek.cpp (Demonstrates seeking records in binary files).

```
//================================================================
// Seek.cpp -- Demonstrates seeking records in binary files
// To compile:
//    bcc -c bstream
//    bcc seek bstream.obj
// To run:
//    seek
// Copyright (c) 1996 by Tom Swan. All rights reserved.
//================================================================

#include <iostream.h>
#include <stdlib.h>
#include "bstream.h"

#define FILENAME "Tbclass.dat"

class TAnyClass {
  int x;
  int y;
  friend ostream & operator<< (ostream &, TAnyClass &);
  friend istream & operator>> (istream &, TAnyClass &);
  friend bofstream & operator<< (bofstream &, TAnyClass &);
  friend bifstream & operator>> (bifstream &, TAnyClass &);
public:
  TAnyClass(): x(0), y(0) { }
  TAnyClass(int X, int Y): x(X), y(Y) { }
};

int main()
{
  TAnyClass a(0,1), b(2,3), c(4,5), d(6,7), e(8,9);

  bofstream bofs("Abcde.dat");
  if (!bofs) {
    cerr << "Error: unable to create Abcde.dat" << endl;
    exit(1);
  }
  bofs << a << b << c << d << e;
  bofs.close();

  TAnyClass aa, bb, cc, dd, ee;
  bifstream bifs("Abcde.dat");
  if (!bifs) {
    cerr << "Error: unable to open Abcde.dat" << endl;
    exit(2);
  }

//  bifs >> aa >> bb >> cc >> dd >> ee;

  streampos rn = 3;  // Record number
  bifs.seekg(sizeof(TAnyClass) * rn);
  bifs >> aa;
  cout << aa;

  rn = 2;  // Number of records to seek backwards
  bifs.seekg(-(sizeof(TAnyClass) * rn), ios::cur);
  bifs >> bb;
```

274

```
  cout << bb;

  rn = 1;  // Number of records to seek from end of file
  bifs.seekg(-(sizeof(TAnyClass) * rn), ios::end);
  bifs >> cc;
  cout << cc;

  rn = 4;  // Number of records to seek from beginning of file
  bifs.seekg((sizeof(TAnyClass) * rn), ios::beg);
  bifs >> dd;
  cout << dd;

  bifs.seekg(0);

  return 0;
}

ostream & operator<< (ostream &os, TAnyClass &c)
{
  os << "x == " << c.x << endl;
  os << "y == " << c.y << endl;
  return os;
}

istream & operator>> (istream &is, TAnyClass &c)
{
  cout << "Enter value for X: ";
  is >> c.x;
  cout << "Enter value for Y: ";
  is >> c.y;
  return is;
}
```

Using TAnyClass, the program constructs and initializes a few objects to store in a disk file:

```
TAnyClass a(0,1), b(2,3), c(4,5), d(6,7), e(8,9);
```

It then opens a binary output stream, and writes the objects to disk:

```
bofstream bofs("Abcde.dat");
if (!bofs) {
  cerr << "Error: unable to create Abcde.dat" << endl;
  exit(1);
}
bofs << a << b << c << d << e;
bofs.close();
```

To read the objects from disk into memory, the program defines some additional variables of type TAnyClass, and opens the file for input using the bifstream class:

```
TAnyClass aa, bb, cc, dd, ee;
bifstream bifs("Abcde.dat");
if (!bifs) {
  cerr << "Error: unable to open Abcde.dat" << endl;
  exit(2);
}
```

275

Then a single input file stream statement reads the objects back from disk:

```
bifs >> aa >> bb >> cc >> dd >> ee;
```

However, rather than sequentially read all data from the file, we want to seek and read *specific* records at random, as you might need to do in a database file of names and addresses. For example, to seek to record number 3, define a `streampos` variable and call the input file stream object's inherited `seekg` member function like this:

```
streampos rn = 3;   // Record number
bifs.seekg(sizeof(TAnyClass) * rn);
```

This positions the internal file pointer to the first byte of record number 3. Because record number 0 is the first record in the file, the following statements read and display the *fourth* record:

```
bifs >> aa;
cout << aa;
```

Executing these statements sets object aa's two integer data members to 6 and 7, the values stored in record number 3. After this step, the internal file pointer is automatically advanced to the *next* record. To seek two records backward from that point, pass a negative offset to `seekg` and specify the `ios::cur` seek direction:

```
rn = 2;   // Number of records to seek backwards
bifs.seekg(-(sizeof(TAnyClass) * rn), ios::cur);
bifs >> bb;
cout << bb;
```

Before executing this code, the file is positioned at record number 4. Seeking two records back positions the internal file pointer to record number 2. Reading that record sets object bb to (4,5).

It's sometimes useful to seek backward from the end of the file. As when seeking backward from other locations using `ios::cur`, you must use a negative offset with `ios::end`:

```
rn = 1;   // Number of records to seek from end of file
bifs.seekg(-(sizeof(TAnyClass) * rn), ios::end);
bifs >> cc;
cout << cc;
```

This loads cc with the last record in the file, regardless of how many records the file holds. Running this fragment sets object cc to (8,9).

The most common operation is to seek forward from the beginning of the file. Because we know the file has five records, seeking to record number 4 positions the internal file pointer to the file's last record. This loads the last record (8,9) into dd:

```
rn = 4;   // Number of records to seek from beginning of file
bifs.seekg((sizeof(TAnyClass) * rn), ios::beg);
bifs >> dd;
cout << dd;
```

To reset the file to its beginning, perhaps to prepare for sequentially rereading data from the first record, seek to record number 0:

```
bifs.seekg(0);
```

> **TIP**
>
> In the preceding sections, I purposely left out error checks to conserve space. Use the file stream `eof` member function to detect whether the internal file pointer is positioned at the end of the file, from which it would be a mistake to read data.

Other File Stream Techniques

Here are a few other miscellaneous file stream techniques you won't use every day, but might find handy.

Opening and Closing File Objects

Constructing file stream objects in busy programs that work on multiple files can penalize a program's performance. In such cases, you can construct the objects ahead of time and use them later to open and create files.

To construct an output file stream, but *not* associate that stream with a file, define the object like this:

```
ofstream ofs;
```

The `ofs` file stream object is not connected to a file, and you can't use the object in an output file stream. To write to or create a file using the object, call its `open` member function:

```
ofs.open("Newfile.dat");
if (!ofs) exit(1);  // Exit if any errors are detected
```

Or, you can specify `open_mode` constants. For example, use a statement like this to overwrite and truncate an existing file:

```
ofs.open("Newfile.dat", ios::out | ios::trunc);
```

You can then write to the file and close it:

```
ofs << "First line" << endl;
ofs << "Second line" << endl;
ofs << "Last line" << endl;
ofs.close();
```

Construct unopened input file stream objects in a similar way. First define an `ifstream` class object, specifying no parameters to the constructor:

```
ifstream ifs;
```

Later in the program, call the object's `open` member function to open an existing file and read its contents:

```
ifs.open("Newfile.dat");
if (!ifs) exit(1);
while (!ifs.eof()) {
  ifs.getline(buffer, BUFLEN, '\n');
  cout << buffer << endl;
}
ifs.close();
```

After calling the `close` member function, you can reuse the file stream objects `ofs` and `ifs` to read and write other files.

Getting a File Descriptor

I might be asking for trouble by mentioning this subject, but it's possible to obtain a file stream object's internal file descriptor—sometimes called a *file handle*. After getting this value, you can use it to read and write to the file by calling operating system subroutines. If you decide to use this technique, you probably should abandon all hope of porting your programs to other systems. But the method might be useful at odd times and strange places.

An object of the `filebuf` class provides low-level services to `ifstream` and `ofstream`. Those two file-stream classes declare a member function to return a pointer to their `filebuf` object:

```
filebuf *rdbuf();
```

Use the resulting pointer to call low-level `filebuf` member functions. For example, on my system, member function `fd` returns a file handle, represented as an integer. To use the function, and to keep the code simple, include the fstream.h header and define a macro to call `fd`:

```
#include <fstream.h>
#define FD(s) (((s).rdbuf())->fd())
```

You can then construct a file stream object and use the macro to obtain the file's handle:

```
ifstream ifs("Anyfile.txt");
cout << "Descriptor == " << FD(ifs) << endl;
```

The second line writes the file handle's value to the standard output—assuming, however, that `fd`'s return type can be reduced to a native C++ type.

Reading and Writing from the Same File

All of the sample listings in this chapter distinguish between input and output files. With many C++ compilers, however, you can construct a single file stream object that you can use for reading and writing to the same file without having to close the file between input and output operations.

One way to perform read and write operations on a single file opened in binary mode is to combine this chapter's `bofstream` and `bifstream` classes into a new class, `bfstream`, derived from the `fstream` class.

Listing 8.19, Bfstream.h, and Listing 8.20, Bfstream.cpp, declare and implement the `bfstream` class, which you can use to read and write records stored in binary files. A test program follows the two listings.

Listing 8.19. Bfstream.h (Declares the `bfstream`, binary file, class).

```
//=============================================================
// Bfstream.h -- Declares the bfstream, binary file, class
// Copyright (c) 1996 by Tom Swan. All rights reserved.
//=============================================================

#ifndef __BFSTREAM_H
#define __BFSTREAM_H        // Prevent multiple #includes

#include <iostream.h>
#include <fstream.h>

// Binary input and output file stream

class bfstream: public fstream {
  friend bfstream & operator>> (bfstream &, signed char &);
  friend bfstream & operator>> (bfstream &, unsigned char &);
  friend bfstream & operator>> (bfstream &, signed short &);
  friend bfstream & operator>> (bfstream &, unsigned short &);
  friend bfstream & operator>> (bfstream &, signed int &);
  friend bfstream & operator>> (bfstream &, unsigned int &);
  friend bfstream & operator>> (bfstream &, signed long &);
  friend bfstream & operator>> (bfstream &, unsigned long &);
  friend bfstream & operator>> (bfstream &, float &);
  friend bfstream & operator>> (bfstream &, double &);
  friend bfstream & operator>> (bfstream &, long double &);

  friend bfstream & operator<< (bfstream &, signed char);
  friend bfstream & operator<< (bfstream &, unsigned char);
  friend bfstream & operator<< (bfstream &, signed short);
  friend bfstream & operator<< (bfstream &, unsigned short);
  friend bfstream & operator<< (bfstream &, signed int);
  friend bfstream & operator<< (bfstream &, unsigned int);
  friend bfstream & operator<< (bfstream &, signed long);
  friend bfstream & operator<< (bfstream &, unsigned long);
  friend bfstream & operator<< (bfstream &, float);
  friend bfstream & operator<< (bfstream &, double);
  friend bfstream & operator<< (bfstream &, long double);
public:
  bfstream(const char *fn)
    : fstream(fn, ios::in | ios::out | ios::binary) { }
  void writeBytes(const void *, int);
```

continues

279

Listing 8.19. continued

```
  void readBytes(void *, int);
};

inline bfstream & operator<< (bfstream &bofs, signed char q)
{
  bofs.writeBytes(&q, sizeof(signed char));
  return bofs;
}

inline bfstream & operator<< (bfstream &bofs, unsigned char q)
{
  bofs.writeBytes(&q, sizeof(unsigned char));
  return bofs;
}

inline bfstream & operator<< (bfstream &bofs, signed short q)
{
  bofs.writeBytes(&q, sizeof(signed short));
  return bofs;
}

inline bfstream & operator<< (bfstream &bofs, unsigned short q)
{
  bofs.writeBytes(&q, sizeof(unsigned short));
  return bofs;
}

inline bfstream & operator<< (bfstream &bofs, signed int q)
{
  bofs.writeBytes(&q, sizeof(signed int));
  return bofs;
}

inline bfstream & operator<< (bfstream &bofs, unsigned int q)
{
  bofs.writeBytes(&q, sizeof(unsigned int));
  return bofs;
}

inline bfstream & operator<< (bfstream &bofs, signed long q)
{
  bofs.writeBytes(&q, sizeof(signed long));
  return bofs;
}

inline bfstream & operator<< (bfstream &bofs, unsigned long q)
{
  bofs.writeBytes(&q, sizeof(unsigned long));
  return bofs;
}

inline bfstream & operator<< (bfstream &bofs, float q)
{
  bofs.writeBytes(&q, sizeof(float));
  return bofs;
}
```

```
inline bfstream & operator<< (bfstream &bofs, double q)
{
  bofs.writeBytes(&q, sizeof(double));
  return bofs;
}

inline bfstream & operator<< (bfstream &bofs, long double q)
{
  bofs.writeBytes(&q, sizeof(long double));
  return bofs;
}

inline bfstream & operator>> (bfstream &bifs, signed char &q)
{
  bifs.readBytes(&q, sizeof(signed char));
  return bifs;
}

inline bfstream & operator>> (bfstream &bifs, unsigned char &q)
{
  bifs.readBytes(&q, sizeof(unsigned char));
  return bifs;
}

inline bfstream & operator>> (bfstream &bifs, signed short &q)
{
  bifs.readBytes(&q, sizeof(signed short));
  return bifs;
}

inline bfstream & operator>> (bfstream &bifs, unsigned short &q)
{
  bifs.readBytes(&q, sizeof(unsigned short));
  return bifs;
}

inline bfstream & operator>> (bfstream &bifs, signed int &q)
{
  bifs.readBytes(&q, sizeof(signed int));
  return bifs;
}

inline bfstream & operator>> (bfstream &bifs, unsigned int &q)
{
  bifs.readBytes(&q, sizeof(unsigned int));
  return bifs;
}

inline bfstream & operator>> (bfstream &bifs, signed long &q)
{
  bifs.readBytes(&q, sizeof(signed long));
  return bifs;
}

inline bfstream & operator>> (bfstream &bifs, unsigned long &q)
{
  bifs.readBytes(&q, sizeof(unsigned long));
```

continues

Listing 8.19. continued

```
  return bifs;
}

inline bfstream & operator>> (bfstream &bifs, float &q)
{
  bifs.readBytes(&q, sizeof(float));
  return bifs;
}

inline bfstream & operator>> (bfstream &bifs, double &q)
{
  bifs.readBytes(&q, sizeof(double));
  return bifs;
}

inline bfstream & operator>> (bfstream &bifs, long double &q)
{
  bifs.readBytes(&q, sizeof(long double));
  return bifs;
}

#endif  //  __BFSTREAM_H
```

Listing 8.20. Bfstream.cpp (Implements the bfstream class).

```
//================================================================
// Bfstream.cpp -- Implements the bfstream class
// To compile:
//    bcc -c bfstream
// Copyright (c) 1996 by Tom Swan. All rights reserved.
//================================================================

#include "bfstream.h"

void bfstream::writeBytes(const void *p, int len)
{
  if (!p) return;
  if (len <= 0) return;
  write((char *)p, len);
}

void bfstream::readBytes(void *p, int len)
{
  if (!p) return;
  if (len <= 0) return;
  read((char *)p, len);
}
```

The Bfstest.cpp program in Listing 8.21 demonstrates how to use the bfstream class. The program includes the bfstream.h header, and declares a class TAnyClass, similar to the class you examined elsewhere in this chapter.

Listing 8.21. Bfstest.cpp (Tests the bfstream binary file stream class).

```cpp
//================================================================
// Bfstest.cpp -- Tests the bfstream binary file stream class
// To compile:
//    bcc -c bfstream
//    bcc bfstest bfstream.obj
// To run:
//    bfstest
// Copyright (c) 1996 by Tom Swan. All rights reserved.
//================================================================

#include <iostream.h>
#include <stdlib.h>
#include "bfstream.h"

#define FILENAME "ABCDE.DAT"

class TAnyClass {
  int x;
  int y;
  friend ostream & operator<< (ostream &, TAnyClass &);
  friend istream & operator>> (istream &, TAnyClass &);
  friend bfstream & operator<< (bfstream &, TAnyClass &);
  friend bfstream & operator>> (bfstream &, TAnyClass &);
public:
  TAnyClass(): x(0), y(0) { }
  TAnyClass(int X, int Y): x(X), y(Y) { }
};

inline bfstream & operator<< (bfstream &bfs, TAnyClass &q)
{
  bfs << q.x;
  bfs << q.y;
  return bfs;
}

inline bfstream & operator>> (bfstream &bfs, TAnyClass &q)
{
  bfs >> q.x;
  bfs >> q.y;
  return bfs;
}

int main()
{
  TAnyClass a(0,1), b(2,3), c(4,5), d(6,7), e(8,9);
  TAnyClass aa, bb, cc, dd, ee;

  // Construct output file stream object bfs
  bfstream bfs(FILENAME);
  if (!bfs) {
    cerr << "Error: unable to create " << FILENAME << endl;
    exit(1);
  }

  // Write records to file
  bfs << a << b << c << d << e;
```

continues

Listing 8.21. continued

```cpp
  // Reset file to beginning, read and display records
  bfs.seekg(0);
  bfs >> aa >> bb >> cc >> dd >> ee;
  cout << aa << bb << cc << dd << ee;

  // Seek record number 3 and change it
  TAnyClass x(123,456);                  // Construct new object
  long rn = 3;                           // Define record number
  bfs.seekp(sizeof(TAnyClass) * rn);     // Seek to record #3
  bfs << x;                              // Write object to file

  // Seek to record number 3 again and read it
  TAnyClass y;                           // Construct empty object
  bfs.seekg(sizeof(TAnyClass) * rn);     // Seek to record #3
  bfs >> y;                              // Read object from file
  cout << endl << "Modified record:" << endl;
  cout << y;

  // Make sure other records are undisturbed;
  bfs.seekg(0);
  bfs >> aa >> bb >> cc >> dd >> ee;
  cout << aa << bb << cc << dd << ee;

  // Close file object
  bfs.close();

  return 0;
}

ostream & operator<< (ostream &os, TAnyClass &c)
{
  os << "x == " << c.x << endl;
  os << "y == " << c.y << endl;
  return os;
}

istream & operator>> (istream &is, TAnyClass &c)
{
  cout << "Enter value for X: ";
  is >> c.x;
  cout << "Enter value for Y: ";
  is >> c.y;
  return is;
}
```

The only difference between this program's TAnyClass class and the earlier version is the bfstream references in the overloaded operator functions. Use the following statements to construct a few objects of the class, and write them to a file named Abcde.dat:

```cpp
TAnyClass a(0,1), b(2,3), c(4,5), d(6,7), e(8,9);
bfstream bfs("Abcde.dat");
if (!bfs) {
  cerr << "Error: unable to create Abcde.dat" << endl;
```

```
   exit(1);
}
bfs << a << b << c << d << e;
```

Define a few more objects to hold data read from the file:

```
TAnyClass aa, bb, cc, dd, ee;
```

Then, using the same bfs file stream object, reset the file to its beginning and read the file's records like this:

```
bfs.seekg(0);
bfs >> aa >> bb >> cc >> dd >> ee;
cout << aa << bb << cc << dd << ee;
```

To rewrite data at random in the file, seek to a specific record by calling the stream's seekp member function. For example, these four lines change record number 3 (the *fourth* record in the file) to a new TAnyClass object:

```
TAnyClass x(123,456);              // Construct new object
long rn = 3;                       // Define record number
bfs.seekp(sizeof(TAnyClass) * rn); // Seek to record #3
bfs << x;                          // Write object to file
```

To read a specified record by number, call the stream's seekg member function; then use an input stream statement to load the data from disk into an object of the appropriate type:

```
TAnyClass y;                       // Construct empty object
bfs.seekg(sizeof(TAnyClass) * rn); // Seek to record #3
bfs >> y;                          // Read object from file
```

Close the bfstream object in the usual way by calling close():

```
bfs.close();
```

A Few New Keywords

Following are some new miscellaneous keywords recently added to ANSI C++, and newly supported by Borland C++ 5.

bool

C and C++ have never had an explicit Boolean true-or-false data type—until now, that is. (Named after George Boole, *Boolean* is always properly capitalized.) As every C and C++ programmer knows, to create a logical true-or-false variable, you can use the int data type:

```
int done;
```

You'll probably also need two constants, TRUE and FALSE, defined as follows (and traditionally always in uppercase):

```
#define FALSE 0
#define TRUE 1
```

285

None of this is necessary any longer, although these techniques still work as before. Beginning with Borland C++ 5, you can now declare a Boolean variable:

```
bool done;
```

To initialize done, assign to it one of the predefined constants true or false. You don't need to define these constants, and they must be in lowercase. Constant true internally equals 1; false equals 0. Use the constants to assign values to Boolean variables:

```
done = true;
done = false;
bool forever = true;
```

The third statement defines a Boolean variable, forever, and initializes it to true. You may also declare Boolean functions, parameters, and so on. Here's a sample prototype for a function that returns true or false, and requires a Boolean argument:

```
bool Continue(bool PromptUser);
```

Use Boolean variables and functions in conditional expressions, just as you have done with int logical variables in the past:

```
while (Continue(true)) {
... // do something
}
if (!done) cout << "I'm not done yet!" << endl;
if (done) exit(0);
```

explicit

Use the explicit keyword to force calls to a required class constructor. An example illustrates the problem that explicit can solve. Consider the following class:

```
class TAnyClass {
  int value;
public:
  TAnyClass(int n) { value = n; }
  TAnyClass(const char *ns) { value = atoi(ns); }
  int GetValue(void) { return value; }
};
```

TAnyClass declares two constructors, one that requires an int argument and another that requires a char pointer to a null-terminated string. Each constructor assigns its parameter to the private value data member. The second constructor calls the standard atoi function in stdlib.h to convert its string parameter to an integer. You can define variables of TAnyClass and display their values with statements such as

```
TAnyClass v1 = 123;
TAnyClass v2 = "96";
cout << "v1 == " << v1.GetValue() << endl;
cout << "v2 == " << v2.GetValue() << endl;
```

The values 123 and "96" are *implicitly* converted into objects of their class types. To *explicitly* state that such values must only be class objects, and thus preventing the implicit conversions, preface the constructor declarations with the `explicit` keyword. Here's the revised class declaration:

```
class TAnyClass {
  int value;
public:
  explicit TAnyClass(int n) { value = n; }
  explicit TAnyClass(const char *ns) { value = atoi(ns); }
  int GetValue(void) { return value; }
};
```

The preceding v1 and v2 variable declarations now produce compilation errors:

```
Cannot convert 'int' to 'TAnyClass' in function main()
Cannot convert 'char *' to 'TAnyClass' in function main()
```

Because the class constructors are `explict`, you may assign only `TAnyClass` object values with statements such as

```
TAnyClass v1 = TAnyClass(123);
TAnyClass v2 = TAnyClass("96");
TAnyClass v1(123);
TAnyClass v2("96");
TAnyClass v3 = v1;
TAnyClass v4 = v2;
```

mutable

Declaring a member function `const` promises the compiler that the function makes no changes to an object's data members. This is a particularly valuable technique to use for functions that return class data member values, but that should not alter any data in class objects. For example, consider this typical class:

```
class TAnyClass {
  int value;
  const char *message;
public:
  TAnyClass(): value(0), message(NULL) {  }
  int GetValue(void) const;
};
```

Member function `GetValue` is declared `const`. This produces a compilation error if `GetValue` attempts to modify any data members in `TAnyClass`. Implementing the function as follows does not work:

```
int TAnyClass::GetValue(void) const
{
  value = 123;  // ???
  message = "A new string assignment";  // ???
  return value;
}
```

The compiler generates the following error messages for the assignment statements in the function:

```
Cannot modify a const object in function TAnyClass::GetValue() const
Cannot modify a const object in function TAnyClass::GetValue() const
```

Although this technique is useful for preventing functions from modifying class data members, it is often too much of an all-or-nothing affair. Until recently, there was no way to selectively permit const member functions to assign values to specific data elements on a case by case basis. For example, suppose you want GetValue to return the value data member, and to guarantee that value will not be changed, but you also want the function to assign a new value to the message character pointer. There was no way to do this with const functions in the past. Now, starting with Borland C++ 5, you can preface a data member with the mutable keyword, which tells the compile to permit const functions to modify those members. Redeclare the class as

```
class TAnyClass {
  int value;
  mutable const char *message;
public:
  TAnyClass(): value(0), message(NULL) {  }
  int GetValue(void) const;  // Can change message but not value
};
```

Function GetValue can now assign a string to message, but it still is not permitted to modify value. You could also declare value to be mutable:

```
mutable int value;
```

However, if all of a class's data members are mutable, there's no good reason to use const functions.

typename

Use the typename keyword instead of class in a template placeholder expression. For example, following is the max function template described elsewhere in this chapter:

```
template<class T> T max(T a, T b)
{
  if (a > b)
    return a;
  else
    return b;
}
```

The word class here seems to confuse many programmers because it does not refer to a C++ class, but rather, it is a generic term that means "any typename." Apparently realizing this, the powers that be have added a new keyword, typename, which you can use instead of class. For example, you can change the preceding template header to

```
template<typename T> T max(T a, T b)
```

You may mix `typename` and `class` in the same template declaration:

```
template<typename T, class C>
C AnyFunction(T t1, C c1) {
...
}
```

This indicates that `T` and `C` are placeholders for data types to be defined elsewhere in the program. `AnyFunction` returns an object of type `C`, and takes arguments of type `T` and `C`.

> **TIP**
>
> As a useful, though optional, convention in templates, you might use typename to refer to any old type and class to refer to an object of a C++ class.

Odds and Ends

All computer languages have valuable features that are rarely used. You probably won't employ the following techniques often, but then again, you might find one or more of these C++ odds and ends to be just what you need.

Huge Arrays

You can now declare huge arrays in 16-bit and in 32-bit applications. In 16-bit programs, preface the array declaration with `far`. For example, to create an array of 60,000 characters (bytes), use this global declaration:

```
char far bigArray[60000L];
```

The array must be global or static to insert it into the data segment. You can't do this inside a function because there isn't enough room on the stack to accommodate huge arrays.

To create an array larger than 64K, replace `far` with `huge` in the declaration. For example, this creates a 100,000-byte array:

```
char huge biggerArray[100000L];
```

Using the 32-bit compiler (Bcc32.exe), you can declare huge arrays directly without using `far` and `huge`:

```
char bigArray[60000L];       // 32-bit applications only
char biggerArray[100000L];   // 32-bit applications only
```

Declarations in Conditional Expressions

Starting with Borland C++ 5.0, you may declare variables in `while`, `if`, and `switch` conditional expressions. (This does not apply to `do-while` statements, however, because their conditional expressions follow the statement block.) For example, the compiler now accepts this syntax, formerly not allowed:

```
while (bool keepGoing = AFunction()) ... ;
```

This defines `keepGoing` strictly for use within the `while` statement block. Outside of that block, `keepGoing` does not exist. The new syntax is equivalent to, but obviously a lot simpler than

```
bool keepGoing = AFunction();
while (keepGoing) {
  // ...
  keepGoing = AFunction();
}
```

except that in this case, `keepGoing` is defined for the entire function in which this code exists.

You may define variables of other types in conditional expressions, as long as the expression evaluates to true or false. Presumably, `AFunction` eventually does something that ends the loop—in this case, for example, setting `keepGoing` `false`. To try the preceding `while` loop, insert this function into a program:

```
// Returns false when static n becomes >= 10
bool AFunction()
{
  static int n = 0;
  cout << "n == " << n << endl;
  n++;
  if (n < 10)
    return true;
  else
    return false;
}
```

Classes versus Structs

A `class` and a `struct` are functionally equivalent except for one tiny, but important, detail. By default, the members of a `struct` are public; in a `class`, they are private. Because of this relationship, a `class` can inherit a `struct`—a technique that is valuable for creating object-oriented class wrappers for structures such as in a C library. For example, suppose the library has a `struct` defined as

```
struct TAnyStruct {
  int x;
  int y;
};
```

The x and y members are public by default. To create an object-oriented wrapper, a class can inherit `TAnyStruct` like this:

```
class TAnyClass: public TAnyStruct {
  int z;
public:
  TAnyClass() { x = 0; y = 0; z = 0; }
  void Display(void) {
```

```
    cout << "x == " << x << endl;
    cout << "y == " << y << endl;
    cout << "z == " << z << endl;
  }
};
```

The class inherits the x and y members, which retain their public status. To make them private members, change public to private in the class declaration.

Pointers to Member Functions

You can address class member functions with pointers, but not in the same way you can address common functions. Member functions are called in reference to objects of a class, and they receive an undeclared this pointer. For these reasons, addressing member functions with pointers requires new techniques.

A member function pointer is bound to its class name. For example, for a class TFirstClass, you might declare a pointer to a member function like this:

```
double (TFirstClass::*myfnptr)(void);
```

This states that myfnptr addresses a TFirstClass member function that requires no input and returns a value of type double. To declare myfnptr as a pointer to a member function that returns void and has two int parameters, write its declaration as

```
void (TFirstClass::*myfnptr)(int, int);
```

These declarations do not specify which member function myfnptr addresses, only the form of the function that may be assigned to the pointer variable. It's still necessary to create an object of the class and to assign the address of a class member of the appropriate form to the pointer. Listing 8.22, Mfnptr.cpp, shows the basic steps required to define and use pointers to member functions.

Listing 8.22. Mfnptr.cpp (Demonstrates pointers to member functions).

```
//============================================================
// Mfnptr.cpp -- Demonstrates pointers to member functions
// To compile:
//    bcc mfnptr
// To run:
//    mfnptr
// Copyright (c) 1996 by Tom Swan. All rights reserved.
//============================================================

#include <iostream.h>
#include <iomanip.h>

class TFirstClass {
private:
  int count;
```

continues

Listing 8.22. continued

```
public:
  TFirstClass() { count = 0; }
  int Access(void);
};

int (TFirstClass::*myfnptr)(void);

void main()
{
  int i;
  TFirstClass fc;

  cout << endl << "Call Access the normal way:" << endl;
  for (i = 0; i < 9; i++)
    cout << setw(8) << dec << fc.Access();
  cout << endl << endl
       << "Call Access via the member function pointer" << endl;
  myfnptr = &TFirstClass::Access;
  for (i = 0; i < 9; i++)
    cout << setw(8) << dec << (fc.*myfnptr)();
  cout << endl << endl
       << "Member function pointer and a dynamic instance" << endl;
  TFirstClass *fp = new TFirstClass;
  for (i = 0; i < 9; i++)
    cout << setw(8) << dec << (fp->*myfnptr)();
}

int TFirstClass::Access(void)
{
  return count++;
}
```

The single-line declaration following the TFirstClass declaration states that myfnptr is a pointer to a TFirstClass member function. The function requires no arguments and it must return an int value. The program may assign the address of any such matching function to the pointer, and then use the pointer to call that function.

For example, function main declares a TFirstClass object fc. The program then calls the class's Access member function for object fc using the expression

```
fc.Access();
```

That shows the common method for calling class member functions. (Access merely increments and returns a private data member, just to give the program something to do.)

Next, the program shows another way to call Access through the use of the member function pointer, myfnptr. To initialize the pointer, the program assigns to myfnptr the address of the Access member function in TFirstClass:

```
myfnptr = &TFirstClass::Access;
```

Alternatively, you can declare and initialize a member function pointer using a single statement like this:

```
int (TFirstClass::*myfnptr)(void) = &TFirstClass::Access;
```

Either way, when calling a member function using a pointer, you must follow two rules:

1. Refer to an object of the class.
2. Surround the function call with parentheses.

For example, if n is an `int` variable and `fc` is a `TFirstClass` object, the following statement copies to n the result returned by `Access`, which is addressed by `myfnptr`:

```
n = (fc.*myfnptr);
```

The period and asterisk symbol `.*` is called the *pointer-to-member* operator and is used to dereference a member function pointer for a class object. The parentheses around (`fc.*myfnptr`) are required because the function-call operator `()` has higher precedence than the pointer-to-member operator. The preceding expression is exactly equivalent to

```
n = fc.Access();
```

You can also call member functions via pointers when objects are addressed by other pointer variables. For example, in Mfnptr.cpp, near the end of function `main`, a statement assigns to pointer `fp` the address of a `TFirstClass` object created dynamically by `new`:

```
TFirstClass *fp = new TFirstClass;
```

Following this statement, the expression

```
(fp->*myfnptr)();
```

in the subsequent output stream statement calls the `Access` member function for the object addressed by `fp`. The triple character symbol `->*` is a variation of the pointer-to-member operator. Again, the extra parentheses are needed because `()` has higher precedence than `->*`. The preceding expression is exactly equivalent to

```
fp->Access();
```

In addition to addressing member functions with pointers, it's also possible to address other public data members. For example, if `TFirstClass` had a public `double` member named `balance`, you could define a pointer to that member as

```
double TFirstClass::*dataPtr;
```

As declared, pointer `dataPtr` can address any public `double` data member in class `TFirstClass`. To initialize the pointer, use a statement such as

```
dataPtr = &TFirstClass::balance;
```

Or you could define the pointer and assign the address of the `balance` member in one easy motion:

```
double TFirstClass::*dataPtr = &TFirstClass::balance;
```

Either way, `dataPtr` now addresses the `balance` member in `TFirstClass`. Actually, `dataPtr` does not hold the address of a memory location; instead, it holds the offset where the `balance` member is stored in a `TFirstClass` object. It is therefore necessary to refer to the addressed data member through a class object. These statements, for instance, initialize and display `balance`'s value:

```
fc.balance = 1234.56;
cout << endl << "Balance=" << fc.*dataPtr;
```

The notation `fc.*dataPtr` is similar to the notation used to call a member function, and it uses the pointer-to-member operator `.*`. The expression does not require extra parentheses, however, because it contains no conflicting operators.

Static Members

A *static member function* typically performs a global action or initializes global data for all objects of a class. To declare a static member function, precede a normal class member function declaration with the keyword `static`.

```
class TAnyClass {
public:
  static void GlobalInit(void);
  ...
};
```

Static member functions such as `GlobalInit` may not be virtual. Implement the static member function as you do others, prefacing the function name with the class name and a scope resolution operator:

```
void TAnyClass::GlobalInit(void)
{
  // Statements to perform
}
```

The static member function may perform any statements; however, it does not receive a `this` pointer, and it cannot access any data or function members in the class. A program calls a static member function by referring, not to an object, but to the class itself:

```
TAnyClass::GlobalInit();  // Call GlobalInit() static function
```

Presumably, a static member function like `GlobalInit` performs actions that affect all future and present objects of type `TAnyClass`.

Classes can also declare static data members. For example, in the class

```
class TAnyClass {
private:
  static char c;  // Static data member
```

8

```
public:
  char GetC(void) { return c; }
};
```

member c is declared as a private static char variable. (Static data members also can be protected or public.) Due to its static nature, only one instance of TAnyClass::c exists regardless of how many TAnyClass objects the program defines. Somewhere, the program must define and initialize the static member, usually with a global definition such as

```
char TAnyClass::c = 'q';
```

In effect, c is a global variable that is accessible only to TAnyClass member functions. It is hidden from other statements. To use the static data, you might define an object x and call the class GetC member function, which displays the character 'q':

```
TAnyClass x;
cout << x.GetC();  // Displays static c data member
```

Placing Objects at Specific Addresses

You might occasionally need to store an object at a specific location, perhaps in a global buffer. Such objects persist beyond the scope of their declarations and are sometimes called "persistent objects."

Listing 8.23, Persist.cpp, demonstrates how to store an object at a specific address. The program also shows how a statement can call a destructor—an uncommon technique that may be necessary to delete objects that are created by an overloaded new operator that bypasses the default memory allocator.

Listing 8.23. Persist.cpp (Demonstrates persistent objects).

```
//=============================================================
// Persist.cpp -- Demonstrates persistent objects
// To compile:
//    bcc persist
// To run:
//    persist
// Copyright (c) 1996 by Tom Swan. All rights reserved.
//=============================================================

#include <iostream.h>

class TPersist {
private:
  int x, y;
public:
  TPersist(int a, int b) { x = a; y = b; } // Constructor
  ~TPersist() { x = 0; y = 0; }  // Destructor
  void *operator new(size_t, void *p) { return p; }
  friend ostream& operator<< (ostream &os, TPersist &p);
};
```

continues

Listing 8.23. continued

```
char object[sizeof(TPersist)];

void main()
{
  TPersist *p = new(object) TPersist(10, 20);
  cout << *p << endl;
  cout << "Address of object == " << &object << endl;
  cout << "Address of *p      == " << &(*p) << endl;
  p->~TPersist();  // Explicit call to destructor
// p->TPersist::~TPersist();  // Required in Borland C++ 3.1
}

ostream& operator<< (ostream& os, TPersist &p)
{
  os << "x == " << p.x << ", y == " << p.y;
  return os;
}
```

Class TPersist overloads operator new in an unusual way. Rather than allocate memory to a pointer, the overloaded operator simply returns its void pointer parameter p. The program uses new to store a TPersist object in a global buffer named object. The expression new(object) calls the overloaded new and passes the char buffer object's address as an argument. Because the overloaded operator simply returns p, this strange-looking statement in effect assigns object's address to p and also calls the TPersist constructor to initialize the newly allocated object in the buffer.

The program displays the address of the object character buffer, and also the address of the object in the buffer. The addresses are the same, which shows that the object is stored in a predetermined location.

A good exercise is to run Persist.cpp in Turbo Debugger. Inspect the object buffer and single step the code by pressing F8. After the first statement in main executes, you'll see the values 10 and 20 stored in the global buffer—proving that the overloaded new bypasses the default memory allocator.

The program also demonstrates how to call a destructor for an object addressed by a pointer. Because of the way this program bypasses the normal memory allocator, this extra step is necessary to prevent deleting the global object buffer as though it were a dynamic memory block. At the same time, the destructor must be called to perform any cleanups for class objects. C++ doesn't recognize the scope of the object stored at an explicit address in the buffer, so it can't call the object's class destructor automatically, because as far as C++ is concerned, such an object is never destroyed.

Call a virtual or nonvirtual destructor as demonstrated in the listing:

```
p->~TPersist();
```

In Borland C++ 3.1, this statement required the class name and a scope resolution operator. You may also use this alternate form in later compiler versions:

```
p->TPersist::~TPersist();  // Required in Borland C++ 3.1
```

Again, executing an explicit call to a destructor in Turbo Debugger is instructive. If you try this, you'll see the destructor's inline statements reset the global object's data members to zero.

Initializing Class Object Members

As many of this book's listings demonstrate, a constructor typically initializes data members for an object of a class. For example, the following TAnyClass declares two int data members x and y. An inline class constructor initializes those members by setting them to zero:

```
class TAnyClass {
private:
  int x, y;
public:
  TAnyClass() { x = 0; y = 0; }
  ...
};
```

Alternatively, you can initialize data members as though they had constructors, writing the constructor this way:

```
class TAnyClass {
private:
  int x, y;
public:
  TAnyClass(): x(0), y(0) { }
  ...
};
```

This form of the TAnyClass constructor assigns zero to x and y just as the inline statements did in the previous example. The compiled code is the same for both forms, but the second form specifies *initializers* for data members before the body of the constructor is executed. (In this example, the constructor's body is empty.)

The technique of using initializers is essential to initialize class object data members of another class. For example, suppose TAnyClass owns a data member object of class TNewClass, and that TNewClass's constructor requires an integer parameter:

```
class TNewClass {
  int x;
public:
  TNewClass(int n) { x = n; }
  ...
};
```

If TAnyClass declares a data member of type TNewClass, TAnyClass's constructor must initialize that object. Because constructors can't be called directly, the object must be initialized using an initializer:

```
class TAnyClass {
private:
  int x;
  TNewClass z;   // Object data member
public:
  TAnyClass(int n): z(n)   // Initialize z
    { x = n; }             // Initialize x
  ...
};
```

Member x is type int as before. Member z is an object of class TNewClass. TAnyClass's constructor declares an int parameter n, which is used to initialize z before executing any statements in the constructor. Inside the constructor, an assignment stores the value of n in x. In a class with multiple object data members, you can initialize them in a list separated with commas:

```
class TAnyClass {
private:
  int x;
  TNewClass a, b, z;   // Three object data members
public:
  TAnyClass(int n): a(n), b(n), z(n)   // Initialize a, b, and z
    { x = n; }                         // Initialize x
  ...
};
```

Nested Class Declarations

Items other than data and function members can nest inside class declarations. A class can declare a typedef symbol, a struct, or even another class. These *nested class declarations* are sometimes useful for providing declarations closely related to a specific class. Nested class declarations also permit two or more classes to declare identically named items that are distinguished by their respective class names.

For example, you can use a nested typedef to export a data type from inside a class. The following class, TAnyClass, uses typedef to declare CLASS_COUNTER as an alias for int:

```
class TAnyClass {
public:
  typedef int CLASS_COUNTER;   // Nested typedef declaration
  static CLASS_COUNTER ClassCount;   // Static variable
public:
  TAnyClass() { ClassCount++; }
  ~TAnyClass() { ClassCount--; }
};
```

The class also declares a static CLASS_COUNTER variable named ClassCount. To define memory for this variable, the program needs a global declaration such as

```
TAnyClass::CLASS_COUNTER TAnyClass::ClassCount;
```

The class name prefaces the data type and variable name. Because TAnyClass provides the typedef CLASS_COUNTER, the program can define the variable ClassCount without any direct knowledge of the variable's underlying data type. For instance, with no extra help from the program, the class itself can count the number of its own constructed objects:

```
TAnyClass *cp1, *cp2, *cp3;   // Declare class-object pointers
cp1 = new TAnyClass;          // Construct class objects
cp2 = new TAnyClass;          //    "         "         "
cp3 = new TAnyClass;          //    "         "         "
cout << "There are " << TAnyClass::ClassCount << " objects" << endl;
```

The final statement displays 3. Here again, the class name prefaces the reference to ClassCount.

Complex nested declarations are also possible. A class can declare an inner struct:

```
class TAnyClass {
public:
  struct ClassStruct {
    int x;
    int y;
  };
};
```

The program can then define an object of ClassStruct using a statement such as

```
TAnyClass::ClassStruct k;
```

Use k as you would a non-nested struct:

```
k.x = 1;
k.y = 2;
```

Extending these concepts further leads to a *nested class declaration*—one class declared inside another. Here's an example:

```
class TAnyClass {
public:
  class ClassClass {
    int x;
    int y;
  public:
    ClassClass() { x = 1; y = 2; }
    int GetX(void) { return x; }
    int GetY(void) { return y; }
  };
};
```

In this declaration, TAnyClass declares an inner class named ClassClass. A program might define an object k of the nested class and use it like this:

```
TAnyClass::ClassClass k;
cout << "k.x == " << k.GetX() << endl;
cout << "k.y == " << k.GetY() << endl;
```

Other kinds of nested class declarations such as enumerated constants are also possible. The key to using nested class declarations is to remember always to preface references to nested items with the class name and a scope resolution operator. Other than this rule, you can use most nested class declarations as you do unnested ones.

The Fast this Option

Borland C++ 3.1 introduced an important optimization, now called the fast this option, that can greatly increase performance of object-oriented programs. As you know by now, class member functions receive an undeclared this pointer, which addresses the object for which the member function is called. Defining a variable of a class named TAnyClass:

```
TAnyClass anyvar;
```

and calling a TAnyClass member function:

```
anyVar.AnyFunction();
```

passes to AnyFunction a this pointer that addresses anyvar. Literally speaking, this is how member functions address data members in class objects.

To avoid wasting time and memory, Borland C++ can pass this in a register, thus saving the time it takes to push this onto the stack and, inside member functions, to refer to the stacked this pointer. Known as the *fast* this *option,* this simple yet effective code optimization can make a world of difference in performance, especially in programs that can call many small member functions—a typical case for most object-oriented applications.

16-bit this pointers are passed in register si. 32-bit this pointers are passed in ds:si, and the compiler automatically saves and restores ds as needed. To engage the fast this option, compile the program from a DOS prompt with option -po. You might, for instance, use the command

```
bcc -po myprog
```

You can also select a fast this option by using the IDE's *Options\Project\Compiler\Code Generation* command, and selecting the fastthis check box.

> **NOTE**
>
> Like all optimization techniques, the fast this option doesn't guarantee faster code. One obvious negative effect is the elimination of si as a register variable. For best results, test the effects on your code with and without a fast this option.

Namespaces

Sooner or later, every programmer runs into the problem of identifier conflicts. For instance, after three months developing an application, you decide (or are forced by management) to use a new third-party subroutine library. Unfortunately, that library's function and other identifiers conflict with dozens of your own carefully chosen names. Until recently, unless you were lucky to have the library source code, your only solution was to globally search and replace all conflicting symbols—not exactly a welcome prospect.

Namespaces neatly solve this problem. By wrapping your symbols in a namespace, you in effect preface all symbols with a secret name, which can be anything you like. For example, if you declare a namespace as

```
namespace MYSPACE {
  int x;
}
```

integer x lives within the namespace MYSPACE. Any other variables named x in the program, or in another namespace, do not conflict with this one. To refer explicitly to a variable in a namespace, use a scope resolution operator:

```
MYSPACE::x = 123;
```

You may nest namespaces to provide a hierarchy of spaces that might, in some cases, help compartmentalize numerous symbols in a large function or class library:

```
namespace OUTER {
  int x;
  namespace MIDDLE {
    int x;
    namespace INNER {
      int x;
    }
  }
}
```

Each of the three x variables lives in its own namespace, and therefore, there are no conflicts among them. Refer to each variable by qualifying it with its namespace names:

```
OUTER::x = 1;
OUTER::MIDDLE::x = 2;
OUTER::MIDDLE::INNER::x = 3;
```

Creating Namespaces

Function and class libraries should be wrapped in namespaces to help prevent identifier conflicts. For instance, the standard C++ template library introduced in Chapter 10, "Mastering the Standard Template Library," is wrapped in the namespace std. It's probably best to use a unique name such as your name or your company's name, as Listing 8.24, Namespac.cpp, demonstrates.

Listing 8.24. Namespac.cpp (Demonstrates namespaces).

```
//================================================================
// Namespac.cpp -- Demonstrates namespaces
// To compile:
//    bcc namespac
// To run:
//    namespac
// Copyright (c) 1996 by Tom Swan. All rights reserved.
//================================================================

#include <iostream.h>

namespace FOREIGNER {
class TAnyClass {
public:
  int q;
  TAnyClass() { q = 0; }
};
}  // namespace FOREIGNER

namespace TSWAN {

class TAnyClass {
  int x, y, z;
public:
  TAnyClass() { x = 0; y = 0; z = 0; }
  void SetXYZ(int X, int Y, int Z) {
    x = X; y = Y; z = Z;
  }
  void Display(void) {
    cout << "x == " << x << endl;
    cout << "y == " << y << endl;
    cout << "z == " << z << endl;
  }
};

void main()
{
  TAnyClass v1;
  v1.SetXYZ(123, 234, 345);
  v1.Display();
  FOREIGNER::TAnyClass v2;
  cout << "v2.q == " << v2.q << endl;
}

} // namespace TSWAN
```

The program declares two classes, each named TAnyClass. The first class is declared within the namespace FOREIGNER. The second is declared within the namespace TSWAN. The FOREIGNER namespace illustrates a typical situation in which a module imports library functions and classes that conflict with symbols in the program. Because TSWAN's symbols are wrapped in a unique namespace, however, there is no conflict and the program compiles normally.

Use the scope resolution operator to refer to symbols in a specific namespace. The current namespace is the default. The following defines an object of TSWAN's TAnyClass:

```
TAnyClass v1;
```

To refer to the FOREIGNER's class, preface it with the namespace identifier:

```
FOREIGNER::TAnyClass v2;
```

Notice that in the listing, the closing brace on the last line ends the namespace.

> **NOTE**
>
> You may redefine a namespace that already exists. Doing so *extends* the namespace; it does not replace it. Any new declarations in the new namespace are added to the existing namespace's symbols.

Creating Namespace Aliases

You may create aliases to namespaces, redefining them for use in your program. There are two reasons for doing this: to reduce typing (providing an abbreviation for a long namespace name, for example), and also to resolve the rare case where two namespace names conflict. For example, suppose a function library defines the namespace BOZO_THE_CLOWN_SOFTWARE, in which TAnyClass is defined:

```
namespace BOZO_THE_CLOWN_SOFTWARE {
  class TAnyClass {
  public:
    void Func(char c) { cout << c << endl; }
  };
} // namespace BOZO_THE_CLOWN_SOFTWARE
```

Rather than type long-winded declarations such as

```
BOZO_THE_CLOWN_SOFTWARE::TAnyClass v1;
```

you can define a shorter namespace alias. Insert this statement into your program:

```
namespace BOZO = BOZO_THE_CLOWN_SOFTWARE;
```

Now, instead of clowning around, you can preface declarations with the shorter BOZO:

```
BOZO::TAnyClass v1;
```

Using the using Directive

Rather than typing namespace qualifiers such as

```
BOZO_THE_CLOWN_SOFTWARE::TAnyClass v1;
```

303

or defining an alias, you can insert a using directive into a program that tells the compiler to use a namespace's identifiers by default. For example, insert this statement:

```
using BOZO_THE_CLOWN_SOFTWARE::TAnyClass;
```

You can then use TAnyClass without qualification:

```
TAnyClass v2;
```

If necessary, you can still resolve any identifier conflicts by using the namespace qualifier. You would have to do that, for example, if the program also declares TAnyClass.

You may not use the using directive inside classes. For example, this does not compile:

```
// Move using declaration to here
class TAnotherClass {
  using BOZO_THE_CLOWN_SOFTWARE::TAnyClass;  // ???
  TAnyClass vx;
};
```

Move the using directive ahead of the class, and the program will compile. However, there is one exception to this rule. You may insert a using directive into a class to overload an inherited function in a derived class. For example, suppose you have a base class with a member function named Show that displays a string passed as a constant character pointer:

```
class TBaseClass {
public:
  void Show(const char *cp) {
    cout << "String = " << *cp << endl;
  }
};
```

You want to derive a new class and overload Show to display an integer parameter. Normally, a derived class would *inherit* Show. To overload the function, insert a using directive in the derived class

```
class TDerivedClass: public TBaseClass {
public:
  void Show(int k) {
    cout << "Integer = " << k << endl;
  }
  using TBaseClass::Show;  // Overloads Show
};
```

The using directive redeclares the original member function in the derived class, thus overloading Show to take integer and string parameters. You can now use the derived class as follows

```
TDerivedClass anObject;
anObject.Show("A string");  // Calls TBaseClass.Func
anObject.Show(123);         // Calls TDerivedClass.Func
```

Insert those statements into a main function and compile the preceding class declarations. Comment out the using directive to view the compilation errors you receive due to the ambiguity of the inherited Show's parameters. Overloading the function with using fixes the problem and allows the program to compile.

Runtime Type Information

Runtime type information (RTTI) gives you exactly what its name implies—information about object data types at runtime. You can use runtime type information to compare the types of objects, and to obtain strings that describe them.

The `typeid` operator returns an object of the `typeinfo` class that describes the type of an object. You can use `typeid` with objects of simple types such as `int` and `double`, and you can use it with classes, structures, arrays, and other types of your own making. You can also use `typeid` to compare data types for equivalence (equal and not equal) and to compare their names alphabetically.

> **NOTE**
>
> In past versions of Borland C++, the `typeinfo` class was named `Type_info`. The Typeinfo.h header file still defines this obsolete spelling, but for ANSI C++ compatibility, you should use `typeinfo` in new programs.

To use `typeid`, include the Borland C++ Typeinfo.h header. The operator returns an object of the `typeinfo` class, which provides member functions that you can call. One of those functions is `name`. Use it to display the name of an object's data type:

```
int count;
cout << typeid(count).name() << endl;
```

This output statement displays *int,* the name of `count`'s data type. You can also compare object types using code such as

```
int i;
int j;
if (typeid(i) == typeid(j))
  cout << "i and j are the same type" << endl;
```

Or, use the `!=` operator to test where object types are not equal:

```
if (typeid(i) != typeid(j))
  cout << "i and j are not the same types" << endl;
```

You also can call the `before` function to determine whether a type's name is alphabetically ahead of another type's (the syntax is awkward and of questionable value, and you could more easily compare the strings returned by `name`—still, the following is how you are *supposed* to compare type names lexically):

```
if (typeid(i).before(typeid(d)))
  cout << "i's type name is lexically before d's type name";
```

If, for some reason, `typeid` cannot provide a `typeinfo` object—when fed a dereferenced null pointer, for example—the operator is supposed to throw an exception of type `Bad_typeid`. When using `typeid`, then, you should provide a `catch` statement to trap this error.

Listing 8.25, Typeinfo.cpp, demonstrates how to use the typeid operator.

Listing 8.25. Typeinfo.cpp (Demonstrates the typeid operator).

```
//================================================================
// Typeinfo.cpp -- Demonstrates the typeid operator
// To compile:
//    bcc typeinfo
// To run:
//    typeinfo
// Copyright (c) 1996 by Tom Swan. All rights reserved.
//================================================================

#include <iostream.h>
#include <string.h>
#include <typeinfo.h>

class TAnyClass {
public:
  TAnyClass(int c) { count = c; }
private:
  int count;
  virtual void f() { return; }
};

#pragma warn -use

void main()
{
  char c;
  int i;
  double d;
  TAnyClass a(1);
  TAnyClass *pa = new TAnyClass(2);

  cout << "Name : " << typeid(c).name() << endl;
  cout << "Name : " << typeid(i).name() << endl;
  cout << "Name : " << typeid(d).name() << endl;
  cout << "Name : " << typeid(a).name() << endl;
  cout << "Name : " << typeid(pa).name() << endl;
  cout << "Name : " << typeid(*pa).name() << endl;
  cout << "Name : " << typeid(typeid(i)).name() << endl;

  cout << endl;  // Start new display line

// It is necessary to use name() only once in an
// output stream statement as the following demonstrates.

  if (typeid(c) != typeid(d)) {
    cout << typeid(c).name() << " and ";
    cout << typeid(d).name() << " are not equivalent." << endl;
  }

// Compare common and dynamic objects of same types
  if (typeid(a) == typeid(*pa))
    cout << "a and *pa are objects of the same types" << endl;
```

```
// Demonstrate Bad_typeid exception handling
  try {
    cout << endl;
    cout << "Using a dereferenced null pointer typeid" << endl;
    TAnyClass *p;  // Define a pointer to class with virtual func
    p = 0;   // Assign null to the pointer
    cout << typeid(*p).name() << endl;  // Throws exception
  }
  catch (Bad_typeid x) {
    cout << "Exception Bad_typeid caught" << endl;
    // ... exit program or take other action here
  }

  delete pa;
}
```

The program displays the names of several objects. Closely examine these two statements, which use the pa pointer to a TAnyClass object:

```
cout << "Name : " << typeid(pa).name() << endl;
cout << "Name : " << typeid(*pa).name() << endl;
```

The typeid operator correctly identifies pa as a pointer of type TAnyClass*. It also correctly identifies the *dereferenced* pointer, *pa, as type TAnyClass.

The following statement displays *typeinfo,* the name of the class data type of the object that typeid returns:

```
cout << "Name : " << typeid(typeid(i)).name() << endl;
```

Because name uses a static character buffer, you should not call it more than once in an output stream statement. For example, this code does not display the correct type names:

```
if (typeid(c) != typeid(d))
  cout << typeid(c).name() << " and "
       << typeid(d).name() << " are not equivalent." << endl;
```

To fix the problem, divide the output statement into two statements as shown in the listing:

```
if (typeid(c) != typeid(d)) {
  cout << typeid(c).name() << " and ";
  cout << typeid(d).name() << " are not equivalent." << endl;
}
```

Passing a dereferenced pointer to typeid throws a Bad_typeid exception, but only if the pointer is bound to a class that declares at least one virtual function. For example,

```
TAnyClass* p = 0;
cout << typeid(*p).name() << endl;  // Throws exception
```

throws an exception because, in order to discern type addressed object's type, the compiler must evaluate the typeid expression at runtime. However, if a pointer addresses a simple typed object or an instance of a class with no virtual functions, no exception is thrown:

```
int *p = 0;
cout << typeid(*p).name() << endl;  // Does not throw an exception
```

In this case, the compiler knows the addressed type and it does not evaluate the `typeid` expression. Thus no code is generated to throw the exception. Even so, when using `typeid` with pointers, it's a good idea to wrap statements in a `try-catch` block to nab this exception as the listing demonstrates.

Choosing a `string` Class

Borland C++ 5 provides two string classes. The class described in this section is the same as in past compiler versions. Chapter 11 describes how to use the new ANSI C++ standard string class template.

> **NOTE**
>
> In new programs, especially if portability is a goal, you should use the newer ANSI C++ standard string template instead of the one described here.

Borland's `string` class is designed to be compatible with `char*` strings and null terminated string arrays. Using the `string` class is easy, and this section is not a complete reference to its considerable talents. (You don't really need me to explain what `string::length` does, do you?)

To gain the most from `string`, use it as you do any other data type. Assign it values, compare `string` objects, allocate memory for them, and delete them when no longer needed. You can also call a variety of `string` functions. Simply include the Cstring.h header and start using the class. Listing 8.26 demonstrates some basic `string` techniques.

> **TIP**
>
> Include the Cstring.h header to use Borland's `string` class. The similarly named String.h header declares standard C and C++ string functions that operate on null-terminated strings addressed by `char*` pointers and in `char` arrays. You may include either or both headers without conflict in the same modules.

Listing 8.26. String.cpp (Demonstrates Borland's string class).

```
//=================================================================
// String.cpp -- Demonstrates Borland's string class
// To compile:
//    bcc string
```

```
// To run:
//    string
// Copyright (c) 1996 by Tom Swan. All rights reserved.
//===============================================================

#include <iostream.h>
#include <cstring.h>

void main()
{
// Common string variables
  string s1;
  string s2 = "Initialized string";
  string s3(s2);

// Dynamic string variables
  string *sp1;
  sp1 = new string("Initialized dynamic string object");
  string *sp2 = new string(s2);
  string *sp3 = new string(*sp2);

// Display string values
  cout << "s1 ......... = " << s1 << endl;
  cout << "s2 ......... = " << s2 << endl;
  cout << "s3 ......... = " << s3 << endl;
  cout << "*sp1 ........ = " << *sp1 << endl;
  cout << "sp2->c_str() = " << sp2->c_str() << endl;
  cout << "*sp3 ........ = " << *sp3 << endl;

// Convert a string to all uppercase/lowercase letters
  s3.to_upper();
  cout << "s3.to_upper() = " << s3 << endl;
  s3.to_lower();
  cout << "s3.to_lower() = " << s3 << endl;
}
```

You can define string variables as you do other kinds of objects:

```
string s1;
string s2("Initialized string");
```

The first statement defines an uninitialized string, s1. The second defines a string object initialized with a literal character string. You can also write the second line as

```
string s2 = "Initialized string";
```

You can assign one string to another:

```
s1 = s2;
```

And, you can compare strings with the usual operators:

```
if (s1 == s2)      // Or <, >, <=, >=, !=, etc.
  DoSomething();
```

You can concatenate strings by adding them up (add these lines to the sample listing):

```
string a, b, c;
a = "Apple ";
```

309

```
b = "Peaches ";
c = "Pumpkin pie";
string d = a + b + c;
cout << d << endl;
```

That code sets string object d to the single string Apple Peaches Pumpkin pie, joined from the other three strings, a, b, and c.

Other member functions in the string class search for string patterns and return copies of strings for a variety of parameters. You can, for example, request an index for the first character of a substring located in a string:

```
string x("abcdefg");
string y("cde");
int index = x.find(y);   // Find y in x
cout << index << endl;
```

That code sets index to 2, the position in x that contains the substring, "cde".

To convert a string class object to a C-style, null-terminated string, call the c_str function—for example, if you need to call a function declared as

```
void f(char *s);   // Function that requires a C—style string argument
```

You can't pass a string object to f because string is not equivalent to a pointer of type char*. You can, however, pass the function the address of the string object's contents by calling c_str:

```
string anyString("Any character string");   // Construct string object
f(anyString.c_str());   // Pass equivalent C-style string to function
```

This technique is especially useful in Windows, which has numerous functions that require char* arguments.

There's plenty more to the string class, but as I mentioned, most functions are intuitive. (See Chapter 11 for information on the ANSI C++ standard string template.) The key is to use Borland's string as you do other data types. In most cases, you'll need to consult your references only for special needs. Following, however, are two sections that describe aspects of the string class that are important to know.

Copy-on-Write Technology

When two or more string objects are equal in value (two strings, for example, that each equal the character string "Apple"), only one copy of that string object is stored in memory. Internally, the string class uses a *reference count* to keep track of how many copies of itself are in use. When you delete a duplicated string object, memory is freed only if the object's reference count indicates that this is the only copy.

Changing a string's value *in any way* causes a new `string` object to be created. In other words, any *write* operations on a `string` object may cause a new string object to be constructed. *Read* operations that merely examine a string's value do not create a new object.

This *copy-on-write* method saves memory, but you need to be aware of its consequences. Assignments and other operations that change a `string` object's value may cause memory to be allocated for a new string. All of this happens automatically, but if your RAM budget is tight, you need to be aware that the `string` class may allocate memory on its own.

Strings and the Paranoid Programmer

String objects are stored in memory using a *hash table*. A *hash function* gives a value based on a string's contents that the `string` class uses to find strings in memory, or to find empty table locations to store new strings.

The use of a hash table keeps programs running fast—it's a far better method for searching string data than, for example, using a linked list or an array of pointers. Unfortunately, however, it's possible for any hash function to give the *same* value for two different objects. This problem is rare, and you may never experience any trouble, but it doesn't hurt to be a teensy bit paranoid about the possibility of a conflict.

To reduce your paranoia, call the `set_paranoid_check` function with an argument of 1. Pass 0 to the function to reset to let-it-all-hash-out behavior. Call `get_paranoid_check` for the current setting. For example, given the `string` object `schizoid`, you can set its paranoia check to 1 with the statement:

```
schizoid.set_paranoid_check(1);
```

Any operations involving a search for `schizoid`'s value in memory are immediately followed by a character-by-character comparison of the located string. This comparison is carried out by the standard C and C++ string function, `strcmp`, declared in the standard library header file String.h. If the comparison fails, the search continues until a match is found. I could find no information on what happens if *no* match is ever found, but in theory, that supposedly can't happen.

TIP

No hash function is perfect, and it's possible, though extremely unlikely, that some poor programmer's `string` object will someday, when least expected, refer to the wrong data. The `set_paranoid_check` function ensures (knock on wood) that no such errors can occur.

Summary

- Classes can declare a copy constructor, which C++ calls when an object initializes another object of the same class, when an object is passed to a function's value parameter, and when a function returns a class object.

- Classes can overload the assignment operator, which C++ calls when an object of a class is assigned to another already constructed object of that same class.

- I/O streams are provided as classes derived from ios and declared in Iostream.h. Four I/O stream objects are provided: cin, cout, cerr, and clog. The ios class and derivatives define input (>>) and output (<<) stream operators for all built-in C++ data types.

- I/O stream manipulators, declared in Iomanip.h and Iostream.h, make it possible to format input and output in I/O stream statements. You can also write your own manipulators.

- Classes can overload I/O stream operators to provide input and output capabilities for class objects. Programs can use objects of these classes in I/O stream statements.

- Templates are useful for creating general-purpose functions and classes for which actual implementation details are supplied by the templates' users.

- Other C++ features covered in this chapter include pointers to member functions, static member functions, placing objects at specific addresses, calling destructors directly, initializing class object members, nesting class declarations, and engaging the fast this option.

- Relatively new C++ keywords discussed in this chapter include bool, true, false, explicit, mutable, typename, namespace, and using.

- You can now declare huge arrays in 16- and 32-bit applications. Use the far and huge qualifiers in 16-bit applications. Declare the array with long integer constants. You may not define huge arrays as automatic variables in functions.

- C++ now permits variable declarations inside while, if, and switch conditional expressions.

- Classes and structs are equivalent except that a struct's members are public by default; a class's members are private. You can use this fact to derive a class from a struct.

- Namespaces eliminate identifier conflicts that often arise from using third-party function and class libraries.

- Borland's string class provides an easier-to-use alternative to common null-terminated, also called C-style, strings. Include the Cstring.h header to use the string class. Chapter 11 describes how to use the newer standard C++ string template.

Exercises

8.1 Given a class named TFruit and an object orange of type TFruit, use orange to initialize a new object named grapefruit.

8.2 Write the prototype for a copy constructor in the hypothetical TFruit class from Exercise 8.1.

8.3 Write an overloaded assignment operator for the TFruit class from Exercise 8.1.

8.4 Write a program that uses the min template function declared in this chapter's header file, Minmax.h.

8.5 Create a database of 100 random integers using the TDatabase template class declared in this chapter's header file, Db.h. Use a for loop and output stream statement to display the object's values in 8-character columns.

8.6 Define two Borland string-class variables, each named aString. Use namespaces to eliminate the identifier conflict between the two equally named objects.

PART

Class Libraries

9

Mastering Borland's Template Class Library

Borland's template class library provides *container* classes that you can plug into programs for managing all sorts of data collections. Like conventional arrays and lists, container classes are general-purpose vessels for storing data. Container classes are object-oriented, however, and you can extend them through inheritance and virtual functions to accommodate many different types of objects and tasks.

This chapter introduces Borland's template class library, which has several varieties of containers and related classes.

> **NOTE**
>
> Borland has announced that it will not further develop its container class library, officially known as BIDS (Borland International Data Structures). However, many existing programs use BIDS, which the current compiler fully supports. In fact, BIDS is still used internally by OWL. And although it is possible to have a program that uses the new STL containers and OWL, it is very difficult and not recommended. For new programs, and especially when portability is important, Borland recommends that you use the ANSI C++ standard template library as explained in the next chapter rather than BIDS.

Borland C++ 3.1 provided two forms of the BIDS library—one with common classes and one with C++ templates. Beginning with version 4.0, Borland C++ now provides only the template classes, which are more versatile, although they require some additional effort to use. If you don't know how to program with templates, you might want to review that information in Chapter 8, "Advancing Your C++ Knowledge," before continuing.

You may use the BIDS container class library in DOS, EasyWin, and Windows applications, in 16- and 32-bit object code. For simplicity, this chapter's sample listings run as DOS or EasyWin programs, but the techniques explained are applicable to all target platforms.

> **NOTE**
>
> The original class library is provided in subdirectory obsolete, located in the path C:\bc5\include\classlib, and implemented in C:\bc5\lib\obsolete.lib. Use these classes only to compile existing programs. Use the template library or the ANSI C++ standard templates for new code.

Introducing Template Container Classes

With BIDS, you can store any kind of data objects in containers, and you can select from a variety of storage methods. For example, you might store objects in a vector (an array of juxtaposed values), or you could use a linked list. Containers *hide* their implementation details so you can change how a container stores data without having to rewrite your code. With container classes, you select the best storage methods for your application, and you can easily change those methods later.

ADTs and FDSs

A container class is an *abstract data type* (ADT). It provides an *abstraction* of a data-storage method. A stack, for example, is an ADT with functions such as Push and Pop for storing and retrieving data in a stack-like manner. The internal implementation of those functions is independent of the concept of a stack. You can create a stack using a vector, or you can use a linked list. A stack is merely a programming method—an abstraction—that has nothing to do with the stack's internal storage details.

Vectors and lists, however, are inseparable from their internal structures. They are therefore referred to as *fundamental data structures* (FDS). Loosely defined, an FDS is any structure that can be used to implement an ADT. You can implement a stack class (the ADT), for example, using a linked list (the FDS). Or, you could implement a stack using a different fundamental type.

> **NOTE**
>
> Just to confuse you, no doubt, C++ gurus call arrays *vectors*. Actually, however, the terms are not synonymous. A vector is a fundamental data structure that stores objects next to each other. An array is an abstraction that provides random access to objects through the indexing operator, [ ]. As a container, an array might be implemented using a vector, a list, or another fundamental storage mechanism.

Every container class combines one ADT and one FDS. The resulting class name might be something like TArrayAsVector. From its name, you know this container is an array (an ADT) that is implemented as a vector (the FDS). The initial T stands for "type."

Borland's container-class library provides a variety of ADT and FDS templates, plus several other classes. To use a container class, you specify the type of data to store using the general form TClass<T>, where <T> represents your data type. TStackAsList<long>, for example, specifies a stack container class that can store long objects on a linked list. TQueueAsVector<MyDataType> creates a queue container class that can store objects of MyDataType using a vector for the internal storage mechanism.

Containers can hold simple objects (ints, floats, and so on), structured data (arrays, strings, and structs), and class objects. You can store data objects directly in containers, or you can store pointers to objects. Containers can own their objects, and delete them automatically, or you can retain object ownership. You can even store containers in other containers. The data-storage possibilities are nearly limitless.

How To Create a Container

A simple example demonstrates how to use container classes. First, include one or more header files from the C:\bc5 subdirectory, include\classlib. For example, to use a stack container, include Stacks.h:

```
#include <classlib\stacks.h>
```

Next, construct a container object from one of the header's classes such as TStackAsVector. Look up the class constructor in your *Borland ObjectWindows Reference*:

```
TStackAsVector(unsigned max = DEFAULT_STACK_SIZE);
```

The constructor for this class indicates that you may specify an optional maximum stack size or use a default value defined in classlib\Resource.h. You also need to provide the template with the type of data you want to store. For example, to construct a stack container for double objects, use a statement such as

```
TStackAsVector<double> myStack(100);
```

The definition creates a container named myStack from the TStackAsVector class template, capable of storing up to 100 double values. Most containers automatically grow to accommodate more data, and limits such as 100 in this example merely determine the container's initial size—they don't necessarily limit a container to holding a fixed number of objects.

After constructing a container, you can store and retrieve its data by calling one or more member functions, some of which might be inherited from ancestor classes. Listing 9.1, Stacked.cpp, demonstrates some of the functions you can use with the TStackAsVector container.

> **NOTE**
>
> You may compile Stacked.cpp as a DOS or an EasyWin application. In either case, however, you must link the program to a compiled class library, Bidsx.lib (*x* represents a memory model). For example, to compile Stacked.cpp from a DOS prompt, enter the command
>
> ```
> bcc stacked bidss.lib
> ```
>
> As I mentioned, BIDS stands for *Borland International Data Structures*. There are different BIDS library code files for each memory model, indicated by the final letter of the filename: S (small), C (compact), M (medium), L (large), H (huge), or F (flat 32-bit).
>
> To compile the program as an EasyWin application, click the right mouse button, or press Alt+F10, and select TargetExpert. Set *Target Type* to *EasyWin* and use the *Large* or *Small Target Model* (other memory models will work too, but *Large* is usually the best choice for Windows applications). Be sure to enable the *Class Library* checkbox under *Standard Libraries*. Compile other sample programs in this chapter similarly.

Listing 9.1. Stacked.cpp (Demonstrates TStackAsVector).

```
//===============================================================
// Stacked.cpp -- Demonstrates TStackAsVector
// To compile:
//   bcc stacked bidss.lib
// To run:
//   stacked
// Copyright (c) 1996 by Tom Swan. All rights reserved.
//===============================================================

#include <iostream.h>
#include <classlib\stacks.h>

// Construct global container object
TStackAsVector<double> myStack(100);

void main()
{
  double d;
  bool done = false;

// Prompt for values and push onto the stack
  while (!done && !myStack.IsFull()) {
    cout << "Enter double value (0.0 to quit): ";
    cin >> d;                // Get value from user
    if (d == 0.0)
      done = true;           // Exit the while loop
    else
      myStack.Push(d);  // Push d onto stack
  }

// Display some information about the stack
  int n = myStack.GetItemsInContainer();
  cout << endl << "Number of objects: " << n << endl;
  if (n > 0)
    cout << "Top of stack: " << myStack.Top() << endl << endl;

// Pop values from stack and display
  while (!myStack.IsEmpty())
    cout << myStack.Pop() << endl;
}
```

Run the program and enter several floating-point values. When you enter 0, the program displays the number of items on the stack and the top object's value. The program pops and displays the stack's values, which empties the stack before the demonstration ends. Because a stack is a last-in, first-out (LIFO) data structure, values come out in reverse-entry order. Figure 9.1 shows a sample program run.

Call IsFull to determine whether a stack contains its initial maximum number of objects. Call IsEmpty to determine whether a stack is empty. You should normally call IsFull before pushing a new object onto the stack:

```
if (!myStack.IsFull())
  myStack.Push;
```

Figure 9.1.

Sample output from Stacked.cpp.

```
Enter double value (0.0 to quit): 9.9
Enter double value (0.0 to quit): 3.14159
Enter double value (0.0 to quit): -88.55
Enter double value (0.0 to quit): 4.32
Enter double value (0.0 to quit): 6.9
Enter double value (0.0 to quit): 0

Number of objects: 5
Top of stack: 6.9

6.9
4.32
-88.55
3.14159
9.9
```

Variable d is a double variable. It does *not* have to be a class object that is derived from a supplied base class, as was necessary with the old object-based library. Because all containers in the new library are templates, *they mold to the type of data you want to store.*

To retrieve a value, call Pop, which removes one object from the stack. Pop returns an object of the type stored in the container. This might be a copy of an object, or a pointer to a dynamic object, depending on the type of container. Usually, you should call IsEmpty to prevent popping an empty stack:

```
if (!myStack.IsEmpty())
  d = myStack.Pop();
```

If you merely want to examine the top of the stack, call Top, which returns a copy of, or a pointer to, the object most recently pushed, but does not remove that object. Again, it's wise to call IsEmpty to prevent accessing an empty stack, which has no top object:

```
if (!myStack.IsEmpty())
  d = myStack.Top();
```

Call GetItemsInContainer for a count of the number of objects the stack holds. This is always safe:

```
int n = myStack.GetItemsInContainer();
```

Most container classes have similarly named functions such as GetItemsInContainer. Learn the functions in one container, and you get the others for free. Only stacks, of course, have functions such as Push, Pop, and Top.

Template Naming Conventions

The library's numerous class names may seem overwhelming at first, and because many classes are derived from others, you often need to read about several classes to learn what one does. For example, TStackAsVector defines only a constructor. The class's ancestor, TMStackAsVector, defines other functions such as Push, Pop, and Top. You have to read about both classes to learn what TStackAsVector can do.

NOTE

Class names that begin with TM provide a memory manager for a container. Use these classes only if you need to provide a custom memory manager—but more on this later.

A good knowledge of container class names will help you hack through the weeds in the library's documentation jungle. Most important is to become familiar with class naming conventions. Remember this rule:

Container class names indicate their capabilities and interrelationships.

Initially, container class names may seem as understandable as punk-rock lyrics, but take each name apart and you'll discover that they follow a sensible plan. In general, container class names follow this format:

```
T [preface] [ADT] [AsFDS] [suffix]
```

All class names begin with the letter T, meaning "type." An optional preface modifies how the class stores data—whether to sort (S) objects, for example, or to store them indirectly (I) as pointers. Next comes the name of an ADT such as Array or Stack. If the word As follows, then the container is implemented using the specified FDS, which might be List, DoubleList, or another fundamental type. Finally, an optional suffix refers to a supporting class type. Some classes, for instance, end with Iterator, which tells you this class performs iterative operations on a container's data.

Not all classes in the library follow this naming convention perfectly. Some classes are not even containers—they might, for instance, be fundamental structures used to implement containers. Other classes play mere supporting roles. You also will not find every combination of ADTs and FDSs. There is, for example, no TStackAsHashTable class because it's senseless to implement a stack (a sequentially accessed data type) using a hash table (a random-access data structure).

Table 9.1 lists the library's abstract data types and shows their header files. The table also lists the fundamental data structures that are used to implement each container. A Deque, for example, can be implemented as DoubleList or Vector. From the table, you can expect to find container classes named TDequeAsDoubleList and TDequeAsVector. You would not expect to find TDequeAsHashTable. No container uses the BinarySearchTree structure.

Table 9.1. Abstract Data Types (ADT).

ADT	Header	Binary-SearchTree	Double-List	Hash-Table	List	Vector
Array	arrays.h					•
Bag	bags.h					•

Table 9.1. continued

ADT	Header	Binary-SearchTree	Double-List	Hash-Table	List	Vector
Deque	deques.h		•			•
Dictionary	dict.h			•		
Queue	queues.h		•			•
Set	sets.h					•
Stack	stacks.h				•	•

Table 9.2 lists the same information in Table 9.1, but shows fundamental data structure headers and their applications. Use the table to select containers implemented with a certain fundamental structure. For example, Table 9.2 indicates that only Stack containers are implemented using a List, and therefore, you can expect to find a class named TStackAsList in the library. The table also shows that Vector is the busiest fundamental structure, used to implement six different types of containers.

Table 9.2. Fundamental Data Structures (FDS).

FDS	Header	Array	Bag	Deque	Dictionary	Queue	Set	Stack
BinarySearchTree	binimp.h							
DoubleList	dlistimp.h			•		•		
HashTable	hashimp.h				•			
List	listimp.h							•
Vector	vectimp.h	•	•	•		•	•	•

Table 9.3 extends the ADT and FDS names from Tables 9.1 and 9.2 with several storage modifiers. Specify a modifier after the initial T in the class name. For example, TIStackAsVector refers to an *indirect* stack container class, implemented using a vector. Indirect containers store pointers to objects. Without the I modifier—as in TStackAsVector, for example—a container stores object data directly. Add S for automatic sorting. The TSArrayAsVector class, for instance, is a sorted array of objects, implemented using a vector. The TISArrayAsVector class is a sorted array of *pointers to objects,* implemented using a vector.

Table 9.3. Storage modifiers.

Modifier	Purpose
C	Counted
I	Indirect (no I = direct)

Modifier	Purpose
IS	Indirect sorted
M	Memory managed
MC	Memory managed counted
MI	Memory managed indirect
MIC	Memory managed indirect counted
MIS	Memory managed indirect sorted
MS	Memory managed sorted
S	Direct sorted

Classes with an M modifier provide memory management for like-named containers. (I call these *class M containers,* probably because I've watched too many *Star Trek* reruns.) The TMQueueAsVector class, for example, provides memory management for the TQueueAsVector class. The only reason to use a class M container class is to replace the standard memory manager with your own. Most programmers will rarely, if ever, need to do that.

Class M containers use the default allocator class, TStandardAllocator, defined in ALLOCTR.H. This class uses the stock new, new[], delete, and delete[] operators, which, in Borland C++, call the standard C library functions, malloc and free. If you must provide your own allocator, create a class with the same member functions as TStandardAllocator and implement those functions to allocate and delete memory as you wish.

You could, for example, reserve a block of memory at the start of your program and use a custom allocator to ensure that all container objects are stored in that block. (See Persist.cpp and discussion in Chapter 8 for some applicable techniques.) This might be useful to guarantee the availability of storage space for some kinds of objects—those used in a critical error-recovery procedure, for instance, which might be called for an out-of-memory condition that has made standard memory allocation methods unusable.

> **NOTE**
>
> Sorted containers must be able to compare their objects. Direct-storage containers must also be able to copy objects. C++ obfuscators tell you, "Objects must have meaningful copy and comparison semantics." This means you might have to supply a copy constructor for a class, and overload equals (==) and less-than (<) operators.

As you browse through the container library, you will come across some additional classes that end with one of three suffixes (I call these *class type modifiers,* but there's no official term for them). Classes that end with Element provide list-object wrappers. There are only two such classes: TMDoubleListElement and TMListElement. They make it possible to create lists of objects that don't have pointer fields. You never have to use Element classes in abstract data type containers. They are used only by fundamental data structures.

Another class type modifier, Imp, stands for Implementation. In general, classes that end with Imp are fundamental data structures that are used in the construction of abstract containers. TDoubleListImp, for example, implements a double-linked list. You may use Imp classes to construct your own containers, but this requires a good understanding of the class internals. In most cases, you are better off using an abstract container such as TDequeAsDoubleList rather than TDoubleListImp on which the abstract container is based.

A third and final class type modifier, Iterator, refers to a class that provides iterative services for a like-named container or fundamental structure. An iterator provides access to all of a container's objects. TDequeAsVectorIterator, for example, provides an iterator for objects in a TDequeAsVector container. Iterator classes that end with Imp provide iterative services for fundamental structures. TDoubleListIteratorImp, for instance, provides the implementation of an iterator for objects in a TDoubleListImp structure.

Finally, there's one class, TShouldDelete, that marches to a different drummer. As its name suggests, this special class indicates whether a container should delete the objects it contains, or whether you accept that responsibility. See "Object Ownership" in this chapter for more information about this class.

Developing Class Consciousness

After you become familiar with class naming conventions and the general library layout, you're ready to begin storing data in containers. The following sections explain some key techniques in using containers and selecting from the library's many features.

Direct and Indirect Containers

Regardless of the container type, an important decision to make is whether to store objects indirectly (by pointer) or directly (by copying). Containers with I in their names, such as TIQueueAsVector, store objects indirectly as pointers. Containers with no I (TQueueAsVector, for example) store objects directly. Listing 9.2, Direct.cpp, demonstrates how to use direct and indirect containers.

Listing 9.2. Direct.cpp (Demonstrates direct and indirect containers).

```
//===============================================================
// Direct.cpp -- Demonstrates direct and indirect containers
// To compile:
//    bcc direct bidss.lib
// To run:
//    direct
// Copyright (c) 1996 by Tom Swan. All rights reserved.
//===============================================================
```

```
#include <iostream.h>
#include <cstring.h>
#include <classlib\arrays.h>

// Direct and indirect string containers
TArrayAsVector<string> dStrings(10);
TIArrayAsVector<string> iStrings(10);

void main()
{
  bool done = false;  // while-loop control variable
  int i;              // for-loop control variable
  string s;           // Input string object
  char buf[81];       // Input character buffer

  while (!done) {
    cout << "Enter a string: ";       // Prompt for string
    cin.getline(buf, sizeof(buf));    // Input into buffer
    s = buf;                          // Convert to string object
    if (s.length() == 0)              // Check if length is zero
      done = true;                    // If yes, end while loop
    else {                            // ...else...
      dStrings.Add(s);                // Add to direct container
      iStrings.Add(new string(s));    // Add to indirect container
    }
  }

  // Display direct container objects
  cout << endl;
  cout << "Direct string array" << endl;
  for (i = 0; i < dStrings.GetItemsInContainer(); i++)
    cout << dStrings[i] << endl;

  // Display indirect container objects
  cout << endl;
  cout << "Indirect string array" << endl;
  for (i = 0; i < iStrings.GetItemsInContainer(); i++)
    cout << *iStrings[i] << endl;
}
```

The program defines two containers that can store objects of the Borland string class, defined in Cstring.h. This statement, for example, creates a container that can store string objects directly:

```
TArrayAsVector<string> dStrings(10);
```

The following statement, which looks similar, but selects a different class, creates a container that can store pointers to dynamic strings created by new:

```
TIArrayAsVector<string> iStrings(10);
```

The two containers, dStrings and iStrings, offer identical functions and capabilities. They differ only in that dStrings makes a copy of an inserted string; iStrings saves a pointer to a string object.

The program next prompts you to enter a string, which is placed in a char buffer. After using the buffer to construct a string object, s, the program inserts it into dStrings by calling the container class's Add function:

```
dStrings.Add(s);
```

The Add function inserts a new object into an array container. Not all container classes have an Add function, but all have at least one method for inserting objects. To insert a string into the other container, iStrings, the program uses this statement:

```
iStrings.Add(new string(s));
```

It is not correct to pass the address of s to the indirect container's Add function. The string variable s is a temporary object, which is allocated space on the program's stack. Passing that object's address to an indirect container is likely to cause all sorts of problems when the container is destroyed. The moral is this: *when using indirect containers, always know where your objects are.* A good course of action, as shown here, is to use new to create a dynamic object of a string for inserting in a container.

Because the sample containers are arrays, they offer a GetItemsInContainer function that reports the number of stored strings. The program uses this function in a for loop to display the objects in the direct container:

```
for (i = 0; i < dStrings.GetItemsInContainer(); i++)
  cout << dStrings[i] << endl;
```

Displaying the objects in the indirect container is nearly the same, but requires dereferencing the array elements because they are pointers:

```
for (i = 0; i < iStrings.GetItemsInContainer(); i++)
  cout << *iStrings[i] << endl;  // Note dereference *
```

> **TIP**
>
> Delete the asterisk from the preceding statement, recompile, and run the program. It now displays the address of each object because the compiler evaluates iStrings[i] as a string pointer.

Iterators

An iterator provides an alternate method for accessing a container's objects. Iterators are available for abstract containers such as arrays and queues, and also for fundamental structures such as lists and vectors.

Using an iterator, you can "walk through" the objects in a structure without removing them. Normally, for example, only the top object in a stack is available for inspection, and to obtain other objects, you have to remove them by calling Pop. With an iterator, however, you can "walk the stack" to perform operations on the stack's contents.

A simple example demonstrates how to use an iterator to walk through the objects in a queue. As in Direct.cpp, Listing 9.3, Iterate.cpp, stores a collection of string objects indirectly, but this time, in a container of the TIQueueAsDoubleList class.

Listing 9.3. Iterate.cpp (Demonstrates iterators).

```
//================================================================
// Iterate.cpp -- Demonstrates iterators
// To compile:
//   bcc iterate bidss.lib
// To run:
//   iterate
// Copyright (c) 1996 by Tom Swan. All rights reserved.
//================================================================

#include <iostream.h>
#include <cstring.h>
#include <classlib\queues.h>

// Define global indirect-string, queue container
TIQueueAsDoubleList<string> iQueue;

void main()
{
// Insert a few strings into the queue
  iQueue.Put(new string("Line up"));
  iQueue.Put(new string("for the"));
  iQueue.Put(new string("Magical"));
  iQueue.Put(new string("Mystery"));
  iQueue.Put(new string("Tour"   ));

// Define indirect-string iterator for iQueue
  TIQueueAsDoubleListIterator<string> iterator(iQueue);

// Use iterator to "walk the queue"
  cout << "\nWalk the queue using an iterator:" << endl;
  cout << "-------------------------------" << endl;
  while (iterator != 0) {
    cout << *iterator.Current() << endl;
    iterator++;
  }

// Use standard method to extract queue's objects
  cout << "\nExtract queue objects:" << endl;
  cout << "-------------------------------" << endl;
  while (!iQueue.IsEmpty()) {
    string *p = iQueue.Get();
    cout << *p << endl;
    delete p;
  }
}
```

For the container, the program defines a global object, iQueue. The container is indirect (its class name begins with TI), and therefore, it stores pointers to string objects:

```
TIQueueAsDoubleList<string> iQueue;
```

As I mentioned, it's usually best to use new for creating dynamic objects to be stored indirectly in containers. To add some strings to the queue, the program passes new's pointers to Put, a member of all queue containers. Put for queues is analogous to Add for arrays.

```
iQueue.Put(new string("Magical"));
iQueue.Put(new string("Mystery"));
```

Next, the program constructs an iterator of a class designed for use with TIQueueAsDoubleList. To form the class name, add Iterator to its end:

```
TIQueueAsDoubleListIterator<string> iterator(iQueue);
```

That's a mouthful and a half, and to reduce confusion, it's often useful to invent a shorter alias with a typedef statement such as

```
typedef TIQueueAsDoubleListIterator<string> TIterator;
```

This typedef directive states that, from now on, TIterator is a synonym for the preceding gobble-dygook. The container definition is now much prettier (and is a lot easier to read):

```
TIterator iterator(iQueue);
```

Either way, the definition constructs an iterator object of type TIQueueAsDoubleListIterator<string>. Passing iQueue to the iterator's constructor links it to that container. Operations involving iterator are performed on iQueue's data.

For example, the expression iterator.Current returns the current object from iQueue—the first such object initially. If the container is empty, the iterator returns a null pointer (or a null reference for direct-storage containers).

When used in an expression, an iterator object returns a value of type int. It can do that because iterator classes overload the int operator. Thus, when an iterator object is used in an expression that evaluates to int, the program calls the overloaded int operator function for that value. If this value is zero (false), you know that the iterator has finished scanning the container's data.

You can use iterator functions and values to "walk the queue," displaying the container's objects in their stored order:

```
while (iterator != 0) {  // Uses overloaded int() operator
  cout << *iterator.Current() << endl;  // Gets current object
  iterator++;              // Increments iterator to next object
}
```

All iterators implement ++ operators (postfix and prefix varieties). As the preceding fragment demonstrates, you can use the expression iterator++ (or ++iterator) to increment the iterator object to the next object in the container. The ++ operators return an object of the container's type, a fact that you can use to write efficient loops. Reset the iterator by calling its Restart function and define a string pointer, p:

```
iterator.Restart();  // Reset iterator to first object
string *p;           // Define a string pointer
```

You can now write a `while` loop (or another kind) to walk the container:

```
while (p = iterator++)   // Get current object and advance iterator
  cout << *p << endl;    // Display object addressed by p
```

The `while` loop's control expression assigns the address of the current `string` object to `p`, and advances the iterator to the next object. Upon reaching the last object, the control expression evaluates to zero, ending the loop. A simple output stream statement displays each `string` object.

If you compiled the preceding code, you probably received a warning about a "possibly incorrect assignment" because the compiler recognizes = as a possible mistake for ==. The single equal sign is correct, however, because we want to *assign* the iterator's return value to p. If the warning bothers you, change the preceding code to the following, which is exactly equivalent, though a bit harder to read:

```
while ((p = iterator++) != 0)
  cout << *p << endl;
```

All iterators have at least a constructor, a `Restart` function, and overloaded `int` and `++` operators. Some iterators also provide functions for special uses. Array iterators, for example, overload `Restart` with two parameters:

```
void Restart(unsigned start, unsigned stop);
```

Pass index values to `Restart` to begin an iteration over a restricted range of objects in an array container.

Object Ownership

Storing objects in containers is not at all like storing candy in a dish. Candy is easy. You dump it in, take out a piece, eat it, and it's gone. Container objects require more care to use (but are less fattening). You may have to know whether dynamic objects were created by `new`, or whether they exist temporarily on the stack or globally in a data segment. You may have to determine if an object is a copy of another, or if it's the Real McCoy. Class objects might also need destructors, especially if they address other dynamic structures. In such cases, you must be sure that the destructor is called, and that your objects are properly destroyed at the correct times.

These concerns lead to the question of whether a container should *own* the objects it stores. In general terms, when a container owns its objects, the container can delete them automatically when the objects are removed. When a container does not own its objects, it's your responsibility to delete them as necessary.

How To Specify Object Ownership

Specify object ownership by constructing an indirect container such as `TIArrayAsVector` and calling functions inherited from `TShouldDelete`. For example, consider this indirect container, which stores pointers to `string` objects:

```
TIArrayAsVector<string> stuff(100);
```

To determine whether `stuff` owns its objects (it does by default), call `OwnsElements`, inherited from `TShouldDelete`:

```
cout << stuff.OwnsElements() << endl;
```

`OwnsElements` returns true (1) if the container owns its objects, or false (0) if not.

To change a container's ownership, pass true or false to a second, overloaded, `OwnsElements` function, which returns `void`. It's probably a good idea to define `TRUE` and `FALSE` constants to keep your intentions clear:

```
#define TRUE 1
#define FALSE 0
...
stuff.OwnsElements(FALSE);  // Disable object ownership
```

> **NOTE**
>
> Because Borland has frozen the BIDS library, classes and functions do not use the newer `bool` data type, or the constants `true` or `false`. All true-and-false functions and variables are of type `int`.

Turning ownership off for the `stuff` container tells it *not* to delete its objects automatically. To enable automatic deletion, pass `TRUE` to `OwnsElements`:

```
stuff.OwnsElements(FALSE);
```

By the way, you can't do any of this with direct-object container classes, which are not derived from `TShouldDelete`. If you construct a direct-object container like

```
TArrayAsVector<string> stuff2(100);
```

you cannot change `stuff2`'s object-ownership with

```
stuff2.OwnsElements(TRUE);  // ???
```

Compiling that statement generates the error "'OwnsElements' is not a member of 'TArrayAsVector<string>'" because direct-object container classes are not derived from TShouldDelete. You can specify ownership rules only for indirect containers—those that store pointers to objects.

How To Use Object Ownership

After specifying whether an indirect container owns its objects, you may call member functions to remove, and optionally delete, one or more objects in the container. Listing 9.4, Owner.cpp, demonstrates some of these basic techniques.

Listing 9.4. Owner.cpp (Demonstrates object ownership).

```
//================================================================
// Owner.cpp -- Demonstrates object ownership
// To compile:
//    bcc owner bidss.lib
// To run:
//    owner
// Copyright (c) 1996 by Tom Swan. All rights reserved.
//================================================================

#include <iostream.h>
#include <cstring.h>
#include <classlib\arrays.h>

// Define type name aliases
typedef TIArrayAsVector<string> TContainer;
typedef TIArrayAsVectorIterator<string> TIterator;

// Function prototype: displays container contents
void ShowMe(const char *msg, TContainer &cr);

void main()
{
  TContainer *cp;      // Container pointer
  string s("Tulips"); // A string object

  // Construct container and display its ownership rule
  cp = new TContainer(10, 0, 10);
  cout << endl;
  cout << "Array owns objects: ";
  if (cp->OwnsElements())
    cout << "TRUE" << endl;
  else
    cout << "FALSE" << endl;

  // Add some string objects to the container
  cp->Add(new string("Tip"));
  cp->Add(new string("Toe"));
  cp->Add(new string("Through"));
  cp->Add(new string("The"));
  cp->Add(&s);  // !!!Dangerous!!! See text.
  ShowMe("Original array:", *cp);

  // Detach and destroy an object by index
  cp->Detach(2, TShouldDelete::Delete);
  ShowMe("After Detach(2, Delete)", *cp);

  // Detach and do NOT destroy a nonglobal object
  cp->Detach(&s, TShouldDelete::NoDelete);
  ShowMe("After Detach(&s, NoDelete)", *cp);

  // Detach and possibly destroy last object
  int n = cp->GetItemsInContainer();
  cp->Detach(n - 1, TShouldDelete::DefDelete);
  ShowMe("After Detach(n - 1, DefDelete)", *cp);

  // Remove and possibly destroy all objects
  cp->Flush();
```

continues

Listing 9.4. continued

```
  ShowMe("After Flush()", *cp);

  // Delete the container. Does NOT destroy objects???
  delete cp;
}

// Display contents of container cr, passed by reference
void ShowMe(const char *msg, TContainer &cr)
{
  TIterator iterator(cr);   // Construct iterator for container
  string *sp;               // Addresses container objects

  cout << endl << msg << endl;              // Display message
  cout << "Items in container = ";          // Display message
  cout << cr.GetItemsInContainer() << endl; // Display num items
  while ((sp = iterator++) != 0)            // Loop on iterator
    cout << " " << *sp;                     // Display items
  cout << endl;                             // Start new line
}
```

To reduce confusingly long declarations, the program defines two type aliases. TContainer is defined as an indirect string array, implemented using a vector. TIterator is an iterator for that container. The program defines a pointer to TContainer, and uses new to construct the container object:

```
TContainer *cp;
cp = new TContainer(10, 0, 10);
```

After displaying whether the container that cp addresses owns its objects (it does by default), the program adds some string objects with statements such as

```
cp->Add(new string("Tip"));
```

Notice that the program also passes the address of a temporary string object, s, which is stored on the system stack:

```
cp->Add(&s);  // !!!
```

This is a *very* dangerous practice that is best avoided. If you must add nonglobal objects by address to an indirect container, however, you can do so safely by following the advice in this section. Most important, you must not allow the container to delete the object. Doing that might link a portion of the stack into the heap's free-memory pool, an error that will almost surely vaporize the stack and heap (not to mention the program) by allocating memory on top of function return addresses.

To detach an object from the container, the program executes this statement:

```
cp->Detach(2, TShouldDelete::Delete);
```

The first argument, 2, indicates that the *third* object should be detached from the container. Other objects are moved up to take the deleted object's place. The second argument, TShouldDelete::Delete, specifies that, regardless of ownership, this object should be deleted.

You can also elect not to delete an object, regardless of the container's ownership setting. This is necessary, for example, to detach the nonglobal `string` object from the container:

```
cp->Detach(&s, TShouldDelete::NoDelete);
```

You must execute a similar statement for *every* nonglobal object in an indirect container before calling any other function that might delete that object. For instance, if the program did not first detach the nonglobal s, this statement would most likely corrupt the heap:

```
cp->Flush();
```

Calling `Flush` deletes all objects that a container owns. To avoid flushing your code down the drain, if the container addresses any nonglobal objects, either disable ownership or detach the objects beforehand.

You can also write statements that delete objects on the condition that the container owns them. For example, the program deletes the last object, indexed by integer n, with this statement:

```
cp->Detach(n - 1, TShouldDelete::DefDelete);
```

Passing `DefDelete` to `Detach` tells the function to delete the removed object, but only if the container owns it. If the container does not own its objects, the statement removes the object, but does not delete its memory.

Finally, the sample program deletes the container, which was allocated memory by `new`:

```
delete cp;
```

You might expect that statement also to delete all owned objects left in the container. In my not-so-humble opinion, indirect containers probably *should* do that, but they don't. To be sure that every object is properly deleted, you can take one of two corrective measures:

1. Call `Flush` before deleting the container.
2. Derive a new container class and write a destructor that calls `Flush`.

The first solution, used in the sample program, is easy, but if you forget to call `Flush`, your program can develop a nasty memory leak. The second solution ensures that destroying a dynamic container always calls `Flush`. To try out this technique, declare a new class template in Owner.cpp:

```
template <class T> class TIMyArrayAsVector :
  public TIArrayAsVector<T> {
public:
  TIMyArrayAsVector(int upper, int lower = 0, int delta = 0) :
    TIArrayAsVector<T>(upper, lower, delta) { }
  ~TIMyArrayAsVector() { Flush(); }
};
```

The template class, `TIMyArrayAsVector`, calls its ancestor constructor. A destructor calls `Flush`, with a default argument of `DefDelete`. A container constructed of this class automatically deletes its owned objects when the container is destroyed.

If you make the preceding change to Owner.cpp, also revise the `typedef` alias for `TContainer` to the following. The modified program then uses the new derived class.

```
typedef TIMyArrayAsVector<string> TContainer;
```

> **TIP**
>
> Introducing a derived class into a program often requires modifying all former uses of that class's ancestor. With an alias such as `TContainer`, however, you can update an entire program to use a new class by changing a single `typedef` declaration. In this sense, you can think of `typedef` aliases as data type constants. Use them as you do other constants to simplify program maintenance.

Using Abstract Data Types

Following are a few notes about member functions you can call for various container classes. There are too many functions to cover them all here, but I have tried to choose those that are most generally useful.

For reference, each section specifies the header that declares classes of a certain type. Include one or more of these headers to use their classes.

Arrays (arrays.h)

Array containers are similar to C-style arrays, such as `char` buffers, but can store any objects or pointers. Unlike common arrays, array containers are dynamic—they resize automatically to accommodate more information. Like C arrays, array containers provide indexed access to objects through the `[]` indexing operator. Table 9.4 lists the library's array containers.

Table 9.4. Array containers.

Container	Description
TArrayAsVector	Arrays (indexed collections)
TSArrayAsVector	Sorted arrays
TIArrayAsVector	Indirect arrays
TISArrayAsVector	Indirect, sorted arrays

Construct a 10-element `string` array like this:

```
TArrayAsVector<string> array(10);
```

I'll use Borland's string class for the data type of most objects in this section, but you can use any other types as well. You can optionally specify an array's lower index. This, for example, creates a nine-element array with indexes from 2 to 10:

```
TArrayAsVector<string> array(10, 2);
```

Specify an optional *delta* value as a third argument:

```
TArrayAsVector<string> array(99, 0, 25);
```

This definition creates an array that can initially store up to 100 string objects, indexed from 0 to 99. The array automatically expands by 25 additional elements at a time—if, for example, you add more than 100 elements to the container.

Call Add to insert an object into the next available array position:

```
array.Add(string("Abcdefg"));
```

Or, call AddAt to insert an object and move others (if any) upward:

```
array.AddAt(string("Abcdefg"), 6);
```

Use indexing expressions to access array elements:

```
cout << array[6] << endl;
```

To delete an object, call Destroy:

```
array.Destroy(4);   // Destroy object at array[4]
array.Destroy(s);   // Destroy string matching s
```

Calling Destroy removes *and deletes* the object. Call Detach to remove objects, but not destroy them:

```
array.Detach(5);
```

With indirect containers (those with class names that have an I in them), if object-ownership is enabled, to detach and destroy an object, pass a second argument to Detach. If that argument is DefDelete, then the object is deleted only if the container owns it:

```
array.Detach(5, TShouldDelete::DefDelete);
```

Three other class member functions help you write code for processing the objects in an array container. These functions are

- ForEach: Passes the address of each object, and an optional pointer argument, to a function of type IterFunc.
- FirstThat: Returns a pointer to the first object in the container for which a user-supplied function of type CondFunc returns true.
- LastThat: Returns a pointer to the last object in the container for which a user-supplied function of type CondFunc returns true.

Listing 9.5, Array.cpp, demonstrates how to use these three functions, which many other types of container classes also provide.

Listing 9.5. Array.cpp (Demonstrates ForEach, FirstThat, and LastThat).

```
//================================================================
// Array.cpp -- Demonstrates ForEach, FirstThat, and LastThat
// To compile:
//    bcc array bidss.lib
// To run:
//    array
// Copyright (c) 1996 by Tom Swan. All rights reserved.
//================================================================

#include <iostream.h>
#include <classlib\arrays.h>

// Function prototypes
void ShowOne(long &i, void *);
int GreaterThan(const long&i, void *value);
int LessThan(const long&i, void *value);

// Construct array container of long values
TArrayAsVector<long> array(10);

void main()
{
  long value;       // Passed to GreaterThan and LessThan
  long *vp;         // Holds result of FirstThat and LastThat

  // Add some values to the container
  array.Add(100);
  array.Add(200);
  array.Add(300);
  array.Add(400);
  array.Add(500);

  // Use ForEach to display objects in array
  cout << "Array contents:" << endl;
  array.ForEach(ShowOne, 0);

  // Demonstrate FirstThat search
  value = 350;
  vp = array.FirstThat(GreaterThan, &value);
  if (vp) {
    cout << endl;
    cout << "First value greater than " << value;
    cout << " = " << *vp << endl;
  }

  // Demonstrate LastThat search
  vp = array.LastThat(LessThan, &value);
  if (vp) {
    cout << endl;
    cout << "Last value less than " << value;
    cout << " = " << *vp << endl;
  }
}
```

```
// Display one object value i; void * not used
void ShowOne(long &i, void *)
{
  cout << i << endl;
}

// Return true if i is greater than addressed value
int GreaterThan(const long&i, void *value)
{
  return i > *(long *)value;
}

// Return true if i is less than addressed value
int LessThan(const long&i, void *value)
{
  return i < *(long *)value;
}
```

In the sample program, the following statement displays array's values by calling the container class's ForEach function. That function calls another, ShowOne, for each object in the array.

```
array.ForEach(ShowOne, 0);
```

You could replace the second argument, 0, with the address of some other data to pass to ShowOne. There is no such data in this example. You may name ShowOne something else, but it must return void and declare two parameters:

```
void ShowOne(long &i, void *);
```

- The first parameter is of type T &—a reference to an object of type T—which, in this example, is long.
- The second parameter is a generic pointer of type void *, which receives the second argument passed to ForEach.

To search an array container, you can call one of two other functions, FirstThat and LastThat. Their names suggest their purposes. FirstThat returns true for the first object (searching from low to high indexes) that satisfies a condition. LastThat returns true for the last object (searching from high to low indexes) that satisfies a condition.

In either case, specify a condition by supplying a CondFunc function as the program's two examples demonstrate:

```
int GreaterThan(const long&i, void *value);
int LessThan(const long&i, void *value);
```

You may name these functions anything you like, but they must return int values, and they must declare two parameters:

- The first parameter must be of type const T &—a constant reference to an object of type T—which in this example, is const long.
- The second parameter must be a generic pointer of type void *, which receives the value passed in the second argument to FirstThat or LastThat.

The program calls `FirstThat`, passing the `GreaterThan` function by address along with a second value, also passed by address. `FirstThat` calls `GreaterThan` for each object in the container until the function returns true.

```
vp = array.FirstThat(GreaterThan, &value);
```

Similarly, `LastThat` calls `LessThan` for each object until that function returns true:

```
vp = array.LastThat(LessThan, &value);
```

Bags (bags.h)

Think of a bag as—well, a *bag*. It's a general-purpose container that stores collections of objects in no particular order, like groceries thrown into a paper bag. The only way to get an object out of a bag is to specify its value. You also can search bags, flush them, and perform a few other operations demonstrated here. Table 9.5 lists the library's bag containers.

Table 9.5. Bag containers.

Container	Description
TBagAsVector	Bags (arbitrary collections)
TIBagAsVector	Indirect bags

When using bags, the most important decision to make is whether you want paper or plastic. (Just kidding.) Listing 9.6, Bag.cpp, demonstrates some of the functions that you can call for bag containers.

Listing 9.6. Bag.cpp (Demonstrates bag containers).

```
//================================================================
// Bag.cpp -- Demonstrates bag containers
// To compile:
//    bcc bag bidss.lib
// To run:
//    bag
// Copyright (c) 1996 by Tom Swan. All rights reserved.
//================================================================

#include <iostream.h>
#include <cstring.h>
#include <classlib\bags.h>

// Function prototype
void Show(const char *msg);
```

```
// Construct default-size indirect bag of string pointers
TIBagAsVector<string> bag;

void main()
{
  char buffer[81];  // Input string buffer

  // Stuff some strings into the bag
  bag.Add(new string("Dog"));
  bag.Add(new string("Cag"));
  bag.Add(new string("Bird"));
  bag.Add(new string("Elephant"));
  bag.Add(new string("Whale"));
  bag.Add(new string("Dolphin"));
  bag.Add(new string("Pelican"));

  Show("Original bag");

  // Prompt and search for an object to delete
  cout << "Enter object to delete: ";
  cin.getline(buffer, sizeof(buffer), '\n');
  string findMe(buffer);

  // Search bag and delete object or display error message
  if (bag.HasMember(&findMe)) {
    string *sp = bag.Find(&findMe);
    if (sp) {
      cout << endl << "Deleting " << *sp << endl;
      bag.Detach(sp, TShouldDelete::NoDelete);
      cout << *sp << " is deleted";
      delete sp;
    }
  } else {
    cout << "Object not found" << endl;
  }

  Show("Contents after deletion");

  // Set ownership and flush bag's objects
  bag.OwnsElements(true);
  bag.Flush();
}

// Display a message and show bag's contents
void Show(const char *msg)
{
  TIBagAsVectorIterator<string> iterator(bag);
  string *sp;

  cout << endl << msg << endl;
  cout << "Number of objects: ";
  cout << bag.GetItemsInContainer() << endl;
  while ((sp = iterator++) != 0)
    cout << *sp << endl;
  cout << endl;
}
```

Constructing bags and inserting objects into them is the same as for arrays. Call `Add` to insert an object into a bag:

```
bag.Add(new string("Dog"));
```

To locate an object in a bag, you have to search for it. Call `HasMember` to determine whether a value is stored in a bag. For example, after prompting you for a string, `findMe`, the program calls `HasMember` to determine whether the string is in the bag:

```
if (bag.hasMember(&findMe)) {
  // ...
}
```

Or, you call `Find` to locate an object:

```
string *sp = bag.Find(&findMe);
```

The program wouldn't have to call both `HasMember` and `Find`—I did that just to show their differences.

Bag classes also provide `Detach` and `Flush` functions, which work the same as the ones you've already seen. Indirect bag classes are derived in part from `TShouldDelete`, and as the program demonstrates, you can call the inherited `OwnsElements` to change a bag's object ownership setting. Bags normally own their objects, so the sample statement is redundant.

Deques (deques.h)

The word *deque* is a phonetic abbreviation for *double-ended queue*. Think of a deque as a kind of train track, open at both ends. You can roll objects into a deque from the front or back, and you can switch them out from either end. See also "Queues" in this chapter.

In classic deques, you are not permitted access to objects in between the ones at the ends. A deque container class, however, provides `ForEach`, `FirstThat`, and `LastThat` functions, which work the same as their counterparts in arrays. You can also construct iterators to walk objects in a deque. To play by the rules, however, you should access only the first and last objects stored in a deque.

Table 9.6 lists the library's deque containers.

Table 9.6. Deque (double-ended queue) containers.

Container	Description
TDequeAsVector	Deques (double-ended queues)
TIDequeAsVector	Indirect deques
TDequeAsDoubleList	Deques as double lists
TIDequeAsDoubleList	Indirect dequeus as double lists

Deques are frequently of value in scheduling, and for creating versatile lists that you can manipulate from either end. As vectors, large deques might waste memory, because in most applications, deques tend to grow and shrink greatly in size. Potentially large deques, then, might be better implemented as lists, using a type such as TDequeAsDoubleList.

Listing 9.7 demonstrates some of the functions you can call for deque containers.

Listing 9.7. Deque.cpp (Demonstrates deque containers).

```
//================================================================
// Deque.cpp -- Demonstrates deque containers
// To compile:
//    bcc deque bidss.lib
// To run:
//    deque
// Copyright (c) 1996 by Tom Swan. All rights reserved.
//================================================================

#include <iostream.h>
#include <cstring.h>
#include <classlib\deques.h>

// Function prototype
void Show(const char *msg);

// Define indirect deque of strings as double list
TIDequeAsDoubleList<string> deque;

void main()
{
  string *sp;  // Holds results from GetLeft and GetRight

  // Insert strings at left
  deque.PutLeft(new string("One"));
  deque.PutLeft(new string("Two"));
  deque.PutLeft(new string("Three"));
  deque.PutLeft(new string("Four"));

  // Insert strings at right
  deque.PutRight(new string("Five"));
  deque.PutRight(new string("Six"));
  deque.PutRight(new string("Seven"));
  deque.PutRight(new string("Eight"));

  Show("Original contents");
```

continues

Listing 9.7. continued

```
    // Display leftmost string in deque
    cout << "Leftmost object = ";
    cout << *deque.PeekLeft() << endl;

    // Display rightmost string in deque
    cout << "Rightmost object = ";
    cout << *deque.PeekRight() << endl;

    // Remove leftmost string from deque
    sp = deque.GetLeft();
    delete sp;
    Show("After removing head");

    // Remove rightmost string from deque
    sp = deque.GetRight();
    delete sp;
    Show("After removing tail");

    // Delete remaining strings
    deque.Flush();
}

// Display message and show deque contents
void Show(const char *msg)
{
    TIDequeAsDoubleListIterator<string> iterator(deque);
    string *sp;

    cout << endl << msg << endl;
    cout << "Number of objects: ";
    cout << deque.GetItemsInContainer() << endl;
    while ((sp = iterator++) != 0)
      cout << " " << *sp;
    cout << endl << endl;
}
```

As with most container classes, deques have unique functions to insert, inspect, and remove objects. To insert objects at the left end, call `PutLeft`. To insert objects at the right, call `PutRight`:

```
deque.PutLeft(new string("One"));
deque.PutRight(new string("Five"));
```

> **NOTE**
>
> The terms *left* and *right* are conceptual—they are just words that distinguish the two ends of a deque. There are, of course, no "left" and "right" directions in memory.

To inspect, but not remove, objects at either end of a deque, call `PeekLeft` and `PeekRight`. In the sample program, these functions are dereferenced because the deque object indirectly stores strings as pointers:

```
cout << *deque.PeekLeft() << endl;
cout << *deque.PeekRight() << endl;
```

To remove an object from a deque, call GetLeft or GetRight. The object is never deleted, even for deque containers that own their objects (sp is a string pointer in this example):

```
sp = deque.GetLeft();
sp = deque.GetRight();
```

Deque classes support many functions that you have already seen such as ForEach, FirstThat, LastThat, Flush, and GetItemsInContainer. They work the same as their counterparts in other classes.

Dictionaries (assoc.h, dict.h)

With a dictionary class, you create *associative containers* that store values identified by keys. You can search the dictionary for a given key's associated value.

You could create associative containers using other classes—arrays, linked lists, and sets, for example. A dictionary class is advantageous, however, because it stores keys in a *hash table,* which can be searched quickly.

Unlike other container classes, dictionary objects cannot be any types. They must be *association objects,* constructed from one of the TxAssociation classes listed in Table 9.7a.

Table 9.7a. TxAssociation classes.

Class	Key	Value
TDDAssociation	Direct	Indirect
TDIAssociation	Direct	Indirect
TIDAssociation	Indirect	Direct
TIIAssociation	Indirect	Indirect
TMDDAssociation	Memory managed class for TDDAssociation	
TMDIAssociation	Memory managed class for TMDIAssociation	
TMIDAssociation	Memory managed class for TMIDAssociation	
TMIIAssociation	Memory managed class for TMIIAssociation	

After selecting a TxAssociation class, you can create objects of that class and insert them into a dictionary container. The dictionary must be an object of a class from Table 9.7b. A direct dictionary stores copies of TxAssociation objects. An indirect dictionary stores pointers to TxAssociation objects. The keys and values in either case may be directly or indirectly stored.

Table 9.7b. Dictionary containers.

Container	Description
TDictionaryAsHashTable	Dictionaries (associative collections)
TIDictionaryAsHashTable	Indirect dictionaries

An association class such as TIDAssociation relates a key (K) with value (V). The key and value may be of any types, and either or both may be directly or indirectly stored. All association classes perform identical services, but for different combinations of keys and values.

Listing 9.8, Dict.cpp, demonstrates how to use associations to create a small antonym dictionary. Run the program and enter one of the listed keyword strings (Day, Girl, Up, Water) for its antonym.

Listing 9.8. Dict.cpp (Demonstrates association and dictionary classes).

```
//=============================================================
// Dict.cpp -- Demonstrates association and dictionary classes
// To compile:
//   bcc dict bidss.lib
// To run:
//   dict
// Copyright (c) 1996 by Tom Swan. All rights reserved.
//=============================================================

#include <iostream.h>
#include <cstring.h>
#include <classlib\assoc.h>
#include <classlib\dict.h>

// Declare class for keys, derived from string
class TKey: public string {
public:
  TKey() : string() { }
  TKey(const char *s) : string(s) { }
  unsigned HashValue() const { return hash(); }
};

// Declare class for values, also derived from string
class TValue: public string {
public:
  TValue() : string() { }
  TValue(const char *s) : string(s) { }
};

// Try to make this program a little more readable
typedef TDDAssociation<TKey, TValue> TAssoc;
typedef TIDictionaryAsHashTable<TAssoc> TDict;
typedef TIDictionaryAsHashTableIterator<TAssoc> TIter;
```

```
// Function prototype
void ShowKeys();

// Define globlal dictionary container
TDict antonyms;

void main()
{
  char buffer[81];
  TAssoc *searchKey;
  TAssoc *ap;

  string::set_case_sensitive(0);  // Turn off case sensitivity

  // Insert a few associations into the container
  antonyms.Add(new TAssoc("Girl"  , "Boy"  ));
  antonyms.Add(new TAssoc("Water" , "Land" ));
  antonyms.Add(new TAssoc("Day"   , "Night"));
  antonyms.Add(new TAssoc("Up"    , "Down" ));

  ShowKeys();

  // Prompt for a search key
  cout << "Enter key: ";
  cin.getline(buffer, sizeof(buffer), '\n');
  cout << endl;

  // Construct association object from user entry
  searchKey = new TAssoc(buffer, 0);

  // Search for association and display if found
  ap = antonyms.Find(searchKey);
  if (ap)
    cout << "Antonym = " << ap->Value() << endl;
  else
    cout << "Key not found" << endl;

  // Flush all association objects from the dictionary
  antonyms.Flush(TShouldDelete::Delete);
}

// Use iterator to display keys in dictionary
void ShowKeys()
{
  TIter iterator(antonyms);
  TAssoc *p;

  cout << endl << endl;
  cout << "Number of associations = ";
  cout << antonyms.GetItemsInContainer() << endl;
  cout << endl << "Keys in database: ";
  while ((p = iterator++) != 0)
    cout << "  " << p->Key();
  cout << endl << endl;
}
```

The sample listing derives two classes, TKey and TValue, from the Borland string class. You don't have to use class objects for keys and values, but in most cases, this is the best and easiest approach.

The TKey class must provide a function named HashValue. It also must have two constructors: a default (with no parameters) and an alternate with a parameter of the type of data that represents a search key. The key does not have to be a string as it is here—you can create keys of any types.

If you don't want to use a class for key objects, you must instead provide a global HashValue function defined as

```
unsigned HashValue(K &keyRef);
```

Either way—as a class member or a global function—HashValue returns an unsigned value based on keyRef, a reference to an object of your key's data type (K), TKey in this case. Ideally, HashValue should return a *unique* value for all possible keys, but that ideal is rarely achieved. If too many keys produce the same hash value, however, searches degenerate to linear scans, which can greatly degrade performance.

TIP

When debugging a hash-table driven dictionary, it's often useful to program a temporary HashValue function that returns the same value for all possible keys. This tests the search engine's ability to handle clashes of equal hash values for different keys, and can also provide you with worst-case performance data.

In the sample listing, HashValue simply calls the hash function inherited from the string class. This provides a (probably unique) hash value created from the characters in a string. If you don't want to use this default hash value, replace HashValue with your own function.

NOTE

Borland does not specify the algorithm used by the string::hash function, but it appears to simply exclusive-OR character values in the string.

An association's value can also be any type, but again, a class is often the most convenient. In the sample listing, TValue is derived from string, and it provides two constructors, similar to those in TKey. Unlike keys, however, value classes do not need a HashValue function.

For better readability, the program defines three aliases for the following template class data types:

```
typedef TDDAssociation<TKey, TValue> TAssoc;
typedef TIDictionaryAsHashTable<TAssoc> TDict;
typedef TIDictionaryAsHashTableIterator<TAssoc> TIter;
```

The first line states that TAssoc is an alias for the preceding template declaration, which associates a key and value of the TKey and TValue classes. The TDDAssociation class specifies that keys and values are stored directly. The second line states that TDict is an alias for the preceding dictionary declaration, which specifies TAssoc as its data type. Objects of that type are stored indirectly as pointers in a dictionary of the resulting class. The third line states that TIter is an alias for the preceding template declaration, which creates a class suitable for constructing iterators to access a dictionary's contents.

The aliases simplify the programming for dictionary, association, and iteration objects. The following line, for example, hides its inner complexity beneath the skirts of the TDict alias to create an associative container named antonyms:

```
TDict antonyms;
```

Without aliases, the equivalent declaration is a confusing mess of class names and template brackets:

```
TIDictionaryAsHashTable<TDDAssociation<TKey, TValue>> antonyms;
```

The antonyms container stores pointers to association objects, addressed by a pointer such as

```
TAssoc *searchKey;
```

To add association objects to the dictionary, the program executes statements such as

```
antonyms.Add(new TAssoc("Girl", "Boy"));
```

The statement uses new to create a TAssoc object with the specified key and value strings. Literal strings are acceptable here because the TKey and TValue class constructors specify parameters of type const char*.

To search for a key and value in a dictionary, first construct an object of the association data type, TAssoc in this example:

```
searchKey = new TAssoc(buffer, 0);
```

The buffer argument is an array of char that holds the key that you enter when prompted. The 0 argument sets the value portion of the association to null. A search requires an association object that has only a key, not a value.

To find a key, call Find for the dictionary object. Pass the association search value as an argument. Find returns a value of the type stored in the dictionary, in this case, TAssoc*, assigned to pointer ap:

```
ap = antonyms.Find(searchKey);
```

If ap is not null, it addresses the TAssoc object that contains the specified key. Display the associated value by calling the Value function like this:

```
cout << "Antonym = " << ap->Value() << endl;
```

You can also access the association's key with ap->Key. To delete all dictionary associations before the program ends, call Flush:

```
antonyms.Flush(TShouldDelete::Delete);
```

Notice also how function ShowKeys in the sample program uses an iterator to display the database's keys. Except for the expression p->Key, which is specific to association objects, the programming is nearly identical to other iterations in this chapter. Iterators provide all containers with standard-access methods, even for complex structures such as associative dictionaries.

Queues (queues.h)

If you happen to be British, you probably know what a queue is, but bear with me while I bring my compatriots up to speed.

Americans *line up* at ticket windows; the British *queue up*. A queue is simply a collection in which people—or objects in a computer program—enter at one end and exit from the other.

Good analogies of classic queues are difficult to find, but paratroopers about to leap out of an airplane come close. The first trooper in line is the first out—a queue is a first-in, first-out (FIFO) data structure. Once you have entered the queue, the only way to depart is to jump out the other end. *Yeehah!*

Table 9.8 lists the library's queue containers.

Table 9.8. Queue (FIFO) containers.

Container	Description
TQueueAsVector	Queues (FIFO collections)
TIQueueAsVector	Indirect queues
TQueueAsDoubleList	Queues as double lists
TIQueueAsDoubleList	Indirect queues as double lists

You may create direct or indirect queues that are implemented as vectors or as double lists. In general, you should use vectors only for relatively short queues that do not vary much in size. Use a double list for large queues, or for those that must accommodate a wide range of objects.

Queues are often used to schedule events so that oldest actions (those inserted earliest) are performed first. For example, in a database, complex search expressions could be organized into a queue that specifies which searches to complete before others.

Listing 9.9, Queue.cpp, demonstrates some of the functions you can call for queue containers.

Listing 9.9. Queue.cpp (Demonstrates queue containers).

```
//=================================================================
// Queue.cpp -- Demonstrates queue containers
// To compile:
//    bcc queue bidss.lib
// To run:
//    queue
// Copyright (c) 1996 by Tom Swan. All rights reserved.
//=================================================================

#include <iostream.h>
#include <cstring.h>
#include <classlib\queues.h>

// Define global queue container
TIQueueAsDoubleList<string> queue;

void main()
{
  string *sp;      // Pointer to string object
  int count = 1;   // For numbering output

  cout << endl;
  cout << "MBC2 Production schedule" << endl;
  cout << "------------------------" << endl;

  // Insert string objects into queue
  queue.Put(new string("Finish manuscript"));
  queue.Put(new string("Edit chapters"));
  queue.Put(new string("Review page proofs"));
  queue.Put(new string("Write cover copy"));
  queue.Put(new string("Make last minute changes"));
  queue.Put(new string("Take a vacation"));

  // Remove objects from queue, display, and delete
  while (!queue.IsEmpty()) {
    sp = queue.Get();
    cout << count++ << " : " << *sp << endl;
    delete sp;
  }
}
```

The program defines a queue container for indirectly storing string objects using a double list as the fundamental data structure:

```
TIQueueAsDoubleList<string> queue;
```

351

To use a vector instead, change that line to the following and recompile. No other changes are needed—a good demonstration of how, with container classes, you can easily change internal storage mechanisms without revising any other code.

```
TIQueueAsVector<string> queue;
```

Call Put to insert objects into a queue. This differs from a deque, a "double-ended queue," in which you can insert objects at either end:

```
queue.Put(new string("Review page proofs"));
```

Call Get to extract an object from a queue. The returned object is always the oldest—that is, the one inserted earliest (sp is a string object pointer):

```
sp = queue.Get();
```

Queue classes support several functions that work the same as their counterparts in other classes you have examined. These functions are FirstThat, LastThat, ForEach, Flush, GetItemsInContainer, IsEmpty, and IsFull.

You can also create iterators of types such as TQueueAsDoubleListIterator for accessing all of a queue's objects. This is a nonstandard way to use a queue, but it's a useful technique in special circumstances. Use queue iterators as demonstrated in other listings in this chapter—Deque.cpp, for example.

Sets (sets.h)

C's lack of a *set* data type is widely noted as one of the language's major drawbacks. Other languages such as Pascal make it easy to create sets, typically represented as bitmaps, one bit for each object in a set. This makes sets highly efficient data structures. With sets, for example, you can represent a program's options, a graphic object's color values, or other data in a very small space.

In C, you can use bit-field structures to represent data collections in a similar way, but you have to provide the necessary programming. C can pack bits into structs, but it has no special operators for evaluating set expressions. Bit-field structures also tend to be nonportable.

Unfortunately, the C++ container library's set classes do little to correct the lack of a built-in set data type and the deficiencies of bit-field structures. Set containers do not represent their contents as bit patterns. They are, in fact, merely bags in which duplicate objects are not allowed. You can add and remove objects from set containers, and you can determine whether an object is a member of a set, but that's about it. Operators usually associated with sets—union (+), intersection (*), and difference (-), for example—are strangely lacking. Of all the container classes in the BIDS library, sets are the weakest and least useful.

Table 9.9 lists the library's set containers.

Table 9.9. Set containers.

Container	Description
TSetAsVector	Sets (unique collections)
TISetAsVector	Indirect sets

Use set classes as you do bags. You may construct a set of direct or indirect objects. For example, the following set can store pointers to string objects:

```
TISetAsVector<string> movieSet;
```

Call Add to insert objects into a set:

```
movieSet.Add(new string("Jurassic Park"));
```

If the inserted object already exists, Add has no effect. An object is either a member of a set, or it's not. By definition, a set cannot have any duplications.

Call HasMember, inherited from bag classes, to determine whether an object is a member of a set. Define an object of the proper type:

```
string video("The Birds");
```

Then, call HasMember to determine whether the object is in the set:

```
if (movieSet.HasMember(&video))
{
  cout << "You're in luck." << endl;
  cout << video << " is in your library" << endl;
}
```

IsEmpty returns true for an empty set. IsFull returns true for a full set, which is somewhat ridiculous, as there is no way (other than specifying an initial size in bytes) to predetermine a set's extent. How then, can a set be "full?" That is, how can the set represent a complete range of values when there's no way to inform the set what those values are?

As you can probably tell, set classes are my least favorite in the BIDS library, and in practice, I don't use them. So, let's move on to the library's final (and far more useful) abstract container—the stack.

Stacks (stacks.h)

If there's a classic data structure that's most intimately identified with computers, it's a stack. As you undoubtedly know, your PC's processor has a stack register, which it uses to pick up previously saved addresses for returning from function calls. Programs also pass data to and from functions on the system stack.

Stacks are not limited, however, to their use by a computer's processor. They also come in handy for storing objects of many kinds. Stacks are last-in, first-out (LIFO) containers. You *push* objects onto a stack, and you *pop* them off the stack's top. The most recently pushed object is always the next to be popped.

Table 9.10 lists the library's stack containers.

Table 9.10. Stack (LIFO) containers.

Container	Description
TStackAsVector	Stacks (LIFO collections)
TIStackAsVector	Indirect stacks
TStackAsList	Stacks as linked lists
TIStackAsList	Indirect stacks as linked lists

An earlier example, Stacked.cpp, demonstrated some of the functions you can call for stack classes. See "How to Create a Container" in this chapter for more information on using the classes in Table 9.10.

Summary

- Borland's template class library—also known as the BIDS, for Borland International Data Structures—offers a variety of container classes for storing data objects in many different ways. Version 3.1 provided two libraries—one based on classes, and one based on templates. Beginning with version 4, Borland C++ now provides only the more-versatile template classes. (The old classes are still available, but you should not use them for new code.)

- Borland has stated that it will not further develop the BIDS classes. You may use the library, however, as described in this chapter. Borland recommends for new programs, and to ensure portability, that you use the newer ANSI C++ templates described in the next chapter.

- You may use the template class library in DOS, EasyWin, and Windows programs. Both 16- and 32-bit versions are supported.

- An abstract data type (ADT) provides an abstraction of a data storage method—a stack, for example.

- A fundamental data structure (FDS) provides an internal representation for storing data—a linked list, for example.

- Abstract containers combine one ADT with one FDS. A class such as TArrayAsVector implements an abstract array using a vector for the internal storage mechanism.

- To make full use of the library, you should become familiar with template naming conventions, described in this chapter. All class names begin with T, and are followed by prefaces, ADTs, FDSs, and suffixes that describe the nature of each class. Not all combinations of ADTs and FDSs are provided.

- The container class library has classes for creating abstract containers such as arrays, bags, deques, dictionaries, queues, sets, and stacks.

- The library also provides classes for implementing internal data structures used by abstract containers: binary search trees, double lists, hash tables, lists, and vectors.

- Direct containers store copies of their objects. Indirect containers store pointers to objects.

- Iterators can "walk" the objects in a container. Use iterators to gain read-only access to a container, or a fundamental structure's, data.

- The TShouldDelete class specifies whether an indirect container owns its objects. If so, the container can delete those objects automatically when the objects are removed. You can choose to always delete objects, to never delete them, or to delete them only if the container owns them.

- Only indirect containers are derived in part from TShouldDelete. Direct containers are not derived from TShouldDelete. You never specify object-ownership for direct-storage containers.

10

CHAPTER

Mastering the Standard Template Library

Until recently, one of the drawbacks of C++ has been its reliance on the standard C function library, which does not take advantage of enhancements such as classes, templates, inline code, and exceptions. Although the standard C library provides many useful functions, they are intimately tied to specific data types, which makes the library less than ideally versatile. For example, although standard string functions can search for patterns in null-terminated strings, it's virtually impossible to adapt the functions' algorithms to search other types of data structures.

The C++ standard template library (STL), a comprehensive collection of data structures and algorithms developed by Alexander Stepanov and Meng Lee at HP Labs, is the newest salvo in the battle to create a standard C++ library. The STL has recently been accepted by the ANSI/ISO standards committee for inclusion in the standard C++ library. Borland's implementation of the STL plus other components comes from Rogue Wave Software.

At the moment, the STL is but a piece of a larger whole, which continues to evolve and grow. Eventually, the full standard C++ library will encompass the STL, iostreams, memory management via new and delete, a basic string template, exceptions, and other features such as mathematical classes and numerical limits. By basing your code now on standard C++ library capabilities, you will be better prepared to update your code for future releases of Borland C++ and other ANSI C++ compatible compilers.

In time, the STL is expected to lose its identity as it merges with the full standard C++ library, through which standard C functions will still be available. However, ANSI and Borland C++ have not yet reached this advanced stage in their evolution, so in this chapter, I'll treat the STL as a separate entity.

To compile the listings in this chapter, you must use the 32-bit command line compiler, Bcc32.exe, or you must select a 32-bit output target with the IDE's TargetExpert.

> **TIP**
>
> To ensure future portability, use the container classes and algorithms described in this chapter rather than the Borland International Data Structures (BIDS) explained in the preceding chapter. Also, use the basic string class (see the next chapter) instead of Borland's string class.

The Standard Template Library

The first key feature of the STL is the separation of data structures from algorithms that operate on data. For example, because the STL's sort algorithm is completely generic, you can use it with virtually any collection of data, including lists, vectors, and common C++ arrays.

The second key feature of the STL is that it is not object oriented. There are few class hierarchies in the library, which relies much more heavily on templates than on encapsulation, inheritance, and polymorphism—OOP's three main anchors. At first, the lack of OOP in the

STL may seem to be a drawback, but its low-level nature gives the library its true generality. Also, because the STL is not object oriented, it tends to produce smaller code files that also run fast due to the heavy use of inline code.

> **NOTE**
>
> You should be aware that, at the time of this writing, the STL implementation only works in 32-bit. Support for 16-bit was initially planned but never fully implemented; therefore, compiling the STL examples in 16-bit mode will generally result in numerous compiler warnings and an executable that aborts with General Protection Faults (GPF). If you compile in 16-bit mode with debug information, an internal compiler error will result.

STL Components

The STL provides a large number of template classes and functions that you may use in OOP and in non-OOP applications. All of its approximately 50 algorithms are completely generic, and are not tied to any specific data types. The three essential library components are as follows:

- *Iterators* are similar to pointers that provide access to data elements. A pair of iterators can define a range of data elements in a container.
- *Containers* are data structures such as lists, vectors, and deques provided as template classes. You typically access a container's data elements using iterators, which the containers generate.
- *Algorithms* are function templates that operate on data. For example, algorithms can sort data in a vector, or search a list of objects. The functions possess no special knowledge of the types and structures of data on which they operate, a fact that makes the use of standard algorithms completely generic.

Along with the STL, Rogue Wave's implementation of the standard C++ library also provides miscellaneous components. These features include exceptions for error handling, mathematical and numeric limits classes, and a string class template. However, because these are all new features in Borland C++ 5, I'll discuss them together in this and the next three chapters.

Header Files

Standard C++ library headers drop the usual .h extension. For example, to include the library's algorithms, insert the statement

```
#include <algorithm>
```

Borland C++ automatically chops the specified header to eight characters, applies .h, and reads the Algorith.h file in the BC5\Include path. However, on the source code level, these details are unimportant, and as a result of this new header style, source-code files are more portable to other operating platforms that permit long filenames or use different extensions such as .hpp.

> **NOTE**
>
> When the standard C++ library becomes a reality, all standard headers will conform to the new no-extension style.

Table 10.1 lists the headers to include for various container data structures. This is not a complete list, and I'll introduce other headers at the appropriate times throughout this chapter.

Table 10.1. Header files and container classes.

#include	*Container classes*
<bitset>	bitset
<deque>	deque
<list>	list
<map>	map, multimap
<queue>	queue, priority_queue
<set>	set, multiset
<stack>	stack
<vector>	vector, vector<bool>

Iterators

Iterators provide access to data values, and also can define ranges for cycling through multiple data elements. Iterators closely resemble pointers. In fact, a pointer *is* an iterator. Container classes also can generate iterators for passing to algorithms that operate on the container's data. As with pointers, you must dereference an iterator to "get to" its data using the * operator. To peruse a collection of data, increment an iterator with the ++ operator. If this advances the iterator beyond the last value in a container, the iterator assumes the *past-the-end* value, which is equivalent to a null pointer. Dereferencing an iterator that equals the *past-the-end* value is never allowed.

Because iterators and algorithms are general in nature, it is not possible to use iterators in multi-threaded code. However, this is not a severe drawback because you can wrap iterators in classes for safe multi-threaded access to data. For example, an iterator cannot safely access a multi-user database. But a class that encapsulates the iterator can provide a member function that locks the data file (or a range of data), uses the iterator, and then unlocks the file for other users.

Apply the ++ operator to advance an iterator to the next data element in a collection, or to the *past-the-end* value. In a range of data defined by two iterators, incrementing the first iterator must eventually cause it to reach the second iterator, which may refer to a value in the container or the *past-the-end* value.

> **WARNING**
>
> The standard C++ library does not ensure that one iterator is reachable from another. For example, when sorting a range of data, if you specify two iterators from *different* structures (two lists, for instance), the second iterator is not reachable from the first, and your code will surely suffer and die. This is one of the prices we pay for the STL's complete generality. *Algorithms in the STL do not guard against dumb mistakes.*

Introducing Iterators

There are five types of iterators:

- *Input iterators* provide read-only access to data.
- *Output iterators* provide write-only access to data.
- *Forward iterators* provide read-write, forward (incrementing) access to data.
- *Bidirectional iterators* provide read-write, forward-backward (incrementing and decrementing) access to data.
- *Random-access iterators* provide read-write, random movement through data.

Iterators lower in this list derive from those higher up, and this is one of the few places in the STL where you'll find a class hierarchy. As a consequence of these derivations, you may use forward iterators where an algorithm calls for an output or an input iterator. You may use bidirectional iterators in place of forward, output, or input iterators. You may use random-access iterators in algorithms requiring a bidirectional iterator.

Pointer Iterators

To demonstrate how to use an iterator—which in its simplest form is merely a C++ pointer—consider how you might use the standard find algorithm to search an array of integers. Listing 10.1, Iterdemo.cpp, shows how to do that with an iterator.

Listing 10.1. Iterdemo.cpp (Demonstrates iterators).

```
//===============================================================
// Iterdemo.cpp -- Demonstrates iterators
// To compile:
//    bcc32 iterdemo
// To run:
```

Listing 10.1. continued

```
//    iterdemo
// Copyright (c) 1996 by Tom Swan. All rights reserved.
//================================================================

#include <algorithm>
#include <iostream>

using namespace std;

#define SIZE 100

int iarray[SIZE];

void main()
{
  iarray[20] = 50;
  int* ip = find(iarray, iarray + SIZE, 50);
  if (ip == iarray + SIZE)
    cout << "50 not found in array";
  else
    cout << "50 found in array";
}
```

All standard template library programs must include a using namespace statement for the pre-defined symbol std. This avoids any possible conflicts between STL names such as sort with names in your existing code, and as a result, you should be able to start using STL containers and algorithms without having to make any modifications to your program files. Simply add the following statement near the beginning of each module (a good place is after the module's #include directives):

```
using namespace std;
```

After that statement, the Iterdemo.cpp program defines an array of 100 integer values, and then uses the find algorithm to search the array for the value 50:

```
int iarray[SIZE];
int* ip = find(iarray, iarray + SIZE, 50);
```

The program passes three arguments to find. The first two arguments are iterators. Because C++ arrays are actually pointers, the expression iarray *points to* the first data value in the array. The second iterator, iarray + SIZE, equals the *past-the-end* value—one element past the end of the array. The third argument is the value to locate, 50. The find algorithm returns an iterator of the same kind as its first two arguments, in this case an integer pointer, assigned to integer-pointer ip. To determine whether find was successful, the program tests ip against the *past-the-end* value:

```
if (ip == iarray + SIZE) ...
```

If this expression is true, then the iterator equals the *past-the-end* value, and the search argument was not found. Note that it is *not* correct to test whether ip is null:

```if (ip == NULL) .... // ??? Don't do this!```
```

You dereference iterators just as you do pointers. For example, you can display the results returned by `find` using an output stream statement:

```
cout << "Value found == " << *ip << endl;
```

Container Iterators

Although simple pointers are iterators, it is more common to use iterators generated by a container class. These iterators are used in *exactly* the same way as just demonstrated, but you'll usually call a container function such as `begin` or `end` to obtain iterators for a specific collection of data. (With some containers, you can also call `rbegin` and `rend` to obtain reverse iterators for specifying a range of elements in reverse order.) Listing 10.2, Vectdemo.cpp, demonstrates the fundamentals of using container classes and iterators.

Listing 10.2. Vectdemo.cpp (Demonstrates vectors and iterators).

```
//================================================================
// Vectdemo.cpp -- Demonstrates vectors and iterators
// To compile:
//    bcc32 vectdemo
// To run:
//    vectdemo
// Copyright (c) 1996 by Tom Swan. All rights reserved.
//================================================================

#include <algorithm>
#include <vector>

using namespace std;

vector<int> intVector(100);

void main()
{
  intVector[20] = 50;
  vector<int>::iterator intIter =
    find(intVector.begin(), intVector.end(), 50);
  if (intIter != intVector.end())
    cout << "Vector has value " << *intIter << endl;
  else
    cout << "Vector does not contain 50" << endl;
}
```

The program defines a vector of 100 `int` values using the standard `vector< >` container-class template. For demonstration, the first statement in `main` assigns 50 to the vector at indexed position 20. (Vectors closely resemble arrays, but are more powerful as you will discover in Chapter 12.) The next statement constructs an iterator and calls `find`. Examine this statement closely:

```
vector<int>::iterator intIter =
    find(intVector.begin(), intVector.end(), 50);
```

The iterator `intIter` is defined using the `iterator` type of the `vector<int>` container-class template. This makes `intIter` valid for accessing the container's data values. The program passes to `find` two other iterators provided by the container's `begin` and `end` functions. The `begin` function returns an iterator to the container's first element. The `end` function returns the *past-the-end* value. Together, the two iterators define the range of data in the container to search for the value 50. The program assigns `find`'s result to `intIter`. Following this, if `intIter` does not equal the *past-the-end* value, then the search value was found:

```
if (intIter != intVector.end())...  // True if search value was found
```

USING CONTAINER CLASS TEMPLATES

Those without much experience with class templates may find the syntax in the preceding example confusing. If so, break it into steps, and use `typedef` to simplify long-winded expressions. For example, you can use `typedef` to define an iterator data type:

```
typedef vector<int>::iterator TIterator;
```

This specifies that `TIterator` represents the type of iterator created by the `vector<int>` container class. Using the newly defined type, you can define an iterator variable such as `intIter` to which you assign `find`'s return value:

```
TIterator intIter =
  find(intVector.begin(), intVector.end(), 50);
```

Constant Iterators

You may assign values to dereferenced iterators (but not to output-only iterators). The following statement assigns 123 to the `intVector`'s first data value.

```
vector<int>::iterator intIter = intVector.begin();
*intIter = 123;  // Okay for all except output-only iterators
```

This is equivalent to using the indexing operator to assign vector data values:

```
intVector[0] = 123;
```

Iterators may be constant to prevent statements from changing their values. Preface the iterator declaration with `const` to create a constant iterator:

```
const vector<int>::iterator intIter = intVector.begin();
*intIter = 123;  // ??? Compiler error
```

This assignment produces the compiler error, "Cannot modify a const object." If the container is constant, all iterators to the container's data are automatically constant, whether the iterators are declared explicitly `const` or not.

Types of Iterators

In this section, you examine each type of STL iterator. Because using iterators requires an understanding of subjects such as containers and algorithms not yet introduced, you may want to reread this section after finishing the next three chapters.

Input Iterators

An input iterator is the most general type. Input iterators at a minimum can be compared with != for inequality, dereferenced with * to access data values, and incremented with ++ to advance to the next value in a sequence or to the *past-the-end* value.

The STL's `find` algorithm demonstrates these most basic of iterator operations. The algorithm is defined as a function template:

```
template <class InputIterator, class T>
InputIterator
  find(InputIterator first, InputIterator last, const T& value)
```

`InputIterator` and `T` are placeholders that you supply. The `find` algorithm returns the value `InputIterator`. The algorithm also requires a search value as a constant reference `T`. Iterator `first` addresses the first value in the data collection; iterator `last` addresses the final value *plus one* in the collection. (This value might be the *past-the-end* value.) The use of templates and the `InputIterator` and `T` placeholders makes it possible to write the body of `find` in a completely generic way that does not depend on the type or structure of the data sequence:

```
{
  while (first != last && *first != value)
    ++first;
  return first;
}
```

In English, the `while` statement loops as long as the first iterator does not equal the last, and if the dereferenced `first` iterator does not equal the search argument `value`. The loop simply increments the `first` iterator to the next value in sequence, and the function returns the `first` iterator that either equals the search argument or the second iterator (which might equal the *past-the-end* value). The algorithm is completely general, and it can search a list, a vector, or a data collection of any kind.

In the preceding example, notice that, if the search argument is not located, incrementing `first` *must* eventually cause it to equal the `last` iterator. Thus if `first` and `last` refer to values in different containers, this algorithm potentially never ends. There is no way for the compiler to guard against this situation without compromising the STL's general versatility. That's your responsibility.

Output Iterators

An output iterator is write-only by default, and is typically used to copy data from one location to another. For example, the `copy` algorithm can transfer one or more values from one data structure to another. This works even if the data structures are different, although they must be able to store the same types of values, or provide for their conversion.

For example, suppose you define an array of `double` values that you want to transfer to a `vector<>` data structure, perhaps to take advantage of a vector's ability to grow at runtime. Listing 10.3, Outiter.cpp, demonstrates how to use output iterators with the `copy` algorithm.

Listing 10.3. Outiter.cpp (Demonstrates output iterators).

```
//================================================================
// Outiter.cpp -- Demonstrates output iterators
// To compile:
//    bcc32 outiter
// To run:
//    outiter
// Copyright (c) 1996 by Tom Swan. All rights reserved.
//================================================================

#include <algorithm>
#include <vector>

using namespace std;

double darray[10] =
  {1.0, 1.1, 1.2, 1.3, 1.4, 1.5, 1.6, 1.7, 1.8, 1.9};

vector<double> vdouble(10);

void main()
{
  vector<double>::iterator outputIterator = vdouble.begin();
  copy(darray, darray + 10, outputIterator);
  while (outputIterator != vdouble.end()) {
    cout << *outputIterator << endl;
    outputIterator++;
  }
}
```

The program defines an array of 10 double values, initialized to 1.0, 1.1, … 1.9. It also defines a vector large enough to hold 10 double values. The first statement in main declares and initializes a vector iterator, outputIterator, equal to the first value in the vector as returned by the begin() member function:

```
vector<double>::iterator outputIterator = vdouble.begin();
```

Passing outputIterator to the copy algorithm transfers the values from the common array to the vector container:

```
copy(darray, darray + 10, outputIterator);
```

The first two arguments to copy are input iterators, which define the range of source values. The third argument is the output iterator, which specifies the transfer's destination. Following this statement, the program uses a while loop to display the values in the vector, using the iostream output statement:

```
cout << *outputIterator << endl;
```

When using the copy algorithm, it is your responsibility to ensure that the destination is large enough to hold the transferred values.

TIP

Use iterators to ensure that a destination container is large enough to hold values from a source container. For example, you can define the vdouble vector in Outiter.cpp using a pair of iterators that define the range of the source, darray. This guarantees that vdouble will be large enough to hold the values in the specified range:

```
vector<double> vdouble(darray, darray + 10);
```

Forward Iterators

A forward iterator can read and write data values, and can be incremented to the next value in a sequence. As their name implies, however, forward iterators cannot be decremented. The replace algorithm uses two forward iterators and is defined as

```
template <class ForwardIterator, class T>
void replace (ForwardIterator first,
              ForwardIterator last,
              const T& old_value,
              const T& new_value);
```

Use replace to change to new_value all values equal to old_value in the range first to last. For example, given the vdouble vector in the Outiter.cpp, this replaces all values equal to 1.5 with the value of *pi:*

```
replace(vdouble.begin(), vdouble.end(), 1.5, 3.14159);
```

NOTE

When I mention a range such as `first` to `last`, the second iterator always refers to a value *that is one past the last value in the range*. This may be a valid data element, or the *past-the-end* value.

Bidirectional Iterators

Bidirectional iterators can be incremented and decremented, a requirement of some algorithms in the standard library. The `reverse` algorithm, for example, requires two bidirectional iterator arguments:

```
template <class BidirectionalIterator>
void reverse (BidirectionalIterator first,
              BidirectionalIterator last);
```

Use `reverse` to reverse the values in a container—for example, after sorting a container in low to high order, you can reverse it to produce a high-to-low ordering. In some circumstances, this might be faster than resorting the container in cases where both orderings are needed. For example, to reverse the values in the `vdouble` vector from Outiter.cpp, you could use the following statement:

```
reverse(vdouble.begin(), vdouble.end());
```

Random Access Iterators

Random access iterators can access data in any order, and can be used to read and write data values. (Common C++ pointers are random access iterators.) The standard library's sorting and searching algorithms use random access iterators, which also have the capability of being compared using relational operators.

The `random_shuffle` algorithm specifies two random access iterators to define a range of values in a sequence. Using this algorithm scrambles the values within the range. The algorithm is defined as

```
template <class RandomAccessIterator>
void random_shuffle (RandomAccessIterator first,
                      RandomAccessIterator last);
```

To randomize the order of values in the `vdouble` vector from Outiter.cpp, insert this statement into the program:

```
random_shuffle(vdouble.begin(), vdouble.end());
```

Iterator Techniques

Following are some additional techniques that you will find useful for working with iterators.

Iostreams and Iterators

Many of this book's listings use iostreams to read and write values. For example, an output statement such as

```
cout << "Value == " << value << endl;
```

writes a label, a value, and a new-line manipulator to the standard output.

With iterators, there's another way to use iostreams and standard algorithms. The key to the technique is that an input or output iostream object can be *converted* into an iterator. Thus any algorithm that can accept an iterator argument can work with iostreams. For example, Listing 10.4, Outstrm.cpp, demonstrates how to use an output stream iterator to display a container's contents.

Listing 10.4. Outstrm.cpp (Demonstrates output stream iterators).

```
//=================================================================
// Outstrm.cpp -- Demonstrates output stream iterators
// To compile:
//    bcc32 outstrm
// To run:
//    outstrm
// Copyright (c) 1996 by Tom Swan. All rights reserved.
//=================================================================

#include <algorithm>
#include <iostream>
#include <vector>

using namespace std;

void Display(vector<int>& v, const char* s);

void main()
{
// Construct vector and fill with random integer values
  vector<int> collection(100);
  for (int i = 0; i < 100; i++)
    collection[i] = random(1000);

// Display, sort, and redisplay
  Display(collection, "Before sorting");
  sort(collection.begin(), collection.end());
  Display(collection, "After sorting");
}

// Display label s and contents of integer vector v
void Display(vector<int>& v, const char* s)
{
  cout << endl << s << endl;
  copy(v.begin(), v.end(),
    ostream_iterator<int>(cout, " "));
  cout << endl;
}
```

The `main` program defines a vector of 100 integers and fills it with random values. A local `Display` function shows the vector's contents before and after sorting, using the standard `sort` algorithm.

Function `Display` demonstrates how to use an output stream iterator. The statement

```
copy(v.begin(), v.end(),
  ostream_iterator<int>(cout, " "));
```

calls the `copy` algorithm—the same one you already examined—to transfer the vector's contents to the standard output. This is a marvelous demonstration of the versatility of algorithms in the STL! The third argument to `copy` is an output iterator, in this case one created from the standard library's `ostream_iterator< >` template, specifying `int` as the object's data type. The program uses this iterator's two-argument constructor to specify `cout` as the output stream object, and a blank as the separator to insert between values. To display values one per line, you can change the iterator argument to

```
ostream_iterator<int>(cout, "\n")
```

The next program, Listing 10.5, Readchar.cpp, demonstrates how to use input and output stream iterators to read and display the contents of a text file.

Listing 10.5. Readchar.cpp (Reads text file using iostreams and iterators).

```
//================================================================
// Readchar.cpp -- Reads text file using iostreams and iterators
// To compile:
//    bcc32 readchar
// To run:
//    readchar readchar.cpp
// Copyright (c) 1996 by Tom Swan. All rights reserved.
//================================================================

#include <iostream>
#include <fstream>
#include <algorithm>

using namespace std;

int main(int argc, char *argv[])
{

// Check if user supplied a filename
  if (argc <= 1) {
    cerr << "Error: filename missing" << endl;
    exit(1);
  }

// Open the input file stream
  ifstream ifs(argv[1], ios::in);
  if (!ifs) {
    cerr << "Error: unable to open " << argv[1] << endl;
    exit(2);
  }
```

```
// Turn off "eat white space" flag
  ifs.unsetf(ios::skipws);

// Copy input stream to output stream using iterators
  copy(istream_iterator<char, ptrdiff_t>(ifs),
       istream_iterator<char, ptrdiff_t>(),
       ostream_iterator<char>(cout));

  return 0;
}
```

The first step is to construct an input file stream object of type `ifstream`, declared in the `<fstream>` header file. In this case, the program uses `argv[1]` as a filename, which lets you enter a filename on the DOS command line, but you could just as well use a string buffer or constant. If the input stream object, named `ifs`, is created successfully, the program resets the `ios::skipws` (skip white space) flag so that spaces and new line control codes are not thrown out.

With these preliminaries out of the way, a single call to the standard `copy` algorithm reads the entire file and transfers it to the standard output. In this case, all arguments to `copy` are iostream iterators. Carefully examine this statement:

```
copy(istream_iterator<char, ptrdiff_t>(ifs),
     istream_iterator<char, ptrdiff_t>(),
     ostream_iterator<char>(cout));
```

The first argument to `copy` is an object of the `istream_iterator` template, which requires two type names. The first is the type of value to be input, in this case, `char`. The second type represents the distance between iterators (`ptrdiff_t` is the default, and is predefined in the library). This input iterator specifies `ifs`, the input file stream object, as the constructor's argument. As a result, this first iterator argument to `copy` represents the beginning of the input file.

The second argument to `copy` is also an input stream iterator, of the same type as the first. However, empty parentheses construct this object using the `istream_iterator`'s default constructor. This represents the end-of-file. As a result, the two iterators refer to the file's contents just as two iterators might refer to the range of values in a vector or list.

> **TIP**
>
> Remember, the `istream_iterator`'s default constructor creates an input stream iterator that represents the end of file value, and as such must never be dereferenced.

The third and final argument to `copy` is an output stream iterator object. To the `ostream_iterator< >` template the program specifies `char` as the output data type and `cout` as the output stream object. Together, this single statement copies the input file stream from the first and last input iterator to the standard output.

Insertion Iterators

To insert values into a container, you normally use an *insertion iterator.* These are also called *adaptors* because they adapt or convert a container into an iterator that you can pass to an algorithm such as `copy`. For example, in a program that defines a list and a vector each containing `double` values:

```
list<double> dList;
vector<double> dVector;
```

a single `copy` statement can insert the values from the vector into the front of the list using a `front_inserter` object:

```
copy(dVector.begin(), dVector.end(), front_inserter(dList));
```

There are three types of insertion iterators:

- *Front inserters* insert objects into the front of a data collection—for example, at the head of a list.
- *Back inserters* insert objects at the end of a collection—for example, at the end of a vector, an operation that might cause the vector to grow in size.
- *Inserters* insert data ahead of any location in a data collection.

Using an inserter may cause other data in a container to move in position, thus invalidating any existing iterators for those values. Inserting a value into a vector, for instance, causes other values to move aside to make room. However, insertions in structures such as lists are efficient and do not cause data to move.

Typically, a plain `inserter` is used following a search of a data structure to locate the position of a particular value. The insertion is then made ahead of that location. Listing 10.6, Insert.cpp, demonstrates how to use the three types of insertion iterators.

Listing 10.6. Insert.cpp (Demonstrates insertion iterators).

```
//================================================================
// Insert.cpp -- Demonstrates insertion iterators
// To compile:
//    bcc32 insert
// To run:
//    insert
// Copyright (c) 1996 by Tom Swan. All rights reserved.
//================================================================

#include <algorithm>
#include <list>

using namespace std;

int iArray[5] = { 1, 2, 3, 4, 5 };

void Display(list<int>& v, const char* s);
```

```
void main()
{
  list<int> iList;

// Copy iArray backwards into iList
  copy(iArray, iArray + 5, front_inserter(iList));
  Display(iList, "Before find and copy");

// Locate value 3 in iList
  list<int>::iterator p =
    find(iList.begin(), iList.end(), 3);

// Copy first two iArray values to iList ahead of p
  copy(iArray, iArray + 2, inserter(iList, p));
  Display(iList, "After find and copy");
}

void Display(list<int>& a, const char* s)
{
  cout << endl << s << endl;
  copy(a.begin(), a.end(),
    ostream_iterator<int>(cout, " "));
  cout << endl;
}
```

The program defines a global integer array containing the sequence 1, 2, 3, 4, 5. A copy statement transfers those values into a list container using a front_inserter object. This causes the original data to be inserted at the head of the list, thus reversing the value order and creating the list 5, 4, 3, 2, 1. Change front_inserter to back_inserter to insert the values in their original order. (Note: You cannot use a front_inserter on a vector.)

Next, the program uses the find algorithm to search the list for the value 3. The statement

```
list<int>::iterator p =
  find(iList.begin(), iList.end(), 3);
```

constructs an iterator p for a list<int> container, to which the program assigns the result of find. After this statement, p refers to the value 3 in the list, or if that value does not exist in the collection, p equals the *past-the-end* value.

Finally, the program again calls copy using a plain inserter object, constructed from iList, the container into which the insertion is to be made, and p, the location of that insertion.

TIP

Try changing the search argument to find to a value not in the list—99, for example. Because this sets p to the *past-the-end* value, the final copy statement appends the first two values from iArray onto the end of the list rather than in the middle.

Iterator Functions

Here are two functions that you will find useful for working with iterators:

- advance increments or decrements an iterator a specified number of times.
- distance returns the number of operations required to increment or decrement an iterator by a certain amount.

Suppose you have the following list container:

```
list<int> iList;
```

You can use find to locate a value in the list. This searches for the value 2:

```
list<int>::iterator p =
  find(iList.begin(), iList.end(), 2);
```

Use advance to increment the list iterator p two values ahead:

```
cout << "p == " << *p << endl;
advance(p, 2);  // same as p++, p++
cout << "p == " << *p << endl;
```

Pass to advance an iterator and positive integer equal to the number of increment operations to perform. This value must be positive for forward-moving iterators; it can be negative for bidirectional and random-access iterators.

Use distance to determine the number of increment or decrement operations required to move an iterator from one value to another, or to the *past-the-end* value. For example, the following fragment sets k to the number of elements from p to the end of iList:

```
int k = 0;
distance(p, iList.end(), k);
cout << "k == " << k << endl;
```

> **WARNING**
>
> The distance function is iterative—that is, it *accumulates* a value in its third argument, k in the example. You must therefore initialize k before passing it to distance. *Failing to initialize this argument for* distance *can produce incorrect results.*

Functions and Function Objects

In the standard library, functions are known as *algorithms*, which implies that they have a more general purpose than other functions. Standard functions are implemented as templates, or template classes (called function objects) with overloaded function operators, which you can use to perform a wide variety of actions on data in containers. This section describes how to use the different types of standard library functions and function objects.

Functions and Predicates

You will frequently need to perform operations on data held in containers. The standard library provides algorithms such as `accumulate` and `for_each` for operating on data elements. For example, given a vector of `double` values

```
vector<double> vdouble;
```

you can write a function to perform an operation such as this one, which multiplies a double value by 10:

```
void AFunction(double& rd)
{
  rd *= 10;
}
```

To perform this function on the vector's contents, pass the function to `for_each` using a statement such as

```
for_each(vdouble.begin(), vdouble.end(), AFunction);
```

Another type of function is called a *predicate.* This is a function that returns a `bool` or an `int` true or false value. Use predicate functions with algorithms such as `find_if`, which returns an iterator to a value for which a predicate function returns true. For example, to search for the first negative value in a vector, you could write a predicate function `IsMinus` that returns true if an integer value passed as a reference argument is less than zero:

```
bool IsMinus(const int& ri)
{
  return ri < 0;
}
```

You can then define a vector of type `int`, and assign integer values using indexing expressions:

```
vector<int> vint(5);
vint[0] = 4;
vint[1] = 18;
vint[2] = -9;
vint[3] = 100;
vint[4] = -2;
```

To search the `vint` vector for the first negative value, call `find_if` and pass the predicate function by name:

```
vector<int>::iterator j =
  find_if(vint.begin(), vint.end(), IsMinus);
if (j == vint.end())
  cout << "No negative values found" << endl;
else
  cout << "Result of find == " << *j << endl;
```

The `find_if` algorithm applies the predicate function, `IsMinus`, to each element in the specified range, in this case, to the entire `vint` container. After this, if `j` equals `vint.end()` (the *past-the-end* value), the array contains all positive values; otherwise, the program displays the located value by dereferencing `*j`.

10

Function Objects

Rather than pass a function by name to various algorithms, you will often need to pass a *function object* instead, which allows for greater versatility. For example, a function object can maintain a reference to a collection of data, define static variables, member functions, and so on. Another reason to use a function object is speed. Because its code is expanded inline, the results may be faster than they would be by calling a function repeatedly for a lengthy iteration.

Technically, a function object is any struct or class that overloads the function operator, ( ). The standard library defines several such objects including `plus`, `minus`, `times`, `greater`, `greater_equal`, and others. A useful function, which you will often use with function objects, is `accumulate`. By default, `accumulate` sums the values in a data collection. Include the `numeric` header to use `accumulate`:

```
#include <numeric>
```

Consider how you might apply `accumulate` on a vector of integers, defined as

```
#define MAX 10
vector<int> v(MAX);
```

Fill the vector with some values on which to operate:

```
for (int i = 0; i < MAX; i++)
  v[i] = i + 1;
```

To sum the values in vector v, call `accumulate` like this:

```
int sum = accumulate(v.begin(), v.end(), 0);
```

Argument 0 represents an initial value for the accumulation. When summing values, this should normally be zero. However, by applying a function object, you can use `accumulate` to produce the product of a series, that is, its factorial:

```
int product = accumulate(v.begin(), v.end(), 1, times<int>());
```

In this case, because the operation to apply is multiplication, the initial value must be 1. The function object, `times<int>()`, provides `accumulate` with the means to multiply integer values.

> **NOTE**
>
> If you try the preceding code, compile with BCC32 so that `int` values are large enough to hold the product.

One particularly useful type of function object is called a *generator*. This kind of function has a memory—that is, it "remembers" a value from a previous call. A good example is a random number generator, which uses its previous return value to compute the next value in a random sequence.

An algorithm such as random_shuffle, which you examined earlier in the chapter, can accept a function that produces a number at random. You might use this capability to experiment with alternate random sequence algorithms, or for testing purposes. For example, you could designate a function that simply returns the same value repeatedly or an ordered series to test worst-case behavior of an application using random numbers.

Listing 10.7, Randfunc.cpp, demonstrates how to use a function object to pass a random sequence generator to the random_shuffle algorithm.

Listing 10.7. Randfunc.cpp (Demonstrates function objects).

```
//==============================================================
// Randfunc.cpp -- Demonstrates function objects
// To compile:
//    bcc32 randfunc
// To run:
//    randfunc
// Copyright (c) 1996 by Tom Swan. All rights reserved.
//==============================================================

#include <iostream>
#include <algorithm>
#include <vector>

using namespace std;

// Data to randomize
int iarray[10] = {1, 2, 3, 4, 5, 6, 7, 8, 9, 10};
vector<int> v(iarray, iarray + 10);

// Function prototypes
void Display(vector<int>& vr, const char *s);
unsigned int RandInt(unsigned int n);

void main()
{
  Display(v, "Before shuffle:");
  random_shuffle(v.begin(), v.end(), ptr_fun(RandInt));
  Display(v, "After shuffle:");
}

// Display contents of vector vr
void Display(vector<int>& vr, const char *s)
{
  cout << endl << s << endl;
  copy(vr.begin(), vr.end(), ostream_iterator<int>(cout, " "));
  cout << endl;
}

// Return next random value in sequence modulo n
unsigned int RandInt(unsigned int n)
{
  return random(n);
}
```

The program defines an array, iarray, of 10 integer values, and then uses that array to initialize a vector of the same size. By the way, this shows an alternative way to copy a common array into a vector container. The statement

```
vector<int> v(iarray, iarray + 10);
```

defines v as a vector of int values, and passes a pair of iterators that define the range of source values in iarray. This selects the appropriate vector template constructor to initialize the vector using the values from the array.

Function RandInt provides an unsigned integer at random within the range of $0 \ldots n - 1$. In this example, the function merely calls the standard random function, but in another application, you might replace RandInt with another random-number algorithm (the next listing suggests a way to do this).

This statement passes the new RandInt function to random_shuffle:

```
random_shuffle(v.begin(), v.end(), ptr_fun(RandInt));
```

Passing RandInt directly by name doesn't work because the algorithm expects to receive a pointer to a binary function. The object ptr_fun is predefined in the STL as an instance of the pointer_to_unary_function template. The term "unary function" means a function that receives one argument and returns a value, all of user-specified types. The STL also defines pointer_to_binary_function, also instantiated as object ptr_fun, for functions that require two arguments and return a value.

The next program, Listing 10.8, Fiborand.cpp, demonstrates a more sophisticated use for function objects. The program is a good example of how a function object can define entirely fresh behavior for standard algorithms, in this case, teaching the random_shuffle function how to use a Fibonacci random number generator.

> **NOTE**
>
> For more information about how the Fibonacci random number generator works, see my article *Algorithm Alley* in *Dr. Dobb's Journal*, January 1994.

Listing 10.8. Fiborand.cpp (Defines Fibonacci random number function object).

```
//============================================================
// Fiborand.cpp -- Defines Fibonacci random number function object
// To compile:
//    bcc32 fiborand
// To run:
//    fiborand
// Copyright (c) 1996 by Tom Swan. All rights reserved.
//============================================================

#include <iostream>
#include <algorithm>
```

```
#include <vector>

using namespace std;

// Data to randomize
int iarray[10] = {1, 2, 3, 4, 5, 6, 7, 8, 9, 10};
vector<int> v(iarray, iarray + 10);

// Function prototype
void Display(vector<int>& vr, const char *s);

// The FiboRand template function-object class
template<class Arg>
class FiboRand : public unary_function<Arg, Arg> {
  int i, j;
  Arg sequence[18];
public:
  FiboRand();
  Arg operator()(const Arg& arg);
};

void main()
{
  cout << "Fibonacci random number generator" << endl;
  cout << "using random_shuffle and a function object" << endl;
  Display(v, "Before shuffle:");
  random_shuffle(v.begin(), v.end(), FiboRand<int>());
  Display(v, "After shuffle:");
}

// Display contents of vector vr
void Display(vector<int>& vr, const char *s)
{
  cout << endl << s << endl;
  copy(vr.begin(), vr.end(),
    ostream_iterator<int>(cout, " "));
  cout << endl;
}

// FiboRand class constructor
template<class Arg>
FiboRand<Arg>::FiboRand()
{
  sequence[17] = 1;
  sequence[16] = 2;
  for (int n = 15; n > 0; n--)
    sequence[n] = sequence[n + 1] + sequence[n + 2];
  i = 17;
  j = 5;
}

// FiboRand class function operator
template<class Arg>
Arg FiboRand<Arg>::operator()(const Arg& arg)
{
  Arg k = sequence[i] + sequence[j];
  sequence[i] = k;
  i--;
  j--;
  if (i == 0) i = 17;
  if (j == 0) j = 17;
  return k % arg;
}
```

379

To insert the new random-number generator into the program, we need a class that encapsulates various items. This particular generator is an excellent example of how a function object "remembers" previous invocations. In this case, class `FiboRand` maintains a sequence of 18 values (index [0] is ignored) and two index variables i and j that must retain their values between calls to the generator. Encapsulating these items in a class is a neat solution, and creates a truly modular generator that could be used in any situation requiring random sequences.

The `FiboRand` class is derived from the `unary_function` template, using the declaration:

```
template<class Arg>
class FiboRand : public unary_function<Arg, Arg>
```

`Arg` is the user-specified type. The class requires two member functions—a constructor to initialize a `FiboRand` function object and an overloaded function `operator()`. The constructor (see its implementation near the end of the listing) prepares the internal `sequence` array and assigns starting values to i and j. The operator member function uses and alters these values, and returns an `Arg` value at random. The algorithm assumes only that `Arg` values can be added.

Passing an instance of the `FiboRand` class template creates a function object that `random_shuffle` can use. Simply construct the object specifying a type for `Arg` as follows:

```
random_shuffle(v.begin(), v.end(), FiboRand<int>());
```

Binder Function Objects

A *binder* creates a function object from another function object f and an argument value v. The function object must be binary—that is, it must accept two arguments a and b. There are two binder objects in the standard library:

- `bind1st` creates a function object that applies value *v* to the first function argument, a.
- `bind2nd` creates a function object that applies value *v* to the second function argument, b.

The purpose of the two binders will be clearer from an example. Listing 10.9, Binder.cpp, demonstrates how to search a list of values using `bind1st`.

Listing 10.9. Binder.cpp (Demonstrates `bind1st` binder).

```
//==============================================================
// Binder.cpp -- Demonstrates bind1st binder
// To compile:
//    bcc32 binder
// To run:
//    binder
// Copyright (c) 1996 by Tom Swan. All rights reserved.
//==============================================================

#include <iostream>
#include <algorithm>
#include <list>
```

```
using namespace std;

// Data
int iarray[10] = {1, 2, 3, 4, 5, 6, 7, 8, 9, 10};
list<int> aList(iarray, iarray + 10);

void main()
{
  int k = 0;
  count_if(aList.begin(), aList.end(),
    bind1st(greater<int>(), 8), k);
  cout << "Number elements < 8 == " << k << endl;
}
```

The program defines an array of 10 integers, which are used to initialize a linked list container. Algorithm `count_if` counts the number of elements in the list that satisfy a certain condition. This is done by binding a function object with an argument, and passing the resulting function object to `count_if`'s third parameter. The algorithm deposits the resulting count in the fourth argument, `k`, which must be initialized to zero as shown in the listing.

Carefully examine the binder expression:

```
bind1st(greater<int>(), 8)
```

This constructs an object, of the `binary_function` template, that combines another function object (`greater<int>()`) with an argument value, 8. Because the program uses `bind1st`, that value is applied to the function's first argument, thus creating an object that computes the result of the expression:

```
8 > q
```

where q is one of the container's values. Despite appearances, then, this statement

```
count_if(aList.begin(), aList.end(),
  bind1st(greater<int>(), 8), k);
```

actually counts the number of values in `aList` that are *less than* 8 (or, technically speaking, the number of values for which 8 is greater). To make the statement count the number of values that are greater than 8, replace the `count_if` and output statement with

```
count_if(aList.begin(), aList.end(),
  bind2nd(greater<int>(), 8), k);
cout << "Number elements > 8 == " << k << endl;
```

Because `bind2nd` is now used, the resulting function object performs the expression

```
q > 8
```

where q is a value from the container. Thus the modified statement counts the number of elements greater than 8.

381

Negator Function Objects

A *negator* creates a function object from another function object but having the opposite effect. Where the original function returns true, the negator object returns false.

There are two negators in the standard library, not1 and not2. Pass any unary function object to not1. Pass any binary function object to not2. Negators are often used in conjunction with binders to create function objects with a negated logic.

You might use a negator to search a list of values. (Use a copy of the preceding program, Binder.cpp, to test the following code fragments.) Construct an iterator start for the list<int> class and assign to start the result of find_if, which searches the list looking for a matching condition:

```
list<int>::iterator start =
  find_if(aList.begin(), aList.end(),
  bind2nd(greater<int>(), 6));
```

That condition is specified here using a function object constructed by bind2nd. Thus start equals the first value in the list greater than 6, or it equals aList.end(). Display this value with

```
if (start != aList.end())
    cout << "start == " << *start << endl;
```

To perform the opposite search—that is, to look for the first value that is *not* greater than 6—construct another function object using not1 like this:

```
not1(bind2nd(greater<int>(), 6)
```

You must use not1 in this instance because bind2nd returns a unary_function object. Use not2 to create a function object from any binary_function object.

Summary

- The C++ Standard Template Library (STL) is a comprehensive collection of data structures and algorithms recently adopted into ANSI C++.

- The STL is expected to merge with the full ANSI C++ standard library and lose its identity. Meanwhile, this and the next few chapters treat the STL as a separate entity.

- Two features characterize the STL: the separation of data structures from algorithms and its non-object-oriented nature.

- *Iterators* are similar to pointers that provide access to data elements. A pair of iterators can define a range of data elements in a container.

- *Containers* are data structures such as lists, vectors, and deques provided as template classes. You typically access a container's data elements using iterators, which the containers generate.
- *Algorithms* are function templates that operate on data. For example, algorithms can sort data in a vector, or search a list of objects. The functions possess no special knowledge of the types and structures of data on which they operate, a fact that makes the use of standard algorithms completely generic.

11

CHAPTER

Mastering Standard Strings

It seems that everybody and their uncles' brothers (plus a certain computer-book author) have at one time or another written a string class template. Many of these authors have optimistically promoted their strings as *standard* or as *closely resembling the coming ANSI C++ standard string-class template.*

Finally, these battles among string enthusiasts are over. The standard C++ library now provides a standard string-class template that promises to put a lid on string library propagation once and for all. Following is an in-depth look at the standard string template's capabilities. To use standard strings, insert the following include statement into your program (*do not append .h to the filename*):

```
#include <string>
```

To compile the listings in this chapter, you must use the 32-bit command line compiler, Bcc32.exe, or you must select a 32-bit output target with the IDE's TargetExpert.

> **NOTE**
>
> Including the `<string>` header makes the standard C++ string templates and `typedefs` available, and imports standard C null-terminated string functions such as `strcpy` and `strtok`. You do not also have to include `<string.h>` to use standard C string functions.

Introducing String Templates

A standard string object is a sequence of characters, which you can access individually using the indexing operator [ ]. A standard string is similar to a vector, but the string class provides many more operations specific to string-handling tasks. For this reason, the standard library implements its string templates separately from other data structures. In other words, strings are not derived from the vector container class as you might suppose.

On the technical level, the standard string template is named `basic_string`, and all string objects are constructed from this fundamental class template. Characters may be 8- or 16-bits wide, which means that `basic_string` potentially supports any language's character set, from English to Japanese.

To simplify the use of the `basic_string` template, the standard library defines two `typedefs`: `string` and `wstring`. In all cases, you should define string objects using one of these two `typedefs`—it's highly unlikely you'll even need to use `basic_string` directly. The `string` template provides 8-bit *narrow* character strings. The `wstring` template provides 16-bit *wide* character strings. String objects may be as large as memory allows. All string operations are the same for `string` and `wstring` objects, and you can convert from one type to the other simply by recompiling. For simplicity in this chapter, I'll use `strings` rather than `wstrings` in the sample listings.

Declaring String Objects

There are many ways to declare string objects, which are far more versatile than the arrays of char so often used in C and C++ programs. Include the <string> header; then declare a string variable. This creates an empty string

```
string AnyString;
```

to which you might assign string values, function return values, and so on. Following are three other ways to declare and initialize string objects:

```
string s1("Stringing in the rain");
string s2 = "Any string of yours is a string of mine";
string s3(s1);
```

As these examples show, you can initialize a string object from a literal string constant, or you can assign a string constant to a string object. You can also initialize a new string object using another string. Listing 11.1, Sdeclare.cpp, demonstrates a variety of additional methods you can use to declare string objects. You must compile this program using the 32-bit compiler, bcc32, or by specifying a 32-bit output target in the IDE.

Listing 11.1. Sdeclare.cpp (Declares string objects in various ways).

```
//=============================================================
// Sdeclare.cpp -- Declares string objects in various ways
// To compile:
//    bcc32 sdeclare
// To run:
//    sdeclare
// Copyright (c) 1996 by Tom Swan. All rights reserved.
//=============================================================

#include <iostream>
#include <string>
#include <vector>

using namespace std;

void ShowString(const char* s, const string& sr);

string sEmpty;
string sFromLiteral("Stringing in the rain");
string sFromString(sFromLiteral);
string sFromAssign = "A string in time saves mine";
string sFilled(40, '#');
//Following should reserve 64-char string, but it doesn't
//string sReserve("Short and sweet", 64);
//Use following statement instead and assign literal string *
string sReserve(64, '\0');
string sPartial(sFromAssign, 9, 7);

char buffer[5] = { 'a', 'b', 'c', 'd', 'e' };
string sFromPointers(buffer + 1, buffer + 5);
```

continues

Listing 11.1. continued

```
vector<char> cVector(buffer, buffer + 5);
string sFromIterators(cVector.begin(), cVector.end());

void main()
{
  ShowString("sEmpty", sEmpty);
  ShowString("sFromConst", sFromLiteral);
  ShowString("sFromString", sFromString);
  ShowString("sFromAssign", sFromAssign);
  ShowString("sFilled", sFilled);
  sReserve = "Short and sweet";      // * Assign literal string
  ShowString("sReserve", sReserve);
  ShowString("sPartial", sPartial);
  ShowString("sFromPointers", sFromPointers);
  ShowString("sFromIterators", sFromIterators);
}

void ShowString(const char* s, const string& sr)
{
  cout << s << " : " << sr << endl;
  cout << " len:" << sr.length();
  cout << " siz:" << sr.size();
  cout << " cap:" << sr.capacity();
  cout << endl;
}
```

Specify an integer value and a `char` to declare and fill a string with that many characters:

```
string sFilled(40, '#');
```

This creates a 40-character string filled with hatch marks (some people call them pound signs, although on old text terminals, I believe they were Klingon warships). To reserve extra space in a string, you should be able to specify a literal string value and an integer:

```
string sReserve("Short and sweet", 64);
```

The resulting string object should be 15-characters long (the length of the literal string), but with the capacity to hold up to 64 characters. Reserving space for strings this way improves efficiency by limiting memory reallocations for strings that need to grow beyond their current capacity. Unfortunately, however, this is not what happens—instead, the compiler incorrectly sets sReserve's length, size, *and* capacity to 64, resulting in random characters in the string. As a workaround, you can assign nulls to a string of the capacity you want, and then assign the literal string:

```
string sReserve(64, '\0');
...
sReserve = "Short and sweet";  // Length = 15, capacity = 64
```

Because this requires an extra statement, it is less than ideal, but it works. You can also specify a range of characters to initialize a new string:

```
string sPartial(sFromAssign, 9, 7);
```

This creates sPartial using seven characters beginning with the character at sFromAssign[9]. The result in this example is a string equal to *in time*.

You can also use iterators to create string objects. There are two basic forms. The first constructs a string from a character buffer, or from a portion of a buffer:

```
char buffer[5] = { 'a', 'b', 'c', 'd', 'e' };
string sFromPointers(buffer + 1, buffer + 5);
```

The expressions buffer+1 and buffer+5 are iterators (in the form of char pointers), which define the range of characters in the original buffer to use for initializing the string object. In this example, the resulting string, *bcde,* begins with the second character in buffer. Note that buffer+5 equals the buffer's *past-the-end* value.

You can also use iterator functions such as those provided by a container class template. For example, the following constructs a string object from a vector of characters, initialized from the preceding buffer:

```
vector<char> cVector(buffer, buffer + 5);
string sFromIterators(cVector.begin(), cVector.end());
```

This is an excruciatingly convoluted method to construct a string object, but it demonstrates the wide variety of methods available. You can create a string object using just about any imaginable collection of characters.

Reading and Writing Strings

You can use iostream statements to read and write string objects. For example, this writes a string to the standard output file:

```
string s("Write me right out");
cout << s << endl;
```

You can input strings using similar statements:

```
cout << "Enter a string: ";
cin >> s;
```

However, this reads only the first word of input because white space (blanks, tabs, end of line markers, and so on) terminate the input. To read an entire string including blanks and controls, use the getline function, provided in the <string> header. For example, the statement

```
string s;
getline(cin, s, '\n');
```

reads text from the standard input to a string object. Specify three arguments to getline: an istream object reference (cin), a string object (s), and an input terminator ('\n').

Other input terminators are allowed. For instance, use '\t' to terminate input when a tab control code is encountered. Listing 11.2 shows how to use getline to read a text file using string objects.

11

Listing 11.2. Rstrings.cpp (Reads a text file using string objects).

```
//==============================================================
// Rstrings.cpp -- Reads a text file using string objects
// To compile:
//    bcc32 rstrings
// To run:
//    rstrings
// Copyright (c) 1996 by Tom Swan. All rights reserved.
//==============================================================

#include <iostream>
#include <fstream>
#include <string>

using namespace std;

void main()
{
  string s;

  ifstream ifs("Rstrings.cpp", ios::in);
  while (ifs.good()) {
    getline(ifs, s, '\n');
    cout << s << endl;
  }
}
```

Just to keep things short, the program reads its own text file using an `ifstream` (input file stream) object. The call to `getline` specifies `ifs` as the input stream, `s` as the string object to hold each line of the file, and a new-line character as the line delimiter.

To parse a file into words, specify a blank as the delimiter:

```
getline(ifs, s, ' ');
```

Getting the Facts

Strings provide many functions that you can call to obtain factual information such as the length of a string object. Table 11.1 lists these functions and their return values.

Table 11.1. String-fact functions.

Function	Returns	Description
size	size_type	Size of string in characters
length	size_type	Length of string in characters
capacity	size_type	Capacity of string in characters
max_size	size_type	Maximum potential capacity of string
resize	void	Resize and optionally fill string
reserve	void	Reserve additional capacity
empty	bool	Returns true if string length is zero

The `size`, `length`, and `capacity` functions return values of type `size_type`, an integer of a type dependent on the program's memory model. A string's `size` and `length` are always the same. Its `capacity`, however, equals the maximum potential size of the string that will not require a memory reallocation. For example, if the string's length is 12 and its capacity is 24, you can append another 12 characters before the string's internal buffer needs to be reallocated. (Such reallocations occur automatically as needed, but it's best to avoid forcing too many of these time-wasting operations to occur.)

A string's `max_size` equals its potential maximum size. Depending on the operating system and memory model, this might be as large as all available memory, or at least as large as the largest contiguous block. In any case, a string's size, length, and capacity can never exceed `max_size`.

Call the `resize` function to expand or contract a string's size. For example, this changes a string's size and length to 64 characters without disturbing the string's content, as long as it is shorter than the new capacity:

```
s.resize(64);  // Upsize to 64 characters
```

If the specified value is smaller than the string's current size, its length is downsized:

```
s.resize(10);  // Downsize to 10 characters
```

However, this does not alter the string's capacity or size in memory, only its current length in characters. To reduce the string's physical size, create a new string object.

To expand a string and fill its extra space with a character (the default fill character is a blank), use the statement

```
s.resize(64, '@');  // Upsize s and fill extra space with @ characters
```

Call reserve to expand a string's capacity without altering its current length:

```
s.reserve(128);
```

This does not change the string's size, but it reallocates the internal string buffer to the new specified capacity up to the limit specified by `max_size`.

Finally, call `empty` to determine if a string size is zero:

```
if (s.empty()) ...
```

This is generally faster than testing whether size or length equal 0.

The `resize` and `reserve` functions, along with others not yet introduced, throw an exception of type `length_error` if the resulting string's length exceeds `max_size`. You might want to catch this error in function main, or you can embed calls to `resize` and `reserve` and other string functions in a try-catch block:

```
try {
  aString.reserve(128);
}
catch (length_error e) {
  cout << "*** Length Error: " << e.what() << endl;
}
```

Using String Operators

The usual assignment, comparison, and some mathematical operators are defined for string templates. You can assign one string to another:

```
string newString;
string oldString = "Old";
newString = oldString;    // Copies oldString to newString
```

You can assign a literal string to a string object:

```
string stringObject;
// ...
stringObject = "Literal string";
```

And you can also assign a character to a string object, which is converted into a string with that character and a length of 1:

```
string charString;
// ...
charString = 'Q';   // Sets charString equal to the string "Q"
```

However, don't try the following—you cannot declare and initialize a string object with a character (apparently because characters evaluate to integer values, and this is therefore ambiguous):

```
string charString = 'Q';  // ??? Does not compile
```

Use the + and += operators to concatenate (join) two strings. For example, this appends text to the end of an existing string object named colors:

```
string colors = "red";  // Initialize colors string
colors += " blue";      // Append blue to colors
colors += " green";     // Append green to colors
```

Use the + operator to concatenate two strings, creating a temporary string object that you can assign to another string or use in another statement:

```
string first = "First", second = "Second";
string third = (first + second);
cout << (first + second + third) << endl;
```

Strings also provide the subscript operator [ ], which you can use to access a string's individual characters. This statement

```
cout << aString[4] << endl;
```

displays the fifth character in aString. (It's the fifth because aString[0] is the first.) This is equivalent to calling a string object's at function. For example, this statement has the same effect as the preceding one:

```
cout << aString.at(4) << endl;
```

Indexing outside of a string's length throws an `out_of_range` error. To trap this error, embed all indexing operations and calls to `at` in a `try-catch` block:

```
try {
  cout << alphabet[100] << endl;
  cout << alphabet.at(100) << endl;
}
catch (out_of_range e) {
  cout << "*** Range Error: " << e.what() << endl;
}
```

Because 100 is larger than `alphabet`'s size, the program displays the error message

```
*** Range Error: position beyond end of string
```

Calling String Functions

Various string member functions perform operations such as appending new text to string objects and finding patterns embedded in strings. Some functions such as `find` duplicate standard algorithms. Although you can apply some of the standard algorithms to string objects, the native methods are generally faster and you should use them whenever possible.

Table 11.2 lists the functions described in this and the next two sections. All functions except `swap`, which returns `void`, return a reference of type `basic_string&`. You may use these functions in output stream statements, pass them to other functions that declare string parameters, or assign them to string variables.

Table 11.2. String member functions (all return `string&`).

Function	Description
append	Appends text from one string onto another
assign	Assigns text from one string to another
insert	Inserts text from one string into another
remove	Removes text from strings
replace	Replaces text in strings
substr	Returns a substring of a string
swap	Swaps two strings

To try these functions, first define two string objects in a small test program:

```
#include <string>
...
string aString;
string alphabet = "Abcdefghijlkmnopqrstuvwxyz";
```

I'll use these definitions throughout this section to demonstrate string functions. Call append to add text to the end of an existing string. There are several variations. For example, this appends alphabet onto the end of aString:

```
aString = "Alphabet: ";
aString.append(alphabet);
```

You can also append a literal string:

```
aString.append(" == The End! ==");
```

Or you can specify a starting index and number of characters. The following statement appends up to six characters from alphabet starting with the fifth character:

```
aString.append(alphabet, 4, 6);  // 4=starting index, 6=count
```

Use the assign function to assign a new string, or portions of a string, to any string object. Call the function for the object to which you want to make the assignment. Declare two strings as you did for append:

```
string aString;
string alphabet = "Abcdefghijlkmnopqrstuvwxyz";
```

Then call assign using one of the following styles. Comments show the resulting strings:

```
aString.assign(alphabet);        // aString = "Abc...xyz"
aString.assign(alphabet, 2, 6);  // aString = "cdefgh"
aString.assign(alphabet, 20);    // aString = "uvwxyz"
aString.assign('@');             // aString = "@"
aString.assign(8, '*');          // aString = "********"
```

The first line assigns one string object to another, in this case replacing aString with a copy of alphabet's text. The second statement assigns six characters to aString starting at alphabet[2]. The next assigns characters to aString starting from alphabet[20] to the end of the alphabet string. Pass a char constant to create a single-character string. Pass an integer and a char constant to create and fill a string with the specified number of characters.

You can also pass a pair of iterators to assign. For example, this code assigns a portion of a char array to a string object:

```
char buffer[26];
strcpy(buffer, alphabet.c_str());
aString.assign(buffer + 5, buffer + 10);  // aString == "fghij"
```

The second line shows how to access a string object as a null-terminated array of char. The string's c_str() function returns a const char* to the string object's text as a C-style string. You may not make assignments or any other changes to the resulting string.

You may also pass a pair of iterators from any data structure that contains character data. This, for example, copies characters from a vector to a string object:

```
vector<char> v(buffer, buffer + 26);
aString.assign(v.begin(), v.end());  // aString == "Abc...xyz"
```

These and other string functions can throw out_of_range or length_error exceptions. Use try-catch blocks to trap these errors, as in this example:

```
try {
  aString.assign(alphabet, 100);  // Force exception with bad index
}
catch (out_of_range e) {
  cout << "*** Range Error: " << e.what() << endl;
}
catch (length_error e) {
  cout << "*** Length Error: " << e.what() << endl;
}
```

To swap two strings, call the swap member function for either of them:

```
s1.swap(s2);  // Swaps strings s1 and s2
s2.swap(s1);  // Same as preceding statement
```

The next two sections, "Inserting and Deleting Strings" and "Copying Strings," discuss the remaining functions in Table 11.2: insert, remove, replace, and substr.

Inserting and Deleting Strings

To insert characters into strings, and to delete portions of strings, call the insert and remove string member functions. Combine the two functions by calling replace, which performs an insertion followed by a removal.

The insert function is similar to the vector data structure's insert method. The remove function is similar to the vector's erase. Removing a portion of a string may change its length, but not its capacity. To alter the physical size of a string following a removal, copy it to another string object.

Use insert to insert text anywhere in a string. For example, the code

```
string s1 = "It's a life";
string s2 = "It's a beautiful day";
s1.insert(7, s2, 7, 10); // s1 == "It's a beautiful life"
```

sets string s1 to It's a beautiful life. The first parameter is the index where the insertion is to be made; next is the source string object to insert, followed by an index into that source string, and ending with a count of the characters to insert from the source into the destination.

The following code fragment uses insert and remove to insert a filename into an error message:

```
string errString = "Error: @ not found";
int k = errString.find('@');
errString.remove(k, 1);  // k==index; 1==count
errString.insert(k, "Filename.xxx");
```

The second statement calls the find member function to locate the index position of the at-sign character. The program then removes that character and inserts a filename. A single call to replace does the same job with less work:

```
errString.replace(k, 1, "Filename.xxx");
```

Pass an index k plus a count (1 in the example) to replace that many characters at the specified position. The function throws an out_of_range exception if the index is greater than the string's size.

You can also pass iterators to insert, remove, and replace. These can be iterators generated by a data structure's begin and end functions (or rbegin and rend reverse iterator functions), a string object's begin, end, rbegin, or rend functions, or pointers into a char array. Here are some sample statements using iterators. Comments show the resulting strings:

```
#include <vector>
#include <string>
// ...
vector<char> alphaVect(alphabet.begin(), alphabet.end());
string s = "========";          // s == "========"
s.insert(s.begin() + 4, '@');   // s == "====@===="
s.insert(s.begin() + 4, 3, '$'); // s == "====$$$@===="
s.insert(s.begin(),             // s == "defgh====$$$@===="
  alphaVect.begin() + 3, alphaVect.begin() + 8);
```

Using the alphabet string from earlier examples, the program constructs a vector of characters and a string, s, with eight equal signs. The first argument to insert is the iterator in the destination string where the insertion is to be made. You can insert a single character, or a count of characters, or you can specify two more iterators to copy a range of characters into the source string.

Copying Strings

Member function copy transfers a string object's characters, or a portion of those characters, to a memory buffer, usually an array of char. Given this string object

```
string alphabet = "Abcdefghijklmnopqrstuvwxyz";
```

the following code inserts the first three characters from alphabet into a char buffer:

```
char buffer[40];
alphabet.copy(buffer, 3);
buffer[3] = 0;              // buffer = "Abc"
```

Function copy does not insert a null terminator into the buffer. Another form copies a count of characters from a starting index. This code

```
alphabet.copy(buffer, 6, 3);
buffer[6] = 0;             // buffer = "defghi";
```

copies into buffer six characters from alphabet starting with the character at alphabet[3]. Again, it is your job to insert any required null. The reason copy doesn't do this for you is so you can use the function to replace portions of char arrays with string data. For example, this statement

```
alphabet.copy(buffer, 3, 4); // buffer = "efgghi";
```

copies into buffer three characters from alphabet starting at alphabet[4]. Given the preceding code, this overwrites buffer's first three characters, resulting in the string efgghi.

Another way to copy portions of strings is to call the `substr` function. Unlike `copy`, however, `substr` returns a `basic_string` object (*not* a reference). Use `substr` in output stream statements. These output stream statements display substrings from the `alphabet` string:

```
cout << alphabet.substr(20) << endl;    // "uvwxyz"
cout << alphabet.substr(6, 8) << endl;  // "ghijklmn"
```

The first statement displays a substring of `alphabet` starting with the twenty-first character to the end of the source string. The second statement displays eight characters starting with `alphabet[6]`. You can also assign `substr` to another string object:

```
string s = alphabet.substr(10, 5);  // s = "klmno";
```

Converting to Null-Terminated Strings

As I mentioned, you can call a string object's `c_str` function to obtain a `const char` pointer to the object's text as a C-style, null-terminated array of `char`. You may not assign text or modify this array in any way. This text is a copy of the string's data, with the character `traits::eos()` (usually NULL) appended to the end.

> **NOTE**
>
> The `traits` object is a user-defined parameter passed to the `basic_string` template to create the `string` and `wstring` typedefs. It is one of these types:
>
> ```
> string_char_traits<char>       // string
> string_char_traits<wchar_t>    // wstring
> ```
>
> The `string_char_traits` structure, defined in the `<string>` header file, defines various string attributes such as the end of string character (`eos`) and various standard inline functions such as `length` and `copy`. You will probably not have to use `string_char_traits` in programs, but if you want to learn more about how `basic_string` functions operate, this is the structure to study.

Another method to get to a string object's internal buffer is to use the `data` function. This function returns the same result as `c_str` with one difference. If the string object's size or length is zero, `data` returns NULL. Function `c_str` returns `traits::eos()`, which specifies the end of string character. Usually, this is NULL, but it may be another character to support a nonstandard string format.

Here are some sample statements that use `c_str` and `data`:

```
const char* cp;
cp = alphabet.c_str();
```

Or you can use `data` to do the same:

```
cp = alphabet.data();
```

Either way, the statements declare and initialize a character pointer, cp, to the alphabet string object as a null-terminated string. Assignments to cp are forbidden:

```
cp[5] = 'Q';  // ??? Error: Can't modify a const object
```

To modify the string, you must first copy it to a buffer:

```
char cbuf[10];
strncpy(cbuf, cp, 9);
cbuf[9] = 0;
cbuf[5] = 'Q';
```

Comparing Strings

Compare strings naturally by using logical operators, as in the following example:

```
if (s1 == s2) ...  // Do if s1 equals s2
if (s1 < s2 ) ...  // Do if s1 is less than s2
if (s1 >= s2) ...  // Do if s1 is greater than or equal to s2
if (s1 != s2) ...  // Do if s1 is not equal to s2, etc.
```

Such expressions call the basic_string template's compare method, which provides additional parameters that you can use to compare portions of strings. There are three basic forms of compare, all of which return an integer result:

```
int result, pos, count;
string s1, s2;
...
result = s1.compare(s2, pos, count);
result = s1.compare("Literal string", pos);
result = s1.compare("Literal string", pos, count);
```

The result is less than zero if s1 < s2, zero if s1 = s2, and greater than zero if s1 > s2. In addition, pos and count receive default values so you can use statements such as

```
result = s1.compare(s2);
result = s1.compare("Literal string");
```

To try compare, create a test program that includes <string> and insert the following code into function main. Define two strings and some integer variables:

```
string s1 = "ABCDEFG";
string s2 = "ABCDEFGHIJKLMNOP";
int result;
int pos = 2;
int count = 8;
```

Then, use compare as follows. Comments indicate the results:

```
result = s1.compare(s2, pos, count);        // result > 0 (s1 > s2)
result = s1.compare("CDEFG", pos);          // result = 0 (s1 = s2)
result = s1.compare("CDEFG", pos, count);   // result < 0 (s1 < s2)
```

The first line compares s2 and `count` characters of s1 starting at s1[pos]. The second line compares a literal string and s1[pos] to the end of s1. The third line compares a literal string and `count` characters of s1 starting at s1[pos].

Searching Strings

The `basic_string` template provides two fundamental search functions: `find` and `rfind`. The first searches a string from its beginning; the second searches a string in reverse, starting at its end. The functions return the index in the source string where a substring is found, or if no matches are found, they return a value greater than the length of the string. (Tests indicate that the *no-match* value equals the string's capacity, at least for Borland C++ 5.0, but this fact should not be taken as gospel for all ANSI C++ compilers.)

The following code fragments demonstrate how to use `find` and `rfind`.

```
string alphabet = "Abcdefghijklmnopqrstuvwxyz";
cout << alphabet.find("klmnop") << endl;
cout << alphabet.rfind("def") << endl;
cout << alphabet.find("White elephant") << endl;
cout << alphabet.rfind("White elephant") << endl;
```

The first output statement displays 10, the index of the string `klmnop` in the `alphabet` string object. The second output statement displays 3, the index of `def`. In this case, however, `rfind` searches the string from back to front. The final two statements display a value greater than the length of `alphabet`, indicating the `White elephant` was not found.

Of course, as you probably expect, you can search for string objects as well as literal strings:

```
string search = "mnop";
cout << alphabet.find(search) << endl;
```

This displays 12, the index of `mnop` in `alphabet`. As you can with `compare`, you may also specify a starting position to begin the search:

```
cout << alphabet.find(search, 4) << endl;
```

This looks for the `search` string starting at `alphabet[4]` and moving forward. You can specify a count of characters to search, but for some strange reason, you can do so only with a C-style string, not a string object. This searches six characters of `alphabet`, looking for `mnop`, starting with `alphabet[4]`.

```
cout << alphabet.find("mnop", 4, 6) << endl;
```

But this does not compile (a minor, but annoying omission in the `basic_string` template):

```
cout << alphabet.find(search, 4, 6) << endl;  // ???
```

You can also search for individual characters:

```
cout << alphabet.find('y') << endl;
```

Other string search functions locate the first character from a character set, represented as a string. For example, given this `alphabet` string object

```
string alphabet = "abcdefghijklmnopqrstuvwxyz";
```

the following statements display the values shown in comments:

```
cout << alphabet.find_first_of("aeiou") << endl;        // 0
cout << alphabet.find_last_of("aeiou") << endl;         // 20
cout << alphabet.find_first_not_of("aeiou") << endl;    // 1
cout << alphabet.find_last_not_of("aeiou") << endl;     // 25
```

Function `find_first_of` locates the index of the first occurrence of any characters in the string `aeiou`. Function `find_last_of` locates the last such index. The reverse functions, `find_first_not_of` and `find_last_not_of`, locate the first or last non-matching character in `alphabet`.

You can also specify a starting index, for example, to continue a search. The following code snippet locates the indexes of all vowels in the `alphabet` string:

```
cout << "Find all vowels in alphabet" << endl;
int p = alphabet.find_first_of("aeiou");
while (p < alphabet.size()) {
  cout << p << endl;
  p = alphabet.find_first_of("aeiou", p + 1);
}
```

Summary

- A standard string object is a sequence of characters that can be accessed individually with the indexing operator. Strings are similar to vectors, but the `basic_string` template is not derived from the `vector` container class.

- Include <string> (no trailing .h) to use standard strings. Two `typedefs`, `string` and `wstring`, construct 16-bit (narrow character) and 32-bit (wide character) string objects respectively.

- Call native `string` and `wstring` functions whenever possible. Although you can use standard algorithms with string objects, the native functions are generally faster.

- A string's `length` equals the number of characters it contains. Its `size` is always equal to its `length`. A string's `capacity` is the maximum size to which a string can grow without requiring a memory reallocation. A string's `max_size` represents its largest possible size and capacity.

- The usual logical and assignment operators are defined for string objects. You can also call the compare function to compare two strings.

- String member functions such as `append`, `assign`, `insert`, `remove`, `replace`, and others perform a variety of string operations.

- Call the `c_str` member function to obtain a constant `char` pointer to a null terminated C-style string, for example, to pass a string object to a function that requires a `const char*` argument. You may not modify the data addressed by the pointer returned by `c_str`.

- Search strings for substrings and characters using `find` and `rfind`. Search for sets of characters using `find_first_of`, `find_last_of`, `find_first_not_of`, and `find_last_not_of`.

12

Mastering Standard Containers

The standard library provides 10 container data structures in the form of class templates. Because they are templates, the containers automatically mold themselves to accommodate any type of data you need to store. To access data in a container, you instantiate one or more iterators of the class's `iterator` type, using the techniques explained in the preceding chapter. The use of iterators makes containers completely general in nature—you can store objects in them, pointers to objects, and even other containers to create multilevel structures.

To compile the listings in this chapter, you must use the 32-bit command line compiler, Bcc32.exe, or you must select a 32-bit output target with the IDE's TargetExpert.

> **NOTE**
>
> Some of the methods in this chapter require template member functions, a feature that few, if any, C++ compilers support. The STL, which is still in its evolutionary stages, uses this feature, and because Borland C++ 5 does not yet support template member functions, you may experience problems compiling some of the example code in this chapter.

Introducing Containers

Table 12.1 lists the standard library's 10 container class templates arranged in order of complexity.

Table 12.1. Standard container class templates.

Class template	Description
vector	Linear sequence, similar to a C++ array
list	Double-linked list
deque	Double-ended queue
set	Associative array of unique keys. A special form of set capable of holding binary values is called a *bit set.*
multiset	Associative array of possibly duplicated keys
map	Associative array of unique keys and values
multimap	Associative array of possibly duplicated keys and values
stack	Last-in-first-out (LIFO) data structure
queue	First-in-first-out (FIFO) data structure
priority_queue	Critical-event-ordered queue or vector

Following are some key rules and regulations about containers that you should keep in mind:

- A container may store any type of data, including fundamental objects such as ints and doubles, strings, structs, class objects, and pointers. However, a container cannot store references.

- An object's copy constructor handles that object's insertion into a container. By overloading the assignment operator and providing a copy constructor, you gain total control over container insertions. This control is valuable, for example, in managing the effects of operations such as copying one container to another.

- Containers automatically allocate and release memory as needed for object storage.

- A vector can grow to accommodate new data, but it cannot automatically shrink in size. Other containers such as lists, deques, and sets can grow and shrink as needed.

- When a program destroys a container, it first calls any destructor for its owned objects. You can therefore safely destroy a container without first removing its contents.

- The preceding rule does not hold true when a container stores pointers to objects. In that case, it is your responsibility to destroy the addressed objects or to free any allocated memory.

TIP

For safe, automatic destruction of objects addressed by pointers stored in containers, see "Pointers in Containers" in the next chapter.

Vector

A vector is like a smart array that maintains size information and can grow to make room for storing more data. Vectors provide random access to their data through the C++ subscript operator ([ ]). They also provide a number of useful member functions you can call.

Vectors shine at providing immediate access to all data elements. It takes no longer to access the last element in a vector container than it does the first. However, because elements in a vector are stored physically together, insertions into the middle of a vector cause other elements to move, which takes time proportional to the number of those elements. Insertions at the end of a vector are efficient, unless the insertion requires the vector to expand. Also, when a vector expands, its data must be copied to another memory block. Thus vector expansions may temporarily require more than twice the amount of occupied memory. If your program does a lot of insertions, you may want to use a list or another memory-efficient data structure.

12

Declaring Vectors

Here are some different ways to construct vectors.

```
#include <vector>
...
vector<int> vint1;
vector<string> vstr1(10);
vector<double> vdouble1(100);
```

The first statement constructs an empty vector that can hold values of type int. It's rarely useful to construct empty vectors this way—instead, you'll normally specify an initial size as the next two statements demonstrate. The first of these constructs a vector, vstr1, of 10 string objects. The second constructs a vector, vdouble1, of 100 double values.

You may store any type of data in a vector. However, any structures require

- A default constructor
- A copy constructor
- A destructor
- Address-of operator
- Assignment operator

You need to implement the last two items only if the compiler can't provide them by default. Listing 12.1, Tcoord1.h, shows an example of a bare-bones class that you can use as a guide to creating structures for storing in vectors.

Listing 12.1. Tcoord1.h (Declares class for vector data).

```
//===============================================================
// Tcoord1.h -- Declares class for vector data
// Copyright (c) 1996 by Tom Swan. All rights reserved.
//===============================================================

class TCoord {
  int x, y;
public:
  TCoord(): x(0), y(0) { }      // Default constructor
  TCoord(const TCoord& arg)     // Copy constructor
    { x = arg.x; y = arg.y; }
  ~TCoord() { }                 // Destructor
};
```

Given the TCoord class declaration, you can create vectors of class objects and pointers to those objects:

```
vector<TCoord> coordArray(100);      // Array of 100 TCoord objects
vector<TCoord*> coordPointers(100);  // Array of 100 TCoord pointers
```

Use subscripting to assign and refer to data in vector containers:

```
vstr1[1] = "Value: ";
vdouble1[10] = 3.14159;
cout << vstr1[1] << vdouble1[10] << endl;
```

In addition to an initial size, you also can specify a value to insert into every vector slot. For example, this creates a vector of 32 int values, all initialized to -1:

```
vector<int> vint2(32, -1);
```

You may also construct vectors using iterators. For instance, this code

```
int iarray[24];
vector<int> vint3(iarray, iarray + 24);
vector<int> vint4(vint3.begin(),vint3.end());
```

constructs two vectors. The first, vint3, is given the values from the integer array, iarray. The second, vint4, specifies vint3's begin and end iterators to use for constructing the vector and initializing its contents.

Using Vectors

The *size* of a vector equals how many elements it stores. If vdouble1 is a vector of 100 double values, this statement

```
cout << "Size of vdouble1 = " << vdouble1.size() << endl;
```

displays 100. A vector's *capacity* indicates how large the vector may become before a memory allocation is needed to store more data:

```
cout << "Capacity = " << vdouble1.capacity() << endl;
```

A vector's max_size function returns the upper limit on a vector's size and capacity, usually equal to the largest memory block available:

```
cout << "Max_size = " << vdouble1.max_size() << endl;
```

You can alter a vector's capacity without affecting its current size by calling the reserve function. This is a memory-efficient way to avoid frequent memory allocations in cases where you can determine in advance how many values you will ultimately store in the container. For example, this statement

```
vdouble1.reserve(250);
```

changes vdouble1's capacity to 250, but its size remains the same.

The standard library treats Boolean vectors as a special superset of the vector template. Define a Boolean vector like this:

```
vector<bool> vbool(16);
```

That creates a vector, `vbool`, of 16 true or false values. Use subscript expressions to assign values to vector elements:

```
vbool[0] = true;
vbool[1] = false;
```

You can also specify an initial value. For example, this creates an eight-element vector of `bool` values initialized to `true`:

```
vector<bool> binit(8, true);
```

Note that a vector's size equals the number of values it contains, which is not the same as its size in bytes. The following statements display 16, the vector's size in elements, and 24, its size in bytes, respectively:

```
cout << "Size = " << vbool.size() << endl;
cout << "Bytes = " << sizeof vbool << endl;
```

Vector values are interpreted as 1 (true) or 0 (false). The following statement therefore displays 1 0, not the words `true` and `false`.

```
cout << vbool[0] << " " << vbool[1] << endl;
```

> **NOTE**
>
> A Boolean vector is *not* a packed array of bits. See also "Bit Sets" in this chapter for another way to store bit values in containers.

Calling Vector Functions

Vector's provide a number of useful member functions. Call `assign` like this

```
vdouble1.assign(10, 1.0);
```

to erase the first 10 values in a vector and assign 1.0 to those values. Use the `front` and `back` functions to inspect the first and last vector elements:

```
cout << "First = " << vdouble1.front() << endl;
cout << "Last = " << vdouble1.back() << endl;
```

Three functions you'll probably use more often than others are `erase`, `resize`, and `insert`. To demonstrate these functions, define a vector of six integers as follows:

```
int ia[6] = { 1, 2, 3, 4, 5, 6 };
vector<int> sixints(ia, ia + 6);
```

Erasing a vector element moves any other elements upwards. For example, you might call the standard `find` algorithm to locate a particular value to erase:

```
vector<int>::iterator p = find(
  sixints.begin(), sixints.end(), 3);
sixints.erase(p);
```

Because `erase` does not change the size of the vector, the resulting element values are 1, 2, 4, 5, 6, 6. Call resize to remove the now duplicated final value:

```
sixints.resize(5);
for (int i = 0; i < sixints.size(); i++)
  cout << sixints[i] << endl;
```

Call `insert` to insert a new value into a vector, and move other values down. This statement

```
sixints.insert(sixints.begin() + 2, 99);
```

inserts the value 99 ahead of the value at location `sixints[2]`. Given the original series 1 2 3 4 5 6, the vector now contains 1 2 99 3 4 5 6.

Use the `pop_back` and `push_back` functions to use a vector as a stack. This pushes the value 123 onto the end of the vector:

```
sixints.push_back(123);
```

Remove the last element by calling `pop_back()`:

```
sixints.pop_back();
```

This is equivalent to erasing the last element and resizing the vector. Exchange two vectors by calling the `swap` function for one of the containers and pass the other as an argument. This swaps vector `v` and `sixints`:

```
vector<int> v(6);
sixints.swap(v);
```

The `flip` function is defined only for `vector<bool>` containers. It toggles all values in a Boolean vector from false to true and vice versa:

```
vector<bool> tf(8);
tf.flip();
```

List

Lists are linear collections of doubly linked elements. That is, each element contains two pointers that can address two other elements. This organization makes lists extremely efficient storage vessels. Regardless of its arrangement of elements, a list container takes only as much space as necessary (plus a smidgen more for the double links). Also, because the elements of a list do not have to be stored physically together, a list can potentially hold more information than a vector. Lists are excellent at storing data in fragmented memory caused by prior deletions that divide available memory into smaller chunks.

Insertions and deletions from lists are absolutely efficient. It takes no more time to delete the first item in a list than it does the last. Also, deleting items from the middle of a list makes that element's memory available for other data. There are no holes in a list.

However, lists are poor choices when you need rapid access to data—by searching for matching values, for example. Searches are linear, and therefore take time proportional to the number of examined elements. If you need random access to data, you might want to use a vector instead of a list. If you need the benefits of a list and random access (you want your cake and eat it too), consider using a set, a map, or a priority_queue.

Declaring Lists

Here are some different ways to construct list containers:

```
#include <list>
...
list<int> intList1;
list<int> intList2(10);
list<double> intList3(10, 3.14159);
```

The first declaration creates an empty list that can store int values. The second creates a list with 10 int values that are not initialized. The third constructs a list of 10 double values initialized to 3.14159.

You may store any type of data or pointer in a list. However, any structures require the following items:

- A default constructor
- A copy constructor
- A destructor
- Equality operator (==) (must be const)
- Less-than operator (<) (must be const)
- Address-of operator (*)
- Assignment operator (=)

You must explicitly declare the constructors and destructor. Overload the four operators only if necessary. For example, if memberwise assignment is good enough for the class (that is, it contains no pointers to dynamically allocated objects), you don't have to overload the assignment operator. Listing 12.2, Tcoord2.h, shows a bare-minimum class for objects to be stored in a list. Your class may of course provide other members and operators.

Listing 12.2. Tcoord2.h (Declares class for list data).

```
//=============================================================
// Tcoord2.h -- Declares class for list data
// Copyright (c) 1996 by Tom Swan. All rights reserved.
//=============================================================

class TCoord {
  int x, y;
public:
  TCoord(): x(0), y(0) { }                    // Default constructor
```

```
  TCoord(const TCoord& arg)                  // Copy constructor
    { x = arg.x; y = arg.y; }
  ~TCoord() { }                              // Destructor
  bool operator== (const TCoord& arg) const  // Equality operator
    { return (x == arg.x) && (y == arg.y); }
  bool operator< (const TCoord& arg) const   // Less-than operator
    { return (x < arg.x) && (y < arg.y); }
// Alternate constructor (optional)
  TCoord(int X, int Y): x(X), y(Y) { }
};
```

Given the TCoord declaration, you can declare lists of class objects and pointers:

```
list<TCoord> coordList(10);       // List of 10 TCoord objects
list<TCoord*> coordPointers(10);  // List of 10 TCoord pointers
```

Insert a TCoord object into the coordList container with a statement such as

```
coordList.insert(coordList.begin(), TCoord(4, 5));
```

When the list is destroyed, the container calls the TCoord destructor for every element. Insert a pointer to a TCoord object with a statement like this:

```
coordPtrs.insert(coordPtrs.begin(), new TCoord(4, 5));
```

In this case, because the container stores pointers, it is your responsibility to call any required destructors. For example, to remove a listed element requires two statements:

```
delete coordPtrs.front();
coordPtrs.remove(coordPtrs.front());
```

The first statement deletes the memory allocated to the first element in the list. The second statement removes the now invalid pointer to that element.

Using Lists

To determine the number of elements in a list, call the size function. Try this. First define a list container and fill it with some values:

```
list<int> anyList;
for (int i = 0; i < 10; i++)
  anyList.insert(anyList.end(), i);
```

Call empty and size to determine if the list is empty, or if not, to display the number of elements:

```
if (anyList.empty())
  cout << "List is empty" << endl;
else
  cout << "List has " << anyList.size() << " elements" << endl;
```

There are several other ways to insert elements into a list container. You can use the insert function as shown in preceding examples, or you can call push_front and push_back to insert elements at the beginning or end of the list. Define and fill the list as before; then add elements to its head and tail with code such as

411

```
list<int> anyList;
for (int i = 0; i < 10; i++)
  anyList.insert(anyList.end(), i);
anyList.push_back(1234);
anyList.push_front(4321);
```

TIP

To display the integer list contents for the examples in this section, include the `<algorithm>` header and use the following copy statement:

```
copy(anyList.begin(), anyList.end(),
    ostream_iterator<int>(cout, " "));
```

To insert multiple elements, use a statement like this:

```
anyList.insert(anyList.begin(), 4, -1);
```

That inserts four values equal to -1 at the head of `anyList`.

WARNING

With integer lists, don't accidentally reverse the order of the values in the preceding example. The following statement causes a serious bug:

```
anyList.insert(anyList.begin(), -1, 4);  // ??? Don't do this!
```

That attempts to insert the value four, minus one times, which seems to hopelessly confuse the `insert` function—another example of how lax the standard library is at preventing logical errors.

You'll often perform a search followed by an insertion of a new value into a list. Use the standard `find` algorithm as in this code fragment:

```
list<int>::iterator p =
  find(anyList.begin(), anyList.end(), 8);
anyList.insert(p, -2);
```

First define an iterator (named `p` in the sample) for the appropriate type of list. Call `find`, specifying as arguments a pair of iterators for the range of values to inspect and the value to find (8 in the example). Then, call `insert` with the resulting iterator to insert a value (-2 here) ahead of the located one. Note that if 8 is not in the list, `p` is set to the *past-the-end* value, and the insertion is made at the end of the list. This code operates correctly even if the list is empty.

There are several different methods for removing elements from a list. Call `erase` to remove a specific element—following a search for a value, as in the following example:

```
list<int>::iterator p =
  find(anyList.begin(), anyList.end(), 7);  // Find 7
if (p != anyList.end())  // If search was successful,
  anyList.erase(p);      // remove element at p
```

This, and other removal techniques, delete any memory allocated to list elements automatically and also call a destructor if one is defined. If the list contains pointers, however, memory management is your responsibility.

You can use an alternate form of `erase` to remove all elements in a range. Often, you'll do this after searching for a specific element, as in this example:

```
list<int>::iterator p =
  find(anyList.begin(), anyList.end(), 7);
anyList.erase(p, anyList.end());
```

The `find` algorithm searches for the value 7 in `anyList`. After that, the program passes the resulting iterator p and the list's *past-the-end* value to erase all elements from the one equal to 7 to the end of the list.

Lists are often used as stacks and queues where elements are pushed and popped from the front or end of the list. Remove the first element of a list by calling `pop_front`. Remove the last by calling `pop_back`. For example, this loop displays and removes all elements from `anyList`:

```
while (!anyList.empty()) {
  cout << anyList.front() << endl;
  anyList.pop_front();
}
```

Replace `front` with `back` and `pop_front` with `pop_back` to delete elements in reverse order, like a snake eating itself from tail to head.

Call the remove function to remove all elements equal to a specified value. For example, this statement

```
anyList.remove(-1);
```

removes from `anyList` all values equal to -1.

> **NOTE**
>
> The `remove_if` member function removes an element if it satisfies a certain condition. However, this and a few other functions are not available in Borland's STL implementation. This is due to the use of template member functions in the library, a feature that very few C++ compilers support. Borland C++ can't be faulted here—the library designers are guilty of using a feature that is so new, it barely exists.
>
> The standard library provides alternate non-template functions for many such member templates. However, `remove_if` has no non-template counterpart. In place of functions such as this, see the next chapter on standard algorithms. Chances are there's an algorithm that will do the same job as the missing member function.

Finally, here's a unique function—in fact, its name is `unique`. Call it to remove all but one of every duplicate value in a list. For example, create a list and insert a series of duplicate adjacent values:

```
list<int> anyList;
for (int i = 0; i < 10; i++) {
  anyList.insert(anyList.end(), i);
  anyList.insert(anyList.end(), i);
}
```

This inserts into `anyList` the sequence 0, 0, 1, 1, ..., 9, 9. Remove the duplicated values by calling `unique`:

```
anyList.unique();
```

After that, `anyList` contains the sequence 0, 1, ..., 9. The list does not have to be sorted, but the duplicated values must be adjacent.

Calling List Functions

As with all container data structures, lists provide several member functions that perform highly specialized jobs. Use `assign` to erase a list's current contents and copy values from another source such as a common C++ array. Define a list and fill it with some values:

```
list<int> anyList;
for (int i = 0; i < 10; i++)
  anyList.insert(anyList.end(), i);
```

To replace `anyList`'s values, call `assign` with a pair of iterator arguments. For example, these statements define a buffer of four integer values, remove any values in `anyList`, and insert the buffer's values in their place:

```
int buffer[4] = { 10, 20, 30, 40 };
anyList.assign(buffer, buffer + 4);
```

Alternatively, you can assign a count of values to a list. The following statement, for example, removes all values from `anyList` and assigns four values equal to -1.

```
anyList.assign(4, -1);
```

TIP

Call `assign` to initialize a list of a certain size. For example, if you know you will need to insert 100 values into a list, it might be faster to use `assign` to prepare the list, and then use a dereferenced iterator to copy new values to list elements. Define a list and use `assign` to initialize it to 10 values:

```
list<int> iList;
...
iList.assign(10, 0);
```

Use an iterator to assign values to the list elements. Since these values are already linked in the list, the following code is potentially faster than allocating new storage for each inserted list element:

```
list<int>::iterator iter;
int count = 1;
for (iter = iList.begin(); iter != iList.end(); iter++)
  *iter = count++;   // Assign value to list element at iter
```

Call reverse to reorder a list from front to back. If anyList contains the sequence 10, 20, 30, 40, this statement:

```
anyList.reverse();
```

converts the list to 40, 30, 20, 10. Call sort to sort a list of values into ascending order:

```
anyList.sort();
```

The sort member function uses the default less-than operator for the values in the list. Pass a binary function template such as greater_equal to sort in the other direction:

```
anyList.sort(greater_equal<int>());
```

> **NOTE**
>
> The preceding example doesn't yet work in Borland C++ 5.0 due to the lack of template member functions, a feature that almost no C++ compilers support.

Merge one list into another with the merge function. For example, define two lists:

```
int buf1[4] = { 10, 20, 30, 40 };
list<int> list1(buf1, buf1 + 4);
int buf2[4] = { 15, 25, 35, 45 };
list<int> list2(buf2, buf2 + 4);
```

To merge list2 into list1, execute the statement

```
list1.merge(list2);
```

The resulting list1 contains the sequence 10, 15, 20, 25, 30, 35, 40, 45. This also removes all values from list2. As a beneficial side effect, removing the merged values from their source list prevents more than one list from addressing the same dynamic objects in memory, which would cause a serious bug when those objects are deleted.

To alter the order of merged list elements, pass a function object such as greater_equal:

```
list1.merge(list2, greater_equal<int>());
```

> **NOTE**
>
> The preceding example doesn't yet work in Borland C++ 5.0 due to the lack of template member functions, a feature that almost no C++ compilers support.

A *splice* is a special form of insertion function. Given the preceding definitions for list1 and list2, this statement inserts all values from list2 into the beginning of list1, and also removes all values from list2:

```
list1.splice(list1.begin(), list2);
```

To splice a single value from one list to another, use code such as

```
list1.splice(list1.begin(), list2,
  find(list2.begin(), list2.end(), 35));
```

This locates the value 35 in list2, and passes to splice the resulting iterator returned by find. This moves the value 35 from list2 to the head of list1. The following demonstrates a third way to splice lists:

```
list1.splice(list1.begin(), list2,
  find(list2.begin(), list2.end(), 25),
  list2.end());
```

In this case, find returns an iterator to the value 25. Passing this and a second iterator moves all values in that range from list2 to list1. The original values are removed from list2.

> **NOTE**
>
> You cannot pass lists to the standard sort algorithm because it requires random-access iterators. Lists provide only bidirectional iterators, and therefore, the list template provides its own specialized sort member functions. The sorting functions are stable—that is, equal elements maintain their original relative order after sorting.

Deque

The standard deque—short for "double-ended queue"—is not exactly the same as the classic data structure of the same name. A deque container combines the features of a vector with a list. In this sense, a deque is a list for which indexing operations are allowed.

Deques are advantageous for algorithms requiring access to the front and rear of lists. A classic deque operates like a stack mixed with a queue, in which you can push and pop elements at either end of a list. The standard deque also permits insertions anywhere in the container, although middle insertions are not as efficient as with plain lists. Insertions and deletions at a deque's beginning or end are highly efficient.

Declaring Deques

Here are some different methods for declaring deque data structures:

```
#include <deque>
#include <string>
...
deque<string> d1;
deque<double> d2(10);
deque<int> d3(12, -1);
```

The first statement creates an empty deque of string objects. The second creates a 10-element list of double values. The third creates a deque with a dozen integer values initialized to -1.

Using Deques

You'll normally use the push_front and push_back functions to insert elements into deques. For example, this constructs a deque of strings named fruits and inserts four string objects:

```
deque<string> fruits;
fruits.push_front("Apple");
fruits.push_back("Banana");
fruits.push_front("Pear");
fruits.push_back("Orange");
```

The resulting list is Pear, Apple, Banana, Orange. Display these values and remove them from the deque using the pop_front function:

```
while (!fruits.empty()) {
  cout << fruits.front() << endl;
  fruits.pop_front();
}
```

Or, change front to back and pop_front to pop_back to display and remove elements in the reverse order.

> **TIP**
>
> The pop_front and pop_back functions do not return elements from the deque—they merely remove those elements. Use front and back as demonstrated to access elements at the head and tail of a deque container.

Calling Deque Functions

Deque functions such as at, assign, insert, erase, size, and swap are the same as those functions in the vector and list templates. Refer to those structures in this chapter for more information.

Deques possess one unique ability over lists—indexing. Classically, you should access deque elements only at the head and tail of the list, but the standard container also permits indexing as in this example, which displays a deque's contents:

```
for (int i = 0; i < fruits.size(); i++)
  cout << fruits[i] << endl;
```

Set and Multiset

A set is a collection of unique values. A multiset is a collection of possibly non-unique values. Sets of either type are automatically maintained in order, as defined by a default or explicit function object. Insertions and deletions are optimized, and searches for values in sets are fast. Sets are unlimited in size. Values in sets are called *keys*.

Set and multiset containers resemble bags in other container class libraries such as Borland's data structures. You are not restricted to using sets in their strict mathematical sense. For this reason, it's helpful to think of sets and multisets as magic sacks that can contain and quickly retrieve any types of values. Programs can also quickly determine whether a value is in a set, or how many of those values are in a multiset.

However, sets and multisets are not good for linear or random access operations. You cannot sort a set or multiset, and there are few member functions defined for these templates. If you just want to stuff objects in a handy location, and get them back fast, a set or multiset may be the right tool; otherwise, you should consider using another container class.

> **NOTE**
>
> All information in this section applies to sets and multisets, but for simplicity, I'll use sets in the example programs. The only difference between the two structures is that sets store only unique values; multisets can store possibly duplicated values.

Declaring Sets

Sets are a bit more complex to declare than other containers. In addition to specifying the type of data to store in a set, you also must define a function object for maintaining set values in order. For this reason, it's usually best to use a `typedef` statement that defines the set's parameters. For example, this statement

```
typedef set<int, less<int> > TSet;
```

defines a set data type named `TSet` that can store `int` values and that uses the `less<int>` function object to maintain those values in order.

TIP

When using declarations such as the previous one, insert a space between the two greater-than symbols. Otherwise, you will receive the warning "Use '> >' for nested templates instead of '>>'." Even though the code compiles with Borland C++, some other C++ compilers will interpret >> as a right shift operator and give an error for statements such as

```
set<int, less<int>> setx; // ??? No space between >> ???
```

Given the preceding definition, you can now declare set container objects using statements such as

```
#include <set>
...
TSet emptySet;
```

That creates an empty set. To insert initial values into a set, declare it like this:

```
int buf1[4] = { 2, 4, 6, 8 };
TSet set1(buf1, buf1 + 4);
```

This uses the `TSet typedef` name to define `set1` using the four values from the array, `buf1`. Without the `TSet` name, the definition is more complex. For example, the following statement is exactly equivalent to the preceding definition:

```
set<int, less<int> > set2(buf1, buf1 + 4);
```

Carefully examine this statement. It defines `set2` as a set of `int` values, using the `less<int>` object as the comparison function. The initial values for the set are taken from the integer array, passed to the set constructor as the two iterators `buf1` and `buf1+4`.

You can also define a set using the values from another set. For example, this defines `set3` using copies of the values from `set1`:

```
TSet set3(set1.begin(), set1.end());
```

Using Sets

There's only one insertion method, appropriately named `insert`. Because sets are always ordered, you can't insert values at specified locations—you simply toss values into sets without concern about where those values go. To demonstrate set insertions, use a `typedef` statement as before, but this time specify `double` as the type of values to insert:

```
#include <set>
...
typedef set<double, greater<double> > TSet;
```

Also, to make it easier to display the values of a set, define an output stream operator that uses the copy algorithm and an output stream iterator to display set values:

```
#include <algorithm>
...
ostream& operator<<(ostream& os, const TSet& s)
{
  copy(s.begin(), s.end(),
    ostream_iterator<TSet::value_type>(os," "));
  return os;
}
```

Next, define a set to hold double values:

```
TSet valueSet;
```

To insert values into the set, use statements such as

```
valueSet.insert(3.14159);
valueSet.insert(4.5);
double n = 2.5 * 5.2;
valueSet.insert(n);
```

Because you defined an output stream operator for TSet objects, you can use simple statements such as these to display the values in valueSet:

```
cout << "ValueSet" << endl;
cout << valueSet << endl;
```

TIP

Sets are ordered using the defined function object, in this example, greater<double>. The preceding statement therefore displays the values from high to low order. Change greater to less to order the set's values from low to high.

Remove values from a set by calling the erase function. You can erase a specific value:

```
valueSet.erase(4.5);
```

Or, you can specify a pair of iterators. This erases all values from the set:

```
valueSet.erase(valueSet.begin(), valueSet.end());
```

Remove a range of values by searching for them, using the find member function. This is a bit tricky:

```
TSet::iterator p1 = valueSet.find(4.5);
TSet::iterator p2 = valueSet.find(3.14159);
p2++;  // !!!
valueSet.erase(p1, p2);  // Iterator order is critical!
```

The first two statements call find to locate the values 4.5 and 3.14159, setting two iterators, p1 and p2, to those values. The program then increments p2 to include the second value in the range of those to remove, and calls erase to complete the removal.

It's vital to get the iterator order right. The preceding code assumes that set values are ordered from high to low. If not, the program will hang!

TIP

Don't use the standard `find` algorithm with sets. Because sets are automatically ordered, the `find` member function is faster.

You can insert class objects into sets. This requires some careful programming as Listing 12.3, Tcoord3.h, demonstrates.

Listing 12.3. Tcoord3.h (Declares class for set data).

```
//===============================================================
// Tcoord3.h -- Declares class for set data
// Copyright (c) 1996 by Tom Swan. All rights reserved.
//===============================================================

class TCoord {
  int x, y;
public:
  TCoord(): x(0), y(0) { }                   // Default constructor
  TCoord(const TCoord& arg)                  // Copy constructor
    { x = arg.x; y = arg.y; }
  ~TCoord() { }                              // Destructor
  bool operator== (const TCoord& arg) const  // Equality operator
    { return (x == arg.x) && (y == arg.y); }
  bool operator< (const TCoord& arg) const   // Less-than operator
    { return (x < arg.x) && (y < arg.y); }
// Alternate constructor (optional)
  TCoord(int X, int Y): x(X), y(Y) { }
// Member functions
  int GetX() const { return x; }
  int GetY() const { return y; }
};

typedef set<TCoord, less<TCoord> > TCoordSet;

ostream& operator<<(ostream& os, const TCoord& c)
{
  cout << "(" << c.GetX() << "," << c.GetY() << ")";
  return os;
}

ostream& operator<<(ostream& os, const TCoordSet& s)
{
  copy(s.begin(), s.end(),
    ostream_iterator<TCoord>(os, "\n"));
  return os;
}
```

The header file defines a class, TCoord, which can store a pair of integer values that might represent a graphics coordinate. The file also declares TCoordSet as a set of TCoord objects, using the less<TCoord> object for the comparison function. This detail requires the class to overload the less-than operator, which must be const as must be the overloaded equality operator.

In addition, output stream operators are overloaded for TCoord and TCoordSet objects. Armed with these declarations, you can write a program to store TCoord objects in a set. Include these header files:

```
#include <algorithm>
#include <set>
#include "tcoord3.h"
```

And define a set container, coords, of type TCoordSet:

```
TCoordSet coords;
```

To insert some TCoord objects into the set, use the following statements in function main:

```
coords.insert(TCoord(1,2));
coords.insert(TCoord(2,3));
coords.insert(TCoord(4,5));
coords.insert(TCoord(6,7));
```

Because stream output operators are defined for TCoord and TCoordSet objects, it's a simple matter to display the values in the set:

```
cout << "Coordinates" << endl;
cout << coords << endl;
```

On screen, that displays

```
Coordinates
(1,2)
(2,3)
(4,5)
(6,7)
```

You receive these same results regardless of the order of insertions. Try mixing up the previous insert statements to see this effect. The set order is automatically maintained using the overloaded less-than operator for the TCoord class.

Calling Set Functions

Set functions are few and far between. You can use traditional operations such as union and set intersection with set and multiset objects, but you can also do so for *any* ordered collection of values. The next chapter covers algorithms such as these, so I won't go into them here.

You can't sort a set (nor would you want to). Set iterators are constant, so you also can't assign values to dereferenced iterator objects.

One useful function, count, determines how many elements of a particular value are in a set or multiset. For example, this defines a multiset of integers:

```
int buffer[6] = { 2, 4, 6, 4, 8, 4 };
multiset<int, less<int> > multi(buffer, buffer + 6);
```

Because it's a multiset, the container may have duplicated keys. To display the number of 4s in the set, use a statement such as

```
cout << "Number of 4s = " << multi.count(4) << endl;
```

You also can use count to determine whether an element value is in a set or multiset. For example, this code checks whether multi contains a 6:

```
if (multi.count(6) > 0)
  cout << "Multi has a 6" << endl;
```

This is equivalent to, but faster than, the following code, which uses the find member function to search for a specific value.

```
if (multi.find(6) != multi.end())
  cout << "Multi has a 6" << endl;
```

The find function returns an iterator, which if equal to the *past-the-end* value, indicates the specified argument (6 here) is not in the set.

Bit Set

A bitset combines the features of a set with those of a vector. However, unlike other containers in the standard library, the bitset template does not provide iterators. Instead programs use subscript expressions to access bit values in bitset objects. Internally, a bitset object is implemented as a packed array of binary values, which makes this container ideal for representing on-off and true-false data collections in the smallest space possible. You can also use bitwise logical operators to perform surgery on the bit values in bitset objects.

Don't confuse bitsets with Boolean vectors. The following constructs a vector that can hold true and false values:

```
vector<bool> vectorOfBool(16);
```

That's *not* the same as a packed array of bits, which you can create using the bitset template:

```
bitset<16> setOfBits;
```

> **NOTE**
>
> Some documents incorrectly identify bitset as bit_set with an embedded underscore. The correct name is bitset.

Declaring Bit Sets

Create `bitset` containers by specifying the number of bits in brackets rather than a data type, as you normally do with other containers. Here's an example:

```
#include <bitset>
...
bitset<32> setOfBits;
```

The `setOfBits` container has room for 32-bit values. These are packed efficiently, as you can prove with a couple of output statements:

```
cout << "size = " << setOfBits.size() << endl;
cout << "size of = " << sizeof setOfBits << endl;
```

The first line displays 32—the number of bits that `setOfBits` can store. The second statement displays 4, the size in bytes of the `setOfBits` object.

> **NOTE**
>
> The size in bytes of a `bitset` object is based on the size of an integer. Thus even a `bitset` with eight bits will occupy four bytes when compiled for a 32-bit memory model.

You can also construct `bitset`s using a string as the initializer. For example, this statement

```
bitset<8> bitString("11001010");
```

creates the `bitString` container with eight bit values, initialized with the digits in the string argument.

Using Bit Sets

Use subscript expressions to access the bits in a `bitset` container. For example, this displays the bit at index 4 in `bitString`:

```
cout << bitString[4];
```

Use a similar subscript expression in an output stream template to create a function that can display `bitset` values. The header file in Listing 12.4, Bitout.h, declares the function.

Listing 12.4. Bitout.h (Declares bitset output stream function).

```
//================================================================
// Bitout.h -- Declares bitset output stream function
// Copyright (c) 1996 by Tom Swan. All rights reserved.
//================================================================

#include <iostream>
#include <bitset>
```

```
template<class T>
ostream& operator<<(ostream& os, T& t)
{
  for (int i = t.size() - 1; i >= 0; i--)
    cout << t[i];
  return os;
}
```

WARNING

The order of bits in a bitset may be dependent on the implementation; therefore, although the function in Bitout.h works correctly for Borland C++ 5, there is no guarantee that this same function will be portable to other C++ compilers.

Include the header in a program, and define a couple of bitsets.

```
#include "bitout.h"
bitset<32> setOfBits;
bitset<8> bitString("11001010");
```

You can then display their values in output stream statements:

```
cout << "setOfBits = " << setOfBits << endl;
cout << "bitString = " << bitString << endl;
```

Calling Bit Set Functions

Call the any function to test whether at least one bit in a bitset equals 1. For example:

```
if (bitString.any())
  cout << "at least one bit in bitString equals 1" << endl;
else
  cout << "no bits in bitString are set" << endl;
```

Test individual bits by calling the test function. For example, this code displays a message if bit 6 in bitString equals 1:

```
if (bitString.test(6))
  cout << "bitString[2] equals 1" << endl;
```

Set bits to 1 by calling the set function. With no arguments, set assigns 1 to all bit values; with an integer argument k, set assigns 1 to bitset[k]:

```
setOfBits.set();    // Set all bits equal to 1
setOfBits.set(8);   // Set setOfBits[8] equal to 1
```

You can also assign values using subscript expressions:

```
setOfBits[12] = 1;
```

To set bits to 0, call `reset`. Like `set`, there are two forms:

```
setOfBits.reset();     // Set all bits to 0
setOfBits.reset(12);   // Set setOfBits[12] to 0
```

Toggle bits on and off by calling the `flip` function. Here are two flippant examples:

```
setOfBits.flip();     // Toggle all bits
setOfBits.flip(12);   // Toggle setOfBits[12]
```

Call `count` to determine how many bits in a `bitset` container are set to 1. This displays the count of bits in `setOfBits` equal to 1:

```
cout << "count = " << setOfBits.count() << endl;
```

Call `to_ulong` to convert a `bitset` into an equivalent long integer value. For example, this displays the decimal value of the bit pattern in `setOfBits`:

```
unsigned long v = setOfBits.to_ulong();
cout << "setOfBits as long = " << v << endl;
```

Call `to_string` to convert a `bitset` into a string, which you can, for example, assign to a string variable:

```
string s = setOfBits.to_string();
cout << "setOfBits as string = " << s << endl;
```

You can apply all the usual C++ bitwise logical operators on `bitset` containers. Table 12.2 lists these operators and their effects.

Table 12.2. Bit set logical operators.

Operator	Effect
~	Bitwise NOT
&	Bitwise AND
¦	Bitwise OR
^	Bitwise Exclusive OR (XOR)
<<	Shift left
>>	Shift right

Following are some sample statements that perform bitwise logical operations on `bitset` containers. First define some `bitset`s:

```
bitset<8> b1("10110110");
bitset<8> b2("01001001");
bitset<8> b3("00001111");
bitset<8> b4;
```

Then try these statements:

```
b4 = (b1 & b2);    // AND
b4 = (b1 | b2);    // OR
b4 = ~b1;          // NOT
b4 = (b2 ^ bitset<8>("11111111"));  // XOR
b4 = b1 << 4;      // SHL
b4 = b1 >> 4;      // SHR
```

> **NOTE**
>
> The preceding examples do not yet work in Borland C++ 5 due to the lack of template member functions, a feature that almost no C++ compilers support.

Map and Multimap

The `map` and `multimap` templates are *associative containers* that store keys and associated values. The two templates are identical in all respects but one: keys in `maps` must be unique; keys in `multimaps` may be duplicated. In use, `map` and `multimap` containers are similar to vectors, which provide a subscript operator. However, unlike a vector, indexing a map or multimap structure performs a lookup on that key value. Also, you may use *any* data object as the indexing key, including strings, integers, floating point values, and others.

Maps and multimaps are ideal for applications that require dictionaries or other small associative databases. The structures automatically maintain their elements in key order, which makes searches fast, regardless of the type of key. It must be possible to compare key values using the less-than operator. Except for that requirement, any type of key is okay.

Declaring Maps

Declaring map and multimap containers takes a bit more effort than other data structures. You must provide three elements:

- A key type
- A value type
- A comparison function object

> **NOTE**
>
> Although I use the `map` container in the following examples, all operations apply equally to `multimap` structures.

Imagine that you need to create an associative array of strings and integer values. You can declare the map like this:

```
map<string, int, less<string> > relation;
```

That creates `relation` as a `map` data structure. The key is a string, the value is an integer, and the `less` function object is used to maintain value order in the structure. However, to insert values into the container, you need to construct string-integer objects. Because the type of that object is provided by the `map` template, it's best to use two `typedef` declarations that simplify the syntax:

```
typedef map<string, int, less<string> > TRelation;
typedef TRelation::value_type TValue;
```

The first declaration states that `TRelation` is a map data type with a string key associated with an `int` value. The `less` object performs key comparisons. The second declaration states that `TValue` is the data type of objects to insert in the `map`. The `map` template provides this type as `value_type`. Armed with these type definitions, you can construct a `map` container of type `TRelation`, and insert `TValue` objects using code such as

```
TRelation relation;
relation.insert(TValue(string("Label1: "), 1));
relation.insert(TValue(string("Label2: "), 2));
relation.insert(TValue(string("Label3: "), 3));
```

Using Maps

Listing 12.5, Scores.cpp, demonstrates how to use a map to create a database of person names and score values. The program also shows how to write output stream functions for maps and their data values.

Listing 12.5. Scores.cpp (Demonstrates the map container).

```
//===============================================================
// Scores.cpp -- Demonstrates the map container
// To compile:
//    bcc32 scores
// To run:
//    scores
// Copyright (c) 1996 by Tom Swan. All rights reserved.
//===============================================================

#include <iostream>
#include <string>
#include <map>

using namespace std;

typedef map<string, double, less<string> > TScores;
typedef TScores::value_type TValue;

ostream& operator<< (ostream& os, const TValue& r)
{
```

```
  cout << r.first << " :: " << r.second;
  return os;
}

void main()
{
  TScores scores;

  scores.insert(TValue(string("Barbara"), 85.5));
  scores.insert(TValue(string("Peter"),   78.9));
  scores.insert(TValue(string("Flo"),     98.0));
  scores.insert(TValue(string("Xavier"),  87.3));

  cout << "Scores:" << endl;
  TScores::iterator it = scores.begin();
  while (it != scores.end()) {
    cout << *it << endl;
    it++;
  }
}
```

NOTE

Using a prerelease copy of Borland C++ 5.0, the Scores.cpp does not compile correctly. Also see Borland's example listing in the Stl.hlp online help file under the index heading "map," which produces this same error. See this book's Readme.txt file for any updates on this problem.

The program uses two `typedef` declarations. `TScores` represents a map of string keys and double values. `TValue` represents the type of those object pairs.

Two output stream functions illustrate one way to display `map` objects. You can use these same functions with any values stored in `map` and `multimap` structures. Just rename the `typedef` declarations. The first function displays the key and value of a `TValue` object. The elements are available through the `first` and `second` iterators, provided by the `map` template. Thus `r.first` gives the key of the `TValue` reference `r`; `r.second` gives the value associated with that key. The second output stream function uses the standard `copy` algorithm to output all objects in a `TScores` map structure.

As the main program shows, these declarations greatly simplify the syntax of the code. Simply define a container of type `TScores`, and insert `TValue` objects. Each such object is composed of a string key and a floating point score. Thanks to the overloaded output stream operators, displaying the resulting map is simplistic.

Another way to get to the data in a `map` is to use subscript expressions with key indexes. For example, to display Peter's score, you can use the statement:

```
cout << "Peter's score = " << scores["Peter"] << endl;
```

Unlike a vector, a map is indexed using any key value, in this case a string. This performs a search of the container's association objects, and returns the value associated with the specified key. For example, to display Tom's score, you can use this statement:

```
cout << "Tom's score = " << scores["Tom"] << endl;  // ???
```

However, because Tom is not in the original database, this has the unfortunate effect of adding Tom to the map. At the same time, it displays Tom's score as zero. If this isn't the effect you want, call the map's find function to search for Tom, and display his score only if he is in the map:

```
TScores::iterator p = scores.find("Tom");
if (p == scores.end())
  cout << "Tom isn't in the database" << endl;
else
  cout << "Tom's score = " << scores["Tom"] << endl;
```

The find member function returns an iterator to a located value. If the iterator equals the map's end function (that is, the *past-the-end* value), then the search was not successful. Since at this point you have an iterator to the located object, you can replace the final statement with

```
cout << "Tom's score = " << *p << endl;
```

Or, you can refer to the value of the object at p through the first iterator. This statement is equivalent to the preceding one:

```
cout << "Tom's score = " << *p.second << endl;
```

Keys are constant; their associated values are modifiable. For example, you can change an element's value with a simple assignment:

```
scores["Flo"] = 76.7;  // Change value for Flo to 76.7
```

Call erase to remove elements from a map. Pass an index key as an argument. This erases Flo's entry:

```
scores.erase("Flo");
```

You can also search for keys and pass the resulting iterator to erase:

```
TScores::iterator p =
  scores.find("Peter");   // Get iterator to Peter's element
if (p != scores.end())    // If the search was successful,
  scores.erase(p);        // erase Peter's element
```

Remember to call the find member function for map and multimap containers rather than the standard algorithm. Locate two iterators and pass them to erase to remove a range of values:

```
TScores::iterator p1 = scores.find("Peter");
TScores::iterator p2 = scores.find("Xavier");
if ((p1 != scores.end()) && (p2 != scores.end()))
  scores.erase(p1, ++p2);
```

Be careful to perform the searches in key order. If, for example, you search the preceding key's in the opposite order, the program will develop a serious bug. Notice also that to erase the range of elements from Peter up to *and including* Xavier, the program must increment the second iterator.

Calling Map Functions

Like other containers, the `map` and `multimap` data structures provide useful member functions. Two are standard issue:

- `size` returns the number of elements in the container.
- `empty` returns true if the container has no elements.

> **NOTE**
>
> The `lower_bound` and `upper_bound` member functions are not available in Borland's STL implementation due to the lack of member function templates.

A cute trick is to use the `count` function to determine whether a specific key is in a database. This works for map and multimap structures:

```
if (scores.count("Peter") > 0)
  cout << "Peter is in the database" << endl;
```

Using `count` to search a container is faster than calling `find` because `count` does not return an iterator.

Stack

There are three kinds of stack containers. One is constructed using a `vector`; another is made from a `deque`; a third is based on a `list`. A vector stack stores all elements together in memory. A deque or list stack stores elements on a double-linked list. Except for the difference in storage methods, all kinds of stacks provide the same operations.

Stacks are useful in many algorithms. They are especially good for storing and retrieving information in a certain processing order—the results of subexpression evaluations in an electronic calculator, for example. A stack is a last-in, first-out (LIFO) data structure. Elements in a stack must support less-than and equality operators. Except for that requirement, you may store any type of data in a stack.

Whether to base a stack on the `vector`, `deque`, or `list` containers depends on your application. Because a `vector` stores elements together, it provides rapid access to data but it does not use memory efficiently. For example, deleting all elements from a vector stack does not reduce the container's size. Deque and list stacks are also fast, since elements are always inserted and removed from the end of the list. They are memory efficient, and deleted memory is available for other uses.

Declaring Stacks

Include at least two header files to use stack containers. For example, to create a vector-based stack, use these statements:

```
#include <stack>
#include <vector>
```

Include the `<deque>` or `<list>` (or both) headers to create list-based stacks. To create a stack container, specify the type of data to store and the type of underlying structure to use. For example, this

```
stack<int, vector<int> > iStack;
```

creates a stack that can store integer values and that uses an integer vector for its storage mechanism.

You can also construct stacks of structs and class objects. For example, include one of the Tcoord.h header files from this chapter and create a stack of coordinates with code such as

```
#include "tcoord2.h"
...
stack<TCoord, deque<TCoord> > coordStack;
```

The resulting stack can store TCoord objects using a double-linked deque for the underlying storage mechanism.

Using Stacks

Call the push member function to insert a value onto the top of the stack. This is the only allowable method to insert values:

```
for (int i = 1; i <= 10; i++)
  iStack.push(i);
```

Call the top function to examine the current element on the top of the stack. Call the pop function to remove that element. For example, given the preceding code, the following displays the integer values 10 down to 1 and depletes the stack:

```
while (!iStack.empty()) {
  cout << iStack.top() << endl;
  iStack.pop();
}
```

Calling Stack Functions

Stacks provide few member functions in addition to push, pop, and top. Call the size function to determine how many elements a stack contains. Call empty to determine if the stack has no elements. For example:

```
if (iStack.empty())
  cout << "Stack is empty";
else
  cout << "Stack has " << iStack.size() << " elements" << endl;
```

Queue

There are two types of queue containers. One is based on a list; another on a deque. Both types of queues provide the same operations. A queue is a first-in, first-out (FIFO) data structure, like a line at the post office. Unless you cheat, you enter at the back of the line and exit at the front.

Queues are often used for scheduling applications—for example, a phone messaging system that routes callers in the order received, or a work scheduler that assigns jobs as they come in. Elements stored in queues must support less-than and equality operators. Except for those requirements, you may store any type of data in a queue.

Declaring Queues

Declare queues similar to the way you declare stacks. Include the <queue> header plus either the <list> or <deque> headers, depending on how you want to construct the queue. For example, this creates a queue of integer values using an integer list as the underlying container:

```
#include <queue>
#include <list>
...
queue<int, list<int> > iQueue;
```

As you can with stacks, you can also construct queues using structs or class objects. For example, include one of the TCoord class header files from this chapter and use the following code to construct a queue of those objects.

```
#include <deque>
#include "tcoord2.h"
...
queue<TCoord, deque<TCoord> > suzyQueue;
```

The resulting suzyQueue can store TCoord objects using a deque as the underlying data structure.

Using Queues

Use queues similar to the way you use stacks. Declare the queue:

```
queue<int, list<int> > iQueue;
```

Then insert values by calling push:

```
for (int i = 1; i <= 10; i++)
  iQueue.push(i);
```

Inspect the element at the front of the queue by calling the front member function. Remove that element by calling pop. The following code uses both functions to display and remove a queue's values:

```
while (!iQueue.empty()) {
  cout << iQueue.front() << endl;
  iQueue.pop();
}
```

Compare this with the example for stacks. The queue displays and removes the values in insertion order; the stack reverses that sequence.

Calling Queue Functions

Call the back function to inspect the most recently inserted value in a queue. For example:

```
cout << "Last item inserted = " << iQueue.back() << endl;
```

The queue template provides only a few other functions. As in most containers, empty is true if the queue has no elements and size returns the number of elements. Use them like this:

```
if (iQueue.empty())
  cout << "Queue is empty";
else
  cout << "Queue has " << iQueue.size() << " elements" << endl;
```

Priority Queue

Priority queues are similar to stacks or queues, but always maintain data elements in a critical order. Regardless of insertion order, the most critical data elements are removed from the container before less critical ones. Criticality is determined by applying the less-than operator to element pairs, or by a user-supplied comparison function. Elements that satisfy the comparison are moved to the front of the queue for every push or pop operation.

There are two kinds of priority queues. One is based on a vector. The other is constructed from a deque. A vector priority queue is generally faster, but less memory efficient. A deque priority queue uses memory more efficiently, and may be smaller than one based on a vector.

Priority queues are useful in applications that prioritize data. A good example is a to-do list. Items labeled with low numbers (1-Clean oven, 2-Sweep garage) have less priority than items with higher numbers (8-Cash paycheck, 9-Call mother). You insert items into the list in no particular order. They come out based on their assigned priorities.

Declaring Priority Queues

Include the `<queue>` and either the `<vector>` or `<deque>` (or both) header files, and declare a priority queue similar to the way you declare stacks and queues:

```
#include <queue>
#include <vector>
...
priority_queue<int, vector<int>, less<int> > pQueue;
```

That constructs a priority queue that can store integer values using an integer vector as the underlying storage container. In addition, the `less` function object (this is the default) is used to maintain element order.

You can also construct priority queues of structs or class objects, but usually, you'll need to give some thought to how elements should be prioritized. An example in the next section demonstrates how to do this.

Using Priority Queues

In use, a priority queue is similar to a stack. Call the `push` function to insert values. For example, the following code inserts into the `pQueue` container 10 values selected at random:

```
for (int i = 0; i < 10; i++)
  pQueue.push(random(100));
```

Call `top` to inspect the element with the highest priority. Call `pop` to remove that element. This displays and removes the data in `pQueue` in high-to-low order:

```
while (!pQueue.empty()) {
  cout << pQueue.top() << endl;
  pQueue.pop();
}
```

Listing 12.6, Todo.cpp, demonstrates how to create a priority queue of class objects. The program creates a prioritized "to do" list of jobs that need doing.

Listing 12.6. Todo.cpp (Demonstrates priority queues).

```
//==============================================================
// Todo.cpp -- Demonstrates priority queues
// To compile:
//    bcc32 todo
// To run:
//    todo
```

continues

Listing 12.6. continued

```cpp
// Copyright (c) 1996 by Tom Swan. All rights reserved.
//===============================================================

#include <iostream>
#include <string>
#include <queue>
#include <deque>

using namespace std;

// Items to store in priority queue
class Item {
  int weight;      // Priority
  string item;     // Description
public:
  Item(): weight(0), item("") { }
  Item(int w, string s): weight(w), item(s) { }
  int GetWeight() const { return weight; }
  string GetItem() const { return item; }
  bool operator< (const Item& arg) const
    { return weight < arg.weight; }
};

// Display an Item object
ostream& operator<< (ostream& os, const Item& r)
{
  cout << "(" << r.GetWeight() << ") " << r.GetItem();
  return os;
}

priority_queue<Item, deque<Item>, less<Item> > todo;

void main()
{
  todo.push(Item(1, "Clean oven"));
  todo.push(Item(8, "Cash paycheck"));
  todo.push(Item(2, "Sweep garage"));
  todo.push(Item(9, "Call mother"));

  cout << "The most critical item is:" << endl;
  cout << todo.top() << endl;

  cout << endl;
  cout << "Removing items in critical order:" << endl;
  while (!todo.empty()) {
    cout << todo.top() << endl;
    todo.pop();
  }
}
```

To base the priority queue on a memory-efficient double-linked list, the program includes the <queue> and <deque> header files. Class `Item` represents the data to store in the queue. The class declares an integer weight and a string item, which describes the job to do. Item objects with higher weights have priority over other items.

The most important element of the `Item` class is its overloaded less-than operator. The priority queue calls this function to maintain elements in order of their weight values.

The program constructs the priority queue with the statement:

```
priority_queue<Item, deque<Item>, less<Item> > todo;
```

This creates `todo` as a container that can store `Item` objects using a `deque` as the underlying storage mechanism. The container uses the `less` function object for `Item` objects to maintain element order.

Call `push` to insert `Item` objects into the queue:

```
todo.push(Item(1, "Clean oven"));
```

The program calls `top` to display the most critical item, and also calls `empty`, `top`, and `pop` to display and remove items in their critical order.

To modify that order, you have several options. You can simply reverse the order of weight comparisons in the `Item` class's overloaded operator function:

```
bool operator< (const Item& arg) const
  { return arg.weight < weight; }
```

Or, you can overload the greater-than operator:

```
bool operator> (const Item& arg) const
  { return weight > arg.weight; }
```

And specify the `greater` function object in the container declaration:

```
priority_queue<Item, deque<Item>, greater<Item> > todo;
```

It's up to you to define an appropriate comparison function that makes sense for the type of data you store in the priority queue. This data does not have to be of an integer type. It could be a string or another type, provided only that it can be comparable with a less-than or greater-than operator.

Calling Priority Queue Functions

Priority queues have the fewest member functions of all standard containers. In addition to push, pop, and top, call size to determine how many elements a priority queue contains. Call empty to determine if a priority queue has no elements. For example:

```
if (pQueue.empty())
  cout << "Priority queue is empty" << endl;
else
  cout << "Priority queue has " << pQueue.size()
       << " elements" << endl;
```

Summary

- The standard library provides 10 container data structures in the form of class templates.

- Standard containers can store data of any type (but not references). They also can store pointers to data, but in that case, memory management is your responsibility.

- The 10 standard containers are vector, list, deque, set, multiset, map, multimap, stack, queue, and priority_queue. In addition, the library provides a special kind of set, called a *bit set,* that can store binary 1 and 0 values.

- In many cases, you access data in containers by using iterators. Some containers such as vectors also provide random access to data using the subscript operator.

- Container templates provide member functions that you can call to perform specialized operations such as popping data from a stack, or inserting objects into a list. In general, when a container provides a member function, it's best to use it rather than a standard algorithm that might perform a similar function.

- The next chapter describes how to use iterators and containers with many of the standard algorithms in the library.

13

CHAPTER

Mastering Standard Algorithms

Standard algorithms sort, merge, search, copy, and perform other magic on containers and data. Algorithms work with all types of data structures, and they simplify common programming tasks. For example, the sort algorithm can operate on a list or a vector regardless of the type of data the container holds. Also, because standard algorithms are not object-oriented, they carry out their duties equally well in OOP and conventional applications.

The standard library provides every algorithm as a generalized function template that defines the algorithm's name, a return type or void, and any parameters. Extensive use of inline code keeps algorithms running fast without sacrificing versatility. To use most algorithms, you simply define any required data types and provide one or more iterators that define a range of data objects on which to operate. Using this information, the compiler constructs a function that performs the required task on that data.

To compile the listings in this chapter, you must use the 32-bit command line compiler, Bcc32.exe, or you must select a 32-bit output target with the IDE's TargetExpert.

The Algorithms

The Algorithm.h header file defines all standard algorithm function templates. In every module that uses one or more standard algorithms, include the header file, minus its .h extension, using the directive

```
#include <algorithm>
```

Usually, you'll also include one or more other headers that define container class templates such as vectors, deques, and lists. Simply include all of the headers you need, in any order. Because the linker automatically binds the resulting program with any required object-code modules, you don't have to specify any linkage options or library filenames.

In the following sections are examples of all algorithmic categories in the standard library. So you can more easily find the topics you need, I arranged the categories in alphabetic order. However, some algorithms depend on information introduced in preceding sections, so on the first time through, you should probably read these sections in order. The chapter ends with advice on standard-library exception handling and pointers in containers.

> **NOTE**
>
> Because of the large number of example programs in this chapter, many of which contain duplicated code, to save space, this chapter does not include complete listings. Instead, I describe significant portions of the programs as needed to demonstrate most standard algorithms in the library. Of course, all programming examples are on the CD-ROM, ready to compile and run. See the beginning comments in each listing for compilation instructions. Example program filenames are shown immediately after each of the following section headers.

MASTERING STANDARD ALGORITHMS

13

Accumulating

Example program: Accum-ex.cpp

An accumulation is an arbitrary operation that combines a collection of data in some specified fashion. For example, a simple accumulation sums a list or an array of integers, or calculates a combined product or factorial. The `accumulate` algorithm is defined as

```
ContainerType accumulate (InputIterator first, InputIterator last,
  ContainerType initial [, BinaryFunction ] );
```

Two iterators define a range of data objects. The initial argument provides a starting value for the accumulation. This should be 0 for addition operations, and 1 for multiplication. You can optionally specify a binary function object, which will be applied over the data set.

To demonstrate how to use `accumulate`, the example program defines a container with a few floating point values:

```
double data[5] = { 1.2, 3.4, 5.6, 7.8, 9.10 };
vector<double> array(data, data + 5);
```

To sum the values in the array, the program calls `accumulate` like this:

```
double sum = accumulate(
  array.begin(), array.end(), 0.0);
```

The first two arguments are iterators that define the range of data objects on which to operate. The third argument is the starting value for the accumulation. By default, `accumulate` applies the plus operator (+) to the starting value and all values in the defined range, one after the other. The function returns the resulting value, assigned here to the double variable, `sum`.

To perform a different type of accumulation, you can optionally provide a function object as the fourth argument. For example, this code multiplies all values in the array:

```
int product = accumulate(
  array.begin(), array.end(), 1.0, times<double>());
```

The `times` function argument is defined in the `<functional>` header, which the program must include. Specify a data type to the template (`double` here), and append to the argument the function call operator (the empty parentheses). This tells `accumulate` to call the overloaded `operator()` function in the times class, which performs the arithmetic operation. Notice that because this function is a multiplication, the starting value must be `1.0` not zero.

Copying

Example program: Copy-ex.cpp

There are two copy algorithms. The first copies a range of data objects from an input source to an output destination, in a forward direction:

```
OutputIterator copy (InputIterator first, InputIterator last,
  OutputIterator result);
```

Two iterators specify the range of source data objects to copy. A third iterator specifies the starting location of the destination container.

The second copy algorithm, `copy_backward`, does the same but copies from the end of a range of data into a structure in a backward direction:

```
BidirectionalIterator copy_backward
  (BidirectionalIterator first, BidirectionalIterator last,
  BidirectionalIterator result);
```

To use the algorithms, define some containers as the example program demonstrates:

```
int data[10] = { 1, 2, 3, 4, 5, 6, 7, 8, 9, 10 };
vector<int> a(data, data + 10);
vector<int> b(10);
```

Then use the following statement to copy the integer values from vector a to vector b:

```
copy(a.begin(), a.end(), b.begin());
```

Specify the range of source data as a pair of iterators. Specify the destination as a single iterator. The destination must be large enough to hold the copied data, or you can use an insertion iterator (see "Operating on Sets" in this chapter for instructions).

To copy in the reverse direction, use `copy_backward` and specify the end of the destination container:

```
copy_backward(a.begin(), a.end(), b.end());
```

You can also use copy to display a container's data objects. For example, the following statement displays the integer values in vector b by specifying an output stream iterator as the destination argument:

```
copy(b.begin(), b.end(),
  ostream_iterator<int>(cout, " "));
```

Counting

Example program: Count-ex.cpp

Use the count and count_if algorithms to determine how many objects of a specified value are in a container. The count algorithm requires two input iterators, a constant value to search for, and an integer variable to hold the resulting count:

```
void count (InputIterator first, InputIterator last,
  const T&, Size &);
```

The example program defines a vector and fills it with 100 integer values selected at random:

```
vector<int> a(100);
randomize();
for (int i = 0; i < 100; i++)
  a[i] = random(1000);
```

A `for` loop calls the `count` algorithm to find the most-repeated value in the container:

```
for (int i = 0; i < 100; i++) {
  int v = *(a.begin() + i);      // Assign search value to v
  int k = 0;                     // Initialize result (must do!)
  count(a.begin(), a.end(), v, k); // Set k to number of values v in a
  if (k > sum) {
    sum = k;        // Save current maximum sum
    value = v;      // Save associated search value
  }
}
```

The program assigns each successive value from vector a to an integer variable v. The resulting count, k, is initialized to zero before the program calls count to set k to the number of values v in the vector.

> **TIP**
>
> You may call count repeatedly to produce a computed sum. For example, the example program could call count several times to find the total number of 1s, 2s, 3s, and 4s or other values. As a consequence, however, you *must* initialize count's final parameter (k in the example) to zero, or the result will be incorrect.

The other counting algorithm, `count_if`, counts a number of specified values that satisfy a Boolean predicate function:

```
void count_if (InputIterator first, InputIterator last,
  Predicate, Size &);
```

To use the algorithm, first define the predicate. In most cases, it's best to create a template class such as

```
template<class Arg>
class is_even : public unary_function<Arg, bool>
{
public:
  bool operator()(const Arg& arg1) { return (arg1 % 2) == 0; }
};
```

You can use the is_even class with any data type for which the modulo expression arg1 % 2 is zero if the argument value is even. For example, to count the number of even values in vector a, call count_if like this:

```
int numEvens = 0;
count_if(a.begin(), a.end(), is_even<int>(), numEvens);
```

Filling

Example program: Fill-ex.cpp

Use the `fill` and `fill_n` algorithms to stuff values into containers, or to initialize a non-empty data structure. The first algorithm requires two iterators and a value to insert in that range of data elements:

```
fill(ForwardIterator first, ForwardIterator last,
  const T& value);
```

The `fill_n` algorithm requires a single iterator where filling is to begin, a count, and a value to use for the fill operation:

```
void fill_n(OutputIterator first, Size n, const T& value);
```

To demonstrate the algorithms, the example program defines and initializes a vector with these statements:

```
int data[10] = { 1, 2, 3, 4, 5, 6, 7, 8, 9, 10 };
vector<int> a(data, data + 10);
```

To replace the values 2 through 9 with 99, the program executes the statement

```
fill(a.begin() + 1, a.end() - 1, 99);
```

The first two arguments define the range of values to fill, skipping the container's first and last elements.

Use `fill_n` to fill a structure with a certain number of values:

```
fill_n(a.begin() + 2, 6, 0);
```

This statement assigns zero to the six values starting with the third element in the vector. You can also use an insertion iterator to insert new values into a structure. For example, this inserts into the backside of vector a three values equal to 22:

```
fill_n(back_inserter(a), 3, 22);
```

Finding

Example program: Minmx-ex.cpp

There are several algorithms for finding elements that match certain criteria. (See also "Searching" in this chapter for related functions.) Of these algorithms, `min` and `max` are the simplest:

```
const T& max(const T& a, const T& b [, Compare ] );
const T& min(const T& a, const T& b [, Compare ] );
```

Unlike most algorithms, which operate on containers using iterators to access data elements, these two functions compare a pair of values passed by reference. The functions return a reference to the maximum or minimum of the two arguments. You may optionally provide a comparison function object. To demonstrate the algorithms, the example program defines two variables:

```
double v1 = 123.45;
double v2 = 543.21;
```

The following assigns to a third variable, v3, the lesser of the two test values:

```
double v3 = min(v1, v2);
```

Use max to find the greater value:

```
v3 = max(v1, v2);
```

You can also specify a function object for comparing two values. For example, using the greater template with min finds the greater of two values:

```
v3 = min(v1, v2, greater<double>());
```

Normally, you'll use this trick only when comparing complex objects that require special comparison logic. You could, for example, construct a function object of your own class design. See the preceding chapter, and also "Operating on Sets" in this chapter, for suggestions on how to write a function object that you can pass to max and min.

NOTE

As do all standard algorithms, min and max use the less-than operator (<) to compare two values. But this seemingly simple fact can lead to unexpected results. For example, you might imagine that the following statement finds the smaller of two values:

```
v3 = max(v1, v2, less<double>());   // ???
```

Actually, however, this statement finds the *maximum* value because max is already programmed to compare v1 and v2 using the less-than operator. Overloading that operator as shown here is therefore equivalent to the function's default operation.

Locate the maximum and minimum values in a container by calling the max_element or min_element algorithms, defined as

```
ForwardIterator max_element (ForwardIterator first,
  ForwardIterator last [, Compare ] );
ForwardIterator min_element (ForwardIterator first,
  ForwardIterator last [, Compare ] );
```

Each function requires a pair of iterators that define the range of data to search. Note that the functions return an iterator to the located value, which might equal the *past-the-end* value if the container is empty. To demonstrate the functions, the example program defines a vector of 10 integer values:

```
int data[10] = { 1, 2, 3, 4, 5, 6, 7, 8, 9, 10 };
vector<int> a(data, data + 10);
```

To hold the function results, the program also defines an iterator for the type of container:

```
vector<int>::iterator result;
```

The following statement locates the maximum element in the vector:

```
result = max_element(a.begin(), a.end());
```

This locates the minimum element:

```
result = min_element(a.begin(), a.end());
```

In both cases, because the result is an iterator, you must use the dereference operator to obtain the resulting value:

```
cout << "result = " << *result << endl;
```

> **TIP**
>
> The `max_element` and `min_element` algorithms are intended for use with unordered containers, and therefore they are not especially fast. With a sorted container, or with an automatically ordered map or a set, you can more quickly locate the minimum and maximum values simply by accessing the container's first and last elements.

Finding Duplicates

Example program: Dup-ex.cpp

To find consecutive duplicate data elements in a container, call the `adjacent_find` algorithm:

```
ForwardIterator adjacent_find(
  ForwardIterator first, ForwardIterator last [, Predicate pred]);
```

This can be useful for creating unique data sets. The example program defines a vector with some duplicate values:

```
int data[14] = { 1, 2, 3, 3, 3, 4, 5, 6, 6, 6, 7, 8, 9, 10 };
vector<int> a(data, data + 14);
```

The program calls `adjacent_find` to locate the first element in the duplicated values (the threes and sixes in the sample data). The algorithm returns an iterator, which equals the *past-the-end* value if the sequence has no adjacent duplications. A simple `while` loop calls the vector's `erase` function to remove duplicate values, leaving the sequence 1, 2, ... 10 in the vector:

```
vector<int>::iterator iter =
  adjacent_find(a.begin(), a.end());
while (iter != a.end()) {
  a.erase(iter);
  iter = adjacent_find(a.begin(), a.end());
}
```

Lexically Comparing

Example program: Lex-ex.cpp

This one's a tongue twister. Call `lexicographical_compare` to compare elements in two data structures. The function is most useful with character data, but it is fully generalized and you can use it with any structure that contains elements that can be compared with the less-than operator. The function returns true if one structure is less than another based on a comparison of its individual elements. It returns false if the structure is greater than or equal to another. The function is defined as

```
bool lexicographical_compare
  (InputIterator first1, InputIterator last1,
   InputIterator first2, InputIterator last2 [, BinaryFunction ] );
```

Supply two pairs of iterators to the data elements to be compared. Optionally provide a function object that returns true if an element is less than another. Here's how to use the function to compare two lists of characters. First, define the list structures:

```
char s1[] = "George Washington";
char s2[] = "Abraham Lincoln";
list<char> name1(s1, s1 + sizeof s1 - 1);
list<char> name2(s2, s2 + sizeof s2 - 1);
```

The name1 and name2 structures are double-linked lists with a character for each element. The following statement compares the two lists, setting result to true if name1 is less than name2, or to false if name1 is greater than or equal to name2:

```
bool result = lexicographical_compare(
  name1.begin(), name1.end(),
  name2.begin(), name2.end());
```

Merging

Example program: Merge-ex.cpp

There are two forms of merging algorithms. One merges the elements in one data structure with another and deposits the results in a third container. Another merges data within the same container. Let's take a look at the second and easier-to-use algorithm:

```
void inplace_merge (BidirectionalIterator first,
  BidirectionalIterator middle,
  BidirectionalIterator last [, BinaryFunction ] );
```

Use `inplace_merge` to merge the data within a single container. The example program defines a list of integers with even and odd sequences:

```
int d1[9] = { 2, 4, 6, 8, 1, 3, 5, 7, 9 };
list<int> list1(d1, d1 + 9);
```

Calling `find` locates the first odd value:

```
list<int>::iterator middle = find(
    list1.begin(), list1.end(), 1);
```

To perform the merge, the program passes the resulting iterator plus two others as arguments:

```
inplace_merge(list1.begin(), middle, list1.end());
```

The first and third iterators reference the full range of data elements. The second iterator (middle) designates the first element of the second sequence. The result is the set of values 1, 2, ..., 9 in the list.

To merge two sequences into a third, use the `merge` algorithm. For example, define two lists, one with even and another with odd values:

```
int d2[4] = { 2, 4, 6, 8 };
int d3[5] = { 1, 3, 5, 7, 9 };
list<int> list2(d2, d2 + 4);
list<int> list3(d3, d3 + 5);
```

Also define a third structure to hold the merged data. Be sure to create a structure that is large enough to contain both sets of input data. In this example, I also initialize the list elements to zero:

```
list<int> list4(list2.size() + list3.size(), 0);
```

Call `merge` to combine the two input lists into the final destination:

```
merge(list2.begin(), list2.end(),
  list3.begin(), list3.end(), list4.begin());
```

After this statement, `list4` contains the sequence 1, 2, ..., 9.

> **TIP**
>
> Merging is a stable operation. That is, after merging, any duplicated elements retain their relative orders.

Operating on Sets

Example program: Set-ex.cpp

The set container does not provide operators such as union, intersection, and others. This is because sets are merely ordered containers of arbitrary data. For that reason, the standard library provides general algorithms to perform logical operations on ordered containers. You may use these algorithms with sets, but you may use them also on vectors, lists, and any other ordered containers.

The four basic set algorithms are `set_union`, `set_intersection`, `set_difference`, and `set_symmetric_difference`. These all take the general form shown here for `set_union`:

```
set_union (InputIterator1 first1, InputIterator1 last1,
  InputIterator2 first2, InputIterator2 last2,
  OutputIterator result [, Compare comp]);
```

A related algorithm, named `includes`, determines whether a set of elements is a subset of another data set:

```
bool includes (InputIterator1 first1, InputIterator1 last1,
  InputIterator2 first2, InputIterator2 last2 [, Compare comp]);
```

To demonstrate these algorithms, the example program defines a string list using the `typedef` declaration:

```
typedef list<string> TSet;
```

The program then creates and sorts lists of strings using code such as

```
TSet colors1;
colors1.push_back("Red");
colors1.push_back("Orange");
colors1.sort();
```

See the listing for other similar color sets. Call `includes` with two pairs of iterators to determine if one set is a subset of another:

```
if (includes(
  colors2.begin(), colors2.end(),
  colors1.begin(), colors1.end()))
    cout << endl << "colors1 is a subset of colors2" << endl;
```

Call `set_union` to form the union of two sets:

```
set_union(
  colors1.begin(), colors1.end(),
  colors3.begin(), colors3.end(), colors4.begin());
```

The first two pairs of iterators define the range of values in the two sets to be combined. The final argument is an iterator to the starting location in the destination container, which must be large enough to handle the results. If it is not convenient to predetermine the destination container's size, you can use an insertion iterator for the fourth argument. For example, define a string-list (`TSet`) of colors, and also define an object of the `insert_iterator` template (you can add this code to the example program):

```
TSet colorsX;
insert_iterator<TSet> ins(colorsX, colorsX.begin());
```

The second line defines `ins` as an insertion iterator object, which can insert new values into the destination container `colorsX`, starting at the beginning of the structure. Use the `ins` iterator to construct a set union:

```
set_union(
  colors1.begin(), colors1.end(),
  colors3.begin(), colors3.end(), ins);
```

As a result of the insertion iterator argument, `set_union` inserts into the `colorsX` container the union of the `colors1` and `colors3` data sets. See the listing for other set operations, which use similar arguments.

Performing Arbitrary Functions

Example program: For-ex.cpp

At times, you'll need to perform an arbitrary function of your own making on the data elements in a container. Use the for_each algorithm to apply the function to every data object in a specified range:

```
void for_each(
  InputIterator first, InputIterator last, Function f);
```

The only firm rule is that the specified function must not alter the collection by adding or deleting values. Except for this restriction, the function may perform any operation. Usually, it's best to create a class that overrides the function-call operator (a pair of empty parentheses). Write the class like this:

```
template <class T>
class Times: private unary_function<T, void>
{
  T multiplier;
public:
  Times(const T& m): multiplier(m) { }
  void operator()(const T& arg)
    { cout << arg * multiplier << endl; }
};
```

This template class is derived from unary_function, which provides for an overloaded operator() member function that receives one argument of type T and returns void. The class constructor assigns a multiplier to a private variable. Its function-call member displays a data object's value times this multiplier, and starts a new line on the standard output.

To use the function class, construct some objects of the Times data type:

```
Times<int> t1(1), t2(2), t10(10);
```

Pass the objects to for_each along with a pair of iterators to perform the class's overloaded function-call operation:

```
for_each(array.begin(), array.end(), t1);
for_each(array.begin(), array.end(), t2);
for_each(array.begin(), array.end(), t10);
```

These statements display three lists of data in the array, first multiplied by 1, then by 2, and finally by 10. The original data in the array is undisturbed.

Randomizing

Example program: Rand-ex.cpp

It always interests me that, in such an orderly and methodical business as computer programming, randomness intrigues programmers like no other subject. For example, one of the algorithms that most programmers study early in their careers shuffles a simulated deck of cards.

This algorithm has other more practical uses. For example, a randomizer might prepare test data for a simulation, or it could scramble a set of data prior to sorting with a method that exhibits worst-case behavior with a partially ordered data set.

Call the `random_shuffle` algorithm to scramble the elements in a range of data defined by a pair of iterators:

```
void random_shuffle(
  RandomAccessIterator first, RandomAccessIterator last);
```

You may use this algorithm only with vectors, deques, and pointer data. Never apply it to an ordered container such as a set.

The example program creates an array of 100 values with the statements

```
vector<int> array;
for (int i = 0; i < 100; i++)
  array.push_back(i);
```

The program then scrambles the values in the array by calling `random_shuffle` like this:

```
random_shuffle(array.begin(), array.end());
```

Removing

Example program: Remov-ex.cpp

Call one of four removal algorithms to remove values from a container. Due to the general nature of containers and algorithms in the standard library, the results may not be exactly as expected. For instance, after removing data from a container, you'll usually have to also erase values left over from the removal operation. The example program demonstrates how to handle this situation.

The program begins by defining an array of 10 integers, initialized to the sequence 1, 2, ..., 10:

```
int data[10] = { 1, 2, 3, 4, 5, 6, 7, 8, 9, 10 };
vector<int> array(data, data + 10);
```

Call `remove` to remove the value 6 from the array. The algorithm is defined as

```
ForwardIterator remove (
  ForwardIterator first,  ForwardIterator last,
  const T& value);
```

The algorithm returns an iterator, which you should save as the example program demonstrates:

```
vector<int>::iterator start =
  remove(array.begin(), array.end(), 6);
```

The iterator, `start`, is of the iterator data type as defined by the `vector<int>` class. The purpose of this iterator becomes obvious when you examine `remove`'s result. After calling the algorithm, the container holds the sequence:

```
1 2 3 4 5 7 8 9 10 10
```

The algorithm moves up the values 7 through 10, but it doesn't clean up after itself. Consequently, you must also erase the now duplicated 10 at the end of the array. Do this by calling the container's erase function, using the iterator returned by remove:

```
array.erase(start, array.end());
```

Call the similar remove_if algorithm to remove all data values that satisfy an arbitrary specification:

```
ForwardIterator remove_if(
  ForwardIterator first, ForwardIterator last,
  Predicate pred);
```

As the example program shows, create a class template with an overloaded operator() function for the Predicate argument. For example, the following class determines whether an integer argument is even:

```
template<class T>
class is_even: public unary_function<T, bool>
{
public:
  bool operator()(const T& x){ return (x % 2) == 0; }
};
```

The class is derived from unary_function, which provides for an operator() member function that receives one argument of type T, and returns bool. As programmed here, the function returns true if the argument is evenly divisible by 2.

To apply is_even to a set of data, pass an object of the class template to remove_if. For example, this statement removes all even values from the array:

```
start = remove_if(array.begin(), array.end(), is_even<int>());
```

As before, save the returned iterator (for convenience, the program uses the already defined start iterator). Use this iterator to erase values in the array left over from any removals:

```
array.erase(start, array.end());
```

> **TIP**
>
> It is not necessary to test whether the start iterator equals the *past-the-end* value. Even if it does (which indicates that no removals were made), the preceding statement still works correctly by performing no actions on the array's data elements.

The remove_copy and remove_copy_if algorithms are similar to remove and remove_if, but deposit their resulting values in a destination container:

```
OutputIterator remove_copy(
  InputIterator first, InputIterator last,
  OutputIterator result, const T& value);
OutputIterator remove_copy_if(
  InputIterator first, InputIterator last,
  OutputIterator result, Predicate pred);
```

The example program demonstrates how to use `remove_copy`. The program defines two vectors:

```
vector<int> invec(data, data + 10);
vector<int> outvec(invec.size(), 0);
```

Vector `invec` is initialized to the sequence 1, 2, ..., 10. Vector `outvec` is the same size as `invec`, but its values are initialized to zero. To create a new vector minus the value 8, call `remove_if` as follows:

```
start = remove_copy(
  invec.begin(), invec.end(), outvec.begin(), 8);
```

The only difference from `remove` is the addition of a third iterator that designates the starting location in the destination container. The original container (`invec`) is not altered in any way.

TIP

You may specify an insertion iterator if it is not convenient to predetermine the destination container's size. See "Operating on Sets" in this chapter for instructions.

Removing Unique Elements

Example program: Uniq-ex.cpp

Call the `unique` algorithm to remove all duplicated values from a set of data. The algorithm is similar to `remove` in that it does not clean up values left over by moving other values upwards in a container. You must therefore follow `unique` with an erasure to throw away those leftovers. The standard library defines `unique` as

```
ForwardIterator unique(
  ForwardIterator first, ForwardIterator last);
```

To demonstrate `unique`, the example program defines an array and fills it with duplicated values:

```
vector<int> array;
for (int i = 1; i < 9; i++)
  for (int j = 1; j <= i; j++)
    array.push_back(i);
```

This creates the sequence:

```
1 2 2 3 3 3 4 4 4 4 5 5 5 5 5 6 6 6 6 6 6
7 7 7 7 7 7 7 8 8 8 8 8 8 8 8
```

To remove all duplicated values, and to erase leftovers from any such removals, the example program executes the following two statements. The start iterator indicates the new end of the data set, which is used to erase values from that location to the container's end.

```
vector<int>::iterator start =
  unique(array.begin(), array.end());
array.erase(start, array.end());
```

To copy a set of data and remove any duplications, but not disturb the original container, call the unique_copy algorithm. It is the same as unique, but adds a third iterator to the destination. Use an insertion iterator if you cannot predetermine the destination container's size. The library defines unique_copy as

```
OutputIterator unique_copy(
  InputIterator first, InputIterator last,
  OutputIterator result);
```

Replacing

Example program: Rep-ex.cpp

Replace values in a container with the replace, replace_if, replace_copy, and replace_copy_if algorithms. The example program demonstrates how to use replace and replace_if, defined as

```
void replace(
  ForwardIterator first, ForwardIterator last,
  const T& old_value, const T& new_value);

void replace_if(
  ForwardIterator first, ForwardIterator last,
  Predicate pred, const T& new_value);
```

The other two algorithms are similar, but accept a third iterator to a destination container for depositing the algorithms' results. To demonstrate the algorithms, the example program defines a vector of integers:

```
int data[10] = { 2, 4, 6, 2, 8, 2, 1, 2, 2, 9 };
vector<int> array(data, data + 10);
```

A call to replace sets to zero every value equal to 2:

```
replace(array.begin(), array.end(), 2, 0);
```

Use the replace_if algorithm to replace values that satisfy a certain condition. For example, you can define an is_even class template (see "Removing" in this chapter), and pass an object of that class to the algorithm:

```
replace_if(array.begin(), array.end(), is_even<int>(), 0);
```

The statement replaces all even values in the array with zero.

Searching

Example program: Find-ex.cpp

The `find` and `find_if` algorithms search a container for a specified value. See also "Finding" in this chapter for related algorithms. The standard library defines the algorithms as

```
InputIterator find(
  InputIterator first, InputIterator last, const T& value);

InputIterator find_if(
  InputIterator first, InputIterator last, Predicate pred);
```

The example defines some data to search:

```
int data[10] = { 1, 2, 3, 4, 5, 6, 7, 8, 9, 10 };
vector<int> array(data, data + 10);
```

To locate the value 6, call `find` and assign the function's return value to an iterator of an appropriate type. The easiest way to ensure that you use the correct type of iterator is to define it using the `iterator` data type provided by the `vector< >` template:

```
vector<int>::iterator start =
  find(array.begin(), array.end(), 6);
```

You might use this iterator to erase all data from the container starting with the value 6:

```
array.erase(start, array.end());
```

Call `find_if` to search a container for a value that matches an arbitrary specification. Using the `is_even` class template (see "Removing" in this chapter), the following code locates the first even value in the array and removes all values from that one to the end of the container:

```
start = find_if(array.begin(), array.end(), is_even<int>());
array.erase(start, array.end());
```

> **TIP**
>
> Don't apply `find` or `find_if` to ordered data collections such as sets and maps. Instead, call the member functions provided by these template classes to search for data elements.

Sorting

Example program: Sort-ex.cpp

If there's a subject dear to every programmer's heart, it's sorting. Finally, there's a standard algorithm that can sort the data in any container (although, of course, you shouldn't use the algorithm on ordered collections such as sets and maps). The standard library defines `sort` as

```
void sort(
  RandomAccessIterator first, RandomAccessIterator last);
```

The example program shows how to sort an associative array of objects of the class in Listing 13.1.

Listing 13.1. TData class (Extracted from Sort-ex.cpp).

```
class TData
{
  string s;  // String data
  int n;     // Associated integer data
  friend ostream& operator <<(ostream &os, const TData& d);
public:
  TData(): s(""), n(0) { }
  TData(const char* S, const int N): s(S), n(N) { }
  bool operator< (const TData& d) const
    { return n < d.n; }    // For sorting on the integer data
//   { return s < d.s; }  // For sorting on the string data
};

// Output a TData object
ostream& operator <<(ostream &os, const TData& d)
{
  os << "(" << d.n << "): " << d.s;
  return os;
}
```

The TData class defines private string and integer variables, and it also provides two overloaded operators. The first, operator<<, is a friend function that displays the integer and string data in one TData object. The second overloaded function, operator<, compares two data objects, returning true if this->n is less than an argument d.n. (Use the alternate statement, commented-out in the listing, to compare two TData objects on their string members.)

To define an associative array of TData objects, the example program constructs the vector:

```
vector<TData> array;
```

It then inserts some objects into the array. Each object is composed of a string and an integer value (pretend they are test scores):

```
array.push_back(TData("Loretta", 85));
array.push_back(TData("Brandy",  67));
array.push_back(TData("Camille", 99));
array.push_back(TData("Carmen",  92));
array.push_back(TData("Anne",    88));
array.push_back(TData("Betty",   94));
```

Call sort to arrange the data objects:

```
sort(array.begin(), array.end());
```

Because the objects' `TData` class provides an overloaded less-than operator, the resulting list is ordered on the objects' integer members:

```
(85): Loretta
(67): Brandy
(99): Camille
(92): Carmen
(88): Anne
(94): Betty
```

Enable the commented statement in the `TData` class, and delete or comment-out the preceding statement. Recompile and run to arrange the objects on their string data:

```
(67): Brandy
(85): Loretta
(88): Anne
(92): Carmen
(94): Betty
(99): Camille
```

> **TIP**
>
> You can more quickly sort a list by calling that class's `sort` member function. However, for sorting vectors, deques, and even ordinary arrays, you'll find the standard `sort` algorithm quick and easy to use.

In collections that have duplicated values, if you must maintain those objects' relative positions, call the `stable_sort` algorithm like this:

```
stable_sort(array.begin(), array.end());  // Alternate method
```

This method is generally slower than sort, so don't use it unless absolutely necessary. You might call `stable_sort`, however, to sort a collection two or more times on different fields—for example, to sort a name and address database by state and by some other attribute such as ages or sex.

Other Topics

Following are some miscellaneous tips and techniques for pointers and exception handling that you may find useful in applications that use standard algorithms.

Exception Handling

Example program: Excpt-ex.cpp

The standard library supports exception handling. However, because of the general nature of containers and algorithms, there are not many places that throw exceptions—the standard library does little to prevent common errors. In fact, a search of header files shows that only bitset and string structures use exceptions to report errors.

Still, you should use exceptions (especially with strings) to help build robust applications. Table 13.1 shows the standard exception class hierarchy. All standard library classes and functions, including standard strings, throw only these exceptions. Be aware, however, that other non-standard classes such as those in the ObjectWindows library can throw other types of exceptions not listed here.

Table 13.1. Standard exception classes.

Base class	Derived class	Sub-derived class
exception		
	logic_error	
		domain_error
		invalid_argument
		length_error
		out_of_range
	runtime_error	
		range_error
		overflow_error

The class exception is the ancestor of all other classes. There are two main classes derived from exception: logic_error and runtime_error. A logical error is one that typically occurs due to a mistake in the source code, such as indexing a string beyond its end. A runtime error is one that occurs during a program operation, such as running out of memory during an insertion that causes an attempted expansion of a data structure.

To use exception handling, surround your code in try-catch statements. For example, include the <string> header file and try these statements:

```
string s("Never-never land");
s.remove(100, 10);  // ???
```

The program purposely passes an out-of-range index, 100, to the string class's remove member function. This sends the code into outer space, and halts the program with an "abnormal termination" message. A try-catch statement prevents this unhappy occurrence:

```
string s("Never-never land");
try {
  s.remove(100, 10);
}
catch (out_of_range e) {
  cout << e.what() << endl;
}
```

Now, the program itself catches the exception, and displays the message "string index out of range." This demonstrates how to catch a specific exception. To catch all standard exceptions, replace out_of_range with any of the classes in Table 13.1. For example, use exception to catch every possible standard exception.

Listing 13.2, Allex-ex.cpp demonstrates how to catch all standard exceptions in function main. This technique ensures that the program will not end prematurely due to an unhandled exception—at least those thrown by the standard library and listed in Table 13.1.

Listing 13.2. Allex-ex.cpp (Demonstrates catching all standard exceptions).

```
//===============================================================
// Allex-ex.cpp -- Demonstrates catching all standard exceptions
// To compile:
//   bcc32 allex-ex
// To run:
//   allex-ex
// Copyright (c) 1996 by Tom Swan. All rights reserved.
//===============================================================

#include <string>

using namespace std;

void Run();

void main()
{
  for (;;) {
    try {
      Run();
      cout << "No errors detected." << endl;
      return;
    }
    catch (exception e) {
      cout << e.what() << endl;
    }
  }
}

void Run()
{
  int index;
  string s("Never-never land");

  cout << "Before string = " << s << endl;
  cout << "Enter index: ";
  cin >> index;
  s.remove(index, s.length() - index);
  cout << "After string  = " << s << endl;
}
```

The program uses a "do-forever" loop in function main that calls a subfunction, Run, which performs the program's actions. The loop repeats until Run returns normally, at which time the program ends with the message "No errors detected." Run the program and enter 100 or another out-of-range index value. The program displays an error message, and repeats the prompt for a correct value. Enter a legal index value such as 12 to end.

Pointers in Containers

Until now, I've avoided the subject of storing pointers in data structures. You may certainly do this, and all containers and algorithms are perfectly happy with pointers as they are with actual data objects.

However, when you store pointers in containers, you assume responsibility for memory allocations and deletions. A common error is to erase pointers from containers without first deleting any memory allocated to those pointers. This will cause a gradual loss of available memory, a serious situation that might eventually shut down the program faster than Yellowstone National Park during a budget crisis.

Listing 13.3, Point-ex.cpp, demonstrates how to store pointers to string objects in a vector. You can use similar techniques with other data objects, pointers, and containers. The program also demonstrates the correct way to delete pointers and their addressed data from a vector.

Listing 13.3. Point-ex.cpp (Demonstrates storing pointers in containers).

```
//==============================================================
// Point-ex.cpp -- Demonstrates storing pointers in containers
// To compile:
//    bcc32 point-ex
// To run:
//    point-ex
// Copyright (c) 1996 by Tom Swan. All rights reserved.
//==============================================================

#include <iostream>
#include <string>
#include <vector>

// Define vector of string pointers
vector<string*> array;

void main()
{
// Insert some dynamic string objects into the array
  array.push_back(new string("The point of this"));
  array.push_back(new string("code is to store"));
  array.push_back(new string("pointers to string objects"));
  array.push_back(new string("in a container."));

// Display the data in the vector
  for (int i = 0; i < array.size(); i++)
    cout << *array[i] << endl;

// Delete and erase the string objects and pointers
  for (int j = 0; j < array.size(); j++)
```

```
    delete array[j];
  array.erase(array.begin(), array.end());
}
```

The program defines an array of string pointers, and uses statements such as the following to create dynamic strings and store their pointers in the array:

```
array.push_back(new string("The point of this"));
```

This inserts into the array the string-pointer that new returns. To get to the dynamic strings addressed by the container's pointers, use a dereference expression as in the following output statement, which displays the string indexed by integer i:

```
cout << *array[i] << endl;
```

Never erase any pointers from a container without first deleting their addressed memory. The sample program shows the correct way to manage the container, using a for loop to delete all memory allocations and then calling the erase member function to delete the pointers from the array. If you forget to delete the pointers, the erasure will leave the memory allocations stranded on the heap, causing a gradual loss of available memory.

Because standard containers can automatically delete only objects, but not pointers, another solution to the problem of storing pointers in containers is to wrap the pointers inside a class. The class holds onto the pointer as a private variable, and its destructor can delete any memory allocated to the pointer when the container deletes the object. Listing 13.4, Wrap-ex.cpp, demonstrates the basics of writing a wrapper class and storing it in a container.

Listing 13.4. Wrap-ex.cpp (Demonstrates wrapper class for pointers).

```
//============================================================
// Wrap-ex.cpp -- Demonstrates wrapper class for pointers
// To compile:
//    bcc32 wrap-ex
// To run:
//    wrap-ex
// Copyright (c) 1996 by Tom Swan. All rights reserved.
//============================================================

#include <iostream>
#include <string>
#include <vector>

template <class T>
class wrapper
{
  T* xp;      // Pointer to dynamic object
public:
  wrapper(): xp(0) { }           // Default constructor
  wrapper(T* x): xp(x) { }       // Parameterized constructor
```

continues

461

Listing 13.4. continued

```
 ~wrapper() { delete xp; }       // Destructor
  T& get() const { return *xp; }  // Access to private data
};

// Use a typedef declaration to simplify the code
typedef wrapper<string> TWrap;

// Array of wrapper-class objects
vector<TWrap> array;

void main()
{
// Construct some wrapper objects
  TWrap a(new string("Using a wrapper class"));
  TWrap b(new string("provides automatic"));
  TWrap c(new string("memory management for"));
  TWrap d(new string("pointers in containers."));

// Insert the objects into the array
  array.push_back(a);
  array.push_back(b);
  array.push_back(c);
  array.push_back(d);

// Display the data in the vector
  for (int i = 0; i < array.size(); i++)
    cout << array[i].get() << endl;

// Erasing wrapper objects deletes addressed strings
  array.erase(array.begin(), array.end());
}
```

The wrapper class is a template that stores a pointer (xp) to a dynamic variable of type T. The class requires a default constructor to satisfy the expectations of the standard container. The second constructor saves in xp a pointer created by new. A destructor ensures that this variable is properly deleted when the wrapper object is destroyed. To provide access to the internal pointer's data, member function get returns a reference to an object of type T. Together, these features effectively hide the pointer inside the wrapper object. As far as the container is concerned, a wrapper is just another object—the container requires no special knowledge that this object actually contains a pointer to a dynamic object in memory.

To make the wrapper class easier to use, the program declares the type definition:

```
typedef wrapper<string> TWrap;
```

This states that TWrap is a wrapper class that stores a pointer to a string object. Using the type definition, the program creates a vector of TWrap objects:

```
vector<TWrap> array;
```

This is equivalent, but easier on tired eyes and minds, to the following:

```
vector<wrapper<string> > array;
```

In function `main`, the program constructs some wrapper objects with statements such as

```
TWrap a(new string("Using a wrapper class"));
```

and then stuffs the wrapper object into the vector:

```
array.push_back(a);
```

Calling `get` provides access to the data addressed by the hidden pointer:

```
cout << array[i].get() << endl;
```

Unlike the preceding example (Point-ex.cpp), the new program can safely erase the wrapper objects from the array. This calls the objects' class destructor, which automatically deletes the dynamic strings. It is no longer necessary to delete the strings before erasing the array, and in fact, doing so would be an error.

NOTE

The standard library provides an `auto_ptr` class that is supposed to simplify storing pointers in containers. The class is similar to the `wrapper` class in the preceding listing, but it ensures that only one `auto_ptr` object addresses the same dynamic object in memory. The class also provides safe exception handling for the `new` operator. However, despite these lofty goals, the `auto_ptr` class is awkward to use, and its complexity vastly outweighs its minor benefits. (A friend at Borland told me he thinks `auto_ptr` is a "half-vast" idea.) Internally, the class requires member function templates, which few (if any) C++ compilers implement. Worse, the class's constructors use questionable techniques in order to satisfy the one-dynamic-allocation-per-object requirement. For these reasons, I recommend that you run, don't walk, away from `auto_ptr` objects. Storing pointers in containers as explained in this chapter isn't *that* difficult, and as the preceding listing demonstrates, you can easily wrap your pointers in a class of your own making if you need automatic memory management.

Summary

- The standard library provides numerous algorithms in the form of template functions. Algorithms are completely generalized, and most can work with all types of data, pointers, and containers.

- In most cases, you pass iterators to algorithms to define a range of data objects on which to operate.

- Algorithms possess no information about the containers on which they operate. This makes algorithms extremely versatile, but also means that some kinds of operations require careful programming. For example, deleting objects from a container merely moves other objects into the deleted space. You still must erase the objects left over from such deletions.

- The standard library fully supports exception handling. However, because standard algorithms do little to guard against common mistakes, not many places in the standard library actually throw exceptions. Those that do throw exceptions are guaranteed to throw only the exceptions listed in Table 13.1.

- Containers may store pointers to data; however memory management is then your responsibility. Specifically, you must delete any allocated memory assigned to pointers before erasing those pointers from a container. To regain automatic memory management, you can create a wrapper class that maintains your pointers, and then store objects of the class in the container.

- Avoid the standard auto_ptr class. Despite its lofty goals, this class is difficult to use and its small benefits don't warrant its internal complexity.

IV

PART

Windows
Development

Introducing OWL

The ObjectWindows library, or OWL, has come a long way since its introduction in Borland C++ 3.1 as an object-oriented class library for Windows programming. With plenty more meat on its original bare-bones skeleton, OWL 5.0 now provides a mature body of classes and related tools for 16- and 32-bit Windows developers.

Most significant in OWL's portfolio is a new emphasis on 32-bit programming for Windows 95 and Windows NT, collectively known as Win32. OWL encapsulates common controls, the shell interface, OLE, graphics, and other Win32 features, all of which greatly simplify Windows programming. If you've written Windows code the old way—that is, using only C-style techniques—you'll be pleasantly surprised at how easy it is to write robust applications using OWL's numerous classes, which encapsulate just about all corners and cubbyholes in the overwhelmingly extensive Windows API (application programming interface).

This chapter introduces OWL 5.0 fundamentals, and demonstrates common tasks for 16- and 32-bit Windows applications. The next chapter explains 32-bit programming techniques that require Windows 95 or Windows NT. Other chapters in this part show how to write OLE client and server applications using OWL's Object Component Framework (OCF) classes.

> **NOTE**
>
> OWL's version number, 5.0, is now the same as the compiler's. The previous version was 2.5. There are no intermediate versions.

The ObjectWindows Library

You can write conventional Windows programs with Borland C++, but due to Windows' event-driven nature, OWL's classes and Windows naturally fit together. OWL programs tend to be shorter, easier to understand, and most importantly, easier to maintain than Windows programs written conventionally in C. I've written Windows applications using both methods; but given a choice, I prefer OWL. Why struggle when you don't have to?

> **TIP**
>
> I recommend using OWL for new applications instead of Microsoft's Foundation Classes (MFC), which Borland C++ 5.0 supports but does not provide on disk. See chapter 24, "Compiling MFC Applications." To obtain the MFC library, you must purchase Microsoft's Visual C++.

The original 1.0 version of the ObjectWindows Library—I'll call it OWL from now on—was a paragon of simplicity. It encapsulated only a minimum of the Windows API (application programming interface), essentially the portions that dealt with event-driven programming. OWL 1.0 simplified message handling, dialog boxes, and window management. But other common aspects of Windows software development such as menus and graphics commands mostly required standard Windows techniques.

OWL 1.0 relied on a unique feature in Borland C++ 3.1 called *dynamically dispatchable virtual tables,* or DDVTs. These tables made it possible for a program to call *response functions* for class objects when certain events occur. For example, with an appropriate entry in a DDVT, a window object could receive a message and automatically call a response function to provide programming for that message. DDVTs were not restricted to Windows applications—any event-driven operating system could, in theory, make use of dynamic function tables.

OWL 2.0, introduced in Borland C++ 4.0, completely changed OWL's design. No longer a minimalist library, OWL 2.0 encapsulated most of the Windows API. As before, a variety of classes simplified the programming of windows, dialog boxes, and other standard interface elements. But the new OWL 2.0 went the extra mile, adding classes for graphics, device contexts, common dialogs, and a host of other items.

OWL 2.0 also eliminated the need for DDVTs in message handling, a change that has percolated up to the current release. Although this change results in more complex source code—rather than specify a simple entry in a DDVT, for example, you now have to use a set of macros to link class objects to messages—the modification allows OWL source code to conform to ANSI C++ specifications. This makes OWL versions 2.0 through 5.0 potentially portable to other platforms and ANSI C++ compilers.

OWL 5.0 furthers the previous versions' renaissance in Windows class library programming. This newest version, available in Borland C++ 5.0, encapsulates the Win32 API for Windows 95 and Windows NT 32-bit programming. You may still use OWL for 16-bit Windows application development, but for best results, you should target your applications for a true 32-bit platform. This chapter's example programs use techniques that apply to 16- and 32-bit Windows programming. The next chapter covers 32-bit OWL programming topics.

> **NOTE**
>
> Borland C++ 5.0 continues to support DDVTs, but OWL no longer uses them. If you have OWL's source code files from an earlier release, you can compile old-style programs with the new compiler. It's probably best, though, not to write new programs that use DDVTs.

Developing Windows Applications with OWL

The best way to learn how to use OWL is to examine a sample program, OwlWelc, which is a kind of Windows version of the Welcome.cpp program listed way back in Chapter 3. The program doesn't do much—it simply welcomes you to Windows programming, and it shows the basic format, parts, and pieces of an OWL application.

> **NOTE**
>
> The programs in this chapter (and others in this part) consist of several files, all of which are stored on disk in subdirectories. The files for the OwlWelc application, for example, are located in Source\C14\Owlwelc. There are two ways to compile the sample programs. Using the IDE, change to the program's subdirectory, load the .ide project file using *File/Open,* and then press Ctrl+F9 to compile and run. If you prefer to use command-line tools, from a DOS prompt, change to an example directory and type **make** to compile, using the supplied Makefile. If you did not install Borland C++ in the default directory, C:\BC5, you must modify all pathnames in .ide and Makefile files before compiling.
>
> Run the resulting .exe code file as you do other programs. If you are using Windows 95, you can run applications by typing their names at a DOS prompt. Or, select the executable code file using the Explorer, File Manager, Program Manager, or a similar utility.

Owlwelc's Files

The demonstration program consists of several files. In this book's previous edition, the first file, Owlwelc.def in Listing 14.1, is needed only for 16-bit Windows 3.1 applications. Called a *linker definition file,* it specifies the program type, runtime memory segment options, and the sizes of a local heap and stack. The local heap and stack are part of the program's data segment. Windows also provides a global heap where applications can create dynamic variables by using the C++ new operator.

You do not need to use a linker definition file for 32-bit Windows 95 and NT programming, although you may do so. And even for most 16-bit applications, Borland C++ options and features replace many of the commands in linker definition files, which other compilers such as Microsoft C/C++ and Visual C++ require. Except for the heap and stack sizes, for instance, you can use the default definition file (which is the same as Owlwelc.def) in most OWL applications. For these reasons, this file is not on disk, and you don't need it to compile the program.

Listing 14.1. Owlwelc.def.

```
EXETYPE WINDOWS
CODE PRELOAD MOVEABLE DISCARDABLE
DATA PRELOAD MOVEABLE MULTIPLE
HEAPSIZE 4096
STACKSIZE 5120
```

The heap and stack sizes shown for Owlwelc.def are adequate minimums for 16-bit Windows applications. 32-bit Windows programs use a minimum of one megabyte for each setting.

The next two listings, 14.2 (Owlwelc.rh) and 14.3 (Owlwelc.rc), list the program's *resources.* In Windows programs, resources are stored in binary form in a program's .exe code file. They specify the contents of menus, dialog boxes, bitmaps, strings, accelerator (hot) keys, and other items. Using resources is optional—you could create the same types of objects using program statements. For example, it's possible to create a dialog box by calling Windows functions. But it's easier and more memory efficient to create dialog boxes with a resource editor, and load the resource into memory as needed.

I used the internal resource editor in the Borland C++ IDE to create the resources for the programs in this chapter. This is equivalent to the formerly stand-alone Resource Workshop (RW), provided with Borland C++ up through version 4.5, which is also provided with version 5.0 for Windows 3.1 users. I removed comments and adjusted indentations in the resulting .rh and .rc files for printing here. But the files are essentially equivalent to those that the IDE resource editor created.

Each resource requires an identifier that a program uses to refer to that resource. Resource identifiers—also called *resource names*—can be strings or integers. I prefer to use integer identifiers, which load faster and take less memory. However, string resource names potentially cause fewer conflicts, especially in resources to be shared among multiple applications.

Owlwelc.rh, Listing 14.2, defines the sample program's resource identifiers. The .rh filename extension, for *resource header*, isn't required, but it distinguishes the file's contents from a program's other .h headers.

Listing 14.2. Owlwelc.rh (Declares resource constants for Owlwelc program).

```
//==============================================================
// Owlwelc.rh -- Declares resource constants for Owlwelc program
// Copyright (c) 1996 by Tom Swan. All rights reserved.
//==============================================================

#define ID_MENU 100
#define CM_TEST 101
```

The ID_MENU constant in Owlwelc.rh identifies the program's menu resource as the integer 100. The exact value doesn't matter as long as all resources of the same type (all menus, all dialogs, and so on) are uniquely identified.

The CM_TEST constant identifies a *resource component,* in this case, a command named *Test* inside the menu. Resource components must be identified by integers, not strings.

> **TIP**
>
> Adopt a naming convention so that you can distinguish among resource identifiers and components. I preface all resource identifiers with ID_. I preface resource components according to their use (CM_ for command, for example). The exact convention doesn't matter as long as you choose a style and use it consistently.

To create resources, you can write commands in a *resource script* such as the example in Listing 14.3, Owlwelc.rc. You can create and edit resource script files using any text editor, including the one in the IDE. You can also use the IDE's resource editor to visually construct and maintain resources, create the script file, and then make minor changes to the resulting text.

Listing 14.3. Owlwelc.rc (Declares resources for Owlwelc program).

```
//================================================================
// Owlwelc.rc -- Declares resources for Owlwelc program
// Copyright (c) 1996 by Tom Swan. All rights reserved.
//================================================================

#include "owlwelc.rh"
#include <owl\window.rh>

ID_MENU MENU
{
 POPUP "&Demo"
 {
  MENUITEM "&Test...", CM_TEST
  MENUITEM "E&xit", CM_EXIT
 }
}
```

Owlwelc.rc begins by including two resource header files. The first included file, Owlwelc.rh, defines the program's resource identifiers. The second file is supplied with OWL, and it defines standard identifiers for window objects. In this case, I want to use a standard *Exit* command, which OWL defines as CM_EXIT.

As in C and C++ programs, use angle brackets to include a file from a default pathname; use double quotes to include a file in the current directory. For example, the designation `<owl\window.rh>` refers to the Window.rh file in the OWL subdirectory inside BC5's default path for include files—usually C:\BC5\Include. The quoted expression `"owlwelc.rh"` refers to the Owlwelc.rh file in the current directory.

Following its included files, Owlwelc.rc defines a menu resource. Because you can more easily use the visual resource editor to create menus, I won't go into the script commands here. Besides, they are fairly obvious. Double-click on the Owlwelc.rc filename in the project window, and select the ID_MENU identifier to open the menu editor and view how the menu will appear in the compiled application.

The preceding three files merely set the stage for the main act: the program's source code module. Listing 14.4, Owlwelc.cpp, shows the basic layout of an OWL application. You'll examine the code in microscopic detail under "Owlwelc's Operation" following the listing and compilation instructions.

Listing 14.4. Owlwelc.cpp (Demonstrates ObjectWindows (OWL) programming).

```
//===========================================================
// Owlwelc.cpp -- Demonstrates ObjectWindows (OWL) programming
// Copyright (c) 1996 by Tom Swan. All rights reserved.
//===========================================================

#include <owl\applicat.h>
#include <owl\framewin.h>
#pragma hdrstop
#include "owlwelc.rh"

// ==========================================================
// The application's main window
// ==========================================================

class TDemoWin: public TFrameWindow {
public:
  TDemoWin(TWindow* parent, const char far* title);
protected:
  void CmTest();
DECLARE_RESPONSE_TABLE(TDemoWin);
};

// Create response table declared for class
DEFINE_RESPONSE_TABLE1(TDemoWin, TFrameWindow)
  EV_COMMAND(CM_TEST, CmTest),
END_RESPONSE_TABLE;
```

continues

Listing 14.4. continued

```
// Constructor
TDemoWin::TDemoWin(TWindow* parent, const char far* title)
  : TFrameWindow(parent, title),
    TWindow(parent, title)
{
  AssignMenu(ID_MENU);
}

// Menu command function
void
TDemoWin::CmTest()
{
  MessageBox("OWL Welcome -- By Tom Swan",
    GetApplication()->GetName());
}

// ============================================================
// The application class
// ============================================================

class TDemoApp: public TApplication {
public:
  TDemoApp(const char far* name)
    : TApplication(name) {};
  void InitMainWindow();
};

// Initialize the program's main window
void
TDemoApp::InitMainWindow()
{
  MainWindow = new TDemoWin(0, "Welcome to ObjectWindows");
}

#pragma argsused

// Main program
int
OwlMain(int argc, char* argv[])
{
  TDemoApp app("OwlWelc");
  return app.Run();
}
```

Compilation Options

There are as many ways to compile Windows programs as there are stars in the sky. Well, maybe there aren't *that* many options, but there are enough to produce mass confusion among beginning Windows developers. Following are some compilation tips for the Owlwelc program that you can also use to compile other OWL applications.

The first question is whether to use the IDE or DOS-prompt command-line tools. It's hard to recommend one over the other, but if you are the kind of person who likes to have total control over all aspects of your programs, the command-line route is probably right for you. If you are more interested in fast results, the IDE may better suit your needs. I use both methods, but I tend to prefer the command-line environment.

Because Windows programs are composed of multiple files, in the IDE, you must create a *project* that specifies the program's components. Projects are complex databases that describe all aspects of a program, from module dependencies to output target platforms.

Configure a project using the IDE's *TargetExpert* command. For example, use the *File|Open* command to open the Owlwelc.ide project file on this book's CD-ROM. This creates the *Project* window shown in Figure 14.1 (the directory in the window's caption bar may be different on your display).

Figure 14.1.

The Owlwelc.ide project window.

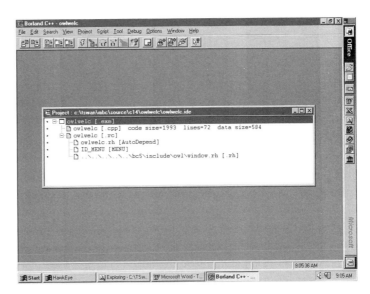

The first line of the sample project file specifies an *output target*. This is the file to create—in this case, an executable code file with the filename extension .exe. Single-click the right mouse button on Owlwelc.exe, or highlight that line and press Alt+F10, to open a floating popup menu, from which you can select various commands to configure this program. Select *TargetExpert* to open a dialog of target options (see Figure 14.2).

Following are some tips for configuring Owlwelc and other OWL projects:

- Set *Target Type* to *Application (.exe)*. All Windows application code files are of this type.

- Set *Platform* either to *Windows 3.x (16)* for 16-bit applications, or to *Win32* for Windows 95, NT, or Win32s applications. (Win32s is a subset of the full Win32 operating system. It permits Windows 3.1 to run 32-bit code, but not as well as a true 32-bit operating system.)

- OWL programs must specify *OWL* under *Frameworks.* This automatically selects *ClassLibrary,* which OWL uses. You can't turn off this automatic selection.

- You may optionally select BWCC to use Borland Windows custom controls in 16-bit application. BWCC enhances the look and feel, and also the operation, of buttons, check boxes, and other controls. Win32 applications use 3D-style controls (*CTL3D*) by default.

- To conserve disk and memory space, specify *Dynamic* linkage for libraries. This setting loads the library DLLs into memory as needed, and also permits applications to share library functions. All of OWL, for example, is provided as a DLL. If you run one, two, or a dozen dynamically linked OWL applications at the same time, they all share the same DLLs in memory.

- Loading DLLs takes time, so you can speed a program's startup by changing *Dynamic* to *Static.* With this setting, all of OWL (or at least the parts your program uses), the container class library, and the runtime library are copied into the program's compiled .exe code file. Multiple applications receive their own private copies of these libraries, which the applications cannot share. You should carefully consider whether a tiny speed increase warrants this much wasted memory and disk resources.

- With *Dynamic* linkage, you may use only the *Large* memory model for OWL programs. With *Static* linkage, you may use the small, medium, or large models. OWL programs cannot use the compact or tiny memory models; 32-bit programs for Windows 95 or Windows NT (Win32) use the flat memory model, which gives applications access to all free memory. There are no other memory models available for 32-bit operating system platforms.

- Enable the *Diagnostic* check box to add debugging features that halt programs and display error messages for common mistakes such as not initializing a required parameter.

- After selecting the options you want, click OK or press Enter to close the TargetExpert dialog. Press Ctrl+F9 to compile and run a project. Or, use other commands in the *Project* menu, and run the resulting .exe code file as you do other Windows programs.

- To compile from the DOS command line is even simpler. Just change to the directory that contains the program's files and type **make**. If you receive errors, load the file named Makefile into your favorite text editor and change any pathnames to match your installation.

Figure 14.2.

Target Expert dialog for Owlwelc.

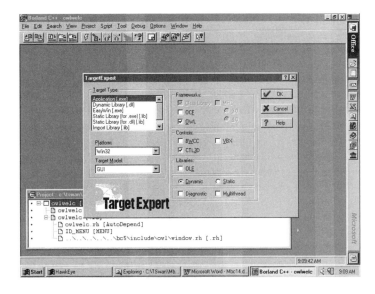

Instead of editing Makefile with a text editor, you can open the program's .ide project file, make any changes you need with commands in the Options menu (and also in the Target Expert dialog), and then regenerate Makefile using the *Project/Generate makefile* command.

Owlwelc's Operation

After compiling and running Owlwelc, you should see the window in Figure 14.3. You can move and resize the window, zoom it to full screen or shrink it to an icon, and open its system menu. To close the window, and thus end the Owlwelc program, select that menu's *Exit* command or press Alt+F4.

The program displays a small menu with two commands: *Test*, which creates the message dialog shown in Figure 14.4, and *Exit,* which ends the program. You can also use other standard ways to end the program—press Alt+F4, for example, or select the *Close* button at far right in the window's title bar.

The program's source file, Owlwelc.cpp in Listing 14.4, shows the basic steps for writing OWL programs. The first step is to include the OWL header files for any classes the program needs. Usually, you'll need at least the two headers shown: Applicat.h and Framewin.h.

Figure 14.3.
Owlwelc's bare-minimum window.

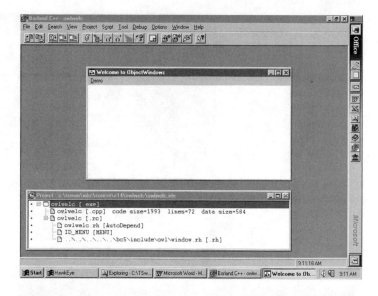

Figure 14.4
Message dialog displayed by OWLWELC's Test command.

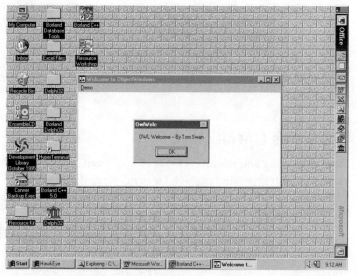

The directive, #pragma hdrstop, tells the compiler to stop collecting precompiled header information from this point on. All headers that precede the directive are stored in precompiled form in a file, usually ending with .csm (short for *compiled symbols*). All headers that follow the directive are not precompiled. The compiler can reload precompiled header information faster than it can recompile the header text, so using precompiled headers greatly speeds compilation, but only after the first time you compile the program.

Most OWL applications have at least two class objects, one of type TFrameWindow and another of type TApplication. To use these classes, derive new ones as shown in the listing, and add the functions and data members you need. For example, for the program's main window, I derived a new class, TDemoWin from TFrameWindow. For the application object, I derived TDemoApp from TApplication.

The TDemoWin class represents the style and operation of the program's main window. The class needs a constructor (named TDemoWin in the class's public section) to initialize an object of this class. (In a moment, I'll explain how to create this object.) The class also declares a function, CmTest, for the program's *Test* command.

Near the end of the TDemoWin class is the following macro in uppercase:

```
DECLARE_RESPONSE_TABLE(TDemoWin);
```

The macro—one of several in OWL—adds various declarations to the class for building a table of function addresses related to Windows messages. (In OWL 1.0, you would use a DDVT entry in place of the macro.)

Following the class declaration is another macro, which creates the actual table declared for the class. This macro ends in an integer value that specifies how many ancestor classes there are for this one. In this case, there's only one, so DEFINE_RESPONSE_TABLE1 is the correct macro to use.

Inside the response table definition is another macro that associates the CmTest function in the class with the CM_TEST command constant—the same one that was used to identify this menu resource component.

Notice that there's no entry for the CM_EXIT command because that one is understood automatically in the TFrameWindow class.

Further into the listing is the TDemoWin constructor, which performs two duties. It calls its ancestor classes (both of them, because TFrameWindow is virtually derived from TWindow), and it calls AssignMenu to assign the program's menu resource identifier to the window.

The `CmTest` function is an ordinary C++ class member function. It calls the Windows API `MessageBox` to display the dialog in Figure 14.4. Don't hunt for the statement that calls `CmTest`—there isn't one. The program calls it automatically by using the function's entry in the class's response table when you select the *Test* command. This is a good example of *event-driven programming*—in Windows, events, not program statements, direct the program's overall flow.

The `TDemoApp` class shows the basic form for an application class, which you might think of as an envelope that surrounds the program instance. Derived from `TApplication`, `TDemoApp` declares a constructor and overrides an inherited member function, `InitMainWindow`.

Turn to `InitMainWindow` next in the listing, and you'll discover the statement that creates the program's main window. This is an object of the `TDemoWin` class, constructed by the new operator, and passed two arguments: zero (representing a null pointer because this window has no parent window object) and a string for the window caption.

The rest of the listing is a function, `OwlMain`, which resembles the `main` function in a non-Windows C or C++ program. Like `main`, `OwlMain` returns an `int` value and receives two arguments: `argc` equals the number of command-line arguments (such as filenames or options) passed to the program; `argv` is an array of string pointers to those arguments.

Because `OwlMain` in this example doesn't use its two arguments, I preceded the function with the directive `#pragma argsused`, which prevents the compiler from issuing a warning about the unused parameters. (Although the parameters are unused, `OwlMain` still receives them, and you must declare them.)

> **NOTE**
>
> Command-line arguments aren't used as widely in Windows as they are under DOS, but they are still available. You can, for example, use the Program Manager or Windows 95 Start menu's *Run* command to run a program by entering a command such as `myprog filename -x`. This passes the two options, `filename` and `-x`, to `myprog.exe`. The Explorer and File Manager utilities also use command-line arguments to pass filenames to programs—such as when you double-click a text filename to open it in the Notepad.

`OwlMain` performs two essential services. First, it constructs an object to represent the application. In this example, the object is of the class `TDemoApp`, which is derived from `TApplication`. The string passed to this object's constructor represents the program's name. It can be any string, but is usually the same as the module's filename minus its .exe extension.

`OwlMain` also calls the application object's `Run` function, inherited from `TApplication`. As you might imagine, this runs the program. `OwlMain` returns the integer value that `Run` passes back, though Windows ignores this value. You see it in Turbo Debugger, however, and might use the value to indicate error codes, but it has no other significance.

Device-Independent Graphics

One of the most practical benefits in Windows is *device-independent graphics.* The Windows GDI, or *graphics device interface,* operates independently of any specific output device. You call the same GDI functions to display graphics on-screen or to print figures on paper. As long as a device provides a suitable software driver, GDI functions can use that device.

The next program, Sketch, demonstrates how to use the GDI in OWL programs. Sketch also shows more about message-response handlers. Listing 14.5, Sketch.rh, declares resource identifiers for the program's menu. Listing 14.6, Sketch.rc, is the resource script that defines the menu's commands. Listing 14.7, Sketch.cpp, is the program's main module.

Listing 14.5. Sketch.rh (Declares resource constants for Sketch program).

```
//============================================================
// Sketch.rh -- Declares resource constants for Sketch program
// Copyright (c) 1996 by Tom Swan. All rights reserved.
//============================================================

#define ID_MENU 100
#define CM_ERASE 101
```

Listing 14.6. Sketch.rc (Declares resources for Sketch program).

```
//============================================================
// Sketch.rc -- Declares resources for Sketch program
// Copyright (c) 1996 by Tom Swan. All rights reserved.
//============================================================

#include <owl\window.rh>
#include "sketch.rh"

ID_MENU MENU
BEGIN
  POPUP "&Demo"
  BEGIN
    MENUITEM "&Erase", CM_ERASE
    MENUITEM "E&xit", CM_EXIT
  END
END
```

Listing 14.7. Sketch.cpp (Demonstrates mouse handling techniques).

```
//============================================================
// Sketch.cpp -- Demonstrates mouse handling techniques
// Copyright (c) 1996 by Tom Swan. All rights reserved.
//============================================================
```

continues

Listing 14.7. continued

```
#include <owl\applicat.h>
#include <owl\framewin.h>
#include <owl\dc.h>
#pragma hdrstop
#include "sketch.rh"

// ================================================================
// The application's main window
// ================================================================

class TSketchWin: public TFrameWindow {
  bool dragging;    // True if clicking and dragging the mouse
  TClientDC* cdc;   // Pointer to client-window device context
public:
  TSketchWin(TWindow* parent, const char far* title);
protected:
  void CmErase();
  void EvLButtonDown(UINT modKeys, TPoint& point);
  void EvMouseMove(UINT modKeys, TPoint& point);
  void EvLButtonUp(UINT modKeys, TPoint& point);
  void EvLButtonDblClk(UINT modKeys, TPoint& point);
DECLARE_RESPONSE_TABLE(TSketchWin);
};

DEFINE_RESPONSE_TABLE1(TSketchWin, TFrameWindow)
  EV_COMMAND(CM_ERASE, CmErase),
  EV_WM_LBUTTONDOWN,
  EV_WM_MOUSEMOVE,
  EV_WM_LBUTTONUP,
  EV_WM_LBUTTONDBLCLK,
END_RESPONSE_TABLE;

// Constructor
TSketchWin::TSketchWin(TWindow* parent, const char far* title)
  : TFrameWindow(parent, title),
    TWindow(parent, title)
{
  AssignMenu(ID_MENU);
  dragging = FALSE;
}

// Erase drawing in window
void
TSketchWin::CmErase()
{
  Invalidate();    // "Window needs updating"
  UpdateWindow();  // "Do it now!" (optional but faster)
}

// Note: The commented /*modKeys*/ parameters in the next three
// functions eliminate warnings from the compiler that these
// items are not used.

// Respond to mouse-click WM_LBUTTONDOWN message
// Begin mouse click-and-drag operation
void
TSketchWin::EvLButtonDown(UINT /*modKeys*/, TPoint& point)
```

```
{
  if (!dragging) {
    dragging = TRUE;
    SetCapture();
    cdc = new TClientDC(HWindow);
    cdc->MoveTo(point);
  }
}

// Respond to mouse-move WM_MOUSEMOVE message
// Leave trail behind mouse as user drags it
void
TSketchWin::EvMouseMove(UINT /*modKeys*/, TPoint& point)
{
  if (dragging)
    cdc->LineTo(point);
}

// Respond to mouse-release WM_LBUTTONUP message
// End click-and-drag operation
void
TSketchWin::EvLButtonUp(UINT /*modKeys*/, TPoint& /*point*/)
{
  if (dragging) {
    ReleaseCapture();
    delete cdc;
    dragging = FALSE;
  }
}

// Respond to mouse double-click WM_LBUTTONDBLCLK message
// Erase any drawing in window
void
TSketchWin::EvLButtonDblClk(UINT /*modKeys*/, TPoint& /*point*/)
{
  CmErase();
}

// ===============================================================
// The application class
// ===============================================================

class TSketchApp: public TApplication {
public:
  TSketchApp(const char far* name)
    : TApplication(name) {};
  void InitMainWindow();
};

// Initialize the program's main window
void
TSketchApp::InitMainWindow()
{
  MainWindow = new TSketchWin(0, "Click and Drag the Mouse");
}

#pragma argsused
```

continues

Listing 14.7. continued

```
// Main program
int
OwlMain(int argc, char* argv[])
{
  TSketchApp app("Sketch");
  return app.Run();
}
```

Sketch includes the OWL header file, Dc.h, which declares *device context* classes. A device context is an internal object in Windows that connects GDI functions to a specific device. Think of it as a kind of universal plug that joins software and hardware. For example, when drawing in a window, a program uses a display device context. When printing, the program uses a printer device context. The device context frees the program from dependency on specific hardware devices.

In OWL programs, various classes declared in Dc.h represent device contexts. To call GDI functions, you construct an object of one of these classes and you call the functions for that object. For example, to draw a line in a window's client area, first construct an object of the TClientDC class:

```
TClientDC* cdc;
cdc = new TClientDC(HWindow);
```

The HWindow argument refers to a window object's handle, which is available in any function of a class derived from TWindow. After creating the device context, call any GDI function in reference to that object. For example, to draw a line from the coordinates (10,10) to (100,125), you could use these statements:

```
cdc-->MoveTo(10, 10);
cdc-->LineTo(100, 125);
```

Delete the device context object when you are done with it:

```
delete cdc;
```

Sketch performs those steps in response to various messages received by the program's window. To see how this works, examine the window's class, TSketchWin, derived from TFrameWindow. The class declares a constructor and five protected member functions. Each of these functions is associated with a message that Windows generates for specific events such as mouse clicks and movements.

To program the message response functions, the class declares that it uses a response table, just as Owlwelc did. That table is then defined, again as in Owlwelc, using five macros (see the uppercase text following the class declaration). The EV_COMMAND macro relates the CmErase function with the CM_ERASE menu command identifier. As a result, when you select the *Erase* command, the program calls CmErase.

The other four message-response functions refer to specific messages and do not require any arguments. EV_WM_LBUTTONDOWN refers to the message, WM_LBUTTONDOWN, which as you can probably guess, Windows issues in response to a left mouse-button click. EV_WM_MOUSEMOVE refers to the WM_MOUSEMOVE message, which Windows issues when the mouse moves.

All such messages in Windows have corresponding response-table macros, prefaced with EV_. To respond to a message, simply insert it into a response table as shown, and add an appropriate member function to the class.

Each of those member functions must have the correct form, and each is named the same as the macro, but in upper- and lowercase, and missing _WM_. For example, the member function for EV_WM_LBUTTONDOWN is named EvLButtonDown. It takes a little while to get used to these naming conventions, but after you master them, you'll appreciate the clarity they lend to the source code.

In this case, the four mouse message response functions receive the same types of arguments. The UINT (unsigned integer) modKeys contains flags that indicate whether a key such as Alt is pressed along with a mouse event. Sketch ignores these values. The TPoint object reference contains the coordinate of the mouse cursor at the time of the event.

Sketch's message-response functions draw lines when you click and drag the mouse. To distinguish between clicking-and-dragging and normal mouse movements, the program sets to true or false a private bool flag, dragging. When you click the left mouse button, function EvLButtonDown sets the flag true, and calls the Windows function, SetCapture, which directs future mouse messages to this window. The function also constructs a device context object and positions the internal display coordinate by calling MoveTo for the mouse's position in point.

> **NOTE**
>
> In prior versions, OWL defined BOOL as an uppercase true or false macro. Starting with Borland C++ 5.0, Boolean functions and variables now use the lowercase ANSI C++ bool data type for true and false values. The uppercase macro is still supported, but you should no longer use it in new code.

Upon moving the mouse, function EvMouseMove checks whether dragging is true. If so, the function calls LineTo for the device context object addressed by cdc. This draws a line from the location set by MoveTo to the mouse's new position, which causes the mouse to leave a trail behind.

When you release the mouse button, function EvLButtonUp calls ReleaseCapture, undoing the effect of the earlier call to SetCapture. This function deletes the device context object and sets dragging to false, ending the click-and-drag operation.

Another message-response function, `EvLButtonDblClk`, erases the window when you double-click the left mouse button. This function calls `CmErase`, the same function that is also called in response to selecting the program's *Erase* menu command. (I purposely programmed Sketch this way to hammer home the fact that you may call menu-command functions as you can any other.)

Function `CmErase` shows how to erase a window's contents. First, it calls the Windows `Invalidate` function, which tells Windows that this window is invalid—that is, its contents need updating. Windows performs this update by issuing a `WM_PAINT` message, which by default erases the invalid portion. Normally, however, `WM_PAINT` messages are low in priority, and are issued only when no other messages are pending for a window. To force the window to be updated immediately, you may call `UpdateWindow` as shown here. Usually, this improves display performance.

Using Turbo Debugger for Windows

A good way to learn more about how Sketch and other OWL programs work is to run them under control of Turbo Debugger for Windows (TDW). You can run TDW independently as you do other applications, but you can run it more easily from the IDE by using the *Tool\Turbo Debugger* command.

Many times, however, it's more convenient to use the GUI debugger built into the IDE. The GUI debugger is less capable than the stand-alone Turbo Debugger, but is still highly useful for investigating how programs work—or, when chasing bugs, how they *don't* work.

After successfully compiling and trying Sketch, run the IDE debugger and try a few experiments. These tips will help guide you through your own future debugging sessions. Open the Sketch.cpp file, and then follow these numbered steps:

1. Set a breakpoint on the only statement in `EvLButtonDblClk`. The simplest method is to click the left mouse button while pointing to the extreme left of the statement. Or, you can use the *Debug\Add breakpoint* command. Or, click the right mouse button and select *Add breakpoint* from the floating popup menu. After setting the breakpoint, press Ctrl+F9 to run the program. Draw a sample sketch and double-click the left mouse button. The debugger halts the program when OWL calls the function in response to the mouse event. The program halts *before* executing the statement for which the breakpoint is set.

2. You can set similar breakpoints in other response functions (or whatever functions you need to inspect). Try setting a breakpoint on the first statement in function `EvLButtonDown`. Run the program by again pressing Ctrl+F9 and click the mouse pointer in the window.

3. The program should halt inside the EvLButtonDown function. When the IDE appears, inspect the point structure passed to the function. To do that, move the text cursor to any character in point (it doesn't matter which instance of that variable you use), and select the *Debug* menu's *Inspect* command. You should see point in the resulting dialog, but if not, type it in. Press Enter or select OK to close the dialog and inspect point's contents. An inspection window (see Figure 14.5) shows the structure's x and y member values. Use these same steps to inspect the values of any variable, but only if that variable is in scope.

4. Press Ctrl+F9 again to run the program, and exit normally. This will put you back in the IDE.

Figure 14.5.

Inspecting the point structure with the IDE's debugger.

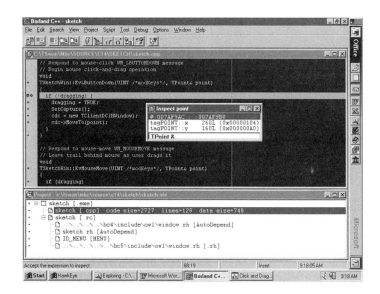

Using WinSight

Another useful debugging tool is an all new 32-bit version of the WinSight utility, which displays messages for any or all running applications. Figure 14.6 shows WinSight32's window behind the Sketch program's.

Tracing a program's message flow is a great way to learn how Windows works, and it also can provide clues for hunting bugs. To use WinSight32, after compiling and running this chapter's Sketch program, run WinSight32 as you do other applications or select it from the *Tools* menu, and then follow these numbered steps:

1. Select the *Spy\Find Window* command and slowly move the mouse pointer to Sketch's window. Click the left mouse button to select the window. You may have to shuffle the windows so you can see them. As you move the mouse from window to window, WinSight32 shows each window's handle and other information. Use *Spy\Open Detail* to see more facts about selected windows.

2. After selecting Sketch's window, use the *Messages\Options* command to limit tracing to Mouse messages. You can trace all messages, but doing so produces reams of data and can slow system performance to a crawl. In most cases, it's best to limit tracing to a small number of message types.

3. Make sure that *Message Trace* is selected (has a checkmark next to it) in the *View* menu.

4. Also make sure that *Selected Windows* in the *Messages* menu has a checkmark next to it. If not, select that command.

5. Select the *Start!* command to begin tracing messages for the selected window. Move the mouse back to Sketch's window and click to bring the window forward. (For best results, adjust the Sketch and WinSight32 windows so that you can see both on-screen.) Click and drag the mouse inside Sketch to draw a shape. As you do, WinSight32 shows you the messages that Windows generates for mouse-click and mouse-move events.

6. To stop tracing, select the *Stop!* command, which replaces *Start!* while tracing.

Figure 14.6

WinSight32 inspecting Sketch's message flow.

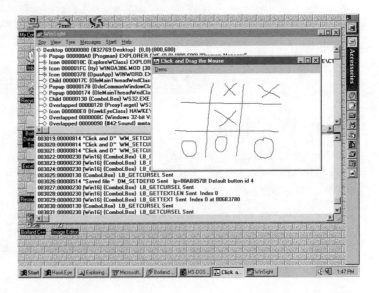

> **NOTE**
>
> WinSight32 traces messages received via the Windows functions, `GetMessage` and `SendMessage`. The utility can't trace messages, such as `WM_INITDIALOG`, passed directly to the program's functions.

Using WinSpector

Borland C++ 5.0 includes another debugging utility, WinSpector (see Figure 14.7). Use WinSpector to inspect conditions that exist after a program halts with a general protection (GP) fault. These errors are also called UAEs, or Unrecoverable Application Errors. They are typically caused by a program that attempts to read or write memory beyond the application's defined boundaries, or that executes an illegal instruction code. When Windows receives a UAE, it displays a system error message and halts the offending program. Windows 3.1 and earlier versions often halted or became confused by some kinds of UAEs. Windows 95 and NT do a far better, but still not perfect, job of protecting the operating system due to a serious program error. You should do everything possible to locate and repair the causes of any UAEs you receive. WinSpector can help you find the trouble spots.

Figure 14.7.
The WinSpector utility.

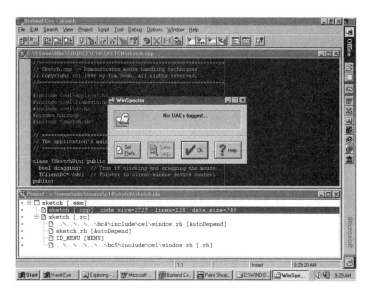

When developing Windows programs, it's probably best to start WinSpector and leave it running in the background for the entire session. To do this automatically, insert the program's .exe code file into the StartUp menu or folder.

When a system-level error occurs, WinSpector awakens. While the trail of the GP fault is still warm, the program quickly takes a snapshot of various conditions, register values, and other system-level elements, all of which might help you to determine where your code went awry. Double-click on WinSpector's icon to display a report on recent errors.

Use the *Set Prefs* button to select WinSpector's options. You can write information about trapped conditions to a log file, append new information to old logs (probably the best choice to keep a history list of goings on), and set other options to dump stack frame information, add your own comments, and so on.

Deciphering the contents of a WinSpector snapshot requires a great deal of knowledge about Windows, DOS, and PC internals. If you don't comprehend a WinSpector log file, you probably aren't ready to use the information anyway. In fact, if you are just getting started with Windows programming, WinSpector's reports might be more confusing than helpful. Even for advanced programmers, a WinSpector snapshot (called a *core dump* in programming's ancient days) still provides only vague clues about a bug. The reports don't tell you what statements in your code committed a crime. They just show you what the victim looks like after the dirty deed has been done.

> **NOTE**
>
> At one point, WinSpector was called Dr. Frank, and its icon resembled Dr. Frankenstein's infamous monster. For a short time, a version of Dr. Frank was available on CompuServe, but Borland deleted the free program when the company decided to include WinSpector with Borland C++. Personally, I liked the name Dr. Frank better—after all, debugging Windows code can provide you with more chills than a horror film. At Borland, however, less ghoulish heads prevailed, and Dr. Frank became WinSpector. (Officially, that's "spector" as in "inspector," but the true story behind the program's new name is that "WinSpector" is phonetically, if not literally, the specter of its formerly monstrous self.)

Menus, Icons, and Other Resources

Resources are structures that describe the attributes of various on-screen elements. Resources include menu commands, dialog boxes, buttons, check boxes, icons, and keyboard "hot key" accelerators. You design all of these and other resources separately, and then combine them with your compiled program.

There are many ways to accomplish that same end. In the early days of Windows programming, developers created resources with text-file script commands. A resource compiler such as Microsoft's Rc.exe translated these .rc script files into .res binary resource files, and then bound the result into the compiled program's .exe image.

Borland C++ 3.1 introduced Borland's own resource compiler, Brc.exe. Use the program as you do Rc.exe—that is, enter a command such as `brc myfile.rc` to compile a resource script. Enter `brc` alone for a list of command-line options. Brc calls two other code files, Brcc.exe and Rlink.exe, which together are functionally equivalent to Microsoft's Rc.exe utility. Unlike Rc, however, Brc can bind multiple resource (.res) files into an executable code file, and the Borland program also does a better job of detecting resource ID conflicts. For compiling 32-bit resources to be bound into Win32 code files, use the Brc32.exe utility.

You can still write resource scripts in these old-fashioned ways, but it's much easier to use a tool such as Borland's Resource Workshop (RW), now integrated into version 5.0's IDE (see Figure 14.8). With this visual resource editor, you construct your resources on-screen as you want them to appear. You then can create an .rc script file or a compiled .res binary file, ready for attaching to your code.

Figure 14.8.
Design resources with the IDE's resource editor, which replaces the formerly stand-alone Resource Workshop.

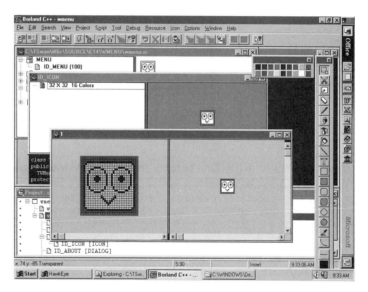

It's also possible to add .rc script text files to a project, in which case the IDE compiles the resource commands into a binary .res file. The IDE can compile .rc script files directly; it doesn't require brc.exe or brc32.exe to be online. If you compile with the command-line compiler, you must run Brc.exe or Brc32.exe to bind a resource file to your compiled code. In fact, you must run one of these programs *even if your program does not use any resources.*

The next program uses resources to construct a pull-down menu and an About-Box dialog—a common place to insert a copyright notice or other miscellaneous information about the program (see Figure 14.9). Several files make up the demonstration, including Listing 14.8, Wmenu.rh (the resource header file), and Listing 14.9, Wmenu.cpp (the program's source text). In addition to these two files, on the CD-ROM you'll find Wmenu.ico (About-Box and desktop icon image), Wmenu.ide (project file), and Wmenu.rc. As you are probably realizing, there are many component files that go into producing a typical Windows application.

Figure 14.9.

Wmenu's main window and About-Box dialog.

Listing 14.8. Wmenu.rh (Declares resource constants for WMenu program).

```
//==============================================================
// Wmenu.rh -- Declares resource constants for WMenu program
// Copyright (c) 1996 by Tom Swan. All rights reserved.
//==============================================================

// Resource ID values
#define ID_MENU 100
#define ID_ABOUT 100
#define ID_ACCELERATORS 100
#define ID_ICON 100

// Menu-command ID values
#define CM_DEMO_NEW 101
#define CM_DEMO_EXIT 102
#define CM_HELP_ABOUT 201
```

Listing 14.9. Wmenu.cpp (Demonstrates menu-command techniques).

```cpp
//================================================================
// Wmenu.cpp -- Demonstrates menu-command techniques
// Copyright (c) 1996 by Tom Swan. All rights reserved.
//================================================================

#include <owl\applicat.h>
#include <owl\framewin.h>
#include <owl\dialog.h>
#pragma hdrstop
#include "wmenu.rh"


// ================================================================
// The application's main window
// ================================================================

class TWMenuWin: public TFrameWindow {
public:
  TWMenuWin(TWindow* parent, const char far* title);
protected:
  void CmDemoNew();
  void CmDemoExit();
  void CmHelpAbout();
DECLARE_RESPONSE_TABLE(TWMenuWin);
};

DEFINE_RESPONSE_TABLE1(TWMenuWin, TFrameWindow)
  EV_COMMAND(CM_DEMO_NEW, CmDemoNew),
  EV_COMMAND(CM_DEMO_EXIT, CmDemoExit),
  EV_COMMAND(CM_HELP_ABOUT, CmHelpAbout),
END_RESPONSE_TABLE;

// Constructor
TWMenuWin::TWMenuWin(TWindow* parent, const char far* title)
  : TFrameWindow(parent, title),
    TWindow(parent, title)
{
  AssignMenu(ID_MENU);
  Attr.X = GetSystemMetrics(SM_CXSCREEN) / 8;
  Attr.Y = GetSystemMetrics(SM_CYSCREEN) / 8;
  Attr.H = Attr.Y * 6;
  Attr.W = Attr.X * 6;
}

// Respond to Demo|New menu command
void
TWMenuWin::CmDemoNew()
{
  MessageBox(
    "Demo|New command selected!",
    "Message Box Dialog",
```

continues

Listing 14.9. continued

```
      MB_ICONINFORMATION ¦ MB_OK);
}

// Respond to Demo¦Exit menu command
void
TWMenuWin::CmDemoExit()
{
  CloseWindow();
}

// Respond to Help¦About menu command
// Display About-box dialog
void
TWMenuWin::CmHelpAbout()
{
  new TDialog(this, ID_ABOUT)->Execute();
}

// ================================================================
// The application class
// ================================================================

class TWMenuApp: public TApplication {
public:
  TWMenuApp(const char far* name)
    : TApplication(name) {};
  void InitMainWindow();
};

// Initialize the program's main window
void
TWMenuApp::InitMainWindow()
{
  MainWindow = new TWMenuWin(0, "OWL Menu Demonstration");
  MainWindow->Attr.AccelTable = ID_ACCELERATORS;
  MainWindow->SetIcon(this, ID_ICON);
}

#pragma argsused

// Main program
int
OwlMain(int argc, char* argv[])
{
  TWMenuApp app("WMenu");
  return app.Run();
}
```

In addition to its usual duty of creating the program's main window, the TWMenuApp class's InitMainWindow function now performs two more services. To implement *accelerator keys*—otherwise known as hot keys that you can press to issue commands—the program assigns an accelerator resource table's identifier, ID_ACCELERATORS, to the AccelTable member in the Attr structure. This structure describes the application's *attributes.* The program also calls the Windows SetIcon function to assign a desktop icon for display when you minimize the program's window.

Wmenu's window class, TWMenuWin, is similar to others you've seen. It declares three response functions for the program's menu commands, two of which show how to display a dialog box.

The TWMenuWin class constructor also demonstrates how to open a program's window in a certain size and position. To do that, assign values to the X, Y, H, and W members of the Attr structure. The values are up to you—for fun, WMenu calls the Windows function GetSystemMetrics to obtain the screen X (SM_CXSCREEN) and Y (SM_CYSCREEN) limits. The program manipulates these values to position the window centered and in a relative size regardless of display resolution.

Function CmDemoNew, called when you select the *New* command, calls the Windows MessageBox to display a message. This is a handy function to use for informal messages, warnings, and other simple notes. You can specify a combination of icons and buttons using MB_ constants, listed in a Windows API reference or online help file. As shown here, the dialog displays an information icon and OK button (see Figure 14.10).

Figure 14.10.
Message box displayed by WMenu.

Function CmHelpAbout, called when you select the *About* command, shows how to display a modal dialog box, created in the program's resources. Open Wmenu.rc and inspect the dialog. This statement constructs an object of the TDialog class, declared in Dialog.h, which the program includes, and calls that object's `Execute` member function. `ID_ABOUT` identifies the dialog resource; `this` refers to the window object that owns the dialog window:

```
(new TDialog(this, ID_ABOUT))-->Execute();
```

You can use this same method to bring up any dialog box. You don't have to delete the object—that happens automatically when you close the dialog window.

Windows and Graphics

In addition to providing a graphical user interface, Windows gives programmers a rich library of device-independent graphics functions. Collectively known as the Graphics Device Interface (GDI), these functions work independently of any specific output device. This means you can use the same `Rectangle` function to draw rectangles in windows and also to print rectangles on paper, or perhaps draw them on a plotter.

As I mentioned in the discussion of the Sketch program, a key concept in Windows graphics is the device context, represented in OWL programs by an object of a class such as `TClientDC`. The next program demonstrates a similar, but different, way to paint a window's contents using a `TPaintDC` object, which is derived from the general-purpose device context class, `TDC`.

When a window or a portion of a window requires updating, Windows issues a `WM_PAINT` message, which OWL intercepts and, in response, calls an event-handler function named `EvPaint`. This function prepares a device context, and calls another virtual function, `Paint`. This gives you two ways to paint graphics in windows. You can provide your own `EvPaint` event handler, or you can provide a replacement for `Paint`. Either way, Windows calls your function whenever the window needs updating—to redraw its contents, for example, when another covering window moves aside.

Listing 14.10, Grdemo.cpp, demonstrates how to write an event-handler `EvPaint` function. Following the discussion of the listing, I'll explain how to use the somewhat easier `Paint`. The methods are nearly equivalent, but I prefer to define my own `EvPaint` event handler, as this gives me full control over `WM_PAINT`'s response. The program's other text files, Grdemo.rh and Grdemo.rc, are similar to others of those types listed before, and are not included here. They are, of course, provided on disk along with the Grdemo.ide project file for opening in the IDE.

Listing 14.10. Grdemo.cpp (Demonstrates window painting).

```
//================================================================
// Grdemo.cpp -- Demonstrates window painting
// Copyright (c) 1996 by Tom Swan. All rights reserved.
//================================================================

#include <owl\applicat.h>
#include <owl\framewin.h>
#include <owl\dc.h>
#include <owl\gdiobjec.h>
#include <owl\point.h>
```

```
#include <owl\color.h>
#pragma hdrstop
#include "grdemo.rh"

// ================================================================
// The application's main window
// ================================================================

class TGrDemoWin: public TFrameWindow {
  TPen blackPen, redPen, greenPen, bluePen;
  TBrush blueGreenBrush;
public:
  TGrDemoWin(TWindow* parent, const char far* title);
  void DrawEllipse(TDC& dc, TRect& cr);
protected:
  void EvPaint();
  void EvSize(UINT sizeType, TSize &size);
DECLARE_RESPONSE_TABLE(TGrDemoWin);
};

DEFINE_RESPONSE_TABLE1(TGrDemoWin, TFrameWindow)
  EV_WM_PAINT,
  EV_WM_SIZE,
END_RESPONSE_TABLE;

// Constructor
// Note how private member class objects are constructed
TGrDemoWin::TGrDemoWin(TWindow* parent, const char far* title)
  : TFrameWindow(parent, title),
    TWindow(parent, title),
    blackPen(TColor::Black),          // Construct private
    redPen(TColor::LtRed),            //   member-object
    greenPen(TColor::LtGreen),        //   pens and brush.
    bluePen(TColor::LtBlue),
    blueGreenBrush(TColor::LtCyan)
{
  AssignMenu(ID_MENU);
}

// Draw a filled, outlined, colored ellipse
// Demonstrates that other functions can draw shapes
// dc == reference to a TDC device-context object
// cr == reference to client window dimensions class object
void
TGrDemoWin::DrawEllipse(TDC& dc, TRect& cr)
{
  TColor foreground(255, 0, 128);
  TColor background(0, 128, 255);
  TPen pen(foreground);
  TBrush brush(background);
  dc.SelectObject(pen);
  dc.SelectObject(brush);
  TPoint origin((cr.right / 4) * 3, cr.bottom / 4);
  TSize size(cr.right / 5, cr.bottom / 5);
  TRect dimensions(origin, size);
  dc.Ellipse(dimensions);
  dc.RestorePen();
```

continues

497

Listing 14.10. continued

```
  dc.RestoreBrush();
}

// Respond to WM_PAINT messages
void
TGrDemoWin::EvPaint()
{
// Construct a device context object
  TPaintDC dc(*this);

// Get client area dimensions
  TRect cr;                             // Define rectangle
  GetClientRect(cr);                    // Set cr to client area

// Erase window background
  TBrush whiteBrush(TColor::White);     // Create white brush
  dc.FillRect(cr, whiteBrush);          // Paint window white

// Shrink a copy of rectangle cr 10 pixels on all sides
  TRect outline(cr);                    // Construct copy of cr
  outline.Inflate(-10, -10);            // Shrink copy

// Draw a red rectangle using dimensions in TRect outline
  dc.SelectObject(redPen);              // Use red pen in dc
  dc.Rectangle(outline);                // Draw the rectangle

// Draw a black rectangle the "hard way"
  dc.SelectObject(blackPen);            // Use black pen in dc
  dc.Rectangle(25, 25, 150, 175);       // Draw the rectangle

// Draw a green rectangle using TPoint arguments
  TPoint p1(20, 20);                    // Construct a couple of
  TPoint p2(60, 80);                    //  TPoint objects.
  dc.SelectObject(greenPen);            // Use green pen in dc
  dc.Rectangle(p1, p2);                 // Draw the rectangle

// Draw a filled rectangle using TPoint and TSize arguments
  TPoint p3(30, 90);                    // Construct TPoint object
  TSize s(48, 32);                      // Construct TSize object
  dc.SelectObject(bluePen);             // Use blue pen in dc
  dc.SelectObject(blueGreenBrush);      // Use blue-green brush
  dc.Rectangle(p3, s);                  // Draw the rectangle

// Draw colored lines
  for (int i = 0; i < 3; ++i) {
    // Construct line start and stop points
    TPoint startLine(cr.right / 2 + i * 8, cr.bottom / 2);
    TPoint stopLine(startLine.x, cr.bottom - 20);
    if (i == 0)
      dc.SelectObject(redPen);          // Use red pen in dc
    else if (i == 1)
      dc.SelectObject(greenPen);        // Use green pen in dc
    else
      dc.SelectObject(bluePen);         // Use blue pen in dc
    dc.MoveTo(startLine);               // Move to start of line
```

```
      dc.LineTo(stopLine);                    // Draw to end of line
  }

// Restore original pen and brush in the device context
  dc.RestorePen();
  dc.RestoreBrush();

// Call a program function to draw an ellipse
// It's okay to pass the TPaintDC object, dc, to
// the function's TDC& parameter because TPaintDC is
// derived from TDC.
  DrawEllipse(dc, cr);
}

// Respond to WM_SIZE message
// Forces window to be redrawn completely if its size changes
void
TGrDemoWin::EvSize(UINT sizeType, TSize &size)
{
  TFrameWindow::EvSize(sizeType, size);  // Default actions
  Invalidate();  // Force update of window's client area
}

// ============================================================
// The application class
// ============================================================

class TGrDemoApp: public TApplication {
public:
  TGrDemoApp(const char far* name)
    : TApplication(name) {};
  void InitMainWindow();
};

// Initialize the program's main window
void
TGrDemoApp::InitMainWindow()
{
  MainWindow = new TGrDemoWin(0, "Paint Demo");
}

#pragma argsused

// Main program
int
OwlMain(int argc, char* argv[])
{
  TGrDemoApp app("GrDemo");
  return app.Run();
}
```

Grdemo's window class, TGrDemoWin, defines three pens and one brush, which the program uses to paint colorful shapes in the main window as Figure 14.11 shows. This display probably won't win any prizes down at the art gallery, but even so, the program's source code demonstrates key graphics techniques that you'll need to create your own graphical output.

Figure 14.11.
GrDemo's display.

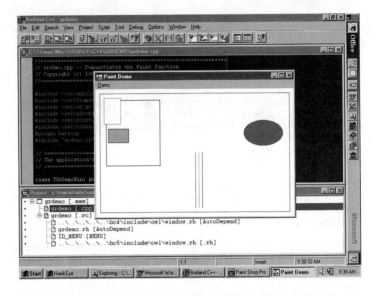

The class also defines a constructor, and a DrawEllipse function, which I'll come back to in a moment. Two protected event-handler functions respond to Windows messages. EvPaint responds to WM_PAINT, issued when all or a portion of the program's window becomes *invalid*—that is, in need of redrawing. EvSize responds to WM_SIZE, issued when the window's size changes so that the program can resize its graphics. Not all programs need to do this, but in this case, I want the graphics to maintain their sizes and positions relative to the window's size and shape. The response table following the class declaration associates the window messages with the event-handler functions.

The TGreDemoWin constructor initializes the pen and brush variables, using TColor class color values such as LtRed and LtCyan. TPen variables draw foreground patterns and outlines. TBrush variables draw backgrounds and fill shapes with colors and patterns. You don't have to create pens and brushes as variables—you can also construct them on the fly as needed. But creating them in advance helps boost program speed, which often suffers in complex graphical displays. When it comes to graphics, even a tiny bit of extra speed may make a critical difference in usability.

Skip down to the EvPaint function. To provide a device context for drawing on-screen, the function begins by creating a variable of the TPaintDC class. The argument *this associates the device context with the program's main window.

> **NOTE**
>
> In an EvPaint event handler, or in a Paint function (to be explained later in this section), a device context is often called a *display context*. The terms are frequently used as synonyms, but strictly speaking, a display context is merely a specific type of device context.

To erase the window's background to white, EvPaint obtains the client area's dimensions by calling GetClientRect. Next, the program prepares a TBrush object initialized to TColor::White. It then passes the client area rectangle and the brush to the device context object's FillRect function. Use this technique to fill a window with any color, or to paint rectangular backgrounds.

Rectangles such as cr of type TRect come in handy for all sorts of uses. To shrink or expand a rectangle's dimensions, call its Inflate function. Pass negative values to shrink the rectangle. Pass positive values to expand it. Or, you can mix negative and positive arguments to expand in one direction and shrink in the other. TRect objects are not visible; they merely define areas for drawing shapes. For example, passing the outline rectangle to the device context's Rectangle function draws a visible rectangle. The two statements

```
dc.SelectObject(redPen);        // Use red pen in dc
dc.Rectangle(outline);          // Draw the rectangle
```

first select the redPen object for use in the display context. The second statement uses that pen to draw a rectangle outlined in red, with an interior equal to the default brush color—the same as the window's background. You may select only one pen or brush, or other objects, into a device context. Selecting another automatically disposes of any currently selected object.

> **TIP**
>
> Unlike in conventional C programming, you don't have to delete pen and brush objects, and you don't have to remove them before releasing a device context. The TPaintDC class takes care of these messy details automatically.

You don't have to use a TRect object to draw rectangles and other shapes. As the next statements demonstrate, you can also pass literal or variable coordinates to Rectangle and to other shape-drawing functions:

```
dc.SelectObject(blackPen);          // Use black pen in dc
dc.Rectangle(25, 25, 150, 175);     // Draw the rectangle
```

Alternatively, you can create TPoint objects, which define single coordinate positions in a window. Pass two of them to Rectangle to draw a box with the upper-left and lower-right corners at the specified locations.

Fill a rectangular area by selecting a brush object into the device context, and then calling Rectangle. Notice that in this case, the program calls yet another overloaded Rectangle function—one that takes TPoint and TSize arguments to define the shape's position and its width and height.

> ### NOTE
>
> All of this just demonstrates how many different ways are available to draw shapes. Other shape-drawing functions such as `Ellipse` and `RoundRect` are similarly overloaded to the hilt. Look them up online to find the many types of arguments they accept.

To draw lines, call the `MoveTo` and `LineTo` functions for a device context. `MoveTo` sets an internal starting location; `LineTo` connects a line from that spot to a specified point. In the demonstration, I use `TPoint` objects to define these locations, but you also can pass literal coordinates to `MoveTo` and `LineTo`.

When you are finished using a device context, it's a good idea to restore any pens and brushes selected by calling a *Restore* function such as `RestorePen` and `RestoreBrush`. These steps are not strictly required, but they help prevent strange on-screen bugs, which might arise by leaving a pen or brush of unknown colors in the device context.

Just before ending, `EvPaint` calls another program member function, `DrawEllipse`. This demonstrates that you may pass a `TPaintDC` object such as `dc` to the function's `TDC&` parameter. `TPaintDC` derives from `TDC`, so this is okay, and it's a good trick to remember. Because `DrawEllipse` accepts a more general `TDC` parameter, the function can potentially draw on any valid device context. The *same* function, in other words, can print on paper as well as it can draw on-screen. Just pass the appropriate device context to the function.

> ### TIP
>
> A well-written Windows program performs all graphical output operations in functions such as `DrawEllipse`. `EvPaint` or `Paint` can call the functions to draw output in a window. The program can also prepare other types of device contexts, and call the same functions to print, plot, or output graphics to any device for which it is possible to obtain a device context.

Examine the `DrawEllipse` function in Grdemo.cpp. The function prepares `TColor`, `TPen`, and `TBrush` objects to define various display colors. It selects the pen and brush objects into the device context, and also prepares some other objects to specify drawing locations and dimensions. Finally, the program calls `Ellipse` to draw the elliptical shape. Notice especially that the function restores the device context's original pen and brush objects before returning.

Member function `EvSize` shows the correct way to redraw graphics when the window's size changes. Call the inherited `EvSize` first; then call the Window's `Invalidate` function. This invalidates the entire window, causing Windows to issue a `WM_PAINT` message and, consequently, redraw the window.

Instead of writing an EvPaint event-handler function as GrDemo demonstrates, you can override the window class's virtual Paint function. OWL programs call this function when a window receives a WM_PAINT message. The function receives three arguments:

- TDC& dc—A reference to a device context object of the TDC class. To draw in a window, call GDI functions in reference to this object.

- bool erase—A true or false value that indicates whether the window (or its invalid portion) requires erasure.

- TRect& rect—A structure of the TRect class, a descendent of the Windows RECT struct, containing the upper-left and lower-right corners of an imaginary rectangle, which describes the area in which to draw.

In many cases, you can simply draw into a window using the supplied device context and ignore the other parameters passed to Paint. Windows automatically clips output to the portion of a window that requires drawing, so you don't have to limit drawing to that location. You can instead draw all of a window's contents and let Windows clip the results to the portion that's actually needed.

Writing a Paint function is easy. On disk, file Painter.cpp in the Grdemo directory is a copy of the Grdemo.cpp listing, but with a Paint function in place of the EvPaint event handler. To use Paint, declare it publicly in your window class. For example, you can rewrite TGrDemoWin as follows (to save space here, ellipses mark unchanged sections):

```
class TGrDemoWin: public TFrameWindow {
...
public:
...
  virtual void Paint(TDC& dc, bool erase, TRect& rect);
...
};
```

Do not define an EV_WM_PAINT entry in the window's response table—TFrameWindow already does that. Implement Paint in exactly the same way as you did EvPaint, but with one key difference—use the device context passed to Paint's dc parameter instead of creating your own TPaintDC object:

```
void
TGrDemoWin::Paint(TDC& dc, bool erase, TRect& rect)
{
// Use dc parameter instead of creating a TPaint object
//   TPaintDC dc(*this);  // Delete this statement!
...
}
```

DLLs and Custom Controls

A Dynamic Link Library, or DLL, is a kind of runtime programming library—a module of functions that multiple programs can share. Only one copy of a DLL ever exists in RAM, no matter how many programs use it. You might also use DLLs for multilanguage programming. As soon as they are compiled, DLLs are available to all Windows programs—provided, that is, that the DLL conforms to expected data formats such as floating-point representations.

One intriguing use for DLLs is in custom controls. You can design a control, compile it to a DLL, and then plug the control into a dialog box just as you can buttons, check boxes, scroll bars, and other built-in controls. In the next few listings, you'll implement a sample DLL with a pie-shaped control, useful in a status dialog that you might include in an installation utility or in any program that performs lengthy activities. Figure 14.12 shows a sample dialog with the custom pie-shaped control indicating the elapsed time of a dummy test operation.

Figure 14.12.

A custom control DLL in service.

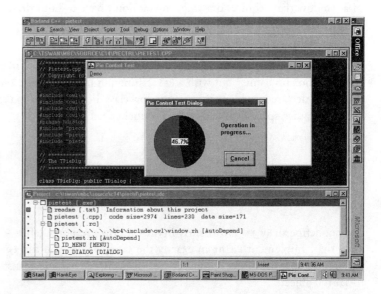

The first of several related listings is Listing 14.11, Piectrl.h, the DLL's header file. Several `#define` statements define constants as `WM_USER` plus values from zero to three. These are called *user-defined messages*—those that programs use to communicate with the DLL's control window. Two other constants, `PIE_BACKCOLOR` and `PIE_FORECOLOR`, serve as selectors for the `WM_CTLCOLOR` message, which the control sends to host programs to request color values. In that way, each program that uses the DLL can color the custom control differently.

NOTE

To compile the custom pie control and its test program, change to the Piectrl subdirectory, and type build at a DOS prompt. Or, using the IDE, you can load the Piectrl.ide and Pietest.ide projects in that order, and compile the DLL and test program separately. Due to a bug in the IDE, if you regenerate the make files on this book's CD-ROM in the C14\Piectrl directory, the Build.bat program may not work correctly. If you cannot compile the application from a DOS prompt, either use the IDE to compile the two .ide project files, or edit the Pietest.mak file (created by the IDE), and locate the following statement:

```
CompLocalOptsAtW16_pietestdexe = -ml -WS -H"owl\pch.h"
```

Then change it to the following:

```
CompLocalOptsAtW16_pietestdexe = -ml -WS
```

Listing 14.11. Piectrl.h (Declares constants for Piectrl DLL).

```
//================================================================
// Piectrl.h -- Declares constants for Piectrl DLL
// Copyright (c) 1996 by Tom Swan. All rights reserved.
//================================================================

#define PIE_SETLIMIT (WM_USER + 0)
#define PIE_GETLIMIT (WM_USER + 1)
#define PIE_SETINDEX (WM_USER + 2)
#define PIE_GETINDEX (WM_USER + 3)
#define PIE_BACKCOLOR 100
#define PIE_FORECOLOR 101
```

Because the DLL is designed for use with 16- and 32-bit Windows programs, it requires a linker-definition file. As Listing 14.12, Piectrl.def, shows, the first line, LIBRARY PIECTRL, tells the linker to create a .dll rather than an .exe code file.

Listing 14.12. Piectrl.def (Linker definition file).

```
LIBRARY PIECTRL
EXETYPE WINDOWS
CODE PRELOAD MOVEABLE DISCARDABLE
DATA PRELOAD MOVEABLE SINGLE
HEAPSIZE 1024
```

Listing 14.13, Piectrl.cpp, shows the DLL's source module. To compile the DLL, load its project file into the IDE (Piectrl.ide is supplied on this book's accompanying disk) and press F9. You can't run a DLL. You have to write another program to load and use the library.

Listing 14.13. Piectrl.cpp (Implements custom pie control DLL).

```cpp
//================================================================
// Piectrl.cpp -- Implements custom pie control DLL
// Copyright (c) 1996 by Tom Swan. All rights reserved.
//================================================================

#include <windows.h>
#include <stdio.h>
#include <string.h>
#include <math.h>
#include "piectrl.h"

#define CLASS_NAME "PieCtrl"   // Custom control class name
#define EXTRA_BYTES 4          // Extra bytes in window instance
#define PIE_LIMIT 0            // Offset to instance Limit value
#define PIE_INDEX 2            // Offset to instance Index value

// Function prototypes
double Radians(double w);
BOOL RegisterPieCtrl(HANDLE hInstance);
void Paint(HDC DC, HWND hWindow);

// Function prototype
LONG FAR PASCAL PieWndFn(HWND hWindow, UINT wMsg, UINT wParam,
  LONG lParam);

// Global variable
HANDLE hModuleInstance = NULL;

// Return radians in angle w
double Radians(double w)
{
  int iw = floor(w);
  return (abs(iw % 360) * M_PI / 180.0);
}

// Register the custom control window with Windows
BOOL RegisterPieCtrl(HANDLE hInstance)
{
  WNDCLASS w;   // Windows "window class" structure

  w.cbClsExtra = 0;
  w.cbWndExtra = EXTRA_BYTES;
  w.hbrBackground = 0;
  w.hIcon = 0;
  w.hInstance = hInstance;
  w.hCursor = LoadCursor(0, IDC_ARROW);
  w.lpfnWndProc = PieWndFn;
  w.lpszClassName = CLASS_NAME;
  w.lpszMenuName = 0;
  w.style = CS_HREDRAW | CS_VREDRAW | CS_GLOBALCLASS;
  return RegisterClass(&w);
}

// Paint pie control
void Paint(HDC DC, HWND hWindow)
{
  RECT r;
```

```
  HBRUSH brush;
  WORD tHeight, center;
  double dLimit, dIndex;
  int xEnd, yEnd, xStart, yStart;
  double percent, dRadius, endAngle, startAngle = 270.0;
  char s[20];

  SaveDC(DC);
  GetClientRect(hWindow, &r);
  if (r.right > r.bottom)
    r.right = r.bottom;
  else if (r.bottom > r.right)
    r.bottom = r.right;
  dRadius = r.right;
  center = r.right / 2;
  dLimit = SendMessage(hWindow, PIE_GETLIMIT, 0, 0);
  dIndex = SendMessage(hWindow, PIE_GETINDEX, 0, 0);
  percent = dIndex / dLimit;
  sprintf(s, "%0.1f%%", (percent * 100.0));
  endAngle = startAngle + (percent * 360.0);
  xEnd = center + floor(dRadius * cos(Radians(endAngle)));
  yEnd = center + floor(dRadius * sin(Radians(endAngle)));
  xStart = center + floor(dRadius * cos(Radians(startAngle)));
  yStart = center + floor(dRadius * sin(Radians(startAngle)));
  brush = (HBRUSH) SendMessage(GetParent(hWindow),
    WM_CTLCOLOR, DC, MAKELONG(hWindow, PIE_BACKCOLOR));
  SelectObject(DC, brush);
  Pie(DC, r.left, r.top, r.right, r.bottom,
    xEnd, yEnd, xStart, yStart);
  if (dLimit != dIndex) {
    brush = (HBRUSH) SendMessage(GetParent(hWindow),
      WM_CTLCOLOR, DC, MAKELONG(hWindow, PIE_FORECOLOR));
    SelectObject(DC, brush);
    Pie(DC, r.left, r.top, r.right, r.bottom,
      xStart, yStart, xEnd, yEnd);
  }
  tHeight = HIWORD(GetTextExtent(DC, s, 1));
  SetTextAlign(DC, TA_CENTER);
  TextOut(DC, center, center - tHeight / 2, s, strlen(s));
  RestoreDC(DC, -1);
}

// Pie control "window function" i.e. message dispatcher
LONG FAR PASCAL PieWndFn(HWND hWindow, UINT wMsg, UINT wParam,
  LONG lParam)
{
  long result = 0L;
  PAINTSTRUCT ps;

  switch (wMsg) {
    case WM_CREATE:
      SendMessage(hWindow, PIE_SETLIMIT, 100, 0);
      SendMessage(hWindow, PIE_SETINDEX, 0, 0);
      break;
    case WM_GETDLGCODE:
      result = DLGC_STATIC;
```

continues

507

Listing 14.13. continued

```
      break;
    case WM_PAINT:
      BeginPaint(hWindow, &ps);
      Paint(ps.hdc, hWindow);
      EndPaint(hWindow, &ps);
      break;
    case PIE_SETLIMIT:
      if (GetWindowWord(hWindow, PIE_LIMIT) != wParam) {
        SetWindowWord(hWindow, PIE_LIMIT, wParam);
        InvalidateRect(hWindow, NULL, FALSE);
        UpdateWindow(hWindow);
      }
      break;
    case PIE_GETLIMIT:
      result = GetWindowWord(hWindow, PIE_LIMIT);
      break;
    case PIE_SETINDEX:
      if (GetWindowWord(hWindow, PIE_INDEX) != wParam) {
        SetWindowWord(hWindow, PIE_INDEX, wParam);
        InvalidateRect(hWindow, NULL, FALSE);
        UpdateWindow(hWindow);
      }
      break;
    case PIE_GETINDEX:
      result = GetWindowWord(hWindow, PIE_INDEX);
      break;
    default:
      result = DefWindowProc(hWindow, wMsg, wParam, lParam);
      break;
  }
  return result;
}

// Windows Exit Procedure (WEP) for DLLs
int FAR PASCAL WEP(int nSystemExit)
{
  switch (nSystemExit) {
    case WEP_SYSTEM_EXIT:
      break;                 // System shut down
    case WEP_FREE_DLL:
      break;                 // DLL released
  }
  UnregisterClass(CLASS_NAME, hModuleInstance);
  return 1;
}

// DLL rough equivalent to a DOS program's main() function
int FAR PASCAL LibMain(HANDLE hModule, WORD /*wDataSeg*/,
  WORD /*wHeapSize*/, LPSTR /*lpszCmdLine*/)
{
  hModuleInstance = hModule;
  return RegisterPieCtrl(hModule);
}
```

The programming near the end of the listing reveals a key difference between DLLs and executable Windows programs. In place of the usual WinMain, a DLL has a LibMain function. When Windows first loads a DLL, it calls this function to initialize the library. Typically, as done here, LibMain saves the DLL's instance handle in a global variable and registers the DLL's window class—in this case, the custom pie-control window.

> **NOTE**
>
> This use of the word "class" is unrelated to its meaning in C++ programming. A *window class* is a structure that Windows recognizes as a description of a window's general characteristics.

Function RegisterPieCtrl near the beginning of the listing registers the window class. Several statements assign values to a WNDCLASS structure, passed by address to the Windows RegisterClass function. The class name, *PieCtrl*, the value of the CLASS_NAME macro, specifies the name that a dialog box or other window can use to reference the custom control. Registering the window class makes its design parameters available to any and all programs.

The only remaining job is to respond to messages passed to the control's window function— that is, the function charged with receiving the control window's messages and taking appropriate actions. Function PieWndFn handles all messages sent to an instance of the custom pie control window. In listing order, the control's messages are as follows:

- WM_CREATE is called during the control window's initialization. In response to receiving this message, the program sends two other user-defined messages to itself, setting the control's maximum range to 100 and the current index to zero. The "limit" might represent a total time estimate, the number of files to be copied, or some other number of operations to be performed. The "index" is the amount of time or other unit from zero to "limit" that has passed.

- WM_GETDLGCODE returns DLGC_STATIC, telling Windows not to send any keyboard messages to this window.

- WM_PAINT draws the control's shape on demand, calling BeginPaint to initialize a PAINTSTRUCT structure and provide a display context (member hdc in the structure). To avoid cluttering the program with drawing commands, a local function, Paint, draws the control. Finally, EndPaint releases the display context and counters the earlier BeginPaint statement. (OWL takes similar steps in calling a Paint member function in response to a WM_PAINT message. Because this sample DLL does not use OWL, it uses standard Windows programming techniques to paint the window's contents.)

- PIE_SETLIMIT implements one of the control's user-defined messages, in this case setting the maximum limit for the control.

- PIE_GETLIMIT is another user-defined message that returns the current control limit value.

- PIE_SETINDEX sets the control's index, which can range from zero to the current limit.

- PIE_GETINDEX returns the control's current index value.

- Finally, in PIECTRL, function WEP (Windows Exit Procedure) shuts down the DLL. Windows calls WEP when the last exiting program to use the DLL frees it from memory, and also as part of Windows' shutdown sequence. As shown, you can inspect parameter nSystemExit to take different actions for each of these conditions. In this case, the DLL requires no special actions, and you can remove these lines—I included them only to show where you can insert any necessary code in your own DLLs. UnregisterClass deletes the class name from Windows before the DLL disappears from RAM. The function returns the value 1 to indicate a successful disengagement.

That finishes the custom control DLL. Now you need a program to use it. Before writing the code, you need to design a dialog box to hold the custom control. (The accompanying disk includes the complete resource in file Pietest.res.) To create your own dialogs, follow these numbered steps:

1. Start the dialog editor, either by creating a new dialog resource or by selecting an existing one from the current project.

2. Select the *Dialog\Insert New Control* command and enter Custom when prompted for a control type. The dialog editor doesn't recognize the custom pie control, so you have to insert a custom static control into the dialog, and then bind it to the custom control window's class.

3. Size and position the custom control. The control uses the smaller resource dimension to calculate its diameter, so the end result is always circular, even if the static-text item isn't perfectly square.

4. Double-click the mouse pointer inside the static-text item. This opens the control's *Properties* dialog.

5. In that dialog, set *Class* to PieCtrl. Close the dialog and save the project.

You have just associated the dummy static-text control with a window registered under the name PieCtrl. You won't see the actual control. At runtime, in the course of creating the program's dialog, Windows searches for a window class to match each of the dialog's controls, including the custom pie-shaped control. So that Windows finds the custom control's class name (PieCtrl), the host program loads Piectrl.dll, which, as mentioned before, initializes and registers the custom control window class. If the DLL is already in memory, Windows ignores any command to load another copy. Thus, only one copy of the same DLL ever exists in RAM.

Listing 14.14, Pietest.h (resource ID header file), and Listing 14.15, Pietest.cpp (host program), carry out the final steps in the process of using a custom control.

Listing 14.14. Pietest.h (Declares constants for the Pietest program).

```
//===============================================================
// Pietest.h -- Declares constants for the Pietest program
// Copyright (c) 1996 by Tom Swan. All rights reserved.
//===============================================================

#define PIE_CTRL_DLL "PIECTRL.DLL"  // Name of custom control DLL
#define EM_DLLNOTFOUND 1            // DLL not found error code
#define END_TIME 15                 // Max time for test dialog

// Function prototype
void Delay(long mSecs);
```

Listing 14.15. Pietest.cpp (Tests the custom pie control DLL).

```
//===============================================================
// Pietest.cpp -- Tests the custom pie control DLL
// Copyright (c) 1996 by Tom Swan. All rights reserved.
//===============================================================

#include <owl\applicat.h>
#include <owl\framewin.h>
#include <owl\dialog.h>
#include <owl\gdiobjec.h>
#pragma hdrstop
#include "piectrl.h"
#include "pietest.rh"
#include "pietest.h"


// ==============================================================
// The TPieDlg class
// ==============================================================

class TPieDlg: public TDialog {
public:
  TPieDlg(TWindow *parent, TResId resId);
  void Start(WORD endTime);
  void Update(WORD time);
  void CmCancel();
  HBRUSH EvCtlColor(HDC hdc, HWND hWndChild, UINT ctlType);
  BOOL Continue() { return continueFlag; }
private:
  BOOL continueFlag;
  TBrush backBrush, foreBrush;
DECLARE_RESPONSE_TABLE(TPieDlg);
};

DEFINE_RESPONSE_TABLE1(TPieDlg, TDialog)
  EV_COMMAND(IDCANCEL, CmCancel),
  EV_WM_CTLCOLOR,
END_RESPONSE_TABLE;
```

continues

511

Listing 14.15. continued

```cpp
// Construct TPieDlg objects and initialize custom control colors
TPieDlg::TPieDlg(TWindow *parent, TResId resId)
  : TDialog(parent, resId),
    backBrush(TColor(16, 0, 16)),
    foreBrush(TColor(255, 0, 0))
{
  continueFlag = TRUE;
}

// Initialize dialog's pie control values
void TPieDlg::Start(WORD endTime)
{
  SendDlgItemMessage(ID_PIECTRL, PIE_SETLIMIT, endTime, 0);
  SendDlgItemMessage(ID_PIECTRL, PIE_SETINDEX, 0, 0);
  continueFlag = TRUE;
}

// Update pie control and execute background tasks
void TPieDlg::Update(WORD time)
{
  MSG msg;
  SendDlgItemMessage(ID_PIECTRL, PIE_SETINDEX, time, 0);
  while (PeekMessage(&msg, 0, 0, 0, PM_REMOVE)) {
    if (~IsDialogMessage(HWindow, &msg)) {
      TranslateMessage(&msg);
      DispatchMessage(&msg);
    }
  }
}

// Prepare to shut down dialog prematurely
void TPieDlg::CmCancel()
{
  continueFlag = FALSE;
  TDialog::CmCancel();
}

// Respond to control's request for color information
HBRUSH TPieDlg::EvCtlColor(HDC hdc, HWND hWndChild, UINT ctlType)
{
  HBRUSH hbr;
  switch (ctlType) {
    case PIE_BACKCOLOR:
      hbr = (HBRUSH)backBrush;
      break;
    case PIE_FORECOLOR:
      hbr = (HBRUSH)foreBrush;
      break;
    default:
      hbr = TDialog::EvCtlColor(hdc, hWndChild, ctlType);
      break;
  }
  return hbr;
}
```

```
// ================================================================
// The application's main window
// ================================================================

class TPieWin: public TFrameWindow {
public:
  TPieWin(TWindow* parent, const char far* title);
protected:
  virtual BOOL CanClose();
  void CmDemoTest();
private:
  BOOL testing;
DECLARE_RESPONSE_TABLE(TPieWin);
};

DEFINE_RESPONSE_TABLE1(TPieWin, TFrameWindow)
  EV_COMMAND(CM_DEMO_TEST, CmDemoTest),
END_RESPONSE_TABLE;

// Constructor
TPieWin::TPieWin(TWindow* parent, const char far* title)
  : TFrameWindow(parent, title),
    TWindow(parent, title)
{
  AssignMenu(ID_MENU);
  Attr.X = GetSystemMetrics(SM_CXSCREEN) / 8;
  Attr.Y = GetSystemMetrics(SM_CYSCREEN) / 8;
  Attr.H = Attr.Y * 6;
  Attr.W = Attr.X * 6;
  testing = FALSE;
}

// Return true if okay to close window
BOOL TPieWin::CanClose()
{
  if (testing) return FALSE;
  return TFrameWindow::CanClose();
}

// Respond to menu's test command
void TPieWin::CmDemoTest()
{
  TPieDlg * dp;     // Modeless dialog pointer
  unsigned time;    // Local time unit counter
  BOOL finished;    // Operation completed flag

  if (testing)      // Prevent recursion
    return;
  testing = TRUE;                 // Prevent app from ending
  dp = new TPieDlg(this, ID_DIALOG);
  dp->Create();                   // Create window element
  dp->Show(SW_NORMAL);            // Make dialog visable
  dp->Start(END_TIME);            // Initialize custom control
  time = 0;                       // Initialize local time
  finished = FALSE;               // Initialize done flag
```

continues

513

Listing 14.15. continued

```
  while (!finished && dp->Continue()) {
    dp->Update(time);              // Update custom control position
    Delay(500);                    // *** Insert user operation
    MessageBeep(0);                // Optional audible feedback
    if (++time > END_TIME)         // Count time passed and set flag
      finished = TRUE;
  }
  if (dp->IsWindow())              // Close dialog if still open
    dp->CloseWindow();
  delete dp;                       // Delete TPieDlg object
  testing = FALSE;                 // Permit application to end
}


// ================================================================
// The application class
// ================================================================

class TPieApp: public TApplication {
public:
  TPieApp(const char far* name);
  ~TPieApp();
protected:
  virtual void InitMainWindow();
  virtual void DoError(int errorCode);
private:
  HINSTANCE libHandle;
};

// Construct TPieApp application object
TPieApp::TPieApp(const char far* name)
  : TApplication(name)
{
  libHandle = LoadLibrary(PIE_CTRL_DLL);
  if (libHandle < HINSTANCE_ERROR)
    Status = EM_DLLNOTFOUND;
}


// Destroy TPieApp application object
TPieApp::~TPieApp()
{
  if (libHandle >= HINSTANCE_ERROR)
    FreeLibrary(libHandle);
}


// Initialize the program's main window
void
TPieApp::InitMainWindow()
{
  MainWindow = new TPieWin(0, "Pie Control Test");
}

// Handle startup errors
void TPieApp::DoError(int errorCode)
{
  if (errorCode == EM_DLLNOTFOUND) {
    ::MessageBox(0, "Can't find PIECTRL.DLL", "Application Error",
      MB_APPLMODAL | MB_ICONSTOP | MB_OK);
```

```
    exit(errorCode);
  } else
    TApplication::Error(errorCode);
}

// ============================================================
// Miscellaneous functions
// ============================================================

// Wait for approximately mSecs milliseconds
void Delay(long mSecs)
{
  long mark = GetTickCount() + mSecs;
  while (GetTickCount() <= mark) ;
}

#pragma argsused

// Main program
int
OwlMain(int argc, char* argv[])
{
  TPieApp app("PieApp");
  return app.Run();
}
```

The TPieApp class constructor calls LoadLibrary to load Piectrl.dll. If that succeeds, the DLL's custom "PieCtrl" window class is initialized and registered with Windows.

Function CMTest displays the program's modeless dialog box and calls various member functions for the dialog's class, TPieDlg. This class, derived from TDialog, communicates with the custom pie control by sending it messages. Meanwhile, as the dummy operation delay shows, you can call a function or perform any other action while the custom pie control slices itself down to nothing.

Any program that loads a DLL should free that library before ending. TPieApp's destructor demonstrates one way to accomplish this step. Freeing the DLL in the application's destructor ensures that this task is completed no matter how the program ends.

Common Dialogs

Listing 14.16, Common.cpp, demonstrates how to use each of the nine common dialogs first introduced in 16-bit Windows 3.1. Windows 95 replaces these DLL-based dialogs with integrated updates, which look somewhat different, but function in mostly the same ways. Because of this relationship, you can use the same dialog techniques in 16- and 32-bit Windows applications. To experiment with the dialogs, load the Common.ide project file into the IDE and press Ctrl+F9 to compile and run the demo. Select a dialog from the program's *Dialogs* menu, which has seven commands, one for each dialog. There are only seven commands because the *Print* command displays a basic printer dialog, from which you can select two or more additional printer setup dialogs. The exact number of sub-dialogs depends on the printer driver.

515

One of the niftiest common dialogs presents a color palette for selecting and customizing colors. Figure 14.13. shows the common color dialog, which looks a lot more exciting on a color display than it does in black and white here.

Figure 14.13.

Common color dialog.

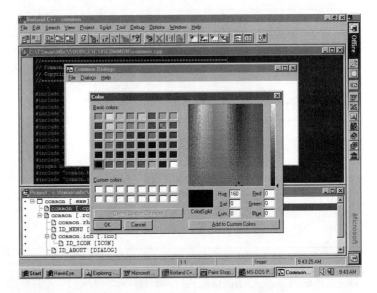

Listing 14.16. Common.cpp (Displays nine common dialogs).

```
//===============================================================
// Common.cpp -- Demonstrates common dialog boxes
// Copyright (c) 1996 by Tom Swan. All rights reserved.
//===============================================================

#include <owl\applicat.h>
#include <owl\framewin.h>
#include <winsys\color.h>
#include <owl\chooseco.h>      // Common color dialog
#include <owl\choosefo.h>      // Common font dialog
#include <owl\opensave.h>      // Common file dialogs
#include <owl\printdia.h>      // Common printer dialogs
#include <owl\findrepl.h>      // Common find & replace dialogs
#include <owl\dc.h>
#include <string.h>
#include <cstring.h>
#pragma hdrstop
#include "common.h"
#include "common.rh"


// ===========================================================
// The application's main window
// ===========================================================

class TCommWin: public TFrameWindow {
public:
  TCommWin(TWindow* parent, const char far* title);
  ~TCommWin();
```

```
protected:
  void CmDialogsColor();
  void CmDialogsFont();
  void CmDialogsOpen();
  void CmDialogsSaveAs();
  void CmDialogsPrint();
  void CmDialogsFind();
  void CmDialogsReplace();
  void CmHelpAbout();
protected:
  LRESULT EvFindMsg(WPARAM, LPARAM);  // Common dialog message
protected:
  // Color dialog members
  TColor color;                    // Selected color
  TColor aColors[NUM_COLORS];      // Custom color array
  // Font dialog member
  LOGFONT font;                    // Logical font
  // File dialog members
  string *fileName;                // Current file name
  char filterStr[MAX_FILTER];      // Wild-card file filters
  // Find and replace dialogs
  TFindReplaceDialog::TData searchData;   // Find/replace info
  TFindReplaceDialog* searchDialog;        // Dialog pointer
  UINT searchCommand;   // Distinguishes find & replace dialogs
DECLARE_RESPONSE_TABLE(TCommWin);
};

// Create response table declared for class
DEFINE_RESPONSE_TABLE1(TCommWin, TFrameWindow)
  EV_COMMAND(CM_DIALOGSCOLOR, CmDialogsColor),
  EV_COMMAND(CM_DIALOGSFONT, CmDialogsFont),
  EV_COMMAND(CM_DIALOGSOPEN, CmDialogsOpen),
  EV_COMMAND(CM_DIALOGSSAVEAS, CmDialogsSaveAs),
  EV_COMMAND(CM_DIALOGSPRINT, CmDialogsPrint),
  EV_COMMAND(CM_DIALOGSFIND, CmDialogsFind),
  EV_COMMAND(CM_DIALOGSREPLACE, CmDialogsReplace),
  EV_COMMAND(CM_HELPABOUT, CmHelpAbout),
  EV_REGISTERED(FINDMSGSTRING, EvFindMsg),
END_RESPONSE_TABLE;

// Constructor
TCommWin::TCommWin(TWindow* parent, const char far* title)
  : TFrameWindow(parent, title),
    TWindow(parent, title)
{
  int i;

  AssignMenu(ID_MENU);
  Attr.X = GetSystemMetrics(SM_CXSCREEN) / 8;
  Attr.Y = GetSystemMetrics(SM_CYSCREEN) / 8;
  Attr.H = Attr.Y * 6;
  Attr.W = Attr.X * 6;

// Initialize color dialog data members
  color = TColor(0, 0, 0);  // Initial color
  for (i = 0; i < NUM_COLORS; i++)  // Set custom colors to white
    aColors[i] = TColor(255, 255, 255);
```

continues

517

Listing 14.16. continued

```
// Initialize logical font data members
  memset(&font, 0, sizeof(font));

// Initialize file name and list-box filters (wild cards)
  fileName = new string;
  if (GetApplication()->LoadString(STR_FILEFILTERS,
      filterStr, sizeof(filterStr)) == 0) {
    memset(filterStr, 0, sizeof(filterStr));
  }

// Initialize find and replace data members
  searchDialog = 0;   // Null doubles as "no dialog" flag
  searchCommand = 0;  // None
}

// Destructor
TCommWin::~TCommWin()
{
  delete searchDialog;  // Delete find/replace dialog if active
}

// DIALOG #1: Common color dialog
void TCommWin::CmDialogsColor()
{
  TChooseColorDialog::TData data;
  TColor tempColors[NUM_COLORS];
  int i;

  for (i = 0; i < NUM_COLORS; i++)
    tempColors[i] = aColors[i];
  data.Flags = CC_RGBINIT | CC_FULLOPEN;
  data.CustColors = tempColors;
  data.Color = color;
  if (TChooseColorDialog(this, data).Execute() == IDOK) {
    color = data.Color;
    for (i = 0; i <= 15; i++)
      aColors[i] = tempColors[i];
  }
}

// DIALOG #2: Common font-selection dialog
void TCommWin::CmDialogsFont()
{
  TChooseFontDialog::TData data;
  LOGFONT tempFont;
  tempFont = font;  // Copy current font
  data.Flags = CF_INITTOLOGFONTSTRUCT | CF_BOTH | CF_EFFECTS;
  data.LogFont = tempFont;
  data.Color = color;  // Selected by Color dialog
  if (TChooseFontDialog(this, data).Execute() == IDOK)
    font = data.LogFont;
}

// DIALOG #3: Common file-open dialog
void TCommWin::CmDialogsOpen()
{
```

```
    TOpenSaveDialog::TData data(
      OFN_FILEMUSTEXIST|OFN_PATHMUSTEXIST,   // Flags
      filterStr,                             // Wild-card filters
      0,                                     // Custom filter
      "",                                    // Initial directory
      "*");                                  // Default extension
    char *tempName = new char[128];
    strcpy(tempName, fileName->c_str());

    data.FileName = tempName;
    if (TFileOpenDialog(this, data).Execute() == IDOK) {
      if (data.Error == 0) {
        delete fileName;
        fileName = new string(tempName);
        // ... Open file here
      }
    }
    delete[] tempName;
}

// DIALOG #4: Common file-save-as dialog
void TCommWin::CmDialogsSaveAs()
{
    TOpenSaveDialog::TData data(
      OFN_OVERWRITEPROMPT|OFN_PATHMUSTEXIST, // Flags
      filterStr,                             // Wild-card filters
      0,                                     // Custom filter
      "",                                    // Initial directory
      "*");                                  // Default extension
    char *tempName = new char[128];
    strcpy(tempName, fileName->c_str());

    data.FileName = tempName;
    if (TFileSaveDialog(this, data).Execute() == IDOK) {
      if (data.Error == 0) {
        delete fileName;
        fileName = new string(tempName);
        // ... Save file here
      }
    }
    delete[] tempName;
}

// DIALOGS #5-7: Common printer, setup, and options dialogs
void TCommWin::CmDialogsPrint()
{
    TPrintDialog::TData data;

    data.Flags = PD_RETURNDC;  // PD_PRINTSETUP for setup dialog
    if (TPrintDialog(this, data).Execute() == IDOK) {
      TPrintDC *prnDC = data.TransferDC();  // new TPrintDC object
      // ... Use prnDC here to print a document
      delete prnDC;  // Delete TPrintDC object when done printing
    }
}

// DIALOG #8: Common find-text dialog
```

continues

519

Listing 14.16. continued

```cpp
void TCommWin::CmDialogsFind()
{
  if (searchDialog) delete searchDialog;   // Prevent duplicates
  searchCommand = CM_DIALOGSFIND;          // Identifies dialog
  searchDialog = new TFindDialog(this, searchData);
  searchDialog->Create();
}

// DIALOG #9: Common replace-text dialog
void TCommWin::CmDialogsReplace()
{
  if (searchDialog) delete searchDialog;   // Prevent duplicates
  searchCommand = CM_DIALOGSREPLACE;       // Identifies dialog
  searchDialog = new TReplaceDialog(this, searchData);
  searchDialog->Create();
}

// Display this program's about-box dialog
void TCommWin::CmHelpAbout()
{
  (new TDialog(this, ID_ABOUT))->Execute();
//  TDialog(this, ID_ABOUT).Execute();  // Alternate method
}

// Respond to find or find-replace message from modeless dialog
LRESULT
TCommWin::EvFindMsg(WPARAM, LPARAM lParam)
{
  if (!searchDialog) return 0;           // No dialog. Exit
  searchDialog->UpdateData(lParam);      // Update flags
  if (searchData.Flags & FR_DIALOGTERM)  // If dialog closing,
    searchCommand = 0;                   // reset searchCommand,
  else {                                 // else...
    char *dialogType;
    if (searchCommand == CM_DIALOGSFIND) // Assign dialogType
      dialogType = "Find";               // string according to
    else                                 // which command user
      dialogType = "Find and Replace";   // selected.
    MessageBox("Search message received", dialogType);
    // ... Or, call your search function here
  }
  return 0;
}


// ================================================================
// The application class
// ================================================================

class TCommApp: public TApplication {
public:
  TCommApp(const char far* name)
    : TApplication(name) {};
  void InitMainWindow();
};

// Initialize the program's main window
void
```

```
TCommApp::InitMainWindow()
{
  EnableCtl3d();  // Enable 3-D controls and dialogs
  MainWindow = new TCommWin(0, "Common Dialogs");
  MainWindow->SetIcon(this, ID_ICON);
}

#pragma argsused

// Main program
int
OwlMain(int argc, char* argv[])
{
  TCommApp app("Common");
  return app.Run();
}
```

As it does for many Windows structures, OWL represents common dialogs using classes. As the Common.cpp listing shows, include one or more header files such as Chooseco.h or Choosefo.h to use common dialogs.

To create a common dialog, construct a data object of type TData, a subclass in each common dialog class. This data object specifies various dialog features such as color values, filename strings, and so on. See function CmDialogsColor for an example.

After assigning various data members, call the dialog object's Execute function, which returns IDOK if the OK button is used to close the dialog window. In that case, you can extract any data values you need from the dialog.

TrueType Fonts

TrueType fonts repair one of the most glaring deficiencies of earlier Windows versions: displaying fonts in the same relative sizes on different display and printer resolutions. TrueType fonts are scaleable vector fonts—they are composed of instructions that explain to an output device how to outline and fill in character patterns. As vectored images, TrueType characters are independent of output resolution. The same TrueType symbols on a low-quality 640×480 display should appear in the same relative sizes (more or less) on a fancy 1024×768 monitor.

Another advantage of TrueType fonts is increased display speed. The first time Windows displays a TrueType font character, it renders the character's pattern as a temporary bitmap in memory. The next time Windows needs that same character, it uses the in-memory bitmap, vastly improving display speed. (It takes far less time to move pixels en masse onto the screen than it does to draw the equivalent lines and filled shapes.) You may have noticed TrueType's two-speed gearshift when using a word processor. Displaying a paragraph with several different fonts the first time takes a few seconds. Displaying that same paragraph again takes only a fraction of the original time because Windows uses the in-memory character bitmaps on the second and subsequent go-arounds.

Figure 14.14 shows a sample display of the next program, Listing 14.17, Ttfont.cpp. The program demonstrates how to select and use TrueType fonts to display text in a window. Load the program's Ttfont.ide project file into the IDE and press Ctrl+F9 to compile and run. Use the program's *Font* menu to open a common font dialog (see Figure 14.15) and select a new font and style.

Figure 14.14.

Sample TrueType-font text as displayed by Ttfont.cpp.

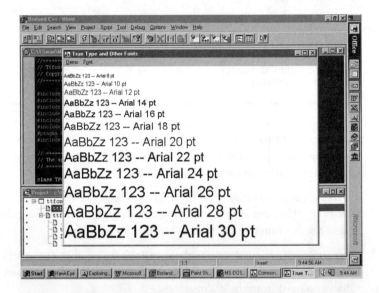

Figure 14.15.

Common font dialog.

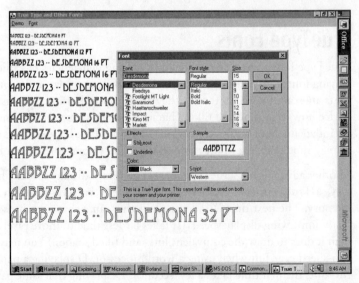

Listing 14.17. Ttfont.cpp (Demonstrates TrueType fonts).

```cpp
//================================================================
// Ttfont.cpp -- Demonstrates TrueType fonts
// Copyright (c) 1996 by Tom Swan. All rights reserved.
//================================================================

#include <owl\applicat.h>
#include <owl\framewin.h>
#include <owl\gdiobjec.h>
#include <owl\choosefo.h>
#include <stdio.h>
#include <string.h>
#pragma hdrstop
#include "ttfont.rh"


// ================================================================
// The application's main window
// ================================================================

class TFontWin: public TFrameWindow {
public:
  TFontWin(TWindow* parent, const char far* title);
  ~TFontWin();
protected:
  void CmFontChoose();
  virtual void Paint(TDC& dc, BOOL erase, TRect& rect);
private:
  TFont *font;
  TColor fontColor;
DECLARE_RESPONSE_TABLE(TFontWin);
};

// Create response table declared for class
DEFINE_RESPONSE_TABLE1(TFontWin, TFrameWindow)
  EV_COMMAND(CM_FONTCHOOSE, CmFontChoose),
END_RESPONSE_TABLE;

// Constructor
TFontWin::TFontWin(TWindow* parent, const char far* title)
  : TFrameWindow(parent, title),
    TWindow(parent, title)
{
  AssignMenu(ID_MENU);
  Attr.X = GetSystemMetrics(SM_CXSCREEN) / 8;
  Attr.Y = GetSystemMetrics(SM_CYSCREEN) / 8;
  Attr.H = Attr.Y * 6;
  Attr.W = Attr.X * 6;
  font = new TFont("Arial", 20);
  fontColor = GetSysColor(COLOR_WINDOWTEXT);
}

// Destructor
TFontWin::~TFontWin()
```

continues

Listing 14.17. continued

```
{
  delete font;
}

// Menu command function
void
TFontWin::CmFontChoose()
{
  TChooseFontDialog::TData data;
  data.Flags = CF_INITTOLOGFONTSTRUCT | CF_BOTH | CF_EFFECTS;
  font->GetObject(data.LogFont); // Copy current font to data
  data.Color = fontColor;
  if (TChooseFontDialog(this, data).Execute() == IDOK) {
    delete font;
    font = new TFont(&data.LogFont);
    fontColor = data.Color;
    Invalidate();
  }
}

// Update display. Paints successive lines using selected font
// and color, starting at 8 points, increasing by 2 points
// for each new line, and stopping at 32 points.
void
TFontWin::Paint(TDC& dc, BOOL /*erase*/, TRect& /*rect*/)
{
  int len, x, y, points;     // Location, length, and text size
  char testString[256];      // Holds text for each line
  int endOfTestString;       // For easily nulling strings
  TSize textExtent;          // Width and height of each line
  int mapModeOldH;           // Saves original dc mapping mode
  HFONT fontH;               // Handle for fonts used for text
  LOGFONT tempFont;          // Describes font characteristics

  x = 10;
  y = 0;
  strcpy(testString, "AaBbZz 123 -- ");
  endOfTestString = strlen(testString);
  font->GetObject(tempFont);   // Copy current font to tempFont
  dc.SetTextColor(fontColor);  // Use color selected in dialog
  dc.SetBkColor(GetSysColor(COLOR_WINDOW));
  // Set graphics mapping to 1 unit = 1/1440 inch,
  // or 1/20 of a typesetting point, equal to 1/72 inch.
  mapModeOldH = dc.SetMapMode(MM_TWIPS);
  points = 8;  // For displaying lines in different point sizes
  while (points <= 32) {
    tempFont.lfHeight = -points * 20;  // At 20 twips per point
    fontH = CreateFontIndirect(&tempFont); // Create line's font
    dc.SelectObject(TFont(fontH));      // No auto delete!
    testString[endOfTestString] = 0;    // Null old font name
    sprintf(&testString[endOfTestString], // Create new text
      "%s %d pt", tempFont.lfFaceName, points); // for this line
    len = strlen(testString);
    textExtent =
      dc.GetTextExtent(testString, len);  // How tall is line?
    y = y + textExtent.cy + 5;     // Adjust Y using char height
    dc.TextOut(x, -y, testString, len);    // Display line
```

```
      DeleteObject(fontH); // Delete font handle; see SelectObject
      points += 2;              // Size of newxt line
    }
  dc.SetMapMode(mapModeOldH);    // Restore saved mapping mode
}

// ================================================================
// The application class
// ================================================================

class TFontApp: public TApplication {
public:
  TFontApp(const char far* name)
    : TApplication(name) {};
  void InitMainWindow();
};

// Initialize the program's main window
void
TFontApp::InitMainWindow()
{
  MainWindow = new TFontWin(0, "True Type and Other Fonts");
}

#pragma argsused

// Main program
int
OwlMain(int argc, char* argv[])
{
  TFontApp app("TTFontApp");
  return app.Run();
}
```

To store the current font and color, the program's TWindow class derivative, TFontWin, includes two data members—font of type TFONT and fontColor of type TCOLOR.

The first of these two types is called a *logical font structure.* It contains various members that describe a font's characteristics. Before using the font to display text, the program requests a handle to a font that most closely resembles the parameters in the logical font structure. If possible, Windows satisfies the requested parameters with an exact match. If the requested font doesn't exist, however, Windows selects another font that, with luck, closely resembles your choice. Although this font-matching scheme seems reasonable, the results are often disappointing. For best results, you should use logical fonts that exactly match those available.

One way to satisfy this goal is to provide users with a font selection dialog. The sample program's CMFontChoose member function provides this service with a common font-selection dialog. The function resembles the one you examined in the preceding section for selecting colors. After initializing a data structure, the function displays the font selection dialog illustrated in Figure 14.15. If the function returns IDOK, it saves the selected logical font and color, and then invalidates the window, causing it to be redrawn by member function Paint.

Examine `Paint` closely. It contains sample statements that show how to display text using TrueType fonts. Select appropriate background and foreground colors and then call `SetMapMode` to change pixel mapping to `MM_TWIPS`.

This special mode maps a graphics display unit to 1/1440 of an inch, equal to 1/20 of a type-setting point, which is about 1/72 of an inch. (The word TWIP is a loose acronym for "twentieth of a point.") With `MM_TWIPS` mapping in effect, you can select font heights using points rather than a fixed number of pixels, causing text to be displayed in about the same relative size regardless of output resolution.

The `while` statement shows how to select a font's point size, commonly expressed as a negative value. Set the logical font to 20 times the desired point size (because there are 20 points in a TWIP). Pass the address of the logical font structure to `CreateFontIndirect` and assign the resulting handle to an `HFONT` variable. Pass this variable and the display context to `SelectObject`, selecting the font for subsequent text output functions such as `TextOut`. When you are done using a font, again select the previously selected font by calling `SelectObject`, and then delete the unneeded font handle. You should also restore the display context's mapping mode.

The remaining statements in the sample program's `Paint` member function calculate the coordinates where lines of text should appear in the window. To calculate text coordinates, call `GetTextExtent`. The function returns a long value. For the selected font and string, the high word of this long value equals the maximum character height. The low word equals the string's length. Using these values (extracted as `cx` and `cy`), you can calculate (x,y) coordinates to pass to `TextOut`. For better control over text location, you might also have to call the Windows functions `SetTextAlign` and `SetTextJustification` (not shown in the sample listing—look these up in the IDE's online help).

Summary

- Borland C++ 5.0 fully supports 16- and 32-bit Windows 3.1, Windows 95, and Windows NT programming. To write Windows applications, you can use the command-line compiler, or the IDE.

- ObjectWindows, or OWL, is Borland's class library for Windows software development. With OWL, you program Windows applications using an object-oriented framework that interfaces with common elements such as graphical windows, dialogs, and controls. OWL 5.0, the newest version, encapsulates most of the Windows 16- and 32-bit API (application programming interface).

- Turbo Debugger for Windows (TDW) resembles the DOS Turbo Debugger (TD). TDW is a Windows application that runs your code, displays variables, sets breakpoints, and performs other tasks that can help you find the causes of bugs. The IDE has a similar built-in GUI debugger.

- WinSight32 is another useful debugging tool. Use WinSight32 to investigate message flow from Windows to and from a program. This does not require the program's source code, so you can use WinSight32 to explore how any program works.

- Faulty program statements might cause Windows to halt a program with a system error. Install WinSpector to trap these errors and display detailed information that might help locate the cause of problems. WinSpector creates a text-file log that you can examine for a detailed error report.

- Most Windows programs have resources such as pull-down menus and dialog boxes. Design these and other resources with the IDE's visual resource editor. This integrated product takes the place of the stand-alone Resource Workshop found in earlier versions. You can also write resource script files and compile them with the Brc.exe or Brc32.exe utilities.

- A display context associates graphics output with a device such as a graphical window on a display monitor, a printer, or a plotter. Call a display context's Graphics Device Interface (GDI) functions to draw lines, shapes, text, and other graphical output.

- A Dynamic Link Library is a collection of functions that many programs can share. Only one copy of a DLL ever exists in memory, regardless of how many programs use the library.

- OWL also supports eye-catching common dialog boxes and display-efficient TrueType fonts.

15

Developing Windows 95 Applications

Despite the growing popularity of Windows 95, relatively few programmers are taking full advantage of what this new operating system has to offer. Many developers are still writing 16-bit applications, using the techniques in the preceding chapter. This permits programs to compile and run under Windows 3.x, Windows 95, and Windows NT, but it ignores the exciting new features available in Windows 95.

To take advantage of these new features, you need to compile your program as a 32-bit application. You also need to use new classes and techniques to modernize your program's user interface to meet Windows 95 guidelines. In this chapter, you explore key Windows 95 programming methods that will help you move up to 32-bit software development. Of course, one chapter cannot cover all that Windows 95 has to offer, but the information here will give you a head start in bringing your code up to speed.

Introducing OWL and Windows 95

OWL 5.0 encapsulates most of the new features in Windows 95, including common controls, dockable toolbars, property-sheet dialog boxes, and WinG graphics. There are class interfaces for APIs such as WinSock, MAPI, MCI, multi-thread processes, and—as advertisers always seem to say on television—much, much more.

The place to start learning about these features is to examine OWL's Windows 95 classes. Read the following notes for the low-down on the most significant new classes in the library. Browsing their online help will give you a quick overview of what you can expect in Windows 95 support. I'll also explain how to prepare Windows 95 projects, which is child's play, but there are a couple of points worth mentioning here.

Windows 95 Classes

OWL 5.0 contains dozens of new classes specifically tailored for Windows 95 software development. Some of these classes, such as TColumnHeader and TSpashWindow produce stunning visual effects. Others such as TMailer, TModuleProc, and TControlEnabler work behind the scenes to take much of the tedium out of creating an interface that meets or exceeds Microsoft's Windows 95 guidelines.

> **NOTE**
>
> Most of the following classes, such as TMailer, require Windows 95. However, OWL 5.0 emulates Windows 95 common controls so you can develop similar-looking dialog boxes for 16- and 32-bit applications. For example, under Windows 3.1, OWL uses its internal code for a TTabControl object, which you can use to display selection tabs in a multi-page dialog window. Under Windows 95, OWL uses the operating system's native tab control.

Windows 95 Support

The following list shows classes that you can use to support the Windows 95 interface. `TMailer` makes it easy to implement electronic mail with a *File|Send* command, one of the required guidelines that all applications must support to earn Win95 logo certification. The `Treg...` classes provide interfaces to the Windows 95 system registry, a repository of information about objects known to the operating system. (Just about every tangible element in Windows 95 can be termed an "object.")

Windows 95 support classes.

`TMailer`

`TRegKey`

`TRegValue`

`TRegKeyIterator`

`TRegValueIterator`

`TRegItem`

`TRegList`

Common Controls

Common controls are the most visible features in Windows 95. OWL's classes in the following list support controls such as column headers, progress and track bars, tab controls, multipage property sheet dialogs, and rich text editors. The `TControlEnabler` class (not actually an encapsulation of a Windows 95 control) helps you to enable and disable controls to prevent their selection—similar to the way you can disable a menu command such as *File|Save* that you don't want users to select at an inappropriate time. The `TPickList` class simplifies list box selection, and resembles OWL's `TInputDialog` class.

Common control classes.

`TColumnHeader`

`TGauge`, `TSlider`, and descendents (for status, progress, and track bars)

`TTabControl`

`TPropertySheet`, `TPropertyPage`

`TRichEdit`

`TControlEnabler`

`TPickList`

Lists and Trees

One of the most vexing problems in designing graphical user interfaces is how to make the most of a limited display's real estate. The classes in the following list help you to prepare graphical and text list and tree windows, and also to split windows into columns. The Windows 95 Explorer demonstrates the intuitiveness of these classes. With little or no instruction, many users easily master the Explorer's tree list of folders (directories) and file list window. Use these classes to add similar organizational tools to your programs' windows.

List and tree classes.

TImageList

TListWindow

TTreeWindow

TSplitterWindow

Graphics and Sound

No doubt about it, we live in a multimedia world, and computer software is headed for future mergers with the world's fast growing informational networks of graphics and sound. The following list shows OWL's classes that you can use to display .avi (Audio Video Interleaved) files and play .wav (Wave) music files. TDibWindow simplifies the display of bitmaps in a window. The TWinGBitmap, TWinGDC, TWinGIdentity, and other TWinG... classes not listed here encapsulate the Win32 GDI for 32-bit graphics. Supporting classes TUIBorder and TUIFace help OWL draw button and other window borders and faces for better-looking 3-D displays. (Borland's BWCC classes and associated dialogs have provided 3-D controls and windows, and these are still available. However, you can choose to create controls and windows using Windows 95 native 3-D effects if you choose, although to my eye, Borland's graphics look more attractive and I prefer using them.)

Graphics and sound classes.

TAnimateCtrl

TMCI, TMCIWaveAudio

TDibWindow

TWinGBitmap, TWinGDC, TWinGIdentity

TUIBorder, TUIFace

Toolbars

If there is any GUI feature that Windows programmers have traditionally struggled with, it's a toolbar of iconic buttons. Finally, it's a snap to add this essential feature to your applications, and also to provide a status bar for messages and keyboard legends showing the status of Ctrl, Caps, and other system keys. Previous versions of OWL supported simplified toolbars, but the new classes in the following list go one step further in creating *dockable* toolbars. With these exciting objects, users can drag a toolbar onto a window to create a floating, resizable, collection of buttons. They can also drag that window or any toolbar to a side border for a vertical toolbar, or drag it to the window's top border for a standard, under-the-menu speedbar (Borland's term for a toolbar). All of these features, which in the past were excruciatingly painful to program, are so simple, the only danger in using them is you may fall asleep while typing the source code.

Toolbar classes.

```
TDockable

TDockableGadgetWindow

TDockableControlBar

TDockingSlip, TFloatingSlip

TToolTip
```

System Services

Other system classes, shown in the following list, provide support for the WinSock API—for serious programming with networks and TCP/IP (which stands for Transmission Control Protocol/Internet Protocol, a phrase worthy of any bureaucracy). The TModuleVersionInfo class provides access to a TModule's VERSIONINFO resource, which you can use to list copyright, product name, and other version information. TModuleProc simplifies the loading and use of DLLs. By using TModuleProc internally, OWL can detect and provide alternate code for a nonexistant DLL such as the Windows 95 common control library.

System service classes.

```
TSocket, TSocketWindow, TService, TServiceWindow, and others

TModuleVersionInfo

TModuleProc
```

Gadgets

I love gadgets, and my kitchen is full of them. One of my favorites is a spring loaded moosher—I call it my mashed potato pogo stick. Computer gadgets are also fun—and provide useful tools such as the three OWL gadget classes in the following list. TTimeGadget displays the current time in various formats. (Don't ask me why there's no TDateGadget, but there isn't.) TMenuGadget displays a popup menu, usually in response to clicking the right mouse button. TModeGadget tracks the state of a virtual key, represented by a constant that begins with VK_.

Gadget classes.

TTimeGadget

TMenuGadget

TModeGadget

Other

The following list shows still more classes, which are new to OWL 5.0 and are particularly useful in developing Windows 95 software. By mixing a THelpFileManager class with TApplication, you can easily provide context-sensitive online help for your programs. TRecentFiles manages a most-recently used (MRU) filename list, typically displayed in the *File* menu. TThread and TSemaphoreSet provide support for multi-threaded applications. (OWL has had multi-thread support for some time, but the code is revised and now works more reliably under Windows 95 and Windows NT.) TSplashWindow simplifies displaying a splash window—a copyright notice and bitmap, for example—during a program's startup before its main window appears. This is not only a nice touch for GUI software, but it also gives users something to watch while the program performs various initializations.

Other classes.

THelpFileManager

TRecentFiles

TThread, TSemaphoreSet

TSplashWindow

Windows 95 Projects

Preparing a Windows 95 project is as easy as baking a pie (one of the premade frozen ones, I mean). Simply select the *File\New* command, and select *Project* from the submenu. Enter or browse to the directory path where you want to store your project's files, and also enter a project name. Then, specify these three settings in the *Target Expert* dialog:

- *Target Type*—Set this to *Application* (.exe).
- *Platform*—Set this to *Win32*. This creates a 32-bit code file for Windows 95 and also for Windows NT.
- *Target Model*—Set this to *GUI*. Select *Console* only for Windows NT non-graphical applications.

In addition to these settings, you'll want to select an appropriate Framework such as *OWL* or *MFC*. I recommend *OWL* for all Windows development. This also automatically includes Borland's class library, which OWL uses internally. Select *OCF* if you are writing OLE applications and want to use the object-component framework library (highly recommended).

Windows 95 controls have a 3-D appearance by default, so you can leave the *Controls* settings disabled. However, you might want to use Borland's BWCC controls, which have a more visually pleasing look than the native controls (at least I think they do). You might also select VBX controls, which Borland C++ supports for 16- and 32-bit development. (VBX controls are normally only for 16-bit applications.) You may optionally select any combination or all of these settings to load the appropriate libraries at runtime.

Enable the *OLE* library only if you are writing an OLE container or server application. This provides your code access to the Borland BOLE dynamic link library.

Finally, choose *Dynamic* to load OWL and other library code at runtime, which takes time (only a little), but conserves disk space and RAM. Choose *Static* to bind OWL and other library code into your application's code file. This balloons your code, and wastes disk and RAM space—however, your application might load faster. Try both settings and compare results if you can't decide which to use.

> **TIP**
>
> Another, and more significant, reason to statically bind library code to an application is to prevent "versionitis"—bugs caused by future or past dynamic link libraries installed on users' computers. By statically linking your application to library code, you ensure that it always uses the correct library version.

Another method for preparing a Windows 95 application is to use AppExpert to create a program shell, which you can then modify. Choose *AppExpert* from the *File\New* submenu, and fill in the pathnames in the resulting *New AppExpert Project* dialog. This is a great way to get a flying start on new software—the resulting application has a toolbar, a standard menu, various classes, printing capabilities, and a print-preview module. You might also use this method simply to explore various Windows 95 and OWL programming techniques that you can extract for your hand-wired applications.

Integrated Resource Editing

Use the *File\New* submenu's *Resource Project* command to begin a new script file for your program's resources. This command replaces the formerly stand-alone Resource Workshop. You can also use the command to create bitmaps, icons, and cursors.

When you select the command, you are presented with the dialog in Figure 15.1. For a new resource project, you may select either the *Resource Script (*.rc)* or *Compiled Resource (*.res)* commands. However—and this is important—you should always create your resources as scripts so you can edit them with a text editor, and also print a backup paper copy.

Figure 15.1.

*Select from this dialog the type
of resource or bitmap project
you want to create.*

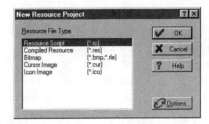

If you create your resources in binary *(*.res)* form only, you will save a tiny bit of compilation time required to translate the text script into the binary resource file. However, you will lose the ability to edit your resources as text (it's so much faster to use the text editor to fix a spelling error for a checkbox or other control than it is to load the entire integrated resource editors). Even more important, you risk losing the ability to rebuild the binary resource file. *For safety, always create resource scripts for your projects.* Use the integrated resource editor's ability to modify .res files directly only if you do not have their source—for example, to extract a bitmap or cursor from a compiled .res code file.

> **NOTE**
>
> Borland C++ 5.0 comes with the complete version 4.52 compiler and related software for Windows 3.1 users who have not yet upgraded to Windows 95 or Windows NT. This older compiler version includes the stand-alone Resource Workshop. You can also run this version of Resource Workshop under Windows 95 or NT, but for 32-bit development, you'll want to use the upgraded integrated resource editors, which provide access to 32-bit controls. A related issue is that OWL 5.0 currently is not compatible with Borland C++ 4.52—you must use OWL 2.5 with that compiler version. However, Borland has hinted privately that they may provide OWL 5.0 backward compatibility for the 16-bit 4.52 compiler in the near future via a software patch or interim upgrade.

Constructing a Windows 95 Application

There's so much glitz and glitter in Windows 95, it's difficult to know where to start introducing the programming techniques you need to write applications. Because AppExpert lays much of the groundwork for many Windows 95 interface features, I'll use it in this section to demonstrate various Windows 95 and OWL techniques. Figure 15.2 shows the display of the finished program you create by performing the following step-by-step instructions.

Figure 15.2.

The completed Windows 95 sample application.

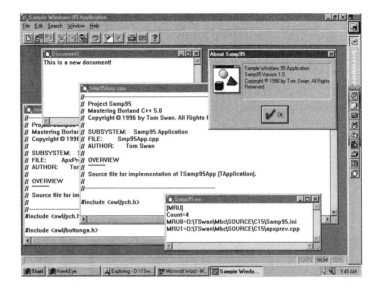

If you want to follow along, create a blank directory (I'll use C:\Samp95, but any name will do), and then carry out these steps:

1. Start the IDE and close the current project and any windows.

2. Select *File|New* and choose *AppExpert* from the submenu.

3. Change to the C:\Samp95 or other blank directory, and enter `Samp95` into the *New AppExpert Project* dialog's *File name* field. Close the dialog by selecting the *Open* button or pressing Enter.

4. You now see the AppExpert Application Generation Options dialog. I'll list only the required and changed settings to recreate this chapter's application, but you are free to experiment with other options on your own.

5. Under *Application*, enable MDI, and *Document/View*. (These are the default settings.)

6. Under *Application:Basic Options*, enable *Help file support*. Retain all other options enabled by default.

7. Under *Application:Advanced Options*, choose Normal for Application Startup State (the default) and select Borland BWCC under Control Style.

8. Under *Application:Admin Options*, enter copyright, author, and company information.

9. I used default settings for the *Main Window* and *MDI Child/View* topics. (However, I changed the main window's title.) You might want to inspect these settings to become familiar with the class names and files that AppExpert generates.

10. When you are satisfied with your choices, select the *Generate* button and read the note box, which confirms the directory path name where AppExpert will create the program's numerous files. Select the *Yes* button or press Enter to create the application.

11. After AppExpert finishes writing its files, you should build the application and play with the resulting shell. This is always a good idea before making changes. Select *Project\Build all* and run the resulting Samp95.exe code file using the Windows 95 Explorer. If you haven't tried AppExpert before, you'll be surprised at the results, which are more complete than you might expect. In fact, the generated program is a respectable text editor in its own right!

12. For future compilations, after making the changes suggested next in this chapter, select *Project\Make all*, which compiles only out-of-date modules.

> **NOTE**
>
> All files for the completed sample Windows 95 application are on this book's CD-ROM in the Source\C15 directory.

Adding a Splash Screen

One of the first "wow" features you'll want to add to your program is a startup splash screen. This gives your program's startup a touch of class, and as I mentioned, also gives users something to watch while the program goes through its initializations. Figure 15.3 shows the splash screen I added to the sample application.

Figure 15.3.
The sample application's splash screen.

OWL's TSplashWindow class makes this job easy. First, you need a bitmap (the 256-color image in the figure comes from Borland's Delphi 2.0). Copy the bitmap file to the project directory and name it Splash95.bmp or another name.

Next, include the Splashwi.h header file. If you are following along, add the following declaration to file Smp95app.cpp, which implements the program's TApplication class, TSamp95App:

```
#include <owl/splashwi.h>
```

Declare a pointer to a TSplashWindow object. For simplicity, I made mine global in file Smp95app.cpp using the statement:

```
TSplashWindow* Splash = 0;
```

The reason for using a global pointer is that the application and main window objects need to refer to the splash window. These objects are implemented in separate modules, making it more difficult for them to share data. Ordinarily, I avoid global variables as much as possible, but in this case, it's a harmless and simple solution.

Next, you need to create the splash window object. The best place to do that is in the application's InitMainWindow function, in this case, in the function declared as

```
void TSamp95App::InitMainWindow()
```

Add the code in Listing 15.1 to that function at its very beginning. I extracted this partial listing from the Smp95app.cpp file. Other listings in this chapter are similarly incomplete—of course the full source listings are on the CD-ROM.

Listing 15.1. From Smp95app.cpp (Creates splash window).

```
void TSamp95App::InitMainWindow()
{
// MBC5
// Create splash window object
//
  int style = TSplashWindow::MakeStatic |
              TSplashWindow::MakeGauge |
              TSplashWindow::CaptureMouse |
              TSplashWindow::ShrinkToFit;
  int timeOut = 3000;
  ::Splash = new TSplashWindow(*new TDib("Splash.bmp"), 400, 300,
    style, timeOut, "Splash95", this);
  ::Splash->Create();
// other programming goes here ...
}
```

First, select the styles you want for the TSplashWindow object. I chose to make my window static (so users can't drag it), to add a progress bar (Borland calls it a gauge), to capture the mouse (so users can't switch to another window), and to shrink the bitmap to fit the window. You might make the window exactly match the bitmap by not specifying ShrinkToFit, but using this option ensures a good-looking window in all display resolutions.

The program next prepares a `timeOut` variable, set to 3000 milliseconds, which keeps the window around for a moment after the main window appears. The `timeOut` value ensures that the splash window disappears eventually, but the window will also destroy itself on sensing a mouse click. The program constructs the `TSplashWindow` object by specifying the bitmap file as a `TDib` object, the window size, the selected styles, the `timeOut` variable, and a title for the window. (This title shows up in Windows' task list, not on screen.) The final argument, the `this` pointer, refers to the application object that owns the splash window.

Finally, after these preparations, you are ready to create and display the splash window. Simply call its `Create` function like this:

```
::Splash->Create();
```

At this stage, when the program executes the modified code, the splash window pops up on-screen, and the program goes about its merry business. The goal now is to update the screen's progress bar as the program performs its initializations and while the user stares in rapt attention at your arty bitmap. There are three basic techniques:

- Modify the main window's constructor.
- Modify the main window's `SetupWindow` function. An MDI application should do this in its client window `SetupWindow` function.
- Create and send a user message to the application, which should perform initializations on receipt of the message.

Each method has its advantages, but the splash-window code is the same in each case. Performing your program's initializations in the main window constructor is an obvious choice, but doing them in `SetupWindow` ensures that a valid window handle is available. This may prevent hard-to-find bugs caused by a deeply nested statement that surreptitiously calls a Windows function requiring the handle. The third choice lets the application window appear behind the splash screen, but may be more work than necessary. (Borland's Splash sample application demonstrates this technique, sending a user-defined message to the application.)

I'll use the second, and most common, method—modifying the main window's `SetupWindow` function to perform the program's initializations and update the splash window progress bar. To add the code to the AppExpert-generated application, open file Smp95mdic.cpp, which implements the MDI application's client window, of the class `TSamp95MDIClient`. Include the splashwi.h header as you did before:

```
#include <owl/splashwi.h>
```

Next, so the linker can resolve references to the global splash window, declare that pointer using the `extern` storage-class modifier:

```
extern TSplashWindow* Splash;
```

Now, this module can access the global pointer defined in the other file. In file Smp95mdic.cpp, locate function `SetupWindow` in the `TSamp95MDIClient` class. Modify that function as shown in Listing 15.2 (for reference, I list the complete function this time).

Listing 15.2. From Smp95mdic.cpp (Implements SetupWindow function).

```
void TSamp95MDIClient::SetupWindow()
{
  // Default SetUpWindow processing.
  //
  TMDIClient::SetupWindow();

  // MBC5
  char buffer[80] = "Setting up client window";
  ::Splash->SetText(buffer);

  // MBC5
  int percentDone = 0;
  while (percentDone <= 100) {
    ::Splash->SetPercentDone(percentDone);
    percentDone += 10;
    uint32 start = GetTickCount();
    while (GetTickCount() - start < 500)
      ;
  }

  // MBC5
  // Enable following code to remove splash window
  // before main window appears
  // delete ::Splash;
  // ::Splash = 0;

  // Accept files via drag/drop in the client window.
  //
  DragAcceptFiles(true);
}
```

As the listing shows, a splash window may display text and a progress bar, which you can update to inform users what's happening during the program's initialization. Here, I call the splash window's SetText function to display the string Setting up client window. (Hint: You might use this same method to display path names for programs that load or scan numerous files during startup.)

To update the progress bar, pass an integer argument with a value from 0 to 100, representing the percentage of work done. For demonstration only, in the sample application, I call the Windows GetTickCount function to create a small delay, and before each such pause, I increment an integer variable by 10. Passing this integer to the splash window's SetPercentDone function updates the progress bar.

You don't have to perform any other chores or cleanups, and SetupWindow can simply end. The splash window will close and delete itself automatically after timing out. How tidy. If you want, though, you may force the window to close by enabling the commented-out statements near the end of SetupWindow. These statements delete the window object and, so the program doesn't accidentally use it, reset the global pointer to null:

```
delete ::Splash;
::Splash = 0;
```

Using the Dockable Toolbar

The sample application, Samp95.exe, sports a *dockable toolbar.* To undock it, click and drag the toolbar anywhere between buttons and drop it inside the program window. This converts the toolbar into a floating window. You can resize this window, and its icons automatically adjust themselves to fit. Or, to once again sail the toolbar into a permanent harbor, drag it to any border—top, left, right, or bottom. When the outline changes to a vertical or horizontal bar, let go of the mouse button and the toolbar docks to its new position.

Dockable toolbars use the TDockable, TDockableGadgetWindow, TDockableControlBar, TDockingSlip, and TFloatingSlip classes, which you can read about in OWL's online help. The sample application's Smp95app.cpp file uses some of these classes (some internally), plus a few others. Listing 15.3 shows the SetupSpeedBar function, which prepares the dockable toolbar object for the sample application.

Listing 15.3. From Smp95app.cpp (Prepares the dockable toolbar object).

```
void TSamp95App::SetupSpeedBar(TDecoratedMDIFrame* frame)
{
  ApxHarbor = new THarbor(*frame);

  // Create default toolbar New and associate toolbar buttons with commands.
  //
  TDockableControlBar* cb = new TDockableControlBar(frame);
  CreateGadgets(cb);

  // Setup the toolbar ID used by OLE 2 for toolbar negotiation.
  //
  cb->Attr.Id = IDW_TOOLBAR;

  ApxHarbor->Insert(*cb, alTop);
}
```

As this code shows, a THarbor object provides a safe port for a dockable toolbar, an object of the TDockableControlBar class. (Being a sailor, I get a kick out of these class names.) The program's InitMainWindow function calls the function in Listing 15.3, passing the application's frame object of class TDecoratedMDIFrame. Use TDecoratedFrame for a non-MDI application.

THarbor is derived directly from TWindow. The class organizes the many tasks required by a dockable toolbar, creating slips (screen areas where the toolbar can dock and not interfere with the window's contents), the insertion and removal of toolbars, and the conversion between floating and securely tied-up toolbars.

After creating the THarbor object, construct a TDockableControlBar object and insert some buttons. The sample application does these jobs with the two statements:

```
TDockableControlBar* cb = new TDockableControlBar(frame);
CreateGadgets(cb);
```

CreateGadgets is a local class function. It calls the toolbar's Insert function to add objects of the TButtonGadget and TSeparatorGadget classes. Statements such as

```
cb->Insert(*new TButtonGadget(CM_EDITCUT, CM_EDITCUT));
cb->Insert(*new TButtonGadget(CM_EDITCOPY, CM_EDITCOPY));
cb->Insert(*new TButtonGadget(CM_EDITPASTE, CM_EDITPASTE));
cb->Insert(*new TSeparatorGadget(6));
```

construct the button and separator objects, and insert them in the toolbar. The CM_ constants specify the bitmap resource identifier and the command to issue when the user selects the button. (AppExpert uses the same constants for both purposes, which looks confusing, but the first constant is a resource ID; the second specifies the WM_COMMAND code the button issues.)

One tricky piece of code enables OLE 2 toolbar negotiation—in other words, the automatic merging of another application's toolbar with this one's. The sample application is not an OLE client or server, but it nevertheless makes this call to prepare for OLE toolbar negotiation:

```
cb->Attr.Id = IDW_TOOLBAR;
```

Finally, to sail the dockable toolbar into her slip, the program calls the harbor object's Insert function, passing the dockable toolbar object and an alignment indicator as arguments:

```
ApxHarbor->Insert(*cb, alTop);
```

You can specify alBottom, alLeft, or alRight for other initial toolbar positions. These constants are members of the TAbsLocation enumeration.

Registering and Unregistering

In the early days of Windows 3.0 (there were earlier versions, but these are best forgotten), software configuration information was stored in one monstrous file named Win.ini. Everything including the kitchen sink was stuffed into that file, and its incomprehensible convolutions were like the twisted plumbing in a many-times renovated old house.

Windows 3.1 "solved" this problem in two ways: The first was to provide functions such as GetProfileString and WriteProfileString, which encouraged software developers to use private .ini files rather than store configuration settings in Win.ini. The second, and more significant, improvement was the introduction of a registration database. Although primarily intended for registering OLE servers, the new registration database gave a glimpse into the future of configuration management in Windows.

Windows 95 carries this concept many steps further. Programs can and still do use initialization files, but they now are expected to register and unregister themselves in the registration database. This is especially important for DDE and OLE applications because other software needs to be able to locate and execute numerous programs to manage compound documents. However, all programs that use file data may register themselves—so that, for example, the Explorer and other program launchers can run the correct program when a user opens a document of a particular type.

543

AppExpert automatically includes all the necessary code required to register and unregister a Windows 95 application. Listing 15.4 shows the two functions that perform these duties.

> **NOTE**
>
> To register an AppExpert-generated program, simply run it. To unregister it, run it using the *Start* menu's *Run* command and enter `program-name unregister`, where `program-name` is the application's code filename. For example, enter `\samp95\samp95.exe unregister` to unregister this chapter's sample application. This undocumented trick causes the program to call function `UnRegisterInfo`, shown in Listing 15.4.

Listing 15.4. From Smp95app.cpp (Registers and unregisters a Windows 95 application).

```
void TSamp95App::RegisterInfo()
{
  TAPointer<char> buffer = new char[_MAX_PATH];

  GetModuleFileName(buffer, _MAX_PATH);

  TRegKey(TRegKey::ClassesRoot,
    "Samp95.Application\\DefaultIcon").SetDefValue(0,
    REG_SZ, buffer, strlen(buffer));
  strcat(buffer, ",1");
  TRegKey(TRegKey::ClassesRoot,
    "Samp95.Document.1\\DefaultIcon").SetDefValue(0,
    REG_SZ, buffer, strlen(buffer));
  strcpy(buffer, "Samp95.Document.1");
  TRegKey(TRegKey::ClassesRoot, ".txt").SetDefValue(0,
    REG_SZ, buffer, strlen(buffer));
}

void TSamp95App::UnRegisterInfo()
{
  TAPointer<char> buffer = new char[_MAX_PATH];

  GetModuleFileName(buffer, _MAX_PATH);

  TRegKey(TRegKey::ClassesRoot,
    "Samp95.Application").DeleteKey("DefaultIcon");
  TRegKey(TRegKey::ClassesRoot,
    "Samp95.Document.1").DeleteKey("DefaultIcon");

  TRegKey::ClassesRoot.DeleteKey("Samp95.Application");
  TRegKey::ClassesRoot.DeleteKey("Samp95.Document.1");
  TRegKey::ClassesRoot.DeleteKey(".txt");
}
```

Use the `TRegKey` class to register and to unregister a Windows 95 application. This and other registration classes are not in the Object Windows library—they are defined in the Registry.h header file in path C:\bc5\include\winsys. This is so you may use these classes in Windows 3.1, Windows 95, and Windows NT GUI and console applications. You can also use the registration classes in programs that do not use OWL.

You register information using base and sub key names. The static function, `ClassesRoot`, provides the base name. You provide the sub key such as *Samp95.Application* and *Samp95.Document.1*. Constructing the `TRegKey` object opens the registration database. You can then call a member function such as `SetDefValue` and `DeleteKey` to insert and remove registration information.

> **TIP**
>
> For more information on the registration classes, read about them in the online help file, Winsys.hlp.

Updating a Recent-File List

Run the sample Windows 95 application (Samp95.exe), and open a couple of text files. Notice that their path names appear in the program's *File* menu. This list is called the most-recently used (MRU) filename list. It makes it easy to reopen files most recently accessed.

Use the `TRecentFiles` class to insert, delete, and manage the MRU list. It's much simpler than doing the menu manipulations by other means. The class is declared in header file Rcntfile.h, which is included in the sample application by including the pch.h header. (This header pulls in most of OWL's class declarations, and speeds compilation by collecting this precompiled information in a .csm compiled symbol file.)

Derive your program's application class using multiple inheritance from `TApplication` and from `TRecentFiles`. For example, Samp95 declares its `TSamp95App` class like this:

```
class TSamp95App : public TApplication, public TRecentFiles {
// ...
}
```

Also define the class's response table, specifying the two base classes and a registered event for the `MruFileMessage` constant:

```
DEFINE_RESPONSE_TABLE2(TSamp95App, TRecentFiles, TApplication)
// ...
  EV_REGISTERED(MruFileMessage, CmFileSelected),
END_RESPONSE_TABLE;
```

`MruFileMessage` is defined in Rcntfiles.h as the string `"MRUFILEMESSAGE"`. You catch this message to respond to a file's selection from the MRU list. For example, Listing 15.5 shows how Samp95 opens a document when you select its name from the *File* menu.

Listing 15.5. From Smp95app.cpp (Opens a document selected from the MRU list).

```
int32 TSamp95App::CmFileSelected(uint wp, int32)
{
  TAPointer<char> text = new char[_MAX_PATH];

  GetMenuText(wp, text, _MAX_PATH);
  TDocTemplate* tpl = GetDocManager()->MatchTemplate(text);
  if (tpl)
    tpl->CreateDoc(text);
  return 0;
}
```

Implementing the MAPI File | Send Command

To earn the right to display the Win95 logo on your application's packaging, the program must meet numerous requirements. (Contact Microsoft for a comprehensive list.) One of these requirements for all programs that do any document processing is to support electronic mail using a *File\Send* command. OWL's TMailer class makes it easy to satisfy this prerequisite.

Declare a pointer to a TMailer object in your application class. For example, the TSamp95App class declares the following public pointer:

```
TMailer* ApxMail;
```

Construct the object in the class's constructor:

```
ApxMail = new TMailer();
```

Don't forget to delete the object in the destructor:

```
delete ApxMail;
```

Because your application might run on a system without electronic mail (MAPI) installed, before attempting to send any documents, you should first call TMailer's IsMAPIAvailable function, which returns true if MAPI is installed. Samp95 does this in function CeFileSend, which determines whether to enable the *File\Send* command. If MAPI is not available, this disables the command and prevents its selection—probably the best all around way to prevent accessing a nonexistent Windows 95 feature. Listing 15.6 shows the code.

Listing 15.6. From Samp95app.cpp (Enables the *File | Send* command if MAPI is installed).

```
void TSamp95App::CeFileSend(TCommandEnabler& ce)
{
  ce.Enable((GetDocManager()->GetCurrentDoc() != 0)
          && ApxMail->IsMAPIAvailable());
}
```

By the way, notice the use of TCommandEnabler, another class new to OWL 5.0. OWL passes to CeFileSend an object of the class. Call its Enable function to enable or disable the associated menu command. In this case, function CeFileSend determines whether to enable the *File\Send* command by testing whether a document is open, and whether MAPI is installed. The corresponding function, CmFileSend, in Listing 15.7, implements the command to mail one or more documents.

Listing 15.7. From Samp95app.cpp (Implements the *File / Send* command).

```
void TSamp95App::CmFileSend ()
{
  // Check to see if a document exists
  //
  TDocument* currentDoc = GetDocManager()->GetCurrentDoc();

  if (currentDoc) {
    TAPointer<char> savedPath = new char[_MAX_PATH];
    TAPointer<char> docName = new char[_MAX_PATH];

    bool dirtyState = currentDoc->IsDirty();

    if (currentDoc->GetDocPath())
      strcpy(savedPath, currentDoc->GetDocPath());
    else
      strcpy(savedPath, "");

    if (currentDoc->GetTitle())
      strcpy(docName, currentDoc->GetTitle());
    else
      strcpy(docName, "Document");

    TFileName tempFile(TFileName::TempFile);

    currentDoc->SetDocPath(tempFile.Canonical().c_str());
    currentDoc->Commit(true);

    currentDoc->SetDocPath(savedPath);
    currentDoc->SetDirty(dirtyState);

    ApxMail->SendDocuments(GetMainWindow(), tempFile.Canonical().c_str(), docName,
false);

    tempFile.Remove();
  }
}
```

The CmFileSend function first checks to see whether a document exists (that is, whether it is open). If so, two TAPointer objects create character buffers to hold the path and document filenames. (Even though CeFileSend disables the *File\Send* command if no document is open, it's still a good idea to double check for a document as shown here. Better safe than sorry.)

The `TAPointer` class template from the standard class library provides a safe pointer to a dynamic array. Using `TAPointer` ensures proper disposal of the memory allocated by new. It also prevents common errors such as aliasing—referencing an object via two pointers, which might cause the program to accidentally delete that object twice. (Use `TPointer` for non-array objects, and also refer to Borland's online help for the related classes, `TEnvelope` and `TAEnvelope`, which provide safe pointers to reference-counted objects.)

The `CmFileSend` function also uses a `TFileName` object. This class, from Borland's class library, can construct a filename from various parts (drive letter, path, and name, for example), and it greatly simplifies filename management. As shown here, for example, specifying the `TFileName::TempFile` enumerated constant constructs a temporary filename, which is needed for sending documents via the MAPI interface.

That action is carried out by calling `SendDocuments` in the `TMailer` class object, addressed here by the `ApxMail` pointer. Windows 95 and MAPI do all the rest of the work. Simply delete the temporary file as shown in the listing after the call to `SendDocuments`.

> **NOTE**
>
> The `TMailer` class encapsulates the entire MAPI DLL. Each member function in `TMailer` corresponds with a MAPI function such as `SendDocuments`. This relationship simplifies communicating with the MAPI interface. For a better understanding of `TMailer`, read up on standard C programming techniques for MAPI. You can then directly translate that programming to `TMailer` functions.

Exploring Other Windows 95 Techniques

Following are notes about several other key Windows 95 programming techniques you may want to add to your programs. For demonstration, I'll refer to Borland's example programs for some of these features. If you haven't installed the examples, you might want to do that before continuing.

Property Sheet Dialogs

Do your users a big favor—don't cram dozens of input boxes, check boxes, radio buttons, and other controls into one giant dialog box. Instead, categorize your program's options into short, but sweet, individual dialogs. Using Windows 95 property-sheet dialog boxes, users can select each category by clicking on a page tab, which resembles the selection tabs in a spiral-bound notebook.

OWL 5.0 provides three main classes to support property-sheet dialog boxes. These are

- `TTabControl`—Simulates a divider that looks like a set of selectable page tabs. You rarely have to use this class directly.

- `TPropertySheet`—Provides a container that encapsulates one or more child windows, each representing a page in the multipage dialog. You typically construct an object of this class and then insert your individual dialog pages.

- `TPropertyPage`—Represents each dialog-box page in a property sheet, selected by a page tab, which the property sheet displays automatically. Usually, you derive a class from `TPropertyPage` and override various functions to control responses to user actions. You need one additionally derived class for each of your dialog's pages.

Borland's Propsht example project, located in the path C:\examples\owl\classes\propsht, demonstrates the basic steps for creating and using a multipage, property sheet dialog. First, create each dialog as an individual resource—just as though you were creating separate dialog boxes. Each dialog resource should be the same size, it should use a 3-D look, and it should include the `WS_CHILD` window style (individual pages in a property sheet dialog are represented as child windows). The dialog resource headers in the .rc script file should be something like this:

```
IDD_WINATTR DIALOG 0, 0, WIZ_CXDLG, WIZ_CYDLG
STYLE DS_3DLOOK ¦ WS_CHILD ¦ WS_VISIBLE ¦ WS_CAPTION
```

It's up to you to decide what kinds of controls you want in each dialog page. However, as I mentioned, it's best to limit the number of controls in any individual page. You may insert buttons, check boxes, or any other controls, just as you do for single-window dialog boxes.

When you are done designing the dialog-box pages, include OWL's Propsht.h and (probably) Commctrl.h header files. Derive a new class from `TPropertyPage`, as Listing 15.8 illustrates. An object of your class will serve as an interface for each page in the multipage dialog.

Listing 15.8. From Propshtx.cpp (Derives a class from `TPropertyPage`).

```
class TPropertyPageDlg : public TPropertyPage {
  public:
    TPropertyPageDlg(TPropertySheet* parent, TResId resId,
                     const char far* title = 0, TResId iconRes = 0,
                     TModule* module = 0):
    TPropertyPage(parent, resId, title, iconRes, module){};

  protected:
    // Virtual methods to handle the Sheet notifications
    //
    virtual    int     Apply(TNotify far&);
    virtual    bool    KillActive(TNotify far&);
```

continues

Listing 15.8. continued

```
    virtual    void    Help(TNotify far&);
    virtual    void    Reset(TNotify far&);
    virtual    int     SetActive(TNotify far&);
    virtual    int     WizBack(TNotify far&);
    virtual    bool    WizFinish(TNotify far&);
    virtual    int     WizNext(TNotify far&);

    TPropertySheet*    GetSheet() const;

  DECLARE_RESPONSE_TABLE(TPropertyPageDlg);
};
```

The virtual function overrides are merely suggestions—you don't have to override them all. Typically, however, you'll want to provide code that performs most of these actions— updating an on-screen window, for example, if the user selects the *Apply* button (which calls the Apply function).

You'll also need a response table and implementations for each function, as the example program shows (see Borland's example file Propshtx.cpp).

Next, for each of your dialog pages, derive an additional class from the one declared in the preceding listing. In the example program, there are two such classes (I list only their declarations here):

```
class TWinAttrDlg : public TPropertyPageDlg {
...
};

class TSamplePageDlg : public TPropertyPageDlg {
...
};
```

Each class is derived from TPropertyPageDlg—the class you derived from OWL's TPropertyPage. You'll need response functions, variables, and other items to correspond to the dialog box controls. For example, TWinAttrDlg declares an event handler that displays a message window when you click on the page's *Background Color* button (it's a faker, however, and it doesn't actually change the background color). The TSamplePageDlg class implements a set of command functions to respond to that page's numerous check boxes and buttons. This demonstrates how, with classes, a program can respond interactively to complex dialog box control selections.

After programming the individual property page classes, you are ready to construct and display the full property-sheet dialog (see Listing 15.9).

Listing 15.9. From Propshtx.cpp (Constructs and displays the full property-sheet dialog).

```
void
TClientWindow::Properties()
{
  TPropertySheet* ps = new TPropertySheet(this, "Options");
  new TWinAttrDlg(ps);
  new TSamplePageDlg(ps);
  ps->Execute();
}
```

First, construct an object of the TPropertySheet class to serve as a container for the individual dialog pages. Assign a title such as *Options*. There is no corresponding dialog box resource for the container—its border, background, and various buttons are created internally.

For each page in the dialog, construct an object of one of your derived classes. Pass to the class constructors the pointer to the TPropertySheet object. For example, the sample program constructs TWinAttrDlg and TSamplePageDlg objects. The individual dialog captions become the text for each selection tab. Finally, to display the whole shebang, call the TPropertySheet class's Execute function. All objects are automatically deleted when the user closes the dialog window. Figure 15.4 and Figure 15.5 show the two pages in the resulting property sheet dialog.

Figure 15.4.

Page one of the property sheet dialog.

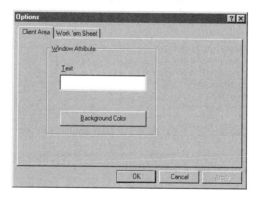

Figure 15.5.

Page two of the property sheet dialog.

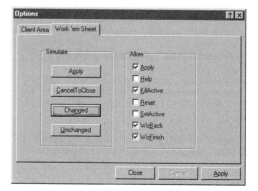

Column Headers

A column header control displays a set of buttons that are the perfect tools for organizing multi-column data lists. For example, Figure 15.6 shows a sample column header from the next sample program, which displays the width of each column.

Figure 15.6.

Sample column header control from the Column example program.

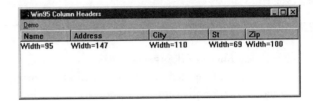

Listing 15.10, Column.cpp, on this book's CD-ROM in the Source\C15\Column directory, demonstrates the basics of constructing and using column headers.

Listing 15.10. Column.cpp (Demonstrates column headers).

```
//================================================================
// Column.cpp -- Demonstrates column headers
// Copyright (c) 1996 by Tom Swan. All rights reserved.
//================================================================

#include <owl\applicat.h>
#include <owl\framewin.h>
#include <owl\colmnhdr.h>
#include <stdio.h>
#pragma hdrstop
#include "column.rh"

const int ColHdrID = 0x100;  // Column header control ID


// ===============================================================
// The application's main window
// ===============================================================

class TDemoWin: public TFrameWindow {
  TColumnHeader*  ColHdr;  // Pointer to column header object
public:
  TDemoWin(TWindow* parent, const char far* title);
protected:
  void EvSize(uint sizeType, TSize& size);
  void SetupWindow();
  void Paint(TDC& dc, bool erase, TRect& rect);
  void ColHdrItemChanged(THdrNotify far&);
DECLARE_RESPONSE_TABLE(TDemoWin);
};

// Create response table declared for class
DEFINE_RESPONSE_TABLE1(TDemoWin, TFrameWindow)
  EV_WM_SIZE,
  EV_HDN_ITEMCHANGED(ColHdrID, ColHdrItemChanged),
```

```
END_RESPONSE_TABLE;

// Constructor
TDemoWin::TDemoWin(TWindow* parent, const char far* title)
  : TFrameWindow(parent, title),
    TWindow(parent, title)
{
  AssignMenu(ID_MENU);
  ColHdr = new TColumnHeader(this, ColHdrID, 0, 0, 0, 0);
  ColHdr->Attr.Style |= HDS_BUTTONS;
}

// Prepare column headers before window becomes visible
void
TDemoWin::SetupWindow()
{
  TWindow::SetupWindow();
  ColHdr->Add(THdrItem("Name"));
  ColHdr->Add(THdrItem("Address"));
  ColHdr->Add(THdrItem("City"));
  ColHdr->Add(THdrItem("St"));
  ColHdr->Add(THdrItem("Zip"));
}

// Handle WM_SIZE message
void
TDemoWin::EvSize(uint sizeType, TSize& size)
{
  TWindow::EvSize(sizeType, size);
  if (ColHdr)
    ColHdr->Layout();
}

// Display column dimensions
void
TDemoWin::Paint(TDC& dc, bool erase, TRect& rect)
{
  char buffer[80];
  int count = ColHdr->GetCount();
  int x = 0;

  for (int i = 0; i < count; i++ ) {
    THdrItem hi;
    ColHdr->GetItem(hi, i, HDI_WIDTH);
    sprintf(buffer, "Width=%i", hi.cxy);
    dc.TextOut(x, 20, buffer);
    x += hi.cxy;
  }
}

// Force repaint when user changes column header width
void
TDemoWin::ColHdrItemChanged(THdrNotify far&)
{
  Invalidate(true);
```

continues

Listing 15.10. continued

```
}

// ============================================================
// The application class
// ============================================================

class TDemoApp: public TApplication {
public:
  TDemoApp(const char far* name)
    : TApplication(name) {};
  void InitMainWindow();
};

// Initialize the program's main window
void
TDemoApp::InitMainWindow()
{
  MainWindow = new TDemoWin(0, "Win95 Column Headers");
}

#pragma argsused

// Main program
int
OwlMain(int argc, char* argv[])
{
  TDemoApp app("OwlWelc");
  return app.Run();
}
```

To add a column header control to a window, include the Colmnhdr.h file:

```
#include <owl/colmnhdr.h>
```

In the window's class, declare a pointer to a TColumnHeader object:

```
TColumnHeader* ColHdr;
```

Next, in the class constructor, create the column header object and assign its style bits:

```
ColHdr = new TColumnHeader(this, ColHdrID, 0, 0, 0, 0);
ColHdr->Attr.Style |= HDS_BUTTONS;
```

So that the control resizes itself correctly if the window size changes, implement an event handler for a WM_SIZE message, and insert the following statement:

```
if (ColHdr)
  ColHdr->Layout();
```

This ensures that the column header always occupies the full width of the window's client area. Initially, the column header control is empty and it looks like a blank bar under the program's menu and tool bars (if it has these objects). To insert a new column into the control, construct an object of the THdrItem class and pass it to the column control's Add function:

```
ColHdr->Add(THdrItem("Name"));
ColHdr->Add(THdrItem("Address"));
```

To remove a column, call `Delete` and specify its index. The first column at left has the index value zero:

```
ColHdr->Delete(index);
```

Change the column width by constructing an object of the `THdrItem` class, and calling `SetItem`. For example, this sets the width of the third column to 150:

```
THdrItem hi;
hi.cxy = 150;
hi.mask = HDI_WIDTH;
ColHdr->SetItem(hi, 2);
```

To find the number of columns, call `GetCount`:

```
int count = ColHdr->GetCount();
```

To get specific information about a column, call `GetItem` along with three parameters: a `THdrItem` object, an integer index (the first column index is zero), and an `HDI_` constant of the type of information you want. For example, the following sets hdrItem.cxy to the width of the third column:

```
THdrItem hdrItem;
ColHdr->GetItem(hdrItem, 2, HDI_WIDTH);
```

> **NOTE**
>
> You can request the height of a column header using constant `HDI_HEIGHT`, but this has the same value as `HDI_WIDTH` and produces no useful information.

There are numerous notification messages your program can use to respond to column header changes and selections. For instance, the sample listing declares the event function, `ColHdrItemChanged`, using the corresponding `EV_HDN_ITEMCHANGED` macro in the window's response table. By this maneuver, the program can respond to changes in a column header—for example, when the user clicks and drags a column border to resize it. The sample program uses this opportunity to invalidate the window, causing function `Paint` to redisplay the column widths.

You might also respond to other messages such as `HDN_BEGINTRACK` and `HDN_ITEMCLICK`. For example, use code such as the following to respond to the user selecting a column button:

```
void
TYourWindow::ColHdrItemClick(THdrNotify far& hdrNotify)
{
  THdrItem hdrItem;  // For getting info about the column selected
  ColHdr->GetItem(hdrItem, hdrNotify.iItem, HDI_LPARAM);
//... Do whatever you want
  Invalidate(false);  // Recommended to update window if needed
}
```

Of Lists and Trees

The image list common control provides a useful method for working with multi-image bitmaps. For example, an animation might pack several image frames into a single bitmap, and then display them in succession similar to the way you flip the pages of a cartoon book.

TImageList, declared in header file Imagelst.h, encapsulates the Windows 95 image list control. Declare a pointer to an object of this class in your window class:

```
TImageList* ImageList;
```

You next construct the object, specifying a bitmap, which might be a program resource. For example, Borland's Drawcell sample application (in the owl\imagelst path) loads a series of chess-piece bitmaps and icon masks using a for loop:

```
for (int i = IDB_WKING; i <= IDB_BPAWN; i++) {
  TBitmap img(*GetModule(), i);
  TBitmap msk(*GetModule(), i+MASK_DELTA);

  if (!ImageList) {
    ImgSize = TSize(img.Width(), img.Height());
    ImageList = new TImageList(ImgSize, true, 10, 10);
    ImageList->SetBkColor(RGB(0xff, 0, 0));
  }
  ImageList->Add(img, msk);
}
```

Each pair of TBitmap objects is added to the ImageList object by calling the class's Add function. Notice also how the ImgSize object (a TSize pointer) is used to specify the image sizes.

To display an individual bitmap frame from the image list, call the Draw function. For example, you might call Draw something like this:

```
ImageList->Draw(index, dc, x, y, ILD_TRANSPARENT);
```

The ILD_TRANSPARENT constant specifies a two-step drawing method that combines an image with its mask, letting any background graphics show through the image's holes. This is the same method used to display transparent icons on the Windows desktop.

The TListWindow object encapsulates another useful list control. Despite its name, the class encapsulates the Windows 95 list *view* control. (OWL already has a TListView class, so Borland used a different name for TListWindow.)

Include the listwind.h header file and declare a TListWindow pointer in your window's class:

```
TListWindow* ListWind;
```

Construct a list view object, perhaps in response to the user clicking a button:

```
ListWind = new TListWindow(this, ListWindId, 40, 40, 400, 200);
ListWind->Attr.Style |= LVS_SHAREIMAGELISTS | LVS_ICON;
ListWind->Create();
```

`ListWindId` should be any unique constant for all active list view controls. Specify the coordinates, width, and height of the control; then assign selected `LSV_` style bits. You can display large or small icons, or list only text. (A good example of the list view control is the Windows 95 Explorer's right window pane.) Finally, unless you are creating the object in the parent window's `SetupWindow` function, you must call the control's `Create` function to create and display the underlying window structure.

Also create a `TImageList` object with the bitmaps that you want to use in the `TListWindow` object. Call the list view's `SetImageList` function to assign these bitmaps. For example, Borland's Listwind example program executes the statement:

```
ListWind->SetImageList(*ImageList, TListWindow::Normal);
```

Also assign text values to each listed item. To do this, prepare a `TListWindItem` object, associate it with its bitmap using a unique integer index, and insert it into the list view:

```
TListWindItem item("Your text");   // Or use a char buffer
item.SetImageIndex(n);             // n == index of associated bitmap
ListWind->InsertItem(item);        // Insert into list view
```

Use the `TTreeWindow` class to create outlines and tree-like lists. This class encapsulates the Windows 95 tree view control. (Again, Borland renamed the class because OWL already has a `TTreeView` class.) A good example of the tree view control is the Windows 95 Explorer's left pane, which shows directory path name hierarchies. Figure 15.7 shows the tree produced by Borland's Treewind example program.

Figure 15.7.

A sample `TTreeWindow` *object.*

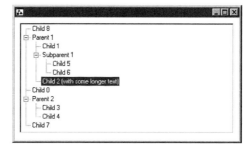

To use `TTreeWindow`, you need two objects—one of that class and one of the `TImageList` class, which specifies the icons to use for the tree view's open and close buttons.

Select the tree display styles you want using the `TTreeWindow`'s `TStyle` nested class. Then create the object and save its pointer. For example, Borland's sample program executes this code:

```
TTreeWindow::TStyle style =
  TTreeWindow::TStyle(TTreeWindow::twsHasLines ¦ TTreeWindow::twsHasButtons);
#if defined(BI_PLAT_WIN32)
  style = TTreeWindow::TStyle(style ¦ TTreeWindow::twsLinesAtRoot);
#endif
TreeWind = new TTreeWindow(this, TreeWindId, 10, 10, 400, 200, style);
```

The next job—in the window's `SetupWindow` function, for example—is to assign string values to parent and child levels of the tree. Construct an object of the `TTreeNode` class by calling the tree view's `GetRoot` function:

```
TTreeNode root = TreeWind->GetRoot();
```

You can now add `TTreeItem` objects to the root:

```
root.AddChild(TTreeItem("New child"));
```

Continue to call `AddChild` for additional nodes. To create a new root, add a child, which has a brief childhood and immediately grows up to become a parent:

```
TTreeNode parent = root.AddChild(TTreeItem("New parent"));
```

Then use the resulting object to add some children:

```
parent.AddChild(TTreeItem("It's a boy child!"));
parent.AddChild(TTreeItem("It's a girl child!"));
```

Detecting Windows Versions

Because many PC users are still running Windows 3.1, you may need to generate 16- and 32-bit versions of your applications. When doing this, it's best to maintain a single set of source code files. The alternative—multiple sets of source code files—tends to breed more bugs than a swamp on a still summer day, and is a nightmare to maintain. However, creating a single source, multitarget project requires you to correctly detect the build platform and the runtime operating system. You must determine

1. Whether the program is being compiled to a 32-bit or a 16-bit code file platform.
2. Whether the program is running under Windows 95, Windows NT, or Win32s layered on a 16-bit version of Windows.

These two goals are not mutually exclusive. To determine build time platforms, use conditional compilation statements along with two defined constants, `BI_PLAT_WIN16` and `BI_PLAT_WIN32`. For example, these statements select sections of source code based on the output target:

```
#if defined(BI_PLAT_WIN16)
  // building for 16-bit code file platform
#elif defined(BI_PLAT_WIN32)
```

```
  // building for 32-bit code file platform
#else
  #error Not a 16- or 32-bit Windows target
#endif
```

To determine the operating system and version at runtime, call static functions in the `TSystem` class, declared in file System.h in the C:\bc5\include\winsys path. (Because the functions are static, you don't have to create a `TSystem` object.) For example, you can use the following statement to detect that a program is *not* running under Windows 95:

```
// Add to OwlMain:
if (!TSystem::IsWin95()) {
  ::MessageBox(0, "Requires Windows 95", "Error",
    MB_ICONSTOP | MB_OK);
  return -1;
}
```

A good place to insert this code is in `OwlMain`, just before calling the application object's `Run` function. Other `TSystem` functions can detect other versions of Windows. However, you can call only some of `TSystem`'s detection functions depending on the program's build platform. For example, a 16-bit application cannot use `TSystem` to detect that it is running on Windows NT. This is by design because a 16-bit application can't perform 32-bit tasks, and therefore detecting Windows NT provides no useful information. However, it is possible for a 16-bit application to detect Windows 95. Likewise, only a 32-bit application can—and needs to— detect that it is running under Win32s layered on top of a 16-bit Windows version.

Listing 15.11 shows how to combine the `BI_PLAT_WIN16` and `BI_PLAT_WIN32` constants to detect the build platform and to properly detect the runtime operating system. Use this hypothetical code (it's not on CD-ROM) as a guide to constructing Windows software that you can compile to 16- and 32-bit code file platforms, *and* that can run under all Windows versions.

Listing 15.11. Detects build and runtime platforms.

```
#if defined(BI_PLAT_WIN16)
  if (TSystem::IsWoW())
    // is Windows on Win32 (Generic Thunking) ;
  if (TSystem::IsWin95())
    // is Windows 95 ;
#endif
#if defined(BI_PLAT_WIN32)
  if (TSystem::IsNT())
    // is Windows NT ;
  if (TSystem::IsWin95())
    // is Windows 95 ;
  if (TSystem::IsWin32s())
    // is Win32 subset layered on Windows ;
#endif
```

Summary

- Windows 95 is fast gaining in popularity, but many programmers are still writing 16-bit applications that do not take advantage of features available only to 32-bit code files. This chapter's information helps you move up to 32-bit software development.

- OWL 5.0 classes encapsulate most of the new features in Windows 95, including common controls, dockable toolbars, property-sheet dialog boxes, and more.

- AppExpert can create an application that demonstrates many features required for Windows 95 logo certification. Using AppExpert is also a good way to learn new OWL programming techniques that you can extract for your own applications.

- This chapter demonstrates numerous Windows 95 and OWL programming techniques such as adding a startup splash window, creating and using dockable toolbars, registering and unregistering an application in the Windows 95 registration database, updating a most-recently used (MRU) file list, and implementing electronic mail using MAPI.

- This chapter also explains other Windows 95 techniques such as property sheet dialogs, the column header control, image lists, and list and tree view controls.

- To support 16- and 32-bit, single-source development, Borland C++ provides the conditional compilation constants BI_PLAT_WIN16 and BI_PLAT_WIN32. Use these constants along with static functions in the TSystem class to determine build and runtime platforms, which will help you to successfully create 16- and 32-bit versions of your programs, while maintaining a single set of source code files.

16
CHAPTER

Introducing OLE and OCF

Joan, who is bucking for a promotion, has a problem. She must produce a new stockholder's report by tomorrow morning, but she's got a promising date in the queue for this evening. Joan works for the Slick Widgets Company and knows that if the stockholders report looks good, she will get that promotion—if the report doesn't impress everyone, her chances for any type of promotion are dismal. Either she finishes that report in record time, or she'll be up all night in front of a computer screen instead of hopping and bopping at the club.

Fortunately for Joan, who prefers partying to slaving over a hot CPU, she is using the latest Windows software. Because her word processor, spreadsheet, and database programs support OLE (Object Linking and Embedding), she can quickly transfer tables, database forms, and other presentation objects to her word processor. With these tools at hand, she should be able to put that report together faster than you can mix a martini.

Joan quickly designs a first draft. On page one, she envisions a graph showing Slick Widgets' profits. She brings up her spreadsheet and designs the graph. The company's profitability figures are actually contained in a database that supports OLE. Using OLE, she easily moves the monthly profit table to the spreadsheet program. Back in the spreadsheet program, she creates a simple graph of the profitability data, and then moves the table (again, using OLE) to the word processor for the final report.

Now, you might say, "OK, so the spreadsheet, word processor, and database program were created by the same software company: they are designed to work together!" Close, but in this example the word processor is from the Smith Word Processor Co., the spreadsheet is from Jones Electronic Spread Sheets, Inc., and the database program comes from the Overloaded With Data Co. None of these companies knows the other (actually, Smith did meet Jones once). *The only common link between these products is that they all support OLE.*

Borland has created a new set of C++ classes for OLE called OCF (ObjectComponents Framework), first introduced in Borland C++ 4.5. This set of classes helps Windows programmers integrate applications and OLE. You can write OLE applications without OCF, but this is so difficult, I can't recommend it even to the hardiest of programmers in the audience.

To interface Windows applications with OLE, Borland has also created a dynamic link library called BOLE.DLL. This DLL makes it easy to interface with OLE version 2 Windows structures. Figure 16.1 shows the relationship between OLE 2, BOLE, and OLE applications that are created using Borland C++ Version 5.

> **NOTE**
>
> Borland has indicated that although they will provide source code for the Bole.dll file (intended to assist developers in debugging their OLE applications), they won't document the Bole.dll interface. However, this won't affect the use of the DLL for most programmers.

Figure 16.1.

Relationship between OLE, BOLE, and ObjectComponents Framework.

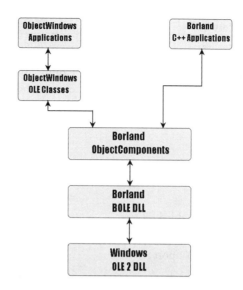

With OWL and Borland C++ 5.0, your applications can support the OLE operations listed in Table 16.1. Although all applications do not have to support all available operations, they do need to support a minimum set. Using AppExpert ensures that your application meets these minimum requirements, even if you don't thoroughly understand what they are.

Table 16.1. OWL's OLE 2 operations.

Operation	Description
Automation controller	The container that sends commands to an automation object. See *Automation servers* for more information.
Automation servers	Exposes server objects to the container so that the container is able to issue commands to the object. The object is usually referred to as an *automation object*. Borland uses the example of a calculator program that exposes its buttons (such as for the numbers and functions), and controls (such as the output window) to the container.

continues

Table 16.1. continued

Operation	Description
Compound file storage	Compound files offer efficient storage for OLE objects and offer advantages for the storage of other non-OLE document items.
In-Place editing	The container's user interface (typically most of the menu selections) can be replaced with the server's user interface.
Linked and embedded containers	Containers that may have either linked or embedded objects.
Linked and embedded servers	Servers that support both linked and embedded objects.
OLE clipboard support	Support at the clipboard level, including interaction with both the Edit menu and the clipboard accelerator keys.
OLE drag and drop	OLE drag and drop supports entire objects, linked and embedded.
OLE user interface support	Support for user-interface functionality, such as menu merging (see *In-Place editing*), pop-up menus, and additional verbs in the container's Edit menu.
Registration	All OLE servers must be registered in the Windows registration file. This process for most server applications is done automatically by code generated by AppExpert.
Type libraries	Type libraries are used to manage the addition of server information to the Windows registration database. Typically, a user would not manually enter information into the registration database, but would merge an application's registration information using the merge command.
Use of Localized strings	Localized strings simplify the process of creating applications that must function in languages other than the native language (such as English) of the developer.

A Few Good Terms

The following small glossary explains OLE terms that you should know for programming OLE applications using OWL and OCF.

- *Server*—An application that provides some data that will be either embedded or linked into a document such as Joan's stockholder's report. A server can be an application such as Microsoft Excel or a specialized DLL that, unlike most DLLs, performs only as an OLE server.

- *Container*—An application that may have one or more OLE objects contained within the container's document. These OLE objects may be either linked or embedded.

- *Linked*—When an OLE object is linked, the container document does not hold a copy of the object's data. Instead, the container has only a representation of the data (perhaps as a bitmap image), and also information about where the actual data can be found—for example, its file pathname. This usually results in a smaller document file because the containing document doesn't include an actual copy of the object's data. However, one disadvantage to a linked document is that, if the object is modified, the container's performance (such as redrawing its window) may be reduced by the time needed to open the original object.

- *Embedded*—An embedded OLE object has both the object's data and presentation placed within the container document. When documents contain embedded objects, the size of the container document is increased by the size of the embedded objects. This can lead to a document becoming quite large, especially if the user doesn't realize how large each embedded object actually is. However, opening the embedded document may be faster than with linked documents.

- *Automation*—This refers to an application that exposes programmable objects to container applications. These objects are called *automation clients*. Typical automation servers insert their menus into the container application's main window whenever their OLE object is selected. The user can then modify the OLE object without the difficulty of switching to a separate application. (See also the sidebar, "OLE Automation.")

- *Drag-and-Drop*—OLE's drag-and-drop functionality is used as a shortcut in copying and pasting data. The same process can be completed using the clipboard's *Copy* and *Paste* facilities. However, with OLE drag-and-drop, you have a much more powerful facility than is supported by the Explorer (Windows 95) or File Manager (Windows 3.1). Those utilities can drag and drop only filenames, while OLE's drag-and-drop capabilities work with complete objects.

- *Render*—An embedded or linked OLE 2 object must be drawn even when it is not active. The process of displaying an inactive OLE 2 object is called rendering.

- *Clipboard*—OLE uses the clipboard to form the bridge between OLE applications. For example, an Excel program places data on the clipboard using special formats that allow OLE programs to access this data using OLE techniques. Despite this enhancement, your application can still use standard clipboard formats without restriction.

OLE AUTOMATION

OLE automation, in which one application menu merges with another for editing a linked or embedded object, provides a glimpse into the future of graphical user interfaces. Someday down the road, instead of using separate applications, we may simply access a common interface that assumes the format, menus, commands, and graphical controls for working with information and documents of various kinds.

This goal is important because it will allow users to focus on the *information* they need rather than on choosing the correct *software* to manipulate data, a requirement that confuses many computer consumers. Especially for new users, selecting hardware is difficult enough. Choosing among software interfaces and data formats is enough to boggle anybody's brain.

But is a one-for-all common interface, built upon the concepts of OLE, merely pie-in-the-sky speculation? Maybe not. Just consider how fast Windows has inspired numerous common interface features among differing applications. As Windows matures (or is replaced by future operating systems), it is likely to inspire and absorb more interface elements into a common design. This will in turn free programmers to concentrate on what their software does rather than how it communicates with end users. OLE automation is the first step in this eventual goal of a truly information-based user interface. We're not there yet, but we're headed in the right direction faster than ever before. You can join in this revolution by making your applications OLE aware.

Creating a Simple OLE Program

One of the nice features that Borland C++ Version 5 has is the capability to create an OLE application using AppExpert. To use this program, you interactively select the features and options you want in your application, and AppExpert uses your selections to create a program shell.

To create an OLE-aware shell, first start AppExpert using the *File\New* submenu. Answer the prompts for a project name and directory. You must provide the project's name, and the default directory (the Borland C++ Version 5 directory) is not appropriate for a project's directory. For reference, the listing files for this chapter are in the directory \...\C16. Use a different, blank directory, to create your own OLE application files. The project name for this program is Basicole.

When you have provided the project's name and directory information and have selected OK, you see the AppExpert main window shown in Figure 16.2. As this figure shows, there are a number of OLE options that you can set for your application. Take a look at these options, and consider how they affect the completed OLE application.

Figure 16.2.

AppExpert's main window.

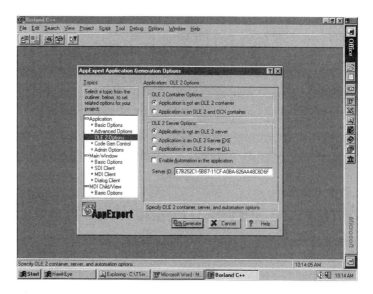

In the *Application/OLE 2 Options* pane of the AppExpert dialog box, there are two group boxes. The first, *OLE 2 Container Options,* contains two radio buttons: *No* and *Container*. If you select *No*, this application will not be an OLE container application. If, however, you select *Container*, this application will function as an OLE container. Notice that it is not necessary for an application to be a server for the application to be a container.

The second group box is labeled *OLE 2 Server Options*. This group box contains three radio buttons: *No*, *Server EXE,* and *Server DLL*. If you select *No*, this application will not be a server application. If you select *Server EXE*, this program will function both as a server and as a standalone program. If you select *Server DLL*, this application will perform as a server; however, it will not be usable as a stand-alone application because it won't have the necessary support to be executable.

Also found on the *Application/OLE 2 Options* pane are two additional controls. The first control is a check box labeled *Enable Automation in the appplication*. If the box is checked, this program will support OLE automation. Note that OLE Automation is different from In-Place editing—some programmers (and users) confuse the two features. OLE Automation allows one program, called the controller, to control another program, called the server. All OLE server applications that you create using AppExpert will support In-Place editing; however, the OLE Automation support is included only if you select the *EnableAutomation in the application* check box.

The second control in the *Application/OLE 2 Options* pane is an edit box where the GUID (Globally Unique ID) is displayed. This edit field is labeled as *Server ID* and will always be initialized to a long string containing hexadecimal digits. The default value in this string is computed using the identifier from your network card (assuming you have one) and the current date and time. The size and method of generation help to ensure that the GUID is unique. The possibility of a duplicate GUID being generated is extremely remote, so in practice you don't have to allow for possible duplications.

Some programmers who are producing a number of related products may want to use sequential GUIDs to their OLE software. If this is important to you, contact Microsoft's developer support group and request a unique GUID number. The number that Microsoft gives you provides a range of 256 possible GUID numbers.

Once you have selected whatever OLE options your application will need, you can set other AppExpert options as necessary. When done setting your AppExpert options, select the Generate button.

What Are Server IDs and Why Have Them?

Server IDs, as noted in the preceding description of AppExpert's *Application/OLE 2 Options* pane, allow Windows to identify each OLE server in the system without having to rely on the server's name or location. When an OLE object is embedded in a container's document, the object's server is not contained as an application name or filename. The GUID string is saved instead. This string is also found in the registration database. Windows then takes care of matching an object's GUID with the actual server. The GUIDs are stored in Windows' registration database.

Figure 16.3 shows the RegEdit program. This program operates as the user interface to the registration database. The RegEdit program (when started with the command `regedit /v`) shows all the entries in the registration database, and the attribute data that is attached to each entry. For users of Windows NT and Windows 95, the registration database contains more information than the OLE object database. However, under Windows 3.*x*, the registration database is primarily used to store information about OLE servers.

> **TIP**
>
> Windows 95 users: Use the Explorer to locate Regedit.exe in your Windows directory and drag it to the desktop using the right mouse button. Release and choose *Create Shortcut(s) Here* from the popup menu. This will make running the Regedit program easier. You might also want to right-click the resulting icon and choose *Properties* to rename it to "Regedit."

In working and reading about OLE applications, you may encounter the term *CLSID* (CLass IDentifier). A CLSID is simply a GUID used to identify a class. Through your work with OLE, you also will encounter, from time to time, the term *UUID* (Universally Unique ID). For all intents and purposes, these terms are one and the same. All refer to the unique GUID.

Figure 16.3.
The Windows 95 RegEdit main window.

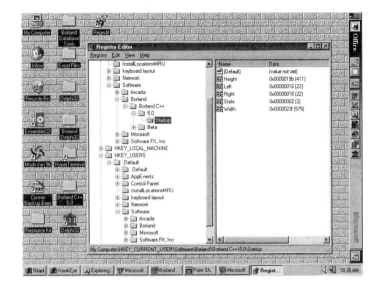

Building Your OLE 2 Program

To build an OLE 2 program, you use the standard Borland C++ build commands. The project that AppExpert created controls the build process, and the files have all the necessary information needed to build the OLE program.

An OLE server must be registered to enable Windows to find the server when a container document references the server's object. This registration is performed automatically by the server—assuming that it is an executable program (.exe) and not a DLL—when it is run for the first time. If your server is built as a DLL, you must register it so that Windows will be able to find the server.

In Windows 3.1, the registration of a DLL server is performed by a registration utility, Regdll, which was included with Borland C++ Version 4.5. Windows 95 does not require this utility.

Once the application is registered, it is not necessary to re-register OLE servers unless there is a change in the system. Changes might include installing a new version of the control, making a new installation of Windows (simply reinstalling Windows will preserve the registration database), or situations in which the registration database has been damaged for some reason.

Debugging Your OLE 2 Program

The first part of debugging an OLE 2 application is to write it and have it compile without any errors or warnings. With OLE 2 applications, it is very important to correct warnings because the OLE 2 environment is much more demanding than for single-task applications.

569

Testing and debugging your OLE 2 applications entails using more advanced techniques than for debugging a typical Windows application. First and foremost, you must be able to determine that the problem is either in the server, the container, or—though unlikely—both. Whenever possible, test your container applications with a proven server (such as Word for Windows or Excel). Likewise, test your server applications with a known good container (again, such as one of the Microsoft Office applications).

Borland supplies several OLE examples with Borland C++ Version 5. These products are found in the directory \bc5\examples\owl\ocf. This subdirectory has several other directories in it, which Table 16.2 describes.

Table 16.2. OLE examples in \bc5\examples\owl\ocf from Borland.

Subdirectory	Description
Mdiole	Contains a multidocument OLE application. This application is contained in two source files and demonstrates a simple OLE application.
Ocxdls	Demonstrates how to use OCF in OWL to create dialog boxes with embedded OCX controls (i.e. 32-bit OLE-aware controls). The example application in this directory requires you to install two sample OCX controls provided with Borland C++ 5. These are *1st Impressions Chart* and *Formula One Spread Sheet*. If you haven't installed these controls, run Setup from the Borland CD-ROM.
Sdiole	Contains a single-document OLE application. This application is contained in two source files and demonstrates a simple OLE application. The Sdiole program is slightly less complex than the Mdiole example. Microsoft has voiced the opinion that future versions of Windows will be more object-oriented and they recommend that applications be designed using the single-document interface wherever possible.
Ttt	Contains a simple Tic-Tac-Toe game. This application is contained completely in a single source file, supplemented with a simple header and resource file. The actual game is very simplistic (any reasonably competent player will either win, if they start first, or play to a draw (if the computer plays first) with this game. If you ignore the actual game strategy in this game, the remaining code shows many of the issues that must be addressed with an OLE 2 server application. The Tic-Tac-Toe game is not able to function as a container.

In addition to the examples listed in Table 16.2, there is another examples directory, \bc5\examples\ocf. This subdirectory has several OLE 2-related example programs, which Table

16.3 lists. The main difference between the examples in this directory and the \bc5\examples\owl\ocf subdirectory is that these example programs are not OWL-based.

Table 16.3. OLE example code in \bc5\examples\ocf from Borland.

Subdirectory	Description
Autocalc	The Autocalc application is an automation server that performs as a simple four-function calculator. Also included is Callcalc, which calls the Autocalc application as an OLE server. This demonstrates the ease of interacting with an automation server.
Localize	This application prints a list of languages and their identifiers.
Regtest	This program tests the process of registering and working with the Windows 95 registration database. The Regtest program tests the following operations: Register, Unregister, File write, Validate, Compare, or Display.
Tutorial	These files correspond with the printed OLE tutorial in the *User's Guide.*

Unlike most of the Borland C++ Version utilities, you must build the utility programs described in Table 16.3 because they are supplied in source format only.

When your server is a stand-alone program (that is, the server is not a DLL), it can be tested as a standard Windows application using normal debugging techniques. For example, you can test the server simply by using the IDE's built-in debugger. When you have debugged the server as a stand-alone application, you can begin the process of debugging the OLE linkage.

Typically, you debug the server by embedding it into a container application. Again, using a container application that is known to work correctly will expedite your debugging process. It is highly frustrating, and possibly futile, to attempt to fix flaws in the container while debugging your server.

When the server is not an executable program (that is, a DLL), the issues of debugging the server are more complex. First, the server must be registered. Without having it registered, it is not possible to actually embed the server's object into a container. When registered and embedded, many of the techniques used in debugging any other DLL are usable. From the beginning of the debugging process, you must also take into consideration the issues of OLE complexity and the process of OLE linkage.

An OLE 2 server actually has two states. The first state is when the server's object has been embedded, but is not active. The user will see the container's object, but won't interact with it directly. The second state is when the user is actually manipulating the object. In this case the object is active, and with In-Place editing support, the container's menu will be updated to display the server's menu. This makes the container resemble the server. You can independently debug each of these states.

571

I suggest that you debug the server in its active state first. Make it work correctly, having it accept the user's input as necessary. When the active state is working acceptably, you can test the server's inactive state. Typically, most OLE objects don't do anything when they are inactive. The exception is an OLE Custom Control, which may actually be able to update the user area—even when the control is inactive.

When an OLE 2 server object is inactive, the container must be able to display (or render) the object. This can be done in a number of ways; however, the most common way is for the server to create a metafile, which is then used to draw the object's rendition. Other rendering methods might include using a bitmap (either a .bmp or a .dib), or some other form of data display.

Compound Files

OLE 2 is an extensive system. It is much more than just a means for two applications to share objects. One problem with embedded and linked objects is how to store the object—and information about the object—in a logical format. A methodology was created called *structured storage*. The structured-storage specification describes the format, but not the medium. Structured storage may describe compound files stored on disk, or simply a block of memory that is shared between two different applications.

Microsoft solved the issue of persistent structured storage by introducing *compound files*. A compound file is, in reality, a file system in a file, comprised of *substorage* objects (which are like a subdirectory) and stream objects (which are like data files). For the remainder of this chapter, I'll use the term *structured storage* for those features that are applicable to all structured storage objects, and I'll use the term *compound files* for those items that apply only to compound files.

Structured storage may have many different *substorage* and *stream* objects, all arranged in a tree-like manner, much like DOS's disk-file directory file structure. Figure 16.4 shows how the contents of a typical structured storage might be arranged. This figure actually shows a compound file that has a single substorage object (called "Player Roster"). The "Player Roster" substorage object has four stream objects ("Dave Valle", "Jay Buhner", "Randy Johnson", and "Ken Griffey Jr."). The root of this compound file also has two additional stream objects ("Coach Listing" and "Document Name").

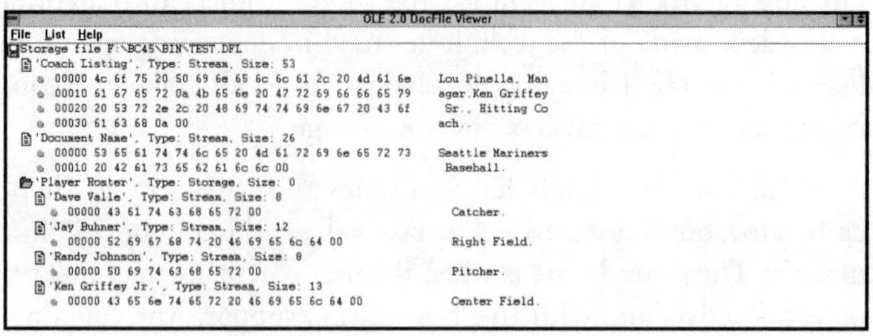

Figure 16.4.

A compound file's internal arrangement.

There are several things that become apparent when viewing this figure. First, a name (either a substorage or stream object) in a structured storage object, such as a compound file, may consist of up to 31 characters, and may also contain embedded spaces. As well, stream objects may be placed at any level, and stream objects may contain any type of data that the application using the compound file wishes to place in the stream.

Following are the main features of structured storage and compound files, which are a primary implementation of structured storage. These features are what make structured storage and compound files so powerful:

- Each structured storage object has a name. This name may be up to 31 characters long, and may contain embedded spaces.
- You may pass both Substorages and streams to other processes. This sharability of structured storage is a very useful feature.
- It is possible to modify a single stream in a structured storage without having to rewrite the entire structured storage. This allows for faster incremental updates.
- It is possible to open a structured storage in the transaction mode. In this mode any modifications made will not be written until committed.

Structured storage also presents a number of problems that you must be aware of. Let's take a closer look at these potential problems, and the methods to handle each situation.

Fragmentation of Compound Files

One problem with disk-based compound files is that, like disks in general, they can become fragmented. The possibility of fragmentation comes when a substorage or a stream is rewritten to a new location, and the original substorage's location becomes vacant. When a compound file becomes fragmented, it must be compressed just like a fragmented disk drive must be compressed.

There are routines that will compress compound files, but they are not easily available. One such routine, called Smasher, can be found in Kraig Brockschmit's book, *Inside OLE, Second Edition*, 1995, published by Microsoft Press. This book is also available on the Msdn Development Library CD.

Listing 16.1 presents a sample function that will compress a compound file. Include a similar routine in your code to add error checking to this type of code.

Listing 16.1. Compress.cpp (Pseudo code for compressing compound files).

```
//===============================================================
// Compress.cpp -- Pseudo code for compressing compound files
// Copyright (c) 1996 by Tom Swan. All rights reserved.
//===============================================================
```

continues

573

Listing 16.1. continued

```c
// Assume: szFile is the name of the file to be compressed

void CompressCompoundFile(char* szFile)
{
// Define work variables
  LPSTORAGE   pNew;           // Pointer to an IStorage interface
  LPSTORAGE   pIOld;          // Pointer to an IStorage interface
  LPMALLOC    pIMalloc;       // Pointer to an IMalloc interface
  STATSTG     StorageStatus;  // A STATSTG structure
  HRESULT     hResult;        // Result handle
  char        szError[129];   // Bit of memory for error messages

// Setup for work

  hResult = CoGetMalloc(MEMCTX_TASK, &pIMalloc);

  if (FAILED(hResult)) {
    return;  // Cannot get memory allocator function handle:
  }

// Check for a compound file

  if (FAILED(StgIsStorageFile(szFile))) {
    wsprintf(szError, "File %s is not a compound file.", szFile);
    MessageBox(szError, "Compound file compressor", MB_OK);
    pIMalloc->Release();
    return;
  }

// Open identified compound file

  hResult = StgCreateDocfile(NULL,
    STGM_CREATE | STGM_READWRITE |
    STGM_DIRECT | STGM_SHARE_EXCLUSIVE, 0, &pINew);

  if (FAILED(hResult)) {
    wsprintf(szError, "Temporary file could not be opened.");
    MessageBox(szError, "Compound file compressor", MB_OK);
    pIMalloc->Release();
    return;
  }

// Open the original file

  hResult = StgOpenDocfile(szFile,
    STGM_READ | STGM_DIRECT | STGM_SHARE_EXCLUSIVE,
    NULL, 0, &pIOld);

  if (FAILED(hResult)) {
    wsprintf(szError, "Can't open original file %s.", szFile);
    MessageBox(szError, "Compound file compressor", MB_OK);
    pINew->Release();
    pIMalloc->Release();
    return;
  }
```

```
    hResult = pIOld->CopyTo(NULL, NULL, NULL, pINew);
    pIOld->Release();

    if (FAILED(hResult)) {
      wsprintf(szError, "Can't copy original file %s.", szFile);
      MessageBox(szError, "Compound file compressor", MB_OK);
      pINew->Release();
      pIMalloc->Release();
      return;
    }
//  pINew is a defragmented copy of pIOld
//  Copy it back over pIOld

    hResult = StgCreateDocfile(szFile, STGM_CREATE |
      STGM_WRITE | STGM_DIRECT | STGM_SHARE_EXCLUSIVE,
      NULL, 0, &pIOld);

    if (FAILED(hResult)) {
      pINew->Stat(&StorageStatus, 0);
      pINew->Release();
      wsprintf(szError, "Can't overwrite %s, new copy = %s,
        szFile, st.pwcsName);
      MessageBox(szError, "Compound file compressor", MB_OK);
      pIMalloc->Free((LPVOID)st.pwcsName);
      pIMalloc->Release();
      return;
    }
// Copy the new compound file over the old one, then delete temp

    pINew->CopyTo(NULL, NULL, NULL, pIOld);
    pIOld->Release();
    pINew->Stat(&StorageStatus, 0);
    pINew->Release();
    OpenFile(StorageStatus.pwcsName, &OpenFileStruct, OF_DELETE);
    pIMalloc->Free((LPVOID) st.pwcsName);
    pIMalloc->Release();

    return;
}
```

The preceding code actually does a bit more than just defragment a compound file: It also gives you an example of the code necessary to manipulate compound files.

Storage Interfaces

There are a number of interface methods to use with OLE structured storage. Table 16.4 shows the interfaces, how they are implemented, and what (a container, server, both, OLE, or something else) would use the interface.

Table 16.4. Storage and memory interfaces.

Interface	Implementor	Used By
IEnumSTATSTG	OLE	The IEnumSTATSTG interface is used when it is necessary to enumerate the IStorage objects. In compound files, the elements would consist of substorages and streams. You would call the IStorage::EnumElements() function to obtain a pointer to a IEnumSTATSTG interface.
ILockBytes	OLE	Although the ILockBytes interface may be used by applications, it is generally used by OLE as a method to manipulate byte arrays that underlie compound files.
IMalloc	OLE	The IMalloc interface is used to manage memory allocations by OLE applications. The IMalloc interface is an important interface, and it is described in more detail below.
IPersist	Object handlers and object applications	The IPersist interface may be used to obtain a given object's CLSID. The IPersistStorage, IPersistStream, and IPersistFile interfaces are all based on the IPersist interface.
IPersistFile	Object applications and (optionally) container applications to support linking to embedded objects and to file-based objects	The IPersistFile interface is used by OLE to load outer-level document objects that reside in files, as opposed to documents that are embedded inside compound documents.

Interface	Implementor	Used By
IPersistStorage	Object handlers and object applications	The IPersistStorage interface is object used by container applications to both read and write native data in compound document objects, which are found in an IStorage interface.
IPersistStream	OLE	The IPersistStream interface is used by container applications to both read and write objects that have been saved in stream storage.
IRootStorage	OLE	The IRootStorage interface is used by container applications to switch the disk files that underlie IStorage objects.
IStorage	OLE	The IStorage interface is used to interface with a structured storage object. The IStorage interface is an important interface, and it is described in more detail below.
IStream	OLE	The IStream interface is used to interface with stream objects found in an IStorage object. You could consider an IStream object to be much like a non-compound file.

The IStorage Interface

As the code in Listing 16.1 shows, you manipulate compound files using a pointer to an IStorage interface object. Listing 16.2 shows the format for the IStorage interface. Use the IStorage interface to interact with structured storage objects.

Listing 16.2. Istorage.cpp (Shows the IStorage interface).

```cpp
//=============================================================
// Istorage.cpp -- Shows the IStorage interface
// Copyright (c) 1996 by Tom Swan. All rights reserved.
//=============================================================

DECLARE_INTERFACE_(IStorage, IUnknown)
{
// *** IUnknown methods ***
  HRESULT QueryInterface (THIS_ REFIID riid, LPVOID FAR* ppvObj);
  ULONG AddRef (THIS);
  ULONG Release (THIS);

// *** IStorage methods ***
  HRESULT CreateStream(THIS_ const char FAR* pwcsName, DWORD grfMode,
    DWORD dwReserved1, DWORD dwReserved2, LPSTREAM FAR*  ppStm);

  HRESULT OpenStream(THIS_ const char FAR* pwcsName, void FAR *pReserved1,
    DWORD grfMode, DWORD dwReserved2, LPSTREAM FAR* ppStm);

  HRESULT CreateStorage(THIS_ const char FAR* pwcsName, DWORD grfMode,
    DWORD dwReserved1, DWORD dwReserved2, LPSTORAGE FAR* ppStg);

  HRESULT OpenStorage(THIS_ const char FAR* pwcsName,
    LPSTORAGE FAR *pstgPriority,
    DWORD grfMode, SNB snbExclude, DWORD dwReserved, LPSTORAGE FAR* ppStg);

  HRESULT CopyTo(THIS_ DWORD dwCiidExclude, IID const FAR *rgiidExclude,
    SNB snbExclude, LPSTORAGE FAR* pStgDest);

  HRESULT MoveElementTo(THIS_ const char FAR* lpszName,
    LPSTORAGE FAR *pStgDest,
    char const FAR* lpszNewName, DWORD grfFlags);

  HRESULT Commit(THIS_ DWORD grfCommitFlags);

  HRESULT Revert(THIS);

  HRESULT EnumElements(THIS_ DWORD dwReserved1, void FAR *pReserved2,
    DWORD dwReserved3, LPENUMSTATSTG FAR* ppenumStatStg);

  HRESULT DestroyElement(THIS_ const char FAR* pwcsName);

  HRESULT RenameElement(THIS_ const char FAR* pwcsOldName,
    const char FAR* pwcsNewName);

  HRESULT SetElementTimes(THIS_ const char FAR *lpszName,
    FILETIME const FAR *pctime,
    FILETIME const FAR *patime, FILETIME const FAR *pmtime);

  HRESULT SetClass(THIS_ REFCLSID rclsid);

  HRESULT SetStateBits(THIS_ DWORD grfStateBits, DWORD grfMask);

  HRESULT Stat(THIS_ STATSTG FAR *pStatStg, DWORD grfStatFlag);

};
```

The `IMalloc` Interface

As the code in Listing 16.2 shows, memory for OLE routines is generally allocated using the `IMalloc` interface functions. Functions in `IMalloc` include the C library-like functions `Alloc`, `Free`, and `Realloc`. Listing 16.3 shows the format for the `IMalloc` interface.

Listing 16.3. Imalloc.cpp (Shows the `IMalloc` interface).

```
//===========================================================
// Imalloc.cpp -- Shows the IMalloc interface
// Copyright (c) 1996 by Tom Swan. All rights reserved.
//===========================================================

DECLARE_INTERFACE_(IMalloc, IUnknown)
{
// *** IUnknown methods ***
  HRESULT    QueryInterface(THIS_ REFIID riid, LPVOID FAR* ppvObj);
  ULONG      AddRef(THIS);
  ULONG      Release(THIS);

// *** IMalloc methods ***
  void FAR*  Alloc(THIS_ ULONG cb);
  void       Free(THIS_ void FAR* pv);
  void FAR*  Realloc(THIS_ void FAR* pv, ULONG cb);
  ULONG      GetSize(THIS_ void FAR* pv);
  int        DidAlloc(THIS_ void FAR* pv);
  void       HeapMinimize(THIS);
};
```

Functions for Substorages and Streams

There are four functions that support interfacing with compound files. Table 16.5 describes these functions.

Table 16.5. Compound file support functions.

Function	Description
OleLoad	The OleLoad function is used to load an embedded or linked object into memory.
OleLoadFromStream	The OleLoadFromStream function is used to load a stream object into memory.
OleSave	The OleSave function is used to save an embedded or linked object from memory.
OleSaveToStream	The OleSaveToStream function is used to save a stream object from memory.

Each of these functions is fully documented in the OLE Help files that are supplied with Borland C++ Version 5.

The Drag-and-Drop Interface

The Windows 95 Explorer and its Windows 3.1 precursor, the File Manager, support a form of drag-and-drop. For example, you can select a filename with the mouse and drag it to a directory or a program. Dropping the filename moves its contents to the directory, or it starts the program with the selected document. However, these types of drag-and-drop actions are unique to the Explorer and File Manager, and they are not related to OLE's concept of drag-and-drop.

OLE's drag-and-drop doesn't deal with filenames. Instead, OLE works in a more general way with objects. An object may be a paragraph from a word processor document, some cells from a spreadsheet, a graph, or perhaps an image. In all cases, a selection is made (generally, part of the originating document is highlighted) and then the mouse cursor is placed inside the selection's area.

Probably the only real hindrance to using drag-and-drop between two applications is that they both must be visible to the user on-screen. For Figure 16.5, it took only a few seconds to select the paragraph and move it to Excel, but I had to shrink both applications so they were simultaneously visible.

Figure 16.5.

Microsoft Excel with a dragged and dropped paragraph from Word for Windows.

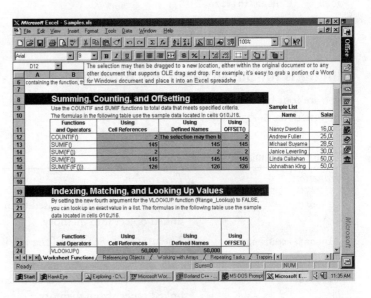

But that's easier said than done! With drag-and-drop, OLE must interact with two applications, and manage the process so that it appears to be simple from the user's viewpoint.

There are two interfaces (and an OLE function) that manage OLE drag-and-drop activity. The next section covers the source's interface, and then the target's interface. It also provides a look at the OLE functions that bind the entire process together.

Drag-and-Drop Source Interface

The drag-and-drop source interface is managed by the IDropSource interface. This interface is comprised of the elements in Listing 16.4.

Listing 16.4. Idrop.cpp (Shows the IDropSource interface).

```
//=============================================================
// Idrop.cpp -- Shows the IDropSource interface
// Copyright (c) 1996 by Tom Swan. All rights reserved.
//=============================================================

DECLARE_INTERFACE_(IDropSource, IUnknown)
{
// *** IUnknown methods ***
  HRESULT QueryInterface (THIS_ REFIID riid, LPVOID FAR* ppvObj);
  ULONG AddRef (THIS);
  ULONG Release (THIS);

// *** IDropSource methods ***
  HRESULT QueryContinueDrag (THIS_ BOOL fEscapePressed,
    DWORD grfKeyState);
  HRESULT GiveFeedback (THIS_ DWORD dwEffect);
};
```

This interface has five functions to manage the drag-and-drop operation at the source. There are two IDropSource methods, QueryContinueDrag and GiveFeedback.

The QueryContinueDrag function determines whether the current drag operation should be continued.

The GiveFeedback function manages the feedback the user gets while dragging an object. This feedback consists of two different aspects: the pointer can change its shape, and the original dragged data may also change its appearance.

Drag-and-Drop Target Interface

The drag-and-drop target interface is managed by the IDropTarget interface. This interface consists of the elements in Listing 16.5.

Listing 16.5. Itarget.cpp (Shows the `IDropTarget` interface).

```
//================================================================
// Itarget.cpp -- Shows the IDropTarget interface
// Copyright (c) 1996 by Tom Swan. All rights reserved.
//================================================================

DECLARE_INTERFACE_(IDropTarget, IUnknown)
{
// *** IUnknown methods ***
  HRESULT QueryInterface (THIS_ REFIID riid, LPVOID FAR* ppvObj);
  ULONG AddRef (THIS);
  ULONG Release (THIS);

// *** IDropTarget methods ***
  HRESULT DragEnter (THIS_ LPDATAOBJECT pDataObject,
    DWORD grfKeyState, POINTL pt, LPDWORD pdwEffect);

  HRESULT DragOver (THIS_ DWORD grfKeyState, POINTL pt,
    LPDWORD pdwEffect);

  HRESULT DragLeave (THIS);

  HRESULT Drop (THIS_ LPDATAOBJECT pDataObject, DWORD grfKeyState,
    POINTL pt, LPDWORD pdwEffect);
};
```

This interface has five functions to manage the drag-and-drop operation at the source. There are four `IDropTarget` methods: `DragEnter`, `DragOver`, `DragLeave`, and `Drop`.

The `DragEnter` function is used to determine whether the target window is able to accept the object being dragged and what effect the object being dragged will have on the target window.

The `DragOver` function provides feedback about the status of the drag-and-drop operation while the cursor is over the potential target application.

The `DragLeave` function removes feedback when either the mouse leaves the target or upon the cancellation of the drag operation.

The `Drop` function causes the dragged data (which is pointed to by the *pDataObject* parameter of `Drop`) to be dropped on the target application.

Drag-and-Drop Functions

OLE provides the `DoDragDrop` function that is used to begin a drag-and-drop operation. This function has four parameters, and returns `HRESULT`. The `DoDragDrop` function prototype is

```
HRESULT DoDragDrop(
  LPDATAOBJECT pDataObject,
  LPDROPSOURCE pDropSource,
  DWORD dwEffect,
LPDWORD pdwEffect);
```

The `DoDragDrop` parameters are

- *pDataObject*—This parameter points to an `IDataObject` interface. You would use the object that *pDataObject* points to obtain information about the data that is being dragged.

- *pDropSource*—This parameter points to an `IDropSource` interface. You would use the object addressed by *pDropSource* to communicate with the dragged object's source during a drag-and-drop operation.

- *dwEffect*—This parameter determines the effects that occur during a drag-and-drop operation. Both *dwEffect* and *pdwEffect* values are from the `DROPEFFECT` enumeration, which defines the values listed in Table 16.6.

- *pdwEffect*—This parameter is a pointer to a `DWORD` value that describes the effects on the source of a drag-and-drop source. If the drag-and-drop operation is canceled, then the value pointed to by this parameter is undefined.

Table 16.6. DROPEFFECT enumerated values.

Value	Definition	Description
DROPEFFECT_NONE	0	The drag-and-drop target is unable to accept the dragged data.
DROPEFFECT_COPY	1	The original data is copied to the target. In the source the data is unmodified.
DROPEFFECT_MOVE	2	The original data is copied to the target, and then deleted from the source.
DROPEFFECT_LINK	4	The original data remains in the source, and a link to the original data is made.
DROPEFFECT_SCROLL	0x80000000	There is a scroll operation occurring. This value is used with one of the other DROPEFFECT values.

Table 16.7 shows the return values from `DoDragDrop`. It is important to check the return values to determine whether the operation was canceled, completed successfully, or failed for some reason.

Table 16.7. DoDragDrop return values.

Return value	Description
S_OK	The drag-and-drop operation has been successfully initiated.
DRAGDROP_S_DROP	The drag-and-drop operation has been successful.
DRAGDROP_S_CANCEL	The drag-and-drop operation has been cancelled.
E_OUTOFMEMORY	There is not sufficient memory to complete the drag-and-drop operation.
E_UNSPEC	The drag-and-drop operation failed. The cause of the failure was not otherwise described.

The usage of the DoDragDrop function is complex, and prior to working directly with this function you should review the Borland C++ Version 5 documentation on OLE 2.

The In-Place Activation and Editing Interface

The final part of this chapter describes the OLE In-Place activation and edit facility. The process of In-Place activation and editing creates a very powerful and user-friendly interface that can greatly enhance the usability of OLE applications. When it is misused, In-Place activation can create a user's nightmare, where the tools and information necessary to complete the editing task are difficult (or even impossible) to access. Throughout the remainder of this chapter, I'll refer to In-Place activation and editing as simply In-Place editing.

MODELESS DIALOGS IN AN IN-PLACE SERVER

When working with OLE, with an object that is being supported using In-Place editing, it is possible for one application to display a modal dialog at the same time as another application has modeless dialogs visible.

To enable the correct behavior for enabling and disabling, the application that wants to display the modal dialog must first call EnableModeless(false). After completion of the dialog, it must then call EnableModeless(true). The object calls IOleInPlaceFrame::EnableModeless and the container calls IOleInPlaceActiveObject::EnableModeless.

In-Place editing allows the container to assume the server's user interface, by allowing the server to replace the container's menu with that of the server.

First, if at all possible, use AppExpert to design your OLE application. Using AppExpert, and the OWL OLE classes, you will have most of the In-Place editing functionality automatically created. You can get additional information about the items described in this section by using the Borland C++ Version 5 on-line help system.

Regardless of how you create your OLE application, it is a good idea to have some idea of how In-Place editing works. In-Place editing is implemented as six interfaces, some structures, and a number of functions.

In-Place Editing Interfaces

There are a number of interfaces that support In-Place editing. These interfaces are listed in Table 16.8. Each of these interfaces offers a number of functions for the OLE 2 application.

Table 16.8. In-Place editing interfaces.

Interface	Description
IOleWindow	This interface is used by both container and object applications. The IOleWindow interface contains the methods used by applications when they need to obtain handles to various windows for In-Place activation. An additional use of the IOleWindow interface is to enter and exit context-sensitive help mode.
IOleInPlaceObject	This interface is used by containers when they must activate (and deactivate) an In-Place object. Your application can get a pointer to the IOleInPlaceObject interface by calling the QueryInterface function.
IOleInPlaceActiveObject	This interface is used to provide a method for communication between In-Place objects and the container application.
IOleInPlaceUIWindow	This interface is used to negotiate border space in either the document or frame window.
IOleInPlaceFrame	This interface is used to control the placement of the composite menu, manage accelerators, manage context-sensitive help, and manage modeless dialog boxes during the In-Place editing process.
IOleInPlaceSite	This interface is used to interact between the container and the server object's In-Place client site.

In-Place Editing Structures

There are three structures that are used to support In-Place editing. These structures are listed in Table 16.9.

Table 16.9. In-Place editing structures.

Structure	Description
OLEINPLACEFRAMEINFO	This structure is used to assist OLE in dispatching keystroke accelerators to the container when an In-Place editing session is active.
OLEMENUGROUPWIDTHS	This structure is used to keep track of the number of menus in each of the menu groups.
BORDERWIDTHS	This structure is used to hold the values used to compute border widths when editing an In-Place object. These borders may be used for toolbars or other purposes as the server may need them.

In-Place Editing Functions

There are four additional functions that are used to support In-Place editing. These functions are listed in Table 16.10. They help the container and the server interact.

Table 16.10. In-Place editing functions.

Function	Description
OleCreateMenuDescriptor	The OleCreateMenuDescriptor function is used to create and return a descriptor for OLE to use when dispatching menu messages and commands.
OleDestroyMenuDescriptor	The OleDestroyMenuDescriptor function is used by the container to free a shared menu descriptor that has been allocated by a call to OleCreateMenuDescriptor.
OleSetMenuDescriptor	The OleSetMenuDescriptor is used to install or remove menu dispatching code from the container's frame window.
OleTranslateAccelerator	The OleTranslateAccelerator is used by the object application, to allow the container to translate its accelerators, which are pointed to by the *lpFrameInfo* parameter.

IsAccelerator	This function is not an OLE support function; however, its operation is closely related to the `OleTranslateAccelerator` function described above. It is necessary for an object application to call `IsAccelerator` to determine whether an accelerator message belongs to the application.

Summary

- This chapter introduces OLE and explains the steps necessary to create an OLE program using AppExpert and the process of building an OLE application.

- GUID, UUID, and CLSIDs are all identifiers used by OLE to identify an OLE server. Generally, a CLISID is a GUID and a GUID is a UUID.

- Some of the issues in debugging an OLE program include the problems of having two different applications interacting with each other. Another problem is the issue of management of objects.

- Compound files are a specific implementation of structured storage. Structured storage defines a methodology of storing information in an hierarchical method.

- OLE supports drag-and-drop techniques; an object may be defined in a server and simply moved using the mouse to drag it.

- In-Place activation and editing allows an embedded object in a server to be edited directly without actually starting the server as a separate application. The server's user interface will actually be merged with the container's user interface while the embedded object is being edited In-Place.

17

CHAPTER

Creating OLE Applications

There's nothing like a little hands-on experience—especially when it comes to learning complex programming techniques such as Object Linking and Embedding. In this chapter, you create two OLE applications, a server and a container. The server "serves" information, which is embedded in the container's document. Together, the two programs demonstrate the minimum programming necessary to create OLE version 2 software.

In both cases, you use AppExpert to create the program's shell. AppExpert creates the basic application, which you modify to produce the final working code. You can write OLE programs from scratch using Borland C++, but with AppExpert, there's no need to go to all that pain and suffering. And even if you don't want to use AppExpert for your own projects, the resulting files contain scads of routines and techniques you can extract for your own purposes.

There are several things that you should keep in mind when writing your versions of these programs:

- First, this chapter provides printed listings only for the source files you modify; you can find the entire project on the CD-ROM in directories C17\Olecntr and C17\Olesvr.

- Second, the CLSIDs (class identifiers) for these programs will differ from the CLSIDs that are generated for your programs when you run AppExpert. This is normal and desirable because the CLSIDs differentiate between multiple server applications.

- Third, these examples are the minimum necessary to get started in OLE programming. You'll need additional code to create a finished server or container application. There just isn't enough room in this chapter to implement a fully functional server and container—if I listed all the necessary files, you would need a forklift to move this book to your desk.

Building an OLE Server

The first OLE application is a server. In this example, you build a *full* server—a program that can function as a stand-alone application as well as a server. By creating a stand-alone server— that is, a server that is an executable program (.exe) and not a dynamic link library (.dll)—you simplify the process of registering the server under Windows.

The initial process for developing your server is simple. First, using the IDE, start AppExpert. Select a new directory and name for your project. I placed my project in the directory C17\olesvr, but you should use a fresh, blank directory. I named the project Olesvr (I always create the project and the project's directory with the same name). Following are the steps I followed:

1. Start AppExpert using the IDE's *File|New* command. Change to your destination directory and enter Olesvr or another title for the project name.

2. After selecting OK in the AppExpert project directory and filename dialog, the next directory displayed is the *AppExpert Application Generation Options* dialog. This dialog allows configuring of the application that AppExpert is generating. You have to change several options for this project.

3. The first option to change is in the *Application* topic. Change the default of MDI (Multiple document interface) to SDI (Single document interface). Figure 17.1 shows the *Application* topic settings.

Figure 17.1.

AppExpert's Application topic settings.

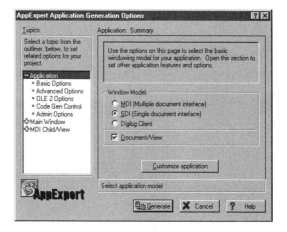

4. Next, you should tell AppExpert that this program is to be an OLE server. Select *Application: OLE 2 Options* and enable the radio button labeled *Application is an OLE 2 Server EXE*. Figure 17.2 shows this dialog page.

Figure 17.2.

AppExpert's Application: OLE 2 Options topic.

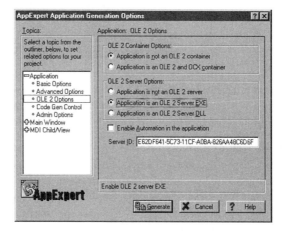

5. Optionally, fill in the *Application: Admin Options* topic of the AppExpert dialog to customize the application's copyright notice, name, and version information.

All topics under the *Main Window* topic should retain their default values. There are no changes needed in these dialog topics, but you might want to inspect the settings just to become fam-iliar with the possibilities. Likewise, because this is a single-document interface, the

MDI Child/View settings have no effect on the generated application. These topics apply only to multiple-document-interface programs.

When you have selected all options, choose the *Generate* button at the bottom of the *AppExpert Application Generation Options* dialog box. AppExpert prompts you for a confirmation that you intend to build this project; when you accept the confirmation, AppExpert generates the application's source code and other files. Figure 17.3 shows the final project loaded into the IDE. The project window lists all source code, header, and resource files generated for the application.

Figure 17.3.
The Olesvr project window.

Now that you have generated the Olesvr program, you must add code to make it a functional OLE server. For example, you'll need statements to paint graphics and you'll want to make other minor adjustments here and there.

Fortunately, you can use both Borland C++ Version 5 and the ClassExpert program to help make most of the necessary changes. First, tackle the program's output. As with any other AppExpert-generated program, the main drawing is done within the view class derived from the TOleView OWL class. The file that implements the view is Olsvrolv.cpp. The derived class is named TOlesvrOleView. Listing 17.1 shows the original file. I modified a few lines so they would fit comfortably on the page, but the file is otherwise unchanged from the one that AppExpert generated.

Listing 17.1. Olsvrolv.cpp (Implements Olesvr's view class).

```
//------------------------------------------------------------------------
//  Project Olesvr
//  Swan Software
//  Copyright © 1996 by Tom Swan. All Rights Reserved.
```

```
//
//  SUBSYSTEM:    Olesvr Application
//  FILE:         OlsvrOlV.cpp
//  AUTHOR:       Tom Swan
//
//  OVERVIEW
//  ~~~~~~~~
//  Source file for implementation of TOlesvrOleView (TOleView).
//
//----------------------------------------------------------------------------

#include <owl/pch.h>

#include "OlsvrApp.h"
#include "OlsvrOlV.h"

#include <stdio.h>


//{{TOlesvrOleView Implementation}}

//
// Build a response table for all messages/commands handled
// by TOlesvrOleView derived from TOleView.
//
DEFINE_RESPONSE_TABLE1(TOlesvrOleView, TOleView)
//{{TOlesvrOleViewRSP_TBL_BEGIN}}
  EV_WM_GETMINMAXINFO,
  EV_OC_VIEWSHOWTOOLS,
//{{TOlesvrOleViewRSP_TBL_END}}
END_RESPONSE_TABLE;


//--------------------------------------------------------
// TOlesvrOleView
// ~~~~~~~~~~
// Construction/Destruction handling.
//
TOlesvrOleView::TOlesvrOleView(TDocument& doc, TWindow* parent)
:
  TOleView(doc, parent)
{
  ToolBar = 0;

  // INSERT>> Your constructor code here.

}


TOlesvrOleView::~TOlesvrOleView()
{
  // INSERT>> Your destructor code here.

}


//
// Paint routine for Window, Printer, and PrintPreview for a TOleView client.
//
```

Listing 17.1. continued

```
void TOlesvrOleView::Paint(TDC& dc, bool erase, TRect& rect)
{
    TOlesvrApp* theApp = TYPESAFE_DOWNCAST(GetApplication(), TOlesvrApp);
    if (theApp) {
        // Only paint if we're printing and we have something to paint,
        // otherwise do nothing.
        //
        if (theApp->Printing && theApp->Printer && !rect.IsEmpty()) {
            // Use pageSize to get the size of the window to render into.
            // For a Window it's the client area,
            // for a printer it's the printer DC dimensions and for print preview
            // it's the layout window.
            //
            TSize   pageSize(rect.right - rect.left, rect.bottom - rect.top);

            TPrintDialog::TData& printerData = theApp->Printer->GetSetup();

            // Compute the number of pages to print.
            //
            printerData.MinPage = 1;
            printerData.MaxPage = 1;

            TOcView*  ocView = GetOcView();

            // Default TOcPart painting
            //
            TRect clientRect = GetClientRect();
            TRect logicalRect = clientRect +(TSize&)ocView->GetOrigin();
              for (TOcPartCollectionIter i(GetOcDoc()->GetParts()); i; i++) {
                TOcPart& p = *i.Current();
                if (p.IsVisible(logicalRect)) {
                  TRect r = p.GetRect();
                  r -= ocView->GetOrigin();
                  p.Draw(dc, r, clientRect);   // Draw the embedded object.
                }
              }

            // INSERT>> Special printing code goes here.

        }
        else {
            TOleView::Paint(dc, erase, rect);

            // INSERT>> Normal painting code goes here.

        }
        dc.TextOut(0, 30, "Olesvr OLE Server");
    }
}


void TOlesvrOleView::EvGetMinMaxInfo(MINMAXINFO far& minmaxinfo)
{
    TOlesvrApp* theApp = TYPESAFE_DOWNCAST(GetApplication(), TOlesvrApp);
    if (theApp) {
        if (theApp->Printing) {
            minmaxinfo.ptMaxSize = TPoint(32000, 32000);
            minmaxinfo.ptMaxTrackSize = TPoint(32000, 32000);
```

```
      return;
    }
  }
  TOleView::EvGetMinMaxInfo(minmaxinfo);
}


bool TOlesvrOleView::EvOcViewShowTools(TOcToolBarInfo far& tbi)
{
  // Construct & create a control bar for show,
  // destroy our bar for hide
  //
  if (tbi.Show) {
    if (!ToolBar) {
      ToolBar = new TDockableControlBar(this);

      TOlesvrApp* theApp = TYPESAFE_DOWNCAST(GetApplication(), TOlesvrApp);
      CHECK(theApp);

      theApp->CreateGadgets(ToolBar, true);
    }

    ToolBar->Create();
    tbi.HTopTB = (HWND)*ToolBar;
  }
  else {
    if (ToolBar) {
      ToolBar->Destroy();
      delete ToolBar;
      ToolBar = 0;
    }
  }

  return true;
}
```

The main view paint routine is the function

```
void TOlesvrOleView::Paint(TDC& dc, bool erase, TRect& rect)
```

which, supplied by AppExpert, has management code but no actual drawing code.

This brings you to your first decision point—your server must do something! For an easy demonstration, you will program your server to draw a five-pointed star, which represents the server's object data. For simplicity, insert a new function in the file, named OurPaint, which does the actual drawing.

> **TIP**
>
> In general, when modifying automatically generated code files, it's often best to insert entire functions and call them from other generated functions instead of modifying individual statements. This way, if you need to regenerate the application, you can more easily reinsert your modifications.

As explained in Chapter 14, Paint receives three parameters: a TDC object reference, a bool variable that tells whether the client area is to be erased, and a TRect object reference that contains the rectangle of the area in the client area to be redrawn. Insert the OurPaint function from Listing 17.2. If you don't feel like typing, copy the function from file Ourpaint.cpp on this book's CD-ROM. Alternatively, you can insert the following #include statement to import the function during compilation:

```
#include "OurPaint.cpp"
```

Listing 17.2. OurPaint.cpp (Implements TOlesvrOleView:: OurPaint function).

```
//================================================================
// Ourpaint.cpp -- Implements TOlesvrOleView:: OurPaint function
// Copyright (c) 1996 by Tom Swan. All rights reserved.
//================================================================

void TOlesvrOleView::OurPaint(TDC& dc, bool /*erase */, TRect& /*rect*/)
{
  TPoint  Points[10];
  HBRUSH  cBrush;
  int     OldFillMode;
  int     FillMode = ALTERNATE;

  cBrush = CreateSolidBrush(RGB(254, 128, 6));
  TRect Clientrect;

  GetWindow()->GetClientRect(Clientrect);

  Points[0].x = (Clientrect.right + Clientrect.left) / 2;
  Points[0].y = Clientrect.top;
  Points[1].x = Clientrect.right;
  Points[1].y = Clientrect.bottom;
  Points[2].x = Clientrect.left;
  Points[2].y = ((Clientrect.bottom + Clientrect.top) / 3) * 1;
  Points[3].x = Clientrect.right;
  Points[3].y = ((Clientrect.bottom + Clientrect.top) / 3) * 1;
  Points[4].x = Clientrect.left;
  Points[4].y = Clientrect.bottom;
  Points[5] = Points[0];

  dc.SelectObject(cBrush);

  OldFillMode = dc.SetPolyFillMode(FillMode);
  dc.Polygon(Points, 6);
  dc.SetPolyFillMode(OldFillMode);
  dc.RestoreBrush();
  DeleteObject(cBrush);
}
```

You must also add a call to OurPaint in the TOlesvrOleView::Paint function. Listing 17.3 shows this modification in bold.

Listing 17.3. Olsvrolv.cpp (Calls `OurPaint`).

```
    }
    // INSERT>> Special printing code goes here.
  }
  else {
    TOleView::Paint(dc, erase, rect);
    // INSERT>> Normal painting code goes here.
    OurPaint(dc, erase, rect);
  }
  dc.TextOut(0, 30, "Olesvr OLE Server");
  }
}
```

Finally, you need to declare the `OurPaint` function prototype in the `TOlesvrOleView` class found in the Olsvrolv.h header file. Listing 17.4 shows the necessary class modification in bold.

Listing 17.4. Olsvrolv.h (Declares `OurPaint` function).

```
class TOlesvrOleView : public TOleView {
  public:
    TOlesvrOleView(TDocument& doc, TWindow* parent = 0);
    virtual ~TOlesvrOleView();

    void OurPaint(TDC& dc, bool erase, TRect& rect);

  private:
    TDockableControlBar* ToolBar;

//{{TOlesvrOleViewVIRTUAL_BEGIN}}
  public:
    virtual void Paint(TDC& dc, bool erase, TRect& rect);
//{{TOlesvrOleViewVIRTUAL_END}}
//{{TOlesvrOleViewRSP_TBL_BEGIN}}
  protected:
    void EvGetMinMaxInfo(MINMAXINFO far& minmaxinfo);
    bool EvOcViewShowTools(TOcToolBarInfo far& tbi);
//{{TOlesvrOleViewRSP_TBL_END}}
DECLARE_RESPONSE_TABLE(TOlesvrOleView);
};    //{{TOlesvrOleView}}
```

Let's review what you have done:

1. You inserted a function, `OurPaint`, into the Olsvrolv.cpp module.
2. You inserted a call to the `OurPaint` function in the `TOlesvrOleView::Paint` function. Thus whenever the window needs updating, the program calls `OurPaint`.
3. You inserted a declaration for `OurPaint` into the `TOlesvrOleView` class in the Olsvrolv.h header file.

Many modifications you make to other automatically generated source code modules will be similar. Now that you have these necessary elements in place, you should compile the project and try running the program.

> **TIP**
>
> For safety, I usually execute *File/Save all* to write any changed files to disk before compiling with *Project/Make all*.

When you run the program, your lucky star shows up in the window's client area. Figure 17.4 shows Olesvr running at this stage.

Figure 17.4.
A star is born—Olesvr running.

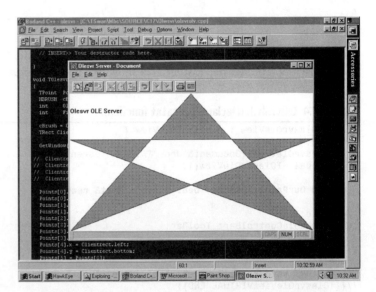

Next, test the Olesvr object by embedding it into a container application. I did this using Microsoft Word 7.0, but any competent OLE container application should work. In the container (Word if you are following along), create a new, blank, document, and select *Insert|Object*. Choose *Olesvr Document Version 1* from the list of available objects. In less than a jiffy, you will see a graphical representation of the server's star. Because the server supports In-Place activation and editing, Olesvr's menu replaces Word's usual menu. This is an automatic, and highly desirable, benefit of using AppExpert. You don't have to add any code to enable In-Place editing in your applications. Neat, huh?

Now click *outside* of the Olesvr object image in the Word document and you will see a number of things happen. First, Word for Windows restores its normal menu. Next, Olesvr's object loses focus, and you will get the normal text cursor. Then a strange thing happens: the star that was so nicely drawn disappears from sight, or depending on your display, the image might be jumbled! What's shooting our star?

TIP

Double-click in the star object image to return to In-Place editing using the Olesvr server application.

This problem demonstrates that it is sometimes necessary to manage the updating of embedded objects in a container. Borland's OCF provides an event handler to take care of this painting of an embedded object. To enable this handler, insert the code from Listing 17.5 into the TOlesvrOleView class in module Olsvrolv.cpp.

Listing 17.5. EV_VIEWPAINT handler.

```
bool TOlesvrOleView::EvOcViewPaint(TOcViewPaint far& vp)
{
  bool result;

  result = TOleView::EvOcViewPaint(vp);

  // INSERT>> Your code here.

  return result;
}
```

The easiest way to insert the EV_VIEWPAINT event handler is to use the IDE's ClassExpert utility. Run it from the *View* menu, and then follow these steps to insert the handler function:

1. Select the TOlesvrOleView class in the left pane of the ClassExpert window.
2. Click on the plus sign to open *Windows Messages* for this class in the right pane. Click on the plus sign to open the subtopic *OLE Messages.*
3. Scroll to the OC_VIEWPAINT macro name, and right-click it to open a popup menu. Select *Add handler* to insert a function for this event, to modify the class's event table, and to declare the necessary function in the class's header file. Notice that a checkmark appears next to OC_VIEWPAINT to indicate that a handler exists for this event.
4. Double-click OC_VIEWPAINT in the right window pane to scroll to its source code in the edit window below. You can then insert any code you need in this handler.

Use similar steps to add event-handlers for other Windows messages, menu-command functions, and notification messages. Browsing through the available functions and macros is also a great way to become familiar with the capabilities of various classes the AppExpert generates.

TIP

Deleting an event handler using ClassExpert is not as easy as adding one. In the right pane of the ClassExpert window, select the handler you want to delete. Right-click the mouse and choose *Delete handler.* Read and close the resulting dialog warning that the handler's source code will not be deleted. Locate that source code, and manually delete its lines from the module. Also remember to delete the function's declaration from its class in the associated header file—you will receive an "unresolved external" error if you forget this step, and the program will not compile until you clean up all traces of the deleted function.

The passed pointer to the TOcViewPaint structure allows your application to access whatever resources are necessary to update the object's client area. The default handler, supplied by OCF, calls the correct paint function based on whether the object is linked or not. The TOleWindow::EvOcViewPaint handler is

```
//
// Ask server to paint itself in the position and dc provided
//
bool
TOleWindow::EvOcViewPaint(TOcViewPaint far& vp)
{
  // paint according to the view paint structure
  //
  TDC dc(vp.DC);
  Pos = *vp.Pos;

  // Paint embedded objects
  //

  bool metafile = dc.GetDeviceCaps(TECHNOLOGY) == DT_METAFILE;
  SetupDC(dc, !metafile);

  if (vp.Linking) {
    PaintLink(dc, true, Pos, *vp.Moniker);
  }
  else if (vp.PaintSelection) {
    PaintSelection(dc, true, Pos);
  }
  else {
    Paint(dc, true, Pos);
    PaintParts(dc, true, Pos, metafile);
  }

  Pos.SetNull;

  return true;
}
```

As this code fragment shows, the TOcViewPaint struct has several members that show the object's status. The TOcViewPaint structure is shown below:

```
struct TOcViewPaint {
// for part adornment painting over part, & painting views
  HDC         DC;
  TRect*      Pos;
  TRect*      Clip;
  TOcAspect   Aspect;
  bool        PaintSelection;  // paint the selection only
  bool        Linking;         // are we doing object linking?
  TString*    Moniker;         // moniker if any
};
```

The TOcViewPaint struct has all the necessary information needed to call the PaintLink, PaintSelection, or Paint. Pay particular attention to the fact that EvOcViewPaint calls TOleWindow::Paint if the TOcViewPaint.Linking and TOcViewPaint.PaintSelection flags are both not set. Remember that TOleWindow::Paint is also called by the supplied Paint function, which is part of your view class.

Of course, Olesvr is a simple program, and there are a number of additional enhancements that you might want to make to create a more finished application:

- Olesvr doesn't properly size its object when it is embedded. It needs to know the size of the area that the embedded object occupies, and then adjust the output to fit this area.

- Olesvr lacks a few usually needed operations. Probably you'll want to set the number of points in the star, the color of the star, the star's outline color, the background, and the polygon fill mode. These activities represent the editing that might be done on an embedded object.

- Olesvr, as a stand-alone application, should implement its file open and save commands. The example in this chapter merely draws an image—a completed program should be able to save that image (or other document data) and load it from a file. A compound file structure would be a good choice for this.

- Olesvr should implement online help, as should all well-written Windows applications.

All in all, Olesvr performs only the bare minimum tasks to qualify as an OLE server application. Figure 17.5 shows an Olesvr object starring in its role as an embedded object in a Word document file (actually, this is the file I am editing as I write these words—kind of a mirror image effect).

Figure 17.5.

An Olesvr object embedded in a Word document.

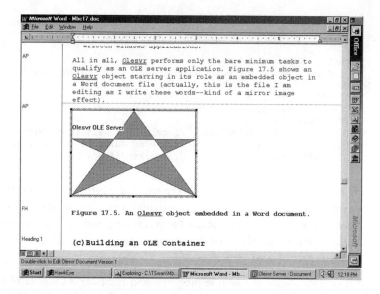

Building an OLE Container

The second application that you build in this chapter is an OLE container. The container is a complete application, and you can use it to embed most any OLE object, including the sample graphical star object in this chapter's server program. Creating a container is by far the easier of the two projects.

Creating a new container is simple. First, start AppExpert from the IDE. Select a new directory and name for your project. I've placed my project in the directory C17\olecntr, and I named the project Olecntr. Here are the steps I followed:

1. Start AppExpert. Change to your project directory and enter a project name. As I mentioned, I used Olecntr for both items.

2. Select OK to close the project directory and filename dialog. You next see the *AppExpert Application Generation Options* dialog. You need to select several options.

3. First, select the *Application* topic, and enable the *SDI (Single document interface)* radio button. This change keeps with Microsoft's intention to make Windows more document oriented, although you can certainly create multiple-document containers using the *MDI* setting.

4. Next, select *Application: OLE 2 Options.* Enable the radio button labeled *Application is an OLE 2 and OCX container.*

5. Optionally fill in the *Application: Admin Options* topic as you did for this chapter's server demonstration, Olesvr. None of these items is required.

6. Once the above modifications have been made, select the *Generate* button. AppExpert prompts you to confirm that you intend to build this project. Answer Yes to create the project and its various and sundry files. Figure 17.6 shows the final Olecntr project window.

Figure 17.6.

The Olecntr project window.

It's a good idea to compile and test the generated application before you make any changes to it, just in case something went wrong or you made any errors in your option selections. Also, compiling the project ahead of time creates binary symbol files, which speed future compilations when you use the *Project\Make all* (F9) command.

You can run the generated container as is—it's a complete application. Do that now, and open a new document with *File\New*. Of course, this isn't a real document, but you can use the resulting blank window to insert objects from OLE servers. For example, from the *Edit* menu select *Insert Object*. This displays the OLE *Insert Object* dialog shown in Figure 17.7.

When you have selected an OLE object (I used Olesvr Document Version 1), choose the OK button to insert it into the container's document. Figure 17.8 shows the final result.

As this demonstration shows, AppExpert creates an OLE container application with all necessary code for accepting an OLE object. Try embedding some other objects such as an Excel worksheet, or a Word paragraph. The automatically generated code implements a complete *Edit* menu, with the usual commands including those related specifically for OLE: *Paste Special, Paste Link, Insert Object, Insert Control, Links, Object,* and *Show Objects*.

603

Figure 17.7.
Olecntr and the OLE Insert Object dialog.

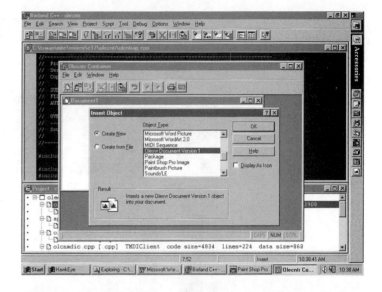

Figure 17.8.
Olecntr with an Olesvr object embedded.

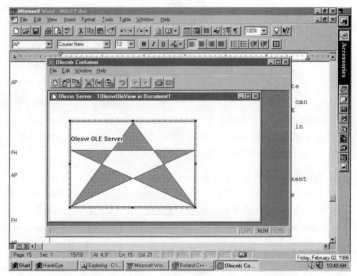

Summary

- The Olesvr application shows what AppExpert creates for you when you develop an OLE server application.

- With OLE server applications, you must add the code to draw the application's object, both in the application when it is running, and as a metafile for the container to render when the object is not active.

- AppExpert creates OLE container applications that are generally (from the viewpoint of OLE) complete. You must add whatever code the application needs to perform its tasks, however.

V

Developer's Toolbox

CHAPTER

18

Managing Projects

The Borland C++ Project Manager is light years ahead of earlier IDE project managers. Originally introduced in Turbo C, a *project* was simply a list of filenames for programs composed of more than one module. Starting with Borland C++ versions 4.0 and 4.5, projects have evolved into sophisticated, hierarchical databases that fully describe application modules and their interrelationships.

This chapter introduces the Borland C++ 5.0 IDE's Project Manager and presents hands-on tutorials you can use to learn its capabilities. The Project Manager is an advanced feature for creating multi-module programs. You can use it to create simple single-file programs (like those in this book's C++ tutorial chapters), but it is most valuable in organizing the many modules that go into producing a typical major software application.

The Project Window

When you open a project file, which ends with the filename extension .ide, you see the project's components, called *nodes,* in the Project window (see Figure 18.1). To follow along, use *File|Open* to open Chapter 14's Sketch.ide project file in the C14\Sketch directory.

Figure 18.1.
The Project window showing the Sketch.ide project.

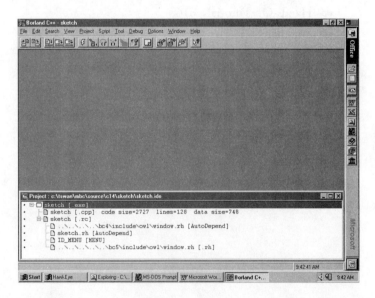

Project nodes are indented to show their dependencies. Each node refers to one file or a resource identifier. In Figure 18.1, for example, the Sketch.exe node (the project's target) depends on the three other nodes, Sketch.cpp, Sketch.rc, and Sketch.def. (Refer to Chapter 14 for descriptions of these files.)

Click a plus sign next to a node to display the other nodes on which it depends. Click a minus sign to collapse a node, and to reduce display clutter. If no plus or minus sign marks a node, it's a leaf, meaning it has no further subnodes.

The Project Manager recognizes drag-and-drop file handling. To add a new node to a project, you can drag its filename from the Windows 95 Explorer to the Project window. Or, you can open a floating popup menu (click the right mouse button) and select *Add node.* Press Del to delete a node. You can also drag nodes to new positions in the Project window, but be careful not to alter the indentation levels of specific nodes.

To move a node to the outer level, drag it to the outermost node, usually ending in the filename extension .exe.

The Project Manager has numerous commands and capabilities, some of which you may never need, depending on the types of programs you write. For example, if you need to create many different target code files, including 16- and 32-bit applications, you can use Style Sheets and Source Pools to organize your program's modules. If, however, you target only a specific operating environment—Windows or DOS, for instance—you may not need these advanced features.

Using Projects

Projects are easy to use. Simply open any .ide project file with the *File|Open* command. Then, to compile and run the program, you can either click on the lightning bolt icon on the IDE's toolbar or press Ctrl+F9. You can also use other toolbar buttons and commands in the *Project* menu to compile projects.

Alternatively, you can also compile the project by using commands in the *Debug* menu. For example, you can press F8 or F7 to compile and begin single stepping a program.

For the projects in this book, it's probably easiest to open their .ide project files and press Ctrl+F9 to compile and run programs. For your own projects, however, and especially those composed of many different files, you may want to use one of two other commands in the *Project* menu. These are as follows:

- *Project\Make all*—Use this command to compile only the minimum number of files necessary. If, for example, a project has three .cpp files and you change only one of them, this command compiles only the changed file to re-create the .exe code file. Usually, this saves time by not recompiling modules that are already up to date.

- *Project\Build all*—Use this command to compile all nodes in a project. If a project has three .cpp files and you change only one of them, this command compiles all three files. Developers usually use this command to generate a finished code file after debugging a new application. You should also use this command when changing a program's target—building an *EasyWin* version of a program, for example, that you previously compiled for DOS.

Project Files

A project file, which ends with .ide, lists the project's nodes and also determines their dependencies. The project file stores filenames, node options, compiler settings, and various other information required to build the project's target. Usually, the target is a code file ending with .exe, but it could be any desired file—a help file, for example, or a function library.

In Borland C++ 3.0 and 3.1 for Windows, project files ended with the filename extension .prj. You may open these older project files with the current IDE, which creates an updated .ide file for the project. However, you cannot create old-style .prj files.

Project Manager

Up to now, I've used the term *compile* to refer to the process of translating a program's text file into a finished executable code file. Actually, compiling is just one part of a complex process of creating an executable program. Each module of a C or C++ program, for example, is first compiled to produce raw object code, stored in files ending with the extension .obj. Those files are then combined by a linker to create the final .exe file.

All of these programs—compilers and linkers—are generally known as *translators.* A compiler translates a text file into raw object code. A linker translates object code files (and also library files containing various runtime functions) into executable code files. A help compiler translates text files into a Windows help file. A resource compiler translates a script into Windows resources (menus, dialogs, and so on).

In a complex project, many different translators might be needed to create a finished program. The Project Manager's main job is to associate each node in a project with a specific translator, which in turn refers to a program on disk (a resource compiler, for example), or a built-in capability in the IDE (the integrated C++ compiler, for instance).

You can display the translators for project nodes. To do that, select *Options\Environment,* choose the *Project View* topic, and enable the *Build translator* check box. Click OK to close the options dialog. This adds the translator name to each project node (see Figure 18.2). For example, in the figure, *LinkTarget* is Sketch.exe's translator. *CppCompile* is Sketch.cpp's translator. The other nodes also have translators. Each translator tells the Project Manager how to process a node.

Figure 18.2.

The Sketch.ide project with Build translators displayed.

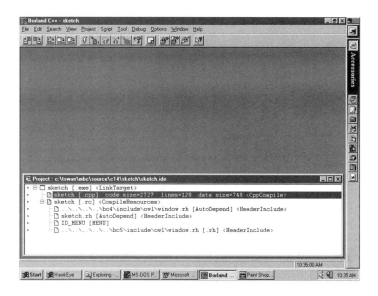

Project-Window Nodes

You are responsible for creating the files associated with many nodes in most projects. For example, a node associated with a file with the extension .cpp is a source code text file that you can create with the IDE's text editor. The fact that a project refers to a node doesn't ensure that the associated file will be created automatically.

Other nodes refer to existing files provided with Borland C++. For example, a node might refer to the header file Windows.h, containing various declarations needed by Windows programs.

613

Figure 18.3.

Types of project nodes.

Still other nodes are created by translators. An object-code node ending with the filename extension .obj, for example, is created by a compiler-translator.

Each node in a Project window is one of the following four types, illustrated by the sample project in Figure 18.3. To follow along, select all *Project View* check boxes using the *Options\Environment* command, including *Show runtime nodes* and *Show project node.*

Project Nodes

The *project node* is the root of the Project window's tree display and represents the entire project. Each project can have only one project node. In Figure 18.3, the project node is shown on the first line, identified as the file Sketch.ide.

Target Nodes

A *target node* represents a node that a translator creates. In most projects, there's only one target node, usually the program's .exe code file. A target node can also be a dynamic link library (.dll), an object code file (.obj), a help file (.hlp), or any other target file created by a translator.

Projects may have multiple target nodes. You can, for example, create 16- and 32-bit target code files for a Windows application. Use the *Project\New target* command to add a new target node to a project.

The project in Figure 18.3 has one target node—the program's executable code file, Sketch.exe, shown indented on the second line. Notice that its translator is *LinkTarget*, which by default calls on Turbo Linker—either Tlink.exe or Tlink32.exe depending on the type of target—to link the program's object-code modules and libraries and create the finished executable code file.

Common Nodes

A *common node* (Borland's documentation simply calls it a *node*) is any file on which a target node depends. The most typical common node is a .c or .cpp text file that contains a program's statements in text form. A translator processes a common node to create an output target.

Figure 18.3 shows two common nodes for the Sketch project: Sketch.cpp and Sketch.rc. If this were a 16-bit application, the project would also refer to the linker definition file, Sketch.def. Each of these common nodes is processed by a different translator (listed in brackets at the end of each line) to create the target node that depends on these files. For example, a .cpp file is translated by *CppCompile*, which normally refers to the IDE's C++ compiler. A resource script file ending in .rc is translated by *CompileResources*, which calls on the IDE's built-in resource compiler.

Runtime Nodes

A *runtime node* is an existing file supplied by Borland or another vendor. Usually, runtime nodes are one of two types: .lib files containing multiple object-code modules, or .obj files containing a single object-code module.

Like common nodes, runtime nodes are typically associated with a target node. A runtime-node translator combines the node with other components to create the target node.

There are five runtime nodes in the Sketch project shown in Figure 18.3. These are C0w32.obj, Owlwfi.lib, bidsfi.lib, import32.lib, and cw32i.lib, all of which are included with Borland C++. To create the Sketch.exe target node, the IDE combines these runtime-node files with other nodes, in this example using the *LinkTarget* translator.

Node Viewers

A node may be associated with one or more *node viewers.* The most common node viewer is the text editor built into the IDE. When you double-click a common node, or when you highlight the node and press Enter, the IDE passes the node's filename to the default viewer for this type of node.

Nodes may be associated with external viewers. Resource script files, for example, which end with the filename extension .rc, may specify an external resource editor such as Resource Workshop (RW) as the default node viewer. Borland C++ 5.0 now includes an integrated resource editor in the IDE, and no longer provides the stand-alone RW.

Resource scripts are plain ASCII text files, and they can also be viewed in the IDE's text editor, an example of an internal viewer. Use the SpeedMenu's *View* command to select between a script's multiple node viewers, or for other nodes that have more than one viewer. For example, highlight Sketch.rc, click the right mouse button, and select *View|Text Edit* to open the file in a text editor window.

Executable code files (usually ending in .exe) can have several viewers. Highlight any executable target file (Sketch.exe, for example) and use the *View* command in the SpeedMenu to run, debug, or debug with Turbo Debugger. These actions provide different views of an executable code file.

Runtime nodes have no viewers. A runtime node such as an object-code file is a binary file, which you cannot view or edit.

Hands-On Tutorials

The Borland C++ on-line and printed documentation lists all Project Manager commands and features. To supplement that information and the preceding introduction, following are several hands-on tutorials that walk you through most Project Manager operations.

Creating a New Project

When you start a new program that you know requires more than one file, the first step is to create a project for that program. (You may create a project file for a single-file program, but it's usually not necessary to do so.) Depending on the type of project, the Project Manager automatically inserts one or more nodes into the project file. You can modify, add to, and delete a project's nodes at any time.

Follow these steps to create a new project for a fictitious program (you don't actually write the program):

1. Use the Windows 95 Explorer to create a new directory for the project files. I'll name it C:\pro, but you can use a different drive and directory. After completing the tutorials in this chapter, you may remove this directory and its files.

2. Select *File|Close project* to close a project window if one is currently open. Also close any other open windows. Always start new projects with a clean slate.

3. Select *File|New,* and choose *Project* from the submenu. This displays the *New Target* dialog box—which is the same as the Target Expert dialog—in Figure 18.4.

4. Click the *Browse* button to open a file dialog, which you can use to change to the C:\pro directory. Enter the project's filename, newproj.ide (or another), and click *OK* or press Enter to close the file dialog. (You can also enter a path and filename directly into the *New Target* dialog, but I find it easier to use the *Browse* button to name a project.) You do not have to enter the .ide filename extension.

5. The project's node and target names do not have to be the same, but they usually are. After entering a path and filename, also enter the project node name under *Target Name.* This will automatically be newproj, but you could specify a different name. (In past Borland C++ versions, you had to enter this name for every new project.)

6. Note that the lower part of the *New Target* dialog resembles the *TargetExpert* dialog you've seen before. You next select the project's target type, platform, and model. You

also select any runtime libraries to be used with the project. For example, set *Target Type* to *Application, Platform* to *Win32,* and *Target Model* to *GUI.* As you make your selections, notice that the default libraries change in the panels to the right. Various targets require different library sets.

7. Also click the *Advanced* button to show the kinds of common nodes that are automatically inserted into the project. Try this button for different target types. You can always insert and delete nodes later, so it's not too important to insert the correct nodes automatically at this stage. (I always use the defaults and make adjustments later.)

8. Make your display resemble Figure 18.4 and select the *OK* button to close the dialog.

9. You now see the *Project* window shown in Figure 18.5. The nodes listed in the project don't yet exist—you still have to create the program's .cpp file, for example. But the new project is ready for use.

10. Save the project by selecting *File|Save.* This creates several files in the current directory, including Newproj.dsw (the IDE's desktop configuration), Newproj.ide (the project file), and Newproj.obr (browser information). These files are not created until you close the project window.

Figure 18.4.
New Target dialog for a new project file.

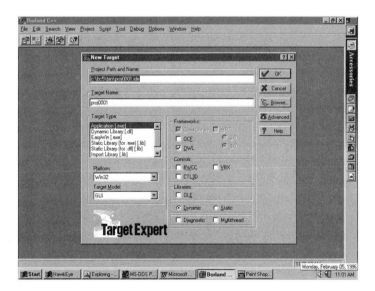

Creating a Multiple-Target Project

Many Windows developers need to create 16- and 32-bit versions of their applications—though Windows 95 is rapidly gaining popularity, there is still a healthy market for 16-bit Windows 3.1 applications. The 16-bit versions, of course, run under all versions of Windows. The 32-bit versions also can run under Windows 3.*x* with the help of Win32s, or as native processes under Windows 95 and Windows NT.

617

Figure 18.5.

Project window with a new project's nodes.

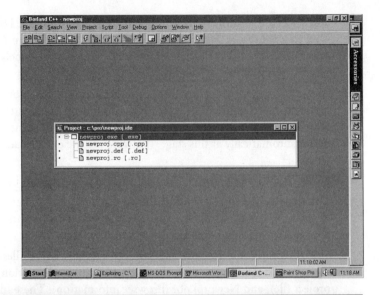

Win32s is a subset of the full Win32 operating system, the collective name for Windows 95 and Windows NT. Win32s adds extensions to Windows 3.x that permit it to run 32-bit applications, but of course, not as well as a true 32-bit operating system.

Follow these steps to create 16- and 32-bit versions of the sample Sketch demonstration program:

1. Copy the SKETCH directory and *only* the following files to another, new directory. I'll name this directory C:\sk2, but you can use a different drive and name. Copy the files Sketch.cpp, Sketch.ide, Sketch.rc, and Sketch.rh.

2. Create two subdirectories in C:\sk2 named Bin16 and Bin32. The 16- and 32-bit Sketch.exe and other target code files will be generated in those directories.

3. In the IDE, use *File|Open* to change to the C:\sk2 directory and open the Sketch.ide project file. (If you were creating a new multi-target project, you would use the *File|New* command and select *Project* from the submenu.) If the project window is not visible, select *View|Project*.

4. Highlight the target node, Sketch.exe, in the Project window. Click the right mouse button to open a floating popup menu, and then select *Edit local options*. This displays the *Project Options* dialog in Figure 18.6. It's the same dialog you get when using the *Options|Project* command, but because you opened it for a target node, any changes you make apply only to that node.

Figure 18.6.

Project Options dialog for a local target node.

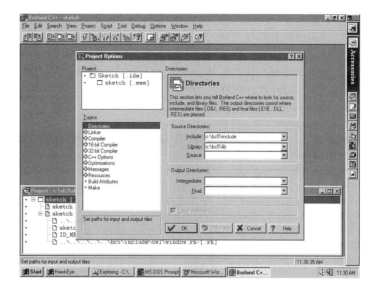

5. Under *Output Directories,* enter Bin32 in the two fields labeled *Intermediate* and *Final.* The intermediate directory holds object code files (usually of type .obj); the final directory holds the target code file (usually of type .exe). You can specify the same or different directories for each type of output file.

6. Select the *OK* button to close the *Project Options* dialog. This completes the creation of the 32-bit target node, the default for the Sketch application.

7. To create a second, 16-bit target for this same program, highlight Sketch.exe in the project window and select the *Project|New target* command. Enter Sketch (do *not* enter a filename extension) into the input dialog *Name* field, and press Enter to open the *New Target* dialog. (This is the same *Target Expert* dialog shown in Figure 18.4.) Set the target type to *Application,* the platform to *Windows 3.x (16),* and the target model to *Large.* Click OK or press Enter to close and accept the new target node.

8. Your project window should now show two Sketch.exe target nodes (see Figure 18.7).

9. Highlight the second Sketch.exe target node, click the right mouse button to open a floating popup menu, and select the *Edit local options* command. Enter the *Intermediate* and *Final* output directory path names as you did before, but this time specify Bin16 for both names. Close the dialog by selecting the OK button.

10. Delete the Sketch.def node from the 16-bit target. In practice, you'll probably use a linker definition file for 16-bit applications; however, for this demonstration, you can use the default file, which the linker automatically includes. Ignore the *No module definition file* warning you receive in the next step.

11. Use *Project\Build all* to compile and link both application targets. (You can also use *Project\Make all*.) This creates two separate Sketch.exe code files, one in the Bin16 and the other in the Bin32 subdirectories. The two program versions are functionally identical, but the one in Bin32 requires Windows 95 or Windows NT (or an installed Win32s subset under Windows 3.1). The version in Bin16 runs under all versions of Windows, including Windows 3.1.

Figure 18.7.

The Sketch.ide project window with 16- and 32-bit target nodes.

> **NOTE**
>
> The preceding tutorial demonstrates how you can create 16- and 32-bit code files using a single set of source code files. You write the code only once. The Project Manager creates both code targets using the same program files. Of course, this also doubles the compilation time, so don't create 16- and 32-bit code files unless you really need to do that!

Creating a Make File from a Project

A Make file is a script that you feed to the Make utility, supplied with Borland C++, to compile and link a program from the DOS prompt. You can easily create a Make file from any project.

Open the .ide project file (the original Sketch.ide file in Chapter 14 will do just fine) and select *Project\Generate makefile*. After a moment or two, you see the Make file's text in an editor window, labeled Sketch.mak. Save this text to the default filename, which you can rename Makefile with no filename extension. Or, use the *File\Save as* command to save Sketch.mak as Makefile. (When you run Make, it looks for a file by that name; however, you can use any filename along with Make's -f command-line option.)

To compile the program using the generated Make file, switch to a DOS prompt and enter this command if you saved the file to Sketch.mak:

```
make -fsketch.mak
```

Or, if you saved the file as Makefile, just enter:

```
make
```

> **NOTE**
>
> Multi-target projects, such as the copy of the Sketch application you made in the preceding tutorial, may not generate correct Make files. If you try to create a Make file for a multi-target application, the IDE warns you that the resulting Make file may not work correctly.

Using the Project Window's SpeedMenu

For practice, highlight each of the nodes in the project window for the Sketch.ide project. Click the right mouse button to bring up a SpeedMenu of commands you can issue for each node. The commands differ for nodes of various types.

You can view, add, delete, make, and build target nodes. For example, after modifying a program module, you can run it through the compiler to check for syntax errors. Rather than translate every node in the project, it is often faster to make or build individual nodes as you work on them.

The lower part of a node's SpeedMenu provides additional commands for editing node properties. You can also select *TargetExpert* to modify a target node—changing it from a 16- to a 32-bit code file, for example, or changing a DOS node to an *EasyWin* application. There are three ways to edit an individual node's properties. Try each of these SpeedMenu commands for the Sketch.cpp common node:

- *Edit node attributes*—Use this command to modify the node's name, and to enter an optional description for display in the Project window. You can also use this command to select a style sheet of default options for this node, and you can change the translator used to build the node's target. (Style sheets are covered in the next section.) Use this command also to change the node type (from .c to .cpp, for example, which ensures a C++ compilation), and to exclude debugging information on a node-by-node basis, which can be useful for conserving memory in very large programs with symbol tables that outstrip Turbo Debugger's capacity.

- *Edit local options*—Use this command to override global project options such as directory settings, compiler options, optimizations, and a host of other goodies. Any changes you make with this command apply only to the selected node. You might, for example, use this command to compile two modules with a different set of optimizations. As the preceding multi-target tutorial demonstrates, you can also specify destination directories for files that a specific translator creates. This can really help organize a large software project by storing object-code files in one directory, executable files in another, and so on.

- *View options hierarchy*—Use this command to generate a report of the options, settings, and properties for each of a project's nodes. You also can modify any listed property by double-clicking it. Although you select this command for a specific node, the resulting dialog provides a view of the entire project from which you can select other nodes. Figure 18.8 shows a sample report for the Sketch.cpp common node.

Figure 18.8.

Options hierarchy dialog for the multi-target Sketch.ide project.

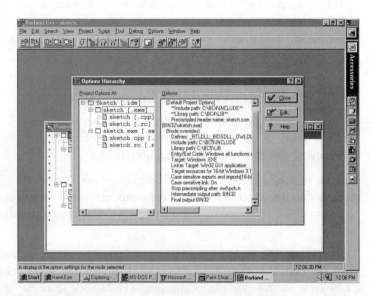

At first, the information in the *Options Hierarchy* dialog may seem overwhelmingly complex. As you become more familiar with Borland C++ options, however, you'll find this dialog useful for quickly checking the properties of individual nodes, and for modifying node options and other properties. For example, select the 16-bit target file, and double-click the Memory model entry in the *Options Hierarchy* dialog. This takes you directly to that setting in the local options page, a faster way of finding this option than using the *Edit local options* command and hunting for the option you want to change.

Using Style Sheets

A *style sheet,* defined as a collection of build options, is similar to a word processor template, which might specify fonts, headers, and other items for certain kinds of documents. To write a personal letter, for example, you select a LETTER template. Similarly, to generate a certain type of program in the IDE, you can select a style sheet of default options. You can also create your own style sheets.

A style sheet provides a starting place for a project's options. You can further modify those options for the project's nodes. Any such changes override the options that the style sheet provides.

Style sheets are easy to use. For practice, open the Sketch.ide project in the temporary C:\sk2 directory (or, if you didn't create that directory, do so now and copy to it the original Sketch files—Sketch.cpp, Sketch.ide, Sketch.rc, and Sketch.rh.) Follow these steps:

1. Select the *Options\Environment* command, and highlight the *Project View* topic. Enable the *Style sheet* check box to view assigned style sheets in the Project window. Close the dialog by clicking *OK* or pressing Enter.

2. To select a style sheet for an output node, highlight one of the Sketch.exe nodes in the Project window, and click the right mouse button to open a SpeedMenu. Select the *Edit node attributes* command. This displays the dialog in Figure 18.9.

Figure 18.9.

Node Attributes dialog for Sketch.exe.

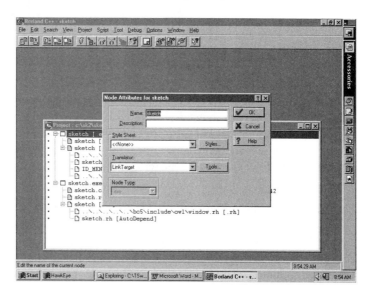

3. Use the dialog's *Style Sheet* list box to select the *Optimized (Speed)* style sheet. Attaching this style sheet to the target code file selects various options that, in theory at least, result in a faster-running program.

4. Click *OK* or press Enter to close the dialog and accept the change to this node. You now see the attached style sheet name in the Project window next to the selected Sketch.exe target.

You can create your own style sheets with any set of options you need. To do that, use the *Options|Style Sheets* command, which displays the dialog in Figure 18.10. You can also access this dialog while editing a node's attributes as just described—click the *Styles* button next to the *Style Sheet* list box (refer back to Figure 18.9).

Figure 18.10.
The Style Sheets dialog.

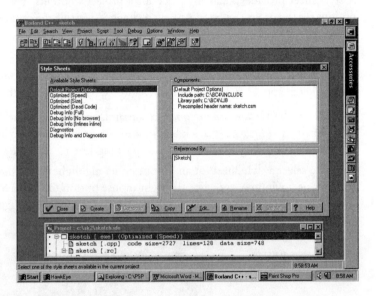

The Style Sheets dialog shows three main pieces of information. At left are the names of available style sheets (the ones shown in Figure 18.10 are provided with Borland C++). The components at top right list in text form the attributes, options, and settings in the selected style sheet. (These settings are in the same form as shown by the *Options Hierarchy* dialog.) At lower right are any nodes that reference the selected style sheet—Sketch.exe, for example, in Figure 18.10.

Use the buttons at the bottom of the dialog to copy, edit, create, rename, and delete style sheets. To preserve default settings, it's a good idea to copy an existing style sheet and modify the copy. Although there may seem to be a lot of commands here, they are mostly intuitive. Selecting the *Edit* button, for example, displays the same options dialogs you have used for other purposes. Choose the options you want to include in this style. You can then attach your style sheet to a project node.

Using Source Pools

A *source pool,* defined as a collection of nodes, simplifies the creation of multi-target projects. In the Sketch project, for instance, the 16- and 32-bit target code files each depend on the same two common nodes, Sketch.cpp and Sketch.rc (refer back to Figure 18.7). This is inconvenient because it requires you to make changes in two places. For example, to add another module to the project, you would have to add the same new node under both target code files.

An easier method that eliminates duplicate nodes is to create a source pool of common nodes. The source pool specifies the common nodes shared by multiple code files. You then use the source pool in place of actual nodes for each target. Any changes to the source pool—adding a new common node, for example—are automatically reflected in all other targets that refer to the source pool. This is similar to the way you use constants in programs. To change a constant, you modify its declared value and recompile. Similarly, to add, subtract, or modify nodes in a multi-target project, you can edit the source pool rather than change multiple references in each node that uses the pool.

Use the following steps to create a source pool named *Sketch pool* for the Sketch project.

> **NOTE**
>
> You might want to make a backup copy of the files in the C:\sk2 directory until you are familiar with the commands in this tutorial. The steps may seem a bit confusing the first time you try them.

1. Open the Sketch.ide project in the C:\sk2 directory.
2. Expand or maximize the Project window so you can see all of its nodes. The window should look similar to Figure 18.11.
3. Select *Project\New target.* Enter *Sketch pool* into the *Target Name* input box, and select *SourcePool* under *Target Type* (see Figure 18.12). Click *OK* or press Enter to accept the new target. This creates the source pool node, which is added after the last entry in the Project window. The following line now appears at the bottom of the window:

   ```
   Sketch pool [SourcePool]
   ```
4. You next insert filenames into the source pool node. Highlight *Sketch pool* in the Project window, and press the Insert key to bring up the *Add to Project List* dialog, a standard file-selection dialog box. You can also use the SpeedMenu's *Add node* command to open this dialog.
5. Change the file filter to *.* (type that and press Enter, or select *All files* from the *Files of Type* control). This displays all files in the current directory.

Figure 18.11.

The Sketch project before adding a source pool node.

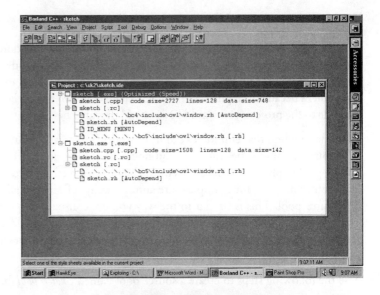

Figure 18.12.

Use the Add Target dialog to create a source pool node.

6. Hold down the Ctrl key while using the mouse to select the two files, Sketch.cpp and Sketch.rc. You can always add and delete from this list later. If you make a mistake, use the Del key to delete the source pool's listed files from the Project window, or highlight the source pool node and press Ins to add other filenames.

7. Click *Open* or press Enter to close the file-selection dialog and accept your selected filenames. The files now appear under the source pool node in the Project window. This completes the creation of the source pool.

8. Next, make a *reference copy* of the source pool under each of the project's target nodes, both named Sketch.exe. Perform these next steps carefully—it's easy (perhaps too easy) to drag nodes from one level to another, and like Humpty Dumpty, a scrambled project file is difficult to put back together again. This is a good time to make a backup copy of the IDE project. (If you do that, close the project, make the copy, and reopen Sketch.ide before continuing.)

9. Highlight the source pool node, *Sketch pool.* Press and hold down the Ctrl key; then using the mouse, drag *Sketch pool* to each of the two target nodes, both named Sketch.exe, and release the mouse button and key. You must click and drag the *Sketch*

pool node *name,* not its icon. *Warning: After each click and drag operation, release and press Ctrl before clicking and dragging again!* If you make a mistake here, it is very difficult to recover—evidence that this aspect of the IDE's Project Manager could stand some additional design work (and an undo command, which is not available). Read the following tip before attempting to click and drag source pool nodes.

TIP

You must press and hold down Ctrl each time before clicking and dragging to create a reference copy of a node. Be sure that the cursor changes to a reference icon (two dog-eared pages with the one behind shown as a dotted outline). If you see a different symbol, move the mouse away from any project node until it changes to a circle with a line through it (the universal symbol for "cancel" or "not"). Release the mouse and key and try again. Also note that previous versions of Borland C++ used the Alt key for this operation.

---

10. You should now see the referenced source pool under each target node. Because the source pool specifies the common nodes shared by each target, you can delete the duplicated actual nodes—they are redundant. Hold down the Ctrl key while you select the two original nodes (Sketch.cpp and Sketch.rc). Press Del to delete these duplicated nodes.

11. Finally, click the plus signs next to each of the two referenced copies of *Sketch pool* under both Sketch.exe nodes. This opens the source pool node trees. Figure 18.13 shows the final Project window.

Figure 18.13.
The Sketch project after adding a source pool node.

If this were a real project, you could now add new modules, change filenames, and make other changes to the source pool's nodes. Those and other changes are automatically reflected in all targets that refer to the source pool.

> **NOTE**
>
> Unlike other nodes, a source pool is never translated. Source pools merely house nodes under one roof, making it easier for multiple targets to refer to shared files, and eliminating duplicated nodes throughout the project.

Summary

- A project is a sophisticated, hierarchical database that fully describes a program's components and their interrelationships. A project file ends with the filename extension .ide.

- In the Borland C++ IDE, the Project window lists the project's components, called nodes.

- Each node in a project is associated with a translator. When you instruct the IDE to *Make* or *Build* a project, the Project Manager passes node filenames to their associated translators.

- A project node represents the entire project. A target node is a node that a translator creates, usually a code file (.exe) or a dynamic link library (.dll). A common node is one on which a target node depends—a .cpp or .c source-code file, for example. A runtime node refers to an existing, binary file such as a function library (.lib) or object-code (.obj) file supplied with Borland C++ (or from another vendor).

- All nodes except runtime nodes may have one or more associated viewers that you can use to view and edit a node's contents.

- A style sheet lists a collection of build options, resembling a template in a word processor. Using style sheets, you can quickly select different sets of options for any node.

- A source pool lists a collection of nodes. You can list multiple common nodes (filenames) under a source pool, and then reference-copy the pool to multiple target nodes that depend on the pool's files. This eliminates duplicate nodes throughout a project with multiple targets that share common files. To create a reference copy of a source-pool node, click and drag its name while holding down the Ctrl key.

19

Mixing C++ and Assembly Language

Despite advances in high-level languages such as C and C++, assembly language continues to play an important role in computer programming. Only with assembly language can a programmer communicate with a computer on its own level—through the language of the processor, often called *machine language* or *machine code.*

Most compiled Borland C++ programs run well enough straight from the compiler; they don't need any help from assembly language. There are times, however, when a sprinkling of low-level code can improve a high-level C++ application. Assembly language can help you to

- Optimize selected critical statements, those on which a program depends most heavily.
- Access hardware at the bit level.
- Implement interrupt service routines (ISRs).

These suggestions are not the exclusive domain of assembly language but are areas where a little native machine code often comes in handy. Borland C++ offers you three ways to use assembly language with C++ programs:

- You can compile a program to an assembly language file.
- You can insert inline asm statements into a program's text.
- You can write external modules assembled by Turbo Assembler (Tasm).

This chapter examines these choices and shows examples of each. Turbo Assembler is available from Borland as a separate purchase.

Function Anatomies

When using assembly language, you take over the compiler's usual task of translating C and C++ statements into machine code. By assuming the role of compiler, you can gain a great deal of control over the final results, but you must accept a tremendous responsibility. Writing assembly language programs is like cooking with atoms and molecules instead of eggs and flour. An assembly language programmer is a kind of software chef. You can mix processor instructions in whatever way you wish, but it's up to you to create a tasty dish.

> **NOTE**
>
> This chapter assumes you are familiar with 80x86 assembly language mnemonics, general purpose registers, segment registers, the stack pointer, bits, bytes, and other low-level concerns. If you are lost already, you might need to study an assembly language tutorial such as my book, *Mastering Turbo Assembler, Second Edition,* and come back to this chapter another time.

Compiling to Assembly Language

Before jumping into your own assembly language functions, it's helpful to look at the code Borland C++ generates. You can also use this method to examine the compiler's output, whether for curiosity's sake or to investigate wayward statements on their most fundamental levels.

Normally, the compiler converts statements directly into processor instructions. Using option -B with the command-line compiler translates a program into an assembly language text file. For a program named Myprog.cpp, the command

```
bcc -B myprog
```

creates Myprog.asm with the compiled output in assembly language form. After compiling, BCC runs Tasm.exe (if installed on a system path) to assemble Myprog.asm into object code, after which it deletes Myprog.asm.

> **NOTE**
>
> I used Bcc.exe for many of this chapter's examples, but you can also use the 32-bit Bcc32.exe compiler if you wish.

You can also insert the line

```
#pragma inline
```

in a program module to achieve the same result. (The #pragma directive gives a private command such as inline to the compiler.)

In the past, the only reason to use the -B option was to assemble inline assembly language statements inserted directly into a C or C++ program. Today, the Borland C++ command-line compiler and the IDE have their own built-in assemblers, which makes -B obsolete except for compiling older programs that use this feature. You can also use -B with -Ename, where name identifies an alternate assembler such as the Microsoft Macro Assembler (Masm).

A related and potentially more valuable option, -S, also generates assembly language output, but does not run Tasm and does not delete the created .asm file. Examining the instructions in this file is a great way to learn how the compiler converts high-level statements to low-level processor code. You can also modify the assembly language text before assembling, perhaps to experiment with a low-level optimization. For a program file, Myprog.cpp, type the command

```
bcc -S myprog
```

to create and retain Myprog.asm. You can edit or examine this file, and then with Tasm.exe in the current path (it's usually stored in C:\tasm\bin, or you can install it in C:\bc5\bin), finish compiling with the command

```
bcc myprog.asm
```

This calls Tasm to assemble the program, and then calls Turbo Linker (Tlink) to link the resulting object code to the appropriate library files, which contain startup and exit code, and also any external references—such as the output stream statement in this example. On screen, you see messages like these:

```
Borland C++ 5.0 Copyright (c) 1987, 1996 Borland International
voidf.asm:
Turbo Assembler  Version 5.0  Copyright (c) 1988, 1996 Borland International
Assembling file:   voidf.ASM
Error messages:    None
Warning messages:  None
Passes:            1
Remaining memory:  345k
Turbo Link  Version 7.1.29.2. Copyright (c) 1987, 1996 Borland International
```

> **NOTE**
>
> The Borland C++ IDE cannot generate assembly language output. To use the techniques described here, you must run the command-line compiler from a DOS prompt. The IDE compiler can, however, compile inline asm statements. Also, some of the version numbers listed here may not match those on your screen. The current version of Tasm is 5.0. You may use version 4.1, however, with this chapter's information.

Functions that Return void

To experiment with the compiler's ability to generate assembly language, use the -S option (you must type a capital S) and compile a program with a simple function that returns void. For example, copy Listing 19.1, Voidf.cpp, from this book's CD-ROM to a directory on your hard drive. At a DOS prompt type

```
bcc -S voidf
```

Listing 19.1. Voidf.cpp (Implements a simple function that returns void).

```
//================================================================
// Voidf.cpp -- Implements a simple function that returns void
// To compile:
//    bcc -S voidf
// Copyright (c) 1996 by Tom Swan. All rights reserved.
//================================================================

#include <iostream.h>
```

```
// The prototype
void f();

// The program
void main()
{
  f();  // Call the function
}

// The function
void f()
{
  int x = 123;
  cout << "x == %" << x << endl;
}
```

Load the resulting Voidf.asm file into your editor or the IDE for examination. Listing 19.2, Voidfm.asm (m for modified), shows the Voidf.asm file's assembly language commands, with extra comments that I added. I also deleted extraneous lines such as debugging information.

Listing 19.2. Voidfm.asm (Commented partial asm output for Voidf.cpp).

```
;==============================================================
; Voidfm.asm -- Commented partial asm output for Voidf.cpp
; Copyright (c) 1996 by Tom Swan. All rights reserved.
;==============================================================
        .286p                       ; Select processor type
_TEXT   segment byte public 'CODE'  ; Start of code segment
        assume  cs:_TEXT,ds:DGROUP   ; Associate segment registers
_main   proc    near                ; Start main() procedure
    ;
    ;      void main()
    ;
     push    bp                      ; Save base pointer register
     mov     bp,sp                   ; Set base equal to stack pointer
    ;
    ;      {
    ;         f();  // Call the function
    ;
     call    near ptr @f$qv          ; Call function f()
    ;
    ;      }
    ;
     pop bp                          ; Restore saved base pointer
     ret                             ; End program
_main   endp                         ; End main() procedure
        assume  cs:_TEXT,ds:DGROUP   ; Set assumptions for f()
@f$qv   proc    near                 ; Start procedure f()
    ;
    ;      void f()
    ;
     enter   6,0                     ; Create stack frame
```

continues

633

Listing 19.2. continued

```
;
;     {
;        int x = 123;
;
    mov word ptr [bp-2],123      ; Assign 123 to local variable
;
;        cout << "x == " << x << endl;
;
    mov ax,word ptr [bp-2]       ; Get value of x into ax
    mov word ptr [bp-4],ax       ; Save in stack frame
    push    0                    ; Push seg of string s
    push    offset DGROUP:s@     ; Push offset of string s
    push    offset DGROUP:_cout  ; Push offset of output object
    call    near ptr @ostream@outstr$qpxct1 ; Output string
    add sp,6                     ; Fix up stack after call
    mov ax,word ptr [bp-4]       ; Get saved value of x
    cwd                          ; ax -> ax:dx
    push    dx                   ; Push 1/2 of double word
    push    ax                   ; Push 1/2 of double word
    push    offset DGROUP:_cout  ; Push offset of output object
    call    near ptr @ostream@$blsh$ql  ; Output x
    add sp,6                     ; Fix up stack after call
    mov word ptr [bp-6],ax       ; Save ax in stack frame
    push    word ptr [bp-6]      ; Push param for function call
    call    near ptr @endl$qr7ostream    ; Output endl
    pop cx                       ; Fix up stack after call
;
;     }
;
    leave                        ; Destroy stack frame
    ret                          ; Return from subroutine
@f$qv   endp                     ; End of procedure f()
_TEXT   ends                     ; End of code segment
_DATA   segment word public 'DATA' ; Start of data segment
s@ label    byte
    db  'x == '                  ; Static string
    db  0                        ; String null terminator
_DATA   ends                     ; End of data segment
_TEXT   segment byte public 'CODE'
_TEXT   ends
    extrn   @ostream@$blsh$ql:near      ; External references
    extrn   @ostream@outstr$qpxct1:near
    extrn   _cout:word
    extrn   @endl$qr7ostream:near
    public  @f$qv                ; Exported function f()
    public  _main                ; Exported function
    end                          ; End of file
```

> **NOTE**
>
> Create your own unmodified assembly language file by compiling Listing 19.1 with the -s option. This creates Voidf.asm, which you can assemble. Because of the deletions I made to the original file, you cannot assemble the modified Voidfm.asm file.

The generated text shows key instructions that you must provide when writing your own assembly language functions. The main function begins with a proc directive, which assigns label _main to this location, a near address. (In other memory models, a function's address might be far.) In assembly language, public symbols such as main have a leading underscore (_main).

The first instruction in main saves the value of register bp on the stack and then sets bp equal to sp, the stack pointer. Register bp addresses items stored on the stack and is typically assigned the stack pointer on entry to a function.

After that, the program calls function f, specifying a near address at label @f$qv. This strange-looking identifier is purposely mangled, a technique that permits non-object-oriented linkers to digest the complex syntax of C++ code. The compiler invents mangled labels as needed. Notice that the original C++ text appears as comments in the assembly language text.

Finally, the main function restores the saved bp register value, and executes a ret instruction. This returns to the startup code that called main. You don't see this code because it is linked from the Borland C++ standard library. However, the startup code assembly language is provided with the compiler.

Next in the listing is the assembly language for function f. Again, a proc directive tells the assembler we are beginning a new procedure. The first task is to prepare the function's stack frame, which is done by an enter instruction that here reserves six bytes on the stack. The zero in this instruction specifies a nesting level (0 for immediate, or no nesting, which is the default in compiled C++ programs).

A mov instruction next deposits the literal value 123 into a word of the space reserved on the stack. Notice how the statement uses bp to address the local variable. This ends the function's preparations.

The rest of the function implements the output stream statement, which displays a literal string, the value of integer variable x, and starts a new display line. Two mov instructions get the value of x from the stack frame, and then save it in a temporary spot at bp - 4. This is apparently done to protect the original variable, but is obviously unnecessary. We can revise similar code to do better—but more on that later.

Three push instructions push the address of the literal string plus the offset address of the cout object onto the stack. Then, a call instruction calls the output stream function, with the purposely (and badly) mangled name shown in the listing.

NOTE

Note that all of the code so far has merely written one string to the standard output. Assembly language, if anything, can seem ponderously tedious at times!

We aren't done yet. After this first part of the output stream statement, the program adds six to the stack pointer, thus canceling the preceding three push instructions. In C++, it is the caller's responsibility to remove parameters from the stack. This is known as the *C calling convention.*

> **NOTE**
>
> In the C calling convention, compiled programs push arguments onto the stack before calling a function. Then, after the function returns, the caller removes the arguments from the stack (accomplished by merely adjusting the stack pointer, not by actually popping the values). In the Pascal calling convention (used, for example, by Microsoft Windows functions), the called function removes arguments from the stack, again by adjusting the stack pointer. The C calling convention permits passing a variable number of arguments to a function, but bloats the object code with stack adjustment instructions. The Pascal calling convention reduces code file size, but permits passing only fixed numbers of arguments to functions (without some tricky finagling, that is). The use of the word "Pascal" in this regard comes from the Pascal programming language, but doesn't necessarily mean the program is written in Pascal. For instance, programs written in C or C++ use the Pascal calling convention to pass arguments to Windows API functions.

The program next retrieves into register ax the saved value of x, which is converted from a word to a double word in the register pair dx:ax. These registers are then pushed onto the stack to feed the value of x to the output stream. Again, the cout object's offset is pushed before the program calls the output stream subroutine. Notice that this is a *different* subroutine than the one used before—apparently, this one is capable of outputting 32-bit integer values.

Following this second call, the program adds six to the stack pointer, removing the pushed parameters. Then, the program implements the final stage in the output statement—starting a new display line. To do that, for reasons that are not entirely clear, the compiled code moves the value of ax into the location [bp-6], which is then pushed onto the stack. I can only surmise that ax holds the offset to the cout object—the push statement before the final call indicates that this must be so; otherwise, the output statement would have no destination. Here again, a different output stream subroutine is called. After this, a pop instruction removes the pushed parameter.

Finally, function f executes a leave instruction, which counters the enter instruction executed at the beginning of the subroutine. A ret instruction returns to the function's caller, in this example, main.

Among other duties, the remaining lines in the file declare external references to output stream subroutines, and the cout stream object. The file also exports as public symbols the mangled name of function f and of main. This permits other modules such as the C++ startup code to link to this one and call the functions.

As you can tell by now, even in this simple example, there's a lot going on below the surface! You should be getting the idea that digging into compiled output is painstaking work. Be sure the results are worth the effort before embarking on similar journeys into your program's lower levels.

Functions that Return Values

When a function returns a value, it does so internally in one of several ways, passing word values in ax, and byte values in al. Functions pass far pointers in registers dx:ax with dx holding the segment and ax holding the offset address components. Floating-point values are passed on the 80x87 math coprocessor stack. Structures are passed directly on the stack. Arrays are passed by address. These aren't the only possible schemes, and the selection of processor and memory model affect how and where values are stored. In 32-bit code, for example, 32-bit registers hold various values.

Many variations of return-value schemes exist. To determine exactly how to handle a specific return type, rather than hunt for notes in various references, simply compile a short example using the -S option and examine the resulting assembly language as explained in the preceding section. It's pointless to memorize a lot of return-value rules, which Borland is likely to change in future compiler releases. Always examine the *actual* output of a sample function before making any assumptions about how low-level compiled code works.

Class Member Functions

Class objects and their class member functions complicate the assembly language story. Take a look at a sample program with a simple class, Listing 19.3, Classf.cpp. Compile with the command

```
bcc -S classf
```

and examine the resulting assembly language statements in Classf.asm.

Listing 19.3. Classf.cpp (Declares and uses a C++ class).

```
//==============================================================
// Classf.cpp -- Declares and uses a C++ class
// To compile:
//    bcc -S classf
// Copyright (c) 1996 by Tom Swan. All rights reserved.
//==============================================================

#include <iostream.h>

class TClass {
public:
```

continues

Listing 19.3. continued

```
    int x;
    void SetX(int n);
    int GetX();
};

main()
{
  TClass q;

  q.SetX(123);
  cout << "q.GetX() == " << q.GetX() << '\n';
  return 0;
}

void TClass::SetX(int n)
{
  x = n;
}

int TClass::GetX()
{
  return x;
}
```

The sample class TClass declares one public data member (int x) and two member functions to set and get the data member's value. Listing 19.4 shows the compiled assembly language output for member function SetX.

Listing 19.4. Compiled assembly language output for member function SetX from Classf.cpp.

```
@TClass@SetX$qi proc     near
    ;
    ;       void TClass::SetX(int n)
    ;
        push    bp
        mov     bp,sp
        push    si
        mov     si,word ptr [bp+4]
    ;
    ;       {
    ;         x = n;
    ;
        mov     ax,word ptr [bp+6]
        mov     word ptr [si],ax
    ;
    ;       }
    ;
        pop     si
        pop     bp
        ret
@TClass@SetX$qi endp
```

As usual in all functions, instructions save bp and set the register equal to the stack pointer sp for addressing values on the stack, in this case, parameter int n. After saving si, the program uses bp to set si equal to the this pointer, passed to all nonstatic class member functions. The this pointer equals, in this case, the offset address of the object for which a statement called a nonstatic member function—here the object q declared back in main. After preparing si to this's value, the program assigns to ax the value at [bp+6], an expression that addresses parameter n on the stack. The program then assigns this value to word ptr [si], an address reference to the first word of object q (addressed by si). Finally, the program restores registers si and bp before the function returns.

The important lesson to learn here is that nonstatic class member functions receive a this pointer to the object for which a statement called those functions. In assembly language, it's up to you to use the this pointer to locate objects for which member functions are called.

Writing Inline Basm Code

Now that you've investigated some sample compiled code in assembly language, you can begin to think about writing your own. You can proceed in two ways. The first choice is to use the built-in assembler (Basm) to insert inline assembly language statements in your program's text. The second option is to write external modules for assembling separately with Tasm into object-code files for linking with your compiled program. This section explains Basm's ins and outs. It's by far the easiest way to add assembly language to C and C++ programs.

Despite its attractive ease of use, however, Basm lacks some of Tasm's advanced capabilities:

- Basm does not have macros.
- Basm cannot assemble 80386- or 80486-specific instructions.
- Basm does not recognize *Ideal mode,* Tasm's enhanced assembly language syntax.
- Basm has only a limited set of assembler directives for reserving memory.

If you need these features, you must use the stand-alone Tasm assembler. Keep in mind, however, that you can use the C and C++ compilers to deal with many situations that require advanced Tasm commands in a stand-alone assembly language program. It's probably best, for example, to reserve space for variables using C and C++ declarations, to which you can refer by name in assembly language statements. If you need to assemble 80386 or 80486 instructions, however, or if you prefer to use Ideal mode, you must use Tasm.

> **NOTE**
>
> If your assembly language statements use any 80186 or 80286 instructions, use the -1 option when compiling with Bcc. If your statements use any protected mode 80286 instructions, use the -2 option.

Writing asm Statements

An inline asm statement injects one or more processor instruction bytes directly into a program's compiled output. Use asm statements to insert snippets of assembly language, perhaps to optimize a critical statement or to access hardware registers. An asm statement has the general form

```
asm mnemonic [operands] [;]
```

The asm keyword comes first, followed by an assembly language mnemonic such as mov or shl. Any required operands come next—one or more register names, for example, or an address reference. An optional semicolon ends the statement, which may also end with a newline. Unlike stand-alone assembly language, semicolons do not begin comments. In stand-alone Tasm modules, for instance, this statement ends with a comment:

```
mov  ax, cx   ; Set ax equal to cx
```

The equivalent inline Basm statement is a little different:

```
asm  mov  ax, cx;  /* Set ax equal to cx */
```

You must use C or C++ comments to document asm statements. A semicolon terminates the statement, but is optional. You could write the preceding statement like this:

```
asm  mov  ax, cx   /* Set ax equal to cx */
```

You can also use C++ comments:

```
asm  mov  ax, cx   // Set ax equal to cx
```

Surround multiple asm statements with braces. Each asm statement is syntactically equivalent to a C or C++ statement, and the rules for forming compound statements apply to asm as they do for if, while, and other constructions:

```
asm {
  push bp        // Save bp on stack
  mov  bp,sp     // Set bp equal to sp
  ...            // Insert other asm statements here
  pop bp         // Restore bp
}
```

You can use semicolons to separate multiple asm statements on one line and save a little space in your program's text. For example, use this popular trick to push and pop selected registers:

```
asm {
  push ax; push bx; push cx; push dx
  ...  // Insert other statements here
  pop dx; pop cx; pop bx; pop ax
}
```

Global asm statements—those appearing outside of any function—assemble to the program's data segment. There's not much call for the technique, but if you want to inject some code into a data segment, you can do so. Just write your asm statements outside of any function implementations.

Local asm statements—those appearing inside a function implementation—are assembled by Basm into the code stream at that position. The compiler prevents most conflicts between Basm's output and nearby C++ statements, but it's wise to examine the output before and after compilation using the -S option to ensure success.

Optimizing Functions

The primary reason for adding assembly language to C++ programs is to improve performance. First, using your own tests—or even better, profiling a program with Turbo Profiler—identify those functions in your program that share a proportionally large amount of the total operating time. Optimizing these critical functions in assembly language might significantly boost your program's performance.

> **NOTE**
>
> Frederick P. Brooks in "The Mythical Man-Month" speculates that all speed problems can be solved by translating from one to five percent of a program into optimized assembly language. Optimizing the rest of the program is likely to produce negligible results.

Consider a simple example, a function MySquare that returns the square of an integer as a long value:

```
long MySquare(int n)
{
  return long(n) * n;
}
```

Use the -S option to compile a program with this function. Listing 19.5 shows the results in assembly language (with explanatory comments added).

Listing 19.5. Mysquare.asm (Assembly for Mysquare function).

```
;=============================================================
; Mysquare.asm -- Assembly for Mysquare function
; For illustration only--don't assemble or compile
; Copyright (c) 1996 by Tom Swan. All rights reserved.
;=============================================================

@MySquare$qi    proc    near
    ;
    ;     long MySquare(int n)
    ;
        push    bp                  ; Save caller's bp register
        mov     bp,sp               ; Address stack with bp
        push    si                  ; Save si (C register var)
        mov     si,word ptr [bp+4]  ; Assign n to si
```

continues

641

Listing 19.5. continued

```
;
;    {
;       return long(n) * n;
;
        mov     ax,si               ; Transfer si (n) to ax
        cwd                         ; ax -> dx:ax
        push    ax                  ; Push 1/2 parameter for mul
        mov     ax,si               ; Restore n into ax
        push    dx                  ; Push 1/2 parameter for mul
        cwd                         ; ax -> dx:ax
        pop     cx                  ; Remove word from stack ?
        pop     bx                  ; Remove word from stack ?
        call    near ptr N_LXMUL@   ; Call multiply subroutine
        jmp     short @2@2          ; Do-nothing jump
@2@2:
;
;    }
;
        pop     si                  ; Restore saved si
        pop     bp                  ; Restore saved bp
        ret
@MySquare$qi    endp
```

There are some obvious inefficiencies in this code, some of which indicate a problem with the original C++ function—but first, let's dig into the assembly language in hopes of understanding the compiler's intentions. After the usual startup instructions that save bp and prepare that register to address data on the stack, the passed parameter n is assigned to si. This register is also saved on the stack in case it is being used elsewhere, possibly as a C++ register variable (not to be confused with a processor register). This *same* value of n is immediately transferred to ax, which brings up the question, "Why not move n directly into ax in the first place?" Apparently the compiled code uses si as a safe place to store n, and thus prevent repeated memory accesses via bp. This is a good optimization in many cases, but here, the compiler seems to have generated many wasteful instructions.

In fact, the entire sequence preceding the call instruction merely converts n from a word to a double word—and worse, those actions are taken twice for the same value. In addition, a jmp instruction uselessly jumps to the very next address, most likely skipping code that in other circumstances would appear at this location.

Compiled code is sometimes strewn with similar inefficiencies, which at first glance appear to be gross errors that a competent assembly language programmer would never make. Keep in mind, however, that unless function MySquare enjoys critical status, these wasteful instructions probably have no perceptible effect on the program's performance.

On the other hand, if MySquare occupies a large proportion of the program's total operating time, optimizing the function for peak performance should produce a profitable payoff. Using the compiler-generated assembly language as a guide, you can rewrite the function with an asm statement as Listing 19.6, Inlinefn.cpp, demonstrates.

Listing 19.6. Inlinefn.cpp (Optimizes MySquare with inline asm statements).

```
//==============================================================
// Inlinefn.cpp -- Optimizes MySquare with inline asm statements
// Copyright (c) 1996 by Tom Swan. All rights reserved.
//==============================================================

#include <iostream.h>

long MySquare(int n);

void main()
{
  int i;
  long array[1000];

  for (i = 0; i < 1000; i++)
    array[i] = MySquare(i);
  for (i = 0; i < 1000; i++)
    cout << "array[" << i << "] = " << array[i] << endl;
}

// Prevent "Function should return value" warning
#pragma warn -rvl

long MySquare(int n)
{
/*
  return long(n) * n;  // type cast is not needed
*/
  asm {
    mov       ax,n
    imul      ax
  }
}

// Restore prevented warning to previous state
#pragma warn .rvl
```

The listing converts function MySquare's original multiplication statement into a comment. When optimizing your own functions, *never delete the original code*. Someday in the future, you might need to port the program to another computer system, perhaps one that does not have an 80x86 processor. Simply remove the comment brackets and delete any asm statements to convert the code back to C or C++.

The function shows MySquare's optimized assembly language. First, the value of parameter n is moved into register ax. You don't have to calculate n's offset address (that is, using an address expression such as [bp+4]). You can simply reference any parameter or variable name and let Basm calculate the appropriate address reference.

An imul instruction multiplies ax times itself with the result placed in dx:ax. These are the registers that the function uses to pass its return value back to its caller.

Evidently, because the modified function does not execute an explicit return, the superfluous `jmp` instruction is also eliminated (determined by examining the listing's compiled assembly language). Unfortunately, however, because of that change, the compiler now warns you that `MySquare` is missing a return statement. Though harmless, the warning is annoying and you can defeat it by using the `#pragma warn` directive as demonstrated in the listing. The directive

```
#pragma warn -rvl
```

turns off the warning. The directive

```
#pragma warn +rvl
```

turns it on. After either such command, you can write

```
#pragma warn .rvl
```

to restore this or another warning to its previous status. You can issue this same warning on the command line using an option such as `-wrvl`. Other warning combinations (there are dozens) are documented in Borland's reference manuals.

After optimizing a function such as `MySquare`, it's wise to examine the final results. To verify the compiler's output, again compile the code using the `-S` option and scan the assembly language. Compile with the command

```
bcc -S inlinefn
```

and examine the resulting Inlinefn.asm file. Here's the entire optimized `MySquare` function as compiled to assembly language (I added the comments):

```
push    bp           ; Save caller's bp register
mov     bp,sp        ; Address stack with bp
mov     ax,[bp+4]    ; Move n into ax
imul    ax           ; ax * ax -> dx:ax
pop     bp           ; Restore saved bp
ret                  ; Return to caller
```

Compare this code with the previous example prior to optimization (refer back to Listing 19.5, Mysquare.asm). The integer parameter is moved directly into `ax` and the superfluous `jmp` instruction is gone. The compiler saves, initializes, and restores `bp`. It also supplies a `ret` instruction.

As you can also see from this small example, optimizing a function takes much time and care. Don't waste *your* critical time optimizing code that already works as fast as necessary.

NOTE

In all fairness to Borland, I have to admit to some shenanigans in the preceding discussions. In this book's early incarnations for Borland C++ 3.1, the compiler's output was not as good as it is in version 5.0. In fact, the compiler now generates tight code that is almost as good as in the optimized Inlinefn.cpp listing. However, for a juicier example, I purposely used a version of Mysquare that would produce code that is not up to par with the compiler's usual output.

I am not being entirely sneaky, though, and even the improved code can stand improvement. Consider again the original Mysquare function, which uses a type cast expression to convert one of its arguments from int to long, thus forcing a long result for the function to return:

```
return long(n) * n;
```

Removing the type cast causes the compiler to generate code that is technically correct, but could lead to a hard to find bug. For example, try this statement:

```
return n * n;
```

When compiled to assembly language, this generates the following code, which is nearly the same as the optimized version in the Inlinefn.asm file, although it needlessly uses an additional register (bx) along with an extra mov instruction:

```
mov     bx,word ptr [bp+4]   ; Move n into bx
mov     ax,bx                ; Also move n into ax
imul    bx                   ; ax * bx -> dx:ax
cwd                          ; ??? Converts ax word to dx:ax double word
```

This is better, but still not perfect. The code could simply load ax and perform the multiplication—bx isn't needed. Additionally, the cwd instruction is also not needed because imul's output is *already* in dx:ax. Worse, the compiled code assumes that a 16-bit result is in ax, and executing cwd to convert that value to a 32-bit quantity throws out the high order portion of the product with the bath water! This, however, is not a bug as you might suspect—the compiler is correct in enforcing a 16-bit multiplication and throwing away the high order portion of the 32-bit result because that, after all, is what the C++ source code specifies. On the other hand, using a type cast to force a 32-bit result produces inefficient compiled code—exactly the sort of situation where some assembly language is needed to squeeze the best performance from the compiled program.

It's amazing what you can learn when you dig deeply into a compiler's output!

Executing Jumps

An assembly language jump instruction such as `jmp` or `jnl` continues a program at a specified address. In stand-alone Tasm programs, labels identify jump-target locations. In Basm, asm jump instructions can transfer control only to C or C++ labels such as targeted by `goto`s. In fact, an asm jump instruction *is* a goto statement.

Because target labels are written in C or C++, they must appear outside of `asm` statements. Suppose, example, you want to insert a copyright notice into the code stream rather than in a data segment where such notice is more likely to be found and modified by a software pirate. You can encode a `jmp` instruction around the text like this:

```
asm {
  jmp L1
  db 13,10,'© 1992,1996 by Tom Swan',0
}
L1:
asm {
  // ... Additional instructions
}
```

The `jmp L1` instruction skips the `db` (define bytes) directive, which inserts a carriage return (13), line feed (10), and copyright string into the code (note the single quotes and explicit NULL termination byte 0 at the end of the string). The target label `L1` appears after the initial asm statement, which might be followed by C and C++ statements or another asm statement as shown here.

You can also use relative jump instructions such as `jnz`, `jl`, and others. If any targets are unreachable by these "near" jump instructions, they abort the program abnormally. For example, if you write

```
asm jne TARGET
```

Basm assembles that instruction (jump if not equal) unchanged only if the distance from this location to TARGET is within –128 and +127 bytes backward or forward. If the target label is located farther away, Basm inserts a jump to the program's abnormal-termination entry point. You can fix this kind of problem by converting the conditional jump to the equivalent code:

```
asm je TEMP
asm jmp TARGET
TEMP:
```

The effect is to skip the unconditional `jmp` instruction if the opposite condition holds. Together, the `je` and `jmp` instructions perform the identical job as the original `jne` jump, but can "hit" targets farther away.

Basm automatically optimizes unconditional `jmp` instructions. If you write

```
asm jmp LABEL
```

and if LABEL refers to an address within -128 and +127 bytes, Basm uses the most efficient 2-byte jmp instruction possible. If the target label is farther away, however, Basm uses a less efficient 3-byte jmp.

You can override these optimizations by prefacing labels with NEAR PTR and FAR PTR. For example, to force a FAR jump to a nearby label, you can write

```
asm jmp FAR PTR LABEL
```

Accessing Variables

In asm statements, you may reference local, global, and register variables by name. You may also refer directly to function parameters. It may be necessary, however, to use WORD PTR and BYTE PTR overrides for loading 16- and 8-bit values into registers. For an int variable or parameter count, the instruction

```
asm mov ax, count
```

is equivalent to

```
asm mov ax, WORD PTR count
```

To move count's first byte into a byte-sized register, you must supply the override:

```
asm mov al, BYTE PTR count
```

Use the similar override DWORD PTR with les instructions and with indirect far calls to load 32-bit pointers—that is, "double word" values.

You may use registers si and di in asm statements without conflicting with register variables. If an asm statement uses si or di, the compiler does not assign register variables to those registers.

Accessing Structure Members

Inline asm statements may refer to structure members by name. You must be careful, however, to consider whether an instruction needs a value (a memory reference) or an address (the member's relative offset).

Suppose you declare a structure TPoint with two int members x and y. Using a typedef (not required in C++, but useful in ANSI C code), you design the struct like this:

```
typedef struct point {
  int x;
  int y;
} TPoint;
```

You next declare a global or local variable cursor of type TPoint:

```
TPoint cursor;
```

In C and C++ statements, the expressions cursor.x and cursor.y refer to cursor's members. In asm statements, you can use similar expressions. For example, this loads into register ax the value of cursor's y member:

```
asm mov ax, WORD PTR cursor.y  // Load y's value into ax
```

To refer to y's offset address relative to the structure's first byte, use the OFFSET keyword:

```
asm mov bx, OFFSET cursor.y  // Load y's offset into bx
```

You can also address structures with registers. Here's how to prepare registers ds:di to address cursor and to load member y's value into ax:

```
asm {
  mov di, OFFSET cursor    // Move cursor's location into di
  mov ax, [di].y           // Move member y's value into ax
}
```

Register ds already addresses the program's global data segment. Only di needs initializing. The compiler assumes y is a member of the TPoint structure, cursor. A conflict might arise, however, if another structure declares a y member. You can resolve the problem by preceding the member with the struct's name in parentheses:

```
asm {
  mov di, OFFSET cursor    // Move cursor's location into di
  mov ax, [di].(TPoint)y   // Tell assembler which struct to use
}
```

Writing External Turbo Assembler Modules

Inline Basm statements are especially appropriate for small optimizations—a few instructions here and there, or a lone function that needs a performance boost. More sophisticated assembly language work requires the additional capabilities of the stand-alone Turbo Assembler, available separately from Borland.

Tasm is a remarkable product that comes with 16- and 32-bit assemblers. Tasm can assemble complete applications written entirely in assembly language. It also boasts a variety of options and directives that range from simple memory reservation instructions to sophisticated macro facilities. Tasm has a kind of class structure, which you can use to write object-oriented assembly language modules. You can even write Windows applications entirely in assembly language (a job not for the faint of heart).

Tasm's main value for C++ programmers, however, is in creating .obj (object code) modules for linking to compiled programs. In a typical scenario, you write and test a prototype C++ function. You then implement the function completely in assembly language to optimize the original code. Remember to use the -s option to provide a starting module that you can modify— this sure beats constructing stand-alone modules from scratch.

As with inline Basm code, external assembly language modules require much care and effort to construct. Be sure the results are worth the trouble; don't convert all or most of your code to assembly language in hopes of better performance. Identify the critical code and concentrate on making that code run as fast as possible.

Using the H2ash and H2ash32 Utilities

One of the most difficult jobs in writing external assembly language modules is developing an interface to a program's data structures. Assembly language isn't designed to accommodate C structures, arrays, strings, and C++ classes, so you may have to use a few tricks for accessing objects of these and other types from assembly language statements.

The utilities H2ash.exe and H2ash32.exe provided with Tasm can help reduce the amount of time you spend answering the question, "How do I access my program's data using assembly language directives and instructions?" I'll refer to both utilities as H2ash from now on—they work the same, but operate on 16- and 32-bit source code files respectively. H2ash converts a C or C++ header file's declarations into an equivalent .ash (assembly language header) file containing equivalent Tasm declarations and equates. You can use these declarations to access your program's data or as guides to writing your own directives.

H2ash supports most C constructs and C++ classes. It expands #include files and can take advantage of Tasm's Ideal mode. Unfortunately, H2ash does not recognize multiple inheritance, virtual base classes, or templates. It also issues warnings for items such as macros that don't translate easily to Tasm directives. Consider H2ash as a guide to, but not the last word on, translating C and C++ declarations to assembly language. Some headers translate to useable .ash files—others are literally reduced to ashes.

If a header file includes other headers, the H2ash utilities need to know the Borland C++ installation paths. The easiest way to satisfy this requirement is to create a configuration file named Turboc.cfg that contains the following commands:

```
-IC:\bc5\include
-LC:\bc5\lib
```

> **NOTE**
>
> For more information about the H2ash utilities, read the text file Tsm-util.txt located in the C:\Tasm\doc directory. (This file might be located in C:\Bc5\doc if you installed Tasm to your Borland C++ directories.)

To learn how to use H2ash, process a few sample header files. For example, consider the Db.h header file from some code I had written for another book. With that file in the current directory (a copy of it is in this chapter's C19 directory, but not listed here), get to a DOS prompt and enter the command

```
h2ash db.h
```

to create a new file Db.ash with equivalent Tasm directives. Because Db.h includes Stdio.h, H2ash converts symbols in that header file as well as those in Db.h. (As H2ash runs, it may warn you from time to time about macros or other items that can't be converted. You can safely ignore these warnings for standard headers.)

Though the results are imperfect, H2ash skillfully translates most items. For instance, Db.h defines these symbolic constants:

```
#define FALSE 0
#define TRUE 1
#define NAMELEN 30
#define ADDRLEN 30
#define CSZLEN 30
#define PHONELEN 13
```

H2ash translates these symbols to the equivalent Tasm directives:

```
FALSE      EQU  0
TRUE       EQU  1
NAMELEN    EQU  30
ADDRLEN    EQU  30
CSZLEN     EQU  30
PHONELEN   EQU  13
```

H2ash also digests more complex declarations. Consider the header file's original struct, which declares members for a sample database record:

```
typedef struct record {
   union {
     long numrecs;
     long custnum;
   } info;
   char name[NAMELEN];
   char addr[ADDRLEN];
   char csz[CSZLEN];
   char phone[PHONELEN];
   double balance;
} Record;
```

Converting this structure to equivalent Tasm directives is difficult by hand, but easy with H2ash. The utility outputs the following equivalent Tasm directives:

```
tag$1      UNION
numrecs    DD     ?
custnum    DD     ?
tag$1      ENDS

record     STRUC
info       tag$1  <>
name       DB     30 DUP ( ? )
addr       DB     30 DUP ( ? )
csz        DB     30 DUP ( ? )
phone      DB     13 DUP ( ? )
balance    DQ     ?
record     ENDS
```

In addition to translating existing names such as numrecs and phone, H2ash creates any needed symbols such as tag$1. It also creates declarations for calling a C or C++ program's prototyped functions:

```
GLOBAL C CreateDB     :NEAR
GLOBAL C OpenDB       :NEAR
GLOBAL C ReadRecord   :NEAR
GLOBAL C WriteRecord  :NEAR
```

Writing External Tasm Modules

The following listings demonstrate how to write an external assembly language module and link it to a C++ program. For this section, you need to purchase and install Turbo Assembler. If you don't have Tasm, skip to the section, "Using Interrupts." Tasm is not provided with Borland C++.

Listing 19.7, Testtime.cpp, calls a function Timer to access the computer's timer count, stored in low memory at address 0000:046C and updated regularly by a BIOS subroutine. Don't compile the program yet. You'll do that later after constructing the external Timer module.

Listing 19.7. Testtime.cpp (Tests Timer function).

```
//==============================================================
// Testtime.cpp -- Tests Timer function.
// *** Requires Turbo Assembler
// To compile:
//    bcc testtime timer.asm
// To run:
//    testtime
// Copyright (c) 1996 by Tom Swan. All rights reserved.
//==============================================================

#include <conio.h>
#include "timer.h"

main()
{
  while (!kbhit()) {
    gotoxy(1, wherey());
    cprintf("%ld   ", Timer());
  }
  getch();   // Throw away keypress
  return 0;
}
```

The program doesn't do much—it just provides a vehicle for testing the Timer function to be written in assembly language. The module includes that function's header, shown here in Listing 19.8, Timer.h.

651

Listing 19.8. Timer.h (Header file for Timer.cpp).

```
//=============================================================
// Timer.h -- Header file for Timer.cpp
// Copyright (c) 1996 by Tom Swan. All rights reserved.
//=============================================================

extern "C" {
  long Timer();
}
```

There's not much to the header, but it performs a valuable service that simplifies importing external assembly language functions into C++ programs. Declaring an external function prototype inside a directive such as

```
extern "C" { }
```

disables a process called *name mangling.* C++ uses name mangling to transform function names into unique strings that permit standard linkers to process object-oriented code. The function name Timer, for instance, is mangled to @Timer$qv. Such names are difficult to read, and even worse to type, and it's probably best to use unmangled external function names in assembly language modules. (The ANSI-C compiler built into Borland C++ does not mangle function names, so this advice applies only to C++ programs.)

> If you must use mangled symbols (perhaps you need to maintain and use a function in C++ and assembly-language forms), write a dummy function that has no instructions and compile with option -S to produce an assembly language file complete with mangled symbols. Use this file as a shell, which you can fill with your function's instructions.

Next comes the assembly language module, which provides the executable instructions for the external Timer function. Listing 19.9, Timer.asm, implements Timer using Tasm's Ideal-mode syntax.

Listing 19.9. Timer.asm (Implements Timer assembly language module).

```
;=============================================================
; Timer.asm -- Implements Timer assembly language module
; Copyright (c) 1996 by Tom Swan. All rights reserved.
;=============================================================

        IDEAL
        MODEL small

        CODESEG
        PUBLIC _Timer

proc    _Timer
        xor     ax, ax                  ; Set ax to 0000
```

```
        mov     es, ax                    ; Set es to 0000
        mov     di, 0046cH                ; Set di to 046C
        mov     ax, [WORD PTR es:di]      ; Get low-order timer
        mov     dx, [WORD PTR es:di+2]    ; Get high-order timer
        ret                               ; Return to caller
endp

end
```

The beginning of the listing shows an important consideration: selecting a memory model. You must use the same memory model for external modules and their host programs. Inside the code segment (started with the CODESEG keyword), declare the external function name in a PUBLIC directive. Preface the public name with an underscore—the C and C++ standard convention for public symbols.

Write the function as you would a stand-alone assembly language subroutine, usually inside PROC and ENDP directives as shown here. It's your responsibility to return any needed values in the appropriate registers, preserve the stack, save and restore registers bp and ds, and take care of other low-level jobs. In this case, the function returns a long int value in the register pair ax:dx. There's no reason to save and restore bp and the stack pointer sp because the function uses no stack-based parameters or variables.

You now possess the necessary components to assemble and compile the example. With Tasm.exe and the Bcc.exe command-line compiler in the system PATH, and with the files Testtime.cpp, Timer.h, and Timer.asm in the current directory, type the command

```
bcc testtime timer.asm
```

at a DOS prompt. The C++ compiler first compiles Testtime.cpp to produce the intermediate object-code file Testtime.obj, and then Bcc.exe runs Tasm to assemble Timer.asm and create Timer.obj. Finally, Turbo Linker joins the object-code files to produce the final output code file, Testtime.exe. Run the program by typing testtime and press any key to stop the repeating timer.

To assemble modules separately, use Tasm's /ml option to generate case-sensitive public symbols (assembly language is normally not case sensitive, but C++ is, so you must use this directive for the linker's benefit). For example, enter the command

```
tasm /ml timer
```

to assemble Timer.asm and create Timer.obj. Next, compile Testtime.cpp separately with the command

```
bcc -c testtime
```

to create Testtime.obj. Finally, link the two object-code modules with the command

```
bcc testtime.obj timer.obj
```

Though not shown in these samples, assembly language modules often need to export data as well as code. Use a DATASEG directive to begin a data segment and specify a public symbol for a global variable:

```
        IDEAL
        MODEL small
        DATASEG             ; Start data segment
        PUBLIC _MyVar
_MyVar  DW      0           ; A wordsize variable
        CODESEG
; ... Insert module's functions here
END
```

In the C++ host, declare MyVar (minus the underscore) in an extern directive:

```
extern int MyVar;
```

You can then use MyVar as though it had been defined in a C++ module. You don't have to use the "C" option in the extern directive as you do with functions because C++ doesn't mangle variable names. It does that only for function identifiers.

To access C++ variables from inside an external assembly language module, use a similar EXTRN directive (and notice that the assembly language word is spelled without a second E). For example, given the global variable

```
int Global;
```

an assembly language module can refer to Global as an external WORD _Global like this:

```
        IDEAL
        MODEL small
        DATASEG
        EXTRN _Global:WORD  ; External word-size variable
; ... Insert other data directives here
        CODESEG
; ... Insert module's functions here
END
```

Using Interrupts

Interrupts tell a program to stop what it's doing, do something else for a while, and then pick up where it left off. A hardware device might generate an interrupt signal to notify the computer of external events such as a keypress or a mouse click. An Interrupt Service Routine (ISR)

19

responds to the interrupt signal and returns to the interrupted program by executing an `iret` (interrupt return) instruction. You can write ISRs in C and C++, but many programmers use assembly language to ensure top speed.

You can also call ISRs with assembly language `int` instructions. (That's int for *interrupt,* not *integer.*) For example, to use a DOS function, programs call the DOS dispatcher using an instruction such as

```
asm int 0x21  // Call DOS function dispatcher
```

Down in a PC's lower reaches is a table of 32-bit address values called *vectors.* Executing a software interrupt instruction causes the 80x86 processor to push registers and flags onto the stack and transfer control to the address stored in the table at the interrupt number's location. Upon receipt of an interrupt signal, the program *vectors* to the ISR subroutine like a car careening around a hidden curve.

Calling DOS Functions

Using the built-in Basm assembler, asm statements can easily call DOS functions. Use the technique illustrated by Listing 19.10, Basmwelc.cpp, which displays the string "Welcome to Basm!$" in two ways: by calling a C function and by calling the DOS print-string subroutine. (I'll explain the purpose of the string's dollar sign in a moment.)

Listing 19.10. Basmwelc.cpp (Calls DOS to output a string).

```
//===============================================================
// Basmwelc.cpp -- Calls DOS to output a string
// To compile:
//    bcc basmwelc
// To run:
//    basmwelc
// Copyright (c) 1996 by Tom Swan. All rights reserved.
//===============================================================

#include <iostream.h>

// Dollar-sign (ASCII$) and null-terminated (ASCIIZ) string
char message[] = "Welcome to BASM!$";

main()
{
  cout << message << endl;  // Display ASCIIZ string
  asm {
    mov ah, 9               // Select DOS function number 9
    mov dx, OFFSET message  // Address ASCII$ string
    int 0x21                // Call DOS via 0x21 interrupt
  }
  return 0;
}
```

All DOS functions have identifying numbers such as 9, the DOS print-string function. This program's `asm` statement loads the DOS function number into register `ah`, assigns to `dx` the offset address of the string's first character, and calls the DOS function dispatcher with the instruction `int 0x21`.

> **NOTE**
>
> Consult a DOS programming reference for other DOS function numbers and their requirements (see "Bibliography").

Due to DOS function 9's unusual requirements, the string must be terminated with a dollar sign character ($), a leftover from DOS's ancestor CP/M operating system. When you run the program, the C++ output stream statement displays the entire string including its dollar sign terminator. The `asm` statement displays the same string, but without the trailing dollar sign.

Calling BIOS Functions

Another set of routines provides I/O services for a PC's hardware components. A collection of ISRs and other subroutines are stored in ROM and are known as the basic input-output system, or BIOS. For the most part, you must call these routines using software interrupt instructions because the subroutine addresses are not necessarily the same in all systems.

> **WARNING**
>
> BIOS routines perform critical hardware operations, including low-level floppy and hard disk drive services. Be extremely careful when calling these routines. The smallest error in calling a BIOS routine can destroy an entire disk full of information. Never call BIOS routines without first backing up all important data.

Listing 19.11, Bigc.cpp, demonstrates how to call a relatively safe BIOS interrupt—in this case, one that changes the shape of the text-screen cursor. From a DOS prompt, compile and run the program to alter your text cursor from its usual skinny appearance to a large size model that's easier to see on a crowded screen. (Reboot to restore the original cursor shape, or under Windows, close and reopen the DOS window.)

Listing 19.11. Bigc.cpp (Changes to a large-model cursor).

```
//=================================================================
// Bigc.cpp -- Changes to a large-model cursor
// To compile:
//    bcc bigc
// To run:
//    bigc
```

```
// Copyright (c) 1996 by Tom Swan. All rights reserved.
//==============================================================

void main()
{
  asm {
    mov ch, 0      // Set cursor top row
    mov cl, 7      // Set cursor bottom row
    mov ah, 1      // Select video BIOS routine #1
    int 0x10       // Call BIOS to change cursor shape
  }
}
```

A single asm statement performs this program's main duty: calling the BIOS video routine to alter the text display's cursor shape. First, mov statements load registers ch and cl with scan-line values, representing the number and position of the horizontal CRT lines that comprise the visible cursor. (If you look closely at the text cursor, you might see these lines on some types of text-screen displays.) Experiment with these two values to construct a variety of cursor shapes.

A third mov instruction loads into register ah the identifying number for the BIOS video ISR's cursor-shape routine. After these preparatory steps, the program calls the BIOS ISR by executing interrupt 0x10, similar to the way the preceding program called the DOS function dispatcher. A large cursor should appear as soon as you run the program. Unfortunately, the cursor may revert back to its former shape due to other programs changing but not restoring the cursor size.

Writing Interrupt Service Routines

In addition to calling DOS and BIOS functions, you can write your own ISRs. To simplify the process, Borland C++ provides an interrupt keyword that converts a void function into an ISR. In C and C++ programs, you write an interrupt function using code declared as

```
void interrupt AnyName(unsigned bp, unsigned di, unsigned si,
                       unsigned ds, unsigned es, unsigned dx,
                       unsigned cx, unsigned bx, unsigned ax,
                       unsigned ip, unsigned cs, unsigned flags)
{
  // ... C++ statements
}
```

The unsigned parameters provide access to register values stored on the stack. In the case of a hardware interrupt, these values should not be disturbed as they represent the interrupted program's state. In fact, for most hardware ISRs, you probably do not need to declare any parameters. Software interrupts, however, typically pass information in registers, accessible in interrupt functions through the listed parameters. You may include only the parameters you need, but you must include them in the order shown. Thus, if your program needs register ax, it still must declare parameters bp through ax.

The compiler adds some of its own code to interrupt functions. In compiled form, interrupt functions begin with this preamble

```
push  ax          ; Save registers
push  bx
push  cx
push  dx
push  es
push  ds
push  si
push  di
push  bp
mov   bp,DGROUP   ; Set bp to data segment address
mov   ds,bp       ; Initialize DS to program's data segment
mov   bp,sp       ; Address local data via bp
```

In addition to saving registers and preparing bp for addressing local variables and parameters, the compiler copies the program's data segment address into ds. This vital step ensures that interrupt functions can locate their program's global data. Remember, a hardware interrupt might be called at any moment, at which time ds might address some other program's data.

The statements in the function come next, followed by cleanup instructions before the ISR ends:

```
pop   bp          ; Restore saved registers
pop   di
pop   si
pop   ds
pop   es
pop   dx
pop   cx
pop   bx
pop   ax
iret              ; Return to interrupted program
```

After restoring register values pushed earlier onto the stack, the function executes iret, which transfers control back to the interrupted program, or in the case of a software interrupt, to the location following an int instruction. Registers and flags saved on the stack by the interrupt signal or instruction are also restored at this time.

Listing 19.12, Multip.cpp, demonstrates how to write and install an interrupt function written with inline asm instructions. You must compile and run this program from a DOS prompt. The program taps into the PC's interrupt 0x1c vector, which normally does nothing but is called on a regular basis by the BIOS function awakened by the system's internal clock. Cycling at approximately 18.2 times per second, interrupt 0x1c gives you a handy hook on which to hang actions to be executed regularly while the rest of the program continues unaware of any interruptions. In Multip.cpp, the interrupt is programmed to display the time at the upper-right corner of the text display while you enter test strings. Press Enter to end the program and remove the ISR from memory.

NOTE

If your computer has a monochrome display adapter, change the `#define` statement value `0xb800` to `0xb000`.

Listing 19.12. Multip.cpp (Demonstrates multiprocessing with interrupts).

```
//===============================================================
// Multip.cpp -- Demonstrates multiprocessing with interrupts
// To compile:
//    bcc multip
// To run:
//    multip (then follow onscreen instructions)
// Copyright (c) 1996 by Tom Swan. All rights reserved.
//===============================================================

#include <stdio.h>
#include <dos.h>
#include <string.h>

#define DISPSEG 0xb800  // Use 0xb000 for monochrome display

// Global variable for saving original 0x1c interrupt vector
void interrupt (far *oldVector)(...);

// Function prototypes
void InitInterrupt(void);
void DoWhateverYouWant(void);
void DeinitInterrupt(void);
void interrupt ShowTime(...);

main()
{
  setcbrk(0);   // Prevent ending program by pressing Ctrl+C
  InitInterrupt();
  DoWhateverYouWant();
  DeinitInterrupt();
  return 0;
}

// Redirect interrupt vector to our own service routine
void InitInterrupt(void)
{
  oldVector = getvect(0x1c);  // Save current vector
  setvect(0x1c, ShowTime);    // Set vector to ShowTime()
}

// ShowTime() runs concurrently with this sample function
void DoWhateverYouWant(void)
{
```

continues

659

Listing 19.12. continued

```c
    int i, done = 0;
    char s[128];

    while (!done) {
        puts("\n\nEnter a string (Enter to quit):");
        gets(s);
        done = (strlen(s) == 0);
        if (!done) {
            for (i = 0; i < 40; i++)
                puts(s);
        }
    }
}

// Restore original interrupt vector before program ends
void DeinitInterrupt(void)
{
    setvect(0x1c, oldVector);
}

// Interrupt 0x1c service routine. Poke time into display.
void interrupt ShowTime(...)
{
    asm {
        xor ax, ax                          // ax <- 0000
        mov ds, ax                          // ds <- 0000
        mov ax, [0x046d]                    // get timer div 256
        mov bx, DISPSEG                     // bx = display addr
        mov ds, bx                          // ds = display addr
        mov word ptr [0x009a], 0x0f07c      // display '¦'
        mov bh, 0x70                        // attribute = reversed
        push ax                             // save timer value
        xchg ah, al                         // ah = timer hi mod 256
        aam                                 // make unpacked bcd
        or ax, 0x3030                       // convert to ascii
        mov bl, ah                          // move digit to bl
        mov [0x0096], bx                    // display 1st hr digit
        mov bl, al                          // move digit to bl
        mov [0x0098], bx                    // display 2nd hr digit
        pop ax                              // restore timer value
        mov cx, 0x0f06                      // calc ax / 4.26
        mul ch                              //    ax <- ax * 15
        shr ax, cl                          //    ax <- ax / 64
        aam                                 // make unpacked bcd
        or  ax, 0x3030                      // convert to ascii
        mov bl, ah                          // move digit to bl
        mov [0x009C], bx                    // display 1st min digit
        mov bl, al                          // move digit to bl
        mov [0x009e], bx                    // display 2nd min digit
    }
}
```

When poking the address of a custom ISR into the PC's interrupt vector table, you should almost always preserve the original vector for restoring later. To save the old vector, declare a variable like this:

```
void interrupt (far *oldVector)(...);
```

In English, this line declares `oldVector` as a far pointer to a void interrupt function that receives a variable number of arguments—represented in C++ as a three-dot ellipsis in parentheses; in ANSI C, as an empty pair of parentheses. To preserve an interrupt vector, assign to `oldVector` the value returned from `getvect`. Call `setvect`, then, to redirect interrupts to your custom routine. Another call to `setvect` restores the saved interrupt vector before the program ends.

The test program prompts you to enter a string, displayed several times in a `for` loop. This code gives the program something to do while the ISR executes in the background—a simple but effective form of multiprocessing using a timer interrupt. Run the program and spend a few minutes typing strings. Despite the fact that function `DoWhateverYouWant` has control, the program's ISR automatically updates the displayed time.

The `ShowTime` ISR uses a single inline `asm` statement to decode the current time, translate the binary coded decimal (BCD) result to ASCII, and poke the digits directly into the display's video buffer. Comments in the listing explain the purpose of each instruction.

It's difficult to imagine a function that is more system-dependent than `ShowTime`, which is unlikely to run correctly on any computer other than a true-blue, 100 percent–compatible IBM PC with a common monochrome or graphics display. The function would certainly fail on nonstandard hardware.

Summary

- Programs written in assembly language are intimately tied to their host machine. Despite this restriction, however, when used skillfully, a little assembly language can go a long way toward optimizing your C++ programs to run as fast as possible in the smallest amount of space.

- With assembly language you can optimize critical statements to run as fast as possible, you can access hardware at the bit level, and you can code interrupt service routines (ISRs) for top speed.

- Use the `-S` option to compile a program to an assembly language text file. Examine the generated file to learn how the compiler translates high-level statements to machine code.

- The primary reason for adding assembly language to programs is to improve the performance of critical code—typically a small percentage of a program's total instructions. Identify your program's critical code (perhaps by using Turbo Profiler), and optimize those instructions with assembly language. Optimizing a program's noncritical code may give little or no performance benefits.

- Borland's built-in assembler (Basm) assembles inline asm statements in C and C++ programs. Terminate an inline statement with a semicolon or a new line. Enclose multiple inline statements in braces.

- Basm lacks sophisticated Tasm features such as macros, 80386 and 80486 instructions, Ideal mode, and advanced directives. Nevertheless, Basm is more than adequate for most assembly language tasks.

- Inline Basm statements recognize C and C++ comments. Unlike stand-alone assembly language programs, Basm comments do not begin with semicolons.

- For more sophisticated assembly language work, write external modules that you assemble with Tasm and link to compiled C and C++ programs. With this method, you can take advantage of Tasm's advanced features such as Ideal mode and macros. You also gain complete control over the low-level instructions in assembled functions. Tasm is sold separately by Borland and is not included with Borland C++.

- Use the H2ash and H2ash32 utilities to simplify translating high-level items, #defines, structures, and other declarations to equivalent assembly language statements.

- Interrupts temporarily halt a program to perform another task. Every interrupt has an identifying number that serves as an index into a table of ISR vectors (addresses) in low memory.

- Hardware devices such as keyboards and a mouse generate interrupt signals, causing the processor to pass control to the associated ISR vector. A hardware interrupt can occur at any time.

- Software ISRs operate like subroutines. Programs call a software ISR with an assembly language int instruction. Call the DOS function dispatcher, for example, with the instruction int 0x21. You can also call BIOS routines using software interrupts, but use extreme caution; the BIOS contains many low-level subroutines that, if misused, can cause the permanent loss of data.

- You can code your own interrupt service routines in C++, but many programmers use assembly language for the best possible performance.

20

CHAPTER

Using Process Control, Optimizations, and Other Tools

Borland C++ supplies a feature-packed toolbox for DOS and Windows developers. This chapter covers several useful tools and techniques for developing projects, including background compilation, code-generation optimizations, the Make utility, memory models, DOS overlays, and miscellaneous C++ classes.

Background Compilation

Borland C++ 5.0's IDE supports multiple-thread processes, which means you can compile programs in the background while you perform other tasks. Of course, you need a fairly fast computer to take full advantage of this feature, but it can be extremely useful. For instance, you can build a large project while you edit other files, create resources, or update your program's documentation.

The term *build process* as I use it here refers to any source translation, including C++ code compilation, object-code linkage, resource compilation, help file creation, and other processes specified in a project. The term *background compilation* is a loose synonym for *build process.*

Configure the IDE's background compilation feature by selecting *Options\Environment.* Choose the *Process Control* topic to display the dialog box shown in Figure 20.1. Use this dialog to modify four categories that affect build-process speed and priorities.

Figure 20.1.
The IDE's Process Control options.

Under the dialog's *Build Process* section, enable the *Asynchronous* check box to turn on background compilation. With this option enabled, you can build a project and at the same time use other IDE tools such as the class Browser, the text editor, and Grep. However, there is one restriction: you cannot debug a program while building another.

> **TIP**
>
> Turn off *Asynchronous* for the fastest build times. However, you then cannot compile in the background.

Also under *Build Process,* select the *Beep on completion* check box to sound an alarm when a project build is finished. If you plan on using background compilation frequently, this option will notify you when the compiler and linker are done.

Choose one of the three radio buttons under *Status Box* to alter the information the IDE reports during a build. Select *None* if you plan on doing frequent background compilations—this speeds the build process a tiny bit, and it reduces screen clutter. Or, select *Status only* for a status box with minimal activity and information. Choose the default, *Full with Statistics,* for the complete ball of wax on build-process information. (Frankly, these options have very little effect on compilation speed, especially on a modern Pentium-based, screaming-demon machine. I can't detect any real difference between these options, so I use *Full* on the theory that the complete story is always better than a digest.)

Two options, *Build priority boost (-2..2)* and *Update interval (milliseconds),* fine-tune background compilation priorities and thus affect the relative speed of multiple processes. The goal in choosing correct settings is to build projects as fast as possible while not producing any noticeable slowdowns in other processes you run. The proper settings depend on your computer's speed, its memory capacity, the operating system, and the types of multiple processes you run. You'll have to play around with these options to find the right values for your system.

Set *Build priority boost (-2..2)* to a value from -2 to +2. The lowest value, -2, gives other foreground processes the maximum amount of time. The highest value, +2, gives the background build process the maximum amount of time. In general, so that foreground processes run at normal speeds, use lower settings on slower computers and higher values on faster systems. You can also modify this setting during compilation with the status box's slide control.

> **NOTE**
>
> If the *Asynchronous* check box is disabled, the *Build priority boost* option has no effect.

Set *Update interval (milliseconds)* to the rate in milliseconds at which the build process updates the status box. Obviously, this option has no effect if you turn off the status box. A larger value may improve the build-process speed somewhat by reducing the number of updates. This will also improve foreground process performance a tiny bit during background compilations. Lower values update the status information more frequently, and therefore may slow the build process.

The final set of process control options are under the *IDE priority* section in the *Process Control* dialog. Choose one of the following radio buttons to alter the time relationship between the IDE and outside processes such as DOS programs and other Windows utilities you run while compiling a project in the background:

- *Low*—Outside processes have top priority over the IDE.
- *Normal*—Outside processes and the IDE share equal time status.
- *High*—The IDE has top priority over outside processes.
- *Realtime*—The IDE has exclusive priority over outside processes, which are halted during the build process.

> **TIP**
>
> Use the *Realtime* setting if you will run only IDE commands during background compilation. However, you should set this option to *Normal* when debugging with the IDE—because the integrated debugger runs in a separate thread, this option affects the internal debugger's speed.

Optimization Options

Borland C++ is an optimizing compiler. This means the command-line and IDE compilers, and also the alternate Intel compiler built into Borland C++, all offer several optimizations that, in many instances, can shrink code size or improve performance. You may optimize DOS and Windows programs using the techniques described here.

Nobody has yet written the perfect compiler. Perhaps no one ever will. Computers are smart, but humans are smarter, and only human programmers are capable of finding the best software solutions to problems.

Although far from perfect, modern compilers do a better job than ever before of generating efficient code. Simply stated, to optimize code, the compiler first translates one or more high-level statements and then examines the generated instructions one byte at a time. In this process, certain patterns emerge. The compiler might discover an assignment of a memory value to a register that's copied back to that same location in the very next instruction. Obviously, the compiler can delete these and other wasteful instructions.

If you were writing your own compiler, you'd want to know why such inefficiencies occur in compiled code. As a programmer, you are mostly interested in having the compiler remove wasteful instructions so that you don't have to rewrite the statements in assembly language. This section describes some of the optimizations you can order Borland C++ to make to your compiled programs and points out some of the pitfalls.

20

When and If To Optimize

Some programmers optimize their programs just before shipping a product. Others optimize at every step along the development path. Which is the right approach for you? In addition to answering that question, you need to choose whether to optimize modules for speed or for size. Small programs tend to run more slowly than large ones, typically because loops (which reduce program size) add significant overhead to a program's total operating time. Small, fast programs are desirable, but in terms of optimization techniques, *small* and *fast* are often incompatible words.

When choosing optimizations, keep the following suggestions in mind:

- Optimizing takes time. In Borland C++, it takes as much as 50 percent longer to compile the same program with speed optimizations than it does without them. It takes about 20 percent longer when optimizing for size. For faster compilation times, turn off all optimizations.

- Optimizations might cause bugs to appear or in some cases might even lead to new bugs. Many programmers continually optimize their code in order to test programs in their final distributed forms. If you wait until the last moment to optimize, the theory goes, a bug might skip your attention. On the other hand, during early prototyping, saving development time is more important than fixing bugs, and you can probably turn off optimizations until later in the development process.

- Try multiple optimization techniques. You might discover that different modules benefit from different optimizations. You might, for instance, optimize some modules for size and others for speed. Be selective.

- Turbo Debugger recognizes optimized code, but be aware that conflicts can arise among statements with bugs, the debugger, and optimized instructions. If a bug won't hold still, try debugging with and without optimizations. Differences in the compiled code might provide useful clues.

- Above all else, use good programming techniques. Don't rely on optimizations to do your job! Your skills as a programmer are the best optimizing tools you have. Use register variables wisely, employ inline functions and inline class member functions, have sound reasons for declaring virtual member functions, and test different algorithms for solving specific problems. The QuickSort algorithm, for example, is not always faster than other sorting methods—despite what text books may have to say on the subject.

TIP

Use the -S option with the command-line compiler to generate assembly language text files, ending in .asm. For insights into the effects of specific optimizations, compile with and without various options and compare the compiler's assembly language output.

Optimizing for Speed or Size

There are two ways to select compiler optimizations: from the command line and from the IDE. From a DOS prompt, enter command-line options in the form -Ox where x represents an optimization letter. That's a capital O, by the way, not a zero. For example, enter this command to compile a program named Test.cpp, optimized for size:

```
bcc -O1 test
```

Optimizations are also available for the 32-bit compiler:

```
bcc32 -O1 test
```

Use -O2 to optimize for speed. To disable all optimizations, use -Od. You can specify multiple options separately or string them together. The expression -Oabc is the same as the three options -Oa -Ob -Oc. You can also enter these and other optimization options into a Turboc.cfg text file. See Appendix B for a complete list of command-line options.

You can also select default optimizations with the IDE's *Options\Project* command. Or, to choose settings for an individual project, open its .ide file, highlight the target code file (its .exe file, usually), click the right mouse button, and choose *Edit local options* from the popup menu. Either way, these commands open the *Project Options* dialog box shown in Figure 20.2. (The figure shows a project window, which is not displayed for default settings selected with the IDE's *Options\Project* command.)

Figure 20.2.

The Project Options dialog's Optimizations topic.

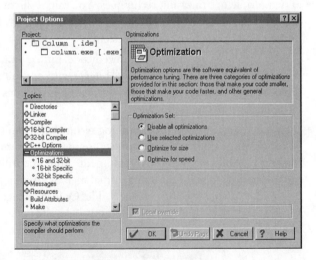

In the *Project Options* dialog, choose the *Optimizations* topic, which offers you four radio buttons:

- *Disable all optimizations*—Turns off all optimizations. Use this setting for the fastest build times.

- *Use selected optimizations*—Enables your selected optimizations. Use this setting for your final build, and also to periodically debug your code with and without optimizations.

- *Optimize for size*—Chooses default optimizations that tend to produce smaller code file sizes, but that might cause the program to run more slowly.

- *Optimize for speed*—Chooses default optimizations that tend to produce faster running times, but that might bloat code file size.

The *Project Options* dialog's Optimizations topic lists three subtopics that you can choose to select individual optimizations. The three subtopics are *16 and 32-bit, 16-bit Specific,* and *32-bit Specific.* The next sections discuss the optimizations for each of these categories.

> **NOTE**
>
> The following settings are found in the IDE's *Project Options* dialog. For reference, however, I also list the equivalent command-line options for each optimization setting.

16- and 32-Bit Optimizations

This subtopic offers three optimizations that apply equally to 16- and 32-bit code generation. The choices are

- *Common subexpressions*—Select one of the three radio buttons to disable common subexpression elimination, or to enable it for local or global processing. The *Global* setting often produces the best results, but because it examines the effects of code over the entire program, it can greatly increase code file size. If this happens, choose the *Local* setting, which restricts the range of this optimization, and thus lowers code file size at the possible expense of some runtime speed. See "Eliminating Common Subexpressions" in this chapter for more information about this optimization technique. Command-line options: -Oc, -Og.

- *Inline intrinsic functions*—Compiles common string and memory function calls as inline code. Because many programs rely heavily on these types of functions, this option can give a tremendous boost in speed, but might also produce an equally shocking increase in code size. See "Inline String Functions" in this chapter for more information. Command-line option: -Oi.

- *Induction variables*—Creates new variables (called induction variables) inside loops for holding results of various subexpressions. For example, the statement a[i] = a[i+1] inside a loop requires two separate, though related, address calculations for accessing an array. Induction variables can optimize this sort of expression by reusing one calculation to formulate another. Command-line option: -Ov.

16-Bit Specific Optimizations

This subtopic offers numerous optimizations that apply only to 16-bit code generation. The choices are

- *Jump optimizations*—Eliminates redundant jump instructions, and also rearranges loops and switch statements, all of which can needlessly waste memory. Command-line option: -O.

- *Loop optimization*—Cuts bytes out of loops by using the processor's string-move instructions (rep and stosx). Command-line option: -Ol.

- *Suppress redundant loads*—Deletes instructions that reload a value into a register that should already equal that value. This optimization may not work in all cases (in code where interrupts might alter registers, for example). Use with care. Command-line option: -Z.

- *Dead code elimination*—Deletes assignments to unused variables. Also deletes memory allocations for variables that are never used. See "Dead Code" in this chapter for more information. Command-line option: -Ob.

- *Windows prolog/epilog*—Suppresses increments and decrements on bp in function prolog and epilog code, attached to functions in Windows 16-bit programs. Not applicable to 32-bit Windows 95 or Windows NT programs. Command-line option: -OW.

- *Global register allocation*—Attempts to globally allocate registers and variables when doing so might result in a speed increase and smaller code size. Command-line option: -Oe.

- *Assume no pointer aliasing*—Tells the compiler to ignore potential effects of aliased pointers. A pointer can become aliased, for example, if the compiled code temporarily transfers an addressed value to a register. If the program subsequently modifies the data addressed by the pointer, the register value and the original data are thrown out of synch. This won't happen if you disable this option; however, enabling it can greatly improve runtime speed. See "Optimizations and Pointer Aliasing" in this chapter for more information. Use with care. Command-line option: -Oa.

- *Invariant code motion*—Attempts to move invariant expressions outside loops. Good programmers perform this optimization instinctively. (Instead of multiplying A*B*C inside a for loop that doesn't affect A, B, or C, you can multiply one time outside of the loop and save time.) Command-line option: -Om.

- *Copy propagation*—Propagates (clones) copies of various values and expressions when their reevaluation would waste time. This option is poorly documented. See "Copy Propagation" in this chapter for more information. Command-line option: -Op.

32-Bit Specific Optimizations

Following are optimizations that you may select only for 32-bit applications. These options are new to Borland C++ 5. The first option is available for Borland C++ and the alternate Intel C optimizing compiler. The second two options are available only with the Intel compiler.

NOTE

Select the Intel C compiler by using the *Options/Project* command and the *32-bit Compiler* topic. Select either of the two radio buttons: *Borland optimizing compiler* or *Intel (C) optimizing compiler.*

- *Pentium instruction scheduling*—Minimizes Pentium and 80x486 processor delays that are caused by certain kinds of address generation interlocks. This optimization also utilizes the Pentium's parallel pipelines feature. Using this optimization might cause debugging anomalies such as mirrored breakpoints (multiple breakpoints in code for which you set only a single breakpoint), and unexpected source-code line jumps during debugging sessions, particularly in code with array indexing expressions. Command-line option: -OS.

- *Cache hit optimizations*—Enables six types of code optimizations that tend to improve the number of processor cache hits, which reduce the number of instruction loads and memory references, and thus improve runtime performance. The six optimizations are labeled: loop interchange, loop distribution, strip mining and preloading, loop blocking, alternate loops, and loop unrolling. This optimization is available only for the Intel C compiler. Command-line option: -OM.

- *Optimize across function boundaries*—Enables five types of interprocedural optimizations that tend to reduce function call overhead. Although applied across function boundaries, the optimizations are restricted to functions within a single module. The five optimizations are labeled: monitoring module-level static variables, inline function expansion, cloning, passing arguments in registers, and constant argument propagation. This optimization is available only for the Intel C compiler, and is disabled for modules containing inline assembly language. Command-line option: -OI.

TIP

The preceding options work best with output code generated for Pentium processors. Using the *Options/Project* command and *32-bit Compiler* topic, choose the *Processor* subtopic and select the *Pentium* or *Pentium Pro* instruction set radio button.

Eliminating Common Subexpressions

A common subexpression typically occurs when you reference the same structure member more than once. Suppose, for example, you have a structure with substructure member v that has an int count member. Given a pointer p that addresses the outer structure, you write an if statement to test whether count's value is in the range 0 to 9:

```
if ((p->v.count >= 0) && (p->v.count < 10))
  // do something
```

In order to address count, the compiler generates code to calculate the structure's address, the offset to member v, and the offset to count. The two common subexpressions, p->v.count, cause the program to repeat this calculation twice to evaluate the full logical expression—a gross waste of time. Experienced programmers eliminate such waste by using a temporary variable:

```
int t = p->v.count;
if ((t >= 0) && (t < 10))
  // do something
```

The compiler's common subexpression eliminator performs this kind of optimization for you. Using the *Options\Project* command and selecting the *Optimizations* topic, you have three choices under the *Common Subexpressions* section in the *16- and 32-bit Optimizations* subtopic: *No optimization, Optimize locally* (-Oc), or *Optimize globally* (-Og). Local suppression works only within compound statement blocks. Global suppression attempts to eliminate common subexpressions from entire functions.

Generally, you should use global suppression for the best speed. This choice, however, can swell code-file size as the compiler creates numerous temporary variables to hold subexpression values. In that case, try switching to local subexpression elimination, which should reduce code-file size but might cause a moderate reduction in performance gain.

Inline String Functions

In theory, Chapter 19's advice about optimizing a program's critical code using assembly language sounds clean and simple. In practice, you might discover your program's critical code is buried deep inside a precompiled library function. Optimizing library functions in assembly language is an unappealing task, but fortunately, there's an alternative—at least for the string and memory functions in Table 20.1. Using a special option, you can have the compiler insert inline code for these functions.

Table 20.1. Potential inline string and memory functions.

alloca	memcpy	stpcpy	strcpy	strncpy
fabs	memset	strcat	strlen	strnset
memchr	rotl	strchr	strncat	strrchr
memcmp	rotr	strcmp	strncmp	

To convert memory and string functions to inline code, use the -Oi command-line compiler option, or select *Inline intrinsic functions* under *Optimizations, 16- and 32-bit topic* in the *Options\Project* dialog. Your program's code files may balloon in size, but they might also run faster if many statements call these common library routines.

Dead Code

Use -Ob (or *Dead code elimination* under the *16-bit Specific* subtopic under *Optimizations* in the IDE) to delete assignments to unused variables. This optimization also eliminates variables assigned values that are never used.

> **NOTE**
>
> Complex macro expansions and conditional compilation instructions might cause dead code to creep into your programs, so it's wise to test the before- and aftereffects of this optimization even if you regularly delete dead-code statements, as careful programmers should do.

A related optimization -Om moves invariant statements outside of loops. If you do something silly like this

```
for (int i = 0; i < 100; i++) {
  count = 100;    // invariant statement
  AnyFunction(i);
}
```

the compiler moves the invariant assignment to count outside of the loop. This optimization is available under the *16-bit Specific* topic in the *Options\Project* dialog.

Optimizations and Pointer Aliasing

Never mention pointer aliasing to a compiler author unless you are prepared to spend the rest of the evening discussing code generation anomalies. Pointers give programmers plenty of trouble; they give optimizing-compiler authors nightmares and hangovers.

When a pointer addresses a variable in memory, if the compiler stores that variable in a register, an assignment via the pointer throws the register and associated memory location out of synch. Recognizing this fact, the compiler normally does not perform subexpression elimination across statements that involve potentially dangerous pointer expressions. It avoids the same traps when performing copy propagation—an optimization technique that "remembers" values assigned to expressions and uses those values instead of repeating the same expressions later.

You can tell the compiler not to take precautions for pointer aliasing by enabling the IDE's *Assume no pointer aliasing* option under the *16-bit Specific* subtopic, or by using the -Oa command-line switch. This tack might put some wind into your code's sails, but it could also sink the ship. Of all the available optimization techniques, assuming that there are no aliased pointers can produce hard-to-find bugs. Use this option with care.

Copy Propagation

Borland's documentation doesn't explain this optimization very well, so I did some investigating in an attempt to understand its effects. From my tests, it appears that copy propagation reuses constants (and, possibly other values) rather than reevaluating some kinds of expressions.

For example, I compiled these three statements:

```
int y = 123;
int x = 321;
x = y + 1;
```

Without any optimizations, the compiler translated that fragment into the following assembly language (I added the comments):

```
mov    si,123              ; Move 123 into register si
mov    di,321              ; Move 321 into register di
lea    ax,word ptr [si+1]  ; Load si + 1 into ax
mov    di,ax               ; Store ax into di
```

The lea (load effective address) instruction does not refer to a memory location as it appears to do—it merely adds register si and the constant 1 and stuffs ax with the result as though this were an address.

With the copy-propagation option -Op, the compiler produced the following output:

```
mov    word ptr [bp-2],123  ; Propagate constant
mov    si,321               ; Move 321 into si
mov    ax,123               ; Move 123 into ax
inc    ax                   ; Increment ax
mov    si,ax                ; Move result into si
```

Two events appear to take place. First, the compiler saves a copy of the constant 123 in memory, apparently for later use even though there is no such use in this example. In addition, the compiler moves a copy of the same constant into ax and increments it.

Moving 123 into ax and incrementing should be faster than using the lea instruction, which apparently, the compiler generates by default in order to produce good compilation speed. It would be even better if the compiler moved 124 into ax and eliminated the increment instruction, but nobody's perfect.

Final Thoughts on Optimization Options

When optimizing your applications, keep the following points in mind:

- Always use good programming methods. Your skill as a programmer is far more important than any optimization technique. Don't rely on the compiler to clean up sloppy code.
- Test the before- and aftereffects of specific optimizations. If an optimization doesn't produce tangible results, don't use it.

- Know *why* you are using a specific optimization—never optimize at random. If you don't care, or if you don't have time for the detective work that's needed to understand what specific optimizations do, compile for smallest code-file size (-O1) or best runtime speed (-O2), whichever matters the most, and let the compiler select option combinations for you.

- During the development of major projects, some experts recommend periodically compiling with optimizations that you will probably select for the finished code. This may reveal bugs caused by specific optimizations. You don't want to be chasing such bugs the day before your disk is scheduled for manufacturing!

- Pay attention to all warnings issued during compilation. Eliminating the source of a warning (deleting unused variables, for example) can help reduce the need for optimizing, and may also help the optimizer run faster by cutting down its workload.

- Use assembly language to fine-tune code only *after* applying all optimizations. Use the -S option with the command line compilers to generate assembly language output for selected functions, and carefully inspect the generated code. Remember that the optimizer processes *compiled* code, not high-level statements, and it may choke on your clever assembly language tricks.

Other Optimizing Techniques

There are several other options and features you can select to alter the runtime performance of your programs. Following are some suggestions you might want to try in the interest of producing the fastest possible code.

Register Variables

With the IDE's *Options|Project* command, select the *Compiler* topic, and choose the subtopic *Code Generation*. This displays a dialog page with a section labeled *Register Variables*. Use it to select from the following three options. I also list the equivalent command-line options:

- *None*—Does not use registers for variables. Command-line option: -r-

- *Register keyword*—Uses registers for variables only if prefaced with the register keyword. (Despite this option's name, register must be lowercase.) Command-line option: -rd.

- *Automatic*—Uses registers for variables whenever possible, not just for those prefaced with the register keyword. This is the default. Command-line option: -r.

To select candidate variables to store in registers, the compiler examines one expression or statement block at a time and attempts to determine the "live range" of all variables within the block's scope. For example, in these hypothetical statements:

```
void f(void)
{
  int y;
```

```
  for (int i = 0; i < 10; i++)
    y += SomeFunction(i);
  int x = SomeOtherFunction(y);
  printf("x == %d\n", x);
}
```

the compiler could store x and i in the same register because these values are not alive concurrently—that is, they are not in use at the same times. Variables y and i would require separate registers because they live in the same statement blocks.

In addition to determining live ranges for variables, the compiler keeps track of any temporary registers that it requires for various instructions. It then performs a *global register optimization* to determine if any free registers remain for storing variables. Registers ax, bx, cx, dx, si, di, and es are available for this purpose (only si and di are preserved across function calls). In the IDE, select *Global register allocation* (see "Size Optimizations" in this chapter), or use the command-line option -Oe. Using option -O2 automatically also selects -Oe.

Another useful register optimization switch is -Z (*Suppress redundant loads* in the IDE's *16-bit Specific* optimizations). With this option, if the compiler detects that a register already has a certain value, it suppresses instructions that would store that same value in that register.

Fast Function Calls

This optimization can give some kinds of programs a tremendous performance boost by passing to functions some argument values in registers instead of pushing those values onto the stack. To have the compiler perform fast function calls whenever possible, select either the *16-bit* or *32-bit Compiler* topics with *Options\Project*, and choose the *Calling Convention* subtopic. Chose the *Register* radio button to enable fast function calls. Use the equivalent -pr option with the command-line compiler.

You can also force specific functions to accept register arguments. Preface the function's name with the _fastcall (one leading underscore) or _ _fastcall (two leading underscores) modifiers:

```
int _ _fastcall square(int n);
```

Be sure to use the same modifier in the function prototype and in its implementation:

```
int _ _fastcall square(int n)
{
  return n * n;
}
```

Because of the _ _fastcall modifier, calls to the square function pass n in a register such as ax instead of pushing the argument value onto the stack. Instead of addressing the parameter on the stack, which takes extra time, the function's compiled code simply uses the register value.

Linker Optimizations

The 16-bit IDE linker and command-line Tlink.exe support four optimizations new to Borland C++ 5.0. To use them, select *Options|Project* and open the *Linker* topic. Highlight the *16-bit Optimizations* subtopic, and then choose one or more of the following check boxes (command-line equivalents are also listed, but note that Tlink.exe uses a slash rather than a dash for command-line options):

- *Chain fixups*—A *fixup* is an address that is resolved at runtime when a program is loaded into memory. This option eliminates duplicate fixup data in the .exe code file, and potentially improves the program's loading time. The option also removes any trailing nulls in data segments, which can simply be allocated and zeroed at runtime. Command-line option: /Oc.

- *Iterate data*—Select this option to have the linker scan your data segments for repeating patterns. The linker compresses these patterns into a descriptor, which is executed at runtime. For example, a block of 80 blanks (such as in a constant string) are compressed to a command that creates this data pattern at runtime. This option can significantly reduce code-file size. Command-line option: /Oi.

- *Minimize segment alignment*—Choose this option to automatically select the smallest possible code-segment alignment, which among other values might be one byte, two bytes, a 16-byte paragraph, a 512-byte block, or as much as a full 64K segment. The default linker alignment is 512 bytes, which corresponds nicely to average disk sector sizes. However, the minimum alignment is dependent on code segment size—a 32K code segment, for instance, can be aligned on a single byte; a 128K code segment can be aligned on a word or larger boundary. By reducing alignment to the minimum possible size, you can greatly reduce your .exe code file's size; however, you might increase load time due to the code file's image crossing disk sector boundaries, resulting in extra disk accesses to load your program into memory. Command-line option: /Oa.

- *Minimize resource alignment*—This optimization is similar to the preceding one, but is applied to resource data segments. Command-line option: /Or.

The preceding optimizations increase linking times, and are best postponed until you build your final application (although, as with all optimization techniques, you should test their effects periodically as you develop your applications). To make these optimizations, the linker first creates a finished .exe code file. It then reopens that file, performs the selected optimizations, and writes the result to a new .exe code file.

Command-Line Tools

Professional programmers use utility programs such as Make, Tlib, Turbo Debugger, command-line compilers, and other tools such as Grep and Touch to make the most of their development systems and to save time. Of all the many utilities that come with Borland C++, these rank highest with the pros. You can use them in DOS and Windows programming, but you must run them from a DOS prompt.

Using Make

Complex programs with dozens of modules are difficult to compile and link by hand. To automate compilation, you can build an IDE project (see Chapter 18, "Managing Projects"), or you can use the DOS command-line Make utility.

Make saves you time and aggravation by issuing only the minimum number of commands that keep an entire project up to date. Suppose you modify four files in a 16-module program. Make examines the dates and times of your program's source and object-code files and automatically recompiles only the four modified files plus any other files on which the modified files depend.

The Borland C++ Make utility reads a text file (called the Make file) that contains compiler and linker commands. Actually, Make can issue any DOS command and it can run most programs and utilities. Typical Make files have three kinds of commands: macros, dependency rules, and DOS command lines:

- *Macros* are optional but save typing and can increase a Make file's clarity. Make-file macros are similar to #defined symbols in a C or C++ program.

- *Dependency rules* state which files depend on others. In Chapter 5, "Investing in Inheritance," for example, the Bench.obj file *depends on* Bench.cpp (refer to Listing 5.2)—if you change Bench.cpp, you must re-create Bench.obj in order to keep the object code file up to date with its source.

- Make issues *DOS commands* when it detects a dependent file that is out of date relative to other files on which the file depends. Typically, Make issues command-line compiler and linker commands, but it can give any valid DOS command.

Listing 20.1, Tbench.mak, is a simple Make file that uses these three concepts to compile and link Chapter 5's Bench.cpp and Tbench.cpp programs (refer to Listings 5.2 and 5.3 in that chapter).

Listing 20.1. Tbench.mak (Make file for Tbench program and class).

```
#================================================================
# Tbench.mak -- Make file for TBench program and class
# To use:
#  Copy to C05 and enter:
#  make -ftbench.mak
# Copyright (c) 1996 by Tom Swan. All rights reserved.
```

```
#================================================================

INCLUDE=c:\bc5\include
LIBRARY=c:\bc5\lib

tbench.exe: tbench.obj bench.obj
  bcc -L$(LIBRARY) tbench.obj bench.obj bidss.lib
tbench.obj: tbench.cpp
  bcc -c -I$(INCLUDE) tbench
bench.obj: bench.cpp bench.h
  bcc -c -I$(INCLUDE) bench
```

Copy Tbench.mak to Chapter 5's source directory (C05) and, at a DOS prompt, change to that directory. Make sure these files are in the directory: Bench.h, Bench.cpp, Tbench.cpp, and Tbench.mak, and then type the command

```
make -ftbench.mak
```

This runs Make and processes the commands in Tbench.mak. If nothing seems to happen, delete the .obj and .exe files in the directory and try again. The program might already be up-to-date, in which case Make correctly performs no actions.

> **NOTE**
>
> If you don't specify a filename with the -f option, Make attempts to read a file named Makefile (with no filename extension) in the current directory.

The first seven lines in Tbench.mak are comments, which begin with #. Make ignores comment lines. The next statements declare two macros, LIBRARY and INCLUDE. Modify the listed pathnames to match your installation. Macros are typically used in expressions such as $(LIBRARY) and $(INCLUDE), which Make replaces with the macros' associated text. You don't have to use macros in Make files, but they can save a lot of typing.

The rest of the example Make file lists dependency rules and commands to issue for compiling and linking the program. This declaration

```
tbench.exe: tbench.obj bench.obj
```

states that Tbench.exe depends on Tbench.obj and Bench.obj. If Tbench.exe's file date and time are earlier than either of the two listed .obj files, or if Tbench.exe does not exist, Make issues the command on the subsequent line, which must be indented by one or more spaces:

```
  bcc -L$(LIBRARY) tbench.obj bench.obj bidss.lib
```

The expression -L$(LIBRARY) expands to -LC:\bc5\lib using the value associated with the LIBRARY macro. The -L option gives the linker the location of any required .lib and .obj files. The statement specifies Bidss.lib, which contains the code for the Timer class. The command links the specified .obj and .lib files to create or re-create Tbench.exe.

679

Similar commands in Tbench.mak keep the program's other files up-to-date. In general, every file on which another depends requires a dependency rule and a DOS command to create that file. These declarations

```
tbench.obj:  tbench.cpp
  bcc -c -I$(INCLUDE) tbench
bench.obj:  bench.cpp bench.h
  bcc -c -I$(INCLUDE) bench
```

keep Tbench.obj and Bench.obj up-to-date. The first line states that Tbench.obj depends on Tbench.cpp. If Tbench.obj's date and time are earlier than Tbench.cpp or if Tbench.obj does not exist, Make issues the command on the subsequent line, which compiles Tbench.cpp to create Tbench.obj using the -c (compile only) option.

The third line in the previous code states that Bench.obj depends on Bench.cpp and Bench.h. If either of those two files' dates and times are more recent than Bench.obj, a change must have been made to one of the text files, and Make issues the command on the next line to compile or recompile the Bench module.

Make sorts out all such dependencies and issues the minimum number of commands in the correct sequence to compile and link an entire project. Try this experiment. After running Make as suggested earlier, load Bench.h into the IDE or another text editor and make an inconsequential change to the file. Save the modified file to disk. Alternatively, you can also type the command

```
touch bench.h
```

to update the file's date and time using the Touch.exe utility. Remember this trick next time you want to rebuild an entire project—use Touch.exe to force all source code modules to become out of date relative to their target executable or object-code files.

Next, from DOS, enter the same Make command you issued earlier:

```
make -ftbench.mak
```

Make now issues commands to compile Bench.cpp and then gives another command to link the resulting object-code files to create Tbench.exe. Next, try a similar experiment, but modify or touch Tbench.cpp. This time, Make determines that Bench.obj is current, so it compiles only Tbench.cpp before linking.

TIP

Another useful command is

```
make -n -ftbench.mak
```

The -n option tells Make to display but not issue commands. Use this option to inspect the commands that Make will give without actually executing those commands. (This is especially useful when debugging a recalcitrant Make file.) You might also rename Tbench.mak to makefile, with no filename extension. You then can just type make to run Make.

Using Tlib

Library files are convenient for storing multiple .obj object-code files, perhaps from a library of common modules. As an added benefit, the linker can extract multiple files from libraries much more quickly than it can read the individual .obj files from disk. Use the Tlib utility to insert and extract .obj files in .lib libraries.

Given the files A.obj, B.obj, and C.obj, combine them into a library named Mylib.lib with this command, entered at a DOS prompt:

```
tlib mylib.lib +a.obj +b.obj +c.obj
```

If Mylib.lib doesn't exist, Tlib creates it. To replace existing modules in a library, use -+ as in

```
tlib mylib.lib -+b.obj
```

> **TIP**
>
> A Make file might include such a command (preceded by at least one blank) to update a library upon recompiling B.obj's source module.

To extract a library file to a new .obj file, use the * command

```
tlib mylib.lib *b.obj
```

To remove a module, use -. To extract and remove a module from a library file, use -*. Use these commands with extreme caution. Keep backup copies of library files from which you remove modules. Once removed, they are gone for good.

Use Tlib's /E option to create an extended dictionary, which helps Turbo Linker (Tlink.exe or Tlink32.exe) load modules quickly. Use the /C option to add mixed case symbols to libraries (two modules, for example, that have symbols such as FALSE, false, and False that differ only in case). Don't use /C or /E for libraries that will be used with other linkers. Use them only with Turbo Linker.

For a list of a library's contents and public symbols, enter either of the following two commands:

```
tlib mylib.lib,con
tlib mylib.lib,temp.txt
```

To print a report, enter

```
tlib mylib.lib,prn
```

You must follow the library name with a comma and output filename for this option to work.

> **TIP**
>
> Use Tlib to find the actual syntax for public symbols in Borland C++ libraries. This can be helpful if you suspect a mistake in the documentation, or if you are having trouble compiling a program. For example, from a DOS prompt, change to C:\bc5\lib, and enter the command
>
> `tlib bidsl.lib,temp.txt`
>
> Load the resulting temp.txt file into the IDE or another text editor to examine the symbols for the large model version of Borland's Data Structure library.

Other Useful Tools

Another useful tool is Grep, which searches for strings in text files at blazing speed. Use Grep to identify files that contain variables, functions, and other symbols. For example, to locate library header files with the word `false`, change to C:\bc5\include and enter

`grep -li false *.h`

The `-li` command means "list filenames and ignore case."

Use the Touch utility to update file dates and times. The command `touch *.*` provides the current date and time for every file in the current directory. Software companies typically use Touch to update files before producing a master disk. The resulting directory looks clean, and any out-of-date files stick out like neon signs.

Finally, if there's a kitchen sink among Borland C++ utilities, Tdump is a virtual bathtub. Undoubtedly the result of torturous object-file investigations conducted by Borland programmers, Tdump rivals *The New York Times* in voluminous output. Enter a command such as

`tdump filename.exe`

for a comprehensive listing of the code file's contents. For example, try the command

`tdump tdump.exe`

for the lowdown on Tdump.exe's executable code layouts. Use Tdump's -v (verbose) option if you really like to read long reports. Type `Tdump` alone for a list of the program's many options. You're on your own with this mostly undocumented tool, but do try it. You might find it useful for uncovering a file's hidden secrets.

Choosing a Memory Model

The great myth about memory models is that, by selecting a larger model, you give your programs extra RAM. Nonsense. All memory is available to all programs in all memory models. A memory model simply changes the *methods* that the compiler and you can use to address data and to call functions. It also affects the organization of data and code in the program's executable code file. A memory model is an addressing scheme, not a memory supplier.

> **NOTE**
>
> Memory models also affect the methods by which 16-bit Windows programs address data and code. Windows 95 and NT programs all use the same, flat memory model, which makes all memory available as one huge block. Here again, though, memory models do not affect the quantity of available memory, only its form of access and code file layout.

The following sections describe each of the Borland C++ seven memory models: tiny, small, medium, compact, large, huge, and flat. Each section illustrates a memory model using a horizontal diagram with lower addresses to the left and higher addresses to the right. These illustrations differ from the standard vertical drawings that ambiguously place addresses at the top or bottom and lead to confusion about whether segments grow up or down. (In some of these illustrations, stacks "grow down" and "shrink up," a confusing mixture of terms.) In this chapter's memory model diagrams, arrows indicate the direction in which segments expand—left toward lower addresses, right toward higher ones. Shaded areas indicate free memory.

The following notes explain more about the parts and labels in this chapter's memory model diagrams:

- The phrase _TEXT segment 'CODE' refers to the symbol and name assigned to a compiled segment, using standard linker terminology. In the linker's lingo, a program's "text" is its code.

- The phrase _DATA segment 'DATA' refers to initialized global data where the program stores global variables. The huge model names data segments 'FAR_DATA'.

- The phrase _BSS segment 'BSS' refers to uninitialized global data.

- The number 64K means "up to 64K." Memory segments may be as small as 16 bytes or as large as 64K (exactly 65,536 bytes). Except for the flat memory model, code and data segments can never be larger than 64K each in any other memory model.

- Segment registers cs, ds, and ss point to the base locations of the program's code, data, and stack segments. In some models, multiple segment registers address the same location. In others, segments are distinct. The stack pointer sp indicates the top of the stack, which moves in the arrow's direction as statements push new data onto the stack and in the opposite direction as statements pop data from the stack. Programs begin with the stack pointer initialized at the highest possible offset address within the stack segment.

- DGROUP is an assembly language term that groups multiple segments into a single segment up to 64K. Some memory models combine the stack, heap, and data segments in DGROUP, thus limiting those segments to a combined total maximum of 64K.

- Programs can access heap memory through the standard malloc function and the C++ new operator. To access far heap memory, you can use far memory allocation functions such as farmalloc. To do the same with new, you can overload the operator to call farmalloc, but it may be just as well to select a model such as large with no far heap, in which case all unused memory is available through malloc and new.

- In models that support multiple data or code segments (or both), the word sfile_... indicates the segment's unique name, created from the module's filename. An ellipsis in these models (medium, large, and huge) indicates that multiple segments of the type at left may appear at this location.

- Near pointers are 16-bit offsets from a segment base. Far pointers are full 32-bit pointers and include segment and offset words. Near functions use similar 16-bit call and ret instructions. Far functions use 32-bit call and retf (far return) instructions. In general, near pointers and functions are faster than their far equivalents.

- In the IDE, the best way to select a memory model is through the *TargetExpert* command, activated with the right mouse button or by pressing Alt+F10 in a module or project window. Different targets permit different memory model selections. For example, you cannot compile tiny Windows programs because the tiny memory model is strictly for old-style .com DOS programs.

- From the command line, you can also select memory models with the -mx option, where x is one of the letters t (tiny), s (small), m (medium), c (compact), 1 (large), or h (huge). For example, the command bcc -ml myprog compiles Myprog.cpp using the large memory model. All modules, including any library routines, must use the same memory model. In some cases, this means you might have to rebuild a library before you can link your program. Also, some libraries require you to use a specific memory model. The 32-bit compiler, Bcc32.exe, has no memory model options because the flat memory model is the only one available to 32-bit applications.

The Tiny Model

The tiny memory model (see Figure 20.3) creates a .com-style program, a relic from MS-DOS's early days originally intended to provide an upgrade path for CP/M applications. (MS-DOS was originally modeled after Digital Research's now obsolete CP/M operating system for 8088-based computers.)

To create a .com file, use a command such as

```
bcc -mt -lt filename.cpp
```

The -mt option selects the tiny memory model. The -lt option tells the linker to use this same model, and to produce a .com executable code file.

Figure 20.3.

The tiny memory model.

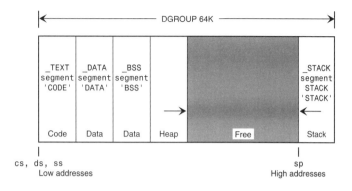

Borland C++ 4.5, using the tiny model, creates a code file ending in .exe that cannot be converted to a .com file. This problem, which did not exist in version 3.1, has been repaired in Borland C++ 5.0.

In the tiny model, every scrap of the program's data, code, stack space, and heap occupy a single memory segment up to 64K long. All pointers and function addresses are near.

Microsoft discourages programmers from creating .com code files, although this model has proven useful for utilities that need to load quickly and conserve disk space. On the other hand, despite their apparently small file sizes, tiny memory model programs always occupy a full 64K segment, if available, even when less memory would do the job. Small memory model programs might therefore occupy less RAM than the equivalent tiny model programs. You cannot use this model for Windows programs.

When compiling .com files, if you do not specify option -lt with Bcc (or /t with Tlink), the linker creates a .exe type code file and displays "Warning: No stack." To complete the compilation, use the DOS Exe2bin utility—for example, type

```
exe2bin myprog.exe myprog.com
```

You might also do this if you are using a different linker. However, it's probably best to have Tlink create .com files directly using the -mt and -lt options with Bcc.exe. Also, starting with Windows 95, Exe2bin is no longer provided with MS-DOS, so you now *must* use Tlink to create .com files.

The Small Model

The small memory model (see Figure 20.4) stores code in a separate segment up to 64K long. Global data, the stack, and the heap occupy one additional segment. Remaining memory is available through far-heap allocation functions.

Figure 20.4.

The small memory model.

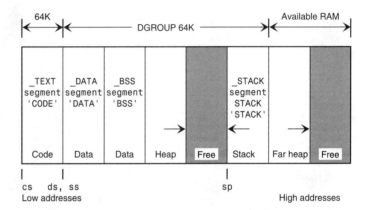

Small model programs are appropriate for short tests, examples (such as many of the non-Windows listings in this book), and utility programs. All pointers and functions are near, giving this model the best possible speed advantages—at least for 16-bit applications. The 16-bit command-line compiler uses the small memory model by default.

This model limits programs to one 64K segment of code, but more importantly, it provides a maximum of 64K for all global data, the heap, and the stack combined. To gain more memory requires using nonstandard far-heap allocation functions, making this model unattractive for writing portable applications that have large data requirements.

The Medium Model

The medium memory model (see Figure 20.5) improves on the small model by permitting multiple code segments, each of which can occupy up to 64K. As with small model programs, global data, the heap, and the stack must fit in one 64K segment, making this model inappropriate for data-intensive programs.

Pointers are near in the medium model, but function addresses are far. Generally, the medium model is best for programs with many functions but only minimum amounts of data. Medium model DOS code segments can be overlays.

Figure 20.5.
The medium memory model.

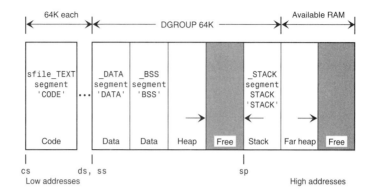

The Compact Model

The compact memory model (see Figure 20.6) might be the all-around best choice for small-to medium-size programs, especially when performance is important. Code and global data have separate segments, each up to 64K long. The stack also has its own segment, and the heap occupies whatever memory remains.

Functions are near in this model, but pointers are far in order to access the potentially large amount of memory on the heap. If your program has a moderate amount of code but needs to work with large amounts of data, the compact model might be the ideal choice.

Figure 20.6.
The compact memory model.

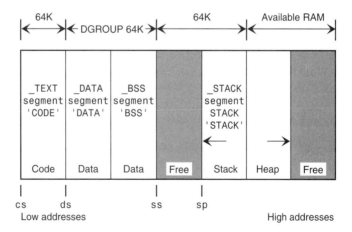

The Large Model

The large memory model (see Figure 20.7) is the same as the compact model but permits multiple code segments. Because of this, large model programs use far functions and far pointers by default.

Figure 20.7.
The large memory model.

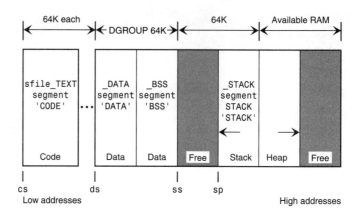

The large model is similar to the model that Borland Pascal programs use. In programs with large amounts of data and many functions, the large model might be the best choice. Of all models, this one tends to take the best advantage of 80x86 segmented memory (in real mode, that is). DOS code segments can be overlays. This is the preferred model for 16-bit Windows programs.

The Huge Model

The huge memory model (see Figure 20.8) extends the large memory model by permitting multiple code and data segments. Programs with massive global data needs and many functions can use this model. Pointers and functions are far by default.

The huge model is useful for programs with many large static arrays or other structures. Even so, individual data segments can be no larger than 64K. DOS code segments can be overlays. You cannot use this model for Windows programs.

Figure 20.8.
The huge memory model.

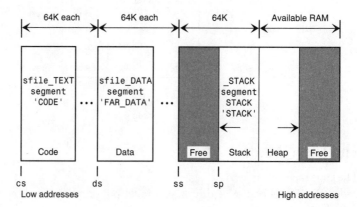

The Flat 32-Bit Model

The seventh memory model, available only to 32-bit Windows 95 and Windows NT programs, is often called the *flat model*. There's no diagram for this one—if there was, it would just be one, large, empty box. In the flat model, memory is not segmented as it is in other models. In the flat memory model, pointers and references are far, 32-bit addresses.

You cannot use the flat memory model in DOS programs. You also must use the 32-bit command-line compiler, or its equivalent built into the IDE. Output from the 32-bit compilers must be linked by (you guessed it) a 32-bit linker. These compilers and linkers produce a new portable executable (PE) code file format. This code file runs only under Win32s, Windows NT, and Windows 95.

> **NOTE**
>
> Don't get the idea that with 32-bit Windows programs your code just sits there all alone in a gigantic memory space. The reality is far more complex, and your program must share memory with other processes and the operating system. The flat model does, however, permit you to create truly massive arrays and other structures.

Near and Far Pointers

Memory models affect the default near and far sizes of pointers and function addresses. Table 20.2 lists the default pointer, function address, and this pointer sizes for Borland C++'s seven memory models. Near pointers are relative to the segment base register ds; near function addresses are relative to the code segment register cs. Near pointers can address code and data within 64K of their segment base. Far pointers include segment and offset values and can directly address any location in a PC's first megabyte of RAM.

Table 20.2. Pointer, function, and this pointer sizes.

Memory Model	Pointer size	Functions	this pointer
Tiny	near	near	near
Small	near	near	near
Medium	near	far	near
Compact	far	near	far
Large	far	far	far
Huge/Flat	far	far	far

In any memory model, you can selectively override near and far default sizes to address data and code in whatever way you wish. You can, for example, declare a far pointer in a small memory model program, which uses near pointers by default. You can also declare functions to be near in a large memory model program, thus improving performance by calling functions with relatively fast `call` instructions that use 16-bit offset addresses. One exception: you can't override the `this` pointer's default near or far status.

> **NOTE**
>
> Be careful when overriding the near and far default sizes of function addresses and pointers. Calls to near functions are possible only from within the same code segment, and near pointers might require you to initialize a segment register. The compiler generates correct code only for default pointer and function address sizes. The results of any overrides are your responsibility.

To override a pointer's default size, declare it with a `near` or `far` keyword. Here are a few samples:

```
double far *dfp;     // Far pointer to a double value
int near *inp;       // Near pointer to an integer
char *c;             // Default size pointer to a char or string
```

In the absence of `near` or `far`, the compiler uses the default size for the current memory model. Using the preceding code, pointer `c` might be near or far depending on the memory model, but `dfp` is always `far`; `inp` is always `near`.

You can also declare huge pointers, which are normalized far pointers with unique segment and offset values. Normalized pointers have offset values in the range of 0 to 15. Declare huge pointers with the `huge` modifier:

```
double huge *p1;     // Huge pointer to a double value
double huge *p2;     // Second huge pointer to a double value
```

Because the compiler normalizes huge pointers, it's safe to compare them in relational expressions. The statement

```
if (p1 < p2)
  DoSomething();
```

executes `DoSomething` if the address value of `p1` is less than the address value of `p2`. You can similarly compare near pointers because these are merely offset values.

You cannot safely compare far pointers, however, because two unnormalized far pointers can differ in value but address the same location! For instance, in hexadecimal, the address values `0000:0010` and `0001:0000` point to the same byte in memory simply by using a different, but logically equivalent, combination of segment and offset values. It's senseless to compare such unnormalized far pointers.

Segment Pointers

An obscure type of pointer, called a *segment pointer,* is a kind of near-and-far hybrid. Declare a segment pointer with the _seg modifier:

```
double _seg *sp;      // Segment pointer to a double value
```

Segment pointers have an assumed offset of 0000, and thus occupy only 16 bits but can address all of a PC's first megabyte of RAM (in 16-byte minimum-size chunks).

Don't confuse segment pointers with pointers declared using one of the segment overrides: _cs, _ds, and _es. Use these overrides to create near pointers as offsets from a nonstandard segment register. For example, to create a pointer dp into the stack, you can declare it as

```
double _ss *dp;      // Pointer to double stored on the stack
```

This pointer's assumed segment register is ss rather than the usual ds. Replace _ss with _cs to address code-segment data, or use _es to create pointers that address data stored relative to es, which you would have to initialize somehow. Beware of these refinements—they are tricky to use correctly. Poking around in the system stack is like traversing a mine field on a pogo stick. You might be better advised to take a safer course (in other words, using standard pointer techniques).

Near and Far Functions

Pointers are not the only kinds of address modifications you can make. You can also declare functions to be near or far independently of a memory model. For a function prototyped as

```
void AnyFunction();
```

the compiler inserts a near ret or a far retf instruction at the function's exit point depending on the current model's default treatment for function addresses. It also uses near or far addresses in calls to the function. To force the compiler to use far addressing, add the far keyword before the function name:

```
void far AnyFunction();
```

You can also force functions to be near:

```
void near AnyFunction();
```

Near functions might be useful in the medium, large, and huge memory models, which use far function calls and returns by default. Compiled calls to near functions require only 16-bit addresses and are somewhat faster than far functions. This is especially true for recursive functions, which perform better and use less stack space when declared to be near.

> **NOTE**
>
> Don't make trouble for yourself by forcing all intersegment function calls to be near. Profile your code to ensure that any modifications to a function's near or far status are truly worth the effort.

DOS-only programs that use the huge memory model give functions the additional task of locating the module's data segment. Each segment in a huge model program has its own private data segment, and thus every function must initialize register ds to address that module's global data. In addition to the usual startup code that prefaces compiled functions, the compiler adds the instructions

```
push ds              ; Save current data segment
mov  ax,X_DATA       ; Assign ax the module's data segment address
mov  ds,ax           ; Move ax into segment register ds
```

The function also executes pop ds before returning to its caller. Functions might suffer a drop in performance from this additional overhead, which you can eliminate by using the large memory model and storing your data on the heap.

Sometimes, functions in other memory models need to initialize ds to locate the program's data. In such cases, use the _loadds modifier in the function's header:

```
void _loadds AnyFunction();
```

The compiler treats this function as it does in huge memory model programs, adding instructions to the function's compiled code to save and initialize ds.

Overlays and VROOMM

VROOMM is the sound that the price of Borland's stock usually makes on Wall Street (but not always in the preferred direction). It's also Borland's *Virtual Runtime Object-Oriented Memory Manager*, otherwise known as the DOS overlay loader. Use VROOMM to load one or more code segments as needed into memory, leaving other code segments on disk. Assuming that not all code segments need to be in memory at once, overlays make it possible to run programs that have more code than available RAM.

VROOMM includes features for storing code overlays in expanded and extended memory. Executable code, however, always runs in a PC's lower 640K of memory. VROOMM is not a DOS extender. It's an overlay manager that you can use to run massive programs in relatively small spaces.

NOTE

Windows has its own flavor of overlays, known as virtual memory. The use of virtual memory is automatic (as long as the user configures it properly). VROOMM applies only to DOS-only applications.

Here are some key observations to keep in mind when using overlays:

- The smallest possible overlay is one code segment. This does not mean, however, that overlays are each 64K long. Overlay segments can occupy anywhere from 16K to 64K, although most fall somewhere in between. Generally, small overlays perform better than large ones. Ideally, all of a program's overlay segments should be similar in size.

- You can overlay only code segments. You cannot overlay data or stack segments or any part of the heap.

- Overlay programs must use the medium, large, or huge memory models. In other words, VROOMM works only with memory models that support multiple code segments (which makes perfect sense because the smallest overlay is a code segment). You cannot overlay tiny, small, or compact programs.

- VROOMM maintains a memory buffer in which code overlays reside on their way in and out of RAM. In the default arrangement, the overlay buffer exists between the stack and far heap in medium model programs (see Figure 20.5) and between the stack and heap in large and huge programs (see Figures 20.6 and 20.7). The default buffer size is about twice as large as the largest overlay segment.

- You can optionally swap overlay segments to expanded or extended RAM. VROOMM makes the process nearly automatic (more on this later). Using these options permits programs to take advantage of extra RAM on modern PCs but still run on RAM-starved PCs of old.

- The overlay manager installs its own control code in private segments. The space that these segments take should pay you back many times in space saved by using overlays. So for all practical purposes, you can ignore VROOMM's overhead.

- VROOMM uses interrupt vector `0x3f` for its dynamic segment loader. Don't touch this interrupt!

- You don't need to take any special actions to call functions in overlay segments. You write your programs the same with or without overlays. VROOMM makes overlay management transparent to programmers—almost transparent, that is. When calling a function in an overlay module, *all currently active functions must be far.* If function A calls function B which calls function C in an overlay segment, A and B must be far or the program will crash. VROOMM walks the stack looking for function return addresses, and it expects those addresses to be far. Using the `near` function modifier in overlay programs, *even in nonoverlay segments,* is extremely hazardous.

- External assembly language functions that are included in overlay object-code modules must be far.

- VROOMM permits multiple overlay segments to occupy memory concurrently. A function in overlay A can call another function in overlay B, which might call yet another function in overlay C. Some other overlay managers permit only one overlay module in memory at a time, thus preventing overlay functions from calling one another. VROOMM does not impose any similar restrictions.

- Never overlay interrupt service routines, critical functions that are called repeatedly, or similar code that must be in RAM at all times or that programs call frequently. Overlaying every one of a program's code segments is usually unwise.

- The stand-alone and IDE Turbo Debuggers support overlays. You debug overlaid programs no differently from others. Use the stand-alone debugger's *View\Module* command to select among a program's multiple code segments.

- Although overlays are not available, nor are they needed, in Windows applications, VROOMM works perfectly well in programs run in a DOS prompt window, and the techniques described here still have much contemporary value.

Writing Overlay Modules

A few simple listings demonstrate how to construct overlay segments and programs. First, Listing 20.2, Root.h, and Listing 20.3, Root.cpp, present a main program that calls three functions, Ov1A, Ov1B, and Ov1C. Each function, to be presented later, exists in a separate overlay code segment.

Listing 20.2. Root.h (Declares three overlay function prototypes).

```
//================================================================
// Root.h -- Declares three overlay function prototypes
// Copyright (c) 1996 by Tom Swan. All rights reserved.
//================================================================

void Ov1A(void);
void Ov1B(void);
void Ov1C(void);
```

Listing 20.3. Root.cpp (Calls the overlay function modules).

```
//================================================================
// Root.cpp -- Calls the overlay function modules
// To compile:
//    bcc -ml -Y root -Yo ovla ovlb ovlc
// To run:
//    root
// Copyright (c) 1996 by Tom Swan. All rights reserved.
//================================================================
```

```
#include <iostream.h>
#include <conio.h>
#include "root.h"

main()
{
  cout << "Enter root program\n";
  cout << "Press Enter to call overlay A...";
  getch();
  OvlA();
  cout << "Press Enter to call overlay B...";
  getch();
  OvlB();
  cout << "Press Enter to call overlay C...";
  getch();
  OvlC();
  return 0;
}
```

Next come the three overlay modules in Listing 20.4, Ovla.cpp, Listing 20.5, Ovlb.cpp, and Listing 20.6, Ovlc.cpp. Nothing in the modules themselves indicates their status as overlays—the source code is no different from any other separate modules.

Listing 20.4. Ovla.cpp (Implements the OvlA function).

```
//=================================================================
// Ovla.cpp -- Implements the OvlA function
// Copyright (c) 1996 by Tom Swan. All rights reserved.
//=================================================================

#include <iostream.h>
#include <conio.h>

void OvlA(void)
{
  cout << "\nWelcome to Overlay A!\n";
  cout << "Press any key to exit Overlay A...";
  getch();
  cout << '\n';
}
```

Listing 20.5. Ovlb.cpp (Implements the OvlB function).

```
//=================================================================
// Ovlb.cpp -- Implements the OvlB function
// Copyright (c) 1996 by Tom Swan. All rights reserved.
//=================================================================

#include <iostream.h>
#include <conio.h>
```

continues

695

20

Listing 20.5. continued

```
void OvlB(void)
{
  cout << "\nWelcome to Overlay B!\n";
  cout << "Press any key to exit Overlay B...";
  getch();
  cout << '\n';
}
```

Listing 20.6. Ovlc.cpp (Implements the `OvlC` function).

```
//===============================================================
// Ovlc.cpp -- Implements the OvlC function
// Copyright (c) 1996 by Tom Swan. All rights reserved.
//===============================================================

#include <iostream.h>
#include <conio.h>

void OvlC(void)
{
  cout << "\nWelcome to Overlay C!\n";
  cout << "Press any key to exit Overlay C...";
  getch();
  cout << '\n';
}
```

You could compile these modules into a single non-overlaid program. To do that from the DOS prompt, enter the command

```
bcc -ml root ovla ovlb ovlc
```

To compile the modules as overlays, use the options -Y and -Yo (a lowercase letter o, not a zero) like this:

```
bcc -ml -Y root -Yo ovla ovlb ovlc
```

You must use the -Y option to compile overlaid modules, and you must select an appropriate memory model, -ml, here. In addition, use the -Yo option to compile selected modules as separate overlay code segments. In this command, ovla, ovlb, and ovlc are compiled and linked as three separate code segment overlays. Root is not an overlay segment. Turn off overlay code generation with -Yo-. Suppose that only ovla and ovlb, but not ovlc, are to be overlays. In that case use the command

```
bcc -ml -Y root -Yo ovla ovlb -Yo- ovlc
```

Normally, options immediately follow bcc. Option -Yo- may appear between filenames on the command line. These options pass to the linker the /o option, which tells Tlink.exe to link in the VROOMM overlay manager from file Overlay.lib (usually stored in C:\bc5\lib). If you run Tlink.exe separately, specify /o to link overlaid modules.

To compile the program using the IDE, use the *Project|Open project* command to open the Root.ide file, on this book's CD-ROM in the C20 directory. Select *Project|Make all* to compile; then switch to a DOS prompt to run the resulting Root.exe program.

> **NOTE**
>
> If you can't build the overlay project with the IDE, highlight the Root.exe target code filename in the Project window, and click the right mouse button or press Alt+F10 to open a popup menu. Select *Edit local options* and check that the *Include* and *Lib* paths are set correctly for your installation.

In general, to build an overlaid application using the IDE, follow these steps:

1. Create a project file for your application. Add all .cpp (or .c) modules to the project, including overlaid and non-overlaid modules.

2. Using *TargetExpert,* set *Target Type* to *Application (.exe),* change *Platform* to *DOS Overlay,* and select a *Target Model*—Medium, Large, or Huge.

3. Optionally specify any libraries your program uses—*BGI,* for example, or the *Class Library.*

4. Back in the Project window, highlight each overlaid module (Ovla.cpp, for instance), and click the right mouse button or press Alt+F10 to open a SpeedMenu. Select *Edit node attributes,* and enable the check box *Overlay this module.* (It's near the bottom of the *Node Attributes* dialog.) Repeat this step for each overlaid module in your program.

Managing the Overlay Buffer

Programs with many small overlay segments might benefit from a larger overlay buffer. To increase the buffer's size, assign a value equal to the buffer size in 16-byte paragraphs to _ovrbuffer in your program's main function. For example, to reserve a 4096-byte buffer for Root.cpp (Listing 20.3), add the following as the first statement in function main:

```
unsigned _ovrbuffer = 256;   // 256 * 16 == 4096 bytes
```

Ignore the warning that "'_ovrbuffer' is assigned a value that is never used...." Or, you can insert #pragma warn -aus to turn off this warning.

Overlays in Expanded and Extended Memory

Look up functions _OvrInitEms and _OvrInitExt in your online help files. They are useful in overlaid programs to enable swapping of code segments to expanded and extended RAM.

All PCs, XTs, and ATs can use expanded, or *page-frame* memory. In this memory system, additional RAM is made available as pages that appear in a *memory window*, a reserved location somewhere in the upper reaches of memory. Commands sent to the memory hardware bring various pages of memory into this window. Call _OvrInitEms to automatically detect and use expanded memory for overlays.

Systems with 80286, 80386, 80486, and Pentium processors can use extended memory, which resides at addresses above the first megabyte of RAM available on all PCs. Extended memory is available only by using the processor's protected mode. Call _OvrInitExt to automatically detect and use extended memory for overlays.

A Few Good Classes

Mixed in with Borland's standard and template class library header files are several classes that you can use in C++ DOS and Windows programs. Although the standard template library provides similar capabilities, these classes are still valuable. Try the following examples on for size. Header paths relative to C:\bc5\include and filenames are listed for reference.

Standard Templates (classlib\stdtempl.h)

Many compilers provide nonstandard min and max functions, which return the minimum and maximum values of two arguments. For example, this sets result to the lesser of two int variables, a and b:

```
int result = min(a, b);
```

The problem with functions like min is that their data types are fixed. You can't pass them your own class objects, structures, or strings. For example, this won't work:

```
string result = max("California", "Florida");  // ???
```

By using templates for min and max, however, you can do exactly that. The templates, defined in Stdtemp.h, mold to whatever data types you want to use.

The header provides three templates: min, max, and range. To use them, declare a function prototype of the forms:

```
const T & min(const T &a, const T &b);
const T & max(const T &a, const T &b);
const T & range(const T &a, const T &b, const T &c);
```

Replace T with your data type. For example, to create a min function that returns the minimum of two long values, type this line outside of any function:

```
const long & min(const long &a, const long &b);
```

Because the min function is a template, you need only provide a prototype that specifies the function's return value and parameter types (all of which must be the *same* type). The compiler uses the prototype to construct a real, inline function, from the template. In other words, the compiler writes the code—you simply specify the function's form as a prototype.

To create a max function capable of returning the alphabetical maximum of two strings, use this statement:

```
const string & max(const string &a, const string &b);
```

A third template, range, creates a function that determines whether a value is between two others. For instance, to create a function that compares int values, add this prototype to your program:

```
const int & range(const int &a, const int &b, const int &c);
```

If c is between a and b, the function returns c. If c is greater than b, it returns b. If c is less than a, it returns a. You can use the function to force c to a value in the range a...b:

```
int a = 1, b = 100;
int c = range(a, b, c); // Define c so that a <= c <= b
```

Listing 20.7, Minmax.cpp, demonstrates the three standard templates, min, max, and range. Compile from a DOS prompt with the command bcc minmax, or compile from the IDE as an EasyWin application.

Listing 20.7. Minmax.cpp (Demonstrates min, max, and range templates).

```
//===============================================================
// Minmax.cpp -- Demonstrates min, max, and range templates
// To compile:
//    bcc minmax
// To run:
//    minmax
// Copyright (c) 1996 by Tom Swan. All rights reserved.
//===============================================================

#include <iostream.h>
#include <cstring.h>
#include <classlib\stdtempl.h>

const long & min(const long &, const long &);
const double & max(const double &, const double &);
const string & max(const string &, const string &);
const int & range(const int &, const int &, const int &);

void main()
```

continues

699

Listing 20.7. continued

```
{
  long along, blong;
  double adouble, bdouble;
  string astring, bstring;
  int aint, bint, cint;

  along = 123456L; blong = 65536L;
  cout << "\nalong = " << along << endl;
  cout << "blong = " << blong << endl;
  cout << "min(a,b) = " << min(along, blong) << endl;

  adouble = 3.14159; bdouble = -55.77;
  cout << "\nadouble = " << adouble << endl;
  cout << "bdouble = " << bdouble << endl;
  cout << "max(a,b) = " << max(adouble, bdouble) << endl;

  astring = "Proteus"; bstring = "Thetus";
  cout << "\nastring = " << astring << endl;
  cout << "bstring = " << bstring << endl;
  cout << "max(a,b) = " << max(astring, bstring) << endl;

  aint = 1; bint = 100; cint = 101;
  cout << "\naint = " << aint << endl;
  cout << "bint = " << bint << endl;
  cout << "cint = " << cint << endl;
  cout << "range(a,b,c) = " << range(aint, bint, cint) << endl;
}
```

Binary-Coded-Decimal Class (bcd.h)

Use the bcd class to construct objects that can represent numeric values in binary-coded-decimal (BCD) form. BCD objects store floating-point values as individual decimal digits. This format eliminates round-off errors in calculations, making the bcd class suitable for business, spreadsheets, accounting, and other applications.

One problem with BCD objects is their speed. Typically, expressions that use floating-point values evaluate faster than similar expressions with BCDs. The bcd class also limits precision to 17 decimal digits, equivalent to the approximate range of 1e+125 to 1e-125.

Listing 20.8, Bcd.cpp, shows how to use the bcd class. It defines an array of bcd values, a sum, and avg. As the program demonstrates, you can use bcd objects as you do variables of built-in numeric classes. You can add, subtract, multiply, and divide bcd objects, and you can output them in stream statements. Compile from a DOS prompt with the command bcc bcd, or compile from the IDE as an EasyWin application.

Listing 20.8. Bcd.cpp (Demonstrates the bcd class).

```
//================================================================
// Bcd.cpp -- Demonstrates the bcd class
// To compile:
//    bcc bcd
// To run:
//    bcd
// Copyright (c) 1996 by Tom Swan. All rights reserved.
//================================================================

#include <iostream.h>
#include <iomanip.h>
#include <bcd.h>
#include <math.h>

#define MAX 10

void main()
{
  bcd array[MAX], sum = 0, avg;
  int i;

  for (i = 0; i < MAX; i++)
    array[i] = (i + 1) * M_PI;

  for (i = 0; i < MAX; i++) {
    sum += array[i];
    cout << "bcd array[" << i << "] == " << array[i] << endl;
  }

  avg = sum / MAX;
  cout << "For " << MAX << " bcd numbers:" << endl;
  cout << "bcd sum == " << sum << endl;
  cout << "average == " << avg << endl;
  bcd rounded = bcd(real(avg), 2);
  cout << "average rounded to 2 places == " << rounded << endl;
}
```

Complex Math Class (complex.h)

I'm not a mathematician, so I have few uses for the `complex` class (in fact, I don't use it at all). Complex numbers, math wizards inform me, are useful for representing otherworldly values such as the square root of -2. The next time I need to do that, I will certainly consider using the `complex` class, demonstrated in Listing 20.9, Complex.cpp. Compile from a DOS prompt with the command `bcc complex`, or compile from the IDE as an EasyWin application.

Listing 20.9. Complex.cpp (Demonstrates the `complex` class).

```
//================================================================
// Complex.cpp -- Demonstrates the complex class
// To compile:
//    bcc complex
// To run:
//    complex
// Copyright (c) 1996 by Tom Swan. All rights reserved.
//================================================================

#include <iostream.h>
#include <complex.h>

void main()
{
  complex number = -2;
  complex result = sqrt(number);
  cout << "complex sqrt(-2) == " << result;
}
```

TDate Class (classlib\date.h)

The TDate and TTime classes are two undiscovered treasures in Borland's class library. After you try the TDate class, you'll undoubtedly want to use it for all dates in your programs. The class has many functions that, for years, uncountable numbers of programmers have reinvented—such as entering dates, displaying dates in a variety of formats, determining the day-of-week for a specific date, and so on.

Listing 20.10, Thedate.cpp, demonstrates some of the properties of this useful class. You must link the compiled object-code to the Bidsx.lib file, where x represents a memory model. Compile from a DOS prompt with a command such as

```
bcc -ml thedate bidsl.lib
```

which compiles the program using the large memory model and links it to that same model of the Borland Data Structure library. Or you can compile from the IDE as an EasyWin application (be sure to enable the *Class Library* check box). When prompted, enter a date in the form mm/dd/yy. Enter your birthday, for example, to find out on what day of the week you were born.

Listing 20.10. Thedate.cpp (Demonstrates the `TDate` class).

```
//================================================================
// Thedate.cpp -- Demonstrates the TDate class
// To compile:
//    bcc -ml thedate bidsl.lib
// To run:
//    thedate
// Copyright (c) 1996 by Tom Swan. All rights reserved.
//================================================================

#include <iostream.h>
```

```
#include <cstring.h>
#include <classlib\date.h>

void ShowDate(const char *msg, TDate &d);

void main()
{
  TDate today;
  ShowDate("Today is ", today);

  TDate dayZero(0,0);
  ShowDate("Day zero is ", dayZero);

  TDate yourDate;
  cout << "\nEnter a date: ";
  cin >> yourDate;
  ShowDate("Your date is ", yourDate);
}

// Display string message and a date
void ShowDate(const char *msg, TDate &d)
{
  cout << endl << msg << d.AsString() << endl;
  cout << "Day of week: " << d.NameOfDay() << endl;
}
```

You can construct TDate objects in various ways. With no arguments, the object is initialized with the current date:

```
TDate today;
```

Alternatively, you can initialize a TDate object by passing its constructor two integer values that represent the day and year. The following statement creates a date object equal to the 135th day of 1975:

```
TDate anyDate(135, 1975);
```

You might think that's a pretty weird way to initialize a date, but if the year is known, a program might store only the day of the year to represent dates. You could then convert the day values into TDate objects as shown here.

More traditional ways to construct TDate objects are

```
TDate(DayTy day, const char *month, YearTy year);
TDate(DayTy day, MonthTy month, YearTy year);
```

The first line constructs a TDate object from a day of month, a month name in string form, and a year. DayTy and YearTy are typedef aliases defined in Date.h. Use these constructors to construct TDate objects such as

```
TDate date1(12, "January", 1925);
TDate date2(15, 6, 1950);
```

After constructing a date object, you can call one of several member functions in the `TDate` class. For example, this displays the day of week for any date:

```
cout << anyDate.NameOfDay() << endl;
```

Check whether a date is valid with code such as

```
if (anyDate.IsValid()) {
  // okay to use anyDate
}
```

You can compare two dates, apply the ++ and -- operators to them, add or subtract two dates, and also add or subtract a specified number of days. With `TDate`, it's simple to create a range of dates:

```
TDate today;
for (int i = 1; i < 10; i++) {
  cout << today.AsString() << endl;
  ++today;
}
```

> **NOTE**
>
> Apparently, `TDate` defines only the prefix form of ++, and therefore, you receive a warning for expressions such as `today++`. Such expressions seem to work correctly, however, and you can probably ignore the warning.

Notice how the fragment calls `AsString` to display the date formatted as a string. You can change that format by calling `SetPrintOption`:

```
TDate::HowToPrint oldHow;
oldHow = today.SetPrintOption(TDate::European);
cout << today.AsString() << endl;
```

In the former code, the date is printed as

```
August 5, 1994
```

In the revised code, the date is printed European style like this:

```
5 August 1994
```

TTime Class (CLASSLIB\TIME.H)

Like `TDate`, the `TTime` class is highly useful, though many Borland C++ programmers may not be aware of its existence. Listing 20.11 demonstrates some of `TTime`'s capabilities. As with the `TDate` class, you must link the program to the proper Bids*x*.lib file where *x* is the memory model you are using. Compile from a DOS prompt with a command such as

```
bcc -ml thetime bidsl.lib
```

or compile from the IDE as an EasyWin application (be sure to enable the *Class Library* check box).

> **NOTE**
>
> Compiling Thetime.cpp produces several errors that have no apparent effect on the resulting code. These errors did not occur in previous releases of Borland C++ 5, and have been reported to Borland as a bug.

Listing 20.11. Thetime.cpp (Demonstrates the `TTime` class).

```
//================================================================
// Thetime.cpp -- Demonstrates the TTime class
// To compile:
//   bcc -ml thetime bidsl.lib
// To run:
//   thetime
// Copyright (c) 1996 by Tom Swan. All rights reserved.
//================================================================

#include <iostream.h>
#include <cstring.h>
#include <classlib\time.h>

void ShowTime(const char *msg, TTime &t);
void Pause(const long secs);

int main()
{
  TTime now;
  ShowTime("Current date and time: ", now);

  TTime anyTime(123456L);
  ShowTime("Any old date and time: ", anyTime);

  cout << "\nPausing for 10 seconds";
  Pause(10);

  return 0;
}

// Display string message and a time
void ShowTime(const char *msg, TTime &t)
{
  cout << endl << msg << t.AsString() << endl;
}

// Use TTime objects to pause for a number of seconds
void Pause(const long secs)
{
```

continues

Listing 20.11. continued

```
TTime start;                    // Initialize start to now
TTime stop(start + secs);       // Initialize stop
SecondTy tick = start.Second(); // Initialize tick variable
while (start < stop) {          // Loop until start >= stop
  start = TTime();              // Update start time to now
  if (start.Second() != tick) { // Check if 1 second passed
    cout << '.';                // Display feedback
    tick = start.Second();      // Update tick variable
  }
}
cout << endl;
}
```

> **NOTE**
>
> The `TTime` class calls the `tzset` ("time-zone set") function defined in the standard Time.h header file, located in C:\bc5\include. This is not the same header that declares `TTime`, located in the Classlib subdirectory. For best results, define an environment variable `TZ` equal to a string that represents the current time zone—`EST5EDT`, for example, for Eastern Standard Time.

Constructing a `TTime` object with no arguments initializes the object to the current time:

```
TTime now;
```

You can also initialize a `TTime` object with the number of seconds that have elapsed since January 1, 1901:

```
TTime anyTime(123456L);
```

Obtain that value for the current time by calling `Seconds`, which returns an object of type `ClockTy`, a `typedef` alias defined in the Time.h header:

```
ClockTy secs;
secs = now.Seconds();
cout << "Number seconds since 1/1/01:  " << secs << endl;
```

> **TIP**
>
> Databases often store times as the value returned by `Seconds`. It's an unambiguous way to represent the current time *and* date in a small space.

Don't confuse the `Seconds` function (plural) with `Second` (singular), which returns a time object's seconds value. Call `Minute` and `Hour` for other time component values. Here's how to display the current time the hard way:

```
TTime now;
cout << "Hour:   " << now.Hour() << endl;
cout << "Minute: " << now.Minute() << endl;
cout << "Second: " << now.Second() << endl;
```

It's a lot easier, however, to display the time in string form by calling the class's `AsString` function:

```
cout << now.AsString() << endl;
```

Besides, by using `AsString`, you receive not only the time, but also the current date. Given that it is February 29, 1996 and way past time for dinner as I write this, the preceding statement displays

```
February 29, 1996 6:19:08 pm
```

Programs can compare two times, add them, and apply the ++ and -- operators as the sample listing demonstrates (see function `Pause`). You can also assign one time object to another, and in general, use `TTime` objects as you do other data types built into C++.

Summary

- The IDE in Borland C++ 5 now supports background compilation. Use the *Options\Environment* command to select the *Process Control* topic for modifying various settings that affect foreground and background processing speed.

- Optimizing compilers revise their generated code in order to remove wasteful instructions. Optimizing takes time, and some programmers postpone optimizing code until just before finishing a program. Other programmers optimize at every stage, on the grounds that the code you distribute tomorrow is the code you should test today.

- You can optimize for speed or size, but not both. Generally, reducing code file size means giving up performance. Extra performance typically causes code file sizes to grow.

- Use the Make utility to automate compilation of multiple-module projects. Make reads a "Make file" (which you can name Makefile with no filename extension) typically containing three types of items: macros, dependency rules, and DOS commands. With a properly constructed Make file, after modifying selected files in a program, a single DOS command such as `make -fmyfile.mak` issues the minimum number of commands required to bring the program's .exe code file up-to-date. If you name your file Makefile, just type **make** to process it.

- Use the IDE's *Project\Generate makefile* command to convert IDE project files to equivalent Make files, which you can use with Make or print for documenting your program's file dependencies.

- Use the Tlib utility to create and manage library .lib files, containing one or more .obj object-code files. The linker can load libraries more quickly than individual .obj files.

- Borland C++ has many other useful tools including Grep (useful for searching text files), Touch (for updating file dates and times), and the wordy, but intriguing, do-it-all, know-it-all utility, Tdump.

- A memory model is an addressing scheme, not a memory supplier. Choosing a larger memory model does not make more memory available to programs; it changes the organization of code and data in memory and on disk, and also selects default methods by which statements access data and call functions.

- Borland C++'s seven memory models are tiny, small, medium, compact, large, huge, and flat.

- In any memory model, you can force pointers and functions to be near or far, and you can use other modifiers to create segment pointers and to load the ds register in functions. The responsibility for mixing near and far addressing techniques is yours.

- VROOMM is Borland's Virtual Runtime Object-Oriented Memory Manager, otherwise known as the overlay loader. Use VROOMM to build overlaid DOS programs that have more code than could possibly fit into RAM at one time.

- Borland's standard and class libraries include several miscellaneous classes. Use min, max, and range templates in place of similar functions often provided by C and C++ compilers. Use the bcd class for binary-coded-decimal numbers; use complex for complex numbers. The TDate and TTime classes represent dates and times, and also provide a wealth of useful functions.

21

Developing Database Applications

New to Borland C++ 5 is a 32-bit edition of the Borland Database Engine (BDE), which is also supplied in a compatible 16-bit version. With the BDE and associated classes, you can use C++ to write local and remote client/server database applications for a variety of database file formats, including Paradox, dBASE, ASCII text, Interbase, Oracle, Informix, Sybase, Microsoft SQL Server, and Open Database Connectivity (ODBC) systems such as Microsoft Access. Because the BDE now supports 32-bit programming, it's the ideal basis for Windows 95 and Windows NT database applications.

In addition to the BDE, Borland C++ 5 provides tools such as the Database Desktop, which you can use to construct new database tables in all supported formats. (A table is roughly equivalent to a file.) Run the BDE Configuration Utility to configure your system, and also to create aliases for database table locations. The use of aliases rather than explicit path and file names makes it possible for applications to access data on different platforms and operating systems, which may use file and directory structures that are incompatible with DOS and Windows.

Together, Borland C++ 5, the IDE for Windows 95 and NT, the BDE, and its supporting tools form a complete database management and development system. You don't need to purchase or install Paradox or any another database product—Borland C++ 5 provides all necessary drivers, tools, and utilities for constructing database tables and for writing applications to enter and access data in those tables.

In this chapter, I introduce database programming using Borland C++ 5, and I explain how to use the supporting non-visual and visual classes, known as *components,* that encapsulate the BDE for object-oriented database software development. Although I used the 32-bit version of the BDE along with Windows 95, the information in this chapter applies also to the 16-bit version.

Introducing the Borland Database Engine

The BDE is the same engine used in Delphi, in Paradox for Windows, and in Visual dBASE for Windows. The current 32-bit BDE, version 3.0, provides consistent methods of access to data sources in a variety of formats. Because your code calls BDE functions rather than executing format-specific database statements, your applications work the same regardless of physical data layouts. This means you can write dBASE interfaces that work equally well with Paradox, remote client/server installations, and other platforms. You can also construct software that accesses data in multiple table formats.

For simpler database forms development, the Borland C++ 5 IDE supports the concept of *live data programming.* With this feature, you can design data entry forms while working with actual database tables, which simplifies testing and maintenance. What you see when you design a database form is what you get when you run the program.

In addition to these elements, the new 32-bit BDE, version 3.0, is fully reentrant and multiple-thread safe. The BDE supports long filenames and preemptive multitasking. All of these features make the 32-bit BDE ideal for writing Windows 95 and Windows NT database applications.

NOTE

Long filenames passed to the BDE may be up to 260 characters in length excluding the terminating null.

Following is a summary of the main features for database programming provided with Borland C++ 5:

- *Borland Database Engine (BDE)*—Provides consistent, low-level, non-object-oriented, access to relational database tables in a variety of formats.

- *BDE Configuration Utility*—Registers database drivers, creates aliases, selects among date and time formats, and configures BDE options.

- *Database Desktop*—Creates database tables and fields, and also edits those structures. Modifies existing database tables, or creates entirely new ones in all supported formats. This utility takes the place of Paradox or another database system, which you do not need to purchase or install in order to develop and use database applications.

- *Non-visual classes*—Encapsulate the BDE's low-level functions for object-oriented database application development.

- *Visual classes*—Provide *components* (special types of classes that I explain in this chapter) that mirror the classes in Delphi 1.0 and 2.0 for constructing data entry forms using Windows 95 and Windows NT. Visual components can use live data to show you exactly how your database forms operate in the finished program. You may use visual components in conventional Windows programming, or with an application framework such as OWL.

NOTE

Installing the BDE stores default configuration information in the path and file \Idapi\Idapi.cfg. In Windows 95, this information is registered as CONFIGFILE01. For example, use the Windows 95 Regedit program to examine the registry entry HKEY_LOCAL_MACHINE/SOFTWARE under Borland/ Database Engine/CONFIGFILE01. If you move the Idapi.cfg file to another location, you must also update the Windows registry.

Interfacing with the BDE

To interface with the BDE, Borland C++ 5 provides a set of non-visual classes that encapsulate BDE functions and data. The classes are structured according to the Common Object Model (COM), which forms the underlying architecture of OLE2. Because of this association, automation controllers such as Excel are compatible with the BDE's class objects.

Also provided is a set of visual classes that support OWL. These classes operate as controls that you can insert into dialog boxes to create data-entry and reporting forms. Because of their special design, visual BDE classes are called *components,* and they mirror the database components in Delphi. This means you can use Delphi to prototype database applications that you later write using C++.

Visual components do not require you to learn OLE—they are automatically OLE-aware— and they also greatly simplify database application development. The components utilize a simplified syntax on a higher, more conceptual level than non-visual components. The only significant disadvantage of visual components is that, in order to use them, you must develop your applications for Windows 95 or Windows NT.

You can write COM/OLE applications with non-visual classes, but this requires you to have a better understanding of OLE and the Common Object Model—both difficult subjects to master. Unless you must develop non-Windows database applications or use COM objects, you will gain much benefit by using visual components and OWL. For that reason, this is the framework I use for the sample programming in this chapter.

> **NOTE**
>
> Some of the instructions in this chapter require the IDE's resource options to be set correctly. To configure your system, select *Options/Environment,* and under the *Resource Editors* topic, highlight *Dialog.* Enable the three check boxes: *Show Control palette, Show Tool palette,* and *Show Property Inspector.*

Non-Visual Database Components

Following are brief descriptions of the non-visual classes that encapsulate the BDE. These classes are used in visual and non-visual database programming, but they have no on-screen appearances at runtime. During an application's design, however, icons represent non-visual components in a form created with the IDE's resource editor. The non-visual components are

- `TBatchMove`—Performs operations on records and tables, such as updating all records that match a specified argument.
- `TBlobField`—A field of indefinite size of a record in a dataset that consists of an arbitrary set of bytes, typically a graphical image such as a bitmap.

- `TDatabase`—Provides additional database services such as server log-ins and local aliases.
- `TDataSet`—The immediate ancestor of `TDBDataSet`.
- `TDataSource`—Connects data-set components such as `TTable` and `TQuery` with data-aware components such as `TDBEdit` and `TDBMenu`. Every database application needs at least one `TDataSource` object.
- `TDBDataSet`—The direct ancestor of `TTable`, `TQuery`, and `TStoredProc`. Most applications use the derived classes `TTable`, `TQuery`, and `TStoredProc` for data-set access rather than `TDBDataSet`. However, functions may pass parameters of this type to operate on all types of data sets and the results of queries.
- `TField`—Provides access to fields in a record.
- `TFieldDef`—Defines the structure of physical fields in records. All `TField` objects do not necessarily have corresponding `TFieldDef` objects. For example, calculated `TField` objects have no physical record fields, and therefore, no `TFieldDef` objects.
- `TFieldDefs`—Holds the `TFieldDef` objects that define the physical fields in a data set.
- `TIndexDef`—Describes the index of a table.
- `TIndexDefs`—Holds the set of all `TIndexDef` objects for a table.
- `TParam`—Defines parameters for `TQuery` and `TStoredProc` objects.
- `TParams`—Holds all parameters for `TQuery` and `TStoredProc` objects.
- `TQuery`—Issues SQL (structured query language) statements to the BDE or to a SQL server.
- `TStoredProc`—Enables applications to execute stored procedures on a database server. Unless you are developing client/server database applications, you probably won't need to use this component. Typical stored procedures include commands for obtaining information on locked processes and the log-on IDs of database users. However, the exact procedures available depend on the server.
- `TStrings`—Not a database component, but used extensively to represent various data values—a list of names, for example, in a `TDBListBox` component.
- `TTable`—Gives applications access to databases through the BDE. This component is usually associated with a `TDataSource` object, which connects the `TTable` with data-aware controls. Most database applications have at least one `TTable` object.

Visual Database Components

Visual database components, interfaced through C++ classes, are actually VBX controls that mirror the visual database components in Delphi versions 1.0 and 2.0. Each visual database component is a data-aware control object that you can insert into a dialog window, also called a database form. To create a database form, you use the IDE's integrated resource editor to construct a dialog window into which you drag the data-aware controls you need. This makes designing data entry forms no more difficult than creating other types of Windows dialog boxes.

Many components resemble the non-data-aware (you might say, data-*blind*) controls on which they are based. For example, the data aware TDBListBox component is similar to a list box control, but the component takes its input from a database table. In fact, the TDBListBox class is subclassed from the Windows LISTBOX structure—not, however, as you might imagine, from the OWL TListBox class. This makes data-aware components available to all Windows frameworks including but not limited to OWL and MFC.

You may freely mix data-aware components with other controls such as buttons and static text items. Although the components are not based on OWL, I've listed the comparable OWL classes for reference. The visual component classes are

- TDBCheckBox—A data-aware TCheckBox component.

- TDBComboBox—A data-aware TComboBox component.

- TDBEdit—A data-aware TEdit single-line text entry component.

- TDBGrid(SSView)—A data-aware text-only TGrid component.

- TDBImage—A data-aware graphical TImage component.

- TDBListBox—A data-aware TListBox component.

- TDBLookupCombo—A data-aware TComboBox component with the capability to search a lookup table.

- TDBLookupList—A data-aware TListBox component with the capability to search a lookup table.

- TDBMemo—A data-aware TMemo multiple-line text-entry component.

- TDBNavigator—A sophisticated database browsing and editing tool. This component is to database programming what a remote control is to a video recorder. Users click the control's buttons to move through database records, insert new records, delete records, and perform other navigational operations.

- TDBRadioGroup—A data-aware TRadioGroup component.

- TDBText—A data-aware read-only text component for displaying database information that you don't want users to be able to edit.

Designing Database Forms

Visual components make designing data-entry forms the easiest part of writing database applications. Additionally, live data saves time by showing you exactly how data will appear in the finished application. Try the following steps for a demonstration of the power of visual components and live data.

> **NOTE**
>
> If the control palette does not appear on screen, before doing step 4, use the *Dialog|Show* command to make the panel visible. Also use this same command, or double-click any component object inserted into a dialog window, to display the property inspector.

1. Select the *File|New* and *Resource Project* commands. Choose *Resource Script* from the *New Resource Project* dialog box. Click the *OK* button.

2. After the noname00.rc window appears, select *Resource|New* and choose DIALOGEX (EX indicates this is a Windows 95 extended control). Click the *OK* button.

3. You now see a blank dialog window. Because it will be used as a data-entry screen, it's commonly called a *database form,* although it is actually no different than any other dialog window. Resize the form as you want, and delete the *Cancel* and *Help* buttons, which aren't needed for this demonstration.

4. Using the *Controls* palette, click the *Data Access* page tab, and click once on the TTable component. (Hint: Rest the mouse cursor for a moment on a component icon for a popup window that tells you the component's name.) Click inside the form to create a TTable object, which is automatically named TTable1. Because this is a non-visual control, the design-time icon that you see in the window is invisible at runtime.

5. Double-click the TTable1 object to open the *Property Inspector* window, which you use to select various component values. Select the *DatabaseName* field, and choose a database alias such as DBDEMOS from the drop-down list. Next, select a table (a .db file, for example) from your chosen database. To do that, highlight the *TableName* field, and select a table file such as Customer.db.

6. You next need a data source object and a control for viewing database records. Insert into the form two components, TDataSource (from the *Data Access* palette) and SSView (from the *Data Aware* palette) objects. These are given the default names TDataSource1 and SSView1 respectively. The TDataSource1 object serves as a go-between for a data set (such as TTable1) and a data control (such as SSView1). Resize the SSView1 object to make more of its grid visible. Move the non-visual controls, TTable1 and TDataSource1, to any convenient positions—their icons are not visible at runtime. (Hint: If a database form is cramped for space, you can position non-visual controls on top of a visual component such as SSView1 with no harmful effects.)

7. Connect the three objects by double-clicking TDataSource1 (the icon with the arrows) and highlighting the *DataSet* field in the *Property Inspector* window. Choose a data set object (TTable1 here) from the drop-down list. This creates a channel through which the data set's records can flow to and from data-aware controls. To provide a visual representation of that data, double-click the SSView1 object and set its Property Inspector's *DataSource* field to TDataSource1.

8. Finally, double-click the TTable1 object and, in the *Property Inspector* window, change the *Active* property to *True*. This tells the IDE to use live data when displaying the finished database form.

9. To try out your design, select the *Dialog\Test Dialog* command, and in a moment, the finished form pops up as it will appear in the running application (see Figure 21.1). Although there *is* no application at this point—you haven't written one line of code— you can view, edit, and scroll the data displayed in the form's grid, a good example of how visual components and live data can greatly aid data entry design. *In many database applications, designing a data-entry form is all the programming you will need!*

Figure 21.1.

Database form with live data.

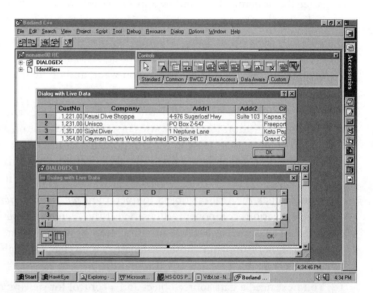

TIP

When testing a database form, if live data does not appear, check that the data set object's *Active* field is set to *True*. If all connections are not completed as you link data set, data source, and data-aware control objects, this field might be reset automatically to *False*—so check its value again before testing.

Components

Before you can write a database application that uses database forms, you need to understand how visual components differ from ordinary C++ classes. A component is a special kind of class that is entirely defined by its input and output. Because of its total independence from outside influences, a component can be written and tested outside of the context in which it is used.

A component's independence also makes it a highly reliable programming tool, even when used by relatively inexperienced programmers. For example, a well-written component might supply a default value for a data member rather than throwing an exception if the program uses that member before being initialized.

Also, because of the component's independence, its internal details are hidden from users. This helps promote code reuse by making future versions of a component more likely to be compatible with existing code. Hiding a component's inner details also ensures that component objects are used in carefully defined ways. This can speed debugging, and even prevent bugs caused by sloppy coding.

Components achieve these objectives through the use and implementation of three key elements in their class designs: *properties, methods,* and *events.* The next section describes these elements.

Properties

Properties are similar to class data members, but are usually related to a runtime action. For example, a change to a component's color property might trigger an event that updates the color of an on-screen graphical object. *Merely assigning a value to a property causes the event to occur.*

You can write code to set property values at runtime, and you also can set initial property values when you design a database form. These values are stored and used automatically as DLGINIT resource data along with the program's other resources. (This data is in hexadecimal, and is difficult if not impossible to edit in text form.)

To set property values when you design a database form, insert a data-aware control such as TEdit and double-click it to open the resource editor's *Property Inspector* (see Figure 21.2). Tab to or click on the field you want to change. There are several types of properties, each with their unique methods for entering or selecting values. For example, to change a caption, enter some text into the *Caption* field. To assign a data source object to a data-aware control, click on a field such as *DataSource* and select an object name from the drop-down list, which opens when you click the down arrow as shown in the figure.

To set a property at runtime, simply assign it a value. For example, to select (highlight) a field's text automatically when tabbing to that field, use a statement such as

```
TDBCompany.AutoSelect = false;
```

This assumes TDBCompany is an object of the TDBEdit class, and refers to a field in the database form (I'll explain how to do that later in this chapter).

Figure 21.2.

The resource editor's Property Inspector.

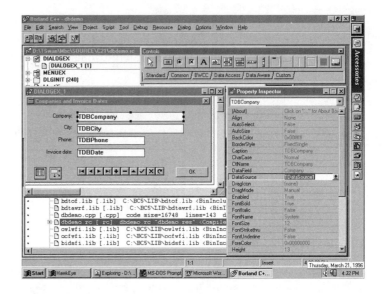

Methods

Methods are class member functions, and they can be void or they can return a value. You call methods in reference to class objects just as you call other class member functions. They are called *methods* mostly because that is the name Delphi uses for member functions.

You normally call methods in reference to data-aware control objects using dot notation. For example, to assign to a TDBEdit control text in a character buffer, you can use a statement such as

```
TDBCompany.SetTextBuf(buffer);
```

Events

Events are similar to Windows message-event handlers. An event, however, might be triggered by a call to a method, or by reading or writing a property value. Events can be triggered also by external actions such as clicking a mouse button or pressing a keyboard key.

All event names begin with On. For example, a component's OnClick event is triggered when the user clicks the mouse on the component's visual representation—to select text in an edit window, for example, or to enable a check box. Much of the programming in database development with visual components involves writing event handlers.

You can also create completely new events, but it's unlikely you'll need to do this unless you are designing custom components. The components in Borland C++ 5 provide all event handlers that you are likely to need for most applications.

There are several steps involved in setting up an event handler. Using visual components takes care of the first requirement: defining the event source. All visual components have event sources such as OnClick and OnEnter already defined—all you have to do is insert a component object into a form and choose the event source you want.

You next have to define two objects: a pointer to a data-aware control, and a sink for that control object. Do this in your database form, which you'll normally derive from TDialog and TVbxEventHandler using multiple inheritance. Here's how such a class might look:

```
class MyDlg: public TDialog, public TVbxEventHandler {
private:
  TDBEdit *DBEdit;  // Pointer to visual component object
  TDBEditNotifySink OnChangeSink;  // Sink for event handler
public:
  MyDlg();  // Constructor
  void OnChangeHandler(TDBEditNotifySink&, TDBEdit&);  // Handler
  DECLARE_RESPONSE_TABLE(MyDlg);  // Response table
};
```

The response table needs to list the class and the two base classes. It doesn't necessarily need any content:

```
DEFINE_RESPONSE_TABLE2(MyDlg, TDialog, TVbxEventHandler )
END_RESPONSE_TABLE;
```

To link the event sink and its handler, initialize the objects as in the sample class's constructor:

```
EventDemoDlg::EventDemoDlg():
  TDialog(0, "Name"),
  DBEdit(new TDBEdit(this, IDC_TDBEdit1)),
  OnChangeSink(TDBEditNotify_MFUNCTOR(*this, &MyDlg::OnChangeHandler))
{
  DBEdit->OnChangeSource += OnChangeSink;
}
```

The constructor first calls the ancestor TDialog constructor, and then initializes the DBEdit pointer to point to a new TDBEdit object. The this argument identifies the control's parent (the database form object), and its resource identifier, and as a result, the control receives its values from its data source. The OnChangeSink object, which you can name anything you like, is initialized using a macro. Borland calls this macro an MFUNCTOR, which links the sink object to a specific control's event. The statement in the sample constructor listed here chains multiple sinks together.

The final step in the process is the easiest—writing the event handler. The function can do whatever you want, so I'll show only the function shell here:

```
void
MyDlg::OnChangeHandler(TDBEditNotifySink&, TDBEdit& te)
{
  // Code to do something with TDBEdit object te
  // upon occurrence of an OnChange event
  Invalidate();  // Update control's appearance (optional)
}
```

Developing Database Applications

Of course, every application is different. But in general, for most database applications, you'll probably need to perform steps such as these:

1. Create a directory for storing database files. Also create a directory for holding the application files. If you prefer, you may use the same directory for both purposes.

2. Use the BDE Configuration Utility to assign an alias to your database directory. For example, you might create an alias such as `WineCellar` for a database stored in the path C:\MyFiles\Database\WineCellar. Later, you can move the database files to another location—even to a network server—without affecting your applications.

3. Use Database Desktop to create database tables and to define fields in those tables. Use the alias in step 2 to refer to your database. You may use any supported file format, but for best results with the BDE and visual components, I recommend selecting *Paradox version 7* from the listed drivers.

4. Design your application's data entry and report forms using the IDE's dialog editor. By using the live data techniques outlined in this chapter, you can enter some sample data into your database at this time; or, you can use Database Desktop to enter some data.

5. Write the code of your application—for example, to calculate fields, to sum numeric columns, to display blobs (Binary Large Objects) as bitmap images, and for other purposes.

> **NOTE**
>
> Components are implemented as VBX controls, and your application must be linked to the Borland C++ VBX support library. To do that, open TargetExpert and select the *VBX* check box under *Controls*. For most database applications, you'll also want to select the OCF framework and OLE library (which is selected automatically when you specify OCF).

Because visual components are actually VBX controls, the program must load and initialize the Visual Basic emulator as part of its startup tasks. Do this by constructing an object of the class `TBIVbxLibrary` in `OwlMain` *before* running the application. For example, you can write `OwlMain` like this:

```
int OwlMain(int, char* [])
{
  TBIVbxLibrary vbxLib;
  return YourApp.Run();
}
```

You can do the same in a conventional Windows program's `WinMain` function.

To catch any exceptions thrown by the application, encase this code in a `try-catch` block. The following more robust `OwlMain` function uses this technique:

```
int OwlMain(int, char* [])
{
  TBIVbxLibrary BiLibrary;
  try {
    fishfactApp app;
    return app.Run();
  }
  catch (xmsg& x) {
    ::MessageBox(0, x.why().c_str(), "Exception", MB_OK);
  }
  return -1;
}
```

Using visual components, you can often construct entire database applications that have no more code than that. In fact, data entry systems, spreadsheet-like browsers, and similar applications may require little or no code. However, you will often need to access values in data-aware components—to copy text from a database record field, for example. The following sample application in Listing 21.1, Dbdemo.cpp, shows the basic methods for constructing and using data-aware visual components in a program's module.

Listing 21.1. Dbdemo.cpp (Demonstrates visual database programming).

```
//===============================================================
// Dbdemo.cpp -- Demonstrates visual database programming
// Copyright (c) 1996 by Tom Swan. All rights reserved.
//===============================================================

#include <owl\pch.h>
#include <vdbt\dbedit.h>
#pragma hdrstop
#include <owl\vbxctl.h>
#include "dbdemo.rh"

// ===============================================================
// Database browser dialog class
// ===============================================================

class TBrowseDlg: public TDialog, public TVbxEventHandler {
public:
  TDBEdit TDBEditCompany;
  TDBEdit TDBEditCity;
  TDBEdit TDBEditPhone;
  TDBEdit TDBEditDate;
public:
  TBrowseDlg(TWindow* parent, TResId resId, TModule* module = 0);
  virtual ~TBrowseDlg();
  void CmOk();
  DECLARE_RESPONSE_TABLE(TBrowseDlg);
};

// TBrowseDlg response table
DEFINE_RESPONSE_TABLE2(TBrowseDlg, TDialog, TVbxEventHandler)
```

continues

Listing 21.1. continued

```
    EV_COMMAND(IDOK, CmOk),
END_RESPONSE_TABLE;

// Constructor
TBrowseDlg::TBrowseDlg(TWindow* parent, TResId resId,
  TModule* module)
:
  TDialog(parent, resId, module),
  TDBEditCompany(this, IDC_COMPANY),
  TDBEditCity(this, IDC_CITY),
  TDBEditPhone(this, IDC_PHONE),
  TDBEditDate(this, IDC_DATE)
{
  // Constructor code goes here
}

// Destructor
TBrowseDlg::~TBrowseDlg()
{
  Destroy();
  // Destructor code goes here
}

// Respond to OK button selection before dialog closes
void
TBrowseDlg::CmOk()
{
  UINT len = TDBEditCompany.GetTextLen();
  LPSTR companyBuf = new char[len + 1];
  TDBEditCompany.GetTextBuf(companyBuf, len);
  MessageBox(companyBuf, "Company selected");
  delete[] companyBuf;
  TDialog::CmOk();
}

// ==============================================================
// The application's main window
// ==============================================================

class TDbDemoWin: public TFrameWindow {
public:
  TDbDemoWin(TWindow* parent, const char far* title);
protected:
  void CmTest();
DECLARE_RESPONSE_TABLE(TDbDemoWin);
};

// Create response table declared for class
DEFINE_RESPONSE_TABLE1(TDbDemoWin, TFrameWindow)
  EV_COMMAND(CM_TEST, CmTest),
END_RESPONSE_TABLE;

// Constructor
TDbDemoWin::TDbDemoWin(TWindow* parent, const char far* title)
  : TFrameWindow(parent, title),
    TWindow(parent, title)
{
```

```
    AssignMenu(ID_MENU);
}

// Menu command function
void
TDbDemoWin::CmTest()
{
  TBrowseDlg* dp = new TBrowseDlg(this, TResId(DIALOGEX_1));
  dp->Execute();
}

// ============================================================
// The application class
// ============================================================

class TDemoApp: public TApplication {
public:
  TDemoApp(const char far* name)
    : TApplication(name) {};
  void InitMainWindow();
};

// Initialize the program's main window
void
TDemoApp::InitMainWindow()
{
  MainWindow = new TDbDemoWin(0, "Visual");
}

#pragma argsused

// Main program
int
OwlMain(int argc, char* argv[])
{
  TBIVbxLibrary bivLib;
  try {
    TDemoApp app("OwlWelc");
    return app.Run();
  }
  catch (xmsg& x) {
    ::MessageBox(0, x.why().c_str(), "Exception", MB_OK);
  }
  return -1;
}
```

Figure 21.3 shows the sample application's database form. The four edit windows are visual components of the TDBEdit class. The bar with the arrows at the lower middle of the dialog window is a TDBNavigator object. By linking this object with the edit fields, this application provides a simple, yet powerful, database browser and editor.

Not shown in Figure 21.3 are the database form's data set and data source objects, which feed data to and from the editor and navigator components. Refer back to Figure 21.2 and you'll see these non-visual components in the dialog window at the lower left corner.

Figure 21.3.
Dbdemo's database form.

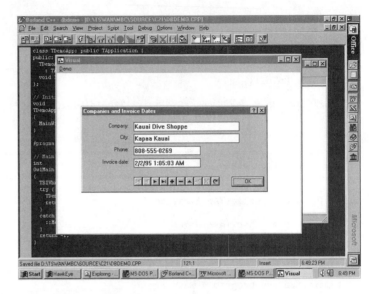

To create this application, I inserted into the form a TTable component, which the IDE named TTable1. This is the first of the two non-visual component icons you can see in Figure 21.2. I set this object's DatabaseName field to DBDEMOS, and then selected Customer.db under TableName. These steps open up the database and a specific table in that database.

Next, to provide a source (data provider) and a sink (data receiver) for data-aware controls in the database form, I inserted a TDataSource component, which the IDE named TDataSource1. Using the Property Inspector, I set this object's *DataSet* field to the first non-visual component, TTable1.

With these two non-visual components in place, I next inserted visual components such as TDBEdit and TDBNavigator. I renamed the edit fields to TDBCompany, TDBCity, and so on for easier reference rather than using the default names TDBEdit1 and TDBEdit2. In each of these data-aware controls, I set *DataSource* to TDataSource1 (the second non-visual component), and selected an appropriate record field such as COMPANY and CITY from the Property Inspector's drop-down lists.

After completing the form's design, I wrote code to perform three key steps, which you'll probably use in most database applications:

- Initialize the VBX library.
- Display the database form.
- Extract a record field and display its text.

Using the method just described, I initialize the VBX library in OwlMain by constructing an object of the TBIVbxLibrary class. This also requires the module to include the <owl\vbxctl.h>

header. Because this header has some non-static declarations, it must follow the #pragma hdrstop directive that halts the collection of compiled symbols into a .csm file.

Displaying the database form is as simple as displaying any other dialog. The components themselves handle opening the database and table, and initializing data-aware controls with information from the data source object. You don't need any code to perform these tasks. Just construct the dialog box object and call its Execute function as shown here:

```
TBrowseDlg* dp = new TBrowseDlg(this, TResId(DIALOGEX_1));
dp->Execute();
```

The final task in a typical database application is accessing specific fields in records. Using visual components, this is no more difficult than accessing information in non-data-aware controls. For each visual component, declare an object in the form's class, as in the sample application, which declares four TDBEdit objects, one for each of the edit fields in the form:

```
class TBrowseDlg: public TDialog, public TVbxEventHandler {
public:
  TDBEdit TDBEditCompany;
  TDBEdit TDBEditCity;
  TDBEdit TDBEditPhone;
  TDBEdit TDBEditDate;
...
};
```

Initialize these objects in the dialog's constructor. For example, the sample application uses these statements:

```
TDBEditCompany(this, IDC_COMPANY),
TDBEditCity(this, IDC_CITY),
TDBEditPhone(this, IDC_PHONE),
TDBEditDate(this, IDC_DATE)
```

This links the objects to the appropriate database form fields, using the control resource identifiers such as IDC_COMPANY and IDC_CITY. The program can now assign property values to the visual component objects, and call their methods. For example, to extract the value of the current *Customer* field when you click the form's *Ok* button, function CmOk executes these statements:

```
UINT len = TDBEditCompany.GetTextLen();
LPSTR companyBuf = new char[len + 1];
TDBEditCompany.GetTextBuf(companyBuf, len);
MessageBox(companyBuf, "Company selected");
delete[] companyBuf;
```

The call to GetTextLen returns the length in characters of the text in the TDBEditCompany object. The program constructs a character array of that size plus one to hold a null terminator, and calls the object's GetTextBuf function to obtain the text—that is, the name of the company in the currently selected record. The user has full control over which record that is by using the navigator tool—no code is required to browse the database. After displaying the selected company name, the program deletes the character array.

Summary

- The 32-bit Borland Database Engine (BDE) is new to Borland C++ 5. With the BDE, you can write local and remote client/server database applications for a variety of database file formats, including Paradox, dBASE, ASCII text, Interbase, Oracle, Informix, Sybase, Microsoft SQL Server, and Open Database Connectivity (ODBC) systems such as Microsoft Access.

- For easy design and maintenance, the Borland C++ 5 IDE supports the concept of *live data programming.*

- To interface with the BDE, Borland C++ 5 provides a set of non-visual classes that encapsulate BDE functions and data. The classes are structured according to the Common Object Model (COM), which forms the underlying architecture of OLE2.

- To provide a simple method for designing database forms in Windows 95 and Windows NT applications, Borland C++ 5 also provides a set of visual classes, called components.

- A component is a special kind of class that is entirely defined by its input and output. The visual components in Borland C++ 5 mirror those in Delphi, which greatly simplifies using Delphi to develop database application prototypes that you will rewrite using C++.

- Components utilize three key elements in their class designs: *properties, methods,* and *events.*

- Because visual components are actually VBX controls, the program must load and initialize the Visual Basic emulator as part of its startup tasks.

22

Customizing the IDE with Object Scripting

All developers have their unique coding styles—in fact, most programmers are fussier than an old maid in a china shop. Braces and comments must look just right, and every line must be aligned just so, or their creative juices dry up like old glue. I tell you this from the experience of one who is truly obsessed with matters of style. When I receive a file from another programmer, I immediately reformat the text to suit my tastes. I can't even begin to understand the program until every line is indented exactly to my liking.

I've often wished that I could automate some of these formatting tasks in the IDE. For instance, why should I have to align my comments? Why can't the IDE do that and other jobs for me? Fortunately, with Object Scripting, a new feature in Borland C++ 5.0, these and many other operations are now possible. By writing and running script files using the IDE's cScript language, which closely resembles C++, you can customize the IDE to create a personalized environment that works exactly as you wish.

This chapter introduces the IDE's Object Scripting capabilities, and explains how to use the example scripts provided with the compiler. I also explain how to write and debug your own scripts using the cScript language. Unlike macro languages found in many text editors and IDEs, cScript is based on C++, so you already know 80 percent of what you need to construct your own scripts. However, because cScript statements are bound into the IDE at runtime, the language differs from C++ in fundamental ways that you need to understand. But more on that later. First, let's take a look at what Object Scripting is and what it can do for you.

Introducing Object Scripting

Object Scripting is a programming system that controls most of the Borland C++ IDE's commands and capabilities. A script is a file containing cScript statements that perform IDE functions. Using cScript, you can write functions, create variables, and read and write files. The cScript language is object-oriented, and you can declare and inherit classes and construct objects with member functions and data. In fact, the IDE itself is represented by one grand object that you can access from your own scripts to perform a variety of commands.

A script begins life as a text file, ending with the extension .spp. You compile this file to create a binary code file ending with .spx, which contains pseudo code (P-Code) that the IDE's script engine interprets at runtime. Scripts are not stand-alone programs—to run a script, you must load it into the Borland C++ IDE.

With scripts, you can perform file operations, run IDE menu commands, create new menus, assign hot keys to functions, display messages, and modify the IDE's startup processes. Most exciting, you can create a script that modifies text in an editor buffer. For example, you might create a script to insert a copyright notice, title, and description header into a source code module. Or, you might design a script to modify selected text. There are numerous global Object Scripting commands and objects you can access, and there's also a full set of example script files that you can explore to learn more about the cScript language and what it can do. I'll explain these topics and more at the proper time, but the place to begin learning how to use Object Scripting is with the IDE's *Script* menu.

The Script Menu

The *Script* menu offers six commands that you can use to run, view, and compile scripts. Use this menu also to install and uninstall the example scripts supplied with Borland C++. Table 22.1 lists and describes the *Script* menu's commands.

Table 22.1. Script menu commands.

Command	Description
Run	Runs a script function. If the script is not loaded, this command loads the script's compiled .spx module into the IDE.
Commands	Lists all script commands currently loaded into the IDE. You can also use this command to select a script function to run.
Modules	Lists available script-file modules, including system scripts, and loaded and unloaded modules. Use this command's extensive dialog box to load, unload, and edit scripts in the default or other script directories. You can choose whether to list only loaded scripts, along with user and system scripts. System scripts built into the IDE are displayed in italic text.
Compile File	Compiles the current editor buffer, which is assumed to contain a script text file ending with the extension .spp. Use this command to create a P-Code .spx file for a script you are writing or modifying.
Run File	Compiles, loads, and runs the current editor buffer, which is assumed to be a script text file. This is the command you'll use most often when writing your own scripts.
Install/Uninstall examples	Installs or uninstalls the example scripts provided with Borland C++. This command works as a toggle.

The easiest way to run a script function is to type its name into the input box displayed by selecting the *Script|Run* command. Do that now and enter the following line (print must be lowercase, exactly as shown—like C++, cScript is case sensitive):

```
print "Fan mail from a flounder"
```

When you press Enter, nothing seems to happen because the print function drowns its output to the IDE's Message window. If that window is closed, select *View|Message* to bring it to the

729

surface. Choose the *Script* page tab. You'll probably see various messages written by other scripts. Scroll to the bottom of the window to see the message you printed.

> **TIP**
>
> To make a script's output easier to find, click the right mouse button while pointing to the *View/Message* window's *Script* page. Select the popup menu's *Delete All* command to clear old messages from the window before you run a new script. Or, just press Crtl+A to select this command from the keyboard. You might also want to maximize the Message window.

In addition to calling global functions such as `print`, you can call class member functions in reference to cScript objects. For example, select *Script|Run* and enter

```
IDE.Message("This is a noteworthy note!");
```

This calls the `Message` function in reference to the IDE object of the `IDEApplication` class. The result is the dialog box shown in Figure 22.1.

Figure 22.1.
Dialog box produced by the
IDEApplication class's
Message function.

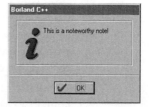

Another way to run a script is to load its .spp file into the IDE, and then select *Script|Run File*. This compiles and runs the current editor buffer as a script, and is probably the method you will use most often to run scripts that you are writing.

To try this command, load the Keyassgn.spp script file from Borland's Script\Examples directory. Select *Script|Run File,* and after compiling the script, press a function key when the script's input dialog box appears. *Don't press Enter, which is interpreted as a valid key.* Instead, use the mouse to select the *OK* button. When I did this, I requested assignments for F3. (I use the Default IDE editor key mappings.) The Keyassign script displayed this text in the message window (click the plus sign to expand the full entry):

```
:Commands assigned to <F3>
  :Editor ->
  :ClassExpert ->
  :Message ->
  :Project ->
  :Desktop -> IDE.SearchSearchAgain();
```

This information tells me that the IDE Desktop object uses key F3 to repeat a search operation.

You can run any script function using the *Script* menu's *Run* and *Run File* commands, but before venturing further, you first you need to become familiar with the available scripts. For that, use the *Script* menu's next two commands.

Script|Commands displays a list of available IDE commands. First, open any text file or create a new text editor window. Then, select *Script|Commands* and, using the resulting dialog shown in Figure 22.2, scroll down to and double-click any command such as *IDE.SpeedMenu()*, and then press the *Run* button. This pops up the IDE's speed menu. Of course it's easier to do that by clicking the right mouse button, but this demonstrates how you can execute IDE operations by calling their script functions. String multiple commands together by double-clicking them in succession and then selecting *Run*—a kind of ad-hoc script macro capability that you might find useful.

Figure 22.2.
Script Commands dialog.

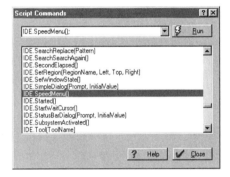

For an even more powerful script command, select *Script|Modules*. This displays the dialog in Figure 22.3. You can use this dialog to load, unload, and edit scripts. You can choose whether to display all scripts, system scripts, or only loaded scripts. You can also browse other directories that contain script files.

Figure 22.3.
Script Modules dialog.

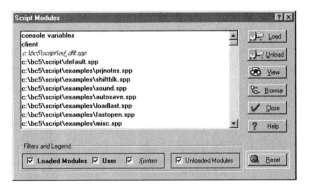

To run your own scripts, use the *Script* menu's next two commands. *Compile File* compiles the current edit buffer into a P-Code .spx file, which you can load and run. *Run File* compiles and runs the current edit buffer—this is the command you'll probably use most often when designing your own scripts. See "Script Construction Techniques" in this chapter for more information on compiling and running scripts.

Finally in the *Script* menu is a command you'll want to execute right away. Select *Install/Uninstall examples* to install the example script files that come with Borland C++. This creates a new menu, *Example scripts,* which lists script files you can select and run. To remove this menu, simply select *Script\Install/Uninstall examples* again. You can repeat the command as often as you wish. See "Running the Example Scripts" in this chapter for more information.

Script Options

There are a few script options you'll want to select, especially for testing your own script files. Select the *Options\Environment* command, and choose the *Scripting* topic. Enable the option *Stop at breakpoint,* so that you can single-step and pause scripts in development. (See "Debugging Scripts" in this chapter for more information about this option.) Enable *Diagnostic Messages* for verbose output in the IDE's message window.

The other two Scripting settings choose startup scripts and set the default script-file path. Enter one or more script function names into *Startup Scripts* to execute scripts automatically when you first start the IDE. Separate multiple script names with semicolons. For example, to enable the fast-open script, which suggests a file to open when you select *File\Open,* enter `fastopen` into the Startup Scripts command.

Enter one or more pathnames into *Script Path* so the IDE looks there for script files. This path is set by default to

```
c:\bc5\script;.;c:\bc5\script\examples
```

Separate multiple paths with semicolons. Notice the middle path—a lone period. This sets the current directory into the default path so you can run your own scripts in their working directories.

Running the Example Scripts

For a list of example scripts provided with Borland C++, after installing Borland's examples as described in the preceding section, select *Script directory* from the *Example scripts* menu. This displays the window in Figure 22.4, which lists the various script files you can load and run. The window also shows which scripts are currently loaded.

Figure 22.4.

Script directory window.

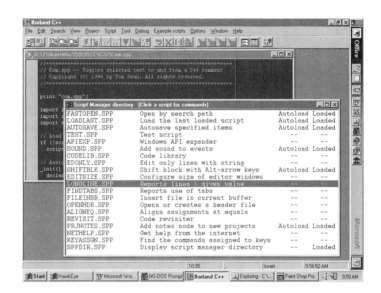

Click the left mouse button on any listed script to display a popup menu of commands. Select a command to load, edit, or unload the highlighted script file. You can also edit the script manager data file, which provides the information for the directory listing. Select that command and enter your script filename following the format explained in the Sppman.dat file. For example, here are the entries for the first two scripts:

```
FASTOPEN.SPP,Open by search path,No menu,1,1
LOADLAST.SPP,Load the last loaded script,E&xample scripts¦&Load last,1,1
```

Each line has a script filename (it cannot have path information), and a description. Use "No menu" if you don't want a script to appear in the *Example scripts* menu. If you do want a menu entry for the script, use the expression on the second line, and separate the menu name from its command using a vertical bar. End the declaration with two integers. The first determines where to (1) autoload or (0) not load the script when the IDE starts. The second integer determines whether to (1) load the script by calling a like-named function in the module (for example, sppman() to load Sppman.spp), or (0) to use the script engine's Load function.

733

For a taste of what the example scripts can do, try the *Align Equals* command in the *Example scripts* menu. First, start a new text editor window, and enter these or similar assignment statements:

```
x = 123;
myVariable = 456;
space = 0;
row = 14;
```

Select each line with the mouse or the Shift-Arrow keys, and then run *Align Equals* by selecting it from the *Example scripts* menu. The script modifies the assignments by aligning the equal signs to the one that is farthest to the right, producing the final text

```
x          = 123;
myVariable = 456;
space      = 0;
row        = 14;
```

TIP

Use hot keys to select example scripts. For example, you can highlight assignment statements and press Alt+XA to run the *Align Equals* script. Later in this chapter, I explain how to attach hot keys to scripts for even easier access.

Table 22.2 lists the scripts installed in the *Example scripts* menu. In addition to these, there are other script files provided with Borland C++ that you can examine to learn more about cScript. These files are in the C:\bc5\script\examples directory (they are not in the main examples directory).

Table 22.2. Scripts in the Example scripts menu.

Script	Filename	Description
Align Equals	Aligneq.spp	Aligns equal signs in all selected lines.
API expander	Apiexp.spp	Expands a word under or to the left of the cursor to a matching API function, including any parameters.
Code library	Codelib.spp	Displays a set of code snippets you can insert into a program. You can add to this set to build a personalized database of programming techniques.
Comment	Comment.spp	Toggles selected block to and from a comment.
Edit only	Edonly.spp	Modifies the current text editor buffer to show only lines that have a matching string.

Script	Filename	Description
Evaluation tips	Evaltips.spp	During debugging session, evaluates text at cursor and displays the result (i.e. a variable value) in a hint window.
Insert file	Fileinsr.spp	Inserts all text from a file into the current edit buffer.
Find tabs	Findtabs.spp	Searches for one or more tab characters files ending with .c, .h, .cpp, .hpp, or .spp. View the Message window for the results of this command.
Key assignments	Keyassgn.spp	Shows commands assigned to various keys. Use it to find whether a hot key is currently unattached.
Load last	Loadlast.spp	Reloads and runs the most recently loaded script.
Long line	Longline.spp	Finds all lines longer than a specified maximum length. View the Message window for the results of this command.
Net help	Nethelp.spp	Provides Internet help via Netscape Navigator. Opens a URL for selected newsgroups, FTP sites, and programming pages.
Open header	Openhdr.spp	Opens a header file ending in .h or .hpp with a filename matching the current edit buffer.
Revisit code	Revisit.spp	Lists files that contain a "revisit code" marker, as specified in file Revisit.cfg. See Message window for results.
Script directory	Sppdir.spp	Displays the script manager's directory, which you can modify by editing the Sppman.dat file.
Test	Test.spp	Provides a test harness that you can use to run script statements, which you can insert into the module's `test()` function. You can then run `test()` using the *Script|Run* command to experiment with your commands.
View locals	Viewlocs.spp	During a debugging session, inspects local variables.

Following are notes on some of the examples I find most useful:

- *Load last*—Press Alt+XL to run the most recently executed script. This is especially handy for rerunning scripts under development.

- *API expander*—Type a partial Windows API function name such as `DefWindow` and run this script with the cursor anywhere on the partial word or to its immediate right. The script looks for a matching function in file Apiexp.dat, which you can edit to insert additional functions (sort the file alphabetically). If the script finds a match, it inserts the full function name plus parameter data types into the text. If you have grown tired of typing long-winded Windows function names, you'll love this script.

- *Code library*—This might be the most useful script in the library. Run it and select a code fragment to insert into the current edit buffer. Edit the Codelib.cfg file to specify path information to locate data files containing the code fragments. For example, see the Codegen.dat file, which contains a sample module comment header and demonstrates the format of a code-fragment data file. Begin each fragment with the symbol `<*>` followed by a description. Spend a day collecting your favorite fragments and module comment headers into this script's data files—you'll more than recover that time as you use this script to automate your favorite programming sequences.

- *Edit only*—Open a *saved* source code file, and run this script. Enter a phrase you want to find in the file—an expression such as `DC->`, for example. Press Enter and wait a moment while the script displays lines containing that text and line numbers. Press Alt+Backspace to undo. Be careful with this one—it appears to modify the existing file! (A better version would output its information to the Message window, or perhaps, to a new edit buffer.)

- *Insert file*—This is a simple script, but it sure beats opening a file, selecting all lines, and cutting and pasting the text into another file. To use the script, first open the file into which you want to insert another; then run the script and specify that file. If you make a mistake, press Alt+X to undo.

- *Open header*—This script merely opens a header file ending in .h or .hpp with the same filename as the current edit buffer, but how handy that is! If, for example, you are editing a file named Neato.cpp, this script opens Neato.h (or Neato.hpp).

- *Revisit code*—As I write programs, I often insert comments to remind me to make a future change to sections that I am not yet ready to complete. This script locates such sections, marked with the C++ comment indicator and a greater-than sign (`//>`). View the Message window for files containing that symbol. This is really handy for finding files that need work in a large, multiple-file project.

In addition to the example scripts, Borland C++ provides the source code for standard scripts used in the IDE. These files are in the C:\bc5\script directory. Table 22.3 lists and describes some of the more interesting standard scripts.

Table 22.3. Standard scripts (partial list).

Filename	Description
Briefex.spp	Provides a selection of functions similar to those in the Brief programmer's editor. Read this file for function names you can enter using the *Script\Run* command.
Edit.spp	Implements the scripts for the IDE's Editor class object. This file makes interesting reading—it contains numerous cScript programming techniques that you'll find useful in your own scripts.
Ed_*.spp	These files implement the IDE's various editor emulations for Brief, Classic IDE, Default IDE, and Epsilon editors. If an emulation doesn't include a feature you need, you can modify and recompile the associated script.
Exscr.spp	Implements the *Script* menu's *Install/Uninstall examples* command. Read this file to learn how to add and remove IDE menu items using scripts.
Ide.spp	Implements top-level IDE commands such as *File\Save* and *Search\Find*. This file shows how to write on event handlers, how to create a new edit buffer, and other techniques. Don't modify this one without careful thought.
Menuhook.spp	Low-level programming used by the Exscr.spp script to insert and remove IDE menu items.
Miscscr.spp	Implements miscellaneous scripts for Windows API functions, accessed though the Miscscr.dll, which is located in C:\bc5\bin. Read this file to learn how to interface a script and a DLL.
Openfile.spp	Implements the local popup menu's *Open source* command, which opens a file using the text at the current cursor position. This file demonstrates numerous cScript techniques such as how to read text at the current cursor position and how to open an editor view window.
Startup.spp	Manages the script engine's entire IDE startup sequence. You can modify this file for new startup operations, but it is probably better to specify one or more startup scripts using the *Options\Environment* dialog. If you do modify the startup script, be sure to save a copy somewhere so you don't lose your changes if you reinstall Borland C++.

Programming with cScript

To write a script, you need to understand how the cScript language differs from C++. See Borland's online help for complete descriptions of operators, statements, variables, classes, and other language elements. In this section, I focus mainly on cScript's features that distinguish it from C++.

cScript is a late-bound, object-oriented language. Late-binding refers to the way compiled scripts are bound into the IDE at runtime rather than linked at compile time, as are C++ modules. Late-binding makes it possible to extend the IDE without recompiling the environment, but it has consequences on data types, variables, and declarations. For example, you cannot declare a type or function forward. Because a script's P-Code is interpreted, all data and code must be defined in advance of their use.

> **WARNING**
>
> cScript statements are case sensitive—myid, myId, and MyId are different identifiers. In fact, you might say that cScript is case *super*-sensitive because references to undeclared objects are ignored during compile time (a consequence of late-binding). If your scripts don't seem to work, check and recheck (then check again) that you have spelled all variables, classes, and functions *exactly* as declared.

cScript statements closely resemble those in C++, and are terminated with semicolons. The usual operators and control statements are available—break, do-while, if, return, continue, else, for, while, and switch—but you declare variables differently. In cScript, a variable's type is determined by its runtime use. Use the declare keyword to create a variable, used here in a sample for loop:

```
declare i;
for (i=0; i < 100; i++) {
// do something
}
```

You can declare and initialize variables with a single statement:

```
declare aNumber = 468;
print aNumber;  // Output appears in Message window
```

You can also declare multiple variables separated with commas:

```
declare v1, v2, v3, row, column;
```

Concatenate strings with a plus sign:

```
print "The number is " + aNumber;
```

This implies that aNumber is converted into a string, which happens due to the context of the variable's use. After running this statement, the Message window shows:

```
The number is 468
```

The `switch` statement differs from C++ in that the controlling and case expressions can be anything you like, such as strings or function calls:

```
switch (myVariable) {
  case 123:
    // Do something and fall through to next case(s)
  case myFunction():
    // Do something else if myFunction() == myVariable
    break; // If here, switch ends
  default:
    // Optional--default if no matching case breaks
}
```

cScript has no structs, unions, or pointers, and therefore, the following operators do not exist:

```
->   *   ->*   .*
```

cScript also does not have `sizeof` and `::` operators, but it does have a few new ones. The *closure operator* (`:>`) is used in *"on"* event handlers (see "Understanding Closure" in this chapter); the *in operator* (`??`) tests whether values are members of arrays and classes.

Strings are similar in cScript and C++, but are limited to 4,096 characters. cScript automatically appends a null to the end of a string as necessary. There's also a `String` class you can use, similar to the standard library's, but capitalized.

There are two types of arrays: *bounded* and *associative*. A bounded array resembles a C++ array, and is declared with a size parameter. Bounded arrays can contain any types of values, and also can expand automatically at runtime. There are two ways to declare bounded arrays:

```
herArray = new array[25];   // Creates new bounded array
array hisArray[25];         // Same as above
```

Those statements create two, 25-element arrays named `herArray` and `hisArray`. Assign values to array positions as you do in C++, but note that because variables are untyped, you can assign any type of value to any array slot. Bounded array indexes are positive integers, beginning with zero. Here are some sample array assignments:

```
herArray[0] = "Sally's array";
herArray[1] = 32;  // Age
hisArray[0] = "Bob's array";
hisArray[1] = 46;  // Age
```

You may declare and initialize a bounded array with parameter expressions in braces, separated with commas:

```
declare four = 4;  // Variables must be preinitialized
initArray[] = {1, 2, "three", four};  // Declare and initialize array
```

Create associative arrays similarly to bounded arrays, but without a size specifier:

```
herArray = new array[];  // Creates new associative array
array hisArray[];        // Same as above
```

Associative array indexes can be any types, but are usually strings. You can assign any data to any array slot:

```
hisArray["Name"] = "Bob";
hisArray["Age"] = 46;
herArray["Name"] = "Sally";
herArray["Age"] = 25;
herArray[0] = hisArray["Name"];
```

Associative arrays are sparse (only referenced indexes exist), but they are slower to use than bounded arrays. If you can calculate an array's size in advance, and if you can use integer indexes, use a bounded array, which will improve the script's speed.

You can expand a bounded array by referencing an out-of-bounds index, but this actually creates a new associative array. For example, if array yourArray has 10 slots, this appears to expand it to 15:

```
yourArray = new array[10];
yourArray[14] = "Expanded array";
```

However, this does *not* cause the array to grow by five more elements. Behind the scenes, cScript attaches an associative array to the end of the bounded array. All assignments outside of the bounded array's declared size go into this associative array. (This may have negative consequences on program speed, and it's best to declare bounded arrays as large as needed in advance.)

Functions in cScript do not have return-type values. Declare a function by name followed by parentheses and statements in braces:

```
noParams() {
  print "Inside noParams";
}
```

Functions may have parameters, which by default are passed by value, as they are in C++. However, parameter types are not specified.

```
byValue(v) {
  v = 123;    // Does not modify caller's variable
}
```

To pass a parameter by reference, preface it with an ampersand (&):

```
byReference(&v) {
  v = 456;    // Modifies caller's variable
}
```

There are some useful built-in functions you can call. For example, FormatString builds strings at runtime, using embedded formatting commands similar to those in the printf standard function. Here's a sample that uses the associative herArray:

```
print FormatString("Sally's age = %1", herArray["Age"]);
```

Running this statement produces the following line in the Message window:

```
Sally's age = 25
```

Unlike with `printf`, embedded variables in FormatString expressions must be integers, which specify the position of the values following the formatting string:

```
print FormatString("v3=%3, v1=%1, v2=%2", v1, v2, v3);
```

The `initialized` function, which returns TRUE or FALSE, tells you whether a variable has been merely declared or if it has been assigned a value. This is especially useful with parameters passed to functions:

```
if (!initialized(anyParam))
  anyParam = "Initial value";
f(anyParam);  // Use parameter
```

> **NOTE**
>
> Unlike in ANSI C++, cScript Boolean constants TRUE and FALSE must be in all uppercase.

The `print` function, as you have seen, prints a string to the IDE's Message window. The command can print multiple expressions separated by commas:

```
print "Error #", errCode, ": ", errMsg;
```

Another especially valuable function, `yield`, makes it possible for users to interrupt a script by pressing the Esc key. It's a good idea to call `yield` from within time-consuming loops:

```
while (!rareCondition()) {
  yield;  // escape loop on Esc
  // do something
}
```

Declaring and Using Classes

cScript Classes resemble those in C++, but there are several key differences that make cScript unique:

- All data and function members are public. There are no `public`, `protected`, or `private` access specifiers.
- Member functions are declared and implemented directly in the class declaration. You cannot implement a class function separately as you can in C++. (Also, cScript lacks the scope-resolution operator `::`.)
- A class may declare parameters. Base class parameters are automatically passed to any derived class parameters of the same names.
- There are no constructors in a cScript class. However, any statements in a class that are not part of a member function are executed when a program creates an object of the class.

- Destructors are the same as in C++ classes. They have the same name as the class and are preceded with a tilde (-). A class may have only one destructor.

- cScript does not support function overloading, and new data and function members completely override inherited data and functions of the same names. However, you may create function chains using `attach`, `detach`, and on event handlers, which produce results similar to C++ function overloading. See "Understanding Closure" in this chapter for details.

- cScript supports only single, not multiple, inheritance.

Class Declarations

Here's a sample class that illustrates the basic format to use for most class declarations:

```
class myClass {
  declare x, y;
  print "myClass object constructed";
  myFunc() {
    print "myFunc executed";
  }
  ~myClass() {
    print "myClass object destroyed";
  }
}
```

Class `myClass` declares two variables, x and y. Because the first `print` statement is not in a member function, it is executed when an object of the class is created. Use statements such as this to initialize class objects, similar to the way you use a constructor in a C++ class. Function `myFunc` is declared and implemented inside the class declaration. The destructor, `~myClass()`, is called when an object of the class is destroyed.

Although cScript classes have no constructors, a class can declare and call its own member functions, and in that way, provide parameterized constructor-like code. For example, consider this class:

```
class Demo {
// Creating a Demo object executes this statement:
  fParams("A string", 10, TRUE);
// Implements the function called by preceding statement:
  fParams(a, b, c) {
    print FormatString("%1 %2 %3", a, b, c);
  }
}
```

Using that declaration, when a script creates a `Demo` object, the script engine executes the statement that calls `fParams` with three arguments—a string, an integer, and a Boolean `TRUE` constant. However, this is not exactly like a C++ constructor because other statements in the script can also call `fParams` after the object is created.

Class Parameters

You can declare parameters in classes, and pass them arguments. Like all cScript variables, the class parameters row and column in this sample class are untyped:

```
class WithParams(row, column) {
  declare r = row;      // Save row in member object r
  declare c = column;   // Save column in member object r
  // Function that later uses r and c
  UseRC() {
    for (r = 0; r < row; r++) {
      // do next row ;
      for (c = 0; c < column; c++)
        // do next column ;
    }
  }
}
```

Class parameters partially make up for the lack of constructors in cScript classes. To construct an object of the WithParams class, pass it argument values like this:

```
declare anObject = new WithParams(25, 80);
anObject.UseRC();  // Call function that uses argument values
```

Class Inheritance

cScript is object-oriented, and it supports class hierarchies, but using only single inheritance. Derive a child class from a base class by typing a colon and the base class name after the derived class declaration. In its simplest form, a derived class declaration looks like this:

```
class Derived(): Base() {
}
```

Class Derived inherits all members of class Base, and all such members are public in the derived class. The declarations are a bit trickier when classes declare parameters. For example, consider this derivation:

```
class Derived(v1, v2, v3): Base(v1, v3) {
}
```

The base class parameters, v1 and v3, are passed through to the derived class's parameters with those same names. Parameter v2 is new to the derived class.

Any overridden members completely replace inherited members of the same name. For example, if a base class has a function aFunc and a data member aVar, this derived class completely replaces those members:

```
class Derived(): Base() {
  declare aVar;  // Overrides Base class aVar
  aFunc() {      // Overrides Base class aFunc
  }
}
```

You may declare nested classes using a syntax such as

```
class Outer() {
  class Inner() {
  }
}
```

Class Inner's scope extends only to Outer, and Inner's name is therefore protected against clashes with another declaration of that same name.

Script Construction Techniques

You create script files the same as you do C++ modules—select *File|New* and choose the *Text Edit* subcommand. Enter cScript statements and save the editor buffer to a file ending with .spp. You can save your own scripts in any directory, but if you want to load them without specifying drive and path information, save or copy your script files to a directory listed in the default *Scripting* path set by selecting *Options|Environment*.

> **TIP**
>
> To enable syntax highlighting for script files, select *Options|Environment* and choose the *Syntax Highlighting* topic. Add `*.spp` to the list of supported filename extensions. For example, the completed list of extensions might look like this (you can separate entries with semicolons or commas):
>
> `*.cpp;*.c;*.h;*.hpp;*.rh;*.rc;*.spp`

A script file's entry point is the beginning of its text—scripts have no main or WinMain functions. Statements outside of any functions execute when the script is loaded, which you can do by any of the means already discussed. After loading a script, you can call its functions by using the *Script|Run* command. Or, you can provide an _init() function, which automatically runs when the script is loaded. Another method is to write a function named the same as the module (myscript() for Myscript.spp, for instance).

Listing 22.1 shows a sample script that you can use as a starting point for your own script files. The sample script also demonstrates how to assign a hot key to a script function. This is probably the best way to add new keyboard commands to the IDE.

> **NOTE**
>
> Follow these steps to compile, load, and run the sample script in Listing 22.1:
>
> 1. Enter or load the Kassign.spp file from disk.
> 2. Select *Script|Run File*. (You won't see any onscreen activity but the IDE *Message* window's *Script* page verifies that the script was compiled and run.)

3. Press Ctrl+X to run the example function. You should see a dialog box with the message, *Example script executed!* Instead of pressing Ctrl+X, you can select *Script/Run* and enter `example()` (you must include the parentheses) to execute that function.

Listing 22.1. Kassign.spp (Assigns hot key to cScript function).

```
//============================================================
// Kassign.spp -- Assigns hot key to cScript function
// Copyright (c) 1996 by Tom Swan. All rights reserved.
//============================================================

print "Kassign script";

import IDE;

_init() {
  declare keybMgr  = IDE.KeyboardManager;
  declare keyboard = keybMgr.GetKeyboard("Editor");
  keyboard.Assign(
    "<Ctrl-X>", "example();", ASSIGN_IMPLICIT_SHIFT);
}

// Example script--press Ctrl+X to run
example()
{
  IDE.Message("Example script executed!");
}
```

The Kassign.spp script demonstrates some important scripting techniques. Use `import` declarations to gain access to objects already loaded. In this case, the program needs to access the IDE object (of the `IDEApplication` class) for the example function's call to that class's `Message` function.

> **NOTE**
>
> By the way, the `import` statement is a good example of late-binding in action. Unlike in C++ programs where external data references are resolved by a linker, the IDE object is bound into the script at runtime. As a consequence, if you misspell IDE as Ide, for example, you'll have no indication that something is wrong until you run the script—the script engine can't produce a compilation error because it doesn't know what kinds of objects will be available when you run the script.

When you run the Kassign.spp script, it executes the two global statements, which print an identifying string to the IDE's Message window and import the IDE object. After executing global statements, the script engine calls a function named `_init`, if such a function exists.

In this example, the _init function declares two variables as references to the IDE's keyboard manager, and then to its "Editor" Keyboard-class object. Call that class's Assign method to attach hot keys to functions. Two strings represent the key sequence and the command to give—this command is the same as you might enter using *Script|Run*. (A semicolon tells the keyboard manager not to attempt to load a script file of this name, but to call a function already loaded.) The constant, ASSIGN_IMPLICIT_SHIFT, indicates that Ctrl-X and Ctrl-x are considered equal. This is the default setting, however, so you don't have to specify the constant as I did.

> **TIP**
>
> To assign hot keys to script functions automatically when you start the IDE, add the script name to the *Startup Scripts* input box using the *Options|Environment* command's *Scripting* topic.

The following sections explain some additional script construction techniques you'll find useful in writing your own scripts.

How To Load and Run Scripts

Scripts do not run exactly the same as programs, and the order of execution of statements and functions may at first seem confusing. This section will help clear the initial confusion you are likely to experience when running your own script files.

When you load a script, the IDE's script engine first executes any global commands that are not inside any functions. It then executes a function named _init, if one exists. When you unload the script, the script engine executes a function named ~() (no name, just a tilde and a pair of empty parentheses). The _init() and ~() functions are similar to a class's constructor and destructor, but they operate on the script-module level.

Listing 22.2 demonstrates these cScript features, and also shows the order of execution for a script module. To make the script's output easier to read, select *Options|Environment* and temporarily turn off the *Scripting* topic's *Diagnostic Messages* option. View the message window and press Ctrl+A to delete any old messages; then open Runorder.spp and select *Script|Run File*.

Listing 22.2. Runorder.spp (Shows cScript module order of execution).

```
//================================================================
// Runorder.spp -- Shows cScript module order of execution
// Copyright (c) 1996 by Tom Swan. All rights reserved.
//================================================================

print "Global statement";

_init()
{
  print "Constructor _init() statement";
```

```
}

~()
{
  print "Destructor ~() statement";
}

runorder()
{
  print "Function runorder() statement";
}
```

After running the script, the Message window shows the following two lines:

```
Global statement
Constructor _init() statement
```

This output illustrates that first, the script engine executed the global print statement. Then, it called the module's _init() function. *These actions occur only when you first load a script module.*

After loading the script, you can run any of its functions by selecting *Script|Run* and entering a function name. For example, select that command now and enter runorder(). You must type the parentheses. The Message window now shows a third line displayed by the runorder function:

```
Function runorder() statement
```

Notice that running the script function does not again execute the global statement and _init function. Those actions occur only when the module is first loaded. However, if the module is not already loaded, then the global actions occur *in addition to the specified function's actions.* To see this important effect, follow these steps:

1. Select *Script|Modules,* and highlight the entry for Runorder.spp.
2. Press the *Unload* button to unload the Runorder.spp script.
3. Press the *Close* button to close the *Script Modules* dialog.
4. View the Message window and press Ctrl+A to delete all old messages.
5. Select *Script|Run* and enter runorder(). (This is the same command you gave before when the module was already loaded.)

Now, when you view the *Message* window's *Script* page, it shows all three lines:

```
Global statement
Constructor _init() statement
Function runorder() statement
```

This experiment demonstrates that the script engine first attempts to run a function already loaded into memory. If that fails, the engine looks for a script file named the same as the function. Finding such a script file, the script engine loads it, executes any global statements, calls an _init function if there is one, and then executes the specified function.

All of this leads to a common misconception—that a script function named the same as the script module is automatically called when you load the script. Not true! Such a function is called only when you or another script executes that function by name, at which time the script engine attempts to load a like-named module unless it is already loaded.

There is one more automatically executed function that Runorder.spp demonstrates—a pseudo destructor named ~(). Use the *Script\Modules* command to unload Runorder.spp as you did before, close the dialog box, and view the Message window. You'll find the following statement, executed by the example script's pseudo destructor:

```
Destructor ~() statement
```

> **NOTE**
>
> If you are following along, reenable the *Scripting* topic's *Diagnostic Messages* option before continuing.

How To Automatically Run a Function

There's another simple, but highly useful, way to automatically run functions when a script is first loaded—simply call those functions using one or more global statements. For example, insert the following function into the Runorder.spp script from the preceding section:

```
otherfun()
{
  print "Function otherfun() statement";
}
```

Next, just below the module's first `print` statement, call the new function. Here are the two lines for reference:

```
print "Global statement";
otherfun();  // Call otherfun() at load time
```

Now, when you load the module using *Script\Run File*, the script engine executes the `print` statement and calls `otherfun`. Both of those actions occur before the script engine calls `_init()`.

> **WARNING**
>
> Never use the foregoing method to automatically call a function named the same as the script module! This will cause a *scripting double whammy error* (at least that's what I call it), which will execute the module's function twice when the unloaded function is run by name. Because this double trouble occurs only when the module is first loaded, it may seem to be an intermittent problem or a bug in the IDE—it's neither.

How To Force a Script Module To Load

Use a variation of the preceding technique to force a script module to be loaded when users select the *Script|Run* command. Simply enter an empty function of the same name as the module. For example, if the script file is named Myscript.spp, enter this function into the file:

```
myscript()
{
}
```

When users enter `myscript()` using the *Script|Run* command, or when Myscript is run by other means (as a startup module, for instance) the script engine will load the Myscript.spp file if it is not already loaded. If it is loaded, the do-nothing function will execute, and of course, will do exactly nothing, which is what we want. Of course, you can use this method only for scripts that do not already have a function named the same as the module, but the trick is especially useful for loading script modules that provide a library of functions.

> ### TIP
>
> If a script is already loaded, and if you make a change to a function named the same as that script, using the *Script|Run* command will execute the old function, *even if you save the changes to the script's text file.* To reload the module, select the *Script|Run File* command, and then try *Script|Run* again. The first time this happens to you, you will understandably wonder if you have found a bug in the IDE, but it's just an unavoidable consequence of late-binding.

How To Prompt for Input

Use code similar to that in Listing 22.3, Input.spp, to prompt users for input. Open the script file, select *Script|Run,* and enter `input()` when prompted. You will see a dialog box that asks you for your age. Go ahead and lie. I promise not to tell.

Listing 22.3 Input.spp (Demonstrates how to prompt users for input).

```
//============================================================
// Input.spp -- Demonstrates how to prompt users for input
// Copyright (c) 1996 by Tom Swan. All rights reserved.
//============================================================

print "Input.spp";

import IDE;

input()
{
  declare value;
  value = IDE.SimpleDialog("Please tell me your age", 124);
  if (value == "")
```

continues

Listing 22.3 continued

```
    return;
  IDE.Message("You entered " + value);
}
```

How To Test for Selected Text

Many scripts operate on selected text in an editor window. Use the method in Listing 22.4, Selected.spp, to determine whether the user has selected some text for processing. The script displays a message dialog that indicates whether any text is selected. Open the script file, select *Script\Run,* and enter selected() to run the test function. Next, select a few lines in the editor window, and repeat the command.

Listing 22.4. Selected.spp (Determines if text is selected).

```
//================================================================
// Selected.spp -- Determines if text is selected
// Copyright (c) 1996 by Tom Swan. All rights reserved.
//================================================================

print "Selected.spp";

import IDE;
import editor;

selected()
{
  declare curView = editor.TopView;
  if (curView.Block.IsValid)
    IDE.Message("Found selected text.");
  else
    IDE.Message("Select some text and rerun script.");
}
```

How To Run a Script from a Script

Use the programming in Listing 22.5, Msgbox.spp, and Listing 22.6, Loader.spp, to create script commands that can load and run another script file. Msgbox.spp is the script we want to load and run by executing another script, Loader.spp. Open Loader.spp, select *Script\Run,* and enter loader() when prompted. You'll see the dialog box displayed by the Msgbox.spp script file.

Listing 22.5. Msgbox.spp (Displays a message).

```
//================================================================
// Msgbox.spp -- Displays a message
// Copyright (c) 1996 by Tom Swan. All rights reserved.
//================================================================

import IDE;
IDE.Message("Module loaded and run");
```

Listing 22.6. Loader.spp (Loads and runs Msgbox.spp script).

```
//================================================================
// Loader.spp -- Loads and runs Msgbox.spp script
// Copyright (c) 1996 by Tom Swan. All rights reserved.
//================================================================

print "Loader.spp";

loader()
{
  declare aModule;
  aModule = load("msgbox.spp");
  if (aModule) {
    run(aModule);
    unload(aModule);
  }
}
```

Loader.spp declares a variable, aModule, and initializes it to the result returned by the load function. This function looks in the default script paths set by the *Options|Environment Scripting* commands, or in the current directory. If load's resulting handle is valid, pass it to the run function as shown. Optionally unload the module after you are done running it. If you don't call unload as shown, the loaded module will remain in memory, which in another case, might be advantageous—if you plan to call several functions in the module, for example.

How To Display Message Dialogs

One of Borland's example scripts simplifies displaying various kinds of message dialogs, and also prompts users for yes and no responses. Listing 22.7 demonstrates how to load and use this example code from the Msg.spp file, located in the C:\bc5\script\examples directory.

Listing 22.7. Message.spp (Demonstrates Borland's msg.spp script).

```
//================================================================
// Message.spp -- Demonstrates Borland's msg.spp script
// Copyright (c) 1996 by Tom Swan. All rights reserved.
//================================================================

print "Message.spp";
```

Listing 22.7. continued

```
import scriptEngine;

if (!scriptEngine.IsLoaded("msg.spp"))
  scriptEngine.Load("msg.spp");

message()
{
// Construct a TMsg object
  declare msg = new TMsg();

// Common message dialogs
  msg.Info("Some important information follows...");
  msg.Warn("You are about to nuke your hard drive!");
  msg.Error("You have just deleted your life history!");

// Yes or no prompts
  declare sTemp = new String;
  sTemp = msg.YesNo("Have you eaten your Wheaties today?");
  if (sTemp == "Yes")
    msg.Info("Go get em tiger!");
  else
    msg.Info("You are such a wimp!");
}
```

Before loading the Msg.spp script, it's a good idea to determine whether that module is already loaded. If you don't do this, the scriptEngine's Load function unloads and then reloads the same script, which is like dumping your ammunition on the ground, putting it back into your pistola, and only then taking your best shot—not a good way to win a duel.

To check if a script is loaded, first import the scriptEngine object. Then, call IsLoaded with the name of the target script in quotes. If IsLoaded is false, you can call Load to load the module.

Next, construct an object of the TMsg class, declared in the Msg.spp script. In reference to the object (msg in the sample listing) call the class's Info, Warn, or Error functions to display a message dialog window with an appropriately selected icon.

The rest of the script demonstrates how to use the TMsg class's YesNo function, which returns a string equal to "Yes" or "No" that indicates which button the user pressed to close the dialog.

How To Peruse a File Directory

Scripts are valuable tools for processing multiple files—to search for uses of a particular function, for example, or to make a global modification to a set of files. Listing 22.8 shows the basic steps for prompting users for a directory, and then scanning the filenames in that path.

Listing 22.8. Scandir.spp (Scans a directory for filenames).

```
//===============================================================
// Scandir.spp -- Scans a directory for filenames
// Copyright (c) 1996 by Tom Swan. All rights reserved.
//===============================================================

print "Scandir.spp";

import IDE;

// Returns TRUE if file extension == .h, .cpp, .spp, or .rc
IsTargetFile(f)
{
  declare s = new String(f);
  s = s.Lower();
  if (s.Index(".h"  ) ||
      s.Index(".cpp") ||
      s.Index(".spp") ||
      s.Index(".rc" ) ) {
    return TRUE;
  }
  return FALSE;
}

// Returns length of filename string f
StrLen(f)
{
  declare s = new String(f);
  return s.Length;
}

// Add your code to process the file
ProcessFile(f)
{
  print f;  // Display in Message window for demo
}

// The main test program
scandir()
{
// Get directory from user
  declare dir;
  dir = IDE.DirectoryDialog(
    "Choose a directory", NULL, IDE.CurrentDirectory);
  if (dir == "") return;
```

continues

753

Listing 22.8 continued

```
// Peruse the path for filenames
  IDE.StartWaitCursor();
  print dir;
  declare f = IDE.FindFirstFile(dir + "\\*.*");
  while (StrLen(f) != 0) {
    if (IsTargetFile(f)) {
      ProcessFile(f);
    }
    f = IDE.FindNextFile();
  }
  IDE.EndWaitCursor();
}
```

The test function shows the main programming for perusing a directory's filenames. Import the IDE object, and call its `DirectoryDialog` function to prompt the user for a directory. This displays a dialog box, and lets users browse directories, change to another drive, and so on. (Tip: You can specify a default string for the edit window in place of the NULL argument in the example code.)

After prompting for a directory, a `while` loop shows how to scan the path for filenames. Call the IDE object's `FindFirstFile` function and save the result in a variable, here named `f`. While the string length of that variable is not zero, process the file and call `IDE.FindNextFile`. This eventually returns all filenames. (Note: Windows 95 long filenames are returned as spelled, including any spaces.)

The test code also demonstrates some miscellaneous scripting techniques you might find useful. The script's `IsTargetFile` function returns TRUE if the passed filename parameter contains one of the specified extensions. Use a similar function to limit processing to files of a specific type. Notice also how the filename null-terminated string is converted to a `String` object so the function can call the `Lower` and `Index` functions.

> **TIP**
>
> The `String` class `Index` function returns zero if the specified substring does not exist in the target string. Otherwise, `Index` returns the substring index *plus one*. Thus, a result of 1 indicates the substring is at the beginning of the target string.

Use the sample script's `StrLen` function to determine the length of a null-terminated string. This small but useful function converts a string argument to a `String` object and returns that object's `Length` value.

How To Modify Selected Text

Modifying text in an editor view is one of the most intriguing operations a script can do. The possibilities are endless—you can insert code snippets, pretty up a source file, create comment headers, modify case of selected text, and automate many other editing chores.

To help you get started writing your own text-editor scripts, Listing 22.9, Com.spp, demonstrates the basic techniques of accessing and changing selected lines in an editor window. To use the script, open Com.spp and select *Script\Run File*. This compiles and loads the script, but doesn't run its main function. You may close the Com.spp file at this point. Next, open or create another file, and enter some lines of text. Select those lines and press Ctrl+Z to convert them into a C++ comment, which the script does by prefacing each line with two slashes (//). Select the same lines and press Ctrl+Z to toggle them back to uncommented text. This script is particularly handy for temporarily removing statements from a program without deleting them, and also for creating large comments composed of several lines or paragraphs.

Listing 22.9. Com.spp (Toggles selected text to and from a C++ comment).

```
//============================================================
// Com.spp -- Toggles selected text to and from a C++ comment
// Copyright (c) 1996 by Tom Swan. All rights reserved.
//============================================================

print "com.spp";

import IDE;
import scriptEngine;
import editor;

// Load Borland's msg.spp script in \bc5\script\examples
if (!scriptEngine.IsLoaded("msg.spp"))
  scriptEngine.Load("msg.spp");

// Assign Ctrl+Z to com() function
_init() {
  declare keybMgr  = IDE.KeyboardManager;
  declare keyboard = keybMgr.GetKeyboard("Editor");
  keyboard.Assign(
    "<Ctrl-Z>", "com();", ASSIGN_IMPLICIT_SHIFT);
}

// Main script: Press Ctrl+Z to run
com()
{
  declare msg = new TMsg();
  declare sTmp = new String();
  declare curView = editor.TopView;

  if (!curView.Block.IsValid) {
    msg.Info("You must first select one or more lines.");
    return;
  }
```

continues

Listing 22.9 continued

```
  declare rowStart = curView.Block.StartingRow;
  declare rowEnd = curView.Block.EndingRow;
  declare i;

  for (i = rowStart; i < rowEnd; i++) {
    curView.Position.Move(i, 1);
    sTmp.Text = curView.Position.Read();
    if (sTmp.Index("//") == 1)
      curView.Position.Delete(2);
    else
      curView.Position.InsertText("//");
  }
}
```

Com.spp uses the techniques explained elsewhere in this chapter for Borland's msg.spp script, and for assigning a hot key to a script function. After checking whether there is any selected text in the current editor view, the script uses the editor object's TopView member to gain access to that text.

TopView is an object of the EditView class, which you can use to perform various editor functions and access properties. Here, for example, the Position object is used to move the cursor, and to delete and insert text. This object is of the EditPosition class, and it is in this class that you will find numerous text operations including searching, inserting files, inserting, and removing text from buffers.

Understanding Closure

No, this is not a tutorial on how to finalize a real estate deal. The term *closure* in cScript refers to techniques for tapping into class functions and enhancing what they do—similar to the way you can inherit and override C++ class member functions to modify their actions.

You create closures in two ways: in a class declaration (the closure applies to all instances of the class), or for a specific class object (the closure affects only that object). Listing 22.10, Cldemo.spp, demonstrates how to create a class-level closure, which is the most obvious use of the technique. I'll explain other variations later in this section. To run the script, compile and load it using *Script|Run File,* and then select *Script|Run* and enter **cldemo()**.

Listing 22.10. Cldemo.spp (Demonstrates cScript closure).

```
//================================================================
// Cldemo.spp -- Demonstrates cScript closure
// Copyright (c) 1996 by Tom Swan. All rights reserved.
//================================================================

print "Closure Demonstration";
```

```
class Base() {
  print "Base object created";
  aFunction() {
    print "Inside Base.aFunction";
  }
  ~Base() {
    print "Base object destroyed";
  }
}

class Derived(): Base() {
  print "Derived object created";
  on this:>aFunction() {
    print "Inside Derived.aFunction event handler";
    return pass();  // Calls Base.aFunction
  }
  ~Derived() {
    print "Derived object destroyed";
  }
}

declare globalObject = new Derived();
on globalObject:>aFunction() {
  print "I have taken control of this function!";
  // pass();
}

cldemo()
{
  declare aDerived = new Derived();  // Create Derived object
  aDerived.aFunction();  // Call on-event handler
  globalObject.aFunction();
}
```

For demonstration purposes, the example script prints notes to the Message window that trace the program's execution. (Temporarily turn off the *Scripting* option's *Diagnostic Messages* to make these notes easier to see.) After running the script and its cldemo function, the Message window displays these lines:

```
Closure Demonstration
Base object created
Derived object created
Inside Derived.aFunction event handler
Inside Base.aFunction
I have taken control of this function!
Derived object destroyed
Base object destroyed
```

For demonstration, the script declares a Base class with a global statement, a function named aFunction, and a destructor. A Derived class inherits Base, and also has a similar set of members. However, to override the inherited aFunction, Derived declares it as

```
on this:>aFunction() {
```

The this pointer is similar to its C++ counterpart—it refers to the object for which a statement makes a call to a class member function. However, to override the function, cScript uses an *on-handler*. This is composed of three parts:

1. The keyword on.
2. A reference to an object or, in a class member function, the this pointer.
3. The cScript closure operator (:>), which to me looks like a smiling bird with its head sideways, but then I'm probably spending too much time answering Internet email.

Declaring an on-handler in a class member function causes the script to call that function instead of an inherited function of the same name. To also call the inherited function, use the cScript pass function as shown. You can optionally return this function as the on-handler's return value, but this is not required if the function doesn't return any value. If you don't call pass, the on-handler completely replaces the inherited function.

> **NOTE**
>
> Technically, it's incorrect to state that an on-handler *overrides* a function. An on-handler actually creates a runtime function chain, an important distinction and another consequence brought to you by late-binding.

Using closure, you may create an on-handler for a specific object of a class. Other objects are unaffected. The syntax is similar, but the programming is outside of any class and function declarations. For example, insert the following statements into Cldemo.spp, just above the cldemo function:

```
declare globalObject = new Derived();
on globalObject:>aFunction() {
  print "I have taken control of this function!";
  // pass();  // Enable to call Derived.aFunction()
}
```

A declare statement constructs a global object of the Derived class. Because this action is global, it takes place only once when the script module is loaded. Also insert this statement into the cldemo function.

```
globalObject.aFunction();
```

This calls the on-handler for the global object, even though that object is of the Derived class, which provides its own on-handler. To call Derived's aFunction, enable the pass statement listed as a commend in the preceding global object's on-handler.

Dynamic On-Handlers

To create dynamic on-handlers that the script itself creates and destroys, use the attach, detach, to, and from keywords along with cScript's closure operator. With dynamic on-handlers, statements can redirect calls to functions based on various conditions such as user commands that occur at runtime.

You normally create a dynamic on-handler in reference to an object so that you can temporarily change what a function does when called in reference to the object. Listing 22.11, Dynamic.spp, demonstrates the basic idea. Open the file and load the script with *Script|Run File*, then select *Script|Run* and enter **dynamic()**.

Listing 22.11. Dynamic.spp (Attaches and detaches an on-handler)

```
//================================================================
// Dynamic.spp -- Attaches and detaches an on-handler
// Copyright (c) 1996 by Tom Swan. All rights reserved.
//================================================================

print "Dynamic.spp";

import IDE;

class AClass() {
  AFunction(objname) {
    print FormatString("%1:%2", objname, "AFunction");
  }
}

class BClass() {
  BFunction(objname) {
    print FormatString("%1:%2", objname, "BFunction");
  }
}

dynamic()
{
  declare a1 = new AClass();
  declare b1 = new BClass();
  a1.AFunction("a1");

  print "attach b1:>BFunction to a1:>AFunction;";
  attach b1:>BFunction to a1:>AFunction;
  a1.AFunction("a1");  // Now calls b1.BFunction
  detach b1:>BFunction from a1:>AFunction;
}
```

The example script declares two classes, AClass and BClass, each with a function: AFunction and BFunction respectively. Each function displays a parameter and identifies itself. The dynamic function declares objects, a1 and b1, of the two classes, and then calls AFunction in reference to object a1.

To change a1's actions for the second such function call, the script executes the attach statement

```
attach b1:>BFunction to a1:>AFunction;
```

This tells the script engine that, from now on, calls to a1.AFunction should instead be routed to b1.BFunction. When the program now calls a1.AFunction, execution is routed instead to the function in BClass, producing these lines in the Message window:

```
a1:AFunction
attach b1:>BFunction to a1:>AFunction;
a1:BFunction
```

To detach a dynamic on-handler, use a detach statement with the same arguments as the associated attach statement. This returns the modified function to its previous operation. The example script detaches BFunction with the statement

```
detach b1:>BFunction from a1:>AFunction;
```

> **TIP**
>
> A class member function can create a dynamic on-handler either for named objects, or for all objects of a class. For example, this statement, if inside a class member function
>
> ```
> attach this:>NewFunction to this:>OriginalFunction;
> ```
>
> redirects calls to OriginalFunction to NewFunction for all objects of the class.

Property Access

Controlling access to data is one of the goals of object-oriented programming. But in cScript classes, because all members are public, it isn't possible to hide data in private and protected sections as you can with C++.

However, using on-handlers that are associated with data members, you can program functions called *getters* and *setters* that control all uses of object data. The following two listings demonstrate this powerful cScript technique.

Listing 22.12, Get.spp, shows how to write a getter, which controls read-only access to a data value. (Important: This does not *make* data read-only—it merely controls all uses of the data that do not change its value.) Compile and load the script using *Script|Run File*, and then select *Script|Run* and enter **get()**. As with many scripts in this chapter, Get.spp directs its output to the IDE's Message window.

Listing 22.12. Get.spp (Demonstrates getters).

```
//================================================================
// Get.spp -- Demonstrates getters
// Copyright (c) 1996 by Tom Swan. All rights reserved.
//================================================================

print "Get.spp";
```

```
import IDE;

class AClass {
// Declare read-only data member
  declare value;
// Implement getter for value
  on this:>value {
    if (!initialized(value))
      value = 10;
    return value;
  }
}

get()
{
  declare anObject = new AClass();
  print FormatString("value = %1", anObject.value);
  anObject.value = 123;
  print FormatString("value = %1", anObject.value);
}
```

For the demonstration, the script declares a class, AClass, with a single data member named value. One use for a getter is to ensure that a data member is initialized. This makes the script more robust, and prevents an error caused by accidentally using an uninitialized object. The class declares value as a common variable. It then provides a getter for value. This looks very much like a function on-handler:

```
on this:>value {
  if (!initialized(value))
    value = 10;
  return value;
}
```

Because of this code, every read-only use of value executes the if statement, which checks whether the data is initialized. If not, the script assigns 10 to value. Skip down to the main program, which prints an uninitialized value, assigns 123 to it, and prints it again. The first line in the Message window indicates that the getter detected the use of the uninitialized value and assigned 10 to it:

```
value = 10
value = 123
```

A *setter* controls write-only access to a value. Here again, a setter doesn't *create* a write-only object; it controls write-only operations that assign values to data members. Listing 22.13 demonstrates how to write a setter. The script is the same as Get.spp, but it now controls all uses of the value data member. Compile and load the script using *Script|Run File,* and then select *Script|Run* and enter set(). View the output in the Message window.

Listing 22.13. Set.cpp (Demonstrates setters).

```
//==============================================================
// Set.spp -- Demonstrates setters
// Copyright (c) 1996 by Tom Swan. All rights reserved.
//==============================================================

print "Set.spp";

import IDE;

class AClass {
// Declare read-only data member
  declare value;
// Implement getter for value
  on this:>value {
    if (!initialized(value))
      value = 10;
    return value;    // Or return pass(); if inherited
  }
// Implement setter for value
  on this:>value(n) {
    if (n < 10 || n > 100)
      IDE.Message("Error: value out of range");
    else
      value = n;
    // pass(n);  // Optional to call inherited function
    // Other statements may go here
  }
}

set()
{
  declare anObject = new AClass();
  print FormatString("value = %1", anObject.value);
  anObject.value = 123;
  print FormatString("value = %1", anObject.value);
}
```

A setter differs from a getter in only one way: setters have a single parameter, which represents the value to be assigned to the data member. For instance, the example's setter for the value data member is declared as

```
on this:>value(n) {
}
```

Because of this code, all assignments to value execute the setter function. Parameter n, which you can name anything you want, is the value to be assigned to the value variable. *It is up to the setter to make this assignment.*

The example script demonstrates the most common use for a setter—limiting assignments to a specific range. When you run the script, you see an error message due to the attempt to assign 123 to value.

To create a read-only data member that cannot be changed, create an empty setter for that member. The setter might display an error message to indicate an illegal assignment to an object.

It's possible with an empty getter to create a write-only data member that can be assigned a value, but that cannot be used in any other way. However, it's hard to imagine a practical use for a write-only object.

Debugging Scripts

You can't use the IDE's built-in Turbo Debugger to debug script. However, you can use the more-or-less equivalent *Script Breakpoint Tool* to track errors in your script files. To use this tool, enable the *Stop at Breakpoint* option using the *Environment|Options* command under the *Scripting* topic. (The option is enabled by default.)

Insert a `breakpoint` command as shown here anywhere in a script file where you want to pause execution:

```
breakpoint;
```

When the script reaches the `breakpoint` statement, it halts and displays the dialog box in Figure 22.5. The dialog tells you the line number where execution halted, and it provides several buttons you can use to continue running, to abort the script, to step over a function call (which is still executed normally, but at full speed), or to step into the function so you can single-step its statements. You can also enter a cScript statement into the dialog's input box, which is executed immediately. This is particularly handy for assigning values to variables during debugging sessions.

Figure 22.5.
Dialog box used when a breakpoint halt occurs.

You probably thought of this one, but I'll mention it anyway: Rather than delete breakpoint statements from scripts, it is far easier simply to disable the *Stop at Breakpoint* option.

Summary

- Object Scripting is a programming system that controls most of the Borland C++ IDE's commands and capabilities.

- A script is a file containing cScript statements that perform IDE functions. Script files end in .spp. The IDE compiles a script to a file ending in .spx, which contains P-Code, interpreted at runtime by the IDE's script engine.

- This chapter explains the Script menu's commands, and also suggests how to use some of Borland's example scripts. Install and remove the examples by selecting the *Script* menu's *Install/Uninstall examples* command.

- The cScript language is object oriented, and it closely resembles C++. However, because scripts are loaded at runtime (late-binding), cScript differs from C++ in several important ways. This chapter explains the differences.

- The term *closure* in cScript refers to techniques for tapping into class functions and enhancing what they do. You create closures in two ways: in a class declaration (the closure applies to all instances of the class), or for a specific class object (the closure affects only that object).

- Use the *Script Breakpoint Tool* to debug your own script files. Enable the *Scripting* option, *Stop at Breakpoint,* and insert one or more breakpoint; statements where you want to pause a running script.

23

Mixing Borland C++ 5 and Delphi 2

Some marriages are made in heaven, but past attempts to hitch together C++ and Pascal have received few if any blessings from above. But now, Borland's new 32-bit Delphi 2.0 with Object Pascal and Borland C++ 5 have finally hit it off, and all signs point to a long-term relationship between these two formerly incompatible languages.

You won't read about this in the *Times'* society columns, but by combining Delphi 2.0 with Borland C++ 5, you can write C++ applications that call functions in object-code files or dynamic link libraries (DLLs) written with Delphi. You can also write Delphi applications that call functions in object-code files and DLLs written in C++. The final results are totally seamless—users won't be able to tell which development system you used to create any particular portion of your software products.

Figure 23.1 shows the Delphi 2.0 and Borland C++ 5 IDEs, projects open in both systems, plus associated files. Peeking through Delphi's background is a Borland C++ project window and status line above the Windows 95 task bar. The completed application—a C++ project that calls a procedure in a Delphi-generated DLL—is running in the upper-right quadrant of this busy display (see the window titled "Calls Delphi DLL procedure" and the message dialog labeled "DelDll").

Figure 23.1.
Borland C++ 5, Delphi 2.0, and an application developed with both systems.

Merging C++ and Object Pascal is not just an academic exercise. There are some real benefits to be gained from combining Borland C++ and Delphi. For example:

- You can use Delphi's Rapid-Application-Development (RAD) environment to quickly prototype applications, which, as time allows, you can selectively convert to C++ so that you can make use of existing C++ libraries and algorithms.
- You can develop and test a stand-alone Delphi application and use the result as the specification for recoding in C++. Because the final project can incorporate portions of

the prototype, you don't have to rewrite the entire application from scratch as you do with some other types of prototype systems. *Users can run the fully working prototype while you develop the final C++ code!*

- You can optimize a Delphi application using C and C++ and even drop into assembly language for highly critical functions.

- You can develop libraries in C++ for Delphi developers. Or if you are a Delphi developer, you can construct components for use in C++ applications. *These are new markets for C++ and Object Pascal software.*

- You can develop user interfaces in Delphi (an area where Delphi's RAD environment really pays off) and code the nonvisual guts of your application in C++. This approach might be ideal for software that uses time-intensive calculations such as modeling, simulations, and other low-level code possibly best written in C++.

- You can develop database applications using a mixture of Delphi and C++. Encapsulations of the Borland Database Engine are nearly identical in both systems' class libraries.

NOTE

Compiling the sample applications in this chapter and on the book's CD-ROM requires Borland C++ 5 and Delphi 2.0 (Developer or Client/Server editions) installed in their default directories. The techniques described here also require Windows 95 or Windows NT 3.51 or later.

Using Delphi in C++ Applications

Follow the methods explained in this section to call functions in Delphi object-code modules or DLLs from a C++ application.

Linking Delphi .Obj Files to C++

The first job is to construct an object-code file using Delphi. The file, which you can link to a Borland C++ project, exports one or more procedures that the C++ application can call. Listing 23.1, DelObj.dpr (located in the Source\DelObj subdirectory on this book's CD-ROM), shows the basic layout of an object-code file written in Delphi's Object Pascal.

Listing 23.1. DelObj\DelObj.dpr (Delphi object-code file project).

```
//================================================================
// Delobj.dpr -- Delphi object-code file project
// Copyright (c) 1996 by Tom Swan. All rights reserved.
//================================================================

unit DelObj;
```

Listing 23.1. continued

```
interface

uses Windows;

// Declare procedure to be exported to C++
procedure DelObj_ShowMessage; cdecl;

implementation

// Implement the procedure to be called from C++
procedure DelObj_ShowMessage; cdecl;
begin
  MessageBeep(0);
  MessageBoxA(0, 'Delphi object-code procedure executed!',
    'DelObj', MB_OK or MB_TASKMODAL);
end;

end.
```

A Delphi object-code file is actually a compiled unit masquerading as a project source code file with the filename extension .dpr (for Delphi Project). Open the Delobj.dpr file using Delphi 2.0. Or if you want to create your own file, follow these steps using Delphi:

1. Close any open project and other windows.

2. Select *File\New Application.* This is necessary to create the project, although you will not construct a Delphi form.

3. Select *File\New* and choose *Unit* from the *New Items* dialog. This adds another page to Delphi's text editor window.

4. Close the text editor's *Unit1* page by selecting its tab and pressing Ctrl+F4 (or click the right mouse button and select *Close Page* from the floating popup menu).

5. Select *File\Save Project As* and save the project in a blank directory. Choose an appropriate name such as Delobj.dpr used for the sample application.

6. Select *Project\Options*, choose the Linker page tab, and under *Linker Output,* enable *Generate Object Files.*

NOTE

Delphi does not create its normal .dof project-options file for separate object-code modules using the methods described here. For this reason, you might have to repeat Step 6 after reopening the project file. If you experience troubles linking the object-code file in your C++ application, double-check with Delphi that you have selected the correct output code format and then recompile the module.

You have now created a bare-bones Delphi project that, when compiled, produces a standard object-code file ending with the extension .obj. This file is compatible with the format expected by most linkers, including, of course, Turbo Linker and the Borland C++ IDE.

The next step is to write the procedures to export from the object-code module. (Refer to the Delobj.dpr listing again.) Change the name of the unit to any appropriate name, usually the same as the compiled module. I used DelObj to indicate that this is an object-code file produced by Delphi.

Add the `Windows` unit to the `uses` directive, which makes Windows API functions available to Object Pascal statements. In the unit's interface section, declare one or more procedures to be called from the C++ application. For example, the sample listing declares `DelObj_ShowMessage` like this:

```
procedure DelObj_ShowMessage; cdecl;
```

I prefaced the procedure name with DelObj and an underscore to indicate in which module this procedure resides, but you can use any other naming convention. You must append the `cdecl` modifier as shown. This is necessary because C and C++ pass parameters from right to left, whereas Object Pascal normally passes them in the other direction. The modifier also disables fast-`this` register parameters, which Delphi uses by default but C++ does not.

Implement the exported procedure as shown in DelObj.dpr. Again, declare the procedure using the `cdecl` modifier. You may call any Windows API function as shown in the demonstration, which beeps the speaker and displays a message box.

> **NOTE**
>
> The sample listing calls `MessageBoxA`, the standard-ASCII message-dialog Windows API function. Under normal circumstances, you would simply call `MessageBox`, which the Delphi linker resolves to `MessageBoxA`, or for a wide-character string argument, to the similar `MessageBoxW`. Those two functions are the *real* Windows API entries—`MessageBox` is just a placeholder.
>
> In Delphi object-code files, you must perform these kinds of translations manually. You cannot call placeholder functions such as `MessageBox` because the C++ preprocessor resolves such calls to either `MessageBoxA` or `MessageBoxW`. The preprocessor never receives the Pascal source code, and to satisfy the C++ linker, you must translate the function calls manually.
>
> There are numerous such cases strewn throughout the Windows API library, and for this reason, combining Delphi object-code files with C++ applications is not the easiest method for mixing the two development systems. (The next section shows a superior approach.) However, if you need to use this technique, you can find the function names you need in the Windows.pas file, located in your Delphi installation path under Source\RTL\Win. It will take a lot of study to figure out which are the right functions to call!

After constructing and compiling the Delphi object-code file, the next job is to write a C++ application to call that file's exported procedures. Listing 23.2 shows how to do this in an OWL Windows application.

Listing 23.2. DelObj\Cppapp.cpp (Calls procedure in a Delphi .obj file).

```
//==============================================================
// Cppapp.cpp -- Calls procedure in a Delphi .obj file
// Copyright (c) 1996 by Tom Swan. All rights reserved.
//==============================================================

#include <owl\applicat.h>
#include <owl\framewin.h>
#pragma hdrstop
#include "cppapp.rh"

// Declare procedure in Delphi object-code file
extern "C" {
  void DelObj_ShowMessage(void);
}

// ============================================================
// The application's main window
// ============================================================

class TDemoWin: public TFrameWindow {
public:
  TDemoWin(TWindow* parent, const char far* title);
protected:
  void CmTest();
DECLARE_RESPONSE_TABLE(TDemoWin);
};

// Create response table declared for class
DEFINE_RESPONSE_TABLE1(TDemoWin, TFrameWindow)
  EV_COMMAND(CM_TEST, CmTest),
END_RESPONSE_TABLE;

// Constructor
TDemoWin::TDemoWin(TWindow* parent, const char far* title)
  : TFrameWindow(parent, title),
    TWindow(parent, title)
{
  AssignMenu(ID_MENU);
}

// Menu command function
void
TDemoWin::CmTest()
{
  DelObj_ShowMessage();  // Calls Delphi object-code procedure
}

// ============================================================
// The application class
// ============================================================
```

```
class TDemoApp: public TApplication {
public:
  TDemoApp(const char far* name)
    : TApplication(name) {};
  void InitMainWindow();
};

// Initialize the program's main window
void
TDemoApp::InitMainWindow()
{
  MainWindow = new TDemoWin(0, "Calls Delphi OBJ procedure");
}

#pragma argsused

// Main program
int
OwlMain(int argc, char* argv[])
{
  TDemoApp app("CppApp");
  return app.Run();
}
```

CppApp is a standard OWL application with a 32-bit GUI output target. Create the Borland C++ project as you normally do, and add the Delphi-generated object-code file as a new node in the C++ project window. (This implies that you must compile the Delphi code first—however, it is theoretically possible to further automate the process by using Make files that run command-line Delphi Dcc32.exe and C++ Bcc32.exe compilers. In that case, the compilation order of individual modules would not matter.)

In the C++ source file, declare the Delphi procedures you want to call. Disable C++ name mangling, which Delphi does not use and cannot duplicate, by encasing the declarations in an extern "C" directive like this:

```
extern "C" {
  void DelObj_ShowMessage(void);
}
```

You don't have to use the directive if your application is written in C. It is needed only for C++ programs, and it permits the C++ linker to find the unmangled Delphi procedure name. Call that function the same way you call C++ functions. For example, see the sample program's CmTest event handler, which executes the following statement:

```
DelObj_ShowMessage();
```

This calls the Delphi procedure when you select the demonstration's *Demo|Test* command. Figure 23.2 shows the resulting window and dialog.

Figure 23.2.

A C++ application that calls a procedure in a Delphi-generated object-code file.

Linking Delphi .Dll Files to C++

Linking a Delphi object-code file to a C++ application as demonstrated in the preceding sections produces the most seamless results—a single .exe code file that contains the entire program. However, because the Delphi source code is not preprocessed by C++, you might have trouble making calls to Windows API functions such as the sample program's use of MessageBox.

A better method that eliminates this kind of trouble exports Delphi procedures in a dynamic link library (DLL). This approach gives you two files to distribute—the Delphi-generated DLL and the finished C++ .exe code file—but the programming is much simpler. This is probably the best all-around method for mixing Delphi code into C++ applications.

Listing 23.3 shows the Delphi project file that creates a DLL for a C++ application to use. Although they perform similar tasks, the format of the DLL module differs significantly from a Delphi-generated object-code file.

Listing 23.3. Deldll\Deldll.dpr (Delphi DLL project).

```
//=============================================================
// Deldll.dpr -- Delphi DLL project
// Copyright (c) 1996 by Tom Swan. All rights reserved.
//=============================================================

library DelDll;

uses
  Windows;

// Implement procedure to be called from C++
procedure DelDll_ShowMessage; cdecl; far; export;
begin
  MessageBeep(0);
  MessageBox(0, 'Delphi DLL procedure executed!',
    'DelDll', MB_OK or MB_TASKMODAL);
end;

// Export procedure from DLL
exports
  DelDll_ShowMessage;

begin
end.
```

Like the object-code file, a DLL is a Delphi project, but you create it differently and a great deal more easily. To re-create the Deldll.dpr project listed here, follow these steps in Delphi:

1. Close any open project and windows.

2. Select *File|New* and choose *DLL* from the *New Items* dialog. This creates a bare library module, which you complete to export procedures to a C++ application.

3. Give the library a name (DelDll in the sample listing) and choose *File|Save Project As*. I named the file DelDll.dpr to identify the project as a Delphi-generated DLL, but any name will do.

Next, program the procedures you want to export to C++. Specify any units the DLL uses (at a minimum, you must list Windows as in the sample). Then, implement each procedure using a declaration such as

```
procedure DelDll_ShowMessage; cdecl; far; export;
```

For clarity, I prefaced the procedure name with the DLL's name and an underscore, but you are free to use any naming convention. The three modifiers after the procedure name specify right-to-left and no fast-this parameters (cdecl), designate a 32-bit address (far), and ensure proper exit and entry code for DLL public functions (export).

The procedure code is free to call any Windows functions. Because the compiled code is linked to a separate DLL code file, the problem with unresolved API function names does not occur as it does for object-code modules. The Delphi linker resolves such calls in the DLL.

Finally, the DLL requires an exports directive with a list of exported function names:

```
exports
  DelDll_ShowMessage;
```

You can also insert statements between the final begin and end keywords to execute startup initializations, or you can leave this section blank as in the demonstration.

Use Delphi's *Project|Build All* command to compile the DLL. You are then ready to write and compile the C++ application. Listing 23.4 shows a sample program that calls the procedure in the Delphi DLL.

Listing 23.4. Deldll\Cppapp.cpp (Calls procedure in a Delphi DLL).

```
//==============================================================
// Cppapp.cpp -- Calls procedure in a Delphi DLL
// Copyright (c) 1996 by Tom Swan. All rights reserved.
//==============================================================

#include <owl\applicat.h>
#include <owl\framewin.h>
#pragma hdrstop
#include "cppapp.rh"

// Declare procedure in Delphi DLL
extern "C" {
```

Listing 23.4. continued

```cpp
  void PASCAL DelDll_ShowMessage(void);
}

// ================================================================
// The application's main window
// ================================================================

class TDemoWin: public TFrameWindow {
public:
  TDemoWin(TWindow* parent, const char far* title);
protected:
  void CmTest();
DECLARE_RESPONSE_TABLE(TDemoWin);
};

// Create response table declared for class
DEFINE_RESPONSE_TABLE1(TDemoWin, TFrameWindow)
  EV_COMMAND(CM_TEST, CmTest),
END_RESPONSE_TABLE;

// Constructor
TDemoWin::TDemoWin(TWindow* parent, const char far* title)
  : TFrameWindow(parent, title),
    TWindow(parent, title)
{
  AssignMenu(ID_MENU);
}

// Menu command function
void
TDemoWin::CmTest()
{
  DelDll_ShowMessage();   // Calls Delphi DLL procedure
}

// ================================================================
// The application class
// ================================================================

class TDemoApp: public TApplication {
public:
  TDemoApp(const char far* name)
    : TApplication(name) {};
  void InitMainWindow();
};

// Initialize the program's main window
void
TDemoApp::InitMainWindow()
{
  MainWindow = new TDemoWin(0, "Calls Delphi DLL procedure");
}

#pragma argsused
```

```
// Main program
int
OwlMain(int argc, char* argv[])
{
  TDemoApp app("CppApp");
  return app.Run();
}
```

Create the C++ application's project as you do any other Windows project. I used OWL for the example, but you can use another class library such as MFC or you can write a "pure" non-object-oriented Windows program. The techniques for accessing a procedure in a Delphi-generated DLL remain the same.

> **TIP**
>
> After you create the C++ project, add the Delphi DLL as a new node in the project window. Select the DLL, and click the right mouse button to open a floating popup menu. Choose the *Edit Node Attributes* command, and set *Translator* to *CreateImportLibrary*. These steps cause the application to automatically load the DLL as needed at runtime—you don't need to write code to do that. However, if you prefer to load the DLL using other methods, you may do so. As long as you follow the declaration conventions detailed in this chapter, you can use a Delphi DLL just as you do any other.

The C++ source code in file Deldll\Cppapp.cpp is nearly the same as the one earlier in this chapter that called a procedure in a Delphi object-code file. However, there are a couple of important differences. First, you must declare the imported functions (the ones in the DLL that the C++ application calls) using the PASCAL modifier as shown here:

```
extern "C" {
  void PASCAL DelDll_ShowMessage(void);
}
```

The extern directive, which is required only in C++ but not C programs, disables mangled function names, which Delphi does not generate. The PASCAL directive is needed because Delphi does not preface public symbols with a leading underscore, as does Borland C++.

Call the Delphi procedure as you do any other C or C++ function. For example, this statement in function CmTest calls the DelDll_ShowMessage function in the Delphi DLL:

```
DelDll_ShowMessage();
```

The result is the message dialog box shown in Figure 23.3.

23

Figure 23.3.
*A C++ application that calls a
procedure in a Delphi-
generated DLL.*

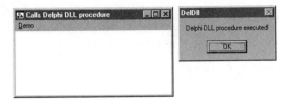

Using C++ in Delphi Applications

Follow the methods explained in this section to call functions in C++ object-code or DLL files
from Delphi applications.

Linking C++ .Obj Files to Delphi

Most readers of this book will want to use the techniques in the preceding sections for importing Delphi object-code and DLL modules into C++ applications. But you can also do the reverse—importing C++ object-code and DLL functions into Delphi applications. The following notes and sample listings show how.

The first step is to create a C++ object-code module that you can bind into a Delphi application. Listing 23.5, Cppobj.cpp, shows the necessary C++ source code.

Listing 23.5. Cppobj\Cppobj.cpp (C++ object-code file project).

```
//===============================================================
// Cppobj.cpp -- C++ object-code file project
// Copyright (c) 1996 by Tom Swan. All rights reserved.
//===============================================================

#include <windows.h>

// Declare function to be exported to Delphi
extern "C" {
  void PASCAL CppObj_ShowMessage(void);
}

// Implement function to be called from Delphi
void PASCAL CppObj_ShowMessage(void)
{
  MessageBeep(0);
  MessageBox(NULL,  "C++ object-code function executed!",
    "CppObj", MB_OK | MB_TASKMODAL);
  return;
}
```

Because the Borland C++ IDE has no object-code project target, you have to use a small trick
to compile the module and create a binary .obj code file. Create a new project using the Borland
C++ IDE, and in the *TargetExpert* dialog, set *Target Type* to *Static Library (for .exe)*. Also make
sure the *Platform* is set to *Win32* and the *Target Model* to *GUI*.

These steps create a target .lib file, which I named Cppobj.lib in the demonstration. Although this library file is never used, it permits the IDE project manager to compile the separate object-code module.

> **TIP**
>
> You don't have to create a dummy library file if you compile the module with the Borland C++ command-line compiler, Bcc32.exe, using the -c (compile only) option.

Use the same syntax in the C++ source code as you do to import a Delphi DLL procedure. For example, the Cppobj.cpp file declares its exported function as

```
extern "C" {
  void PASCAL CppObj_ShowMessage(void);
}
```

As already explained, this declaration disables name mangling, but you don't need to use it if you are writing the module in C. The PASCAL modifier deletes the underscore that C and C++ normally append to public function names. As a convention, I prefaced the function name with its module name and an underscore (CppObj_), but you are free to use a different name if you like.

Implement the C or C++ function as you normally do. In this example, the program calls the Windows API MessageBeep and MessageBox functions to beep the speaker and display a message dialog.

Next, create the Delphi application for linking to the C++ object-code file. Listing 23.6, CppObj\Mainform.pas, shows a sample application that displays a large button. Push it to call the C++ function and display a message.

Listing 23.6. CppObj\Mainform.pas (Calls function in a C++ .obj file).

```
//=============================================================
// MainForm.pas -- Calls function in a C++ .obj file
// Copyright (c) 1996 by Tom Swan. All rights reserved.
//=============================================================

unit MainForm;

interface

uses
  Windows, Messages, SysUtils, Classes, Graphics, Controls,
  Forms, Dialogs, StdCtrls;

type
  TForm1 = class(TForm)
    Button1: TButton;
    procedure Button1Click(Sender: TObject);
  private
```

continues   777

Listing 23.6. continued

```
  { Private declarations }
public
  { Public declarations }
end;

var
  Form1: TForm1;

implementation

{$R *.DFM}

// Load C++ object-code file
{$L CppObj.obj}

// Declare function imported from C++ object-code file
procedure CppObj_ShowMessage; cdecl; far; external;

// Respond to button click
procedure TForm1.Button1Click(Sender: TObject);
begin
  CppObj_ShowMessage;  // Call C++ object-code function
end;

end.
```

Delphi generated most of the application in the sample listing. To write the program, I se-lected *File\New Application.* I saved the unit as Mainform.pas (my usual name for the main unit in a Delphi application) and saved the project as Dellapp.dpr.

> **NOTE**
>
> To compile the Delphi application, you must open the Dellapp.dpr project file. If you open only the Pascal source code file, Mainform.pas, you will not be able to compile and run the full application.

I next inserted a TButton component into the application's form window, and I created a handler for this object's OnClick event. The code for that handler simply calls the function exported by the C++ object-code module:

```
CppObj_ShowMessage;
```

So that the Delphi linker can resolve this call to the C++ function, you must declare it as shown in the listing. You also must load the object-code file during compilation of the Pascal source code. Insert this directive into the form's unit (Mainform.pas in this case) just after the resource-loading directive. For reference, both directives are shown here—Delphi inserts the first one; you type the second:

```
{$R *.DFM}       // Delphi inserts this directive
{$L CppObj.obj}  // You must insert this one
```

The L directive loads an object-code module into a Delphi application, and it also converts that module's information into a form that the Delphi linker can digest. But this step is not enough to import the functions into the application unit. You also have to declare each function using statements such as the following:

```
procedure CppObj_ShowMessage; cdecl; far; external;
```

Insert this and similar statements after the L directive that loads the object-code module containing the external functions. The three directives specify right-to-left parameter passing and no fast-this pointer (cdecl), a 32-bit address (far), and the fact that this procedure is found outside of this and any other units the module uses (external).

With all of these elements in place, the Delphi application can call functions in an external C++ object-code module. Figure 23.4 shows the resulting Delphi form with a large button that when clicked, displays the message dialog programmed in C++.

Figure 23.4.
*A Delphi application that calls
a function in a C++ object-
code module.*

> **NOTE**
>
> Although the preceding techniques work well enough, you might run into difficulties with all but the simplest of C++ object-code modules. For example, the C++ code cannot call any runtime library functions. Except for calls to the Windows API, *your C++ module must provide all needed code!* Even a simple call to a string function will not work because the C++ and Object Pascal runtime libraries are incompatible. Problems involving startup and shutdown sequences could also arise, although because the C++ module is not a program (it doesn't have a main function), this problem is easily avoided (don't call exit, for example). Nevertheless, linking object-code modules into Delphi applications is inferior to the next and final demonstration, which shows how a Delphi application can call functions in C++ DLLs.

Linking C++ .Dll Files to Delphi

The final sample application in this chapter demonstrates how a Delphi application can call a function in a DLL written using Borland C++. This is probably the best all-around method for mixing C++ code into Delphi applications. Because the C++ DLL is fully linked before Delphi uses it, the DLL's functions may call runtime library code and use class libraries such as OWL 5 and standard templates.

The first step in the process is to construct the C++ DLL project. Listing 23.7, Cppdll.cpp, outlines the basic necessities for exporting a DLL function for use in a Delphi application.

Listing 23.7. Cppdll\Cppdll.cpp (C++ DLL project).

```
//================================================================
// Cppdll.cpp -- C++ DLL project
// Copyright (c) 1996 by Tom Swan. All rights reserved.
//================================================================

#include <windows.h>

// Declare function to be exported to Delphi
extern "C" {
  void WINAPI _export CppDll_ShowMessage(void);
}

// Implement function to be called from Delphi
void WINAPI _export CppDll_ShowMessage(void)
{
  MessageBeep(0);
  MessageBox(NULL,  "C++ DLL function executed!",
    "CppDll", MB_OK | MB_TASKMODAL);
  return;
}
```

To create the DLL project using the Borland C++ IDE, select the *File\New* and *Project* commands. Change to your working directory and specify a project name (Cppdll.ide in this case). Next, in the *TargetExpert* dialog, set *Target Type* to *Dynamic Library [.dll]*. Also make sure that *Platform* is set to *Win32* and *Target Model* to *GUI*.

The resulting project will specify .def and .rc nodes along with a .cpp file. You may delete the .def and .rc nodes from the project, although the DLL may use linker-definition commands and resources if necessary for your application.

At a minimum, the C++ DLL source code module (Cppdll.cpp here) should include the Windows.h header file for calling API functions. Declare functions to be exported to Delphi using the syntax shown here:

```
extern "C" {
  void WINAPI _export CppDll_ShowMessage(void);
}
```

As usual, the extern directive disables C++ name mangling, but you don't have to use it if your module is written in C. After any return type (void in the example), insert two modifiers, WINAPI and _export, before the function name.

WINAPI does not identify a Windows API function as the macro's name suggests—it merely deletes the leading underscore that C and C++ normally attach to public function names. Delphi's linker does not recognize this convention. The _export directive ensures that the function is compiled using the proper entry and exit code needed for code exported from a DLL.

Implement the function as shown in the listing. The function's declaration header must use the identical syntax as in the extern "C" directive. The function may call Windows API functions and perform any other tasks. For the demonstration, as in the other sample programs in this chapter, the program calls the Windows MessageBeep and MessageBox API functions.

Compile the project as you normally do, and verify that the directory contains the resulting DLL file (named Cppdll.dll in this case). Next, switch over to Delphi and write your application. Listing 23.8, Cppdll\Mainform.pas, demonstrates the basic methods for calling functions in a C++ DLL.

Listing 23.8. Cppdll\Mainform.pas (Calls function in a C++ DLL).

```
//=============================================================
// MainForm.pas -- Calls function in a C++ DLL
// Copyright (c) 1996 by Tom Swan. All rights reserved.
//=============================================================

unit MainForm;

interface

uses
  Windows, Messages, SysUtils, Classes, Graphics, Controls,
  Forms, Dialogs, StdCtrls;

type
  TForm1 = class(TForm)
    Button1: TButton;
    procedure Button1Click(Sender: TObject);
  private
    { Private declarations }
  public
    { Public declarations }
  end;

var
  Form1: TForm1;

implementation

{$R *.DFM}

// Declare function in C++ DLL
procedure CppDll_ShowMessage; cdecl; far; external 'CppDll';

// Respond to button click
procedure TForm1.Button1Click(Sender: TObject);
begin
  CppDll_ShowMessage;  // Call C++ DLL function
end;

end.
```

Create the Delphi application as you normally do using *File\New Application*. Save the project's form unit as Mainform.pas (or another name), and save the application's project file using a different name (I used Delapp.dpr in the Cppdll directory). Insert the components you need, such as the example's button.

To call an external DLL function, declare it in the form unit's implementation as shown here:

```
procedure CppDll_ShowMessage; cdecl; far; external 'CppDll';
```

This declares the function name, and specifies right-to-left and no fast-this parameters (cdecl), a 32-bit address (far), and the fact that the function is not implemented in this or any other units used by the module. After the external keyword, specify the DLL's filename as a single-quoted string. You do not have to include the .dll filename extension.

The Delphi application can call the DLL's functions as it does any other Pascal procedures. For example, the sample button OnClick event handler executes the following statement to call the function in the C++ DLL:

```
CppDll_ShowMessage;
```

Figure 23.5 shows the Delphi application and the C++ message dialog displayed when you click the form's button.

Figure 23.5.
A Delphi application that calls a function in a C++ DLL.

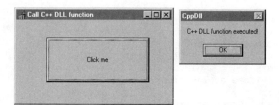

Summary

- Delphi 2.0 and Borland C++ 5 finally make it possible to use a mixture of Object Pascal and C++ in Windows programming.
- Using the techniques described in this chapter, you can write C++ applications that import object-code modules and DLLs written in Delphi. You can also write Delphi applications that link to C++ object-code modules and DLLs developed with Borland C++.
- In most cases, regardless of whether you are developing a C++ or a Delphi application, separate modules containing external functions are best constructed as DLLs. If you must create object-code (.obj) modules, be aware of potential problems summarized in the next two paragraphs.

- Delphi object-code modules are not translated by the C++ preprocessor, and therefore you must resolve any Windows API calls that would normally be transformed invisibly. For example, the Windows `MessageBox` function actually resolves to either `MessageBoxA` or `MessageBoxW`, depending on whether the program passes ASCII or wide-character arguments. Because a Delphi object-code module bypasses the C++ preprocessor, which normally performs such translations, you must do the preprocessor's job manually.

- C++ object-code modules are not fully linked, and therefore, they cannot call functions in the C++ runtime library (RTL). Delphi's RTL is incompatible with the C++ RTL, and Delphi's linker is unable to resolve calls to C++ library functions. However, the C++ object-code module may call Windows API functions because these calls are resolved identically in Delphi and in Borland C++. Another potential, though easily avoided, problem for external C++ object-code modules involves startup and shutdown sequences (if, for example, the module calls `exit`). Such code will cause severe bugs because the C++ startup code is not linked to the separate object-code file.

24

CHAPTER

Compiling MFC Applications

Borland C++ 5 can now compile Windows applications written with the Microsoft Foundation Class (MFC) library. Similar conceptually to Borland's OWL, MFC classes encapsulate most of the Windows API, and many applications have been written using MFC.

This chapter explains how to patch your MFC source code files and recompile the library for use with Borland C++ 5. After applying the patches and recompiling, you can compile existing MFC applications or create new ones using the Borland C++ IDE. You can still use OWL, but you cannot mix OWL and MFC code—you must choose one application framework or the other.

Borland C++ supports MFC versions 3.2 or 4.0. Because I have version 4.0 installed on my system, I have tested the information in this chapter only with this newer MFC release. However, the sample listing is compatible with both versions.

> **NOTE**
>
> To compile MFC applications using Borland C++ 5, you must purchase and install Visual C++. Borland C++ does not include the MFC library files. This chapter assumes you have installed Visual C++ to the default directory, C:\Msdev.

Overview of the MFC Library

The MFC classes are loosely organized into six categories. These categories are

- *Base class*—Most MFC classes derive from one primary base class, `CObject`. Because of this arrangement, most MFC classes are related in some way to one another.
- *Application framework*—The `CWinApp` class encapsulates the activities and requirements of a Windows application. All MFC applications have one, and only one, object of a class derived from `CWinApp`.
- *Visuals*—Numerous MFC classes encapsulate visual objects such as windows, dialog boxes, menus, controls, and other visual elements of a typical Windows application.
- *OLE*—MFC classes provide full support for object linking and embedding and also OCX controls (MFC 4.0 only).
- *Database*—MFC supports ODBC (Open Database Connectivity) programming as well as DAO database support.
- *Miscellaneous*—In addition to its Windows encapsulations, MFC provides a number of miscellaneous classes such as `CString`, `CFile`, and various containers. Many of these classes are not derived from `CObject`.

As in OWL, class member functions handle Windows messages. For this purpose, MFC provides the `CCmdTarget` class. Only classes derived from `CCmdTarget` can receive and respond to Windows messages.

Table 24.1 lists the major classes in the MFC 4.0 hierarchy. Use this table as a starting place for browsing other MFC classes. For example, `CCommonDialog` is the base class for Windows 95 common dialog classes such as `CColorDialog` and `CFileDialog`. You can find documentation on these classes by using the Borland C++ IDE browser and the Visual C++ on-line help files. Another excellent source of MFC information is the Microsoft Developer Network CD-ROM.

Table 24.1. Key MFC classes.

Category	Key MFC Classes
Library Base Class	CObject
Derived from `CObject`:	
Application Architecture	CCmdTarget, CWinApp, CWnd
Arrays	CArray
Control Bars	CControlBar, CSplitterWnd
Control Support	CImageList
Controls	CButton, CEdit, CListBox, etc.
DAO Database Support	CDaoDatabase, CDaoRecordset
Dialog Boxes	CDialog
Exceptions	CException
File Services	CFile
Frame Windows	CFrameWnd
Graphical Drawing	CDC
Graphical Drawing Objects	CGdiObject
Lists	CList
Maps	CMap
Menus	CMenu
ODBC Database Support	CDatabase, CRecordset
Property Sheets	CPropertySheet
Synchronization	CSyncObject
Views	CView
Windows Sockets	CAsyncSocket
Not derived from `CObject`:	
OLE Automation Types	COleCurrency, COleDateTime
OLE Type Wrappers	CFontHolder, CPictureHolder
Runtime Object Model Support	CArchive, CDumpContext, CRuntimeClass

continues

787

Table 24.1. continued

Category	Key MFC Classes
Simple Value Types	CPoint, CRect, CSize, CString, CTime
Structures	CCommandLineInfo
Support Classes	CCmdUI, CWaitCursor, etc.
Synchronization	CMultiLock, CSingleLock
Typed Template Collections	CTypedPtrArray

In addition to its numerous classes, MFC provides a set of global functions that you can call. All of these functions are prefaced with Afx. For example, AfxMessageBox displays a Windows message-box dialog. Apparently, Afx is not an acronym—Af stands for application framework, but the x in these names has no documented meaning.

The MFC library is written using a loose standard of C++, which Borland supports by relaxing many of its normal safeguards. This means you could receive numerous warnings of faulty and nonstandard constructions during compilation of MFC applications. MFC also does not recognize new ANSI C++ features such as the bool data type. Instead, MFC code uses the older BOOL, TRUE, and FALSE macros.

You may call Windows API functions directly from an MFC application. However, because most such functions are encapsulated into class members, to call a Windows API function, preface it with the C++ scope resolution operator. For example, call the API ShowWindow function like this:

```
::ShowWindow(hwnd);   // Calls Windows API ShowWindow
```

Without the leading scope resolution operator, this statement would call the ShowWindow member function.

Preparing the MFC Library

The binary MFC library files supplied with Visual C++ are incompatible with Borland C++ 5. In addition, the MFC source code files contain numerous constructions that Borland C++ does not recognize. For these reasons, you must perform three steps before you can compile MFC applications using Borland C++:

1. Patch the MFC library source code files.
2. Rebuild the MFC library.
3. Copy the modified binary library files to appropriate directories.

After completing these three steps, you can compile existing and new MFC applications using Borland C++ 5. The following notes outline the basic steps, but read the Readme.txt file supplied with the patches for more information—to modify the library sources by hand, for example, if you have already modified them for other purposes.

> **NOTE**
>
> I have tested these steps only with an unmodified copy of MFC 4.0 supplied with Visual C++ 4.0. The patches may not work with other file versions or those supplied with other development systems.

Patching the MFC Library

Applying the patches is the easy part of using MFC with Borland C++ 5. Just run Borland's Setup40.exe utility, which displays a dialog box asking for your Borland C++ and Visual C++ installation directories (see Figure 24.1). Provide these path names and click the Install button to run the patcher.

Figure 24.1.
Borland's MFC patcher.

> **WARNING**
>
> Before patching the MFC source files, you must verify that your MFC version exactly matches the Borland patch utility. Examine the file Afxver_.h in the Msdev\mfc\include directory. For the version 4.0 patches, the 17th line in that file should read as follows:
>
> ```
> #define _MFC_VER 0x0400 // Microsoft Foundation Classes version 4.00
> ```

Do not proceed with patching unless your MFC version exactly matches the Borland patching utility version number!

Patching the MFC library takes only a minute or so. The Setup40.exe utility modifies selected MFC files and also creates a new subdirectory in the path Msdev\mfc\lib\Borland. All new binary files are written to this directory—existing MFC .lib files are undisturbed, and patching MFC does not affect the library's use with Visual C++.

If you have modified your MFC source code files, the automated patch utility may not work correctly. In this case, you might have to apply the patches manually. Notes in Borland's Readme.txt file explain how to do that, but it's probably better just to reinstall the library for the purposes of applying the patches.

All modifications made to MFC source code files are selected by the conditional statement

```
ifdef __BORLANDC__
```

Rebuilding the MFC Library

After patching the MFC source code files, you must rebuild the entire library. You must use Borland's command line Bcc32.exe compiler for this job along with Make files created during the patching process. You can build static, dynamic, and debugging library versions. *Rebuilding will take at least one or two hours and possibly longer depending on your computer's speed and the versions you decide to build.* Fortunately, you can rebuild the libraries in the background while you do other jobs. On my system, I built the non-debugging MFC libraries in about one hour while I ran other programs in the foreground.

Some of the following commands are optional. I've noted the ones that you must perform at a minimum to create a working set of files for use with Borland C++ 5. To conserve space and time, you can build only the non-debugging library files. (You can always build the other files later if you need them.)

To begin rebuilding, from a DOS prompt change the current directory to Msdev\mfc\src. Then, to build the static, non-debugging binary files, enter the command (*this is required*)

```
make -fborland.mak  DEBUG=0
```

You may also build a version with debugging information. This will occupy an additional 50MB of disk space, so don't take this step unless you are sure you will need to trace the library's code. To build the static debugging version, enter the command (the DEBUG macro defaults to 1—you don't have to define it)

```
make -fborland.mak
```

That creates a different file from the preceding command—it doesn't replace the existing non-debugging library. To create a dynamic DLL-based, non-debugging MFC library, enter the command (*this is required*)

```
make -fbfcdll.mak DEBUG=0 LIBNAME=BFC40
```

This creates Bfc40.dll, which contains the dynamic MFC binaries. If you set DEBUG to 1 (or don't assign it any value), the compiler creates additional DLL files with debugging information included. You may optionally construct debugging versions of all other libraries and DLLs by entering the following four commands:

```
make -fbfcdll.mak
make -fbfcole.mak
make -fbfcdb.mak
make -fbfcnet.mak
```

> **NOTE**
>
> Refer to the Borland.mak file copied to the Msdev\mfc\src path during patching. This file's header lists other options you can use to build various versions of the MFC library. For example, you can specify a temporary path for .obj files (to conserve disk space), and you can elect to include browsing information (set BROWSE=1). You can also pass compiler options to Bcc32.exe (set OPT=/x), which might be useful to construct Pentium instruction set binaries or to select various compiler optimizations.

Copying the Modified Files

After patching and rebuilding the MFC library, you must copy the new binary files to appropriate directories. All files are supposed to be written to the Msdev\mfc\lib\borland directory, but when I tried the foregoing commands, a possible bug in the Make files created the DLLs in the path Msdev\mfc\src. Perhaps this bug will be repaired in your patch utility, so check both directories to be sure. Perform these two steps to copy the library files:

1. Copy all library files in the borland directory—those ending with the filename extension .lib—to your Borland C++ 5 lib path, usually C:\Bc5\lib.

2. Copy all .dll files (these might be in the borland or src subdirectories) to C:\Windows\system.

> **NOTE**
>
> You don't have to copy *all* MFC .lib and .dll files—copy only the files you created with Borland's Make files.

24

Creating MFC Projects

If you have been following along, you are now ready to write and compile MFC projects using Borland C++ 5. To be sure you have performed the preceding steps correctly, try to compile an existing application such as one supplied with Visual C++. Next, try the sample application listed at the end of this chapter. The following sections explain both processes.

> **TIP**
>
> You should have a samples directory in your Msdev and Mfc directories—if not, copy the samples from your Visual C++ CD-ROM. If you do this, however, all files will have their read-only attribute bit enabled. Because the Borland C++ IDE will not overwrite a read-only code file, you must disable this setting before compiling the projects. Go to a DOS prompt and change to the Msdev directory, and then enter this command:
>
> `attrib -A *.* /S`

Existing MFC Applications

To compile an existing MFC application, you need to create a Borland .ide project file. For example, perform the following steps to compile the Hello application. On my system, it's in the path \Msdev\samples\mfc\general\hello:

1. Using the Borland C++ 5 IDE, close all open windows, and select the *File\New* command. Choose *Project* from the submenu, and select the *Browse* button. Change to the directory that contains the MFC application files, and enter a project name under *File Name*. For this example, enter `hello` and press Enter to create a project file named Hello.ide.

2. In the *New Target* dialog, disable the *OWL* check box under *Frameworks* and select *MFC*. Also choose the 3.2 or 4.0 radio button to match your MFC version, and select *Dynamic* or *Static* libraries. Select the OK button to close the *New Target* dialog.

3. Delete the .def (linker definition) file from the project. Don't do this, however, if the MFC application has a .def file.

4. Highlight the project target file (Hello.exe if you are following along), and select *Options\Project*. Select the *Directories* topic, and add the path for MFC's include files to the *Source Directories Include* edit window. The final string might look something like this (be sure not to introduce any stray spaces in the string):

   `c:\bc5\include;c:\msdev\mfc\include`

5. You do not have to specify a new path to .lib files, although you could do that if you prefer not to copy MFC's library files to your Borland lib path.

6. Select *Project\Make All* or *Project\Build All* to compile and link the MFC application.

You can run the resulting .exe code file from inside the IDE or open it using the Windows 95 Explorer.

New MFC Applications

If you are able to compile an existing MFC application, you can now use the IDE to create new MFC programs from scratch. Follow these general steps:

1. Close any open windows, and select *File\New*. Choose *Project* from the submenu.

2. Select the *Browse* button and change to the directory where you want to store your application's files.

3. Enter a project name in the *File Name* field. The project manager automatically appends .ide to this name—you do not have to enter a filename extension.

4. In the *New Target* dialog box, set *Target Type* to *Application* (.exe), *Platform* to *Win32*, and *Target Model* to *GUI*.

5. Still in *New Target,* disable the *OWL* check box under *Frameworks* and select *MFC*. Also choose the 3.2 or 4.0 radio button to match your MFC version, and select *Dynamic* or *Static* libraries. You may also elect to include other libraries and options at this time. Select the *OK* button to close the *New Target* dialog.

You now see the IDE's project window with the basic elements of an MFC application (these are the same files as created for OWL projects). You can delete the .def linker definition file, unless you plan to write one.

Open the .cpp node to begin writing your application's source code. Open the .rc node to create your program's resources. Compile and link the MFC program as you do other projects using the *Project\Make All* or *Project\Build All* commands.

MFC Programming Fundamentals

Listing 24.1, Mfcdemo.h, and Listing 24.2, Mfcdemo.cpp, show the fundamental programming required to create an MFC application. To compile and run the program, open the Mfcdemo.ide project file on this book's CD-ROM. Select *Project\Options,* choose the *Directories* topic, and modify the include file path to match your MFC installation. Before you can compile this project, you must have patched and compiled the MFC library as explained in this chapter.

Listing 24.1. Mfcdemo.h (Declares classes for Mfcdemo.cpp).

```
//===============================================================
// Mfcdemo.h -- Declares classes for Mfcdemo.cpp
// Copyright (c) 1996 by Tom Swan. All rights reserved.
//===============================================================

class CDemoApp: public CWinApp {
```

continues

793

Listing 24.1. continued

```
public:
  BOOL InitInstance();
};

class CDemoWnd: public CFrameWnd {
public:
  CDemoWnd();
protected:
  afx_msg void OnPaint();
DECLARE_MESSAGE_MAP()
};
```

Listing 24.2. Mfcdemo.cpp (Implements an MFC application).

```
//================================================================
// Mfcdemo.cpp -- Implements an MFC applicaton
// Copyright (c) 1996 by Tom Swan. All rights reserved.
//================================================================

#include <afxwin.h>
#include "Mfcdemo.h"

// Constructing the demoApp object runs the application
CDemoApp demoApp;

//================================================================
// CDemoApp class member functions
//================================================================

// Create application window
BOOL
CDemoApp::InitInstance()
{
  m_pMainWnd = new CDemoWnd();
  m_pMainWnd->ShowWindow(m_nCmdShow);
  m_pMainWnd->UpdateWindow();
  return TRUE;
}

// Associate Windows message handlers
BEGIN_MESSAGE_MAP(CDemoWnd, CFrameWnd)
  ON_WM_PAINT()
END_MESSAGE_MAP()

//================================================================
// CDemoWnd class member functions
//================================================================

// Constructor
CDemoWnd::CDemoWnd()
{
  Create(NULL, "MFC Demo Application");
}
```

```
// WM_PAINT message handler
void
CDemoWnd::OnPaint()
{
  CRect rect;
  CPaintDC dc(this);

  GetClientRect(rect);
  dc.DrawText("MFC Demo for Borland C++ 5",
    -1, rect, DT_SINGLELINE | DT_CENTER | DT_VCENTER);
}
```

At a minimum, an MFC application requires two derived classes—one to represent the application and another to represent the program's main window. Derive the application class from the MFC class CWinApp, and override its InitInstance member:

```
class CDemoApp: public CWinApp {
public:
  BOOL InitInstance();
};
```

Also derive a class for your program's window, usually from the MFC class CFrameWnd. For example, the demonstration program declares a CDemoWnd class like this:

```
class CDemoWnd: public CFrameWnd {
public:
  CDemoWnd();
protected:
  afx_msg void OnPaint();
DECLARE_MESSAGE_MAP()
};
```

The derived window class must have a constructor, and it should declare any needed Windows message handlers. In this case, the program declares one method to handle WM_PAINT messages for updating the window's contents. The DECLARE_MESSAGE_MAP macro indicates that this class uses an internal table to associate Windows messages and class member functions.

Both of the preceding class declarations are in the Mfcdemo.h header file. You might also declare them directly in the .cpp module, but using a header file is best to keep order among a large application's numerous declarations and implementation files.

The implementation module in this case, Mfcdemo.cpp, implements the MFC application and its window class. Only one MFC header file is required in this simple demonstration, afxwin.h, but a more complex program might include others. Also included is the Mfcdemo.h header that declares this program's two derived classes.

Constructing an object of a class derived from CWinApp initializes and runs the program. You do not have to write the equivalent of a main or WinMain function. (This is not really an advantage; it's just the way MFC works.) This statement, then, initializes and runs the program:

```
CDemoApp demoApp;
```

The CDemoApp class must provide an InitInstance function, which by default simply returns FALSE. This means an MFC application will not have a main window unless your program creates one. Do that by executing the following three statements:

```
m_pMainWnd = new CDemoWnd();
m_pMainWnd->ShowWindow(m_nCmdShow);
m_pMainWnd->UpdateWindow();
```

The first statement constructs the window object using the CDemoWnd class derived from the MFC CFrameWnd class. Call this object's ShowWindow member function to display the window; call its UpdateWindow function to update the window's contents. Notice that these member functions are named the same as Windows API functions. (Reminder: To call the API functions, preface them with a scope resolution operator, ::.)

Return TRUE from your InitInstance function to indicate a successful window creation.

Also declare any message event handlers used by your application class. In this case, CDemoWnd responds to a WM_PAINT message. Construct the association with the OnPaint member function by declaring the event table like this:

```
BEGIN_MESSAGE_MAP(CDemoWnd, CFrameWnd)
  ON_WM_PAINT()
END_MESSAGE_MAP()
```

This is similar to the way you associate Windows messages and member functions in OWL. When the program receives a WM_PAINT message, it calls the OnPaint event handler.

The CDemoWnd class, which represents the program's main window, must have a constructor to initialize objects of the class. The constructor should call the class's Create method as shown, which initializes the object, creates the underlying Windows window element, and provides a window title.

The demonstration program also implements an event handler for a WM_PAINT message. Function OnPaint creates two variables:

```
CRect rect;
CPaintDC dc(this);
```

The CRect class corresponds to the Windows RECT structure (and OWL's TRect class). CPaintDC is similar to OWL's TPaintDC class—it represents a device context for the window display. Calling the DrawText member function in reference to the device context object paints a string of text in the window.

Though complete, the demonstration program listed here barely begins to show the many features in the MFC library. For more information on writing MFC applications, consult the bibliography. Figure 24.2 shows the finished application's window.

Figure 24.2.
Mfcdemo's window.

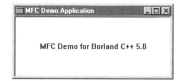

> **NOTE**
>
> Although MFC is a capable class library, I much prefer OWL for new Windows applications. There are many applications written using MFC, and it's good to be able to compile them using Borland C++. But for my new projects, I'll stick to OWL, which offers a superior class design and, more importantly, is fully compatible with the ANSI C++ standard.

Summary

- Borland C++ 5 can now compile Windows applications written with the Microsoft Foundation Class (MFC) library.

- This chapter gives overviews of the MFC classes and lists a sample application you can compile using Borland C++ 5's IDE.

- To prepare MFC for use with Borland C++ 5, you must purchase and install a version of Visual C++ (preferably version 4.0). Borland C++ 5 does not provide the MFC library files.

- After installing Visual C++, you must patch and recompile the MFC library using a Borland utility. Be sure that the utility and MFC version numbers match and then follow the steps outlined in this chapter or in the patch's Readme.txt file.

25

CHAPTER

Jumping Into Java

When I first heard of Java, my reaction was, "Oh, no, not another programming language!" But as I learned more about Java, I knew I could not ignore the impact that this language is sure to have on multiple-platform programming, particularly for interactive information distributed over the Internet. Whether you're a hang-ten network surfer, or just getting your feet wet with this newest facet of the personal computer revolution, you will undoubtedly conclude—as many already have—that Java holds the key to the future of programming over the World Wide Web.

Borland C++ 5 provides you with two Java systems: command-line tools that run from a DOS prompt, and a built-in Java compiler that runs from the IDE. Also provided are Java source code files, library classes, and several demonstration programs. Using these devices, you can write Java programs from scratch, or you can use the IDE's Java AppExpert generator to construct a shell for a Java applet, ready to fill in with your own code.

You must install Java separately from Borland C++ 5. If you haven't done that, before continuing with this chapter, run Setup on the Borland CD-ROM to install Java and its related files. I installed my copy of Java into the directory C:\Bc5\Java, but you can use a different path name if you prefer.

In this chapter, I explain how and why Java came into being, and I suggest some of the ways you might use Java to write multiple-platform software for Internet distribution. I also introduce the fundamentals of programming with Java, and I explain how the language differs from C++. Finally, I show how to write and run a Java class and applet.

> **NOTE**
>
> You do not need an Internet connection to use the information in this chapter. To view Java's Hypertext Markup Language (HTML) document files, however, you must run an Internet browser such as Mosaic or HotJava, or another HTML reader, which Borland C++ 5 does not provide.

Surfing the Interactive Net

Although Java is similar in many ways to C++, and you may be tempted to jump right into Java programming, you'll better understand how to use this new language if you have a good background in the history of the Internet. Like most computer languages, Java was invented to fill a need—in this case, the need for interactive, hardware-independent content in the growing Internet marketplace. In addition, Java is poised to become a key player in future Internet expansions, particularly in the development of the virtual reality modeling language (VRML), which will provide 3D browsing environments for the World Wide Web.

Before digging into the syntax of Java, let's take a quick look at Java's origins and examine some of its potential applications. Then, after you are better acquainted with the purpose and goals of Java, I'll explain how to write and run Java applications.

What Java Does

Although Java has many potential uses, interactive documents are probably in the forefront of this language's applications. For example, suppose that you—a brilliant investment analyst— decide to distribute a document that advises investors on stock market purchases based on long range goals, potential risks, and current portfolios. You know your clients use a variety of computer systems, ranging from PC's to super systems that would strain even the Pentagon's budget. Because these systems run various operating systems, you can't be sure your clients have a specific program such as Excel. All that your clients have in common is access to the Internet. Even writing your own spreadsheet application using C++ is no solution because many of your clients would not be able to run the native code generated by your C++ development system.

Fortunately, you have been experimenting with Java, and you decide to include in your document a Java applet that performs the necessary calculations. Because Java is completely hardware independent, your code will run on any system that has a Java interpreter. Such interpreters are easily implemented and will soon be standard equipment in most Web browsers. Best of all, future documents that you distribute can use the same applet, which can even update itself automatically when your clients access your Web page. You'll never again have to send upgrade notices!

Consider how this approach to software distribution differs from the traditional method of requiring users to purchase specific programs—and an endless supply of upgrades—to view and manipulate formatted data. With Java's help, the document itself provides all the software necessary for viewing and performing actions on the document's data.

This concept that data can provide its own interactive code is the key element in a document-centric, networked environment, which many envision as the real future value of the Internet. Such documents are best modeled using object-oriented programming techniques, and therefore, Java, which is fully object-oriented, is the perfect programming tool in this not-so-futuristic world.

Embedding applets in documents, however, isn't all that Java can do. You may simply want to liven up your Web Page with some splashy animation. After all, it's a visual world, and those who have the most eye-catching Web pages are more likely to capture the attention of network surfers who have time to sample only a few of the thousands of locations they might like to visit. Until now, real-time graphics over the Internet has been impractical due to the slow speed of low-bandwidth telephone lines and modems. Because Java applications run on users' systems, however, they sidestep these limits, and effectively, if not actually, boost apparent data transfer speeds.

Java and the Internet

Java was born in a virtual firestorm that has fanned the smoldering Internet into a raging blaze. The Internet's fast-heating popularity begs for new interactive protocols that will simplify, beautify, and make more practical access to information over the World Wide Web. Java is likely to become that protocol.

In the early days of the Internet, surfing the net required the patience of a monk and the skills of a CIA cryptographer. UNIX gurus may have felt right at home, but most users were put off by the Internet's mysterious and confusing commands.

Then, in 1990 at the CERN particle research laboratory, a new protocol arose for distributing documents that would soon revolutionize the Internet. What later became known as the World Wide Web was actually a remarkably successful attempt to standardize Internet browsing and document retrieval. With the Web, a new basis for distributing and accessing global information was born.

Despite this advance, however, the original software for surfing the Web was text-based, and while it was far better than alternative methods, the software was still difficult to use. The very idea of a World Wide Web may have been revolutionary, but it wasn't until a graphical browsing interface came along that the Web began to realize its full potential as a new medium for the masses.

That graphical interface, named Mosaic, started the ball rolling that led to the Internet's current popularity. Developed at the Illinois National Center for Supercomputing Applications (NCSA), Mosaic was more than just a pretty new face on a computer screen. Layered on top of CERN's Web protocol, Mosaic provided users with an interactive Internet browsing environment. With Mosaic, or one of the hundreds of copycat applications now available, you simply click here, point there, and ride the next wave to whatever catches your fancy—never mind that you may be surfing from one end of the globe to another. From the user's point of view, it's all just a single source of information.

Even so, these hot and heavy developments do little to solve the time-worn problems of information access. Sure, you can download any document to which you have access rights, but unless you have a suitable reader for that document, you're out of luck. Just to give a simple example, my favorite graphics viewer, Paint Shop Pro, supports dozens of file formats, but I still occasionally receive an image file that I cannot view on-screen. Why can't the document itself provide me with a suitable viewer? Why should I have to figure out what software to use?

These are exactly the kinds of questions that Java answers. A Java applet embedded in a graphics document can simply determine whether my system has a suitable file viewer, and if not, provide the necessary software automatically. Or, if the applet detects an older software version, it could automatically update the program on my system. In fact, I may not even be aware that a document has just taught my computer a new graphics-display trick. Java could even update its own interpreter, or provide new Web browsing features as they become available.

JAVA AND SECURITY

Some readers may question the wisdom of a global network that runs and updates code automatically on client systems. Isn't this an open invitation for viruses, Trojan Horses, worms, and other destructive software? While this question is a legitimate concern, Java has numerous built-in safeguards that help prevent hacker abuse. Because a Java program is interpreted, it is more difficult to bury a virus in compiled Java applets than in other native-code applications. The Java interpreter checks Java-compiled code for consistency before running an applet, eliminating the need for external virus detectors. The Java interpreter also determines an application's memory layout at runtime, which provides local control over memory address access. File access restrictions are also easily enforced at the client system level. All of these features will help prevent the spread of destructive time bombs inside legitimate applications. In fact, Java may *reduce* the number of active viruses by providing effective barriers against their proliferation.

Java's Origins

Java was created by a group of Sun Microsystems, Inc. employees, headed by James Gosling. Code-named the Green project, the team's goals were to develop methods for distributing and selling software to consumer electronics companies, and to work on designing new electronics products.

At first, the Green team decided to extend C++, but they soon abandoned this idea in favor of creating an entirely new language. Early attempts were named Oak after a tree outside Gosling's window, but because a trade name search found that Oak was used for another product, and for other unpublicized reasons, the language soon became known as Java. (Perhaps the Green team brewed one pot of java too many that day?)

Developing a new language is no small undertaking, but in hindsight, this proved to be the right decision. C++ is, after all, an extension of C, and again extending this language would only further muddy the waters of C programming, which are anything but crystal clear. For example, a lot of features in C++ duplicate elements found in C—not because those items are desirable, but often merely to provide backward source-code compatibility. For instance, although C++ provides the `class` for object-oriented programming, C++ also fully supports C `structs` even though this adds nothing to the language.

Java's designers recognized a golden opportunity to eliminate these kinds of redundancies and create an idealized, and streamlined, version of C++. As a result, Java uses structured statements similar to those in C++, and it employs a recognizable syntax. Java is also fully object-oriented, unlike C++, which allows programmers to mix OOP with conventional methods. In Java, everything exists in the context of one or more objects.

In the next sections, you take a closer look at Java and how it differs from C++. First, however, you'll want to install your Java tools and run a few sample applications to become acquainted with what this new language can do.

Java and Borland C++ 5

Installing Java provides you with a command-line development system, complete with compiler, interpreter, and debugger. Although you can also create and compile new applications using the Borland C++ IDE, you still must install Java to be able to run programs. If you happen to have a Java interpreter such as HotJava, or a Java-aware version of Mosaic or another Web browser, you can use it to run Java code. In this early stage of Java's young life, however, you may have to try several different approaches to find a combination of software that works for your system.

I explain in this part how to install Java and run its sample applications. Because Borland has announced plans to provide additional Java tools in the future, however, some or all of the information here may be out of date by the time you read it. Check for updates in Readme.txt files on Borland's and this book's CD-ROMs.

The Java Installation

After installing Java, you will find a new subdirectory, aptly named \Java, in your Borland C++ path. Inside \Java are several other directories listed in Table 25.1.

Table 25.1. The Java installation directories.

Directory	Contents
Java\Bin	Executable files including the Java interpreter (Java.exe), compiler (Javac.exe), and debugger (Jdb.exe), plus other utilities such as an applet viewer.
Java\Classes	Various common Java classes, some specific to Borland's installation for Windows 95.
Java\Demo	Demonstration applications.
Java\Doc	Documentation files in HTML format. You must have Mosaic or another Web browser to read these files.
Java\Include	Header files ending in .h, analogous to C and C++ header files.
Java\Lib	Support-classes used by Java applications.
Java\Src	Java library source code files.

The purpose of some of the directories in Table 25.1 requires further explanation. In the Lib subdirectory, you'll find the file Classes.zip. This compressed archive file contains Java's numerous compiled classes stored in the popular Zip format. Java accesses the classes in Classes.zip directly. *Do not unzip or delete this file.*

Installing Java does not create the Src subdirectory. The Src.zip file, which you'll find in the \Java path, contains directory information, but to preserve the long filenames, you must use a Windows 95 compatible program such as WinZip95 to unpack the file. This program is available on most bulletin boards, time-share systems, and of course, over the Internet. You don't have to unpack Src.zip to use and write Java applications, so you can postpone this task until later.

For compiling and running Java applications from a DOS prompt, add your Java\bin directory to the system path. I do this with a small batch file, shown here in Listing 25.1, but you can also modify Autoexec.bat for a more permanent change if you prefer.

Listing 25.1. Javacfg.bat (Configures the PATH for running Java applications).

```
@echo off
rem
rem Javacfg.bat -- Configure PATH for Java
rem
set path=%path%;c:\bc5\java\bin
path
echo.
echo Configured for Java
echo.
```

How To Run a Java Application

After installing Java and configuring your system PATH, open a DOS prompt window and enter java to run the interpreter and display a list of options. You should see the text shown in Figure 25.1.

Next, try to run your first Java application. There are two basic methods. You can load and execute a Class using the Java interpreter, or you can load an HTML document that contains an embedded Java applet. (I'll capitalize Class to distinguish this term's use from a class structure. A "Class" is a compiled Java application, stored in a file ending with the filename extension .class.)

Open a DOS prompt window, and make sure the PATH includes C:\Bc5\Java\Bin, or the directory where you installed Java's executable code files. Change to the ArcTest directory by entering these commands:

```
c:
cd \bc5\java\demo\arctest
```

A directory of the path's files points out a problem that arises from long filenames, which Java uses but DOS does not recognize. Here's a portion of the directory that I received by typing the DOS dir command:

```
ARCTES~1  CLA
ARCTES~1  JAV
EXAMPL~1  HTM
```

Figure 25.1.

The Java interpreter's options.

```
usage: java [-options] class

where options include:
    -help                print out this message
    -version             print out the build version
    -v -verbose          turn on verbose mode
    -debug               enable JAVA debugging
    -noasyncgc           don't allow asynchronous gc's
    -verbosegc           print a message when GCs occur
    -cs -checksource     check if source is newer when
                         loading classes
    -ss<number>          set the C stack size of a process
    -oss<number>         set the JAVA stack size of a
                         process
    -ms<number>          set the initial Java heap size
    -mx<number>          set the maximum Java heap size
    -classpath <directories separated by colons>
                         list directories in which to
                         look for classes
    -prof                output profiling data to
                         ./java.prof
    -verify              verify all classes when read in
    -verifyremote        verify classes read in over the
                         network [default]
    -noverify            do not verify any class
```

DOS replaces long filenames with shorter, uppercase names, ending with a tilde and a number starting with 1. The file you want to execute here is listed as ARCTES~1.CLA, but its actual name is ArcTest.class, which you can discover by viewing this directory with the Windows 95 Explorer. Although you are using DOS to run the Java code, you must enter the longer name minus the .class extension. You cannot enter the shortened version shown by the dir command. *Long filenames are case-sensitive and must be entered exactly as shown.*

Because Java considers Class names to be case-sensitive, to run the application, you must enter the following DOS command exactly as printed here (do not type a filename extension):

```
java ArcTest
```

Figure 25.2 shows the window that appears on-screen. Enter angle values to display filled or outlined arcs, which demonstrate Java's rudimentary graphics commands. If you have trouble closing the application by clicking the window's close button, return to the DOS prompt and press Ctrl+C. This terminates the Java interpreter and closes the application window.

In most cases, rather than run stand-alone applications using the Java interpreter, you will probably embed one or more Java applets in an HTML file for distribution over the Internet.

To load these documents and run the embedded applet requires a different technique. To try it, change to the barchart directory by entering the commands

```
c:
cd \bc5\java\demo\barchart
```

Figure 25.2.

The Java ArcTest class display.

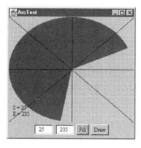

Using the Windows 95 Explorer, view this same directory, where you will find a file named example1.html (in all lowercase). This document contains a command that loads Chart.class, which contains the Java applet. Viewing the HTML document feeds the applet's P-Code to the Java interpreter, which runs the program. To do that, use Java's graphical applet viewer by entering the following command at a DOS prompt (you must type the .html filename extension):

```
appletviewer_g example1.html
```

This displays the sample bar chart window shown in Figure 25.3. You should be able to exit the program by clicking its close button, but if not, get back to the DOS prompt and type Ctrl+C.

Figure 25.3.

The Java BarChart applet display.

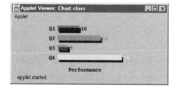

> **NOTE**
>
> In the future—which may have arrived by the time you read this—Web browsers such as Mosaic and HotJava will contain full Java interpreters. You will be able to use these and other programs to load HTML documents and run embedded Java applets. These products, when they become available, will probably work as well or better than the methods described here for running and testing Java programs.

Java Programming

Now that you know where Java fits into the Internet picture, and you have installed your Java tools and tried some sample applications, you are ready to begin learning how to write Java applications. Because most readers of this book are familiar with C++, I'll start by comparing Java and C++. After that, I'll explain how to write a Java Class and an applet.

How Java Differs from C++

Java is a new language, constructed from the ground up, that in many ways resembles C++ but is far simpler in design and implementation. Java is a platform-independent, general-purpose programming language that is fully object-oriented and uses many of the statement forms found in C and C++.

Java's designers based the language on C++, but took the opportunity to get rid of unnecessary baggage, a lot of which originated in C. In particular, Java lacks the following elements found in C and C++:

structs and unions—The `class` is the only structure in a Java application. In fact, Java is fully object-oriented, and everything in an application occurs inside a class.

`#define` *and* `typedef`—There are no macros or type-name aliases in Java.

pointers—The Java interpreter lays out memory at runtime, and performs automatic garbage collection in the background to delete unused objects. Where possible, garbage collection runs as a separate thread. Java does not have a pointer type, nor does it have dereference operators. All objects in Java programs are dynamically allocated.

multiple inheritance—Java classes can inherit from base classes using only single, not multiple, inheritance. The benefits of multiple inheritance, however, are still achievable on the module level.

static arrays—All arrays in Java are actually lists of objects, and must be allocated using the `new` operator. Java supports one- and two-dimensional arrays.

non-member functions—There are no separate functions in a Java application. All functions must be members of a class.

`goto`—Finally, somebody wised up and designed a language without a `goto` command, which I was beginning to think had the evolutionary staying power of the cockroach.

operator overloading—As I mentioned elsewhere in this book, an overloaded operator is merely a syntactical illusion for a function call, so not having operator overloading is no great loss.

null-terminated strings—All strings in Java, including string literals, are objects of the `String` class.

eight-bit characters—Characters in Java are in 16-bit Unicode format.

bool—This is named `boolean` in Java, and is a true literal type, not a substitute for `int`. A `boolean` object may have one of the predefined values, `true` or `false`.

automatic type conversion—Type checking is far stricter in Java than in C++. You must use a type cast expression to convert between data types—to pass a `long` integer value to an `int` parameter, for example.

Java Reserved Words

A legal identifier in Java must begin with a letter, underscore, or dollar sign. Beginning identifiers with underscores and dollar signs—conventions used by library code—is allowed but not recommended. (Errors that lead to identifiers prefaced with one of these two characters may indicate a problem in a library file. This information can be useful during debugging, so it's best not to begin your own identifiers with _ or $.) Identifiers may not contain spaces. They may contain digits. For example, SS6 and LD9 are legal identifiers, but as in C++, more descriptive names will help keep your programs readable.

Identifiers are case-sensitive—`MyVar` and `myVar` are distinct. Common Java convention calls for beginning all identifiers with lowercase letters, regardless of purpose, except for class names, which are capitalized. All uppercase words such as `COUNT` and `MAX_THINGY` are allowed but not recommended, especially if you plan to link in C code, which may define uppercase constants.

Table 25.2 lists Java's reserved key words, which you cannot use for your own identifiers.

Table 25.2. Java reserved key words.

Key words			
abstract	boolean	break	byte
byvalue*	case	catch	char
class	const*	continue	default
do	double	else	extends
false	final	finally	float
for	goto*	if	implements
import	instanceof	int	interface
long	native	new	null
package	private	protected	public
return	short	static	super
switch	synchronized	this	threadsafe
throw	transient	true	try
void	while		
* Currently unused but still reserved			

Writing a Java Program

Listing 25.2, WelcomeToJava.java, shows a simple Java program that displays the message, `Welcome to Java Programming!`. Enter the program using the Borland IDE or another text editor, and save to the suggested long filename. If you have trouble creating this name, save to a temporary file and use the Windows 95 Explorer to rename the file. Make sure C:\Bc5\Java\Bin is in your system PATH, and then enter the following two commands to compile and run the program:

```
javac WelcomeToJava.java
java WelcomeToJava
```

Listing 25.2. WelcomeToJava.java (Demonstrates Java programming).

```
//===============================================================
// WelcomeToJava.java -- Demonstrates Java programming
// To compile:
//    javac WelcomeToJava.java
// To run:
//    java WelcomeToJava
// Copyright (c) 1996 by Tom Swan. All rights reserved.
//===============================================================

class WelcomeToJava {
  public static void main (String args[]) {
    System.out.println("Welcome to Java Programming!");
  }
}
```

The basic Java program consists of a `class` named the same as the module that holds the program's source code. This class must have a `main` member function, which is analogous to the global `main` function in a C or C++ program. Statements in `main` are the first to execute.

Comments in Java source code are the same as in C and C++. You may delimit comments with `/*` and `*/`, or use `//` to begin a comment that extends to the end of the line. In addition, Java supports a new comment style that looks like this:

```
/**
this is a comment
*/
```

The double asterisks are used to create automatic documentation for Java applications, and are typically inserted above member functions.

In the sample listing, the declaration of `main` states that it is a public symbol—that is, it is accessible from outside of the class. The word `static` indicates that this method is unchanged in all instances of the class. The word `void` indicates that the function returns no value.

Though not shown here, classes may have `public`, `protected`, `private`, and `friendly` members. The first three of these access specifiers are the same as in C++. A `friendly` member is accessible to all classes, whether related or not, within the same module.

Getting back to the sample listing, the `main` method receives an array of `String` values, equal to any arguments passed to the program. To display the demonstration program's message, `main` calls the `println` method, which is a member of object `out`, in turn a member of `System`.

> **NOTE**
>
> Member functions are declared and implemented directly in class declarations. Java member functions are not implemented separately from their declarations.

Writing a Java Applet

To demonstrate how to write a Java applet, I converted to Java the Windows Sketch demonstration in Chapter 14, "Introducing OWL." Listing 25.3, Sketch.java, is a complete applet with all the features required for embedding into an HTML document for distribution over the Internet. You might also want to compare the statements with the original Sketch.cpp file (from Listing 14.7) to learn more about the differences between C++ and Java. Figure 25.4 shows the Sketch applet's display with some text that I drew in the window by clicking and dragging the mouse.

Figure 25.4.
Java Sketch applet window.

Listing 25.3. Sketch.java (Implements a Java Sketch-pad applet).

```
//================================================================
// Sketch.java -- Implements a Java Sketch-pad applet
// To compile:
//   1. Load Sketch.ide into Bcw
//   2. Use Project¦Build all or Make all to compile
// To run:
//   1. Open a DOS prompt window
//   2. Add C:\Bc5\Java\Bin to system PATH
//   3. Enter: appletviewer_g Sketch.html
// Copyright (c) 1996 by Tom Swan. All rights reserved.
//================================================================
```

continues

Listing 25.3. continued

```
// Import external classes used by applet

import java.awt.*;
import java.applet.*;
import java.util.Vector;

//===============================================================
// class Sketch
//===============================================================


public class Sketch extends Applet {
  // Construct a blank panel in applet window
  public void init() {
    setLayout(new BorderLayout());
    SketchPanel dp = new SketchPanel();
    add("Center", dp);
  }

  // Exit applet when WINDOW_DESTROY message received
  public boolean handleEvent(Event e) {
    switch (e.id) {
      case Event.WINDOW_DESTROY:
        System.exit(0);
        return true;
      default:
        return false;
    }
  }

  // Entry point. Initialize applet window.
  public static void main(String args[]) {
    Frame frame = new Frame("Java Sketch Pad");
    Sketch sketch = new Sketch();   // Do this only in an applet
    sketch.init();
    sketch.start();
    sketch.add("Center", sketch);
    sketch.resize(300, 150);
    sketch.show();
  }
}

//===============================================================
// class SketchPanel
//===============================================================

class SketchPanel extends Panel {

  boolean dragging;  // True when clicking and dragging mouse
  Vector lines = new Vector();  // Holds lines drawn
  int x1, y1, x2, y2;  // Starting and ending line points

  // Set background color of sketch panel inside applet window
  public SketchPanel() {
    setBackground(Color.white);
  }
```

```
    // Respond to MOUSE and WINDOW_DESTROY events
    public boolean handleEvent(Event e) {
      switch (e.id) {

        // Start a drawing operation on sensing a mouse click
        case Event.MOUSE_DOWN:
          if (!dragging) {
            dragging = true;   // Set dragging flag true
            x1 = e.x;          // Save starting mouse x coordinate
            y1 = e.y;          // Save starting mouse y coordinat
          }
          return true;   // Indicate program has handled message

        // Cancel drawing operation on sensing mouse button release
        case Event.MOUSE_UP:
          dragging = false;
          return true;   // Indicate program has handled message

        // Draw a line on sensing a mouse dragging action
          case Event.MOUSE_DRAG:
          x2 = e.x;   // Save ending mouse x coordinate
          y2 = e.y;   // Save ending mouse y coordinate
          // Add line to lines vector, using a Rectangle object
          lines.addElement(new Rectangle(x1, y1, x2, y2));
          x1 = x2;        // Set start of next line to the
          y1 = y2;        // end of the current line
          repaint();      // Draw all lines in the vector
          return true;   // Indicate program has handled message
        case Event.WINDOW_DESTROY:
          System.exit(0);
          return true;   // Indicate program has handled message
        default:
          return false; // Indicate program has not handled message
      }
    }

    // Repaint sketch pad contents
    public void paint(Graphics g) {
      int n = lines.size();            // Get number of lines in vector
      g.setColor(getForeground());     // Set line drawing color
      g.setPaintMode();                // Select default paint mode
      for (int i = 0; i < n; i++) {
        Rectangle r = (Rectangle)lines.elementAt(i);  // Get line
        g.drawLine(r.x, r.y, r.width, r.height);       // Draw line
      }
    }
}
```

The Sketch.java module imports several classes from the Java library. The statements

```
import java.awt.*;
import java.applet.*;
import java.util.Vector;
```

make available the classes in the AWT (Another Window Toolkit) library, and also the classes for applet development. The third statement imports the Vector class from Java's utility classes. Sketch uses a Vector object to store line coordinates.

An applet requires a class, named the same as the module (Sketch in this case), that is derived from the imported Applet class. The declaration

```
public class Sketch extends Applet {
```

creates a new class named Sketch that inherits the members of Applet. The word `extends` tells Java that Sketch adds new members to the inherited Applet base class.

Inside Sketch, a member function named `handleEvent` calls `System.exit` to end the application on receipt of a `WINDOW_DESTROY` message. This is not a Windows message (although it may be generated by one), but an event that takes place entirely within the Java interpreter. The `switch` statement inside `handleEvent` returns true to indicate that it has successfully handled a message. The function returns `false` to have the interpreter handle a message using default programming.

All Java applications require a `main` member function. Because Sketch is an applet, it creates an instance of its own class, and then calls various member functions as shown in the listing to initialize and run the program, and to size its window. The string `"Center"` is not displayed, but is a command to the interpreter to center the applet's window. Because of Java's system-independent nature, it wouldn't make sense to specify actual display coordinate values. (You'll see other similar strings in Java code such as `"South"` and `"East"` that indicate relative locations of display items.)

Sketch's `SketchPanel` class is derived from `Panel`, another standard Java class. The class's constructor (the member function named the same as the class) sets the background color of the drawing area within the application's window.

Another `handleEvent` function responds to four types of messages: `MOUSE_DOWN`, `MOUSE_UP`, `MOUSE_DRAG`, and `WINDOW_DESTROY`. The programming for these events is obvious, and I heavily commented the lines so you can follow their logic.

To store the line coordinates, the `SketchPanel` class constructs an array of the `Vector` class using the statement:

```
Vector lines = new Vector();  // Holds lines drawn
```

After storing mouse coordinates in four variables—x1, y1, x2, and y2—a simple statement adds a `Rectangle` object to the `lines` Vector:

```
lines.addElement(new Rectangle(x1, y1, x2, y2));
```

The only reason for using a `Rectangle` here is convenience—it has four data members that are suitable for representing the end points of a line. Despite the class name, the Sketch program doesn't draw rectangular shapes.

To paint the window, the program calls the `repaint` function, a standard in visual AWT classes. Calling this function summons the class's `paint` method, which in this case draws lines using the coordinate values collected in the `lines` Vector.

To compile the Sketch application, load its .ide project file into the Borland C++ IDE, and then select the *Project\Make all* or *Project\Build all* commands. This creates the target P-Code file, Sketch.class. Because Sketch is an applet, however, you cannot run that Class using the Java interpreter. Instead, you must embed the applet in an HTML document and use a suitable viewer to test the program's code.

To insert a Java applet into a Web page, simply insert the following command into your HTML document:

```
<APP CLASS="classname">
```

Listing 25.4, Sketch.html, shows a simple document that uses this method to embed the Sketch.class applet in a hypertext document. To run the applet, load its .html file with an applet viewer. For example, enter this command at a DOS prompt:

```
appletviewer_g Sketch.html
```

Listing 25.4. Sketch.html (Hypertext document with embedded Java applet).

```
<title>Java Sketch</title>
<hr>
<applet code=Sketch.class width=400 height=400>
</applet>
<hr>
<a href="Sketch.java">The source.</a>
```

The Java Application Generator

The Borland C++ IDE project manager can construct a bare-bones Java applet shell automatically. Follow these steps to use Borland's Java AppExpert generator:

1. Close any open project and windows.
2. Create a blank directory to hold the project files.
3. Select *File\New,* and choose *Project* from the submenu. (*Do not select AppExpert!*)
4. Click the *Browse* button, and change to the directory you created in step 2.
5. Enter a filename into the *Open Project File* dialog box, and click Ok or press Enter to close this window.
6. Change *Target Type* in the *New Target* dialog to *Java (.class).*
7. Enable the *Launch AppExpert for Java* check box and click the Ok button or press Enter.

After a moment, the project manager will launch the Java application generator (see Figure 25.5). Select the page tab of the item you want to enter, and then choose the options you need. When you are done, click the Save and Exit button to return to the IDE. You can then open the project window's .java and .html nodes to begin programming your application.

815

Figure 25.5.
Borland's Java AppExpert application generator.

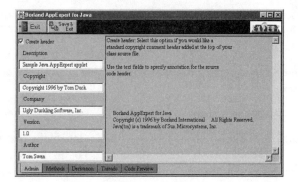

> **NOTE**
>
> Many Java demonstration programs have associated .ide project files that you can open using the Borland C++ IDE. After opening a project, double-click on the .java node in the project window to view the application's source code. You may compile but not run Java applications in the IDE. To run a compiled Java application, switch to a DOS prompt and use one of the techniques described in this chapter.

Summary

- Borland C++ 5 provides two Java systems: a set of command line tools and demonstrations, and a built-in Java compiler you can run using the IDE.

- Java is a new language, constructed from the ground up, that in many ways resembles C++ but is far simpler in design and implementation. Java is a platform-independent, general-purpose programming language that is fully object-oriented and uses many of the statement forms found in C and C++.

- Although you can write all sorts of software using Java, you will usually write small applications, called applets, for embedding into HTML documents distributed over the Internet. In this way, Java provides the Internet with interactive capabilities that would otherwise strain the world's already overloaded, low-bandwidth telephone system. Any Web surfer with a Java interpreter can access your interactive documents and run your Java applets. Best of all, Java code runs on the user's system at nearly the same speed as native code generated by a C or C++ compiler.

26

CHAPTER

Mastering Standard Functions

In this chapter is an alphabetic reference to the most commonly used Borland C++ standard functions. Most sections have these six parts:

1. *Syntax.* The function's prototype as declared in a library header file such as stdio.h. For simplicity, system macros such as _Cdecl and _FARFUNC from header file prototypes are not included. (These and similar macros, if non-null, affect the compiled code but have no bearing on a function's use.)

2. *Include.* One or more header files such as stdio.h that declare the function's prototype, related symbolic constants, structures, and so on. To use a function in your programs, insert a directive such as

   ```
   #include <stdio.h>
   ```

3. *Description.* An explanation of the function's purpose, use, return value, and possible errors.

4. *Parameters.* If the function declares parameters, each is listed here in declaration order. Consult this section for information about the types of arguments you need to pass to a function. Functions with no parameters do not have a Parameters section.

5. *See also.* One or more cross references to other related functions.

6. *Example.* A complete example of the function in a C or C++ program, or a reference to another example that uses this function along with one or more others.

To make room for other new chapters in this book, I reduced the size of this reference by nearly two thirds by deleting obscure and obsolete entries. Deleted functions include those declared in math.h, which are fairly obvious (abs, cos, sin, etc.). I also deleted far versions of functions that have near counterparts (faralloc versus alloc, for instance), and those that begin with underscores, which are generally for internal use by other library functions or have close equivalents (_exit and exit, for example). Functions that remain are generally useful to DOS and Windows developers. No longer listed are functions declared in header files bcd.h, bios.h, complex.h, conio.h, dirent.h, dos.h, float.h, graphics.h, locale.h, math.h, process.h, setjmp.h, signal.h, and utime.h.

Despite these deletions, all examples for all functions are still included on the book's CD-ROM in the Source\C26 directory. Also, the complete unabridged function reference is on disk in the on-line electronic edition of *Mastering Borland C++ 4.5, Second edition.* For these reasons, "See also" notes in the following reference may refer to examples and functions that are not listed here, but are fully documented on disk.

These changes were necessary to keep an already huge *Mastering Borland C++* from straining bookshelves to the breaking point, not to mention the backs of those who have to carry the book around. The result is a streamlined reference that I hope you will find even more useful than in past editions.

abort   Terminate program

Syntax   void abort(void);

Include   STDLIB.H

Description   Writes "Abnormal program termination" to stderr and ends program via _exit(3).

See also   atexit, _c_exit, _cexit, exit, _exit, raise, signal, spawn...

Example
```
/* abort.cpp */
#include <stdio.h>
#include <stdlib.h>
main()
{
  int errorCode;
  printf("Enter error code or 0: ");
  scanf("%d", &errorCode);
  if (errorCode != 0)
    abort();
  else
    puts("No error detected");
  return 0;
}
```

access   Determine file access

Syntax   `int access(const char *filename,int amode);`

Include   IO.H

Description   Determines access mode for a file or directory. Returns 0 if re-
                quested access is allowed, -1 for error; sets global `errno` to `ENOENT` if
                the file doesn't exist, or `EACCES` if access is denied. Typically used to
                detect whether a file or directory exists.

Parameters   `const char *filename` File or path to test.

                `int amode` Mode: 0-exits, 1-executable (ignored), 2-writeable, 4-
                readable, 6-readable and writeable.

See also   `chmod, fopen, fstat, stat`

Example
```
/* access.cpp */
#include <stdio.h>
#include <io.h>
#define FILENAME "access.cpp"
main()
{
  int result;
  result = access(FILENAME, 0);
  if (result == 0)
    puts(FILENAME" exists");
  else
    puts(FILENAME" does not exist");
  return 0;
}
```

alloca   Allocate stack space

Syntax   `void *alloca(size_t size);`

Include   MALLOC.H

Description   Allocates temporary stack space, which might be used for any
                purpose and is similar to space allotted to a local variable. Returns a
                pointer to the reserved space, or null if `size` bytes are not available.
                Allocated space is deleted automatically when the function ends. Do
                not call `alloca()` in an expression passed as an argument to another
                function, because this is likely to corrupt the stack.

Parameters   `size_t size` The number of bytes to allocate.

See also   `malloc`

Example
```
/* alloca.cpp */
#include <stdio.h>
```

```
#include <malloc.h>
#include <string.h>
#define SIZE 128
void f(void);
main()
{
  printf("SP before calling f() == %#x\n", _SP);
  f();
  printf("SP after calling f() == %#x\n", _SP);
  return 0;
}

void f(void)
{
  char *p;
  char dummy[1];
  dummy[0] = 0;   // Ensure proper stack frame
  puts(" Enter function f()");
  printf(" SP before alloca() == %#x\n", _SP);
  p = (char *)alloca(SIZE);
  if (p) {
    printf(" SP after alloca() == %#x\n", _SP);
    strcpy(p, " A string on the stack");
    puts(p);
  }
}
```

asctime   ASCII date and time

Syntax   `char *asctime(const struct tm *tblock);`

Include   TIME.H

Description   Converts to a 26-character string the date and time in a structure addressed by `tblock`. Returns the address of the string, a static variable. Multiple calls to `asctime()` overwrite this variable, and you should copy the converted string for safekeeping.

Parameters   **const struct tm *tblock** See TIME.H for the structure's members. Store date and time information in `tm`, and pass to the function to convert to a string.

See also   `ctime, difftime, ftime, gmtime, localtime, mktime, strftime, stime, time, tzset`

Example
```
/* asctime.cpp */
#include <stdio.h>
#include <time.h>
#include <dos.h>
#include <string.h>
main()
{
  struct tm t;              // time.h date and time structure
  struct time dt;           // dos.h time structure
  struct dosdate_t dd;      // dos.h date structure
```

```
    char ts[26];              // holds result
    gettime(&dt);             // read the current time
    _dos_getdate(&dd);        // read the current date
    t.tm_sec   = dt.ti_sec;        // Seconds
    t.tm_min   = dt.ti_min;        // Minutes
    t.tm_hour  = dt.ti_hour;       // Hour
    t.tm_mday  = dd.day;           // Day
    t.tm_mon   = dd.month - 1;     // Month
    t.tm_year  = dd.year - 1900;   // Year
    t.tm_wday  = dd.dayofweek;     // Day of week
    t.tm_yday  = 0;  // Unused day of year
    t.tm_isdst = 0;  // Unused "is daylight savings time"
    strcpy(ts, asctime(&t));
    puts(ts);
    return 0;
}
```

assert   Abort if assertion fails

Syntax	`void assert(int test);`
Include	ASSERT.H
Description	A macro used for debugging. Tests a condition and aborts program if that condition fails.
Parameters	`int test` True or false expression. If expression is false (zero), function halts program. If expression is true (nonzero), program continues normally.
See also	`abort, exit`
Example	

```
/* assert.cpp */
#include <stdio.h>
#include <assert.h>
#include <stdlib.h>
main()
{
  char buffer[128];
  int testValue;
  printf("Enter test value 0 or 1: ");
  gets(buffer);
  testValue = atoi(buffer);
  assert((testValue == 0) || (testValue == 1));
  puts("Program ending normally");
  return 0;
}
```

atexit   Register exit function

Syntax	`int atexit(void(* func)(void));`
Include	STDLIB.H

Description	Registers an exit function, which runs when the program ends, but before DOS regains control. Programs might call `atexit()` multiple times to register up to 32 exit functions. Returns zero if successful; nonzero if function cannot be registered.
Parameters	`void(* func)(void)` Pointer to exit function that has no parameters.
See also	abort, exit, spawn...
Example	

```
/* atexit.cpp */
#include <stdio.h>
#include <stdlib.h>
void f1(void);
void f2(void);
main()
{
  atexit(f1);  // Register exit function f1()
  atexit(f2);  // Register exit function f2()
  return 0;
}

void f1(void)
{
  puts("Exit function #1");
}

void f2(void)
{
  puts("Exit function #2");
}
```

atoi   ASCII to integer

Syntax	int atoi(const char *s);
Include	STDLIB.H
Description	Converts string to an `int` value. Returns value or zero if string cannot be converted.
Parameters	`const char *s` Pointer to string to convert.
See also	atof, atol, cgets, gets, strtod
Example	

```
/* atoi.cpp */
#include <stdio.h>
#include <stdlib.h>
main()
{
  char buffer[128];
  int result;
  printf("Enter integer value to convert: ");
  gets(buffer);
  result = atoi(buffer);
  printf("Result == %d\n", result);
  return 0;
}
```

atol   ASCII to long

Syntax   `long atol(const char *s);`

Include   STDLIB.H

Description   Converts string to `long` value. Returns value or zero if string cannot be converted.

Parameters   `const char *s` Pointer to string to convert.

See also   `atof, atoi, cgets, gets, strtod, strtol, strtoul`

Example
```
/* atol.cpp */
#include <stdio.h>
#include <stdlib.h>
main()
{
  char buffer[128];
  long result;
  printf("Enter long value to convert: ");
  gets(buffer);
  result = atol(buffer);
  printf("Result == %ld\n", result);
  return 0;
}
```

bsearch   Binary search

Syntax   `void *bsearch(const void *key, const void *base, size_t nelem,`
                    `size_t width, int (*fcmp)(const void *, const void *));`

Include   STDLIB.H

Description   Searches a sorted array using the binary-search algorithm to minimize the number of comparisons required to find a match. Returns zero if search argument is not found; otherwise, returns the matching item's address. When searching an array of duplicate items, a matching item is not necessarily the first in the array. As demonstrated in the example, `bsearch()` requires you to supply a comparison function, similar to that used by `qsort()`. Your function is passed two pointers, A and B, to elements in the array to be searched, and must return -1 if A < B, zero if A == B, or +1 if A > B.

Parameters   `const void *key` Pointer to search key, of the same data type (usually) as the items stored in the array.

                    `const void *base` Pointer to array containing items sorted in low-to-high order.

size_t **nelem** The number of elements in the array.

size_t **width** The size in bytes of each element in the array.

int (*fcmp)(const void *, const void*) Comparison function. See example.

See also   lfind, lsearch, qsort

Example

```
/* bsearch.cpp */
#include <stdio.h>
#include <stdlib.h>
#include <string.h>
char *array[] = {
  "Boston",
  "Chicago",
  "Cincinnati",
  "Los Angeles",
  "Miami",
  "New York",
  "Philadelphia"
};
#define WIDTH (sizeof(array[0]))
#define NELEM (sizeof(array) / sizeof(array[0]))

int Compare(const void *a, const void *b);
main()
{
  char buffer[128];   // Input string buffer
  char **p;           // Result of bsearch()
  char *key;          // Search key pointer
  key = buffer;
  printf("Enter search string: ");
  gets(buffer);
  p = (char **)bsearch(&key, array, NELEM, WIDTH, Compare);
  if (p)
    printf("Found %s\n", *p);
  else
    printf("%s not found\n", buffer);
  return 0;
}

int Compare(const void *a, const void *b)
{
  return stricmp(*(char **)a, *(char **)b);
}
```

calloc   Allocate and clear memory

Syntax   void *calloc(size_t nitems, size_t size);

Include   STDLIB.H

Description Allocates a block of memory up to 64K long on the heap and sets every byte in the block to zero. Returns null if not successful; otherwise, returns the address of the first allocated byte.

Parameters **size_t nitems** Number of items to allocate.

size_t size Size in bytes of one item.

See also farcalloc, free, malloc, realloc

Example
```
/* calloc.cpp */
#include <stdio.h>
#include <stdlib.h>
#define SIZE 128
main()
{
  char *s = (char *)calloc(1, SIZE);
  if (s == NULL)
    puts("Error in calloc()");
  else {
    printf("Enter a string: ");
    gets(s);
    printf("Your string is: %s\n", s);
    free(s);
  }
  return 0;
}
```

chdir Change directory

Syntax `int chdir(const char *path);`

Include DIR.H

Description Change current DOS directory to the path string addressed by parameter path. Returns zero for success and -1 for error, setting errno to ENOENT (path or filename not found).

Parameters **const char *path** Pointer to the path string that may contain drive and directory names. Use double backslashes to separate drive and subdirectory names. Examples of acceptable path strings include `"c:\\"`, `"a:\\backup"`, `"c:\\bc5\\Include"`.

See also _chdrive, getcurdir, getcwd, getdisk, mkdir, rmdir, setdisk

Example
```
/* chdirx.cpp */
/* --------------------------------- */
/* NOTE: Program name changed to avoid */
/* conflict with DOS CHDIR command.    */
/* --------------------------------- */
#include <stdio.h>
#include <dir.h>
main()
{
  char path[128];
  printf("Enter new path: ");
  gets(path);
  if (chdir(path))  // i.e. if not successful
```

```
      perror(path);    // print system error
    return 0;
}
```

chmod   Change file access mode

Syntax   `int chmod(const char *path, int amode);`

Include   SYS\STAT.H

Description   Changes a file's access mode by altering its directory attributes.
Returns 0 for success and -1 for error (see _chmod for errno error
codes).

Parameters   **const char *path** Pointer to filename string that might contain
drive and path information.

int amode One of the three expressions S_IWRITE (write permission),
S_IREAD (read-only permission), or S_IREAD¦S_WRITE (read or write
permission).

See also   access, _chmod, fstat, open, sopen, stat

Example
```
/* chmod.cpp */
#include <stdio.h>
#include <io.h>
#include <sys\stat.h>
#define FILENAME "CHMOD.CPP"
main()
{
  int result;
  printf("Setting %s mode to read and write\n", FILENAME);
  result = chmod(FILENAME, S_IREAD ¦ S_IWRITE);
  if (result)  // i.e. if not successful
    perror(FILENAME);
  return 0;
}
```

chsize   Change file size

Syntax   `int chsize(int handle, long size);`

Include   IO.H

Description   Changes an open file's size. Increasing a file's size with chsize() is
faster than writing dummy blocks after the end of an existing file—a
common trick employed by database systems to reserve disk space
for data. Decreasing a file's size with chsize() truncates the file,
throwing away any information currently stored beyond the file's
new end. The file must be opened with write-permission enabled.
Extended portions of files are filled with null bytes. Returns zero for

success; -1 for error, setting `errno` to EACCESS (access denied) or EBADF (bad file number).

Parameters   `int handle` Handle to file, opened with write-permission enabled.

                      `long size` New size in bytes.

See also   `close, _creat, creat, open`

Example
```
/* chsize.cpp */
#include <stdio.h>
#include <io.h>
#include <sys\stat.h>
#define FILENAME "test.dat"
main()
{
  int handle, result;
  handle = creat(FILENAME, S_IREAD ¦ S_IWRITE);
  if (handle == -1)
    perror(FILENAME);
  else {
    result = chsize(handle, 1024);
    if (result)
      perror("chsize()");
    close(handle);
  }
  return 0;
}
```

clearerr   Reset error indication

Syntax   `void clearerr(FILE *stream);`

Include   STDIO.H

Description   Resets to zero the specified stream's error and end-of-file values. Following a file error, call `clearerr()` to permit further I/O on the stream.

Parameters   `FILE *stream` Pointer to file stream such as returned by `fopen()`.

See also   `eof, feof, ferror, perror, rewind`

Example
```
/* clearerr.cpp */
#include <stdio.h>
main()
{
  char c;
  fread(&c, 1, 1, stdprn);
  printf("Before, ferror() == %d\n", ferror(stdprn));
  clearerr(stdprn);
  printf("After, errno == %d\n", ferror(stdprn));
  return 0;
}
```

clock   Determine processor time

Syntax   `clock_t clock(void);`

Include   TIME.H

Description   Returns a value that represents the amount of time that has passed since a program began running. Returns -1 for systems that lack an internal timer. In Borland C++, but not necessarily on other ANSI C installations, type `clock_t` is a `typedef` alias for a `long int`.

See also   `gettime, time`

Example
```
/* clock.cpp */
#include <stdio.h>
#include <time.h>
#include <dos.h>
main()
{
  clock_t t1, t2, t3;
  t1 = clock();
  delay(500);
  t2 = clock();
  t3 = t2 - t1;
  printf("Clock ticks for 500ms delay == %lu\n", t3);
  printf("500 mx delay in seconds == %f\n", t3 / CLK_TCK);
  return 0;
}
```

close   Close file

Syntax   `int _close(int handle);`
                `int close(int handle);`

Include   IO.H

Description   Closes an open file identified by `handle`. Returns 0 for success and -1 for error.

Parameters   **int handle** File handle such as returned by `open()`.

See also   `creat, creatnew, dup, fclose, open, sopen`

Example
```
/* close.cpp */
#include <stdio.h>
#include <string.h>
#include <io.h>
#include <fcntl.h>
#include <sys\stat.h>
main()
{
  int handle;
  char *fname = strdup(tmpnam(NULL));
  char buffer[128];
```

```
    memset(buffer, 0xff, sizeof(buffer));
    handle = open(fname, O_CREAT, S_IREAD | S_IWRITE);
    if (handle) {
      printf("Writing to file %s\n", fname);
      write(handle, buffer, sizeof(buffer));
      close(handle);
    }
    return 0;
}
```

coreleft   Return unused RAM memory

Syntax

```
unsigned coreleft(void);
unsigned long coreleft(void);
```

Include   ALLOC.H

Description   Returns amount of heap space never before used. This value represents a true picture of available memory only if no objects have been allocated and freed. An accurate tally of available RAM requires walking the heap (see `heapwalk()`). In small memory models, `coreleft` returns an `unsigned` value. In large memory models, `coreleft` returns an `unsigned long` value.

See also   allocmem, brk, farcoreleft, heapwalk, malloc

Example
```
/* coreleft.cpp */
#include <stdio.h>
#include <alloc.h>
main()
{
  printf("coreleft() == %lu", coreleft());
  return 0;
}
```

creat   Create file

Syntax   `int creat(const char *path, int amode);`

Include   SYS\STAT.H, IO.H

Description   Creates new file. If successful, returns nonnegative integer handle for use with other functions—`read()` and `write()`, for example. Returns -1 if an error is detected. Before calling `creat()`, set global `_fmode` variable to `O_TEXT` if creating a text file, or to `O_BINARY` if creating a binary file.

Parameters   `const char *path` Pointer to null-terminated filename string, which may contain a drive and directory paths.

829

int amode Set to S_IWRITE to open file for writing, S_IREAD to open for reading only, or (S_IREAD ¦ S_IWRITE) to open for reading and writing.

See also   close, _creat, creatnew, creattemp, dup, fopen, open, read, write

Example
```cpp
/* creat.cpp */
#include <stdio.h>
#include <io.h>
#include <sys\stat.h>
#include <string.h>
main()
{
  int handle;
  char *fname = strdup(tmpnam(NULL));
  char buffer[128];
  memset(buffer, 0xff, sizeof(buffer));
  handle = creat(fname, S_IREAD ¦ S_IWRITE);
  if (handle) {
    printf("Writing to file %s\n", fname);
    write(handle, buffer, sizeof(buffer));
    close(handle);
  }
  return 0;
}
```

ctime   Convert date and time to string

Syntax   char *ctime(const time_t *time);

Include   TIME.H

Description   Returns a character string representation of the date and time information addressed by pointer time. Use function tzset() (time-zone set) to modify daylight and timezone global variables, which affect ctime()'s result. The function returns a pointer to a static char buffer. Subsequent calls to ctime() use the same buffer, which should be copied using strdup() or a similar string function for safekeeping.

Parameters   **const time_t *time** Pointer to a time_t value, such as returned by the time() function.

See also   asctime, ftime, getdate, gettime, gmtime, localtime, time, tzset

Example
```cpp
/* ctime.cpp */
#include <stdio.h>
#include <time.h>
main()
{
  time_t theTime;
  time(&theTime);
```

```
        printf("The time is %s\n", ctime(&theTime));
        return 0;
    }
```

difftime   Difference between two times

Syntax   `double difftime(time_t time2, time_t time1);`

Include   TIME.H

Description   Returns the difference between `time1` and `time2`. The time interval is system-dependent.

Parameters   **time_t time2** A `long` value such as returned by the `time()` function that is greater than or equal to `time1`.

                 time_t time1 A `long` value such as returned by `time()` that is less than or equal to `time2`.

See also   `asctime, ctime, gmtime, localtime, time, timezone, tzset`

Example
```
/* difftime.cpp */
#include <stdio.h>
#include <time.h>
#include <conio.h>
#include <string.h>
main()
{
  char *s = "How much wood could a woodchuck "
    "chuck if a woodchuck could chuck wood?";
  char buffer[128];
  time_t t1, t2;
  clrscr();
  puts("Type the following sentence.");
  puts("pressing Enter ONLY at the end.");
  gotoxy(1, 10);
  cputs(s);
  gotoxy(1, 15);
  cputs("Enter sentence now:");
  gotoxy(1, 17);
  t1 = time(NULL);
  gets(buffer);
  t2 = time(NULL);
  gotoxy(1, 24);
  if (strcmp(buffer, s) != 0)
    puts("ERROR: Mistakes in typing detected.");
  printf("Typing time == %.1f seconds.\n", difftime(t2, t1));
  return 0;
}
```

dup   Duplicate file handle

Syntax   `int dup(int handle);`

Include   IO.H

Description   Returns a new file handle based on `handle`. Typically used to flush an open file without having to close the file. To use `dup()` this way, first duplicate the file's handle; then close the duplicate, leaving the original handle open. If successful, function returns new file handle and if not successful, it returns -1.

Parameters   **int handle** Handle to open file such as returned by `open()`.

See also   `close, creat, creatnew, _dos_close, _dos_open, dup2, fflush,`
`flushall, fopen, open`

Example
```
/* dup.cpp */
#include <stdio.h>
#include <stdlib.h>
#include <dos.h>
#include <io.h>
#include <string.h>
main()
{
  int handle;     // Original file handle
  int duphandle;  // Duplicate handle
  unsigned num;   // Number of bytes written to disk
  char *fname = strdup(tmpnam(NULL));
  char buf[] = "Write me to disk, please!";
  if (_dos_creat(fname, _A_NORMAL, &handle) != 0) {
    perror(fname);
    exit(1);
  }
  printf("Writing to file %s\n", fname);
  if (_dos_write(handle, buf, strlen(buf), &num) != 0) {
    perror(fname);
    exit(2);
  }
  duphandle = dup(handle);   // Duplicate handle
  if (duphandle != -1)
    _dos_close(duphandle);   // Flush file to disk
  _dos_close(handle);        // File is still open
  return 0;
}
```

ecvt   Convert floating-point number to string

Syntax   `char *ecvt(double value, int ndig, int *dec, int *sign);`

Include   STDLIB.H

Description   Converts specified `double value` to a null-terminated string. Returns address of static buffer, which is overwritten on subsequent function calls. To preserve the returned string, use `strcpy()` or another string function to copy the characters to another location. The same static string buffer is also used (and overwritten) by `fcvt()`.

Parameters   **double value** Floating-point value to convert.

int ndig Number of digit characters desired in the result.

int *dec Pointer to integer, in which ecvt() stores the relative position of the decimal point. (The resulting string does *not* contain a decimal-point character.) A negative value indicates a decimal point to the left of the string's first digit.

int *sign Function sets this integer to zero if value is positive or zero. Sets *sign to nonzero if value is negative.

See also   atof, fcvt, gcvt, sprintf

Example
```
/* ecvt.cpp */
#include <stdio.h>
#include <stdlib.h>
#include <math.h>
#include <string.h>
main()
{
  double value = M_PI;
  char *result;
  int decimal, sign;
  result = strdup(ecvt(value, 10, &decimal, &sign));
  printf("Orignal value == %f\n", value);
  printf("Result string == %s\n", result);
  printf(" decimal      == %d\n", decimal);
  printf(" sign         == %d\n", sign);
  return 0;
}
```

eof   End of file

Syntax   int eof(int handle);

Include   IO.H

Description   Returns true (1) if the file identified by handle is positioned at the file's end. Returns false (0) if the file is not at its end. Returns -1 if an error occurs, and sets errno to EBADF (bad file number).

Parameters   **int handle** Open file handle, such as returned by open().

See also   clearerr, close, feof, ferror, open, perror, read, write

Example
```
/* eof.cpp */
#include <stdio.h>
#include <stdlib.h>
#include <io.h>
main(int argc, char *argv[])
{
  FILE *fp;     // File stream
  int handle;   // Handle to same file
```

```
     char c;        // For reading file content
     if (argc <= 1) {
       puts("No file specified");
       exit(1);
     }
     fp = fopen(argv[1], "r");
     if (!fp)
       perror(argv[1]);
     else {
       handle = fileno(fp);
       do {
         read(handle, &c, 1);    // Read a character
         putchar(c);             // Write to stdout
       } while (!eof(handle));
       fclose(fp);
     }
     return 0;
   }
```

exit   Exit program

Syntax   void exit(int status);

Include   STDLIB.H

Description   Terminates program immediately. Closes any open files, flushes any
                    modified output buffers to disk, and executes any exit functions
                    installed by atexit().

Parameters   **int status** Value to pass back to DOS COMMAND.COM (or to
                    another parent process). Available via DOS errorlevel variable.
                    Note: The example's filename is EXITX.CPP, which avoids a
                    conflict with the DOS EXIT command.

See also   abort, atexit, _exit, keep

Example
```
/* exitx.cpp */
#include <stdio.h>
#include <stdlib.h>
main(int argc, char *argv[])
{
  int i;
  if (argc <= 1) {
    puts("No arguments entered");
    exit(1);
  }
  for (i = 0; i < argc; i++)
    puts(argv[i]);
  return 0;
}
```

fclose   Close stream

Syntax   `int fclose(FILE *stream);`

Include   STDIO.H

Description   Closes an open file stream, such as returned by `fopen()`. If the stream was opened for writing, any modified data held in memory is flushed to disk before closing the file. After closing a file, its `FILE *` value is no longer valid, and must not be used. Returns zero for success; `EOF` for failure.

Parameters   **`FILE *stream`** File stream previously opened by `fopen()` or a similar function.

See also   `close, fcloseall, fdopen, fflush, flushall, fopen, freopen`

Example
```
/* fclose.cpp */
#include <stdio.h>
#include <stdlib.h>
main(int argc, char *argv[])
{
  FILE *fp;
  char buffer[256];
  if (argc <= 1) {
    puts("No file specified");
    exit(1);
  }
  fp = fopen(argv[1], "r");
  if (!fp)
    puts("Error opening file");
  else {
    while (fgets(buffer, 255, fp) != NULL)
      fputs(buffer, stdout);
    fclose(fp);
  }
  return 0;
}
```

fcloseall   Close open streams

Syntax   `int fcloseall(void);`

Include   STDIO.H

Description   Closes all open `FILE *` streams, but not standard I/O files `stdin`, `stdout`, `stdprn`, `stderr`, or `stdaux`. Returns number of streams closed, or `EOF` if an error was detected.

See also   `fclose, flushall, fopen, freopen`

Example   See `_exit`.

835

fdopen   Associate stream with handle

Syntax   `FILE *fdopen(int handle, char *type);`

Include   STDIO.H

Description   Returns a `FILE *` stream for an open file handle such as returned by `creat()`, `dup()`, `dup2()`, or `open()`. Returns null if the file cannot be opened as a stream.

Parameters   `int handle` An open file handle.

                     `char *type` File mode string, identical to `fopen()` mode strings. The specified mode must match the file identified by `handle`. For example, the string `"w"` opens the file for writing. Add `"t"` to a mode string (`"wt"` for instance) to specify text mode; add `"b"` as in `"wb"` for binary mode. In the absence of `"t"` or `"b"`, the file mode is governed by global variable `_fmode`. See `fopen()` for specific string.

See also   `_dos_open, fclose, fopen, freopen, open`

Example
```
/* fdopen.cpp */
#include <stdio.h>
#include <stdlib.h>
#include <io.h>
#include <sys\stat.h>
#include <fcntl.h>
main(int argc, char *argv[])
{
  int handle;  // File handle
  FILE *fp;    // Same file as a stream
  char buffer[256];
  if (argc <= 1) {
    puts("No file specified");
    exit(1);
  }
  handle = open(argv[1], O_RDONLY | O_TEXT, S_IREAD);
  if (handle == NULL)
    puts("Error opening file");
  else {
    fp = fdopen(handle, "rt");  // handle to stream
    while (fgets(buffer, 255, fp) != NULL)
      fputs(buffer, stdout);
  }
  close(handle);
  return 0;
}
```

feof   End of file stream

Syntax   `int feof(FILE *stream);`

Include   STDIO.H

Description   Returns true (nonzero) if the specified file stream's internal pointer
is positioned beyond the file's last byte, usually due to a preceding
I/O operation on the stream. Returns false if the file's internal
pointer is not at the end of the file. Implemented as a macro.

Parameters   **FILE *stream** Any open file stream, such as returned by `fopen()`.

See also   clearerr, eof, ferror, fopen, rewind

Example
```
/* feof.cpp */
#include <stdio.h>
#include <stdlib.h>
main(int argc, char *argv[])
{
  FILE *fp;            // File stream
  char buffer[128];    // For reading text lines
  if (argc <= 1) {
    puts("No file specified");
    exit(1);
  }
  fp = fopen(argv[1], "r");
  if (!fp)
    perror(argv[1]);
  else {
    while (!feof(fp))
      if (fgets(buffer, 255, fp) != NULL)
        fputs(buffer, stdout);
    fclose(fp);
  }
  return 0;
}
```

ferror   Stream error

Syntax   `int ferror(FILE *stream);`

Include   STDIO.H

Description   Returns true (nonzero) if any errors have occurred for the specified
stream. Returns false (zero) if no errors have been detected.

Parameters   **FILE *stream** Any open file stream, such as returned by `fopen()`.

See also   clearerr, eof, feof, fopen, perror, rewind

Example
```
/* ferror.cpp */
#include <stdio.h>
#include <stdlib.h>
#define FNAME "FERROR.CPP"
main()
{
  FILE *fp;
  puts("Opening FERROR.CPP for reading");
  fp = fopen(FNAME, "r");
  if (!fp) {
```

```
    puts("Can't open "FNAME);
    exit(1);
  }
  puts("Attempting to write to file");
  fputs("Force file error", fp);
  if (ferror(fp))
    puts("File stream error detected!");
  fclose(fp);
  return 0;
}
```

fflush   Flush stream

Syntax   `int fflush(FILE *stream);`

Include   STDIO.H

Description   Writes any modified file buffers to disk for the specified stream. Does not close the file. Call this function periodically in any program that keeps output files open for long periods of time. After calling `fflush()`, the file and any in-memory buffers are "in synch."

Parameters   **FILE *stream** Any open file stream, such as returned by `fopen()`.

See also   fclose, flushall, fwrite, setbuf, setvbuf

Example
```
/* fflush.cpp */
#include <stdio.h>
#include <stdlib.h>
#include <string.h>
#include <conio.h>
main()
{
  FILE *inpf, *outf;
char buffer[255];
  char *fname = strdup(tmpnam(NULL));
  outf = fopen(fname, "w"); // Create temporary file
  inpf = fopen("FFLUSH.CPP", "r"); // Open this file
  if (!(inpf || outf)) {
    puts("Error opening files");
    exit(1);
  }
  printf("Writing to %s", fname);
  while (fgets(buffer, 255, inpf) != NULL)
    fputs(buffer, outf);
  printf("\nPress Enter to flush output file");
  getch();
  fflush(outf);
  printf("\nFile is flushed. Closing file.");
  fclose(outf);
  fclose(inpf);
  printf("\nList file %s then delete.", fname);
  return 0;
}
```

fgetc   Get character

Syntax   `int fgetc(FILE *stream);`

Include   STDIO.H

Description   Reads one character from specified stream. Returns character value if successful. Returns EOF if the file's internal pointer is positioned beyond the end of the file. Also returns EOF if any errors are detected.

Parameters   `FILE *stream` Any open file stream, such as returned by fopen(), opened for reading in a text mode.

See also   `fgetchar, fputc, fputs, fread, fwrite, perror`

Example
```
/* fgetc.cpp */
#include <stdio.h>
#include <stdlib.h>
main(int argc, char *argv[])
{
  FILE *fp;  // File stream
  int c;     // Holds each char from file
  if (argc <= 1) {
    puts("No file specified");
    exit(1);
  }
  fp = fopen(argv[1], "r");
  if (!fp)
    puts("Error opening file");
  else {
    while ((c = fgetc(fp)) != EOF)
      fputc(c, stdout);
    fclose(fp);
  }
  return 0;
}
```

fgetchar   Get character

Syntax   `int fgetchar(void);`

Include   STDIO.H

Description   Reads one character from the standard input file stdin. Equivalent to fgetc(stdin). Returns character or EOF if the file pointer is positioned beyond its end, or if an error occurs.

See also   `fgetc, fputchar, getchar`

Example
```
/* fgetchar.cpp */
#include <stdio.h>
#include <stdlib.h>
```

```
#include <string.h>
main()
{
  FILE *fp;  // File stream
  char *fname = strdup(tmpnam(NULL));
  int c;      // Holds characters written to disk
  fp = fopen(fname, "w");  // Create new file
  if (!fp)
    puts("Error writing to file");
  else {
    printf("%s created. Enter text to store in\n", fname);
    printf("file. Press Ctrl+Z and Enter to end.\n");
    while ((c = fgetchar()) != EOF)
      fputc(c, fp);
    fclose(fp);
    printf("\nList %s to see results.\n", fname);
    puts("You may delete this file.");
  }
  return 0;
}
```

fgetpos   Get file pointer

Syntax   `int fgetpos(FILE *stream, fpos_t *pos);`

Include   STDIO.H

Description   Copies the specified file's data pointer to the `fpos_t` variable
                  addressed by `pos`. This value represents the offset in bytes from the
                  beginning of the file to the location where the next I/O operation
                  would take place. Identifier `fpos_t` is defined in Borland C++ as a
                  `typedef` alias for `long`. The function returns zero for success, -1 for
                  failure, and sets `errno` to EBADF (bad file number). The Borland
                  C++ Library Reference specifies error EINVAL (invalid argument),
                  but this error code is rarely seen.

Parameters   `FILE *stream` Any open file stream, such as returned by `fopen()`.

                  `fpos_t *pos` Pointer to a `fpos_t` variable to hold the file's internal
                  pointer.

See also   fseek, fsetpos, ftell, lseek, tell

Example
```
/* fgetpos.cpp */
#include <stdio.h>
#include <stdlib.h>
#define FNAME "FGETPOS.CPP"
void Report(FILE *f, const char *message);
main()
{
  FILE *fp = fopen(FNAME, "r");
  char buffer[256];
  if (!fp) {
    puts("Error opening "FNAME);
```

```
      exit(1);
    }
    Report(fp, "Before reading file");
    fgets(buffer, 255, fp);
    Report(fp, "After reading file");
    fclose(fp);
    return 0;
}

void Report(FILE *f, const char *message)
{
  fpos_t pos;
  puts(message);
  if (fgetpos(f, &pos) != 0) {
    puts("Error accessing file");
    fclose(f);
    exit(1);
  }
  printf(" File position == %ld\n", pos);
}
```

fgets   Get string

Syntax   `char *fgets(char *s, int n, FILE *stream);`

Include   STDIO.H

Description   Reads characters up to and including the next newline character or
at most `n` - `1`. Other characters form a file stream to the location
addressed by `char *s`. Appends a newline character if read plus a
null character to the end of the string. Returns `char *s` for success
and null for failure.

Parameters   `char *s` Pointer to `char` buffer at least `n` bytes long.

`int n` Maximum number of characters including a terminating null
to read into the location addressed by `s`.

`FILE *stream` Any open file stream, such as returned by `fopen()`,
opened for reading in a text mode.

See also   `cgets, fputs, gets`

Example   See `fclose`.

filelength   Get file size

Syntax   `long filelength(int handle);`

Include   IO.H

Description   Returns the size of a file in bytes, or -1 if there is an error.

Parameters   `int handle` File handle such as returned by `open()`.

See also   fopen, lseek, open

Example

```
/* fileleng.cpp */
#include <stdio.h>
#include <stdlib.h>
#include <io.h>
#include <fcntl.h>
main(int argc, char *argv[])
{
  int handle;
  long flen;
  if (argc <= 1) {
    puts("Enter file name to find length\n");
    exit(1);
  }
  handle = open(argv[1], O_RDONLY | O_BINARY);
  if (handle < 0) {
    perror(argv[1]);
    exit(1);
  }
  flen = filelength(handle);
  printf("%s is %ld bytes long.\n", argv[1], flen);
  close(handle);
  return 0;
}
```

fileno   Convert file stream to handle

Syntax   int fileno(FILE *stream);

Include   STDIO.H

Description   Returns a handle for a file stream. Use this function to convert a stream for functions that require a handle.

Parameters   **FILE *stream** Pointer to open file stream.

See also   fdopen, fopen, freopen, open

Example

```
/* fileno.cpp */
#include <stdio.h>
#include <io.h>
char buffer[] = "Write me to stderr using a handle\n";
main()
{
  int handle = fileno(stderr);
  write(handle, &buffer, sizeof(buffer));
  return 0;
}
```

findfirst   Search directory

Syntax   int findfirst(const char *pathname, struct ffblk *ffblk,
                ➥int attrib);

Include	DIR.H, DOS.H
Description	Begins the directory search. Calls DOS function `0x4e`. Returns zero if successful, or -1 if an error is detected or if no files are found.
Parameters	`const char *pathname` Pointer to a path string, which may contain wild card characters `'*'` and `'?'`.
	`struct ffblk *ffblk` Pointer to `ffblk` structure, which may be passed to `findnext()` to continue searching for additional matching files.
	`int attrib` Logical-OR combination of any of the `FA_xxxx` constants declared in DOS.H.
See also	`_dos_findfirst, findnext`
Example	

```
/* findfirs.cpp */
#include <stdio.h>
#include <string.h>
#include <dir.h>
#include <dos.h>
main(int argc, char *argv[])
{
  struct ffblk fb;
  char *path = "*.*";
  int done;
  if (argc > 1)
    path = strdup(argv[1]);
  done = findfirst(path, &fb, FA_NORMAL);
  while (done == 0) {
    puts(fb.ff_name);
    done = findnext(&fb);
  }
  return 0;
}
```

findnext   Continue directory search

Syntax	`int findnext(struct ffblk *ffblk);`
Include	DIR.H
Description	After successfully calling `findfirst()`, you may call `findnext()` to continue searching for additional files. Returns 0 if successful, or -1 if an error is detected or if there are no more matching files.
Parameters	`struct ffblk *ffblk` Pointer to `ffblk` structure filled in by preceding call to `findfirst()`.
See also	`_dos_findnext, findfirst`
Example	See `findfirst`.

flushall   Flush all streams

Syntax   `int flushall(void);`

Include   STDIO.H

Description   Flushes all open file streams, writing to disk any modified data held
in memory buffers. Database applications can call `flushall()`
periodically in the program's main menu loop to ensure that all file
data is written to disk. Leaves file streams open. Returns the current
number of active I/O file streams.

See also   `fclose, fcloseall, fflush, fopen, fwrite`

Example
```
/* flushall.cpp */
#include <stdio.h>
#include <stdlib.h>
#include <string.h>
#include <conio.h>
main()
{
  FILE *inpf, *outf;
  char buffer[255];
 char *fname = strdup(tmpnam(NULL));
 outf = fopen(fname, "w");  // Create temporary file
  inpf = fopen("FLUSHALL.CPP", "r"); // Open this file
  if (!(inpf ¦¦ outf)) {
    puts("Error opening files");
    exit(1);
  }
  printf("Writing to %s", fname);
  while (fgets(buffer, 255, inpf) != NULL)
    fputs(buffer, outf);
  printf("\nPress Enter to flush all files");
  getch();
  flushall();
  printf("\nAll files are flushed.");
  fclose(outf);
  fclose(inpf);
  printf("\nList file %s then delete.", fname);
  return 0;
}
```

fnmerge   Build pathname

Syntax   `void fnmerge(char *path, const char *drive,`
`const char *dir,  const char *name, const char *ext);`

Include   DIR.H

Description   Concatenates the strings addressed by `drive`, `dir`, `name`, and `ext` char
pointers, storing the completed pathname at the location addressed
by `path`. Except for `path`, the component char pointers may be null

or they may address null strings, in which case that component is skipped. Adds a colon to the drive letter unless it is already followed by a colon. Appends a backslash to any directory name and prefaces an extension with a period if necessary. The maximum length of the resulting string, including a null terminator, is defined by the constant MAXPATH declared in DIR.H. (Currently, MAXPATH equals 80.)

Parameters   **char *path** Pointer to a buffer at least MAXPATH bytes long. The resulting path string is stored at this location.

const char *drive Pointer to a drive letter, which may optionally end with a colon.

const char *dir Pointer to one or more directory names, separated by single backslashes, and optionally beginning or ending with a backslash.

const char *name Pointer to a filename of no more than eight characters.

const char *ext Pointer to a file extension of no more than three characters plus an optional preceding period.

See also   fnsplit, _fullpath, _makepath

Example
```
/* fnmerge.cpp */
#include <stdio.h>
#include <dir.h>
main()
{
  char *drive = "C:";
  char *dir = "\\Bc5\\INCLUDE";
  char *name = "DOS";
  char *ext[H];
  char path[MAXPATH];
  fnmerge(path, drive, dir, name, ext);
  printf("Merged path = %s", path);
  return 0;
}
```

fnsplit   Parse pathname

Syntax   int fnsplit(const char *path, char *drive, char *dir, char *name, char *ext);

Include   DIR.H

Description   Separates the components of a pathname string into drive, directory, filename, and file extension. Use constants MAXDRIVE, MAXDIR, MAXPATH, MAXFILE, and MAXEXT, defined in DIR.H, to define char buffers of the correct sizes to hold the function's results. Returns coded `int` value, with bits corresponding to the constants WILDCARDS, EXTENSION, FILENAME, DIRECTORY, and DRIVE. Function results containing one or more of these bits set to one indicate the presence of that component in the original string.

Parameters **const char *path** Pointer to the pathname to be separated. Any missing components (for example, a missing drive letter) are ignored.

char *drive Pointer to string buffer at least MAXDRIVE bytes long. A drive letter and colon are stored at this location.

char *dir Pointer to string buffer at least MAXDIR bytes long. One or more directory names, separated by single backslashes, and beginning and ending with backslashes, are stored at this location.

char *name Pointer to a string buffer at least MAXFILE bytes long. A filename is stored at this location.

char *ext Pointer to a string buffer at least MAXEXT bytes long. A file extension preceded by a period is stored at this location.

See also fnmerge, _fullpath, _splitpath

Example
```
/* fnsplit.cpp */
#include <stdio.h>
#include <dir.h>
main()
{
  char *path = "C:\\bc5\\INCLUDE\\*.H";
  char drive[MAXDRIVE];
  char dir[MAXDIR];
  char name[MAXFILE];
  char ext[MAXEXT];
  int result;
  result = fnsplit(path, drive, dir, name, ext);
  puts("The original path is:");
  printf("  path  : %s\n", path);
  puts("The path's components are:");
  printf("  drive : %s\n", drive);
  printf("  dir   : %s\n", dir);
  printf("  name  : %s\n", name);
  printf("  ext   : %s\n", ext);
  if ((result && WILDCARDS) == WILDCARDS)
    puts("Wild cards detected in path");
  return 0;
}
```

fopen   Open file stream

Syntax FILE *fopen(const char *filename, const char *mode);

Include STDIO.H

Description   Opens an existing file or creates a new one. If it is successful, `fopen()` returns a FILE stream pointer that should be saved in a variable for use with other file functions. Any errors return null.

Parameters   `const char *filename` Pointer to a filename string that may contain drive and directory information, but may not contain any wild cards.

`const char *mode` A pointer to a string equal to one of the modes listed in the following table. Add t to any of these modes to access a text file. Add b for binary files. For example, the mode string `"rb"` opens a file for reading in binary mode. The mode string `"a+t"` opens a text file ready for appending new information to the end of the file. The mode string `"a+t"` is equivalent to `"at+"`.

`fopen()` mode strings.

Mode	Binary	Text	Use
`"r"`	`"rb"`	`"rt"`	Opens an existing file for reading.
`"w"`	`"wb"`	`"wt"`	Creates a new file for writing. Overwrites any existing file of the specified name.
`"a"`	`"ab"`	`"at"`	Opens a file for appending new information to the end of the file.
`"r+"`	`"r+b"`	`"r+t"`	Opens an existing file for reading and writing.
`"w+"`	`"w+b"`	`"w+t"`	Creates a new file for reading and writing. Overwrites any existing file of the specified name.
`"a+"`	`"a+b"`	`"a+t"`	Opens a file for appending new information to the end of the file. If the file does not exist, a new file is created of the specified name.

See also   `creat`, `fclose`, `ferror`, `fread`, `fseek`, `fwrite`, `open`, `perror`, `rewind`, `setbuf`, `setmode`, `strerror`

Example   See `fclose`.

fprintf   Write formatted output

Syntax   `int fprintf(FILE *stream, const char *format[, argument,` ➥`...]);`

Include   STDIO.H

Description Writes formatted text output to a file stream opened for writing or appending in text mode. Returns the number of bytes written to the stream. Returns EOF if any errors are detected. The format string and arguments are identical in format to those used by printf().

Parameters **FILE *stream** Pointer to a file stream such as that returned by fopen(). The function's output is written to this stream.

const char *format Pointer to a format string that may include literal text along with format specifiers prefaced with %, such as %d or &f. See printf() for more information on the many possible formats available.

argument, ... One argument for each format specifier in the format string. The argument's value is converted to text according to the format specifier and inserted into the output text.

See also cprintf, fscanf, fputc, fputs, printf, sprintf

Example
```
/* fprintf.cpp */
#include <stdio.h>
#include <dos.h>
main()
{
  double d = 3.14159;
  char *s = "A string";
  long v = 1234567;
  fprintf(stdout, "Double value == %lf\n", d);
  fprintf(stdout, "String value == %s\n", s);
  fprintf(stdout, "Long value == %ld\n", v);
  fprintf(stdout, "Address of v == %#04x:%#04x\n",
    FP_SEG(&v), FP_OFF(&v));
  return 0;
}
```

fputc   Write character to a stream

Syntax int fputc(int c, FILE *stream);

Include STDIO.H

Description Writes a single character to the specified stream. Returns the value of c for success and EOF for failure.

Parameters **int c** The character value to write.

FILE *stream A stream pointer such as that returned by fopen(). The character is written to this stream.

See also fgetc, fputchar, fputs, putc

Example See fgetc.

fputchar   Put character on stdout

Syntax   `int fputchar(int c);`

Include   STDIO.H

Description   Writes a single character to `stdout`. Returns the value of `c` for success and `EOF` for failure. Defined as `fputc(c, stdout)`.

Parameters   `int c` The character value to write.

See also   `fgetchar, fputc, fputs, putchar`

Example
```
/* fputchar.cpp */
#include <stdio.h>
main()
{
  int c;
  puts("Display the alphabet");
  for (c = 'A'; c <= 'Z'; c++)
    fputchar(c);
  return 0;
}
```

fputs   Put string on stream

Syntax   `int fputs(const char *s, FILE *stream);`

Include   STDIO.H

Description   Writes a null-terminated string of characters to the specified stream. Returns nonnegative value for success and `EOF` for failure.

Parameters   `const char *s` Pointer to a null-terminated string to write to the output stream.

                `FILE *stream` Pointer to a file stream such as that returned by `fopen()`.

See also   `fgets, fprintf, fputc, gets, puts`

Example   See `fclose`.

fread   Read data from stream

Syntax   `size_t fread(void *ptr, size_t size, size_t n, FILE *stream);`

Include   STDIO.H

Description   Reads data from a file stream starting at the current file pointer. After reading data, `fread()` leaves the file pointer positioned after the last byte read. You may call `fseek()` to position the file pointer before reading. `fread()` returns the number of items read. The number of bytes read equals the function result times the number of bytes per item. Returns zero if unsuccessful or if the file pointer is at the end of the file.

Parameters

`void *ptr` Pointer to a destination buffer. Function transfers bytes from the file stream to this location, which must be large enough to hold the requested data.

`size_t size` The size in bytes of one item to be read from the file stream.

`size_t n` The number of items to read.

`FILE *stream` A pointer to an open file stream such as that returned by `fopen()`.

See also

`fopen, fwrite, fprintf, fseek`

Example

```
/* fread.cpp */
#include <stdio.h>
#include <stdlib.h>
int array[100];  // Array of 100 ints equal to zero
main()
{
// Create temporary file in "w+b" mode
  FILE *tempf = tmpfile();
  if (!tempf) {
    perror("Can't open temporary file");
    exit(1);
  }
// Write 100 integers to file
  for (int index = 0; index < 100; index++)
    fwrite(&index, sizeof(int), 1, tempf);
// Read integers into array
  rewind(tempf);
  fread(&array, sizeof(int), 100, tempf);
  puts("Array after reading from disk");
  for (index = 0; index < 100; index++)
    printf("%8d", array[index]);
  rmtmp();  // Close and erase temporary file
  return 0;
}
```

free   Free allocated block

Syntax

`void free(void *block);`

Include

ALLOC.H

Description

Frees a block of memory previously allocated by `malloc()`, `calloc()`, or a similar memory allocator. The memory is returned to the heap for use by subsequent memory requests. After freeing a block, a program must not use that memory.

Parameters   **void *block** Pointer to memory block to be freed. After being passed to free(), the pointer must not be used except to hold the address of freshly allocated memory.

See also   calloc, freemem, malloc, realloc, strdup

Example

```
/* free.cpp */
#include <stdio.h>
#include <stdlib.h>
#include <string.h>
main()
{
  char *original = "An original string";
  char *copy;  // Pointer to copy of original string
// Allocate memory to hold copy of original string
  copy = (char *)malloc(strlen(original) + 1);
  if (copy == NULL) {
    puts("Error allocating memory");
    exit(1);
  }
  strcpy(copy, original);  // Transfer original to copy
  strupr(copy);  // Convert copy to uppercase
  printf("Original == %s\n", original);
  printf("Copy     == %s\n", copy);
  free(copy);  // Free memory occupied by copy of string
  return 0;
}
```

freopen   Associate new file with stream

Syntax   FILE *freopen(const char *filename, const char *mode, FILE *stream);

Include   STDIO.H

Description   Closes a currently open file stream and associates that stream with a new named file. Typically used to redirect stdin, stdout, and stderr streams.

Parameters   **const char *filename** Pointer to the new filename string to be associated with the file stream.

const char *mode Pointer to one of the mode strings listed in the description of fopen(). This is the mode to be used for the newly opened file.

FILE *stream The open file stream to be associated with a new named file.

See also   fclose, fopen

Example

```
/* freopen.cpp */
#include <stdio.h>
```

```
#include <stdlib.h>
#include <string.h>
main()
{
  FILE *outf;
  char *fname = strdup(tmpnam(NULL));
// Redirect stderr to temporary output file
  outf = freopen(fname, "w", stderr);
  if (outf == NULL) {
    puts("Error opening temporary file");
    exit(1);
  }
  fputs("Simulated error message\n", stderr);
  fputs("written to file via stderr.\n", stderr);
  fclose(outf);
  printf("\nList file %s then delete.\n", fname);
  return 0;
}
```

fscanf Scan and format stream input

Syntax   `int fscanf(FILE *stream, const char *format[,address, ...]);`

Include   STDIO.H

Description Reads text from a stream, converting data to binary according to format specifiers embedded in the format string. Values are transferred to the locations specified by the address arguments.

Parameters **FILE *stream** Pointer to open a file stream such as that returned by fopen(). Characters are read from this stream.

const char *format Pointer to a format string that should include one or more format specifiers preceded by %. See scanf() for more information about the allowable specifiers.

address, ... One address pointer for each format specifier. Data is converted from text to binary, and stored in these locations, which must be large enough to hold the expected values.

See also   atof, fprintf, scanf, sscanf, vfscanf, vscanf, vsscanf

Example
```
/* fscanf.cpp */
#include <stdio.h>
main()
{
  double v;
  puts("Enter a floating point value");
  fscanf(stdin, "%lf", &v);  // Note address-of operator!
  printf("Value == %lf\n", v);
  return 0;
}
```

fseek   Reposition file pointer

Syntax   `int fseek(FILE *stream, long offset, int whence);`

Include   STDIO.H

Description Moves a file stream's internal pointer, thus affecting the location of a subsequent read or write operation on the file. Returns zero for success and nonzero for failure.

Parameters **FILE *stream** Pointer to an open file stream such as that returned by `fopen()`.

long offset For binary files, this is the number of bytes to move the file pointer in the direction indicated by `whence`. For text files, this value must be zero or a value returned by `ftell()`. Set `offset` to a negative value to move the file pointer backwards (toward the beginning of the file).

int whence Set to SEEK_SET to move the file pointer `offset` bytes from the beginning of the file. Set to SEEK_CUR to move the file pointer relative to its current position. Set to SEEK_END to move the file pointer a specified number of bytes from the end of the file.

See also   `fgetpos, fopen, fsetpos, ftell, lseek, rewind, tell`

Example
```
/* fseek.cpp ( <- 'p' is 12th character ) */
#include <stdio.h>
#include <stdlib.h>
main()
{
  FILE *inf;
  char c;
// Open text file in binary mode
  inf = fopen("FSEEK.CPP", "rb");
  if (inf == NULL) {
    perror("Unable to open FSEEK.CPP");
    exit(1);
  }
// Seek to 12th byte from file beginning
  if (fseek(inf, 11, SEEK_SET) != 0)
    perror("Error during file seek");
  else {
    fread(&c, 1, 1, inf);
    printf("12th character == %c", c);
  }
  fclose(inf);
  return 0;
}
```

fsetpos   Position file pointer

Syntax   `int fsetpos(FILE *stream, const fpos_t *pos);`

Include   STDIO.H

Description   Restores a file stream's internal pointer to the position returned by a preceding call to `fgetpos()`. Returns zero for success and nonzero for failure.

Parameters   **FILE *stream** Pointer to a file stream such as that returned by `fopen()`.

const fpos_t *pos Pointer to an fpos_t structure prepared by a preceding call to `fgetpos()`.

See also   fgetpos, fseek, ftell, ungetc

Example
```
/* fsetpos.cpp */
#include <stdio.h>
main()
{
  FILE *inf;   // Input file stream
  fpos_t pos;  // File position
  char buffer[128];
  inf = fopen("FSETPOS.CPP", "rb");
  fgets(buffer, 128, inf);
  printf("First string == %s\n", buffer);
  fgetpos(inf, &pos);  // Save current position
  fgets(buffer, 128, inf);
  printf("Second string == %s\n", buffer);
  fsetpos(inf, &pos);  // Restore saved position
  fgets(buffer, 128, inf);
  printf("String after fsetpos == %s\n", buffer);
  fclose(inf);
  return 0;
}
```

fstat   File status

Syntax   `int fstat(int handle, struct stat *statbuf);`

Include   SYS\STAT.H

Description   Use this function to find out information about a file identified by a handle. Returns 0 for success and -1 for failure. Facts about the file are stored in a stat structure, declared in SYS\STAT.H as

```
struct stat
{
  short st_dev;     // Drive number or handle for device (for
                    // example, PRN)
  short st_ino;     // Unused
  short st_mode;    // Mode bit mask using S_xxxx constants
```

```
        short st_nlink;  // Always equal to 1
        int   st_uid;    // Unused
        int   st_gid;    // Unused
        short st_rdev;   // Identical to st_dev
        long  st_size;   // Size of file in bytes (0 for devices)
        long  st_atime;  // Time of most recent file change in
                         // seconds from 1970
        long  st_mtime;  // Identical to st_atime
        long  st_ctime;  // Identical to st_atime
      };
```

Parameters   **int handle** Handle of an open file such as that returned by open().

struct stat *statbuf Pointer to stat structure as listed in Description.

See also   access, chmod, stat

Example

```
/* fstat.cpp */
#include <stdio.h>
#include <stdlib.h>
#include <sys\stat.h>
#include <io.h>
#include <fcntl.h>
#include <time.h>
main(int argc, char *argv[])
{
  char *fname;
  struct stat statbuf;
  int handle, result;
  if (argc <= 1) {
    puts("No file specified");
    exit(1);
  }
  fname = argv[1];
  handle = open(fname, O_RDONLY | O_TEXT);
  if (handle == NULL) {
    perror(fname);
    exit(1);
  }
// Get info about open file associated with handle
  result = fstat(handle, &statbuf);
  if (result != 0) {
    printf("Error getting stats for %s\n", fname);
    exit(1);
  }
  printf("Information about %s\n", fname);
  printf("Drive number  : %d\n", statbuf.st_dev);
  printf("Size in bytes : %ld\n", statbuf.st_size);
  printf("Was updated   : %s\n", ctime(&statbuf.st_atime));
  close(handle);
 return 0;
}
```

ftell   Get file pointer

Syntax   `long int ftell(FILE *stream);`

Include   STDIO.H

Description   Returns a file stream's internal pointer, equal to the offset in bytes from the beginning of a binary file to the byte affected by the next I/O operation. This value can be passed to `fseek()`, for example, to position the file pointer a certain number of bytes ahead or back. You may also use `ftell()` on text files, but the value returned does not necessarily represent a byte offset into the file.

Parameters   **FILE *stream** Pointer to an open file stream such as that returned by `fopen()`.

See also   `fgetpos, fopen, fseek, fsetpos, lseek, rewind, tell`

Example
```
/* ftell.cpp */
#include <stdio.h>
main()
{
  FILE *inf;  // Input file stream
  long pos;   // File position
  char buffer[128];
  inf = fopen("FTELL.CPP", "rb");
  fgets(buffer, 128, inf);  // Read first line of file
  printf("First string  == %s\n", buffer);
  pos = ftell(inf);
  printf("File position == %ld\n", pos);
  rewind(inf);
  pos = ftell(inf);
  printf("Position after rewind == %ld\n", pos);
  fclose(inf);
  return 0;
}
```

fwrite   Write data to stream

Syntax   `size_t fwrite(const void *ptr, size_t size, size_t n,FILE *stream);`

Include   STDIO.H

Description   Writes one or more bytes to a file stream opened in binary mode. For writing to text files, use `fprintf()`, `fputc()`, `fputs()`, or a similar function. Returns the number of items written. The number of bytes written equals the function result times `size`.

Parameters   **const void *ptr** Pointer to source data to be written to the file.

size_t size The size in bytes of one data item.

size_t n The number of data items, each having size bytes, to be written to the file.

FILE *stream Pointer to a file stream opened in binary mode.

See also   fopen, fprintf, fputc, fputs, fread

Example   See fread.

gcvt   Convert floating point to string

Syntax   char *gcvt(double value, int ndec, char *buf);

Include   STDLIB.H

Description   Using the same internal programming as printf() and similar functions that can output double floating-point values in ASCII, gcvt() converts a double value to a null-terminated ASCII string and returns buf. The result, stored at the location addressed by buf, has ndec decimal places in FORTRAN F format:

[+/-] [zeros] [digit...] ['.'] [digit...]

Or if that format cannot accurately represent value, the result is in printf() E style (that is, scientific notation):

[+/-] digit ['.'] [digit...] 'E' sign [digit...]

Parameters   **double value** Floating-point value to convert to ASCII.

int ndec Number of requested decimal places. The result is not guaranteed to have this many digits after the decimal point. A maximum of 18 digits may be requested.

char *buf Pointer to character buffer to hold the result. Allow plenty of space and, after calling gcvt(), use strdup() or a similar string function to trim the result.

See also   ecvt, fcvt, printf, sprintf

Example
```
/* gcvt.cpp */
#include <stdio.h>
#include <stdlib.h>
#include <math.h>
#include <string.h>
#define NDEC 6  // Number of decimal places
main()
{
  double value = M_PI;
  char buffer[128];  // Temporary buffer
  char *copy;  // Pointer to result
  gcvt(value, NDEC, buffer);
// Copy raw string in buffer to heap
```

```
    copy = strdup(buffer);
    if (copy == NULL) {
      puts("Error copying string");
      exit(1);
    }
    printf("Original value == %lf\n", value);
    printf("String == %s\n", copy);
    printf("Length == %d chars\n", strlen(copy));
    free(copy);
    return 0;
  }
```

getc   Get character from stream

Syntax	`int getc(FILE *stream);`
Include	STDIO.H
Description	Returns next character (if any) from the specified input stream. When reading from `stdin`, users must press Enter after typing a character. Returns EOF for an end-of-file error.
Parameters	**FILE *stream** Any file stream opened in text mode for reading.
See also	`fgetc, getch, getchar, getche, gets, putc, putchar, puts, ungetc`
Example	

```
/* getc.cpp */
#include <stdio.h>
main()
{
  char c;
  printf("Input a character: ");
  c = getc(stdin);
  printf("\nCharacter == %c", c);
  printf("\nASCII hex == %#x", c);
  printf("\nASCII dec == %d\n", c);
  return 0;
}
```

getchar   Get character from stdin

Syntax	`int getchar(void);`
Include	STDIO.H
Description	Returns a character value (if any) from `stdin`, or EOF for an end-of-file error. Users must press Enter after typing a character. Implemented as a macro.
See also	`fgetc, fgetchar, getc, getch, getche, gets, ungetc`
Example	

```
/* getchar.cpp */
#include <stdio.h>
```

```
main()
{
  char c;
  printf("Input a character: ");
  c = getchar();
  printf("\nCharacter == %c", c);
  printf("\nASCII hex == %#x", c);
  printf("\nASCII dec == %d\n", c);
  return 0;
}
```

getcurdir   Get current directory for drive

Syntax	`int getcurdir(int drive, char *directory);`
Include	DIR.H
Description	Stores the current directory pathname for any drive at the location addressed by `directory`. Returns 0 for success and -1 for failure.
Parameters	**`int drive`** Drive number. 0-current, 1-A:, 2-B:, and so on.
	`char *directory` Pointer to `char` buffer at least `MAXDIR` bytes long. Function stores current directory pathname at this location.
See also	`chdir, findfirst, findnext, _getdcwd, getcwd, getdisk, mkdir, rmdir`
Example	

```
/* getcurdi.cpp */
#include <stdio.h>
#include <dir.h>
main()
{
  char dir[MAXDIR];
  int cd = getcurdir(0, dir);
  if (cd == 0)
    printf("Current dir == %s\n", dir);
  else
    puts("Error reading current directory");
  return 0;
}
```

getcwd   Get current working directory

Syntax	`char *getcwd(char *buf, int buflen);`
Include	DIR.H
Description	Stores the current directory pathname for the current drive at the location addressed by `buf`. Returns `buf` or null for an error.
Parameters	**`char *buf`** Pointer to `char` buffer at least `buflen` bytes long, including room for the string's null terminator. May be set to null, in

which case `getcwd()` allocates and fills a buffer of `buflen` bytes. Call `free()` to delete this buffer.

int `buflen` Size of the destination buffer in bytes.

See also	`chdir, findfirst, findnext, getcurdir, getdisk, mkdir, rmdir`
Example	

```
/* getcwd.cpp */
#include <stdio.h>
#include <dir.h>
#include <alloc.h>
main()
{
  char *dp;
  dp = getcwd(NULL, MAXPATH);
  if (dp == NULL)
    puts("Error reading directory");
  else {
    printf("Current dir == %s", dp);
    free(dp);
  }
  return 0;
}
```

getdisk   Get current drive

Syntax	`int getdisk(void);`
Include	DIR.H
Description	Returns current disk drive number: 0 for drive A:, 1 for B:, 2 for C:, and so on. Functions `getdisk()` and `_getdrive()` both call `_dos_getdrive()`.
See also	`_dos_getdrive, getcurdir, getcwd, setdisk`
Example	

```
/* getdisk.cpp */
#include <stdio.h>
#include <dir.h>
main()
{
  int drive = getdisk();
  printf("Current drive == %c:\n", 'A' + drive);
  return 0;
}
```

getenv   Get environment string

Syntax	`char *getenv(const char *name);`
Include	STDLIB.H
Description	Returns a pointer to a specified environment variable, or null if the variable can't be found.

Parameters   `const char *name` Pointer to environment variable string—COMSPEC, for example. Function returns this variable's setting if found in the environment.

See also   exec, getpsp, putenv

Example   See exec.

getftime   Get file date and time

Syntax   `int getftime(int handle, struct ftime *ftimep);`

Include   IO.H

Description   Gets a file's date and time as listed in the directory. Returns zero for success and -1 for failure. Fills an `ftime` bit-field structure declared in io.h as

```
struct ftime {
  unsigned ft_tsec  : 5;  // Seconds in two-second intervals
  unsigned ft_min   : 6;  // Minute
  unsigned ft_hour  : 5;  // Hour
  unsigned ft_day   : 5;  // Day
  unsigned ft_month : 4;  // Month
  unsigned ft_year  : 7;  // Year
};
```

Parameters   `int handle` Opens a file handle such as that returned by `open()`.

                 `struct ftime *ftimep` Pointer to an `ftime` structure as listed in description.

See also   open, setftime

Example
```
/* getftime.cpp */
#include <stdio.h>
#include <stdlib.h>
#include <io.h>
main(int argc, char *argv[])
{
  FILE *f;
  ftime ft;
  if (argc <= 1) {
    puts("No filename specified");
    exit(1);
  }
  f = fopen(argv[1], "rb");
  if (!f) {
    printf("Can't open file %s\n", argv[1]);
    exit(2);
  }
  getftime(fileno(f), &ft);
  printf("%s %02d/%02d/%d %02d:%02d\n",
    argv[1], ft.ft_month, ft.ft_day, ft.ft_year,
    ft.ft_hour, ft.ft_min);
```

```
     fclose(f);
     return 0;
}
```

gets   Get string from stdin

Syntax   `char *gets(char *s);`

Include   STDIO.H

Description   Reads characters including whitespace from the standard input until receiving a newline character, which is replaced by null. Successive characters are stored at the location addressed by s. Returns s or null on end of file or any errors. There is no way to specify to gets() the maximum number of characters to read.

Parameters   **char *s** Addresses a buffer large enough to hold expected input. The resulting string is null-terminated.

See also   cgets, ferror, fgets, fopen, fputs, fread, getc, puts, scanf

Example
```
/* gets.cpp */
#include <stdio.h>
main()
{
  char buffer[128];
  printf("Enter a string: ");
  gets(buffer);
  printf("\nYour string is: %s\n", buffer);
  return 0;
}
```

getw   Get integer from stream

Syntax   `int getw(FILE *stream);`

Include   STDIO.H

Description   Gets the next binary integer word value from the specified stream. The file should be opened for reading in binary, not text, mode. Returns EOF on errors or end of file. However, because EOF's value is an integer, you must call feof() to detect an end-of-file condition, and ferror() to detect errors.

Parameters   **FILE *stream** Pointer to a file stream opened for reading in binary mode.

See also   fopen, fread, putw

Example
```
/* getw.cpp */
#include <stdio.h>
```

```
#include <stdlib.h>
main()
{
  FILE *f;
  int w;
  f = tmpfile();
  if (!f) {
    puts("Error opening temporary file");
    exit(1);
  }
  puts("Creating temporary file of 100 integers");
  for (w = 0; w < 100; w++)
    putw(w, f);
  rewind(f);
  puts("Reading temporary file");
  w = getw(f);
  while (!feof(f)) {
    printf("%8d", w);
    w = getw(f);
  }
  return 0;
}
```

gmtime   Greenwich mean time

Syntax

```
struct tm *gmtime(const time_t *timer);
```

Include

TIME.H

Description

Returns a pointer to a static tm structure with a specified local time in seconds from January 1, 1970 converted to Greenwich mean time (GMT). The tm structure, which is overwritten by each call to gmtime(), is declared in TIME.H.

Parameters

const time_t *timer A pointer to a time_t value, such as that returned by the time function. Borland C++ defines time_t as equivalent to long.

See also

asctime, ctime, ftime, localtime, stime, time, tzset

Example

See dostounix.

heapcheck   Check and verify heap

Syntax

```
int heapcheck(void);
```

Include

ALLOC.H

Description

Call heapcheck() to test the validity of allocated and freed memory blocks on the heap. Equivalent to farheapcheck() in large memory model programs. Returns _HEAPEMPTY (1) if there is no heap or _HEAPOK (2) if there is a heap and its memory blocks are verified to be error-free. Returns _HEAPCORRUPT (-1) if any errors are detected.

See also	farheapcheck, heapcheckfree, heapchecknode, heapfillfree, heapwalk
Example	See heapwalk.

heapcheckfree   Check heap free blocks

Syntax	int heapcheckfree(unsigned int fillvalue);
Include	ALLOC.H
Description	After calling heapfillfree() to fill all freed heap memory blocks to a specified value, call heapcheckfree() to verify the heap's stability. If heapcheckfree() returns _HEAPEMPTY (1), there is no heap. If the function returns _HEAPOK (2), then all freed blocks are verified. A return value of _HEAPCORRUPT (-1) indicates a serious error with the heap's structure. A value of _BADVALUE (-3) indicates that a value other than the specified fill value was found in a freed memory block.
Parameters	**unsigned int fillvalue** Value to be compared to values in freed memory blocks. Specify the same value as that passed to heapfillfree().
See also	farheapcheckfree, heapfillfree, heapwalk
Example	

```
/* heapchec.cpp */
#include <stdio.h>
#include <alloc.h>
void Report(const char *s, int result);
main()
{
  int result;
  void *p1 = malloc(1024);
  void *p2 = malloc(1024);
  void *p3 = malloc(1024);
  void *p4 = malloc(1024);
  void *p5 = malloc(1024);
  free(p2);
  free(p4);
  result = heapfillfree(0xffff);
  Report("After filling free blocks with 0xffff", result);
  result = heapcheckfree(0xffff);
  Report("After checking free blocks with 0xffff", result);
  result = heapcheckfree(0);
  Report("After checking free blocks with 0", result);
  free(p1);
  free(p3);
  free(p5);
  return 0;
}

void Report(const char *s, int result)
```

```
{
  printf("%s: ", s);
  switch (result) {
    case _HEAPEMPTY:
      puts("Heap empty");
      break;
    case _HEAPOK:
      puts("Heap is OK");
      break;
    case _HEAPCORRUPT:
      puts("Heap is corrupted");
      break;
    case _BADVALUE:
      puts("Bad value in heap");
      break;
  }
}
```

heapchecknode   Check and verify heap node

Syntax   `int heapchecknode(void *node);`

Include   ALLOC.H

Description Checks the validity of an allocated or freed memory block on the
              heap. Returns _HEAPEMPTY (1) if there is no heap, _HEAPCORRUPT (-1)
              if the heap is corrupted, _BADNODE (-2) if an error is detected in the
              target node or if that node has been deleted and combined with
              another deleted block, _FREEENTRY (3) if the block has been freed and
              no errors are detected, or _USEDENTRY (4) if the block is in use and no
              errors are detected. Note that in the case of a deleted node, a return
              value of _BADNODE does not necessarily indicate a corrupted heap, but
              rather that the memory manager has combined the deleted block
              with another adjacent block.

Parameters **void *node** Pointer to the memory block to be tested.

See also   `farheapchecknode`

Example
```
/* heapnode.cpp */
#include <stdio.h>
#include <alloc.h>
void Report(const char *s, int result);
main()
{
  int result;
  void *p1 = malloc(1024);
  void *p2 = malloc(1024);
  void *p3 = malloc(1024);
  result = heapchecknode(p2);
  Report("After malloc()", result);
  free(p2);
  result = heapchecknode(p2);
```

```
        Report("After free()", result);
        free(p1);
        free(p3);
        result = heapchecknode(p2);
        Report("After freeing all nodes", result);
        return 0;
    }

    void Report(const char *s, int result)
    {
        printf("%s: ", s);
        switch (result) {
          case _HEAPEMPTY:
            puts("Heap empty");
            break;
          case _HEAPCORRUPT:
            puts("Heap is corrupted");
            break;
          case _BADNODE:
            puts("Can't find node");
            break;
          case _FREEENTRY:
            puts("Free node");
            break;
          case _USEDENTRY:
            puts("Used node");
            break;
        }
    }
```

heapfillfree   Fill free heap blocks

Syntax	`int heapfillfree(unsigned int fillvalue);`
Include	ALLOC.H
Description	Fills freed memory blocks (if there are any) with a specified word value. Usually followed by a call to `heapcheckfree()` to verify values stored in freed memory blocks. Also can be used during debugging to make freed blocks easy to find by searching for byte values in memory. Returns `_HEAPEMPTY` (1) if there is no heap, `_HEAPOK` (2) if no errors are detected, or `_HEAPCORRUPT` (-1) if the heap is corrupted.
Parameters	**`unsigned int fillvalue`** Value to be stored in all freed memory blocks.
See also	`farheapfillfree, heapcheckfree`
Example	See `heapcheckfree`.

heapwalk   Access heap nodes

Syntax   `int heapwalk(struct heapinfo *hi);`

Include   ALLOC.H

Description Typically used in a loop to walk the heap by stepping through allocated and freed memory blocks in their linked-list order. Before calling `heapwalk()` for the first time, always call `heapcheck()` to verify that the heap is not corrupted. If `heapcheck()` does not return `_HEAPOK`, do *not* call `heapwalk()`. Returns `_HEAPEMPTY` (1) if there is no heap, `_HEAPOK` (2) if no errors are detected so far, or `_HEAPEND` (5) upon reaching the end of the heap. Fills in members of a `heapinfo` structure declared in ALLOC.H as

```
struct heapinfo
{
  void _FAR *ptr;      // Pointer to node or null
  unsigned int size;   // Size of node in bytes
  int in_use;          // True if allocated; false if freed
};
```

Parameters **struct heapinfo *hi** Pointer to a `heapinfo` structure as listed in description. Set `hi.ptr` to 0 (null) before the initial call to `heapwalk()`; thereafter, pass the same unmodified structure to `heapwalk()` until all blocks are located.

See also   `farheapwalk, heapcheck`

Example
```
/* heapwalk.cpp */
#include <stdio.h>
#include <alloc.h>
void Report(char *s);
long NearHeapSize(void);
main()
{
  void *p1;
  void *p2;
  Report("Before calling malloc()");
  p1 = malloc(1024);
  Report("After allocating 1024 bytes");
  p2 = malloc(1024);
  Report("After allocating another 1024 bytes");
  free(p1);
  Report("After freeing 1024 bytes");
  free(p2);
  Report("After freeing another 1024 bytes");
  return 0;
}

void Report(char *s)
```

867

```
{
  long result;
  puts(s);
  result = NearHeapSize();
  if (result < 0)
    puts("- No near heap or error!");
  else
    printf("- Near heap size = %lu\n", result);
}

// Walk heap and return free space available
long NearHeapSize(void)
{
  unsigned long count;
  struct heapinfo info;

  info.ptr = NULL;
  if (heapcheck() != _HEAPOK)
    return -1L;
  count = coreleft();
  while (heapwalk(&info) == _HEAPOK)
    if (info.in_use == 0)
      count += info.size;
  return count;
}
```

is...   Character classification macros

Syntax

```
int isalnum(int c);
int isalpha(int c);
int isasii(int c);
int iscntrl(intc);
int isdigit(int c);
int isgraph(int c);
int islower(int c);
int isprint(int c);
int ispunct(int c);
int isspace(int c);
int isupper(int c);
int isxdigit(int c);
```

Include   CTYPE.H

Description   These macros return nonzero (true) if character c is a member of a specified set of characters. The macros return zero (false) if the character is not a member of the specified set. The macros are table-driven and very fast. You can undefine one or more function names using #undef to encode them as nonmacro functions. The following table explains the purpose of each macro.

Character classification macros.

Function	Character c is...
isalnum	Alphanumeric (a digit or an uppercase or lowercase letter)
isalpha	Alphabetic (an uppercase or lowercase letter)
isascii	ASCII ($0 \leq c \leq 0x7e$)
iscntrl	ASCII control code (0x7f or 0x00 to 0x1f)
isdigit	A digit from 0 to 9
isgraph	Printable but nonspace ($0x21 \leq c \leq 0x7e$)
islower	A lowercase letter from a to z
isprint	Printable or space ($0x20 \leq c \leq 0x7e$)
ispunct	A punctuation symbol
isspace	A "whitespace" character: space, tab, carriage return, new line, vertical tab, or form feed
isupper	An uppercase letter from A to Z
isxdigit	A hexadecimal digit 0 to 9, A to F, or a to f

Parameters   `int c` The test character.

See also   `toascii, tolower, toupper`

Example
```
/* is.cpp */
#include <stdio.h>
#include <stdlib.h>
#include <ctype.h>
main(int argc, char *argv[])
{
  if (argc <= 1) {
    puts("Enter IS x to determine the");
    puts("nature of character x.");
    exit(1);
  }
  char c = argv[1][0];
  printf("Character %c is:\n", c);
  if (isalpha(c) ) puts("alphabetical");
  if (isascii(c) ) puts("ASCII");
  if (iscntrl(c) ) puts("a control");
  if (isdigit(c) ) puts("a digit");
  if (isgraph(c) ) puts("printable nonspace");
  if (islower(c) ) puts("lowercase");
  if (isprint(c) ) puts("printable including space");
  if (ispunct(c) ) puts("a punctuation mark");
  if (isspace(c) ) puts("a space");
  if (isupper(c) ) puts("uppercase");
  if (isxdigit(c)) puts("a hex digit");
  return 0;
}
```

26

isatty   Check for device type

Syntax   `int isatty(int handle);`

Include   IO.H

Description   Returns nonzero if the hardware device associated with a file handle is a terminal, a console, a printer, or a serial port. Returns zero if the device is none of these types.

Parameters   **`int handle`** File handle such as that returned by open(), or a standard file handle such as stdout.

See also   fileno, open

Example
```
/* isatty.cpp */
#include <stdio.h>
#include <io.h>
main()
{
  int handle = fileno(stdout);
  printf("Standard output (stdout) is ");
  if (!isatty(handle))
    puts("not");
  puts("\na terminal, console, printer, or serial device");
  return 0;
}
```

itoa   Convert integer to string

Syntax   `char *itoa(int value, char *string, int radix);`

Include   STDLIB.H

Description   Converts an int value to a null-terminated string. Returns a pointer to the resulting string.

Parameters   **`int value`** The value to be converted. If value is negative, a minus sign precedes the result only if radix equals 10.

`char *string` A pointer to a char buffer large enough to hold the result. Depending on the radix value, itoa() can return up to 17 bytes.

`int radix` The number base to use for the conversion, from 2 to 36.

See also   atoi, atol, ltoa, ultoa

Example
```
/* itoa.cpp */
#include <stdio.h>
#include <stdlib.h>
main()
{
```

```
        char result[17];
        int value = 23677;
        itoa(value, result, 10);
        printf("value in decimal == %s\n", result);
        itoa(value, result, 16);
        printf("value in hex      == %s\n", result);
        itoa(value, result, 2);
        printf("value in binary  == %s\n", result);
        return 0;
}
```

lfind Linear search

Syntax   void *lfind(const void *key, const void *base, size_t *num,
size_t width, int (*fcmp)(const void *, const void *));

Include   STDLIB.H

Description Searches a table of records using a comparison routine that you must
supply. The table does not have to be sorted. Returns the address of
the first matching record or null if the search key isn't found.

Parameters **const void *key** Pointer to the search key.

const void *base Pointer to the beginning of the table or another
location where the search is to begin.

size_t *num Pointer to a value of type size_t equal to the number
of records in the table to be searched.

size_t width The size in bytes of one record in the table. All records
in the table must be of the same size.

int (*fcmp)(const void *, const void *) Pointer to a comparison
function, which should return zero if the elements addressed by the
two void pointer parameters are equal, or nonzero if the two
elements are unequal. The comparison function needs to examine
records only for equality.

See also   bsearch, lsearch, qsort

Example
```
/* lfind.cpp */
#include <stdio.h>
#include <stdlib.h>
#include <string.h>
#define NUMELEMS 4
typedef char *Pchar;
typedef char **PPchar;
char *cp[NUMELEMS] = {
  "California",
  "Pennsylvania",
  "Arizona",
  "Florida"
```

```
};
int compare(Pchar a, PPchar b);
main()
{
  size_t numelems = NUMELEMS;
  Pchar searchkey = "Arizona";
  PPchar result;
  result = (PPchar)lfind(searchkey, cp, &numelems,
    sizeof(void *), (int(*)(const void*, const
void*))compare);
  if (result)
    printf("Result == %s\n", *result);
  else
    printf("%s not found\n", searchkey);
  return 0;
}

int compare(Pchar key, PPchar b)
{
  return stricmp(key, *b);
}
```

localtime   Convert date and time to structure

Syntax   `struct tm *localtime(const time_t *timer);`

Include   TIME.H

Description   Converts a time value to a static structure of type tm declared in

```
time.h as
struct tm
{
  int tm_sec;    // Seconds
  int tm_min;    // Minutes
  int tm_hour;   // Hour
  int tm_mday;   // Day of month
  int tm_mon;    // Month (1==January)
  int tm_year;   // Year
  int tm_wday;   // Day of week (0==Sunday)
  int tm_yday;   // Day of year (0==January 1)
  int tm_isdst;  // True if daylight savings in effect
};
```

Parameters   `const time_t *timer` Pointer to time_t value such as that returned
by the `time()` function.

See also   asctime, ctime, ftime, gmtime, stime, time, tzset

Example
```
/* localtim.cpp */
#include <stdio.h>
#include <time.h>
main()
{
  time_t thetime;
  tm *timep;
  time(&thetime);
```

```
    timep = localtime(&thetime);
    printf("The time is %02d:%02d\n",
      timep->tm_hour, timep->tm_min);
    return 0;
}
```

lock   Set file-sharing locks

Syntax   `int lock(int handle, long offset, long length);`

Include   IO.H

Description   Locks file regions using functions in DOS 3.0 and higher. Requires
                  DOS's SHARE.EXE code to be loaded. Returns zero for success and
                  -1 for failure, and sets errno to EACCES.

Parameters   **int handle** Handle to a file such as that returned by open().

                  long offset Offset from the beginning of the file, specifying the
                  beginning of the location to lock.

                  long length Number of bytes to lock starting from offset.

See also   fileno, open, sopen, unlock

Example
```
/* lock.cpp */
#include <stdio.h>
#include <stdlib.h>
#include <conio.h>
#include <io.h>
#include <fcntl.h>
#define FILENAME "LOCK.CPP"
void pause(const char *msg);
main()
{
  int handle, lockstatus;
  puts("Opening file");
  handle = open(FILENAME, O_RDONLY | O_BINARY);
  if (handle < 0) {
    printf("Error opening %s\n", FILENAME);
    exit(1);
  }
  pause("lock first byte of file");
  lockstatus = lock(handle, 0, 1);  // Lock first byte of
file
if (lockstatus < 0)
    puts("Error detected. SHARE installed?");
  else {
    puts("First byte of file locked");
    pause("unlock file");
    lockstatus = unlock(handle, 0, 1);  // Unlock first byte
    if (lockstatus < 0)
      puts("Error unlocking file!");
    else
      puts("File unlocked");
  }
```

```
      puts("Closing file");
      close(handle);
      return 0;
    }

    void pause(const char *msg)
    {
      printf("Press any key to %s...", msg);
      getch();
      puts("");
    }
```

locking   File-sharing locks

Syntax int locking(int handle, int cmd, long length);

Include IO.H

Description Locks or unlocks file regions using functions in DOS 3.0 or later versions. Requires SHARE.EXE to be loaded. Returns zero for success and -1 for failure and sets errno to EBADF (bad file number), EACCES (region already locked/unlocked), EDEADLOCK (failure after 10 locking attempts), or EINVAL (bad cmd value or SHARE.EXE not loaded).

Parameters **int handle** Handle to a file such as that returned by open().

int cmd One of the following constants: LK_LOCK or LK_RLCK (attempt to lock region 10 times per second before reporting failure), LK_NBLCK or LK_NBRLCK (attempt to lock region and report failure immediately), or LK_UNLCK (unlock region).

long length Number of bytes to lock starting from offset.

See also fileno, _fsopen, open, sopen

Example
```
/* locking.cpp */
#include <stdio.h>
#include <stdlib.h>
#include <conio.h>
#include <io.h>
#include <fcntl.h>
#include <sys\locking.h>
#define FILENAME "LOCKING.CPP"
main()
{
  int handle, lockstatus;
  long flen;
  printf("Opening %s\n", FILENAME);
  handle = open(FILENAME, O_RDONLY | O_BINARY);
  if (handle < 0) {
    printf("Error opening %s\n", FILENAME);
    exit(1);
  }
```

```
  flen = filelength(handle);
  lockstatus = locking(handle, LK_LOCK, flen); // Lock whole
➥file
  if (lockstatus < 0)
    puts("Error detected. SHARE installed?");
  else {
    puts("Entire file is locked");
    printf("Press any key to unlock and quit...");
    getch();
    puts("");
    lockstatus = locking(handle, LK_UNLCK, flen);  // Unlock
➥file
    if (lockstatus < 0)
      puts("Error unlocking file!");
    else
      puts("File unlocked");
  }
  puts("Closing file");
  close(handle);
  return 0;
}
```

lsearch   Linear search

Syntax
```
void *lsearch(const void *key, void *base, size_t *num,
size_t width, int (*fcmp)(const void *, const void*));
```

Include   STDLIB.H

Description   Like lfind(), lsearch() searches a table for a matching record, but if the target key is not located, lsearch() appends to the end of the table the record addressed by key.

Parameters   See lfind.

See also   bsearch, lfind, qsort

Example
```
/* lsearch.cpp */
#include <stdio.h>
#include <stdlib.h>
#define NUMELEMS 10  // Leave room for additions
double array[NUMELEMS] = { 1.1, 2.2, 3.3, 4.4 };
size_t numelems = 4;
int compare(double *key, double *arg);
void lookup(double key);
void display(const char *msg);
main()
{
  lookup(2.2);  // Look up value in array
  lookup(9.9);  // Look up value not in array
  return 0;
}

int compare(double *key, double *arg)
{
  if (*key == *arg)
```

```
      return 0;
   else
      return -1;
}

void lookup(double key)
{
   double *result;
   printf("\nSearching for %.1lf\n", key);
   display("before");
   result = (double *)lsearch(&key, array, &numelems,
      sizeof(double), (int(*)(const void*, const
void*))compare);
   if (result)
      printf("Result == %.1lf\n", *result);
   display("after");
}

void display(const char *msg)
{
   printf("Array %s. Number elements == %d\n", msg, numelems);
   for (int i = 0; i < numelems; i++)
      printf(" [%.1lf]", array[i]);
   puts("");
}
```

lseek   Move file pointer

Syntax   `long lseek(int handle, long offset, int fromwhere);`

Include   IO.H or STDIO.H

Description   Changes the current file position. Returns the new position as an offset in bytes from the file's beginning, or -1 if any errors are detected, and sets errno to EBADF (bad file handle) or EINVAL (invalid argument).

Parameters   **int handle** File handle such as that returned by open().

long offset Offset in bytes by which to change the current file position. The effect depends on the value of fromwhere. If fromwhere equals SEEK_CUR, offset can be positive to move the current position forward, or negative to move backward.

int fromwhere One of the three constants declared in io.h and stdio.h: SEEK_SET (set new position to file beginning plus offset bytes), SEEK_CUR (set new position to current position plus offset bytes), or SEEK_END (set new position to end of file minus offset bytes).

See also   filelength, fileno, fseek, ftell, open

Example
```
/* lseek.cpp ( <- 'p' is 12th character ) */
#include <stdio.h>
#include <stdlib.h>
#include <io.h>
#include <fcntl.h>
#define SEEKERR -1L
main()
{
  int handle;
  char c;
// Open text file in binary mode
  handle = open("LSEEK.CPP",O_BINARY | O_RDONLY);
  if (handle == NULL) {
    puts("Unable to open FSEEK.CPP");
    exit(1);
  }
// Seek to 12th byte from file beginning
  if (lseek(handle, 11, SEEK_SET) == SEEKERR)
    puts("Error during file seek");
  else {
    read(handle, &c, 1);
    printf("12th character == %c", c);
  }
  close(handle);
  return 0;
}
```

ltoa   Convert long to string

Syntax   `char *ltoa(long value, char *string, int radix);`

Include   STDLIB.H

Description Converts a long value to a null-terminated string. Returns a pointer to the resulting string.

Parameters **long value** The value to be converted. If value is negative, a minus sign precedes the result only if radix equals 10.

char *string A pointer to a char buffer large enough to hold the result. Depending on the radix value, itoa() can return up to 33 bytes.

int radix The number base to use for the conversion, from 2 to 36.

See also   atoi, atol, itoa, ultoa

Example
```
/* ltoa.cpp */
#include <stdio.h>
#include <stdlib.h>
main()
{
  char buffer[33];
  long v = 0xFACEL;
  printf("Original value in hex == %#lx\n", v);
```

```
        ltoa(v, buffer, 2);  // Convert v to binary string
        printf("Value in binary == %s\n", buffer);
        return 0;
      }
```

malloc   Allocate memory

Syntax	`void *malloc(size_t size);`
Include	STDLIB.H or ALLOC.H
Description	Allocates a block of memory from the heap. When you are finished using the allocated memory, pass its pointer to `free()` in order to return that memory to the heap for use by subsequent calls to `malloc()`. The function returns a pointer to the allocated memory, or it returns null if the requested number of bytes is not available.
	In small memory models, the heap consists of addresses from the end of the global data segment to the beginning of the area reserved for the stack. In large memory models, the heap consists of all conventional (not extended or expanded) memory not used by the program's data, code, and stack.
Parameters	`size_t size` Number of bytes to allocate. If `size` equals zero, `malloc()` returns null.
See also	`allocmem, calloc, coreleft, far..., free, heapwalk, realloc`
Example	See `free`.

memccpy, _fmemccpy   Copy characters

Syntax	`void *memccpy(void *dest, const void *src, int c, size_t n);`
	`void far * far _fmemccpy(void far *dest, const void far *src,`
	`  int c, size_t n);`

Include	MEM.H
Description	Copies memory from a source location to a destination until character c is copied, or until n bytes have been copied. Returns the address following c in the destination, or if c was not copied, returns null. Function `_fmemccpy()` is the far-pointer version.
Parameters	`void *dest` Pointer to the destination.
	`const void *src` Pointer to the source.
	`int c` Character that when transferred should end copying.
	`size_t n` Maximum number of bytes to copy.

See also	memchr, memcmp, memcpy, memicmp, memmove, memset
Example	

```
/* memccpy.cpp */
#include <stdio.h>
#include <mem.h>
#include <string.h>
main()
{
  char *source = "Original string";
  char dest[80];
  char *p;
  p = (char *)memccpy(dest, source, 'l', strlen(source));
  *p = NULL;
  printf("Original string == %s\n", source);
  printf("Copy of string  == %s\n", dest);
 return 0;
}
```

memchr, _fmemchr   Search memory for character

Syntax	void *memchr(const void *s, int c, size_t n);
	void far * far _fmemchr(const void far *s, int c, size_t n);
Include	MEM.H
Description	Searches for a character c in a block of memory. If the character is found, memchr() returns its address. If the character is not found, the function returns null. Function _fmemchr() is the far-pointer version.
Parameters	**const void *s** Pointer to memory in which to search for a character.
	int c The character to find.
	size_t n Maximum number of bytes to search, starting at a location addressed by s.
See also	memccpy, memcmp, memcpy, memicmp, memmove, memset
Example	

```
/* memchr.cpp */
#include <stdio.h>
#include <mem.h>
#include <string.h>
main()
{
  char *path = "C:\\bc5\\BIN";
  char *dir;
  printf("Original string == %s\n", path);
  dir = (char *)memchr(path, '\\', strlen(path));
  if (dir)
  printf("Directory == %s\n", dir);
  return 0;
}
```

memcmp, _fmemcmp   Compare memory

Syntax   int memcmp(const void *s1, const void *s2, size_t n);
              int far _fmemcmp(const void far *s1, const void far *s2,
                size_t n);

Include   MEM.H

Description   Compares memory bytes as unsigned char strings, which do not
                  have to be null-terminated. Returns a negative result if the string at
                  s1 is alphabetically less than the string at s2. Returns zero if the two
                  strings are equal. Returns a positive value if the string at s1 is
                  alphabetically greater than the string at s2. Function _fmemcmp() is
                  the far-pointer version.

Parameters   const void *s1 Pointer to the first string of character bytes.

                 const void *s2 Pointer to the second string of character bytes.

                 size_t n Maximum number of bytes to compare.

See also   memccpy, memchr, memcpy, memicmp, memmove, memset

Example
```cpp
/* memcmp.cpp */
#include <stdio.h>
#include <mem.h>
main()
{
  char b1[] = "String #1";
  char b2[] = "String #2";
  int result = memcmp(b1, b2, 6);
  if (result == 0)
  printf("First 6 chars of %s and %s are equal\n", b1, b2);
  return 0;
}
```

memcpy, _fmemcpy   Copy nonoverlapping memory

Syntax   void *memcpy(void *dest, const void *src, size_t n);
              void far *far _fmemcpy(void far *dest, const void far *src,
                size_t n);

Include   MEM.H

Description   Copies an array of bytes from a source to a destination. If any bytes
                  in these two locations overlap, the results are not defined (see
                  memmove()). Function _fmemcpy() is the far-pointer version.

Parameters   void *dest Pointer to the destination.

                 const void *src Pointer to the source.

size_t n Number of bytes to copy from the source location to the destination.

See also memccpy, memchr, memcmp, memicmp, memmove, memset, movedata, movemem

Example
```
/* memcpy.cpp */
#include <stdio.h>
#include <mem.h>
#include <string.h>
main()
{
  char *source = "Original string";
  char dest[80];
  memcpy(dest, source, strlen(source) + 1);
  printf("Original string == %s\n", source);
  printf("Copy of string  == %s\n", dest);
  return 0;
}
```

memicmp, _fmemicmp   Compare memory ignoring case

Syntax
```
int memicmp(const void *s1, const void *s2, size_t n);
int far _fmemicmp(const void far *s1, const void far *s2,
  size_t n);
```

Include MEM.H

Description Same as memcmp() and _fmemcmp(), but ignores case when comparing two strings that do not have to be null-terminated. Function _fmemicmp() is the far-pointer version.

Parameters See memcmp.

See also memccpy, memchr, memcmp, memcpy, memmove, memset

Example
```
/* memicmp.cpp */
#include <stdio.h>
#include <mem.h>
#include <string.h>
main()
{
  char b1[] = "CASELESS COMPARE";
  char b2[] = "caseless compare and extras";
  int result = memicmp(b1, b2, strlen(b1));
  printf("string 1 == %s\n", b1);
  printf("string 2 == %s\n", b2);
  if (result == 0)
    puts("strings begin the same");
  else
    puts("strings differ");
  return 0;
}
```

memmove, _fmemmove   Copy memory

Syntax
```
void *memmove(void *dest, const void *src, size_t n);
void far * far _fmemmove(void far *dest, const void far *src,
size_t n);
```

Include   MEM.H

Description   Copies an array of bytes from a source to a destination. Unlike
`memcpy()`, `memmove()` correctly copies any overlapping bytes in these
two locations. Function `_fmemmove()` is the far-pointer version.

Parameters   **void *dest** Pointer to the destination.

const void *src Pointer to the source.

size_t n Number of bytes to copy from the source to the destination.

See also   memccpy, memchr, memcmp, memcpy, memicmp, memset, movedata, movemem

Example
```
/* memmove.cpp */
#include <stdio.h>
#include <mem.h>
#include <string.h>
main()
{
  char s[] = "      Leading spaces";
  char *p;
  printf("Original string == %s\n", s);
  p = s;
  while (*p == ' ')
    p++;
  if (*p)
    memmove(s, p, strlen(p) + 1);
  else
    s[0] = NULL;
  printf("New string == %s\n", s);
  return 0;
}
```

memset, _fmemset   Set memory

Syntax
```
void *memset(void *s, int c, size_t n);
void far * far _fmemset(void far *s, int c, size_t n);
```

Include   MEM.H

Description   Fills memory with a byte value. Function `_fmemset()` is the far-
pointer version.

Parameters   **void *s** Pointer to the first byte to be filled.

int c Character to store in memory.

size_t n Number of bytes to set to character c, starting with the byte at the location addressed by s.

See also   memccpy, memchr, memcmp, memcpy, memicmp, memmove

Example
```
/* memset.cpp */
#include <stdio.h>
#include <mem.h>
main()
{
  char buffer[80];
  buffer[79] = NULL;
  memset(buffer, '@', 79);
  puts(buffer);
  return 0;
}
```

mkdir   Make directory

Syntax   int mkdir(const char *path);

Include   DIR.H

Description   Creates a new disk directory. Returns zero for success and -1 for failure and sets errno to EACCES (access denied) or ENOENT (no such directory). The EACCES error indicates that the directory already exists. The ENOENT error typically means that a higher-level subdirectory in the path does *not* exist. If path addresses the string "C:\D1\D2\D3", mkdir() can create a directory, D3, in the path C:\D1\D2 only if those nested directories already exist. (Note: To avoid a conflict with the DOS MKDIR command, the example is named MKDIRX.CPP.)

Parameters   **const char *path** Pointer to a null-terminated string specifying the directory name. The string can contain drive and subdirectory information, but only the final directory name in a nested path is created.

See also   chdir, getcurdir, getcwd, rmdir

Example
```
/* mkdirx.cpp */
#include <stdio.h>
#include <stdlib.>
#include <dir.h>
main(int argc, char *argv[])
{
  if (argc <= 1) {
    puts("Enter MKDIRX DIR to create new directory");
    exit(1);
  }
  if (mkdir(argv[1]) == 0)
    printf("%s created", argv[1]);
```

883

```
  else
    printf("%s not created", argv[1]);
  return 0;
}
```

mktemp   Make unique filename

Syntax   `char *mktemp(char *template);`

Include   DIR.H

Description   Returns a pointer to a filename guaranteed to be unique in the
                current directory. Any errors return null.

Parameters   `char *template` Pointer to a null-terminated string that must end
                with six `'X'` characters. The function replaces these characters in the
                original string with the string `"AA.AAA"` and then checks the direc-
                tory for a file of that name. If the string is a unique filename, the
                function returns `template`. For example, if the original string is
                `"QXXXXXX"`, `mktemp()` modifies this string to `"QAA.AAA"` and searches
                for that filename. If the file exists, `mktemp()` modifies the string to
                `"QAA.AAB"` and tries again.

See also   tempnam, tmpfile, tmpnam

Example
```
/* mktemp.cpp */
#include <stdio.h>
#include <dir.h>
main()
{
  char *tempname = "QQXXXXXX";
  if (mktemp(tempname) == NULL)
    puts("Error creating temporary filename");
  else
    printf("Temporary filename == %s\n", tempname);
  return 0;
}
```

mktime   Convert time to calendar format

Syntax   `time_t mktime(struct tm *t);`

Include   TIME.H

Description   Converts members of a `tm` date-and-time structure to a `time_t` value,
                the same type returned by the `time()` function. Returns a `time_t`
                value, which in Borland C++ is equivalent to a `long` integer equal to
                the number of seconds from January 1, 1970 to the specified date
                and time. Allowable dates and times range from January 1, 1970 at
                00:00:00 (that is, at midnight) to January 19, 2038 at 03:14:07. See
                `localtime()` or time.h for the `struct tm` declaration.

Parameters   `struct tm *t` Pointer to a tm structure containing members such as tm_year and tm_hour set to the desired date and time. Out-of-range values are automatically adjusted before converting.

See also   `localtime, strftime, time`

Example
```
/* mktime.cpp */
#include <stdio.h>
#include <stdlib.h>
#include <mem.h>
#include <time.h>
char *dayofweek[7] = {
  "Sun", "Mon", "Tue", "Wed", "Thu", "Fri", "Sat" };
main()
{
  struct tm ts;
  memset(&ts, 0, sizeof(struct tm));
  ts.tm_mday = 31;
  ts.tm_mon = 11;
  ts.tm_year = 99;
  ts.tm_isdst = -1;
  if (mktime(&ts) == -1) {
    puts("Error converting time");
    exit(1);
  }
  printf("Date == %d/%d/%d\n",
    ts.tm_mon + 1, ts.tm_mday, ts.tm_year + 1900);
  printf("Day of week == %s\n",
    dayofweek[ts.tm_wday]);
  return 0;
}
```

movedata   Copy bytes

Syntax   `void movedata(unsigned srcseg, unsigned srcoff, unsigned dstseg, unsigned dstoff, size_t n);`

Include   MEM.H

Description   Copies bytes from a source location to a destination. Works correctly for all memory models. The source and destination addresses must not overlap.

Parameters   `unsigned srcseg` Source segment address.

`unsigned srcoff` Source offset address.

`unsigned dstseg` Destination segment address.

`unsigned dstoff` Destination offset address.

`size_t n` Number of bytes to move from the source to the destination.

885

See also   FP_OFF, memcpy, memmove, MK_FP, movmem, segread

Example

```
/* movedata.cpp */
#include <stdio.h>
#include <mem.h>
#include <dos.h>
#include <string.h>
main()
{
  char b1[80] = "String to be moved";
  char b2[80];
  movedata(FP_SEG(&b1), FP_OFF(&b1),
    FP_SEG(&b2), FP_OFF(&b2), strlen(b1) + 1);
  printf("Original string == %s\n", b1);
  printf("Copy of string  == %s\n", b2);
  return 0;
}
```

movmem   Move memory

Syntax   `void movmem(void *src, void *dest, unsigned length);`

Include   MEM.H

Description   Copies bytes from a source location to a destination. The source and destination addresses can overlap. (Note: Compare the example with `memmove()`'s similar program.)

Parameters   **void *src** Pointer to the source from which bytes are copied.

void *dest Pointer to the destination to which bytes are copied.

unsigned length Number of bytes to copy from the source to the destination.

See also   memcpy, memmove, movedata

Example

```
/* movmem.cpp */
#include <stdio.h>
#include <mem.h>
#include <string.h>
main()
{
  char s[] = "      Leading spaces";
  char *p;
  printf("Original string == %s\n", s);
  p = s;
  while (*p == ' ')
    p++;
  if (*p)
    movmem(p, s, strlen(p) + 1);
  else
    s[0] = NULL;
  printf("New string == %s\n", s);
  return 0;
}
```

open Open a file

Syntax
```
int open(const char *path, int access [, unsigned mode]);
```

Include FCNTL.H, SYS\STAT.H, IO.H

Description Opens a file in a specified mode. The opened file can be read from or written to, depending on the access used.

Parameters **const char *path** Pointer to a null-terminated filename string.

int access One of the FCNTL.H constants O_RDONLY (read only), O_WRONLY (write only), or O_RDWR (read and write) logically ORed with an appropriate combination of the constants O_APPEND (add data to end of file), O_CREAT (create new file), O_TRUNC (rewrite an existing file), O_EXCL (with O_CREAT prevents recreating an existing file), O_BINARY (open in binary mode), or O_TEXT (open as text).

unsigned mode Required only if access includes O_CREAT. Set to one of the expressions S_IWRITE (statements may write to file), S_IREAD (statements may read from file), or S_IWRITE | S_IREAD (statements may read and write file data).

See also close, creat, creatnew, creattemp, dup, dup2, fopen, lseek, lock, _open, read, sopen, write

Example
```cpp
/* open.cpp */
#include <stdio.h>
#include <stdlib.h>
#include <fcntl.h>
#include <sys\stat.h>
#include <io.h>
main(int argc, char *argv[])
{
  int handle;  // File handle
  char c;      // Holds bytes from file
  if (argc <= 1) {
    puts("Filename required");
    exit(1);
  }
  handle = open(argv[1], O_RDONLY | O_BINARY);
  if (handle == -1) {
    perror(argv[1]);
    exit(2);
  }
  printf("\nReading bytes from %s\n\n", argv[1]);
  while (!eof(handle))
    if (read(handle, &c, 1) == 1)
      printf("  %#04x  ", c);
  close(handle);
  return 0;
}
```

26

perror   Print system error message

Syntax	`void perror(const char *s);`
Include	STDIO.H
Description	Following an error by most library functions, call `perror()` to send to stderr a description of the error.
Parameters	**const char *s** Optional string to add to error message. Typically set to the program's filename.
See also	`clearerr`, `_strerror`, `strerror`
Example	See chdir, _open, open

printf   Write formatted output

Syntax	`int printf(const char *format[, argument,...]);`
Include	STDIO.H
Description	Boasting more options than a Mercedes, `printf()` is one of the most capable, if one of the more confusing, functions in the standard library. The `printf()` function's initial argument is a formatting string, which usually contains text interspersed with conversion commands that are replaced with values formatted according to various and complex formulas. Zero or more arguments follow the formatting string, one argument per conversion command. The compiler does not verify the number of arguments or their data types. In other words, all formatting errors (many of which most C and C++ programmers make eventually) are your responsibility to prevent. The function returns the number of characters written to stdout, although this value usually is ignored.

A `printf()` statement might be as simple as

```
printf("Display this string\n");
```

but in this case, it's probably best to call `puts()` instead. A more typical `printf()` statement has at least two parameters—a formatting string and the name of a program variable:

```
printf("Your balance is $%8.2f\n", balance);
```

The statement displays the value of a double variable, balance, formatted in eight columns with two decimal places. The embedded conversion command %8.2f tells `printf()` to send to the standard output balance's formatted value. The \n escape code begins a new line. The other characters in the string are sent literally to stdout. If balance equals 159.72, the statement displays

```
Your balance is $  159.72
```

All formatting conversion commands begin with a percent sign (%) followed by various digits and symbols selected from a smorgasbord of options. Arguments are applied to conversion commands one by one, in left-to-right order. The formatting string conforms to this syntax:

```
% [flags] [width] [.precision] [F¦N¦h¦l¦L] conversion
```

A required percent sign begins a conversion command. Bracketed items are optional. The flags specify justification rules, plus and minus signs, decimal points, trailing zeros, and prefixes in octal or hexadecimal. The width specifies column size, padded with blanks or 0 digit characters. The precision, which must begin with a period, denotes numeric precision for floating-point values or the minimum number of digits for integers. One of several modifiers selects among size-related characteristics: F (far pointer), n (near pointer), h (short int), l (long), or L (long double). The required conversion character selects a data type.

The following sections describe each part of a printf() formatting string. When constructing formatting strings, to avoid confusion, select from one set of options at a time, using the preceding syntax as a guide to the order in which the following notes apply.

'%'   Embedded conversion commands must begin with a percent sign. To insert a percent-sign character into the output, type the symbol twice: %%.

[flags]   Flags are optional. If specified, flags can consist of one or more of the following characters:

Flags for the printf() function.

Flag	Description
–	Left-justifies output. Fills any remaining space to the right with blanks. Default output is right-justified.
+	Prefaces numeric values with a plus or minus sign. Usually, only negative values are prefaced with minus signs.
' '	Displays a blank in front of positive numeric values and a minus sign in front of negative ones. This is the default action, so don't combine a blank flag with +. Do not type the single quotes, only a single blank space.

continues

889

continued

Flag	Description
#	If conversion is x or X, prefaces nonzero arguments with 0x or 0X, respectively. If conversion is o, prefaces result with 0. If conversion is e, E, or f, forces a decimal point to appear in the output (normally one prefaces only nonzero fractions). If conversion is g or G, a decimal point is forced into the output and trailing zeros are *not* truncated as they normally are.

`[width]` Specifies a minimum column width. Normally, any extra space is filled with blanks. If the width value begins with the digit 0, however, any extra space is filled with 0 characters.

The field width also can be the asterisk character, *, which causes the *next* int argument value to be used as the column width—a rare case in which a conversion command requires two arguments. With this command, you specify two values: an integer that represents the minimum width to use, and the value to be formatted within that column width. The width integer comes *before* the value being formatted.

Specifying a 0 width pads output with leading 0s within a variable column width. There is never any danger of specifying fewer columns than are needed to display a value. Columns are enlarged as necessary to ensure that no values are truncated.

`['.'precision]` If a period appears at this location in a formatting string, the next value represents the precision to use for the formatted result. The exact meaning of the precision depends on the type of item being formatted.

An integer value follows the period. The default value is 0—that is, `.0` is the same as specifying no precision. Default precisions are 1 for conversion characters d, i, o, u, x, and X; 6 for e, E, and f; a variable number of significant digits for g and G; and all characters for conversions s and c—that is, strings and characters.

If the conversion character is g or G, the precision represents the maximum number of significant digits in the formatted result. If conversion is e, E, or f, the precision equals the number of decimal places to use, and the final digit is rounded. If conversion is s, the precision stands for the maximum number of characters to use from the string. Precision has no effect on conversion character c (single characters are always displayed). If the conversion character is d, i, o, u, x, or X, at least the number of digits specified by the precision are output, padded at left as necessary with 0 digit characters.

Conversion   The required conversion character tells `printf()` the type of an argument. It is up to you to supply an argument of the expected type. If you use a conversion character g, for example, then the argument must be a floating-point value. Probably the most common cause of problems with `printf()` statements is the application of the wrong type of argument for a specified conversion character.

The following table lists all possible conversion characters, of which only one can be used per command. Case is significant—a lowercase g is not the same as an uppercase G.

Conversion characters for the `printf()` function.

Conversion Character	Description
%	Outputs a percent symbol.
c	A character.
d	A signed decimal.
e	A `double` value to be formatted using scientific notation (for example, 1.0765e+10).
E	Same as e, but inserts an uppercase E into the result.
f	A `double` value to be formatted in decimal format, such as 123.45.
g	A `double` value to be formatted in either scientific or decimal notation. Automatically selects option f or e as needed to give the most accurate results in a reasonably small amount of space.
G	Same as g, but if scientific notation is used, the uppercase letter E appears in the result rather than a lowercase e.
i	Same as d—a signed decimal.
n	Treats the argument value as a pointer to an `int` variable in which `printf()` stores the number of characters written to `stdout` so far. The n conversion does not add any characters to the output.
o	An unsigned octal.
p	A pointer. In tiny, small, and medium memory models, pointers are formatted as offset hexadecimal values. In compact, large, and huge memory models, pointers are formatted as segment and offset hexadecimal values separated by a colon.
s	A null-terminated string. Specify a precision value to restrict output to a maximum number of characters.

continues   **891**

continued

Conversion Character	Description
u	An unsigned decimal.
x	An unsigned hexadecimal using the digits 0, 1, 2, 3, 4, 5, 6, 7, 8, and 9, and the lowercase letters a, b, c, d, e, and f.
X	Same as x, an unsigned hexadecimal, but using uppercase letters A, B, C, D, E, and F.

Parameters   **const char *format** Pointer to a null-terminated string (usually typed as a literal string directly in the printf() statement). The string's characters are passed unchanged to the standard output. Embedded conversion commands in the string (see preceding descriptions) are replaced with values formatted according to the rules for those commands and the argument data types.

argument, ... One or more argument variables, literal values, constants, expressions, pointers, dereferenced pointers, function calls, and so on. At least one argument must be supplied for each conversion command in the preceding format string. Arguments are not checked for number or type, and they are evaluated in left-to-right order.

See also   cprintf, ecvt, fprintf, fread, fscanf, putc, puts, putw, scanf, sprintf, vprintf, vsprintf

Example
```cpp
/* printf.cpp */
#include <stdio.h>
main()
{
    int xint = 123;
    long xlong = 12345678L;
    char xchar = '@';
    char *xstring = "My dog has knees";
    double xdouble = 3.14159;
    long double xlongdouble = xdouble * xdouble;
    puts(  "Sample printf() statements");
    puts(  "VARIABLE            RESULT");
    printf("xint (decimal)  == %d\n", xint);
    printf("xint (hex)      == %#x\n", xint);
    printf("xint (octal)    == %#o\n", xint);
    printf("xlong           == %ld\n", xlong);
    printf("xchar           == %c\n", xchar);
    printf("xstring         == %s\n", xstring);
    printf("xdouble         == %lf\n", xdouble);
    printf("xlongdouble(1)  == %Le\n", xlongdouble);
    printf("xlongdouble(2)  == %Lf\n", xlongdouble);
    return 0;
}
```

putc   Output character to stream

Syntax	`int putc(int c, FILE *stream);`
Include	STDIO.H
Description	Sends a character to a file stream, such as `stdout` or a file opened by function `fopen()`. If successful, `putc()` returns `c`; otherwise, it returns `EOF`. The function is written as a macro.
Parameters	**int c** Character to write to the specified stream.
	FILE *stream Any file stream opened for output.
See also	feof, fopen, fputc, fputch, fputchar, fputs, fwrite, getc, getchar, printf, putch, putchar, putw, vprintf
Example	

```
/* putc.cpp */
#include <stdio.h>
main()
{
  for (int c = 32; c < 127; c++)
    putc(c, stdout);
  return 0;
}
```

putchar   Output character to stdout

Syntax	`int putchar(int c);`
Include	STDIO.H
Description	Same as `putc()` but outputs `c` to `stdout`. Encoded as a macro that executes `putc(c, stdout)`. If successful, `putchar()` returns `c`; otherwise, it returns `EOF`.
Parameters	**int c** Character to write to `stdout`.
See also	putc
Example	

```
/* putchar.cpp */
#include <stdio.h>
main()
{
  for (int c = 32; c < 127; c++)
    putchar(c);
  return 0;
}
```

893

putenv   Add string to environment

Syntax	`int putenv(const char *envvar);`
Include	STDLIB.H

Description   Given an envvar string in the form `"name=value"`, `putenv()` searches for an environment variable name, and if it finds one, it inserts in the environment a pointer to the new string. Case is significant; thus, to `putenv()`, path and PATH are different names. Replaced environment strings are not overwritten or deleted. The function returns zero for success and -1 for failure.

If name is not found, the envvar pointer is appended to the environment. The startup code reserves space for as many as four such attachments. Additional variables cause `putenv()` to expand the environment, in which case the original env pointer passed as the third argument to `main()` becomes invalid.

Parameters   **const char *envvar** Pointer to a null-terminated string in the form `"name=value"`. For best results, pass only global or literal strings to envvar. Automatic string variables or dynamic strings allocated by `malloc()` or similar heap allocators must not be deleted or permitted to go out of scope after being passed to `putenv()`.

See also   `exec...`, `getenv`

Example

```
/* putenv.cpp */
#include <stdio.h>
#include <stdlib.h>
void Display(const char *s);
main()
{
  puts("Before calling putenv()");
  Display("PUTENV");
  putenv("PUTENV=A test string");
  puts("After calling putenv()");
  Display("PUTENV");
  return 0;
}

void Display(const char *s)
{
  char *result = getenv(s);
  if (result)
    printf("%s == %s\n", s, result);
  else
    printf("%s not found in environment\n", s);
}
```

puts   Output string to stdout

Syntax	`int puts(const char *s);`
Include	STDIO.H
Description	Writes to the standard output the specified string plus a newline character.
Parameters	`const char *s` Pointer to a null-terminated string.
See also	`cputs, fputs, gets, printf`
Example	

```
/* puts.cpp */
#include <stdio.h>
main()
{
  puts("Welcome to a program, the primary job");
  puts("of which is to bid you welcome!");
  return 0;
}
```

putw   Output integer to stream

Syntax	`int putw(int w, FILE *stream);`
Include	STDIO.H
Description	Writes an integer to a file stream. Returns w for success and EOF for failure. Because EOF might equal w (both are integer values), call `ferror()` to confirm a suspected `putw()` error.
Parameters	`int w` Integer to write to a file stream.
	`FILE *stream` A file stream such as that opened by `fopen()`.
See also	`fwrite, getw, printf`
Example	See getw.

qsort   Quicksort

Syntax	`void qsort(void *base, size_t nelem, size_t width,`
	`int (*fcmp)(const void *, const void *));`
Include	STDLIB.H
Description	Sorts a table of data elements using the Quicksort algorithm and a user-supplied comparison function.

Parameters
    `void *base` Pointer to the base of the data element array.

    `size_t nelem` Number of elements in the table.

    `size_t width` Size in bytes of a single element.

    `int (*fcmp)(const void *, const void *)` Pointer to a comparison function, to which qsort() passes two pointers that address elements in the table being sorted. The function should return -1 if the first parameter is less than the second, zero if the two parameters are equal, or +1 if the first parameter is greater than the second.

See also
    bsearch, lfind, lsearch

Example

```
/* qsort.cpp */
#include <stdio.h>
#include <stdlib.h>
#include <time.h>
#define SIZE 100
int compare(const void *a, const void *b);
void DisplayArray(void);
int array[SIZE];  // Array of integers
main()
{
  for (int i = 0; i < SIZE; i++)
    array[i] = rand();
  DisplayArray();
  qsort((void *)array, SIZE, sizeof(array[0]), compare);
  DisplayArray();
  return 0;
}

int compare(const void *a, const void *b)
{
  int aint = *(int *)a;
  int bint = *(int *)b;
  if (aint < bint)
    return -1;
  else if (aint > bint)
    return +1;
  else
    return 0;
}

void DisplayArray(void)
{
  puts("");
  for (int i = 0; i < SIZE; i++)
    printf("%8d", array[i]);
}
```

rand   Random number

Syntax
    `int rand(void);`

Include
    STDLIB.H

Description   Returns an integer selected at random from the range zero to
RAND_MAX.

See also   random, randomize, srand

Example
```
/* rand.cpp */
#include <stdio.h>
#include <conio.h>
#include <stdlib.h>
#include <time.h>
main()
{
  puts("Press any key to stop");
  puts("random number generation...");
  randomize();  // Seed generator
  while (!kbhit()) {
    gotoxy(1, wherey());
    printf("%8d", rand());
  }
  getch();  // Throw away keypress
  return 0;
}
```

random   Random number in range

Syntax   int random(int num);

Include   STDLIB.H

Description   Returns an integer selected at random from the range
0 ... num - 1. Encoded as a macro in STDLIB.H.

Parameters   **int num** Upper limit plus one.

See also   rand, randomize, srand

Example
```
/* random.cpp */
#include <stdio.h>
#include <conio.h>
#include <stdlib.h>
#include <time.h>
unsigned long counts[4];
main()
{
  int n;
  double percent;
  unsigned long loops = 0;
  randomize();  // See random number generator
  puts("\nCount frequency of random numbers from 0 to 99.");
  puts("Press any key to stop counting...");
  while (!kbhit()) {
   []= random(100);
    gotoxy(1, wherey());
    cprintf("Random number==%5d  Loops==%lu", n, ++loops);
    if (n < 25) counts[0]++;
    if (n < 50) counts[1]++;
```

```
      if (n < 75) counts[2]++;
      counts[3]++;
   }
   getch();  // Throw away keypress
   puts("\n\n Range  :   Count Percentage");
   puts(   "---------------------------");
   for (n = 0;[]< 4; n++) {
      percent = 100.0 * ((double)counts[n] / loops);
      printf("0 - %d :%8lu == %7.3lf%%\n",
         ((n + 1) * 25) - 1, counts[n], percent);
   }
   return 0;
}
```

randomize   Seed random numbers

Syntax   `void randomize(void);`

Include   STDLIB.H, TIME.H

Description   Randomly seeds the random number generator, causing it to begin a
new random sequence. Calls function `time()`—the reason for
including TIME.H.

See also   rand, random, srand

Example   See rand, random.

read   Read from file

Syntax   `int read(int handle, void *buf, unsigned len);`

Include   IO.H

Description   Reads bytes from a file. Returns the number of bytes read—zero if
attempting to read past the end of the file or -1 for failure.

Parameters   **int handle** Handle to the open file.

                void *buf Pointer to the buffer into which file data is copied.

                unsigned len Maximum number of bytes to read.

See also   _dos_open, _dos_read, fread, fopen, _open, _read, _write

Example   See open.

realloc   Reallocate memory

Syntax   `void *realloc(void *block, size_t size);`

Include   STDLIB.H

Description   Expands or shrinks an existing memory block to a new size, or creates a new block. Copies existing block to a new location if necessary. Returns the address of the modified block and returns null for errors.

Parameters   **void *block** Pointer to block to be resized, such as returned by a preceding call to malloc(). You may set block to null, in which case realloc() attempts to allocate a new block of the specified size.

size_t size The requested size in bytes for the reallocated memory block.

See also   calloc, farcalloc, farmalloc, farrealloc, free, malloc

Example
```cpp
/* realloc.cpp */
#include <stdio.h>
#include <stdlib.h>
main()
{
  void *p1;
  void *p2;
  puts("Allocating 128 bytes");
  p1 = malloc(128);           // Allocate 128 bytes
  if (p1) {
    puts("Resizing block to 256 bytes");
    p2 = realloc(p1, 256);  // Resize to 256 bytes
  }
  if (p2)
    delete p2;   // Delete resized block
  else
    delete p1;   // Or delete original if resizing failed
  return 0;
}
```

remove   Remove file

Syntax   int remove(const char *filename);

Include   STDIO.H

Description   Deletes a named file (if it exists). Returns zero for success and -1 for failure and sets errno to ENOENT (file not found) or EACCES (access denied). Encoded as a macro that calls unlink().

Parameters   **const char *filename** Pointer to null-terminated string that represents the name of the file to be deleted.

See also   chmod, chsize, rename, unlink

Example
```cpp
/* remove.cpp */
#include <stdio.h>
#include <io.h>
#include <sys\stat.h>
```

899

```
main()
{
  char tfname[L_tmpnam];
  tmpnam(tfname);
  printf("Creating temporary file %s\n", tfname);
  int handle = creat(tfname, S_IWRITE);
  if (handle) {
    puts("Closing temporary file");
    close(handle);
  }
  printf("Removing %s\n", tfname);
  remove(tfname);
  return 0;
}
```

rename   Rename file

Syntax   `int rename(const char *oldname, const char *newname);`

Include   STDIO.H

Description   Changes a filename. Can also move a file from one directory to
another (on the same drive only), without causing the file's contents
to be copied. Returns zero for success and -1 for failure and sets
errno to ENOENT (file not found), EACCES (access denied), or ENOTSAM
(not same drive). The example is named RENAMER.CPP to avoid
a conflict with the DOS RENAME command.

Parameters   `const char *oldname` Pointer to existing filename string. Can
contain drive and directory path information but no wild cards.

`const char *newname` Pointer to new filename string. Can contain
drive and directory path information but no wild cards. Any drive
letter must be the same as used for `oldname`. If a different directory is
given, the file is moved to that directory (if it exists) without causing
the file's contents to be copied.

See also   `creat, chmod, chsize, remove`

Example
```
/* renamer.cpp */
#include <stdio.h>
#include <stdlib.h>
main(int argc, char *argv[])
{
  if (argc < 3) {
    puts("Use like DOS RENAME command.");
    puts("ex. RENAME MYFILE.TXT MYFILE.BAK");
    puts("Or, enter a directory to move files.");
    puts("ex. RENAME MYFILE.TXT C:\NEWDIR\MYFILE.TXT");
    exit(1);
  }
  if (rename(argv[1], argv[2]) == -1)
    printf("Error renaming %s to %s\n", argv[1], argv[2]);
```

```
      else
        printf("%s renamed to %s\n", argv[1], argv[2]);
      return 0;
    }
```

rewind Reset file pointer

Syntax	`void rewind(FILE *stream);`
Include	STDIO.H
Description	Resets a file stream's internal position to the beginning of the file. Typically used to reread a file from its first byte, or to prepare for writing new data over the beginning of an existing file. Also clears the file's end-of-file and error flags.
Parameters	`FILE *stream` Pointer to open file stream such as returned by `fopen()`.
See also	`fopen, fseek, fsetpos, ftell`
Example	See `fread`.

rmdir Remove directory

Syntax	`int rmdir(const char *path);`
Include	DIR.H
Description	Deletes named directory, which must have no files and cannot be the current directory or a disk's root directory. Returns zero for success and -1 for failure and sets `errno` to `ENOENT` (directory not found) or `EACCES` (access denied). The example is named RMDIRS.CPP to avoid a conflict with the DOS RMDIR command.
Parameters	`const char *path` Pointer to null-terminated string naming the directory to be removed.
See also	`_chmod, chdir, getcurdir, getcwd, mkdir`
| *Example* | ```
/* rmdirs.cpp */
#include <stdio.h>
#include <stdlib.h>
#include <dir.h>
main(int argc, char *argv[])
{
  if (argc <= 1 ) {
    puts("Enter directory name to remove");
    exit(1);
  }
  if (rmdir(argv[1]) == -1)
``` |

901
```

```
      printf("Unable to remove %s\n", argv[1]);
    else
      printf("%s removed\n", argv[1]);
    return 0;
}
```

rmtmp   Remove temporary files

Syntax   `int rmtmp(void);`

Include   STDIO.H

Description Closes and removes all temporary files previously created by one or
more calls to `tmpfile()`. The current directory must be the same as
when the temporary files were created. Temporary files in other
directories are not removed. Returns the total number of temporary
files closed and removed.

See also   `remove, tmpfile, tmpnam`

Example   See `fread`.

sbrk   Change data segment size

Syntax   `void *sbrk(int incr);`

Include   ALLOC.H

Description Expands or shrinks the size of a program's data segment. Returns
pointer to the former break value (the address following the end of
the data segment). If `sbrk()` fails, it returns -1 and sets `errno` to
`ENOMEM` (not enough memory).

Parameters **int incr** If `incr` is positive, `sbrk()` attempts to expand the data
segment by the specified number of bytes. If `incr` is negative, `sbrk()`
attempts to shrink the data segment by the absolute value of the
specified number of bytes.

See also   `brk, coreleft`

Example
```
/* sbrk.cpp */
#include <stdio.h>
#include <alloc.h>
void Report(const char *msg);
main()
{
  Report("\nBefore expanding data segment to 4K");
  sbrk(4000);
  Report("\nAfter expanding data segment to 4K");
  return 0;
}
```

```
void Report(const char *msg)
{
  puts(msg);
  printf("coreleft() == %ul\n", (unsigned long)coreleft());
}
```

scanf   Get formatted input from stdin

Syntax   `int scanf(const char *format[, address, ...]);`

Include   STDIO.H

Description   Reads text input from stdin, translating input fields to binary according to conversion rules supplied by a format string. Stores the translated values at supplied addresses, usually referring to program variables. Returns the number of input fields successfully scanned, or returns EOF if attempting to read past the input's end of file.

The scanf() function is unforgiving of errors, the most common of which is neglecting to pass the *address* of an argument that follows the format string. Except for arrays (especially char arrays), always apply the & address of operator to arguments passed to scanf(). Between calls to scanf(), it might be necessary to call fflush(stdin) to reset the standard input file after any input errors.

The function's format string conforms to the following rules, expressed in Backus-Naur syntax. The symbol ::= gives a name at left to a set of rules at right. Bracketed items are optional. A vertical bar means "or." The word *blank* stands for a blank character, *literal* for a nonblank character, and *number* for an integer value (in text form).

```
format string ::= [blank] [literal] [conversion rule]
conversion rule ::= % [*] [width] [h ¦ l ¦ L] [N ¦ F] [type]
width ::= number;
type ::= % ¦ c ¦ d ¦ D ¦ e ¦ E ¦ f ¦ F ¦ g ¦ G ¦
         i ¦ I ¦[]¦ o ¦ O ¦ p ¦ s ¦ u ¦ U ¦ x ¦ X ¦ [
```

These rules tell you that format strings can have whitespace characters (blanks), literal text, and conversion rules. Whitespace characters (blanks, tabs, and newline characters) cause scanf() to read and ignore those characters from the input. Non-whitespace characters cause the function to read and ignore matching non-white space characters from the input.

A conversion rule begins with a percent sign (%) and is followed by one or more other optional items in the order shown. Each conversion item is further described in the following sections.

`[*]`	An asterisk suppresses assigning a value to the input field argument.
`[width]`	Maximum number of characters to apply from the input during the translation of the current input field argument. Fewer but no more than this many characters are used in translating the field.
`[h ¦ l ¦ L ]`	Force argument data type to be short int (h), long int (l for all integer arguments), double (l for all floating point arguments), or long double (L for all floating point arguments).
`[N ¦ F]`	Force argument address to be near (N) or far (F).

Type The following table lists conversion type characters, of which one must be supplied for every conversion rule. Case is significant (D and d, for example, specify different conversions).

Conversion characters for scanf() function.

Conversion Character	Description of argument field v
%	No conversion. Read and store a percent character.
c	char *v or char v[n] for a width n.
d	int *v in decimal.
D	long *v in decimal.
e	float *v.
E	float *v.
f	float *v.
g	float *v.
G	float *v.
i	int *v in decimal, octal, or hexadecimal.
I	long *v in decimal, octal, or hexadecimal.
n	int *v set to number of characters so far read from input.
o	int *v in octal.
O	long *v in octal.
p	near *v for tiny, small, and medium memory models in OFFSET format; far *v for compact, large, and huge models in SEGMENT:OFFSET format.
s	char *v to an array of char.

Conversion Character	Description of argument field v
u	unsigned int *v in decimal.
U	unsigned long *v in decimal.
x	int *v in hexadecimal.
X	int *v in hexadecimal.
[	Begin regular expression, a set of characters in square brackets. The conversion rule %[xyz] scans for the characters x, y, and z. A preceding caret (^) means "not." Thus %[^xyz] scans for all characters not equal to x, y, and z. Define character ranges with a hyphen. The rule %[A-Z] scans for uppercase alphabetic characters from A to Z inclusively. You can also string multiple ranges together. The rule %[0-9A-Fa-f] scans for hexadecimal digits 0 through 9, A through F, and a through f. Character ranges must be ordered in ASCII from low to high. The rule %[0-9] specifies the digits 0 through 9; the rule %[9-0] specifies the digits 9 and 0 and a hyphen character (-).

NOTE

Conversion characters e, E, f, g, and G are equivalent for all forms of floating-point values.

Parameters   **const char *format** Pointer to null-terminated string containing one or more conversion rules and other characters as explained in the preceding description. Typically entered as a literal string directly in a scanf() statement.

address, ... Argument addresses, one per conversion rule in the preceding format string. Be sure to supply the *address* of arguments. Pass the int variable x, for example, as &x.

See also   atof, atoi, atol, cscanf, fscanf, getc, gets, printf, sscanf, vfscanf, vscanf, vsscanf

Example
```
/* scanf.cpp */
#include <stdio.h>
main()
{
  int i;
  puts("Enter an integer value in hex");
  scanf("%i", &i);
  printf("In decimal, you entered %d\n", i);
  return 0;
}
```

searchpath   Search system path for file

Syntax   `char *searchpath(const char *file);`

Include   DIR.H

Description   Similar to _searchenv(), but searches for a filename in the current directory and, failing to find the file there, in each directory specified by the PATH environment variable. Returns a pointer to the file's complete pathname, or returns null if the file is not found. The returned string is stored in a static buffer that is reused by each call to searchpath().

Parameters   **const char *file** Pointer to filename string.

See also   _searchenv

Example
```
/* searchpa.cpp */
#include <stdio.h>
#include <dir.h>
main()
{
  char *pathname;
  puts("Searching for BCC.EXE along PATH");
  pathname = searchpath("BCC.EXE");
  if (pathname == NULL)
    puts("BCC.EXE not found");
  else
    puts(pathname);
  return 0;
}
```

setbuf   Enable stream buffer

Syntax   `void setbuf(FILE *stream, char *buf);`

Include   STDIO.H

Description   After opening a file stream (by calling fopen() usually), call setbuf() to attach an I/O buffer to the file. Files are normally buffered (except for nonredirected standard files stdin and stdout). Use this function to cancel buffering, to buffer an unbuffered file, or to use a program variable as a buffer for debugging.

Never call setbuf() after reading or writing to a file or you risk losing data temporarily stored in an existing buffer. Always call setbuf() immediately after opening a file or after calling fseek(). An unbuffered file, however, can be buffered at any time. Also take care that the specified buffer remains valid during the time the file is open.

Parameters	**FILE *stream** An open file such as returned by `fopen()`.
	char *buf Pointer to new buffer to be used for I/O. The buffer must have BUFSIZ (512) bytes. Set `buf` to null to cancel buffering for the file.
See also	`fopen, fseek, setvbuf`
Example	

```
/* setbuf.cpp */
#include <stdio.h>
char buffer[BUFSIZ];
main()
{
  setbuf(stdout, buffer);  // Use our buffer
  puts("Some text for our buffer");
  puts(buffer);  // Displays same string as above
  return 0;
}
```

setdisk   Change current disk drive

Syntax	`int setdisk(int drive);`
Include	DIR.H
Description	Change current disk drive.
Parameters	**int drive** Drive number (0=A:, 1=B:, 2=C:, etc.)
See also	`getdisk`
Example	

```
/* setdisk.cpp */
#include <stdio.h>
#include <dir.h>
main()
{
  setdisk(0); // Change to A:
  return 0;
}
```

setftime   Set file date and time

Syntax	`int setftime(int handle, struct ftime *ftimep);`
Include	IO.H
Description	Change open file's date and time as stored in the directory. Note that, if data is written to a file, closing that file also updates its date and time.
Parameters	**int handle** An open file's handle, such as returned by `open()`.
	struct ftime *ftimep Pointer to `ftime` structure, defined in IO.H.

907

See also   getftime

Example

```
/* setftime.cpp */
/* Change *.BAK file dates and times to 0-00-80 00:00a */
#include <stdio.h>
#include <dir.h>
#include <dos.h>
#include <io.h>
#include <fcntl.h>
#include <stdlib.h>
struct ftime zerodt;  // Zero date and time
main()
{
// *** To enable, remove lines starting here
*******************
  puts("This program resets to 0-00-80 00:00a the dates");
  puts("and times of all *.BAK files in the current
➥directory.");
  puts("Don't run this program unless you are sure you
➥want");
  puts("to reset backup file dates and times!!!");
  exit(1);
// *** End removing lines here
********************************
  struct ffblk fb;
  char *path = "*.BAK";
  int done, handle;
  done = findfirst(path, &fb, FA_NORMAL);
  while (!done) {
    if ((fb.ff_attrib & FA_DIREC) == 0) {
      if ( (handle = open(fb.ff_name, O_RDONLY)) >= 0 ) {
        setftime(handle, &zerodt);
        printf("%s date/time zeroed\n", fb.ff_name);
        close(handle);
      }
    }
    done = findnext(&fb);
  }
  return 0;
}
```

setmem   Fill memory

Syntax   void setmem(void *dest, unsigned length, char value);

Include   MEM.H

Description   Fills memory with a value.

Parameters   **void *dest** Pointer to memory block to be filled.

              unsigned length Size of the memory block in bytes.

              char value Value to store in memory.

See also   calloc, memset, strset

Example

```
/* setmem.cpp */
#include <stdio.h>
#include <mem.h>
#define LEN 64
void Report(unsigned char *p, unsigned len, const char *s);
main()
{
  unsigned char *p = new char[LEN];
  Report(p, LEN, "Before filling");
  setmem(p, LEN, 0xff);
  Report(p, LEN, "After filling");
  delete p;
  return 0;
}

void Report(unsigned char *p, unsigned len, const char *s)
{
  unsigned int c;
  printf("\n\n%s\n", s);
  for (int i = 0; i < len; i++) {
    c = *p++;
    if (c == 0)
      printf("0x00     ");
    else
      printf("%#04x      ", c);
  }
}
```

setmode   Set file mode

Syntax

```
int setmode(int handle, int amode);
```

Include

IO.H, FCNTL.H

Description

Changes an open file's mode to binary or text. Returns previous mode for success and -1 for failure.

Parameters

int handle Open file's handle such as returned by open().

int amode File mode: O_BINARY or O_TEXT.

See also

creat, _dos_open, open

Example

```
/* setmode.cpp */
#include <stdio.h>
#include <io.h>
#include <fcntl.h>
#define FNAME "setmode.cpp"
main()
{
  int handle, c;
  handle = open(FNAME, O_BINARY);
  if (handle)
    if (setmode(handle, O_TEXT) != -1)
      while (!eof(handle))
        if (read(handle, &c, 1))
          putchar(c);
  return 0;
}
```

909

set_new_handler   Operator new error handler

Syntax   `void (* set_new_handler(void (* my_handler)() ))();`

Include   NEW.H

Description   Assigns the address of a user function to be called if new fails to allocate a requested amount of memory. The user function can abort the program, or it can delete some memory (possibly reserved earlier as a safety pool) and return. If the memory request again fails, the handler is again called until the handler ends the program or frees additional memory. The statement `set_new_handler(0)` causes new to return null for memory allocation failures (the default action). Returns the address (null by default) of the previously assigned handler.

Parameters   **void (* my_handler)()** Pointer to a void function requiring no parameters—the function to be called by new. Set to null to reset new to its default action of returning null for memory allocation failures.

See also   `malloc, free`

Example

```
/* set_new_.cpp */
#include <stdio.h>
#include <stdlib.h>
#include <new.h>
void memerr(void);
main()
{
  set_new_handler(memerr);
  for (;;) {
    printf("Allocating 1024 bytes");
    void far *p = new[1024];
    printf(" at %p\n", p);
  }
}

void memerr(void)
{
  fputs("\n\nOut of memory\n", stderr);
  exit(1);
}
```

setvbuf   Assign buffering to stream

Syntax   `int setvbuf(FILE *stream, char *buf, int type, size_t size);`

Include   STDIO.H

Description   Modifies I/O buffering. Buffered I/O stores data in temporary buffers, speeding throughput. Unbuffered I/O (character devices only) reads and writes data one character at a time, which typically gives poor performance but saves memory.

Except for redirected stdin and stdout files, file I/O is normally buffered. Call setvbuf() to attach or to automatically allocate a new program buffer to a file stream. The function returns zero for success and nonzero for failure.

Parameters   `FILE *stream` Open file stream such as returned by fopen(). Or a predefined stream such as stdin or stdout.

`char *buf` Pointer to buffer, usually a char array. If null, setvbuf() allocates a buffer by calling malloc(). Automatically allocated buffers are freed upon closing the file.

`int type` One of the constants _IOFBF (full buffering—input reads full buffer; output writes entire buffer when full), _IOLBF (line buffering—same as full buffering but text output writes entire buffer upon receiving a newline character), or _IONBF (disable buffering).

`size_t size` Size of the new buffer in bytes up to 32767.

See also   fflush, fclose, fopen, fread, fwrite, setbuf

Example
```
/* setvbuf.cpp */
#include <stdio.h>
#include <stdlib.h>
#define FNAME "setvbuf.cpp"
#define SIZE 2048
main()
{
  FILE *f = fopen(FNAME, "rt");
  char buffer[SIZE];
  if (!f) {
    perror(FNAME);
    exit(1);
  }
  if (setvbuf(f, buffer, _IOFBF, SIZE) != 0)
    puts("Unable to attach file buffer");
  else {
    puts("Reading file via buffered I/O...");
    while (!feof(f))
      putchar(getc(f));
  }
  return 0;
}
```

sopen   Open shared file

Syntax   `int sopen(char *path, int access, int shflag[, int mode]);`

Include   FCNTL.H, SYS\STAT.H, SHARE.H, IO.H

911

Description	Similar to open( ), but opens a file to be shared by another process. Returns positive file handle for success and -1 for failure and sets errno to ENOENT (no such file or directory), EMFILE (too many files open), EACCES (access denied), EINVACC (invalid access code).
Parameters	**char *path** Pointer to filename string, which may contain drive and path information.

Parameters **int access** One of the three constants O_RDONLY (read only), O_WRONLY (write only), O_RDWR (read and write) logically ORed with any one or more of the six constants O_APPEND (append to end of file), O_BINARY (open in binary mode), O_CREAT (create new file if it does not exist), O_EXCL (combine with O_CREAT to force error for existing file), O_TEXT (open in text mode), O_TRUNC (truncate file).

int shflag One of the constants SH_COMPAT (compatibility mode—in other words, no flags), SH_DENYNO (permit full read and write access), SH_DENYNONE (same as SH_DENYNO), SH_DENYRD (deny reading), SH_DENYRW (deny reading and writing), SH_DENYWR (deny writing).

int mode Specified only when access includes the O_CREAT option. Either of the two constants S_IWRITE (permit writing) or S_IREAD (permit reading), or the expression S_IREAD ¦ S_IWRITE (permit reading and writing).

See also access, chmod, close, creat, fstat, lock, lseek, open, stat, unlock, unmask

Example
```cpp
/* sopen.cpp */
#include <stdio.h>
#include <stdlib.h>
#include <fcntl.h>
#include <sys\stat.h>
#include <share.h>
#include <io.h>
main(int argc, char *argv[])
{
  int handle;
  char c;
  if (argc <= 1) {
    puts("Enter name of text file to read.");
    puts("ex. SOPEN sopen.cpp");
    exit(1);
  }
  handle = sopen(argv[1], O_RDONLY ¦ O_TEXT, SH_DENYWR);
  if (handle == 0)
    perror(argv[1]);
  else {
    while (read(handle, &c, 1) > 0)
      putchar(c);
    close(handle);
  }
  return 0;
}
```

sprintf   Format values to string

Syntax   `int sprintf(char *buffer, const char *format[, argument, ...]);`

Include   STDIO.H

Description Same as `printf()`, but stores formatted arguments in a user-supplied string buffer. Returns number of bytes inserted into `buffer`, not including a terminating null.

Parameters `char *buffer` Pointer to buffer for storing function's result. The buffer *must* be large enough to hold any possible expansion of the supplied arguments plus a null terminating byte.

`const char *format` Pointer to a formatting string containing whitespace, literal text, and conversion rules (see `printf()`).

`argument, ...` One or more argument values, with at least one argument per conversion rule in the `format` string.

See also   cprintf, fprintf, printf, scanf, vfprintf, vprintf, vsprintf

Example
```
/* sprintf.cpp */
#include <stdio.h>
main()
{
  char buffer[128];
  int i = 123;
  double d = 3.14159;
  char *s = "A string";
  sprintf(buffer, "i==%d  d==%lf  s==%s\n", i, d, s);
  puts(buffer);
  return 0;
}
```

srand   Seed random number generator

Syntax   `void srand(unsigned seed);`

Include   STDLIB.H

Description The statement `srand(n)` seeds the random number generator to produce a random sequence n.

Parameters `unsigned seed` Value to seed random number generator, producing a predictable random sequence (useful for debugging programs that use random numbers). To produce an unpredictable random sequence, set `seed` to a rapidly changing value such as the time of day.

See also   rand, random, randomize

Example

```
/* srand.cpp */
#include <stdio.h>
#include <stdlib.h>
void Display(const char *msg);
main()
{
  srand(9);
  Display("Random numbers for seed == 9");
  srand(9);
  Display("After reseeding with seed == 9");
  srand(2);
  Display("Random numbers for seed == 2");
  return 0;
}

void Display(const char *msg)
{
  puts("");
  puts(msg);
  for (int i = 0; i < 8; i++)
    printf("%8d", rand());
  puts("");
}
```

sscanf   Scan and format string input

Syntax

```
int sscanf(const char *buffer, const char *format[,
    address, ...]);
```

Include   STDIO.H

Description   Same as scanf(), but takes input from a user-supplied string. Returns number of input fields scanned and converted.

Parameters   **const char *buffer** Pointer to string containing input to be scanned.

const char *format Pointer to format string with conversion rules that tell the function how to convert input fields (see scanf()).

address, ... One or more arguments passed by address. The function stores converted fields at these addresses, one per conversion rule in the format string.

See also   fscanf, printf, scanf, vfscanf, vscanf, vsscanf

Example

```
/* sscanf.cpp */
#include <stdio.h>
main()
{
  char *s;
  double d;
```

```
        printf("Enter floating point number: ");
        gets(s);
        sscanf(s, "%lf", &d);
        printf("Input as a string == %s\n", s);
        printf("Input as a double == %lf\n", d);
        printf("Input in scientific notation == %le\n", d);
        return 0;
    }
```

stackavail   Available stack space

Syntax	`size_t stackavail(void);`
Include	MALLOC.H
Description	Returns number of bytes available on the stack, equal to the amount of memory available to `alloca()`.
See also	`alloca, allocmem, coreleft, _dos_allocmem, farcoreleft, heapwalk, segread`
Example	

```
/* stackava.cpp */
#include <stdio.h>
#include <malloc.h>
void f(void);
void Report(const char *msg);
main()
{
  Report("Outside of function");
  f();
  return 0;
}

void f(void)
{
  char buffer[2048];  // Use some stack space
  buffer[0] = 0;      // Prevent compiler warning
  Report("Inside of function");
}

void Report(const char *msg)
{
  puts(msg);
  printf("Stack space == %u bytes\n", stackavail());
}
```

stat   Get file information

Syntax	`int stat(char *path, struct stat *statbuf);`
Include	SYS\STAT.H
Description	Similar to `fstat()`, but uses a filename string rather than an open file's handle to obtain information about a file's status. Returns zero for success and -1 if the specified file is not found.

Parameters	**char *path** Pointer to filename string, which may contain drive and directory information.
	struct stat *statbuf Pointer to a stat structure for storing the function's result.
See also	access, chmod, fstat
Example	

```
/* stat.cpp */
#include <stdio.h>
#include <stdlib.h>
#include <sys\stat.h>
#include <time.h>
main(int argc, char *argv[])
{
  char *fname;
  struct stat statbuf;
  if (argc <= 1) {
    puts("Enter filename");
    puts("ex. STAT stat.cpp");
    exit(1);
  }
  fname = argv[1];
  if (stat(fname, &statbuf) != 0) {
    printf("Error getting stats for %s\n", fname);
    exit(1);
  }
  printf("Information about %s\n", fname);
  printf("Drive number  : %d\n", statbuf.st_dev);
  printf("Size in bytes : %ld\n", statbuf.st_size);
  printf("Was updated   : %s\n", ctime(&statbuf.st_atime));
  return 0;
}
```

stime   Set system date and time

Syntax	int stime(time_t *p);
Include	TIME.H
Description	Change system date and time.
Parameters	**time_t *p** Pointer to time_t value, equal to the number of elapsed seconds since GMT 00:00:00 on January 1, 1970.
See also	asctime, _dos_setftime, _dos_settime, ftime, gettime, gmtime, localtime, settime, time, tzset
Example	

```
/* stime.cpp */
#include <stdio.h>
#include <stdlib.h>
#include <time.h>
#define SECS_PER_HOUR (60 * 60)
main(int argc, char *argv[])
{
```

```
char c;
time_t thetime;
puts("Daylight savings adjustment\n");
if (argc <= 1) {
  puts("Enter + to advance hour; - to retard");
  puts("ex. STIME + or STIME -");
  exit(1);
}
c = argv[1][0];   // i.e. first char of first arg
time(&thetime);
if (c == '+')
  thetime += SECS_PER_HOUR;
else if (c == '-')
  thetime -= SECS_PER_HOUR;
stime(&thetime);
time(&thetime);
printf("The time is %s\n", ctime(&thetime));
return 0;
}
```

stpcpy Copy string to string

Syntax `char *stpcpy(char *dest, const char *src);`

Include STRING.H

Description Copies source string src and its null terminator to a destination string dest. Returns dest + strlen(src).

Parameters `char *dest` Pointer to destination string large enough to hold the result.

`const char *src` Pointer to null-terminated source string.

See also strcpy, strncpy

Example
```
/* stpcpy.cpp */
#include <stdio.h>
#include <string.h>
main()
{
  char src[80] = "abcdefghij";
  char dst[80] = "1234567890";
  printf("Before: src==%s  dst==%s\n", src, dst);
  puts("Calling stpcpy(dst, src)");
  stpcpy(dst, src);
  printf("After : src==%s  dst==%s\n", src, dst);
  return 0;
}
```

strcat, _fstrcat Concatenate strings

Syntax `char *strcat(char *dest, const char *src);`

`char far * far _fstrcat(char far *dest, const char far *src);`

917

Include	STRING.H
Description	Concatenates (joins) a source string src to the end of an initialized destination string dest. Returns dest.
Parameters	**char *dest** Pointer to initialized destination string.
	const char *src Pointer to source string to be copied to the end of the destination string.
See also	stpcpy, strcpy, strncat
Example	

```
/* strcat.cpp */
#include <stdio.h>
#include <string.h>
main()
{
  char src[80] = "abcdefghij";
  char dst[80] = "1234567890";
  printf("Before: src==%s  dst==%s\n", src, dst);
  puts("Calling strcat(dst, src)");
  strcat(dst, src);
  printf("After : src==%s  dst==%s\n", src, dst);
  return 0;
}
```

strchr, _fstrchr   Scan string for character

Syntax	char *strchr(const char *s, int c);
	char far * far _fstrchr(const char far *s, int c);
Include	STRING.H
Description	Searches a string s from front to back for the first occurrence of a character c. Returns a pointer to the character if found and null if not found.
Parameters	**const char *s** Pointer to target string.
	int c Character for which to search. Set to null (ASCII 0) to have strchr() search for a string's null terminator.
See also	strcspn, strrchr, strspn, strstr
Example	

```
/* strchr.cpp */
#include <stdio.h>
#include <string.h>
main()
{
  char src[80] = "abcdefghij";
  printf("String at src == %s\n", src);
  puts("Calling char *p = strchr(src, 'd')");
  char *p = strchr(src, 'd');
```

```
printf("String at p   == %s\n", p);
return 0;
}
```

strcmp   Compare strings

Syntax

```
int strcmp(const char *s1, const char *s2);
int far _fstrcmp(const char far *s1, const char far *s2);
```

Include   STRING.H

Description   Compares two strings. Returns a negative value if s1 < s2, zero if s1 == s2, or a positive value if s1 > s2.

Parameters   **const char *s1** Pointer to first string to be compared.

const char *s2 Pointer to second string to be compared.

See also   strchr, strcmpi, strcoll, stricmp, strncmp, strnicmp

Example
```
/* strcmp.cpp */
#include <stdio.h>
#include <stdlib.h>
#include <string.h>
main(int argc, char *argv[])
{
  char *p;
  if (argc <= 2) {
    puts("Enter two strings to compare");
    puts("ex. STRCMP stringa stringb");
    exit(1);
  }
  int result = strcmp(argv[1], argv[2]);
  if (result < 0)
    p = "is less than";
  else if (result > 0)
    p = "is greater than";
  else
    p = "equals";
  printf("%s %s %s", argv[1], p, argv[2]);
  return 0;
}
```

strcmpi   Compare strings ignoring case

Syntax   int strcmpi(const char *s1, const char *s2);

Include   STRING.H

Description   Same as strcmp() but ignores differences in upper- and lowercase. For compatibility with other C compilers, strcmpi() is implemented as a macro that translates directly to stricmp().

Parameters   See strcmp.

See also   strchr, strcmp, strcoll, stricmp, strncmp, strnicmp

Example

```
/* strcmpi.cpp */
#include <stdio.h>
#include <stdlib.h>
#include <string.h>
main(int argc, char *argv[])
{
  char *p;
  if (argc <= 2) {
    puts("Enter two strings to compare ignoring case");
    puts("ex. STRCMPI stringa stringb");
    exit(1);
  }
  int result = strcmpi(argv[1], argv[2]);
  if (result < 0)
    p = "is less than";
  else if (result > 0)
    p = "is greater than";
  else
    p = "equals";
  printf("%s %s %s", argv[1], p, argv[2]);
  return 0;
}
```

strcoll   Collate strings

Syntax   int strcoll(char *s1, char *s2);

Include   STRING.H

Description   Same as strcmp() but compares two strings using a collating sequence dictated by the current locale. (Borland C++ marginally supports the concept of a locale, and, therefore, this function is provided only for compatibility with other ANSI C compilers.)

Parameters   See strcmp.

See also   localeconv, setlocale, strcmp, stricmp, strncmp, strnicmp, strxfrm

Example

```
/* strcoll.cpp */
#include <stdio.h>
#include <stdlib.h>
#include <string.h>
main(int argc, char *argv[])
{
  char *p;
  if (argc <= 2) {
    puts("Enter two strings to collate");
    puts("ex. STRCOLL stringa stringb");
    exit(1);
  }
```

```
      int result = strcoll(argv[1], argv[2]);
      if (result < 0)
        p = "is less than";
      else if (result > 0)
        p = "is greater than";
      else
        p = "equals";
      printf("%s %s %s", argv[1], p, argv[2]);
      return 0;
    }
```

strcpy   Copy string to string

Syntax

```
char *strcpy(char *dest, const char *src);
char far * _fstrcpy(char far *dest, const char far *src);
```

Include   STRING.H

Description   Copies a source string src and its null terminator to a destination
string dest, overwriting any string in the destination. Returns dest.

Parameters   **char *dest** Pointer to destination, overwritten with a copy of the
source string. The destination string does not have to be initialized.

const char *src Pointer to source string to be copied to the
destination.

See also   stpcpy, strncpy

Example
```
/* strcpy.cpp */
#include <stdio.h>
#include <string.h>
main()
{
  char src[80] = "abcdefghij";
  char dst[80] = "1234567890";
  printf("Before: src==%s  dst==%s\n", src, dst);
  puts("Calling strcpy(dst, src)");
  strcpy(dst, src);
  printf("After : src==%s  dst==%s\n", src, dst);
  return 0;
}
```

strcspn, _fstrcspn   Subset string search

Syntax

```
size_t strcspn(const char *s1, const char *s2);
size_t far _fstrcspn(const char far *s1, const char far *s2);
```

Include   STRING.H

Description   Returns the number of characters from a string s1 that are not also
in a second string s2. Can be used in parsing data entry—counting a

string's initial characters that do not contain a certain punctuation character, for example, or a file extension.

Parameters **const char s1** String in which to search for characters that are not in string s2.

const char s2 String containing characters that stop the incremental search of string s1.

See also strchr, strcspn, strrchr, strspn, strstr

Example
```
/* strcspn.cpp */
#include <stdio.h>
#include <string.h>
main()
{
  char *s = "filename.cpp";
  char *ext = ".cpp";
  printf("Original string s == %s\n", s);
  int result = strcspn(s, ext);
  s += result;
  printf("After calling strcspn s == %s\n", s);
  return 0;
}
```

strdup, _fstrdup   Duplicate string

Syntax char *strdup(const char *s);

char far * far _fstrdup(const char far *s);

Include STRING.H

Description Copies a string to a newly allocated memory block strlen(s) + 1 bytes long. Returns a pointer to the duplicated string. You can delete this string by passing the pointer to free(). Returns null if not enough memory is available for storing the duplicate string.

Parameters **const char *s** Pointer to null-terminated string to be duplicated.

See also malloc, free, strcpy

Example
```
/* strdup.cpp */
#include <stdio.h>
#include <string.h>
#include <alloc.h>
main()
{
  char *s = "abcdefghij";
  char *duplicate;
  printf("Original string == %s\n", s);
  duplicate = strdup(s);
  printf("Duplicate string == %s\n", duplicate);
  free(duplicate);  // Delete duplicated string
  return 0;
}
```

strerror   Create error string

Syntax	`char *strerror(int errnum);`
Include	STDIO.H or STRING.H
Description	Returns a pointer to an error message string identified by `errnum`. Adds a newline character to the end of the string.
Parameters	`int errnum` Error number.
See also	`perror, _strerror`
Example	

```
/* strerror.cpp */
#include <stdio.h>
#include <string.h>
main()
{
  for (int e = 0; e < 21; e++)
    printf("Error #%02d: %s", e, strerror(e));
  return 0;
}
```

strftime   Store date and time in string

Syntax	`size_t strftime(char *s, size_t maxsize, const char *fmt,` `    const struct tm *t);`
Include	TIME.H
Description	Formats the date and time as a string using a conversion rule system similar to `printf()`'s. A format string (`fmt`) contains one or more rules that are replaced by date and time components. The format string can contain other nonrule characters as well. Returns number of characters inserted into the destination string. Conversion rules consist of a percent sign (`%`) and a character from the following table.

Conversion rules for `strftime()`.

Conversion rules	Date and time components
%	Insert percent sign (%)
a	Day of week (abbreviated Sun, Mon, etc.)
A	Day of week unabbreviated
b	Month (abbreviated Jan, Feb, etc.)
B	Month unabbreviated

continues

continued

Conversion rules	Date and time components
c	Date and time in `asctime()` format
d	Day of month (01 to 31)
H	Hour in 24-hour format (00 to 23)
I	Hour in 12-hour format (00 to 12)
j	Day of year (001 to 366)
m	Month number (1 to 12)
M	Minute (00 to 59)
p	AM or PM
S	Second (00 to 59)
U	Week number (00 to 53) (Sunday starts week)
w	Day of week (0 to 6) (Sunday = 0)
W	Week number (00 to 53) (Monday starts week)
x	Date
X	Time
y	Year minus century (e.g. 68 for 1968)
Y	Full year (e.g. 1968)
Z	Time zone name (EST or EDT)

Parameters

`char *s` Pointer to destination string for storing function result.

`size_t maxsize` Maximum number of characters to insert into destination string. Usually set to the size minus one of string s.

`const char *fmt` Pointer to format string containing literal text and conversion rules as explained in the description.

`const struct tm *t` Pointer to a tm structure containing the date and time to be formatted into a string.

See also

asctime, ctime, localtime, mktime, time

Example

```
/* strftime.cpp */
#include <stdio.h>
#include <time.h>
#define SIZE 80
main()
{
  time_t t;
  struct tm *tp;
  char s[SIZE];
  time(&t);
  tp = localtime(&t);
```

```
    puts("");
    strftime(s, SIZE, "The date is %x\n", tp);
    puts(s);
    strftime(s, SIZE, "The time is %X\n", tp);
    puts(s);
    strftime(s, SIZE, "Today is %A\n", tp);
    puts(s);
    return 0;
}
```

stricmp, _fstricmp   Compare strings ignoring case

Syntax	`int stricmp(const char *s1, const char *s2);`
	`int far _fstricmp(const char far *s1, const char far *s2);`
Include	STRING.H
Description	Same as `strcmp()` but ignores case when comparing two strings.
Parameters	See `strcmp()`.
See also	`strcmp, strcmpi, strcoll, strncmp, strnicmp`
Example	

```
/* stricmp.cpp */
#include <stdio.h>
#include <stdlib.h>
#include <string.h>
main(int argc, char *argv[])
{
  char *p;
  if (argc <= 2) {
    puts("Enter two strings to compare ignoring case");
    puts("ex. STRICMP stringa stringb");
    exit(1);
  }
  int result = stricmp(argv[1], argv[2]);
  if (result < 0)
    p = "is less than";
  else if (result > 0)
    p = "is greater than";
  else
    p = "equals";
  printf("%s %s %s", argv[1], p, argv[2]);
  return 0;
}
```

strlen, _fstrlen   String length

Syntax	`size_t strlen(const char *s);`
	`size_t far _fstrlen(const char far *s);`
Include	STRING.H
Description	Returns length of a string—in other words, the number of characters preceding the string's null terminator.

925

Parameters	**const char *s** Pointer to a null-terminated string.
See also	strchr
Example	

```
/* strlen.cpp */
#include <stdio.h>
#include <stdlib.h>
#include <string.h>
main(int argc, char *argv[])
{
  if (argc <= 1) {
    puts("Enter string");
    puts("ex. STRLEN myString");
    exit(1);
  }
  int len = strlen(argv[1]);
  printf("String == %s\n", argv[1]);
  printf("Length == %d character(s)\n", len);
  return 0;
}
```

strlwr, _fstrlwr   Convert string to lowercase

Syntax	char *strlwr(char *s);
	char far * far _fstrlwr(char far *s);
Include	STRING.H
Description	Changes uppercase letters in a string to lowercase.
Parameters	**char *s** Pointer to null-terminated string.
See also	strupr, tolower, toupper
Example	

```
/* strlwr.cpp */
#include <stdio.h>
#include <string.h>
main()
{
  char s[] = "ABCDEFGHIJKLMNOPQRSTUVWXYZ";
  printf("Before conversion s == %s\n", s);
  strlwr(s);
  printf("After conversion s  == %s\n", s);
  return 0;
}
```

strncat, _fstrncat   Concatenate strings

Syntax	char *strncat(char *dest, const char *src, size_t maxlen);
	char far * far _fstrncat(char far *dest, const char far *src,
	size_t maxlen);
Include	STRING.H

Description   Concatenates (joins) up to `maxlen` characters from a source string `src` to the end of an initialized destination string `dest`.

Parameters   `char *dest` Pointer to initialized destination string.

`const char *src` Pointer to source string.

`size_t maxlen` Maximum number of characters to be copied from the source string to the end of the destination string.

See also   `strcat`, `strcpy`

Example
```
/* strncat.cpp */
#include <stdio.h>
#include <string.h>
main()
{
  char src[80] = "abcdefghij";
  char dst[80] = "1234567890";
  printf("Before: src==%s  dst==%s\n", src, dst);
  puts("Calling strncat(dst, src, 5)");
  strncat(dst, src, 5);
  printf("After : src==%s  dst==%s\n", src, dst);
  return 0;
}
```

strncmp, _fstrncmp   Compare partial strings

Syntax   `int strncmp(const char *s1, const char *s2, size_t maxlen);`

`int far _fstrncmp(const char far *s1, const char far *s2,`
  `size_t maxlen);`

Include   STRING.H

Description   Same as `strcmp()`, but compares only up to `maxlen` characters in the two strings.

Parameters   `const char *s1` Pointer to first string.

`const char *s2` Pointer to second string.

`size_t maxlen` Maximum number of characters to compare.

See also   `strcmp`, `strcoll`, `stricmp`, `strnicmp`

Example
```
/* strncmp.cpp */
#include <stdio.h>
#include <stdlib.h>
#include <string.h>
main(int argc, char *argv[])
{
  char *p;
  if (argc <= 3) {
    puts("Enter two strings and a number to compare[]chars");
```

26

```
    puts("ex. STRNCMP stringa stringb 4");
    exit(1);
  }
  int[]= atoi(argv[3]);
  int result = strncmp(argv[1], argv[2], n);
  if (result < 0)
    p = "is/are less than";
  else if (result > 0)
    p = "is/are greater than";
  else
    p = "equal(s)";
  printf("%d chars of %s %s %s", n, argv[1], p, argv[2]);
  return 0;
}
```

strncmpi   Compare partial strings ignoring case

Syntax	`int strncmpi(const char *s1, const char *s2, size_t maxlen);`
Include	STRING.H
Description	Same as `strncmp()`, but ignores the difference between upper- and lowercase letters. Implemented for compatibility with other C compilers as a macro that translates to `strnicmp()`.
Parameters	See `strnicmp`.
See also	`strncmp, strnicmp`
Example	

```
/* strncmpi.cpp */
#include <stdio.h>
#include <stdlib.h>
#include <string.h>
main(int argc, char *argv[])
{
  char *p;
  if (argc <= 3) {
    puts("Enter two strings and a number to compare[]chars");
    puts("ignoring case.");
    puts("ex. STRNCMPI stringa stringb 4");
    exit(1);
  }
  int[]= atoi(argv[3]);
  int result = strncmpi(argv[1], argv[2], n);
  if (result < 0)
    p = "is/are less than";
  else if (result > 0)
    p = "is/are greater than";
  else
    p = "equal(s)";
  printf("%d chars of %s %s %s", n, argv[1], p, argv[2]);
  return 0;
}
```

strncpy, _fstrncpy   Copy partial strings

Syntax

```
char *strncpy(char *dest, const char *src, size_t maxlen);
char far * far _fstrncpy(char far *dest, const char far *src,
  size_t maxlen);
```

Include   STRING.H

Description   Copies up to `maxlen` characters from a source string `src` to a destination string `dst`, overwriting any characters in the destination. If `maxlen` equals the size in bytes of the destination string (and the source string is at least that long), the destination string is not null terminated. If `maxlen` and the length of the source string exceed the size of the destination string, the end of the destination is overwritten, possibly destroying other data or code in memory. To avoid trouble, never set `maxlen` greater than the maximum number of characters that the destination can safely hold.

Parameters   **char *dest** Pointer to destination of at least `maxlen` bytes.

cont char *src Pointer to source string to be copied to the destination.

size_t maxlen Maximum number of characters to copy from the source to the destination.

See also   strcat, strcpy

Example
```
/* strncpy.cpp */
#include <stdio.h>
#include <string.h>
main()
{
  char src[80] = "abcdefghij";
  char dst[80] = "1234567890";
  printf("Before: src==%s  dst==%s\n", src, dst);
  puts("Calling strncpy(dst, src, 5)");
  strncpy(dst, src, 5);
  printf("After : src==%s  dst==%s\n", src, dst);
  return 0;
}
```

strnicmp, _fstrnicmp   Partial caseless compare

Syntax

```
int strnicmp(const char *s1, const char *s2, size_t maxlen);
int far _fstrnicmp(const char far *s1, const char far *s2,
  size_t maxlen);
```

Include   STRING.H

Description Compares up to `maxlen` characters of two strings. Ignores differences between upper- and lowercase letters.

Parameters `const char *s1` Pointer to first string to be compared.

`const char *s2` Pointer to second string to be compared.

`size_t maxlen` Maximum number of characters from both strings to be compared.

See also stricmp, strncmp, strncmpi

Example
```
/* strnicmp.cpp */
#include <stdio.h>
#include <stdlib.h>
#include <string.h>
main(int argc, char *argv[])
{
  char *p;
  if (argc <= 3) {
    puts("Enter two strings and a number to compare[]chars");
    puts("ignoring case.");
    puts("ex. STRNICMP stringa stringb 4");
    exit(1);
  }
  int[]= atoi(argv[3]);
  int result = strnicmp(argv[1], argv[2], n);
  if (result < 0)
    p = "is/are less than";
  else if (result > 0)
    p = "is/are greater than";
  else
    p = "equal(s)";
  printf("%d chars of %s %s %s", n, argv[1], p, argv[2]);
  return 0;
}
```

strnset, _fstrnset   Set characters in string

Syntax char *strnset(char *s, int c, size_t n);
char far * far _fstrnset(char far *s, int c, size_t n);

Include STRING.H

Description Fills a string with one or more characters, stopping upon reaching a null byte in the string.

Parameters `char *s` Pointer to string to be filled.

`int c` Character to store in string.

`size_t n` Maximum number of characters to be filled.

See also memset, setmem, strset

Example

```
/* strnset.cpp */
#include <stdio.h>
#include <string.h>
main()
{
  char s[] = "1234567890";
  printf("Before filling s == %s\n", s);
  puts("Calling strnset(s, '@', 4)");
  strnset(s, '@', 4);
  printf("After filling  s == %s\n", s);
  return 0;
}
```

strpbrk, _fstrpbrk   Scan string for characters

Syntax

```
char *strpbrk(const char *s1, const char *s2);
char far * far _fstrpbrk(const char far *s1,
  const char far *s2);
```

Include

STRING.H

Description

Scans a string for a character from a set of one or more characters. Returns a pointer to the first matching character found, or null if no characters match.

Parameters

const char *s1 Pointer to a string to be scanned.

const char *s2 Pointer to a string containing a set of characters.

See also

strchr, strcmp

Example

```
/* strpbrk.cpp */
#include <stdio.h>
#include <string.h>
main()
{
  char *s1 = "Balance = $341.59";
  char *s2 = "$";
  printf("s1 == %s\n", s1);
  printf("s2 == %s\n", s2);
  puts("Calling char *s3 = strpbrk(s1, s2)");
  char *s3 = strpbrk(s1, s2);
  printf("s3 == %s\n", s3);
  return 0;
}
```

strrchr, _fstrrchr   Scan string reverse

Syntax

```
char *strrchr(const char *s, int c);
char far * far _fstrrchr(const char far *s, int c);
```

Include

STRING.H

931

Description   Same as strrchr(), but searches for the last instance of a given character c in a string s. Returns a pointer to the character if found, or null if not.

Parameters   **const char *s** Pointer to string to be searched.

            int c Character to look for in string.

See also   strcspn, strchr, strpbrk

Example

```
/* strrchr.cpp */
#include <stdio.h>
#include <string.h>
main()
{
  char *s = "FILENAME.CPP";
  printf("s == %s\n", s);
  puts("Calling char *p = strrchr(s, '.')");
  char *p = strrchr(s, '.');
  printf("p == %s\n", p);
  return 0;
}
```

strrev, _fstrrev   Reverse string

Syntax   char *strrev(char *s);

         char far * far _fstrrev(char far *s);

Include   STRING.H

Description   Reverses order of characters in string (except for its null terminator). Possibly useful for searching the ends of long strings for patterns. Reversing two strings, for example, and passing them to strstr() determines whether one string ends with another. Returns s.

          Quote multiword strings passed to the example—type the command **strrev "a multiword string"**.

Parameters   **char *s** Pointer to string to be reversed.

See also   strstr

Example

```
/* strrev.cpp */
#include <stdio.h>
#include <stdlib.h>
#include <string.h>
main(int argc, char *argv[])
{
  if (argc <= 1) {
    puts("Enter string to reverse");
    puts("ex. STRREV your name");
    exit(1);
  }
  printf("Original string == %s\n", argv[1]);
```

```
      strrev(argv[1]);
      printf("Reversed string == %s\n", argv[1]);
      return 0;
   }
```

strset, _fstrset   Set characters in string

Syntax

```
char *strset(char *s, int c);
char far * far _fstrset(char far *s, int c);
```

Include   STRING.H

Description   Assigns character c to all characters in string s, up to but not including the string's null terminator byte.

Parameters   **char *s** Pointer to string to be filled.

int c Character to store in string.

See also   memset, setmem, strnset

Example
```
/* strset.cpp */
#include <stdio.h>
#include <string.h>
main()
{
   char s[] = "1234567890";
   printf("Before filling s == %s\n", s);
   puts("Calling strset(s, '@')");
   strset(s, '@');
   printf("After filling  s == %s\n", s);
   return 0;
}
```

strspn, _fstrspn   Scan string subset

Syntax

```
size_t strspn(const char *s1, const char *s2);
size_t far _fstrspn(const char far *s1, const char far *s2);
```

Include   STRING.H

Description   Returns the number of characters from a string s1 that are also in a second string s2. Can be used in verifying data entry—counting a string's initial characters that are digits, for example.

Parameters   **const char *s1** Pointer to string to be scanned.

const char *s2 Pointer to string containing characters to scan for in string s1.

See also   strcmp, strcspn

Example   /* strspn.cpp */

933

```
#include <stdio.h>
#include <string.h>
main()
{
  char *s = "filename.cpp";
  char *test = "abcdefghijklmnopqrstuvwxyz";
  printf("Original string s == %s\n", s);
  int result = strspn(s, test);
  s += result;
  printf("After calling strspn s == %s\n", s);
  return 0;
}
```

strstr, _fstrstr   Scan string for substring

Syntax
```
char *strstr(const char *s1, const char *s2);
char far * far _fstrstr(const char far *s1,
  const char far *s2);
```

Include   STRING.H

Description Hunts for a string (s2) in another string (s1). Returns address of matching string's first character or null if the substring s2 is not found in s1.

Parameters   **const char *s1** Pointer to string in which to search for the substring addressed by s2.

               const char *s2 Pointer to substring to search for in the string addressed by s1.

See also   strchr, strcmp, strcspn, strspn

Example
```
/* strstr.cpp */
#include <stdio.h>
#include <string.h>
main()
{
  char *s1 = "filename.cpp";
  char *s2 = ".cpp";
  printf("s1 == %s\n", s1);
  printf("s2 == %s\n", s2);
  puts("Calling char *s3 = strstr(s1, s2)");
  char *s3 = strstr(s1, s2);
  printf("s3 == %s\n", s3);
  return 0;
}
```

strtod   String to double

Syntax
```
double strtod(const char *s, char **endptr);
long double _strtold(const char *s, char **endptr);
```

Include	STDLIB.H
Description	Converts a floating point value in string form to a `double` or a `long double` binary value. Returns converted result for success and ± `HUGE_VAL` (`strtod()`) or ± `LHUGE_VAL` (`strtold()`) for errors.
Parameters	`const char *s` Pointer to string containing a floating point value in text, either in decimal (such as `"123.45"`) or in scientific notation (such as `"4.5e-3"`).
	`char **endptr` If non-null, endptr is set to the address of the character *after* the last character in s that participated in the conversion. Use this optional pointer to parse strings for multiple floating point values, perhaps separated by white space, commas, etc.
See also	`atof, printf, sprintf, strtol`
Example	

```
/* strtod.cpp */
#include <stdio.h>
#include <stdlib.h>
#include <string.h>
main(int argc, char *argv[])
{
  if (argc <= 1) {
    puts("Enter double value");
    puts("ex. STRTOD 3.14159");
    exit(1);
  }
  char *endptr;
  double d = strtod(argv[1], &endptr);
  printf("Value in binary == %lf\n", d);
  if (strlen(endptr) > 0)
    printf("Scan stopped at: %s\n", endptr);
  return 0;
}
```

strtok, _fstrtok   Scan string for tokens

Syntax	`char *strtok(char *s1, const char *s2);`
	`char far * far _fstrtok(char far *s1, const char far *s2);`
Include	STRING.H
Description	Divides a source string s1 into tokens (substrings), separated by one or more characters in a second string s2. Typically used to parse parameter lists of tokens separated by commas or other symbols. Returns address of token, or null if no match is found. Call repeatedly, passing the address of a source string s1 on the first call, then setting s1 to null on subsequent calls in order to continue parsing until the function returns null.

Parameters	**char *s1** Pointer to string to be tokenized. *Warning: This function directly modifies the source string by replacing separator characters with nulls.* Set to null to continue parsing the same string.
	const char *s2 Pointer to string containing one or more characters used as token separators in string s1.
See also	strcspn, strspn
Example	

```
/* strtok.cpp */
#include <stdio.h>
#include <string.h>
main()
{
  char s[] = "filename,100,1/1/90";
  char *delimit = ",/";
  printf("Original string == %s\n", s);
  puts("As parsed into tokens:");
  char *p = strtok(s, delimit);
  while (p) {
    puts(p);
    p = strtok(NULL, delimit);
  }
  return 0;
}
```

strtol   Convert string to long

Syntax	long strtol(const char *s, char **endptr, int radix);
Include	STDLIB.H
Description	Converts a long value in string form to a long binary value. The value in the string can be in decimal, octal, or hexadecimal, using standard C formatting (such as recognized by printf(), scanf(), and other similar functions.) Other radixes from 2 to 36 are also recognized. Returns converted result for success and sets a non-null endptr to the address following the last participating character; returns zero for errors and sets a non-null endptr equal to s.
Parameters	**const char *s** Pointer to a string containing a long integer value in text form. Can also contain other characters.
	char **endptr If non-null, endptr is set to the address of the character *after* the last character in s that participated in the conversion. Use this optional pointer to parse strings for multiple long values, perhaps separated by white space, commas, etc.
	int radix Set to a number from 2 to 36 to select a specific radix (number base) for the conversion—for example, use 2 for binary values, 10 for decimals, 16 for hexadecimals, etc. Letters from A to

Z are recognized as numeric symbols for number bases exceeding 10. (Base 16 uses 0 to 9 and A to F, base 17 uses 0 to 9 and A to G, and so on.) Set radix to zero to have the function automatically detect and convert numbers using standard C formatting rules—in other words, decimals begin with a digit, octals begin with the letter o, and hexadecimals begin with 0x or 0X.

See also   atoi, atof, atol, printf, sprintf, strtoul

Example

```
/* strtol.cpp */
#include <stdio.h>
#include <stdlib.h>
#include <string.h>
#define RADIX 0   // Automatic radix detection
main(int argc, char *argv[])
{
  if (argc <= 1) {
    puts("Enter long value");
    puts("ex. STRTOD 0xF96C");
    exit(1);
  }
  char *endptr;
  long l = strtol(argv[1], &endptr, RADIX);
  printf("Value in binary == %ld\n", l);
  if (strlen(endptr) > 0)
    printf("Scan stopped at: %s\n", endptr);
  return 0;
}
```

strtoul   String to unsigned long

Syntax

```
unsigned long strtoul(const char *s, char **endptr, int
radix);
```

Include   STDLIB.H

Description   Same as strtol(), but converts unsigned long values from text to binary.

Parameters   See strtol.

See also   atoi, atof, atol, printf, sprintf, strtol

Example

```
/* strtoul.cpp */
#include <stdio.h>
#include <stdlib.h>
#include <string.h>
#define RADIX 0   // Automatic radix detection
main(int argc, char *argv[])
{
  if (argc <= 1) {
    puts("Enter unsigned long value");
    puts("ex. STRTOUL 98765");
    exit(1);
```

937

```
        }
        char *endptr;
        long l = strtoul(argv[1], &endptr, RADIX);
        printf("Value in binary == %lu\n", l);
        if (strlen(endptr) > 0)
          printf("Scan stopped at: %s\n", endptr);
        return 0;
      }
```

strupr, _fstrupr   Convert string to uppercase

Syntax	`char *strupr(char *s);`
	`char far * far _fstrupr(char far *s);`
Include	STRING.H
Description	Changes lowercase letters in a string to uppercase.
Parameters	`char *s` Pointer to null-terminated string.
See also	`strlwr, tolower, toupper`
Example	

```
/* strupr.cpp */
#include <stdio.h>
#include <string.h>
main()
{
  char s[] = "abcdefghijklmnopqrstuvwxyz";
  printf("Before conversion s == %s\n", s);
  strupr(s);
  printf("After conversion s  == %s\n", s);
  return 0;
}
```

strxfrm   Transform string to string

Syntax	`size_t strxfrm(char *s1, char *s2, size_t n);`
Include	STRING.H
Description	Similar to `strncpy()`, but is said to "transform" up to n characters of one string s1 into another string s2. However, in effect, up to n characters (including a null terminating byte) from the second string s2 are simply copied to s1. Returns number of transformed (copied) characters.
Parameters	`char *s1` Pointer to destination string to be transformed.
	`char *s2` Pointer to source string copied to destination.
	`size_t n` Maximum number of characters to transform.
See also	`strcoll, strcpy, strncpy`

Example

```
/* strxfrm.cpp */
#include <stdio.h>
#include <string.h>
main()
{
  char src[80] = "abcdefghij";
  char dst[80] = "1234567890";
  printf("Before: src==%s  dst==%s\n", src, dst);
  puts("Calling strxfrm(dst, src, 4)");
  strxfrm(dst, src, 4);
  printf("After : src==%s  dst==%s\n", src, dst);
  return 0;
}
```

swab   Swap bytes

Syntax

```
void swab(char *src, char *dest, int n);
```

Include

STDLIB.H

Description

Copies up to n characters, which must be an even number, from a source string src to a destination string dest, and swaps byte pairs while copying. Typically used to convert data between computers that store multibyte values in different orders—when transferring files to 80x86-based PCs that store values of lesser significance at lower addresses, for example, from other systems such as 68000-based Macintoshes that store values of greater significance at lower addresses.

Parameters

char *src Pointer to source data containing an even number of bytes. Though typed as a char *, src can address data of any type. It doesn't have to address a null-terminated string.

char *dest Pointer to destination at least as large as the source data.

int n Maximum number of bytes to copy. Must be an even number.

See also

strcpy

Example

```
/* swab.cpp */
#include <stdio.h>
#include <stdlib.h>
#include <string.h>
main()
{
  char src[] = "Orignal data";
  char dst[80];
  int len = strlen(src);
  if ((len & 1) == 1) {
    puts("Error: Source data length must be even");
    exit(1);
  }
```

```
        printf("Original data  == %s\n", src);
        puts("Calling swab(src, dst, len)");
        swab(src, dst, len);
        printf("Converted data == %s\n", dst);
        return 0;
}
```

system   System command

Syntax   `int system(const char *command);`

Include   STDLIB.H

Description Gives a system command as though typed at a DOS prompt. Loads
and runs COMMAND.COM as a child process using the
COMSPEC environment variable to locate COMMAND.COM's
directory. The function can be used to run another program, in
which case the program's executable code file must be in the current
directory or in any directory listed on the system PATH. Returns
zero for success and -1 for errors and sets errno to E2BIG (command
string too large or contains too many arguments), ENOENT (file or
directory not found), ENOEXEC (error executing child process), or
ENOMEM (not enough memory for operation).

Parameters `const char *command` Pointer to command string. If command is null,
system() returns zero if the environment variable COMSPEC exists;
otherwise, it returns 1. This special case does *not* detect the actual
presence of the COMMAND.COM processor.

See also   exec..., getenv, putenv, _searchenv, searchpath, spawn...

Example
```
/* system.cpp */
#include <stdio.h>
#include <stdlib.h>
#include <conio.h>
main()
{
  puts("Press any key to execute tree command");
  getch();
  system("tree \\");   // Command == tree \
  puts("\nBack from system() tree command");
  return 0;
}
```

tell   Get file position

Syntax   `long tell(int handle);`

Include   IO.H

Description   Returns an open file's current position, equal to the offset in bytes from the beginning of a file where the next I/O operation on that file will occur. Returns -1 for errors.

Parameters   `int handle` Handle to open file such as returned by `open()`.

See also   `fgetpos, ftell, lseek, open`

Example
```
/* tell.cpp */
#include <stdio.h>
#include <stdlib.h>
#include <fcntl.h>
#include <io.h>
main()
{
  int handle; // Input file handle
  long pos;   // File position
  char buffer[128];
  handle = open("TELL.CPP", O_RDONLY ¦ O_BINARY);
  if (handle == -1) {
    puts("Error opening file");
    exit(1);
  }
  pos = tell(handle);
  printf("At start of file, tell() == %ld\n", pos);
  read(handle, buffer, 10);
  pos = tell(handle);
  printf("After reading 10 bytes tell() == %ld\n", pos);
  close(handle);
  return 0;
}
```

tempnam   Temporary filename

Syntax   `char *tempnam(char *dir, char *prefix);`

Include   STDIO.H

Description   Returns the name of a new file guaranteed not to exist in one of several possible directories. The returned name contains complete drive and directory information. Use this name to create a temporary file, which is your responsibility to delete. The temporary filename string is allocated memory by `malloc()`. Call `free()` to delete this memory when you are done using the filename string.

In the course of creating a temporary filename, the function searches up to four directories in this order: a directory assigned to the TMP environment variable, the `dir` argument passed to `tempnam()`, the directory string defined by constant `P_tmpdir` in STDIO.H, or the current directory.

941

P_tmpdir is defined as a null string in Borland C++, thus defaulting to the current directory. In effect, therefore, tempnam() actually searches only three, not four, directories.

Parameters   **char *dir** Pointer to directory string. This directory is searched only if the TMP environment variable is not set, if it refers to a nonexistent directory, or if an error occurs while attempting to create a temporary filename for the TMP directory. Set dir to null to skip searching an explicit directory.

char *prefix A pointer to a string containing up to five characters which may *not* include a period. The temporary filename begins with this text, to which the function adds additional characters to ensure the filename's uniqueness.

See also   free, getenv, mktemp, putenv, tmpfile, tmpnam

Example
```
/* tempnam.cpp */
#include <stdio.h>
#include <alloc.h>
main()
{
  char *fname = tempnam(NULL, "temp");
  printf("Temporary filename == %s\n", fname);
  free(fname);  // Delete temporary name from heap
  return 0;
}
```

time   Get system time

Syntax   time_t time(time_t *thetime);

Include   TIME.H

Description   Returns current date and time expressed as the number of seconds elapsed since GMT 00:00:00 on January 1, 1970. The example is named TIMER.CPP to avoid conflicting with the DOS TIME command.

Parameters   **time_t *thetime** Optional pointer to a time_t variable, in which the current date and time are stored (the same value as returned by the function). Ignored if null.

See also   asctime, ctime, difftime, ftime, gettime, gmtime, localtime, settime, stime, _strdate, strftime, _strtime, tzset

Example
```
/* timer.cpp */
#include <stdio.h>
#include <time.h>
main()
{
  time_t thetime = time(NULL);
  printf("%s\n", ctime(&thetime));
  return 0;
}
```

tmpfile   Open temporary file

Syntax   `FILE *tmpfile(void);`

Include   STDIO.H

Description   Names and creates a temporary file, opened for writing in binary mode. Creates file in the current directory, or if defined, in the directory specified by a TMP or TEMP environment variable. Never overwrites an existing file. The temporary file is automatically deleted when closed or when the program ends. Returns pointer to file stream for success and null for errors.

See also   `fopen, tmpnam`

Example   See `fread`.

tmpnam   Temporary filename

Syntax   `char *tmpnam(char *s);`

Include   STDIO.H

Description   Returns pointer to a temporary filename, guaranteed to be unique in the current directory, or if defined, in a directory specified by the TMP or TEMP environment variables.

Parameters   `char *s` Optional pointer to string buffer at least `L_tmpnam` bytes long in which to store the function result. If s is non-null, `tmpnam()` returns s. If s is null, `tmpnam()` returns the address of static memory that is reused on subsequent calls to `tmpnam()`.

See also   `getenv, mktemp, putenv, tempnam, tmpfile`

Example   See `fflush`.

toascii   Convert int to ASCII

Syntax   `int toascii(int c);`

Include   CTYPE.H

Description	Returns "pure" seven-bit ASCII value by forcing `int c` to the range 0 to 127.
Parameters	`int c` Character to be translated to pure ASCII.
See also	`is...`, `tolower`, `toupper`
Example	

```
/* toascii.cpp */
#include <conio.h>
#include <ctype.h>
main()
{
  int c;
  cprintf("ASCII character values 159 to 255:\r\n");
  for (c = 159; c <= 255; c++)
    putch(c);
  cprintf("\r\n\r\n");
  cprintf("Same values filtered by toascii()\r\n");
  for (c = 159; c <= 255; c++)
    putch(toascii(c));
  return 0;
}
```

tolower   Convert character to lowercase

Syntax	`int tolower(int c);`
Include	CTYPE.H
Description	Returns lowercase equivalent of an ASCII character value c. Affects only alphabetic characters A to Z. Returns other characters unchanged.
Parameters	`int c` ASCII character to be translated. All characters are allowed.
See also	`strlwr, strupr, _tolower, _toupper, toupper`
Example	

```
/* tolower.cpp */
#include <stdio.h>
#include <ctype.h>
main()
{
  char *s = "ABCDEFGHIJKLMNOPQRSTUVWXYZ0123456789";
  printf("s == %s\n", s);
  puts("After tolower()");
  for (int i = 0; s[i]; i++)
    s[i] = tolower(s[i]);
  printf("s == %s\n", s);
  return 0;
}
```

toupper   Convert character to uppercase

Syntax	`int toupper(int c);`
Include	CTYPE.H
Description	Returns uppercase equivalent of an ASCII character value c. Affects only alphabetic characters a to z. Returns other characters unchanged.
Parameters	`int c` ASCII character to be translated. All characters are allowed.
See also	`strlwr, strupr, _tolower, tolower, _toupper`
Example	

```
/* toupper.cpp */
#include <stdio.h>
#include <ctype.h>
main()
{
  char *s = "abcdefghijklmnopqrstuvwxyz0123456789";
  printf("s == %s\n", s);
  puts("After toupper()");
  for (int i = 0; s[i]; i++)
    s[i] = toupper(s[i]);
  printf("s == %s\n", s);
  return 0;
}
```

tzset   Set time zone

Syntax	`void tzset(void);`
Include	TIME.H
Description	Sets the current time zone using the value of an optional environment variable TZ. From DOS, or in a batch file, you can set TZ to a string with a command such as

`set TZ=EST5EDT`

The TZ string, of which the default value is shown here, contains three items: a three-letter abbreviation for the time zone (EST=Eastern Standard Time, PST=Pacific Standard Time, and so on), the number of hours that this time zone differs plus or minus from GMT (Greenwich Mean Time) (EST=5, CST=6, MST=7, PST=8, continental Europe=-1, and so on), and an optional three-letter abbreviation representing the daylight saving time zone (EDT=Eastern daylight saving time, and so on).

Calling tzset() reads the TZ environment variable and sets the values of three global variables accordingly: daylight (true if daylight saving is in effect—that is, if the TZ variable ends with a three-letter suffix such as EDT), timezone (the difference in seconds between local time and GMT), and tzname (an array of pointers to timezone strings—tzname[0] addresses the TZ variable's preface string, such as "EST"; tzname[1] addresses the TZ variable's suffix string, such as "EDT").

See also asctime, ctime, ftime, gmtime, localtime, stime, _strdate, strftime, _strtime, time

Example
```
/* template.cpp */
#include <stdio.h>
#include <stdlib.h>
#include <time.h>
main()
{
  if (getenv("TZ") == NULL)
    putenv("TZ=EST5EDT");
  tzset();
  time_t t = time(NULL);
  printf("Date and time: %s", asctime(localtime(&t)));
  return 0;
}
```

ultoa   Convert unsigned long to string

Syntax char *ultoa(unsigned long value, char *string, int radix);

Include STDLIB.H

Description Converts an unsigned long value to a string.

Parameters **unsigned long value** Value to be converted to a string.

char *string Pointer to char array at least 33 bytes long.

int radix A value from 2 to 36 to use for the converted value's number base.

See also itoa, ltoa

Example
```
/* ultoa.cpp */
#include <stdio.h>
#include <stdlib.h>
main()
{
  unsigned long ul = 987654321L;
  char result[33];
  ultoa(ul, result, 10);
  printf("Value in decimal == %s\n", result);
  ultoa(ul, result, 16);
```

```
      printf("Value in hexadecimal == %s\n", result);
      return 0;
}
```

umask   Set file permissions mask

Syntax   `unsigned umask(unsigned mode);`

Include   IO.H, SYS\STAT.H

Description Sets default file-access permissions for `creat()` and `open()`. Returns
              replaced `mode` value.

Parameters **unsigned mode** Either of the constants `S_IREAD` (permission to read)
              or `S_IWRITE` (permission to write), or the expression (`S_READ |`
              `S_IWRITE`) (permission to read and write).

See also   `creat, open, sopen`

Example
```
/* umask.cpp */
#include <stdio.h>
#include <fcntl.h>
#include <sys\stat.h>
#include <io.h>
#define FNAME "umask.cpp"  // Our own file
main()
{
  unsigned savedmask = umask(S_IREAD | S_IWRITE);
  int handle = open(FNAME, O_TEXT);
  if (handle) {
    printf("%s opened\n", FNAME);
    close(handle);
  } else
    perror(FNAME);
  umask(savedmask);
  // ... Other I/O operations
  return 0;
}
```

ungetc   Return character to input stream

Syntax   `int ungetc(int c, FILE *stream);`

Include   STDIO.H

Description Pushes one character back to an input file stream. The next input
              operation on that same stream—`getc()` or `fgetc()`, for example—
              returns the pushed-back character. Only one such character can be
              pushed onto a file stream at a time. Functions `fflush()`, `fseek()`,
              `fsetpos()`, and `rewind()` delete any pushed-back character. Returns
              c for success and EOF for errors.

26

Parameters **int c** Character to push back to a file stream.

FILE *stream Pointer to an open file stream such as that returned by fopen().

See also fgetc, fread, getc, getchar

Example
```
/* ungetc.cpp */
#include <stdio.h>
#include <string.h>
main()
{
  char s[128];
  puts("Enter a string");
  gets(s);
  if (strlen(s) > 0) {
    printf("Original string == %s\n", s);
    int c = s[strlen(s) - 1];
    printf("Pushing last character %c back to input\n", c);
    ungetc(c, stdin);
    printf("Result from getc() == %c\n", getc(stdin));
  }
  return 0;
}
```

unlink   Delete file

Syntax int unlink(const char *filename);

Include DOS.H or IO.H or STDIO.H

Description Same as remove(). Deletes the named file. (*Unlink* is the UNIX term for *delete file*.) Returns zero for success and -1 for errors; sets errno to EACCES (access denied) or ENOENT (no such file or directory).

Parameters **const char *filename** Pointer to the string representing the name of the file to delete. May contain drive and path information but no wildcards.

See also chmod, remove

Example
```
/* unlink.cpp */
#include <stdio.h>
#include <io.h>
#include <sys\stat.h>
main()
{
  char tfname[L_tmpnam];
  tmpnam(tfname);
  printf("Creating temporary file %s\n", tfname);
  int handle = creat(tfname, S_IWRITE);
  if (handle) {
    puts("Closing temporary file");
    close(handle);
```

```
    }
    printf("Unlinking (removing) %s\n", tfname);
    unlink(tfname);
    return 0;
}
```

unlock Release file-sharing locks

Syntax	`int unlock(int handle, long offset, long length);`
Include	IO.H
Description	Unlocks a lock placed earlier by `lock()`. Requires DOS 3.x and SHARE.EXE installed. Returns zero for success and -1 for errors.
Parameters	**`int handle`** File handle such as that returned by `open()`.
	`long offset` Offset in bytes from the start of the file to the beginning of the locked region.
	`long length` Length of the locked region in bytes.
See also	`lock, sopen`
Example	See `lock`.

va_arg, va_end, va_start Variable arguments

Syntax	`type va_arg(va_list ap, type);`
	`void va_end(va_list ap);`
	`void va_start(va_list ap, lastfix);`
Include	STDARG.H or VARARGS.H
Description	Use these "variable argument" macros to construct functions that accept a variable number of arguments, declared with the three-period ellipsis (. . .). For example, you might declare a function like this:

`void AnyFunction(int FixedParam, ...);`

Function `AnyFunction()` returns `void` and requires at least one `int` argument. The ellipsis indicates that, in addition to `FixedParam`, statements can pass one or more additional argument values of any type (except for values of type `char`, `unsigned char`, and `float`, which are promoted to other types and therefore are not allowed in variable argument lists).

Inside the function, special programming is needed to access these extra parameters. First, declare a variable of type va_list (a pointer to the parameter list), and initialize it with va_start():

```
va_list vap;
va_start(vap, FixedParam);
```

Next, use va_arg() to extract one or more parameters of any type (except the excluded types mentioned earlier). Suppose, for example, that a statement passes two extra int values to the function. You can load these values into local variables like this:

```
int v1 = va_arg(vap, int);
int v2 = va_arg(vap, int);
```

Macro va_arg() requires two arguments: a va_list pointer (vap) and the type of argument to retrieve. If the number of arguments isn't known, use a sentinel to mark the end of the list. You might, for instance, pass a unique value such as -1 to multiparameter functions to end a list of preceding values. You could call the function like this:

```
AnyFunction(10, 9, 8, 7, 6, 5, 4, 3, 2, 1, 0, -1);
```

Assuming by prearrangement that -1 is the end-of-list sentinel, in AnyFunction use a loop to access the parameters:

```
void AnyFunction(int FixedParam, ...)
{
  va_list vap;  // Pointer to variable-argument list
  int v;        // Holds value of each argument
  printf("%d\n", FixedParam);  // Display fixed parameter
  va_start(vap, FixedParam);   // Begin accessing var-arg
list
  while ((v = va_arg(vap, int)) != -1)  // Get one argument
    printf("%d\n", arg);  // Display argument value
  va_end(vap);  // Signal end of list
}
```

The final step in the process passes the initialized vap pointer to va_end() to counter the preceding call to va_start().

Parameters **va_list ap** Pointer to the variable-argument list. Pass to va_start() to initialize, to va_arg() to retrieve the next parameter value, and to va_end() to signal the end of the parameter-retrieval process.

lastfix The address of the last (that is, the rightmost) typed parameter in the argument list. Pass to va_start() only.

type The data type to be returned by va_arg(). Can be different types on successive uses of va_arg(). Cannot be char, unsigned char, or float.

See also   `exec...`, `spawn...`, `v...printf`, `v...scanf`

Example

```
/* va_arg.cpp */
#include <stdio.h>
#include <stdarg.h>
double Average(unsigned num, ...);
main()
{
  double result;
  result = Average(4, 75.5, 89.0, 62.5, 98.0);
  printf("Result = %lf\n", result);
  result = Average(3, 77.7, 88.8, 99.9);
  printf("Result = %lf\n", result);
  return 0;
}

// Return average of a set of double values
// Set num to the number of values that follow
double Average(unsigned num, ...)
{
  va_list vap;
  va_start(vap, num);
  double sum = 0.0;
  for (int i = 0; i < num; i++)
    sum += va_arg(vap, double);
  va_end(vap);
  return sum / num;
}
```

vfprintf   Format output to stream

Syntax

```
int vfprintf(FILE *stream, const char *format, va_list
arglist);
```

Include   STDIO.H

Description   Same as `fprintf()`, but accepts a `va_list` pointer in place of the usual explicit argument values to be formatted to a file stream. Typically used in a function that declares a variable number of parameters (see `va_...()` macros).

Parameters   **FILE *stream** Pointer to a file stream such as that returned by `fopen()`.

                   const char *format Pointer to a format string containing conversion rules and other text, as explained for function `printf()`.

                   va_list arglist A variable-argument list pointer initialized by `va_start()`.

See also   `cprintf`, `fprintf`, `printf`, `scanf`, `sscanf`, `va_arg`, `va_end`, `va_start`, `vfscanf`, `vprintf`, `vscanf`, `vsprintf`, `vsscanf`

951

Example

```
/* vfprintf.cpp */
#include <stdio.h>
#include <stdarg.h>
int MyPrintf(const char *format, ...);
main()
{
  int i = 123;
  double d = 3.14159;
  MyPrintf("int==%d  double=%lf\n", i, d);
  return 0;
}

int MyPrintf(const char *format, ...)
{
  va_list vap;
  va_start(vap, format);
  puts("Inside our own printf()-style function");
  int[]= vfprintf(stdout, format, vap);
  va_end(vap);
  return n;
}
```

vfscanf   Scan and format input from stream

Syntax

```
int vfscan(FILE *stream, const char *format, va_list
arglist);
```

Include

STDIO.H

Description

Same as fscanf() but accepts a va_list pointer in place of the usual address arguments to which values are translated from a file stream. Typically used in a function that declares a variable number of parameters (see va_...() macros).

Parameters

FILE *stream Pointer to a file stream such as that returned by fopen().

const char *format Pointer to a format string containing conversion rules and other text, as explained for function scanf().

va_list arglist A variable-argument list pointer initialized by va_start().

See also

cprintf, fprintf, printf, scanf, sscanf, va_arg, va_end, va_start, vfprintf, vprintf, vscanf, vsprintf, vsscanf

Example

```
/* vfscanf.cpp */
#include <stdio.h>
#include <stdarg.h>
int MyScanf(const char *prompt, const char *format, ...);
main()
{
  int i;
  double d;
  MyScanf("Enter integer and double values: ", "%d %lf", &i,
```

```
➥&d);
  printf("i==%d  d==%lf\n", i, d);
  return 0;
}

int MyScanf(const char *prompt, const char *format, ...)
{
  va_list vap;
  va_start(vap, format);
  printf(prompt);
  int[]= vfscanf(stdin, format, vap);
  va_end(vap);
  return n;
}
```

vprintf   Format output to stdout

Syntax   `int vprintf(const char *format, va_list arglist);`

Include   STDARG.H, STDIO.H

Description   Same as `printf()` but accepts a `va_list` pointer in place of the usual
explicit argument values to be formatted to the standard output.
Typically used in a function that declares a variable number of
parameters (see `va_...()` macros).

Parameters   `const char *format` Pointer to a format string containing conversion rules and other text, as explained for function `printf()`.

`va_list arglist` A variable-argument list pointer initialized by
`va_start()`.

See also   cprintf, fprintf, printf, scanf, sscanf, va_arg, va_end, va_start,
vfprintf, vfscanf, vscanf, vsprintf, vsscanf

Example
```
/* vprintf.cpp */
#include <stdio.h>
#include <stdarg.h>
int MyPrintf(const char *format, ...);
main()
{
  int i = 123;
  double d = 3.14159;
  MyPrintf("int==%d  double=%lf\n", i, d);
  return 0;
}

int MyPrintf(const char *format, ...)
{
  va_list vap;
  va_start(vap, format);
  puts("Inside our own printf()-style function");
  int[]= vprintf(format, vap);
  va_end(vap);
  return n;
}
```

vscanf   Scan and format input from stdin

Syntax   `int vscanf(const char *format, va_list arglist);`

Include   STDARG.H, STDIO.H

Description   Same as `scanf()` but accepts a `va_list` pointer in place of the usual address arguments to which values are translated from the standard input. Typically used in a function that declares a variable number of parameters (see `va_...()` macros).

Parameters   **`const char *format`** Pointer to a format string containing conversion rules and other text, as explained for function `scanf()`.

               `va_list arglist` A variable-argument list pointer initialized by `va_start()`.

See also   `cprintf, fprintf, printf, scanf, sscanf, va_arg, va_end, va_start, vfprintf, vfscanf, vprintf, vsprintf, vsscanf`

Example
```
/* vscanf.cpp */
#include <stdio.h>
#include <stdarg.h>
int MyScanf(const char *prompt, const char *format, ...);
main()
{
  int i;
  double d;
  MyScanf("Enter integer and double values: ", "%d %lf", &i,
&d);
  printf("i==%d  d==%lf\n", i, d);
  return 0;
}

int MyScanf(const char *prompt, const char *format, ...)
{
  va_list vap;
  va_start(vap, format);
  printf(prompt);
  int[]= vscanf(format, vap);
  va_end(vap);
  return n;
}
```

vsprintf   Format output to string

Syntax   `int vsprintf(char *buffer, const char *format, va_list arglist);`

Include   STDARG.H, STDIO.H

Description   Same as `sprintf()`, but accepts a va_list pointer in place of the usual explicit argument values to be formatted to a string buffer. Typically used in a function that declares a variable number of parameters (see va_...() macros).

Parameters   `char *buffer` Pointer to a `char` array large enough to hold the formatted result.

`const char *format` Pointer to a format string containing conversion rules and other text, as explained for the function `printf()`.

`va_list arglist` A variable-argument list pointer initialized by `va_start()`.

See also   cprintf, fprintf, printf, scanf, sscanf, va_arg, va_end, va_start, vfprintf, vfscanf, vprintf, vscanf, vsscanf

Example
```
/* vsprintf.cpp */
#include <stdio.h>
#include <stdarg.h>
int MyPrintf(char *buf, const char *format, ...);
main()
{
  int i = 123;
  double d = 3.14159;
  char buf[80];
  MyPrintf(buf, "int==%d  double=%lf\n", i, d);
  printf("buf contents: %s\n", buf);
  return 0;
}

int MyPrintf(char *buf, const char *format, ...)
{
  va_list vap;
  va_start(vap, format);
  puts("Inside our own printf()-style function");
  int[]= vsprintf(buf, format, vap);
  va_end(vap);
  return n;
}
```

vsscanf   Scan and format input from stream

Syntax
```
int vsscanf(const char *buffer, const char *format,
    va_list arglist);
```

Include   STDARG.H, STDIO.H

Description   Same as `sscanf()` but accepts a va_list pointer in place of the usual address arguments to which values are translated from a `char` buffer. Typically used in a function that declares a variable number of parameters (see va_...() macros).

Parameters   **const char *buffer** Pointer to a char array to be used as the source text.

const char *format Pointer to a format string containing conversion rules and other text, as explained for function scanf().

va_list arglist A variable-argument list pointer initialized by va_start().

See also   cprintf, fprintf, printf, scanf, sscanf, va_arg, va_end, va_start, vfprintf, vfscanf, vprintf, vscanf, vsprintf

Example
```
/* vsscanf.cpp */
#include <stdio.h>
#include <stdarg.h>
int MyScanf(char *buf, const char *format, ...);
main()
{
  int i;
  double d;
  char buf[128];
  printf("Enter integer and double values: ");
  gets(buf);
  MyScanf(buf, "%d %lf", &i, &d);
  printf("i==%d  d==%lf\n", i, d);
  return 0;
}

int MyScanf(char *buf, const char *format, ...)
{
  va_list vap;
  va_start(vap, format);
  int[]= vsscanf(buf, format, vap);
  va_end(vap);
  return n;
}
```

wcstombs   Wide array to multibyte string

Syntax   size_t wcstombs(char *s, const wchar_t *pwcs, size_t n);

Include   STDLIB.H

Description   Translates up to n multibyte characters in a wchar_t (wide-character type) array to a char string. Intended for use with setlocale(), but as currently implemented, simply copies the characters at pwcs to a buffer at s, adding a null-terminating byte if necessary, and has little practical use. Returns the number of characters translated.

Parameters   `char *s` Destination string pointer.

`const wchar_t *pwcs` Pointer to source data, a multibyte character array.

`size_t n` Maximum number of characters to translate.

See also   mblen, mbstowcs, mbtowc, setlocale, wctomb

Example
```
/* wcstombs.cpp */
#include <stdio.h>
#include <stdlib.h>
main()
{
  char s[80];
  wchar_t *pwcs = "Test string";
  wcstombs(s, pwcs, 80);
  printf("s == %s\n", s);
  return 0;
}
```

wctomb   Wide to multibyte character

Syntax   `int wctomb(char *s, wchar_t wc);`

Include   STDLIB.H

Description   Supposedly translates a wide character `wc` to a char pointer destination, returning the number of bytes required to represent the multibyte character in the current locale. As presently implemented, however, simply copies `wc` to the location addressed by `s`, and has little practical use. Returns zero if `s` is null. Returns 1 if `s` is non-null.

Parameters   `char *s` Destination pointer or null.

`wchar_t wc` Character to be translated.

See also   mblen, mbstowcs, mbtowc, setlocale, wcstombs

Example
```
/* wctomb.cpp */
#include <stdio.h>
#include <stdlib.h>
main()
{
  char s[80];
  wchar_t wc = '@';
  int result = wctomb(s, wc);
  printf("result == %d\n", result);
  printf("s[0] == %c\n", s[0]);
  return 0;
}
```

write   Write to file

Syntax   `int write(int handle, void *buf, unsigned len);`

Include   IO.H

Description   General-purpose output function for files identified by an integer handle. Can write text and binary data up to 65,534 bytes at a time. Writes data to the current file position, as set, for example, by `lseek()`. For files opened using the `O_APPEND` option, `write()` sets the internal file pointer to the end of the file prior to each write operation.

Using the function with binary files writes unmodified data. With text files, the function translates line feed control codes to carriage return and line feed pairs—DOS's dual-character end-of-line markers.

Returns the number of bytes successfully written, or -1 for errors and sets `errno` to `EACCES` (access denied) or `EBADF` (bad file handle). For text files, the number of returned bytes counts carriage return and line feed pairs as *one* byte, not two.

Parameters   **int handle** File handle such as that returned by `open()`.

void *buf Pointer to a buffer or other variable containing data to write to the file.

unsigned len Number of bytes to write, starting with the byte addressed by `buf`.

See also   `creat, dup, lseek, open, read, _write`

Example
```
/* write.cpp */
#include <stdio.h>
#include <io.h>
#include <mem.h>
#include <sys\stat.h>
#include <fcntl.h>
char buf[80] = "Introducing\nThe Write Stuff\nby Tom Swan\n";
main()
{
  char fname[L_tmpnam];
  int wresult;
  tmpnam(fname);
  printf("Creating temporary file %s\n", fname);
  int handle = creat(fname, S_IREAD | S_IWRITE);
  if (handle) {
    setmode(handle, O_BINARY);
    puts("Writing data to file");
    wresult = write(handle, buf, sizeof(buf));
    printf("Function wrote %d bytes to file\n", wresult);
```

```
            close(handle);
            setmem(buf, sizeof(buf), 0);   // Erase data buffer
            puts("Reopening file");
            handle = open(fname, O_BINARY, S_IREAD);
            read(handle, buf, sizeof(buf));
            close(handle);
            puts("\nBuffer contents...\n");
            puts(buf);
            remove(fname);
        }
    return 0;
}
```

Character Sets

The following tables show typical character sets for DOS and Windows displays. Table A.1 shows the extended ASCII character set available with DOS text screens. Under Windows, this set is called the Terminal font. Table A.2 shows a typical extended ANSI character set in Windows for the Arial TrueType font. The exact characters you see on-screen depend on your system's hardware and selected font. Unimplemented characters are either blank or shown as empty rectangles.

The tables are arranged in 8 rows of 32 columns and are labeled with hexadecimal numbers. To find the byte value of a character, add its row and column values. For example, a lowercase a in both character sets has the hexadecimal byte value 0x61. A lowercase s has the hex value 0x73.

Table A.1. Extended ASCII characters (DOS).

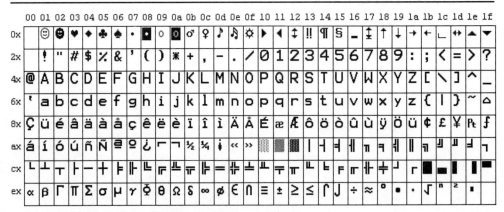

Table A.2. Extended ANSI characters (Windows).

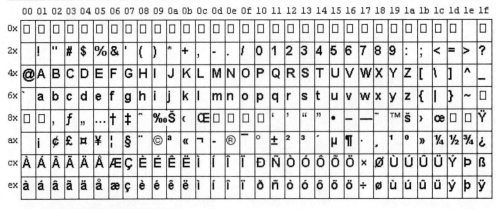

B

Compiler Options

Table B.1. Compiler options.

Option	Default	16-bit only	32-bit only	3.0	3.1	4.5	5.0	Description
@fname				•	•	•	•	Read options from file *fname*.
+fname				•	•	•	•	Use *fname* instead of TURBOC.CFG.
-1		•		•	•	•	•	Enable 80186 instructions.
-1-		•		•	•	•	•	Enable 8088/8086 instructions.
-2	•(bcc)	•		•	•	•	•	Enable 80286 instructions.
-3	•(bcc32)			•	•	•	•	Enable 80386 instructions.
-4			•			•	•	Enable 80486 instructions.
-5			•			•	•	Enable Pentium instructions.
-6			•				•	Enable Pentium Pro instructions.
-a				•	•	•	•	Word alignment.
-a-	•			•	•	•	•	Byte alignment.
-A				•	•	•	•	Limit to ANSI keywords.
-A-	•			•	•	•	•	Enable Borland C++ keywords.
-AK				•	•	•	•	Limit to standard K&R C keywords.
-a*n*						•	•	Align to *n*: 1=byte, 2=word, 4=dword.
-AT				•	•	•	•	Same as -A-.
-AU				•	•	•	•	Limit to UNIX C keywords.

Option	Default	16-bit only	32-bit only	3.0	3.1	4.5	5.0	Description
-b	•			•	•	•	•	Word-size enumerated constants.
-b-				•	•	•	•	Byte-size enumerated constants.
-B				•	•	•	•	Compile to .asm file and assemble.
-c				•	•	•	•	Compile to .obj file; do not link.
-C				•	•	•	•	Enable nested comments.
-C-	•			•	•	•	•	Disable nested comments.
-d				•	•	•	•	Merge duplicate strings.
-d-	•			•	•	•	•	Do not merge duplicate strings.
-dc		•				•	•	Store strings in code segment.
-Dname				•	•	•	•	Define name as null string.
-Dname=str				•	•	•		Define name as string str.
-efname				•	•	•	•	Create linked fname.exe code file.
-Efname				•	•	•	•	Call assembler fname (default=tasm).
-f	•			•	•	•	•	Enable floating-point emulation.
-f-				•	•	•	•	Disable floating-point emulation.

continues

965

Table B.1. continued

Option	Default	16-bit only	32-bit only	3.0	3.1	4.5	5.0	Description
–f287				•	•	•	•	Enable 80287 coprocessor instructions.
–f87				•	•	•	•	Enable 8087 coprocessor instructions.
–Fc				•	•	•	•	Generate COMDEFs (ANSI C only).
–ff	•			•	•	•	•	Enable fast floating point.
–ff–				•	•	•	•	Disable fast floating point.
–Ff				•	•	•	•	Automatically create far variables.
–Ff=size				•	•	•	•	Same as –Ff and set threshold=size.
–Fm				•	•	•	•	Same as –Fc –Ff –Fs.
–fp	•						•	Correct Pentium FDIV flaw.
–Fs				•	•	•	•	Assume ds equals ss.
–gn	• n=255			•	•	•	•	Stop after n warnings.
–G				•	•	•	•	Optimize for speed.
–G–	•			•	•	•	•	Optimize for size.
–h				•	•	•	•	Enable fast huge-pointer arithmetic.

Option	Default	16-bit only	32-bit only	3.0	3.1	4.5	5.0	Description
-H	•			•	•	•	•	Enable precompiled headers.
-H-				•	•	•	•	Disable precompiled headers.
-H"*f*"						•	•	Stop precompiling headers at file *f*.
-H=*fname*				•	•	•	•	Enable precompiled header file *fname*.
-Hc						•	•	Cache precompiled headers.
-Hu				•	•	•	•	Use, don't create, precompiled headers.
-*inum*	•			•	•	•	•	Set maximum identifier length to *num*.
-I*path*				•	•	•	•	Set include-file directories to path.
-Jg	•			•	•	•	•	Template publics; merge duplicates.
-Jgd				•	•	•	•	Template publics; duplicates = error.
-Jgx				•	•	•	•	Template external references.

continues

967

Table B.1. continued

Option	Default	16-bit only	32-bit only	3.0	3.1	4.5	5.0	Description
-j*num*	•			•	•	•	•	Stop after *num* errors.
-k	•			•	•	•	•	Create standard stack frames.
-K				•	•	•	•	Default char is unsigned.
-K-	•			•	•	•	•	Default char is signed.
-K2						•	•	BC++ 3.1 char compatibility.
-l-*opt*				•	•	•	•	Suppress linker option *opt*.
-l*opt*				•	•	•	•	Pass option(s) *opt* to linker.
-L*path*				•	•	•	•	Set library-file directories to *path*.
-mc		•		•	•	•	•	Select compact memory model.
-mh				•	•	•	•	Select huge memory model.
-ml		•		•	•	•	•	Select large memory model.
-mm		•		•	•	•	•	Select medium memory model.
-mm!		•		•	•	•	•	Same as -mm and assume ds !=ss.
-ms	•	•		•	•	•	•	Select small memory model.
-ms!		•		•	•	•	•	Same as -ms and assume ds !=ss.
-mt		•		•	•	•	•	Select tiny memory model.

Option	Default	16-bit only	32-bit only	3.0	3.1	4.5	5.0	Description
-mt!	•			•	•	•	•	Same as -mt and assume ds !=ss.
-M				•	•	•	•	Tell linker to create map file.
-npath				•	•	•	•	Set output directory to path.
-N				•	•	•	•	Enable stack-overflow checking.
-O				•	•	•	•	Optimize unnecessary jumps.
-O1				•	•	•	•	Optimize for smallest size.
-O2				•	•	•	•	Optimize for fastest speed.
-Oa				•	•	•	•	Assume no pointer aliasing.
-Ob				•	•	•	•	Optimize dead code.
-Oc				•	•	•	•	Optimize local common subexpressions.
-Od				•	•	•	•	Disable all optimizations.
-Oe				•	•	•	•	Optimize global register allocation.
-ofname				•	•	•	•	Compile to fname.obj.
-Og				•	•	•	•	Optimize global common subexpressions.

continues

969

Table B.1. continued

Option	Default	16-bit only	32-bit only	3.0	3.1	4.5	5.0	Description
-Oi				•	•	•	•	Inline intrinsic functions.
-OI							•	Optimize across function boundaries (Intel compiler only).
-Ol				•	•	•	•	Optimize loops to REP/STOS.
-Om				•	•	•	•	Optimize invariant code from loops.
-OM							•	Cache hit optimizations (Intel compiler only).
-Op				•	•	•	•	Optimize copy propagation.
-Os				•	•	•	•	Optimize for smaller instructions.
-OS							•	Pentium instruction scheduling.
-Ot				•	•	•	•	Optimize for faster instructions.
-Ov				•	•	•	•	Optimize loop induction variables.
-OW						•	•	Suppress inc bp/dec bp in far functions (16-bit Windows only).
-Ox				•	•	•	•	Optimize for speed (for Microsoft C++ compatibility).

Option	Default	16-bit only	32-bit only	3.0	3.1	4.5	5.0	Description
-p				•	•	•	•	Enable Pascal calling convention.
-pc	•					•	•	Enable C calling convention.
-p-	•			•	•	•	•	Enable C calling convention.
-po						•	•	Use fast this in register.
-pr				•	•	•	•	Enable _fastcall calling convention.
-ps			•			•	•	Enable stdcall convention.
-P				•	•	•	•	Force C++ compile.
-P-	•			•	•	•	•	Automatic C (.c) or C++ (.cpp) compile.
-P-ext				•	•	•	•	C & C++ compile; default extension ext.
-pc						•	•	Enable C calling convention.
-Pext				•	•			C++ compile; default extension ext.
-po	•					•		Enable object-data calling convention.
-Qe	•			•	•			Use all available expanded (EMS) RAM.
-Qe-				•	•			Do not use expanded (EMS) RAM.

Table B.1. continued

Option	Default	16-bit only	32-bit only	3.0	3.1	4.5	5.0	Description
-Qx				•	•			Use extended RAM.
-r	•			•	•	•	•	Enable register variables.
-r-				•	•	•	•	Disable register variables.
-rd				•	•	•	•	Enable declared register variables only.
-R				•	•	•	•	Create ObjectBrowser symbols.
-RT	•					•	•	Enable runtime type information.
-S				•	•	•	•	Compile to .asm file.
-Topt				•	•	•	•	Set assembler option to opt.
-tD						•	•	Create DOS .exe file.
-tDc				•	•	•	•	Create .com file.
-tDe	•			•	•	•	•	Create.exe file.
-Tstr				•	•	•	•	Pass str option to TASM.
-tW	•			•	•	•	•	Compile for Windows (see -W).
-tWC						•	•	Create console .exe file; all functions exportable.
-tWCD						•	•	Create .dll file; all functions exportable.

Option	Default	16-bit only	32-bit only	3.0	3.1	4.5	5.0	Description
-tWCDE						•	•	Create console .dll file; explicit functions exportable.
-tWD						•	•	Create GUI .dll file; all functions exportable.
-tWDE						•	•	Create GUI .dll file; explicit functions exportable.
-tWE						•	•	Create GUI .exe file; explicit functions exportable.
-tWM						•	•	Create multithread 32-bit target.
-tWS						•	•	Create Windows .exe file; smart callback functions.
-tWSE						•	•	Create Windows .exe file; smart callback functions; explicit functions exportable.
-u	•			•	•	•	•	Enable identifier underscores.
-u-				•	•	•	•	Disable identifier underscores.

continues

973

Table B.1. continued

Option	Default	16-bit only	32-bit only	3.0	3.1	4.5	5.0	Description
-U*name*				•	•	•	•	Undefine *name*.
-v				•	•	•	•	Create Turbo Debugger symbols.
-V	•			•	•	•	•	Enable smart C++ virtual tables.
-V0				•	•	•	•	External C++ virtual tables.
-V1				•	•	•	•	Public C++ virtual tables.
-Va				•	•	•	•	Pass class args as temp references.
-Vb				•	•	•	•	Virtual base class ptr size = this size.
-Vc		•		•	•	•	•	No hidden member functions.
-VC						•	•	Calling convention mangling compatibility.
-Vd						•	•	for-loop variable scoping.
-Ve							•	Zero-length empty base classes.
-Vf				•	•	•	•	Enable far C++ virtual tables.
-VF							•	MFC compatibility.
-Vh							•	Treat far classes as huge.
-vi	•			•	•	•	•	Expand inline functions.

Option	Default	16-bit only	32-bit only	3.0	3.1	4.5	5.0	Description
-Vmd				•	•	•	•	Smallest size member pointers.
-Vmm				•	•	•	•	Multiple inheritance mem ptrs okay.
-Vmp				•	•	•	•	Use declared member pointer precision.
-Vms				•	•	•	•	Single inheritance mem ptrs okay.
-Vmv				•	•	•	•	No member pointer restrictions.
-Vo				•	•	•	•	Same as -Va -Vb -Vc -Vp -Vt -Vv.
-Vp				•	•	•	•	Pascal member functions get "this" first.
-Vs				•	•	•	•	Local C++ virtual tables.
-Vt	•			•	•	•	•	BC++ 2.0 virtual table pointers.
-Vv				•	•	•	•	Deep virtual base classes.
-w				•	•	•	•	Disable warnings.
-w-msg				•	•	•	•	Disable warning msg.
-w!						•	•	Return nonzero if warning prevents .obj file creation.

continues

975

Table B.1. continued

Option	Default	16-bit only	32-bit only	3.0	3.1	4.5	5.0	Description
-w*msg*				•	•	•	•	Enable warning *msg*.
-W				•	•	•	•	Windows .obj; all functions exportable.
-WD				•	•	•	•	Windows DLL .obj; all functions exportable.
-WDE				•	•	•	•	Windows DLL .obj; declared functions exportable.
-WE				•	•	•	•	Windows .obj; explicit functions exportable.
-WS				•	•	•	•	Windows .obj; enable smart callbacks.
-WSE						•	•	Create Windows .exe file; smart callback functions; explicit functions exportable.
-x	•					•	•	Enable exception handling.
-xc	•						•	Enable compatible exception handling.
-xd	•					•	•	Enable autodestructor cleanup on exceptions.

Option	Default	16-bit only	32-bit only	3.0	3.1	4.5	5.0	Description
-xf							•	Enable fast exception prologs.
-xp						•	•	Enable exception location information.
-X				•	•	•	•	Disable IDE autodependency information.
-X-	•			•	•	•	•	Enable autodependency information.
-y				•	•	•	•	Add line numbers to symbol table.
-Y				•	•	•	•	Enable code overlays.
-Yo				•	•	•	•	Overlay the following module(s).
-zA*name*				•	•	•	•	Set code class to *name*.
-zB*name*				•	•	•	•	Set BSS class to *name*.
-zC*name*				•	•	•	•	Code segment *name*.
-zD*name*				•	•	•	•	BSS segment *name*.
-zE*name*				•	•	•	•	Far segment *name*.
-zF*name*				•	•	•	•	Far class *name*.
-zG*name*				•	•	•	•	BSS group *name*.
-zH*name*				•	•	•	•	Far group *name*.
-z*name**	•			•	•	•	•	Use default *name* for segment name.

Table B.1. continued

Option	Default	16-bit only	32-bit only	3.0	3.1	4.5	5.0	Description
-zP*name*				•	•	•	•	Code group *name*.
-zR*name*				•	•	•	•	Data segment *name*.
-zS*name*				•	•	•	•	Data group *name*.
-zT*name*				•	•	•	•	Data class *name*.
-zV*name*						•	•	Far virtual segment.
-zW*name*						•	•	Far virtual class.
-z				•	•	•	•	Optimize redundant register loads.

APPENDIX

C

Linker Options

Table C.1. Linker options.

Option	Default	5.0	5.1	6.x	7	Description
/3		•	•	•	•	Enable linking to 32-bit modules
/ax				•	•	Application type: /aa=Windows application, /ap= console application
/A:dd				•	•	.Exe file page alignment
/A=num	512	•	•	•	•	Set segment alignment to num bytes
/B:x				•	•	32-bit image base address (x in hex)
/C		•	•	•	•	Case-sensitive EXPORTS and IMPORTS
/c		•	•	•	•	Case significant public, extern symbols
/d		•	•	•	•	Warn about duplicate library symbols
/e		•	•	•	•	Ignore library extended dictionary
/E				•	•	Enable extended dictionary processing
/En				•	•	Set maximum errors to n before halting link operation
/f				•	•	Do not optimize far calls to near data
/Gn				•	•	Discard nonresident name table
/Gr				•	•	Transfer resident names to nonresident name table
/Gm				•	•	Write mangled identifiers to map file
/i		•	•	•	•	Include uninitialized data segments
/Lpath		•	•	•	•	Search path for library files
/l		•	•	•	•	Add line numbers to map file
/m		•	•	•	•	Create map file with public symbols

Option	Default	5.0	5.1	6.x	7	Description
/n		•	•	•	•	Disable use of default libraries
/o		•	•	•	•	Overlay next modules or libraries
/o-	•	•	•	•	•	Stop linking overlay segments
/oovy		•	•	•	•	Link code segments of class *ovy*
/o#hex	3f	•	•	•	•	Change overlay interrupt to *hex*
/P	•	•	•	•	•	Pack code segments
/P=num	8192	•	•	•	•	Pack code segments up to *num* bytes
/Rk				•	•	Specify RLINK option *k*
/Rv				•	•	Verbose resource binding
Re*x*				•	•	Rename .exe file to *x*
/s		•	•	•	•	Add segment information to map file
/S:x				•	•	Set 32-bit stack size to *x* in hex
/t		•	•	•	•	Link to .com file (tiny memory model)
/Td	•	•	•		•	Link to DOS .exe code file
/Tdc		•	•	•	•	Link to DOS .com file
/Tde	•	•	•	•	•	Link to DOS .exe code file
/Tpd				•	•	Create 32-bit .dll file
/Tpe				•	•	Create 32-bit .exe file
/Tw		•	•	•	•	Link to Windows .exe or .dll file
/Twd		•	•	•	•	Link to Windows .dll file
/Twe		•	•	•	•	Link to Windows .exe file
/v		•	•	•	•	Add Turbo Debugger symbols to output
/wxxx				•	•	Enable/disable warning *xxx*
/x	•	•	•	•	•	Do not create map file
/ye	•	•	•	•	•	Swap to expanded (EMS) RAM
/ye-		•	•	•	•	Do not swap to expanded (EMS) RAM
/yx		•	•	•	•	Swap to 8M maximum of extended RAM

continues

Table C.1. continued

Option	Default	5.0	5.1	6.x	7	Description
/yx+		•	•	•	•	Swap to all available extended RAM
/yxnum		•	•	•	•	Swap to num K of extended RAM

D

Operator Precedence and Associativity

Table D.1. Operator precedence and associativity.

Level	Operators	Evaluation Order
1 (high)	( ) . [ ] -> ::	left-to-right
2	* & ! ~ ++ -- + - sizeof new delete	right-to-left
3	.* -> *	left-to-right
4	* / %	left-to-right
5	+ -	left-to-right
6	<< >>	left-to-right
7	< <= > >=	left-to-right
8	== !=	left-to-right
9	&	left-to-right
10	^	left-to-right
11	¦	left-to-right
12	&&	left-to-right
13	¦¦	left-to-right
14	?:	right-to-left
15	= *= /= += -= %= <<= >>= &= ^= ¦=	right-to-left
16 (low)	,	left-to-right

Operators at the top of the table have higher precedence than operators below. In expressions, beginning with arguments in the innermost set of parentheses (if any), programs evaluate operators of higher precedence before evaluating operators of lower precedence.

Unary plus (+) and unary minus (-) are at Level 2 and have precedence over arithmetic plus and minus at Level 5. The & symbol at Level 2 is the address-of operator; the & symbol at Level 9 is the bitwise AND operator. The * symbol at Level 2 is the pointer-dereference operator; the * symbol at Level 4 is the multiplication operator. In the absence of clarifying parentheses, operators on the same level are evaluated according to their left-to-right or right-to-left evaluation order.

C and C++ Keywords

The following table lists all ANSI C, ANSI C++, and Borland C++ keywords in alphabetical order. These words are reserved for the compiler, and you are not allowed to use them for your own identifiers.

Table E.1. Keywords.

__asm	__cdecl	__cs	__declspec	__ds
__es	__except	__export	__far	__fastcall
__finally	__huge	__import	__interrupt	__loadds
__near	__pascal	__rtti	__saveregs	__seg
__ss	__stdcall	__thread	__try	_asm
_cdecl	_cs	_ds	_es	_export
_far	_fastcall	_huge	_import	_interrupt
_loadds	_near	_pascal	_saveregs	_seg
_ss	_stdcall	asm	auto	bool
break	case	catch	cdecl	char
class	const	const_cast	continue	default
delete	do	double	dynamic_cast	else
enum	explicit	extern	false	far
float	for	friend	goto	huge
if	inline	int	interrupt	long
mutable	namespace	near	new	operator
pascal	private	protected	public	register
reinterpret_cast	return	short	signed	sizeof
static	static_cast	struct	switch	template
this	throw	true	try	typedef
typeid	typename	union	unsigned	using
virtual	void	volatile	wchar_t	while

Answers to
Exercises

Hey, no peeking! Following are answers to all exercises in Chapters 3 through 8, which make up this book's C++ tutorial. Other chapters do not have exercises. Would you believe me if I told you this is because those chapters already have all the answers? I thought not.

NOTE

Except where specifically noted, all files referred to in the following answers are in the Source\Answers directory on the CD-ROM.

Chapter 3

3.1

The solution is nearly identical to program Filter.cpp but calls function `toupper` to convert characters to uppercase before writing them to the standard output with `cout.put`. Function `toupper` is prototyped in Ctype.h in the BC5\Include directory. Compile Toupper.cpp and then from DOS, run the program with a command such as `toupper <toupper.cpp`.

Toupper.cpp (converts input to all uppercase).

```
//===============================================================
// Toupper.cpp -- Converts input to all uppercase
// To compile:
//    bcc toupper
// To run:
//    toupper <toupper.cpp
// Copyright (c) 1996 by Tom Swan. All rights reserved.
//===============================================================

#include <iostream.h>
#include <ctype.h>

void main()
{
  char c;

  while (cin.get(c))
    cout.put((char)toupper(c));
}
```

3.2

Getval2.cpp uses a modified `test` function, which returns the `bool` value `true` if no errors have been detected. If `cin.good` is `false`, then something is wrong with the input stream. In that event, after displaying an error message, `test` clears the stream's state by calling `cin.clear`. It also discards the bad input (which remains in the stream) by repeatedly calling the input stream's get function.

Getval2.cpp (repeatedly prompts for valid input).

```
//================================================================
// Getval2.cpp -- Repeatedly prompts for valid input
// To compile:
//    bcc getval2
// To run:
//    getval2
// Copyright (c) 1996 by Tom Swan. All rights reserved.
//================================================================

#include <iostream.h>

bool test(void);

void main()
{
  double fp;   // A floating point value
  long k;      // A long int value

  do {
    cout << "Enter a floating point value: ";
    cin >> fp;
  } while (!test());
  cout << "Value entered is: " << fp << endl;
  do {
    cout << "Enter an integer value: ";
    cin >> k;
  } while (!test());
  cout << "Value entered is: " << k << endl;
}

bool test(void)
{
  if (!cin.good()) {
    cout << "Error detected" << endl;
    cin.clear();    // Clear error flags
    while (cin.get() != '\n') ;  // Discard bad input
    return false;
  }
  return true;
}
```

3.3

Inline functions are typically stored in header files, as demonstrated by Min.h here. Enter that file separately (or copy it from the CD-ROM's Source\Answers directory). Then, enter, save, and compile Min.cpp, which demonstrates how to use min.

989

Min.h (declares min function).

```
//================================================================
// Min.h -- Declares min function
// Copyright (c) 1996 by Tom Swan. All rights reserved.
//================================================================

inline int min(int a, int b)
{
  if (a <= b)
    return a;
  else
    return b;
}
```

Min.cpp (tests the min function in Min.h).

```
//================================================================
// Min.cpp -- Tests the min function in min.h
// To compile:
//    bcc min
// To run:
//    min
// Copyright (c) 1996 by Tom Swan. All rights reserved.
//================================================================

#include <iostream.h>
#include "min.h"

void main()
{
  int x, y;

  cout << "X? ";
  cin >> x;
  cout << "Y? ";
  cin >> y;
  cout << "min(a, b) == " << min(x, y) << endl;
}
```

3.4

The solution, Minbench.cpp, calls function clock, prototyped in Time.h. Before compiling Minbench.cpp, you might need to adjust const ITERATIONS, set to 5 million loops. This value produces reasonable results for a 100MHz Pentium-based PC but should be set lower to reduce the program's running time for a slower system. Higher values also produce more accurate results. The program includes Min.h from Exercise 3.3 and calls inline min the specified number of times. For comparison, another loop calls a similar non-inline function fmin. Note: If you run this program under Turbo Debugger, the reported times for the inline and non-inline functions are the same, proving that the compiler converts inline functions to normal ones for debugging.

Minbench.cpp (benchmarks inline and non-inline functions).

```
//=============================================================
// Minbench.cpp -- Benchmarks inline and non-inline functions
// To compile:
//   (adjust const ITERATIONS for reasonable running time)
//   bcc minbench
// To run:
//   minbench
// Copyright (c) 1996 by Tom Swan. All rights reserved.
//=============================================================

#include <iostream.h>
#include <time.h>
#include "min.h"

int fmin(int a, int b);
void mark(clock_t &start);
void report(clock_t start, const char *message);

const long ITERATIONS = 5000000L;  // Adjust as necessary

void main()
{
  int z;          // Throw-away integer
  long i;         // For-loop control variable
  clock_t start;  // Starting time for benchmark

  cout << "Testing...";
  mark(start);
  for (i = 0; i < ITERATIONS; i++)
    z = fmin(1, 2);
  report(start, "Normal function calls");

  cout << "Testing...";
  mark(start);
  for (i = 0; i < ITERATIONS; i++)
    z = min(1, 2);
  report(start, "Inline function calls");
  i = z;  // So compiler doesn't complain that z is not used
}

int fmin(int a, int b)
{
  if (a <= b)
    return a;
  else
    return b;
}

void mark(clock_t &start)
{
  start = clock();  // Mark starting time
}

void report(clock_t start, const char *message)
{
  clock_t stop = clock();  // Mark ending time
```

continues

991

continued

```
  cout << endl << message << endl;
  cout << " elapsed time == " <<
    (stop - start) / CLK_TCK << " seconds" << endl;
}
```

3.5

Compile the solution, Abs.cpp, with the DOS command bcc -v abs and then load the code into Turbo Debugger with the command td abs. Set breakpoints at the beginning of each overloaded absolute function, and press F9 to run. As you respond to the program's prompts, the debugger halts the code in each of the overloaded functions. Although the three absolute functions have the same name, the compiler distinguishes among them by their different parameters.

Abs.cpp (demonstrates overloaded functions).

```
//================================================================
// Abs.cpp -- Demonstrates overloaded functions
// To compile:
//    bcc -v abs
// To run in Turbo Debugger:
//    td abs
// Copyright (c) 1996 by Tom Swan. All rights reserved.
//================================================================

#include <iostream.h>

int absolute(int x);
long absolute(long x);
double absolute(double x);

void main()
{
  int ivalue;
  long lvalue;
  double fvalue;

  cout << "Enter integer: ";
  cin >> ivalue;
  cout << " absolute() == " << absolute(ivalue) << endl;
  cout << "Enter long integer: ";
  cin >> lvalue;
  cout << " absolute() == " << absolute(lvalue) << endl;
  cout << "Enter floating point value: ";
  cin >> fvalue;
  cout << " absolute() == " << absolute(fvalue) << endl;
}

int absolute(int x)
{
  if (x < 0)
```

```
      return -x;
  else
      return x;
}

long absolute(long x)
{
  if (x < 0)
    return -x;
  else
    return x;
}

double absolute(double x)
{
  if (x < 0)
    return -x;
  else
    return x;
}
```

3.6

Readstr.cpp uses I/O stream statements and the new operator to read strings into dynamic buffers created on the heap. Note: Some C++ purists would recommend changing #define MAX 3 to a true constant declared as const int MAX = 3;. There's nothing wrong with this technique, but the benefits gained are debatable.

Readstr.cpp (reads strings into dynamic buffers).

```
//================================================================
// Readstr.cpp -- Reads strings into dynamic buffers
// To compile:
//    bcc readstr
// To run:
//    readstr
// Copyright (c) 1996 by Tom Swan. All rights reserved.
//================================================================

#include <iostream.h>
#include <string.h>

#define MAX 3      // Maximum number of strings

char *ReadString(void);

void main()
{
  int i;               // Array index
  char *array[MAX];    // Array of MAX char pointers

  cout << "Enter " << MAX << " strings:" << endl;
  for (i = 0; i < MAX; i++)
    array[i] = ReadString();
```

continued

```
   cout << endl << endl << "Your strings are:" << endl;
   for (i = 0; i < MAX; i++)
     cout << array[i] << endl;
}

char *ReadString(void)
{
   char *p;             // p is a pointer to a char array
   char buffer[128];    // buffer for reading each string

   cin.getline(buffer, sizeof(buffer));
   p = new char[1 + strlen(buffer)];
   strcpy(p, buffer);
   return p;
}
```

3.7

The new program, Reffunc2.cpp, has four main changes: struct customer has a new customer*
pointer field named next, database is a pointer to a list instead of an array, the function
FillDataBase creates a linked list of customer structures, and the reference function BalanceOf
searches the list. Functions main and Currency are unchanged, and the program operates no
differently from before despite the major change to the techniques used to store information.

Reffunc2.cpp (stores double values in a linked list).

```
//===============================================================
// Reffunc2.cpp -- Stores double values in a linked list
// To compile:
//    bcc reffunc2
// To run:
//    reffunc2
// Copyright (c) 1996 by Tom Swan. All rights reserved.
//===============================================================

#include <iostream.h>
#include <stdio.h>
#include <stdlib.h>
#include <string.h>

#define SIZE 10  // Number of records in database
#define SLEN 40  // String length

struct customer {
  char name[SLEN];
  double balance;
  customer *next;  // Pointer to next customer
};

void FillDatabase(void);
const double &BalanceOf(const char *name);
```

```
const char *Currency(double d);

customer *database;   // Array is now a list pointer

void main()
{
  char custname[SLEN];
  bool done = false;

  FillDatabase();
  cout << "Enter 'Customer-X' where X = A, B, C, etc." << endl;
  cout << "Or, press Enter to end program." << endl;
  while (!done) {
    cin.getline(custname, SLEN);
    done = (strlen(custname) == 0);
    if (!done)
      cout << Currency(BalanceOf(custname)) << endl;
  }
}

// Fill database with sample values and display
void FillDatabase(void)
{
  customer *cp;   // Pointer to new customer struct

  randomize();
  for (int i = 0; i < SIZE; i++) {
    cp = new customer;  // Allocate memory for new customer
    if (!cp) {
      cerr << endl << "Out of memory" << endl;
      exit(1);
    }
    strcpy(cp->name, "Customer-X");
    cp->name[9] = 'A' + i;  // "A, B, ..., Z"
    cp->balance = rand() * 0.01;
    cout << cp->name
      << Currency(cp->balance) << endl;
    if (database == NULL) {
      database = cp;          // Create new list
      cp->next = NULL;        // There is no "next" struct
    } else {
      cp->next = database;    // Insert customer into list
      database = cp;          // Change list head to new insert
    }
  }
}

// Return reference to customer balance
const double &BalanceOf(const char *name)
{
  static const double errval = -1;
  customer *cp;

  cp = database;
  while (cp != NULL) {
    if (stricmp(cp->name, name) == 0)
      return cp->balance;
    cp = cp->next;
```

continues

continued

```
  }
  return errval;
}

// Return pointer to formatted string
const char *Currency(double d)
{
  static char buffer[40] = "";
  if (d == -1.0)
    strcpy(buffer, "Error. Enter 'Customer-x'.");
  else
    sprintf(buffer, "  $%8.2f", d);
  return buffer;
}
```

Chapter 4

4.1

Listing Button.cpp shows only one of many possible solutions.

Button.cpp (suggested pushbutton class).

```
//================================================================
// Button.cpp -- Suggested pushbutton class
// To compile:
//    bcc button
// To run:
//    button
// Copyright (c) 1996 by Tom Swan. All rights reserved.
//================================================================

#include <iostream.h>

#define OFF 0
#define ON 1

class TButton {
private:
  int state;                   // Data member
public:
  TButton();                   // Constructor
  TButton(int initialState);   // Overloaded constructor
  int GetState(void);          // Member function
  void SetState(int newState); //    "        "
  void Toggle(void);           //    "        "
  void Display(void);          //    "        "
};

void Show3Buttons(TButton &b1, TButton &b2, TButton &b3);
```

```
void main()
{
  TButton b1;  // Initialized via default constructor
  TButton b2(ON);  // Initialize b2 to ON state
  TButton b3(OFF);  // Initialize b3 to OFF state

  cout << "After initializing three TButton objects" << endl;
  Show3Buttons(b1, b2, b3);
  b1.SetState(ON);
  cout << "After setting b1's state to ON" << endl;
  Show3Buttons(b1, b2, b3);
  b1.Toggle();
  b2.Toggle();
  b3.Toggle();
  cout << "After toggling b1, b2, and b3" << endl;
  Show3Buttons(b1, b2, b3);
}

// Common function to display 3 button references
void Show3Buttons(TButton &b1, TButton &b2, TButton &b3)
{
  cout << " Button b1: ";
  b1.Display();  // Call button's member function
  cout << " Button b2: ";
  b2.Display();
  cout << " Button b3: ";
  b3.Display();
}

// Default constructor
TButton::TButton()
{
  state = OFF;  // Initialize button to OFF state
}

// Alternate constructor
TButton::TButton(int initialState)
{
  state = initialState;  // Initialize button to specified state
}

// Return current button state
int TButton::GetState(void)
{
  return state;
}

void TButton::SetState(int newState)
{
  state = newState;
}

void TButton::Toggle(void)
{
  if (state == OFF)
    state = ON;
  else
    state = OFF;
```

continues

997

continued

```
}

void TButton::Display(void)
{
  cout << "state == ";
  if (state == OFF)
    cout << "OFF" << endl;
  else
    cout << "ON" << endl;
}
```

4.2

The TTime class constructor automatically initializes a class object to the current date and time. So the solution is simple: Just declare a TTime object (today in Dt.cpp) and call the object's Display member function.

Dt.cpp (displays current date and time).

```
//==================================================================
// Dt.cpp -- Displays current date and time
// To compile:
//    bcc -c time6
//    bcc dt time6.obj
// To run:
//    dt
// Copyright (c) 1996 by Tom Swan. All rights reserved.
//==================================================================

#include <iostream.h>
#include "time6.h"

void main()
{
  TTime today;
  today.Display();
}
```

4.3

Add the following line to Dt.cpp after declaring the TTime object today:

```
today.ChangeTime(24 * 60);  // i.e. 24 hours later
```

4.4

The TTime class can already display the day of the week (see Dt.cpp in Exercise 4.2, for example). Day.cpp converts command-line arguments into numeric form, checks for input errors, and assigns a date to a `TTime` class object. Calling that object's `Display` member function displays the day of the week for that date. As a bonus, Day.cpp lists a handy function, `GetMonth`, that converts a month name such as Jan or Apr to an integer value, with January equal to 1, February equal to 2, and so on.

Day.cpp (reports day of week for any date).

```
//================================================================
// Day.cpp -- Reports day of week for any date
// To compile:
//    bcc -c time6
//    bcc day time6.obj
// To run:
//    day Jan 1 2001
// Copyright (c) 1996 by Tom Swan. All rights reserved.
//================================================================

#include <iostream.h>
#include <stdlib.h>
#include <string.h>
#include "time6.h"

const char months[] = "decnovoctsepaugjuljunmayaprmarfebjan";

void CheckDate(int month, int day, int year);
int GetMonth(const char *amonth);
void Error(const char *s);

void main(int argc, char *argv[])
{
  int month, day, year;

  if (argc <= 3)
    Error("Enter a date such as jan 5 1997");
  strlwr(argv[1]);  // Convert month name to lowercase
  month = GetMonth(argv[1]);
  day = atoi(argv[2]);
  year = atoi(argv[3]);
  CheckDate(month, day, year);
  TTime theDate(month, day, year);
  theDate.Display();
}

// Halt with error if any params are bad
void CheckDate(int month, int day, int year)
{
  if ((month < 1) || (month > 12))
    Error("Bad month value");
  if ((day < 1) || (day > 31))
    Error("Bad day value");
  if (year < 1970)
    Error("Bad year value");
}

// Convert monthname string to integer
int GetMonth(const char *amonth)
```

continued

```
{
  const char *s = strstr(months, amonth);
  if (s == NULL)
    Error("Bad month name");
  return (strlen(s) / 3);
}

// Display error message and exit program
void Error(const char *s)
{
  cout << endl << "Error: " << s << endl;
  exit(1);
}
```

4.5

The new TTime constructor and member functions GetSeconds and PutSeconds are written inline, although these could be implemented separately. Use Time6.cpp to compile the new TTime class declaration. (In other words, include Time7.h into Time6.cpp in place of Time6.h.)

Time7.h (declares TTime class version 7).

```
//================================================================
// Time7.h -- Declares TTime class version 7
// Copyright (c) 1996 by Tom Swan. All rights reserved.
//================================================================

#ifndef __TIME7_H
#define __TIME7_H   // Prevent multiple #includes

#include <iostream.h>
#include <time.h>
#include <string.h>

class TTime {
private:
  long dt;   // Date and time in seconds from January 1, 1970
  char *dts; // Date and time as a string
  void DeleteDts(void);   // Delete dts pointer
public:
  TTime();                                   // Constructor
  TTime(int m, int d = -1, int y = -1,       // Constructor
    int hr = -1, int min = -1);

  TTime(long seconds) { dt = seconds; }

  ~TTime();                                  // Destructor
  void Display(void) { cout << ctime(&dt); }

  long GetSeconds(void) { return dt; }
  void SetSeconds(long newSeconds) { dt = newSeconds; }
```

```
    void GetTime(int &m, int &d, int &y, int &hr, int &min);
    void SetTime(int m = -1, int d = -1, int y = -1,
      int hr = -1, int min = -1);
    const char *GetSTime(void);
    void ChangeTime(long nminutes)
      { dt += (nminutes * 60); DeleteDts(); }
};

#endif  // __TIME7_H
```

4.6

Most of the TStr (Type String) class member functions are simple one-statement models and are therefore declared inline. The class is implemented here in separate modules. Tstr.h declares the class. Tstr.cpp implements the destructor and a member function. Testtstr.cpp is a test program that uses the class. Follow compilation instructions in the listings.

Class TStr stores a single private data member, s, a pointer to char. The default constructor TStr sets s to NULL, thus ensuring that s is initialized to a known value for all TStr class objects. An alternate constructor TStr(char *ss); provides a method to initialize a TStr class object to a specific string (see Testtstr.cpp for an example). Member function GetStr returns the value of data member s. Member function PutStr (see Tstr.cpp) deletes any current string addressed by s and then creates a new one by calling the string library function strdup.

The TStr class destructor deletes any addressed string to clean up a TStr class object before it is destroyed. The destructor is implemented in module Tstr.cpp, but you could also write it inline. A useful experiment is to run Testtstr.cpp in Turbo Debugger (use commands bcc -v testtstr tstr and td testtstr). Set a breakpoint on the destructor in module Tstr.cpp and run the program to detect when C++ calls the TStr destructor to delete addressed strings.

Tstr.h (declares the TStr class).

```
//================================================================
// Tstr.h -- Declares the TStr class
// Copyright (c) 1996 by Tom Swan. All rights reserved.
//================================================================

#ifndef __TSTR_H
#define __TSTR_H   // Prevent multiple #includes

#include <string.h>

class TStr {
private:
  char *s;  // Pointer to class object's string
public:
  TStr() { s = NULL; }
  TStr(char *ss) { s = strdup(ss); }
  ~TStr();
```

continues

continued

```
  const char *GetStr(void) { return s; }
  void PutStr(const char *ss);
};

#endif  // __TSTR_H
```

Tstr.cpp. (implements the TStr class).

```
//===============================================================
// Tstr.cpp -- Implements the TStr class
// To compile:
//    bcc -c tstr
// Copyright (c) 1996 by Tom Swan. All rights reserved.
//===============================================================

#include "tstr.h"

// Destructor
TStr::~TStr()
{
  delete s;
}

// Change string to ss
void TStr::PutStr(const char *ss)
{
  delete s;
  s = strdup(ss);
}
```

Testtstr.cpp (tests the TStr class).

```
//===============================================================
// Testtstr.cpp -- Tests the TStr class
// To compile:
//    bcc -c tstr
//    bcc testtstr tstr.obj
// To run:
//    testtstr
// Copyright (c) 1996 by Tom Swan. All rights reserved.
//===============================================================

#include <iostream.h>
#include "tstr.h"

void main()
{
  TStr nullString;
  TStr myName("Tom Swan");
  TStr anyString;
```

```
  anyString.PutStr("Any 'ol string");
  cout << "The three strings are:" << endl;
  cout << " nullString == " << nullString.GetStr() << endl;
  cout << " myName == " << myName.GetStr() << endl;
  cout << " anyString == " << anyString.GetStr() << endl;
  anyString.PutStr(myName.GetStr());
  cout << "After copying myName to anyString" << endl;
  cout << " myName == " << myName.GetStr() << endl;
  cout << " anyString == " << anyString.GetStr() << endl;
}
```

4.7

For simplicity, Rtext.cpp reads a text file of up to 200 lines into an array of TStr class objects. The purpose of this exercise is not to provide a sophisticated file reader but to have you think about the methods for creating multiple class objects in a program. One way to improve the code would be to design a new class object that can store a list or array of strings as a data member. That way, the data representation could change without affecting most of the programming.

Rtext.cpp (reads a text file up to 200 lines).

```
//==============================================================
// Rtext.cpp -- Reads a text file up to 200 lines
// To compile:
//    bcc -c tstr
//    bcc rtext tstr.obj
// To run:
//    rtext rtext.cpp
// Copyright (c) 1996 by Tom Swan. All rights reserved.
//==============================================================

#include <iostream.h>
#include <stdio.h>
#include <stdlib.h>
#include "tstr.h"

void Error(const char *s);

#define MAXSTRINGS 200
TStr sarray[MAXSTRINGS];

void main(int argc, char *argv[])
{
  FILE *inf;
  char buffer[256];
  int index = 0;
  if (argc <= 1)
    Error("Specify text file name to read");
// Open file
  inf = fopen(argv[1], "r");
  if (inf == NULL)
    Error("Can't open file");
// Read file into array of TStr objects
```

continued

```
  while (fgets(buffer, 255, inf) != NULL) {
    sarray[index].PutStr(buffer);
    if (++index >= MAXSTRINGS)
      Error("File too large");
  }
  fclose(inf);
// Display strings in array
  for (int i = 0; i < index; i++)
    cout << sarray[i].GetStr();
}

void Error(const char *s)
{
  puts(s);
  exit(1);
}
```

Chapter 5

5.1

The following program, Screen.cpp, is by no means a complete input-screen designer, but it could serve as a starting place for a more sophisticated utility. Class TText can store and display a string at a specified (X,Y) coordinate, using any foreground or background color as declared in Conio.h. Class TData derives from TText but adds the capability of prompting for new strings. A third class, TScEntry, owns two data member pointers. One pointer addresses an object of type TText and is used to display a label such as Name or Address. A second pointer addresses an object of type TData—the input field where users can enter data associated with this label. You must compile and run this program as a DOS application because EasyWin does not support interactive terminal commands and display colors.

Screen.cpp (implements a sample input-screen designer).

```
//===============================================================
// Screen.cpp -- Implements a sample input-screen designer
// To compile:
//    bcc screen
// To run as a DOS program only:
//    screen
// Copyright (c) 1996 by Tom Swan. All rights reserved.
//===============================================================

#include <iostream.h>
#include <stdlib.h>
#include <string.h>
#include <conio.h>

#define BLANK ' '        // Blank ASCII character
#define MAXLEN 64        // All time input maximum length
```

```
#define FLABEL YELLOW   // Foreground label color
#define BLABEL CYAN     // Background label color
#define FDATA WHITE     // Foreground data color
#define BDATA BLACK     // Background data color

void Error(const char *s);

// Display text with attributes on screen
class TText {
protected:
  int x, y;              // Coordinate
  int fcolor, bcolor;    // Fore and background colors
  char *string;          // Pointer to text string
public:
  TText(int xc, int yc, int fore, int back, const char *s);
  virtual ~TText() { delete string; }
  void PutString(const char *s);
  void Erase(void);
  void Display(void);
};

// Derive a data-entry object from TText
class TData: public TText {
public:
  TData(int xc, int yc, int fore, int back, const char *s)
    : TText(xc, yc, fore, back, s) { }
  const char *GetText(int maxlen);
};

// One screen entry with label and data entry objects
class TScEntry {
protected:
  TText *labelp;  // Pointer to a TText object
  TData *datap;   // Pointer to a TData object
public:
  TScEntry(int xc, int yc,
    const char *labelStr, const char *dataStr);
  ~TScEntry() { delete labelp; delete datap; }
  void Display(void);
  void Edit(void);
};

void main()
{
  TScEntry *screen[3];  // Array of TScEntry objects
  int i;  // screen array index

  clrscr();
  screen[0] = new TScEntry(4, 4, "Name: ", "Tom Swan");
  screen[1] = new TScEntry(4, 6, "Company: ", "Swan Software");
  screen[2] = new TScEntry(4, 8, "Address: ", "Key West FL");
  for (i = 0; i < 3; i++)  // Display screen
    screen[i]->Display();
  for (i = 0; i < 3; i++)  // Edit entries
    screen[i]->Edit();
  for (i = 0; i < 3; i++)  // Delete objects
    delete screen[i];
  gotoxy(1, 24);
}
```

continued

```
// Halt program after displaying error message
void Error(const char *s)
{
  gotoxy(1, 24);
  cout << endl << s << endl;
  exit(1);
}

// Construct a TText object
TText::TText(int xc, int yc, int fore, int back, const char *s)
{
  if (s == NULL)
    Error("Null string pointer passed to TText constructor");
  x = xc;
  y = yc;
  fcolor = fore;
  bcolor = back;
  string = strdup(s);
}

// Change a TText object's string
void TText::PutString(const char *s)
{
  if (s == NULL)
    Error("Null string pointer passed to PutString");
  Erase();
  delete string;        // Delete current string
  string = strdup(s);   // Copy new string to heap
}

// Erase current string display
void TText::Erase()
{
  int len = strlen(string);
  gotoxy(x, y);
  for (int i = 0; i < len; i++)
    putch(BLANK);
}

// Display TText object
void TText::Display()
{
  Erase();                     // Clear area on screen
  gotoxy(x, y);                // Position cursor
  textcolor(fcolor);           // Set foreground color
  textbackground(bcolor);      // Set background color
  cputs(string);               // Display the string
}

// Return new data entry
const char *TData::GetText(int maxlen)
{
  char buffer[MAXLEN + 3];  // Raw input buffer

  if ((maxlen > MAXLEN) || (maxlen <= 0))
    maxlen = MAXLEN;        // Adjust maxlen if necessary
  Erase();                  // Clear entry area
```

```
  gotoxy(x, y);              // Position cursor
  buffer[0] = maxlen;        // Set length for cgets()
  cgets(buffer);             // Get string
  if (buffer[1] > 0)         // If length of input > 0
    PutString(&buffer[2]);   //  insert new string into object
  Display();                 // Make sure display is "right"
  return string;             // Return new or old string
}

// Construct a TScEntry object
TScEntry::TScEntry(int xc, int yc,
  const char *labelStr, const char *dataStr)
{
  int len = strlen(labelStr) + 1;  // Data entry position
  labelp = new TText(xc, yc, FLABEL, BLABEL, labelStr);
  datap = new TData(xc + len, yc, FDATA, BDATA, dataStr);
  if ((labelp == NULL) || (datap == NULL))
    Error("Out of memory in TScEntry constructor");
}

// Display TScEntry's label and data
void TScEntry::Display(void)
{
  labelp->Display();  // Display entry label
  datap->Display();   // Display current data
}

// Edit TScEntry's data (not saved)
void TScEntry::Edit(void)
{
  datap->GetText(30);  // 30 == maximum input length
}
```

5.2

To compile Average.cpp, follow the instructions in the chapter for Tbench.cpp (see Listing 5.3), but replace Tbench with Average. The new program derives a class TAverage from TBench. The TAverage constructor specifies the number of repeated tests to perform (numSets). During each test, the program displays the elapsed time, saved in a private data member, result. TAverage's Display member function displays the average elapsed time by dividing result by sets.

Average.cpp (displays average benchmark test results).

```
//=================================================================
// Average.cpp -- Displays average benchmark test results
// To compile:
//    bcc -c bench
//    bcc average bench.obj bidss.lib
// To run:
//    average
```

continues

continued

```
#include <iostream.h>
#include <stdio.h>
#include "bench.h"

#define NUMTESTS 200000   // 20000 for slower systems
#define NUMSETS 3

class TAverage: public TBench {
private:
  long sets;
  double result;
public:
  TAverage(long numSets): TBench()
    { sets = numSets; result = 0; }
  void Benchmark(long numTests, testfn tf);
  void Report(void);
};

void Testfn(void);

void main()
{
  TAverage test(NUMSETS);

  cout << "Testing sprintf() function" << endl;
  test.Benchmark(NUMTESTS, Testfn);
  test.Report();
}

void Testfn(void)
{
  char buffer[80];
  double d = 3.14159;

  sprintf(buffer, "%lf", d);
}

void TAverage::Benchmark(long numTests, testfn tf)
{
  long numSets = sets;

  while (numSets--) {
    TBench::Benchmark(numTests, tf);
    TBench::Report();
    result += Time();
  }
}

void TAverage::Report(void)
{
  printf("Total elapsed time == %6f sec\n", result);
  printf("Average for %ld sets == %6f sec\n", sets, result / sets);
}
```

5.3

Compile the following three files with the DOS command `bcc tbitset bitset`. Or create and compile an IDE project consisting of the files Bitset.cpp and Tbitset.cpp. Class TBitSet (declared in Bitset.h) stores an unsigned 16-bit value and has various member functions that can set, reset, and extract bits in this value. See comments in the listings for more information about how the class operates.

Bitset.h (declares the TBitSet class).

```
//===============================================================
// Bitset.h -- Declares the TBitSet class
// Copyright (c) 1996 by Tom Swan. All rights reserved.
//===============================================================

#ifndef __BITSET_H
#define __BITSET_H   // Prevent multiple #includes

typedef unsigned int WORD;  // Assumes 16-bit integers

class TBitSet {
private:
  WORD bitset;
protected:
  bool IndexOkay(char n)
    { if (n <= 15) return true; return false; }
public:
  TBitSet() { bitset = 0; }
  void Add(char n);
  void Delete(char n);
  bool HasBit(char n);
  char Extract(char n);
  void Display(void);
};

#endif  // __BITSET_H
```

Bitset.cpp (implements the TBitSet class).

```
//===============================================================
// Bitset.cpp -- Implements the TBitSet class
// To compile:
//    bcc -c bitset
// Copyright (c) 1996 by Tom Swan. All rights reserved.
//===============================================================

#include <iostream.h>
#include "bitset.h"

// Set nth bit in bitset to 1
void TBitSet::Add(char n)
{
  if (IndexOkay(n))
```

continued

```
      bitset |= 1 << n;  // i.e. OR 1 shifted left n times
}

// Set nth bit in bitset to 0
void TBitSet::Delete(char n)
{
  if (IndexOkay(n))
    bitset &= ~(1 << n);  // i.e. AND NOT 1 shifted left n times
}

// Return TRUE if nth bit in bitset == 1
bool TBitSet::HasBit(char n)
{
  if (!IndexOkay(n))
    return false;
  if ((bitset & (1 << n)) != 0)
    return true;
  return false;
}

// Return nth bit in bitset (1 or 0; 9==error)
char TBitSet::Extract(char n)
{
  if (!IndexOkay(n))
    return 9;  // Indexing error
  if (HasBit(n))
    return 1;
  return 0;
}

// Display bitset as a binary value
void TBitSet::Display(void)
{
  for (int i = 15; i >= 0; i--) {
    if (((i + 1) % 4) == 0)
      cout << ' ';
    cout << (int)Extract(i);
  }
}
```

Tbitset.cpp (tests the TBitSet class).

```
//================================================================
// Tbitset.cpp -- Tests the TBitSet class
// To compile:
//    bcc -c bitset
//    bcc tbitset bitset.obj
// To run:
//    tbitset
// Copyright (c) 1996 by Tom Swan. All rights reserved.
//================================================================

#include <iostream.h>
#include "bitset.h"
```

```
void main()
{
  TBitSet bits;

  bits.Add(0);      // Set bits 0, 2, 4, and 15
  bits.Add(2);
  bits.Add(4);
  bits.Add(15);
  bits.Display();   // Display set as a binary value
  bits.Delete(2);   // Reset bit 2
  cout << endl;
  bits.Display();
}
```

5.4

There are four files in the solution listed here. Item.h declares an Item class, which has a private data member that can address an object of this same class. Item's member functions are declared inline. List.h declares class TList, which derives from Item. (This would allow TList class objects to be linked to other TList class objects, although this feature isn't demonstrated here.) List.cpp implements the TList class. Finally, Tlist.cpp demonstrates how to use TList. Compile the test program and its modules by following instructions in the Tlist.cpp listing.

Item.h (declares the Item class).

```
//================================================================
// Item.h -- Declares the Item class
// Copyright (c) 1996 by Tom Swan. All rights reserved.
//================================================================

#ifndef __ITEM_H
#define __ITEM_H      // Prevent multiple #includes

class Item;
typedef Item* PItem;

class Item {
private:
  PItem next;          // Addresses next item
public:
  Item() { next = NULL; }
  virtual ~Item() { }
  PItem GetNext(void) { return next; }
  void PutNext(PItem p) { next = p; }
};

#endif    // __ITEM_H
```

List.h (declares the TList class).

```
//================================================================
// List.h -- Declares the TList class
// Copyright (c) 1996 by Tom Swan. All rights reserved.
//================================================================

#ifndef __LIST_H
#define __LIST_H      // Prevent multiple #includes

#include <stdlib.h>
#include "item.h"

class TList;
typedef TList* PTList;

class TList: public Item {
private:
  PItem anchor;        // Anchors list head
  PItem cip;           // Current item pointer
public:
// Constructor and destructor
  TList(): Item() { anchor = cip = NULL; }
  virtual ~TList();
// Inline member functions
  bool ListEmpty(void)
    { return (anchor == NULL); }
  PItem CurrentItem(void)
    { return cip; }
  void ResetList(void)
    { cip = anchor; }
// Other member functions
  void InsertItem(PItem ip);
  PItem NextItem(void);
};

#endif    // __LIST_H
```

List.cpp (implements the TList class).

```
//================================================================
// List.cpp -- Implements the TList class
// To compile:
//    bcc -c list
// Copyright (c) 1996 by Tom Swan. All rights reserved.
//================================================================

#include <stddef.h>
#include "list.h"

// Destructor. Delete any listed Item objects
TList::~TList()
{
  PItem p;  // Pointer to Item object

  while(anchor) {
    p = anchor;                  // Address item at anchor
```

```
      anchor = p->GetNext();  // Move anchor to next item
      delete p;               // Delete item at p
   }
}

// Insert into list a new Item object addressed by ip
void TList::InsertItem(PItem ip)
{
  if (ip == NULL)         // Ignore request to insert
    return;               //  a NULL item.
  ip->PutNext(anchor);    // Item addresses former anchor
  anchor = cip = ip;      // Anchor and cip address new item
}

// Move current Item pointer to next object
PItem TList::NextItem(void)
{
  if (cip != NULL)          // If list is not empty
    cip = cip->GetNext();   //  set cip to item at right.
  return cip;               // Return current item pointer.
}
```

Tlist.cpp (tests the TList and Item classes).

```
//==============================================================
// Tlist.cpp -- Tests the TList and Item classes
// To compile:
//    bcc -c list
//    bcc tlist list.obj
// To run:
//    tlist
// Copyright (c) 1996 by Tom Swan. All rights reserved.
//==============================================================

#include <iostream.h>
#include "list.h"

class TMyItem : public Item {
private:
  int value;
public:
  TMyItem(int n) { value = n; }
  void PutValue(int n) { value = n; }
  int GetValue(void) { return value; }
};

void ShowList(void);

PTList lp = new TList;

void main()
{
  int i;
```

continues

1013

continued

```
  cout << endl << "After allocating new list";
  ShowList();
  cout << endl << endl << "Insert 10 items into the list";
  for (i = 1; i <= 10; i++)
    lp->InsertItem(new TMyItem(i));
  ShowList();
}

void ShowList(void)
{
  cout << endl << "ITEMS IN LIST: ";
  if (lp->ListEmpty()) {
    cout << "List is empty";
    return;
  }
  lp->ResetList();
  PItem ip = lp->CurrentItem();
  while (ip) {
    cout << ((TMyItem *)ip)->GetValue() << " ";
    ip = lp->NextItem();
  }
  cout << endl;
}
```

5.5

The solution uses the Item and TList classes from Exercise 5.4. File Direct.h declares two classes. TStrItem can store a string (used later to hold filenames). TDirectory derives from TList. Note how simple this class is. All of the list mechanisms are in TList. TDirectory's only job is to read the disk directory and insert filenames in the list of TStrItem objects. Compile the test program Tdirect.cpp by following directions in the listing. Run the program with a command such as tdirect *.cpp to display all .cpp files in the current directory.

Direct.h (declares the TDirectory class).

```
//=================================================================
// Direct.h -- Declares the TDirectory class
// Copyright (c) 1996 by Tom Swan. All rights reserved.
//=================================================================

#ifndef __DIRECT_H
#define __DIRECT_H     // Prevent multiple #includes

#include <string.h>
#include "item.h"
#include "list.h"

class TStrItem;
typedef TStrItem* PTStrItem;

class TStrItem: public Item {
private:
```

```
  char *sp;   // String pointer
public:
  TStrItem(const char *s) { sp = strdup(s); }
  virtual ~TStrItem() { delete sp; }
  virtual const char *GetString(void) { return sp; }
};

class TDirectory: TList {
public:
  TDirectory(const char *wildcard);
  void Display(void);
};

#endif   // __DIRECT_H
```

Direct.cpp (implements the TDirectory class).

```
//================================================================
// Direct.cpp -- Implements the TDirectory class
// To compile:
//   bcc -c direct
// Copyright (c) 1996 by Tom Swan. All rights reserved.
//================================================================

#include <iostream.h>
#include <dir.h>
#include <dos.h>
#include <string.h>
#include "item.h"
#include "list.h"
#include "direct.h"

TDirectory::TDirectory(const char *wildcard)
{
  struct ffblk fb;  // File entry structure
  bool done;        // True when done reading entries

  done = findfirst(wildcard, &fb, FA_NORMAL | FA_DIREC);
  while (!done) {
    strlwr(fb.ff_name);      // Convert name to lowercase
    InsertItem(new TStrItem(fb.ff_name));  // Insert into list
    done = findnext(&fb);    // Do next entry
  }
}

void TDirectory::Display(void)
{
  PItem p;

  ResetList();
  p = CurrentItem();
  while (p) {
    cout << ((PTStrItem)p)->GetString() << endl;
    p = NextItem();
  }
}
```

Tdirect.cpp (tests `TDirectory` by displaying a disk directory).

```
//================================================================
// Tdirect.cpp -- Tests TDirectory by displaying a disk directory
// To compile:
//    bcc -c list
//    bcc -c direct
//    bcc tdirect list.obj direct.obj
// To run:
//    tdirect *.cpp
// Copyright (c) 1996 by Tom Swan. All rights reserved.
//================================================================

#include <iostream.h>
#include "direct.h"

void main(int argc, char *argv[])
{
  char *wildcard;

  if (argc <= 1)
    wildcard = "*.*";
  else
    wildcard = argv[1];
  TDirectory *dp = new TDirectory(wildcard);
  dp->Display();
  delete dp;
}
```

5.6

Class `TNamedDirectory` inherits two base classes, `TStrItem` and `TDirectory`. The new class's constructor passes a string argument to the constructors for each of the base classes. Member function `Display` in `TNamedDirectory` calls `TDirectory`'s `Display` member function to display the directory entries and then calls `GetString` from `TStrItem` to display the original wild card string used to initialize the object. Compile this program by following instructions in the listing and then run the program for a list of all .cpp files in the current directory.

Namedir.cpp (demonstrates multiple inheritance).

```
//================================================================
// Nameddir.cpp -- Demonstrates multiple inheritance
// To compile:
//    bcc -c list
//    bcc -c direct
//    bcc nameddir list.obj direct.obj
// To run:
//    nameddir
// Copyright (c) 1996 by Tom Swan. All rights reserved.
//================================================================

#include <iostream.h>
#include "direct.h"
```

```
class TNamedDirectory: public TStrItem, public TDirectory {
public:
  TNamedDirectory(const char *s)
    : TStrItem(s), TDirectory(s) { }
  void Display(void);
};

void main()
{
  TNamedDirectory dir("*.cpp");
  dir.Display();
}

void TNamedDirectory::Display(void)
{
  TDirectory::Display();
  cout << endl << "Above directory of "
       << GetString() << endl;
}
```

Chapter 6

6.1

Listing Compare.cpp shows the answer. Function main calls a Report function, which compares two blocks of memory in a try-catch statement block. Function CompareBlocks throws an exception of the CompareError class if the standard library function memcmp finds any mismatches. By the way, this is a good example of how you can add exception handling to standard functions that don't support exceptions. Simply wrap the functions in another function (such as CompareBlocks here) that throws one or more exceptions for various error conditions.

Compare.cpp (compares memory blocks using exceptions).

```
//==============================================================
// Compare.cpp -- Compares memory blocks using exceptions
// To compile:
//    bcc compare
// To run:
//    compare
// Copyright (c) 1996 by Tom Swan. All rights reserved.
//==============================================================

#include <iostream.h>
#include <mem.h>

// Function and exception-class declarations
void Report(const char *message);
void CompareBlocks(const void *s1, const void *s2, size_t n);
class CompareError { };
```

continues

continued

```
// Global buffers to be compared
char buffer1[1024];
char buffer2[1024];

void main()
{
// Initialize buffers to hold different contents
  memset(buffer1, 1, sizeof(buffer1));
  memset(buffer2, 2, sizeof(buffer2));
  Report("Before memcpy()");
// Make buffers the same
  memcpy(buffer2, buffer1, sizeof(buffer2));
  Report("After memcpy()");
}

// Display comparison report using try-catch block
void Report(const char *message)
{
  cout << endl << "Comparing buffer1 and buffer2" << endl;
  cout << message << endl;
  try {
    CompareBlocks(buffer1, buffer2, sizeof(buffer1));
  }
  catch (CompareError) {
    cout << "Buffers are not equal" << endl;
    return;
  }
  cout << "Buffers are equal" << endl;
}

// Compare buffers reporting errors as CompareError exception
void CompareBlocks(const void *b1, const void *b2, size_t n)
{
  if (memcmp(b1, b2, n) != 0)
    throw CompareError();
}
```

6.2

Listing Range.cpp implements a function, Range, that throws an exception of the RangeError class for a value that falls outside a specified low to high range. The exception class uses inline functions to initialize its private data members and to display a report of any errors. Function Range throws an exception of the class if value v is not within the range of min to max. This use of exceptions is questionable because there are other, and perhaps simpler, ways to write Range. It could, for example, return a true or false bool value to indicate its results. It is useful, however, to debate the value of exceptions for functions such as Range. An out-of-range value may or may not be exceptional *enough* to warrant the use of exceptions in the code, but that's a determination only you can make.

Range.cpp (uses exceptions to report out-of-range values).

```
//==============================================================
// Range.cpp -- Uses exceptions to report out-of-range values
// To compile:
//    bcc range
// To run:
//    range
// Copyright (c) 1996 by Tom Swan. All rights reserved.
//==============================================================

#include <iostream.h>

// Function prototype
void Range(int min, int max, int v);

// Exception class
class RangeError {
  int low, high, value;
public:
  RangeError(int min, int max, int v) {
    low = min; high = max; value = v;
  }
  void Report() {
    cout << "Error: " << value << " not in range ";
    cout << low << " to " << high << endl;
  }
};

void main()
{
  int v = 50;   // Try also 45, 75, 0

  try {
    Range(0, 100, v);
    Range(50, 100, v);
    Range(0, 50, v);
    Range(1000, 2000, v);   // Comment out for no errors
  }
  catch (RangeError r) {
    r.Report();
    return;
  }
  cout << "No errors detected" << endl;
}

// Throw exception if v is not in range of min to max
void Range(int min, int max, int v)
{
  if ((v < min) || (v > max)) {
    throw RangeError(min, max, v);
  }
}
```

6.3

Listing Concat.cpp implements function StringConcat, which throws an exception if appending a source string to a destination string would exceed a specified maximum length. The function throws an exception of the StringError class, which reports the maximum length and current buffer contents in the event of an error. This use of exceptions is far more appropriate than in the preceding exercise because overflowing a buffer is potentially a much more serious error, which can cause memory problems, than is an out-of-range integer value.

Concat.cpp (concatenates strings using exceptions).

```
//=================================================================
// Concat.cpp -- Concatenates strings using exceptions
// To compile:
//    bcc concat
// To run:
//    concat
// Copyright (c) 1996 by Tom Swan. All rights reserved.
//=================================================================

#include <iostream.h>
#include <string.h>

class StringError {
  const char *bp;     // Buffer pointer
  int maxlen;         // Maximum string length
public:
  StringError(const char *buffer, int n) {
    bp = buffer; maxlen = n;
  }
  void Report() {
    cout << "ERROR: String concatenation length exceeded." << endl;
    cout << "Maximum length = " << maxlen << endl;
    cout << "Current buffer = " << bp << endl;
  }
};

void StringConcat(char *destination, char *source, int maxlen);

#define BUFFERLEN 64
#define STRINGLEN BUFFERLEN - 1

void main()
{
  char buffer[BUFFERLEN];

  buffer[0] = 0;   // Set buffer length to zero
  try {
    StringConcat(buffer, "Message: ", STRINGLEN);
    StringConcat(buffer, "This error message is ", STRINGLEN);
    StringConcat(buffer, "much too long to fit ", STRINGLEN);
// Comment out following two lines for no errors
    StringConcat(buffer, "within the allocated ", STRINGLEN);
    StringConcat(buffer, "buffer!", STRINGLEN);
  }
  catch (StringError e) {
```

```
      e.Report();
      return;
  }
  cout << "No errors detected" << endl;
  cout << "Buffer == " << buffer << endl;
}

void StringConcat(char *destination, char *source, int maxlen)
{
  if (strlen(destination) + strlen(source) > maxlen)
    throw StringError(destination, maxlen);
  strcat(destination, source);
}
```

6.4

Using the Concat.cpp listing from the preceding exercise, to add a declared exception, modify the StringConcat function prototype as follows:

```
void StringConcat(char *destination, char *source, int maxlen)
  throw(StringError);
```

Also modify the implemented function's header to match, but eliminate the terminating semicolon. The declaration indicates that StringConcat may throw an exception of the StringError class, but more importantly, this is the *only* type of exception that StringConcat can throw.

6.5

```
#include <except.h>
...
set_unexpected(your_function_name);
```

6.6

As a function can declare a specific kind of exception (for example, see the answer to Exercise 6.4), it can use the identical format to declare that it throws *no* exceptions of any kind. For example, declare the function like this:

```
void AnyFunction() throw();
```

Appending to the function declaration the keyword throw and an empty set of parentheses indicates that AnyFunction throws no exceptions. According to the ANSI C++ standard, which is somewhat ambiguous on this question, any exceptions that AnyFunction *attempts* to throw will be destroyed before the function returns. However, in this circumstance, Borland C++ aborts the program with an abnormal program termination message. For this reason, you should use this tricky programming with extreme care—or, better yet, don't use it at all.

Chapter 7

7.1

The solution is to make TEngine a friend class of TFuel. That way, TEngine may access TFuel's private level data member. Listing Fuel.cpp demonstrates one possible answer.

Fuel.cpp (demonstrates friends).

```
//===============================================================
// Fuel.cpp -- Demonstrates friends
// To compile:
//    bcc fuel
// To run:
//    fuel
// Copyright (c) 1996 by Tom Swan. All rights reserved.
//===============================================================

#include <iostream.h>

class TFuel {
  friend class TEngine;   // "TEngine may access
private:                  //    TFuel's restricted parts"
  double level;
public:
  TFuel(double n) { level = n; }
};

class TEngine {
private:
  TFuel myFuel;
public:
  TEngine(double n): myFuel(n) { }
  double GetFuelLevel(void)
    { return myFuel.level; }  // Access private data!
};

void main()
{
  TEngine engine(1024);
  cout << "Fuel == " << engine.GetFuelLevel() << " units";
}
```

7.2

Make the following modifications to the program (this partial listing is not on the book's CD-ROM).

Partial—not on the CD-ROM.

```
class TStrOp {
  // ... Other declarations
  friend long operator*(TStrOp a, TStrOp b);
  friend long operator/(TStrOp a, TStrOp b);
};

long operator*(TStrOp a, TStrOp b)
{
  return (atol(a.value) * atol(b.value));
}

long operator/(TStrOp a, TStrOp b)
{
  return (atol(a.value) / atol(b.value));
}
```

7.3

Make the following modifications to the program. Note how `sprintf` is called to reconvert incremented and decremented values back into strings. (This partial listing is not on the book's CD-ROM.)

Partial—not on the CD-ROM.

```
class TStrOp {
  // ... Other declarations
  long operator++();       // Prefix ++x
  long operator++(int);    // Postfix x++
  long operator--();       // Prefix --x
  long operator--(int);    // Postfix x--
};

long TStrOp::operator++()
{
  long t = atol(value);
  sprintf(value, "%ld", (t + 1));
  return t;
}

long TStrOp::operator++(int)
{
  long t = atol(value);
  sprintf(value, "%ld", ++t);
  return t;
}

long TStrOp::operator--()
{
  long t = atol(value);
  sprintf(value, "%ld", (t - 1));
  return t;
}
```

continues **1023**

continued

```
long TStrOp::operator--(int)
{
  long t = atol(value);
  sprintf(value, "%ld", --t);
  return t;
}
```

7.4

The following inline function shows the answer. (This partial listing is not on the book's CD-ROM.)

Partial—not on the CD-ROM.

```
operator double() { return atof(value); }
```

Chapter 8

8.1

Partial—not on the CD-ROM.

```
TFruit orange;
TFruit grapefruit = orange;
```

8.2

Partial—not on the CD-ROM.

```
TFruit(TFruit &copy);
```

8.3

Partial—not on the CD-ROM.

```
void operator=(const TFruit &copy);
```

8.4

To use a template function, all you need to do is declare one or more suitable prototypes, as done in Listing Usemin.cpp for three min() functions.

Usemin.cpp (uses the min template function in minmax.h).

```
//===============================================================
// Usemin.cpp -- Uses the min template function in minmax.h
// To compile:
//    bcc usemin
// To run:
//    usemin
// Copyright (c) 1996 by Tom Swan. All rights reserved.
//===============================================================

#include <iostream.h>
#include "minmax.h"

int min(int a, int b);
double min(double a, double b);
char min(char a, char b);

main()
{
  int i1 = 100, i2 = 200;
  double d1 = 3.14159, d2 = 9.87654;
  char c1 = 'A', c2 = 'z';

  cout << "min(i1, i2) == " << min(i1, i2) << endl;
  cout << "min(d1, d2) == " << min(d1, d2) << endl;
  cout << "min(c1, c2) == " << min(c1, c2) << endl;
  return 0;
}
```

8.5

The TDatabase template class is capable of storing any type of data, including class objects (such as TRecord in the chapter) and also simpler int or double values. The solution defines dbd as a database of 100 integers. A cout.width(8); statement sets output width to eight columns.

Intdb.cpp (creates database of 100 integers at random).

```
//===============================================================
// Intdb.cpp -- Creates database of 100 integers at random
// To compile:
//    bcc intdb
// To run:
//    intdb
// Copyright (c) 1996 by Tom Swan. All rights reserved.
//===============================================================
```

continues

continued

```
#include <iostream.h>
#include <stdlib.h>
#include "db.h"

main()
{
  int rn;   // Record number index

  TDatabase<int> dbd(100);
  cout << endl << endl << "Database of ints" << endl;
  for (rn = 0; rn <= 99; rn++)
    dbd.GetRecord(rn) = rand();
  for (rn = 0; rn <= 99; rn++) {
    cout.width(8);
    cout << dbd.GetRecord(rn);
  }
  return 0;
}
```

8.6

Listing Namespac.cpp shows the answer. Defining each aString object in its own unique namespace eliminates the identifier conflict that would otherwise cause a compiler error.

Namespac.cpp (demonstrates namespaces).

```
//================================================================
// Namespac.cpp -- Demonstrates namespaces
// To compile:
//    bcc namespac
// To run:
//    namespac
// Copyright (c) 1996 by Tom Swan. All rights reserved.
//================================================================

#include <iostream.h>
#include <cstring.h>

namespace SPACE_ONE {
  string aString("This string is in namespace SPACE_ONE");
};

namespace SPACE_TWO {
  string aString("But this one is in namespace SPACE_TWO");
};

void main()
{
  cout << SPACE_ONE::aString << endl;
  cout << SPACE_TWO::aString << endl;
}
```

Bibliography

Brockschmidt, Kraig. *Inside OLE, 2nd Edition*. Microsoft Press, 1995.

Brooks, Frederick P., Jr. *The Mythical Man-Month*. Addison-Wesley Publishing Company, 1982.

Cluts, Nancy Winnick. *Programming the Windows 95 User Interface*. Microsoft Press, 1995.

Ellis, Margaret A., and Bjarne Stroustroup. *The Annotated C++ Reference Manual*. Addison-Wesley Publishing Company, 1990.

Knuth, Donald E., *The Art of Computer Programming. Vol. 1, Fundamental Algorithms; Vol. 2, Seminumerical Algorithms; Vol. 3, Sorting and Searching*. Addison-Wesley Publishing Company, 1973.

Pietrek, Matt. *Windows 95 System Programming Secrets*. IDG Books, 1995.

Sedgewick, Robert. *Algorithms in C++*. Addison-Wesley Publishing Company, 1992.

Stroustrup, Bjarne. *The C++ Programming Language, 2nd Ed*. Addison-Wesley Publishing Company, 1991.

Swan, Tom. *Learning C++*. Sams, 1991.

    — .*Mastering Turbo Assembler, 2nd Edition*. Sams, 1995.

    — .*Mastering Windows Programming with Borland C++ 4*. Sams, 1994.

    — .*Mastering Borland C++ 4.5*. Sams, 1995.

    — .*Foundations of Delphi Development*. IDG, 1995.

Shaw, Robert and Dan Osier. *Teach Yourself MFC in 21 Days*. Sams, 1995.

Williams, Mickey. *Essential Visual C++ 4*. Sams, 1995.

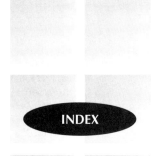

INDEX

Index

C

Add to Your Sams Library Today with the Best Books for Programming, Operating Systems, and New Technologies

The easiest way to order is to pick up the phone and call
1-800-428-5331
between 9:00 a.m. and 5:00 p.m. EST.
For faster service, please have your credit card available.

ISBN	Quantity	Description of Item	Unit Cost	Total Cost
0-672-30858-4		Delphi 2 Unleashed, 2E (Book/CD)	$55.00	
0-672-30914-9		Delphi 2 Developers Guide, 2E (Book/CD)	$59.99	
0-672-30791-X		Peter Norton's Complete Guide to Windows 95	$29.99	
0-672-30762-6		32-Bit Windows Programming (Book/CD)	$39.99	
0-672-30602-6		Programming Windows 95 Unleashed (Book/CD)	$49.99	
0-672-30474-0		Windows 95 Unleashed (Book/CD)	$35.00	
0-672-30902-5		Windows NT 3.51 Unleashed, 3E (Book/CD)	$49.99	
0-672-30611-5		Your Windows 95 Consultant	$19.99	
0-672-30655-7		Developing Your Own 32-Bit Operating System (Book/CD)	$49.99	
0-672-30617-4		The World Wide Web Unleashed	$39.99	
❏ 3 ½" Disk		Shipping and Handling: See information below.		
❏ 5 ¼" Disk		TOTAL		

Shipping and Handling: $4.00 for the first book, and $1.75 for each additional book. Floppy disk: add $1.75 for shipping and handling. If you need to have it NOW, we can ship product to you in 24 hours for an additional charge of approximately $18.00, and you will receive your item overnight or in two days. Overseas shipping and handling adds $2.00 per book and $8.00 for up to three disks. Prices subject to change. Call for availability and pricing information on latest editions.

201 W. 103rd Street, Indianapolis, Indiana 46290

1-800-428-5331 — Orders   1-800-835-3202 — FAX   1-800-858-7674 — Customer Service

Book ISBN 0-672-30802-9

A V I A C O M   S E R V I C · E

The Information SuperLibrary™

Bookstore	Search	What's New	Reference	Software	Newsletter	Company Overviews
Yellow Pages	Internet Starter Kit	HTML Workshop	Win a Free T-Shirt!	Macmillan Computer Publishing	Site Map	Talk to Us

CHECK OUT THE BOOKS IN THIS LIBRARY.

You'll find thousands of shareware files and over 1600 computer books designed for both technowizards and technophobes. You can browse through 700 sample chapters, get the latest news on the Net, and find just about anything using our massive search directories.

All Macmillan Computer Publishing books are available at your local bookstore.

We're open 24-hours a day, 365 days a year.

You don't need a card.

We don't charge fines.

And you can be as LOUD as you want.

The Information SuperLibrary
http://www.mcp.com/mcp/ ftp.mcp.com

CD-ROM Install

What's on the Disc

The companion CD-ROM contains all the source code and project files developed by Tom Swan, plus an electronic version of *Tom Swan's Mastering Borland C++ 4.5*, and the 4.5 source code. The install program will create icons that allow you to install all the CD-ROM material to your hard drive.

Windows 3.1/NT Installation Instructions

1. Insert the CD-ROM disc into your CD-ROM drive.

2. From File Manager or Program Manager, choose Run from the File menu.

3. Type **<*drive*>\setup** and press Enter, where <*drive*> corresponds to the drive letter of your CD-ROM. For example, if your CD-ROM is drive D:, type **D:\SETUP** and press Enter.

4. Installation creates a program manager group named "Mastering Borland C++ 5." To install the CD-ROM material to your hard drive, simply double-click on the icon of your choice.

Windows 95 Installation Instructions

1. Insert the CD-ROM disc into your CD-ROM drive.

2. From the Windows 95 desktop, double-click on the My Computer icon.

3. Double-click on the icon representing your CD-ROM drive.

4. Double-click on the icon titled Setup.exe to run the installation program.

5. Installation creates a program group named "Mastering Borland C++ 5." To install the CD-ROM material to your hard drive, press the Start button and select Programs. Then choose "Mastering Borland C++ 5," followed by the icon of your choice.